# ON THE CONDITION OF LABOR AND THE SOCIAL QUESTION ONE HUNDRED YEARS LATER

*Commemorating the 100th Anniversary of Rerum Novarum, and the Fiftieth Anniversary of the Association for Social Economics*

Edited by

## Thomas O. Nitsch
## Joseph M. Phillips, Jr
## Edward L. Fitzsimmons

Toronto Studies in Theology
Volume 69

The Edwin Mellen Press
Lewiston/Queenston/Lampeter

HN
37
.C3
O54
1994

**Library of Congress Cataloging-in-Publication Data**

On the condition of labor and the social question one hundred years later : commemorating the 100th anniversary of Rerum novarum, and the fiftieth anniversary of the Association for Social Economics / edited by Thomas O. Nitsch.
      p.    cm. -- (Toronto studies in theology ; v. 69)
    Papers from the sixth World Congress of Social Economics, held in Omaha, Aug. 9-11, 1991.
    Includes bibliographical references.
    ISBN 0-7734-9069-8
    1. Church and social problems--Catholic Church--Congresses.
2. Sociology, Christian (Catholic)--Congresses.   I. Nitsch, Thomas
O.  II. Association for Social Economics.  III. Catholic Church.
Pope (1878-1903 : Leo XIII). Rerum novarum.  IV. World Congress of
Social Economics (6th : 1991 : Omaha, Neb.)  V. Series.
HN37.C3O54  1994
261.8'08'822--dc20
                                                  94-17918
                                                  CIP

Edited by
Thomas O. Nitsch, Joseph M. Phillips, Jr., and Edward L. Fitzsimmons.

This is volume 69 in the continuing series
Toronto Studies in Theology
Volume 69 ISBN 0-7734-9069-8
TST Series ISBN 0-88946-975-X

A CIP catalog record for this book is available from the British Library.

The Edwin Mellen Press
Box 450
Lewiston, New York
USA 14092-0450

The Edwin Mellen Press
Box 67
Queenston, Ontario
CANADA L0S 1L0

The Edwin Mellen Press, Ltd.
Lampeter, Dyfed, Wales
UNITED KINGDOM SA48 7DY

Printed in the United States of America

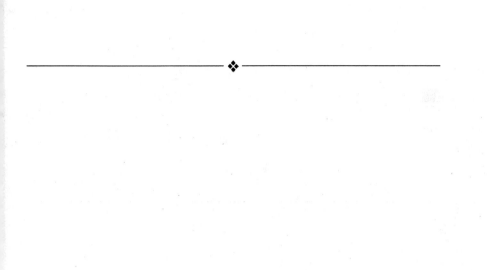

# Contents

# Table of Contents

❖

# Proceedings

# Foreword

It was a pleasure for Creighton University to be cosponsor and host of the Sixth World Congress of Social Economics. Cognizant of the contributions of our Jesuit forebears — Heinrich Pesch in Germany, Ch. Antoine and Valère Fallon in France — to the development and dissemination of the social teaching of the Roman-Catholic Church, it was particularly fitting that we participate in the celebration of the Hundredth Anniversary of *Rerum Novarum: On the Condition of Labor* in this manner.

The Jesuit connection, semicentennial commemoration, and cosponsorship with Marquette University are further established and strengthened when we recognize the founding of the Catholic Economic Association (now Association for Social Economics) in this country by Fathers Thomas F. Divine, S.J., and Bernard F. Dempsey, S.J., both of whom taught at Marquette for many years. Both Jesuits were substantial contributors to the discipline of social economics in its secular and religious forms. From all accounts, the Omaha Congress appears to have been a particular success in continuation of their endeavors.

In publishing these *Papers and Proceedings,* we hope to bring the fruits of the efforts of the participating scholars to a much wider audience interested in the principles and problems of social economy. The work of the conference can be reflected upon today in the light of that "Magna Charta of the Social Order," as Pope Pius XI declared *Rerum Novarum* forty years later in his noted encyclical, *Quadragesimo Anno: On the Reconstruction of the Social Order.* In the "Apostolic Blessing" conveyed to the participants of the conference by the Vatican Secretariat of State (cf. infra), we are informed of the hope expressed by the current pontiff, John Paul II, viz.:

> that the Congress will foster a clearer awareness that "the social message of the Gospel must not be considered a theory, but above all else a basis and a motivation for action" ... on behalf of justice and peace, solidarity and respect for the dignity of all, especially the poor and the most vulnerable members of society.

The quotation is from the recent encyclical *Centesimus Annus* commemorating the centenary of *Rerum Novarum.*

❖

In Creighton University's *Mission Statement* we note, in addition to the University's dedication "to the pursuit of truth in all its forms," the directedness of our comprehensive education "to the intellectual, social, spiritual, and recreational aspects of students' lives and to the promotion of justice." The *Mission Statement* further explains that our "faculty and staff stimulate critical thinking and provide ethical perspectives for dealing with an increasingly complex world." The publication of this volume is another expression of our educational mission.

Rev. Michael G. Morrison, S.J.
President
Creighton University
June, 1993

---------------------------------- ❖ ----------------------------------

# Introduction

## *Thomas O. Nitsch* *

One hundred years and not quite three months prior to the opening of our Sixth World Congress of Social Economics, Pope Leo XIII opened his 'Great Social Encyclical' and later-proclaimed (Pius XI, 1931) "Magna charta of the Social Order,"[1] *RERUM NOVARUM: On the Condition of the Working Classes (RN)*, as follows:

> The ardent thirst for newness, which long ago had begun to agitate peoples, had naturally to pass from the political order to the cognate order of social economy.

This rather literal rendering from the "Authentic Italian Version" (Antonazzi and de Rosa, 1991, p. 77), should serve well to indicate the *nominal* link between the celebrated encyclical letter and our two primary cosponsoring organizations, the International Institute of Social Economics (IISE) and Association for Social Economics (ASE); and, as the pages of their respective organs — the *International Journal of Social Economics (IJSE); Review of Social Economy (RSE)* and *Forum for Social Economics (FSE)* — will attest, the connection is quite *real* as well.[2] Further, as I have attempted to show (Nitsch 1990), Social Economy (ics) — from conception (1736), birth (labor and delivery, 1756-66), baptism (1773), and confirmation (1828-44) — has enjoyed, in its secular-positive form, a history now of a little over two and a half centuries. Roman-Catholic Social Economics (alias, "Christian Political Economy"), the dominant religious-normative form, it might be and has been held, dates its birth to the mid 18-teens, *its* baptism and confirmation coming in the 1830s-40s.

The "Social Question" and "Condition of Labor" also share an intimate nominal and real connection (ibid., passim). Nominally, we have had, for over a century and a half (viz., since 1836), that "question social" and its aliases, "social problem," "labor question," etc.[3] Invariably, and substantively, this has entailed, alternatively but obversely, the growing antagonism between the well-to-do propertied few and the immiserated proletarian masses (Adam Smith's 1:500; Rousseau's those who own but don't work vs. those who work but don't own), more simply the right of (private) property (especially in land), public poverty ("la misère publique"), growing inequality and inequity in the distribution of wealth and material well-being, labor vs. capital ("l'ouvrier" vs. "le capitaliste"), etc. Such, and all the socioeconomic implications and ramifications entailed, have, over the past two full centuries in the occident, constituted what has come to be encoded in the simple rubric of "the Social Question (SQ)."[4] And, it is this SQ to which Roman-Catholic social economics (RCSE) (Christian political economy) has always addressed itself, as both a "critical" discipline and movement — i.e., ideologically and praxeologically — and in that tridimensional, Hegelian-Marxian (*Aufhebung* = "sublation") sense of a "critique," "Kritik," etc. Thus, in theory and in praxis it sought to (1) affirm and preserve whatever in the existing order or dominant system of realities and ideas was good, right and true; (2) negate and abolish whatever therein was bad, wrong and false; and, (3) transcend and supersede that old order or system, thereby, with a new and better one. And, in those earlier days (i.e., from about 1814-53) of what came to be called — perhaps more generically — "social Catholicism," the change sought or otherwise envisioned was essentially "radical," i.e. — to use another word of that day — a "revolution."

This, indeed, completes our (opening) circle; or, alternatively, if we put the SQ and RCSE at the two opposite ends of the base of a triangle and "Revolution" (envisioned and/or invoked) at the apex, of our "triangle." For, the two earlier English renderings (*The Pope and the People, Five Great Encyclicals*, 1939) have our Leonine encyclical opening with "the spirit of *revolutionary* change" gripping and agitating "the nations of the world," and having to pass 'not surprisingly' beyond the political into the cognate economic order (et cf. John Paul II, *CA*, 1991, #5).

## Revolutionary Change and the Congress

When does a revolution begin? How is one measured? What *is* a revolution? We know literally that it is a turnover; an upside-down rearrangement — in our case, of the social order. In the case of Marx's analysis, it means the 180-degree change from private to collective property, from the State as oppressor to the State as liberator and then no State as such or a totally sublated one. Revolution as such does not necessarily imply abrupt and/or violent change; just 180 degrees, root-and-branch, stem-to-stern, "de fond en comble" (Proudhon, Vol. I, p. 5), etc. The one most historic of our experience, of course, is that begun in October 1917. Socioeconomically, it took about 11 years to complete. Now, sixty years later, the new system established thence is itself being overturned by another new order of "'radical' reforms" going under the banner of *perestroika* (Gregory and Stuart 1992, p. 415; Mikhailova 1991, pp. 3-4). But, was "revolutionary change" already in the air? For, hardly had the ink dried on John Paul II's first major social encyclical, *Laborem Exercens (LE)* (September, 1981), than the Pontiff makes a second and even more historic visit to his native Poland, with a noted stare-down of an obviously nervous Communist Party General Secretary and a blessing of the

❖

outlawed Solidarity union and its very "social-Catholic" leader. Nor is there a question of the substantive relationship between the Solidarity uprising *and* the reflections "On Human Work" contained in the significant letter.[5]

Because of the 100th anniversary approaching and those momentous developments going on in the Soviet Union and Eastern Europe, there was little doubt regarding the appearance of another (actually the third) major social encyclical on the part of this Pope. As noted in my own anticipation (Nitsch 1991/1992, pp. 1 and 14, n. 3), such an appearance was earlier forecast in this country by Archbishop Rembert Weakland in February 1985. The question was, what — if only for ceremonial adequacy and dramatic effect — would be the nature of "the (thirst for) revolutionary change(s)" addressed in the forth-coming *Centesimus Annus (CA)* of J.P. II? What would be put forward as the "signs of the times" demanding moral-theological reflection and doctrinal pronouncement at the highest level of official Roman Christendom? With this in mind, the present writer commenced some serious reflections and machinations of his own regarding an appropriate concelebration of that 100th anniversary on the parts, in particular, of the IISE and the ASE, whose semicentennial would occur simultaneously.

It was thus that I rang up Barrie Pettman in Hull on the morning/afternoon of March 15, 1988 to propose a special "Seventh World Congress of Social Economics (WCSE) in Rome in Spring/ Summer of 1991, in commemoration of the 100th anniversary (First Centennial) of *RN* (Leo XIII, May 15, 1891)."[6] As I found him in the throes of virtually single-handedly moving the fifth WCSE from Jerusalem, as originally planned, to York, Barrie conveyed rather effectively his lack of enthusiasm regarding the contemplation of the seventh three years down the road — the sixth, at the time, was being slated for Fresno under John O'Brien's able coordination. Yet, Barrie agreed with and accepted that proposal "in principle." This was further confirmed by his written assurance (March 28, 1988) "that with sufficient advanced planning and organizational effort we can make a go of the 100th anniversary of *RERUM NOVARUM.*" After "in-house" discussions here between the Dean, Department Chairman and myself,[7] the proposal was advanced at the ASE Executive Council meeting in Chicago, April 8, 1988. The focus then was still on the singular commemoration of *RN,* as it remained through the subsequent Spring (1989).

A consultation early on with super-organizer John C. O'Brien promptly produced such questions as "Why Rome?" "Who's there to make the arrangements?" etc. Rome, because it would be magnetic, irresistible! Catholic social economists, philosophers, theologians, et al. would flock there by the droves for such an occasion. And, if not at that time, it later occurred to me that Creighton (Marquette had not yet been approached), being a Jesuit institution, would have some connections and "pull" there, e.g. the Jesuit Curia and Gregorian U. It is obvious whose judgment won the day!

During the Spring-Summer of 1989, consultations were held with the officers of the ASE,[8] Barrie Pettman,[9] and Dean Tom Bausch at Marquette.[10] It was mutually

❖

agreed and understood that (1) the IISE would be the primary sponsor, with the ASE, Creighton and Marquette Universities as cosponsors; (2) this would be the sixth (instead of seventh) WCSE, as John O'Brien would have his hands full organizing the December 1989 meetings of the ASE; (3) Omaha would be the site, Creighton the host institution, and the dates would be August 9-11, 1991; and (4) finances permitting, we should publish all conference papers conforming to appropriate editorial standards.[11] At the same time, it might be noted, Barrie Pettman had indicated in his May 2nd letter, and affirmed at Lake Tahoe, whence, again in his welcoming remarks at the Congress, his desire to retire from the WCSE "concept," and for it to be transferred gradually — via this act of co-sponsorship — to the ASE. In the meantime, on campus here, further consultations had been held with the Chairman and Dean, and the official go-ahead secured from the President, Michael G. Morrison, S.J.[12] Also, a planning/co-ordinating committee had been constituted, to wit: Eugene L. Donahue, S.J., Associate Professor of Business and Society; Edward L. Fitzsimmons, Assistant Professor of Economics; Bryan F. LeBeau, Associate Professor of History and Director of the Creighton Center for the Study of Religion and Society; Joseph M. Phillips and Gerard L. Stockhausen, S.J., Associate Professors of Economics; and, myself, Chair. With dispatch, and following the advice/instructions of the ASE officers consulted in mid-May 1989, as soon as the Lake Tahoe pact has been sealed, a preliminary announcement should go out to — as I thought, anyhow — stake out some turf, given the competition anticipated, which turned out to be keener even than evisaged at that time. Thus, a "Preliminary Announcement" was drafted, with a 'Call for Proposals/Requests' appended. In the late Summer of 1989, accordingly, copies of this "announcement/ call" were posted to appropriate administrators/faculties of all Jesuit and otherwise major Catholic universities and colleges in the United States, Canada, and western Europe. The veritable plethora and wide-ranging variety of Catholic institutions of higher or post-secondary education listed in the most comprehensive directory of the day, coupled with the meager resources available here at the time, precluded our going beyond these limits; and, of course, it is from those quarters that one would expect the greatest demand, i.e. willingness and ability to attend. At the same time, beginning with the Spring of 1990, announcement/calls or "adverts" were included in various issues of the *IJSE, RSE* and *FSE*. An initial announcement and Call for Papers ("Congress will mark *Rerum Novarum* centenary") and reminder/call ("*Rerum Novarum:* 100 years later") appeared in the Autumn 1990 and Spring 1991 issues of our *Center for the Study of Religion and Society* newsletter.

Inquiries began to trickle in; and, on April 1, 1990, a 'response letter' was drafted and addressed to "Colleagues expressing an interest in the 6th WCSE, et al.," providing "Further Information/Details on the Congress." Noting the two latest meeting of the ASE (Atlanta, December 27-30, 1989; Chicago, March 29-31, 1990), it was indicated that the membership and officers had resumed discussions of "the August 1991 WCSE as presented on the announcement/call enclosed." Responding to counsel and instructions received there, the letter proposed — in

❖

both general terms and some detail — a broad range of "topics/themes" for prospective presenters to consider, stipulating that "both orthodox/traditional and heterodox/critical perspectives and analyses thereof are solicited." Some of the topics/ themes proposed were as follows: (1) On the Condition of Labour or the Working Class in General, specifying various national, regional, and continental bases; (2) Affluence, Poverty and the Issue of Income/Wealth Distribution on Particular National, Regional, etc. and Global Bases; (3) Capitalism, Socialism/ Communism and Alternative Systems for Meeting the Problems of the 1990s and Challenges of the 21st Century; (4) the Role of the Institutional Church(es) or Organized Religion(s) in the further Formation, Development and Improvement of Human Economic Society (ies); (5) the Great Social Encyclical Revisited, subtopics ranging from (a) Catholic and Related Socioeconomic Thought in the Pre-*RN* Period, to (e) the Question of Property, viz. the Ownership, Possession, Control and Use of our Natural and Human-made Resources; (6) the Founding and Historical Development of the Catholic Economic Association, whence Association for Social Economics; (7) Current Status, New Directions, Challenges of the ASE: Social Economics and/vs. Socio-Economics, pluralism, vs. unification, divergence vs. convergence; (8) New Dimensions of the Social Question and Social Economy(ics) — the Physical Environment and the Human Household to be Managed Prudently as well as Administered Efficiently — *Homo Faber* and *Homo Oeconomus:* ...the questions of Scarcity and Unlimited Wants re-examined; (9) Beyond Political Economy and Social Economics (and the related "Isms"); (10) Special/Explicit Perspectives, Emphases, etc. — (a) Minority (in the U.S., e.g., African-American, Latino/Chicano, et al.), (b) Marxian/Neo-Marxian, (c) Liberation-theological, (d) other-secular, (e) other-religious; (11) the Conscientious Social Economist and the Standard Bill-of-Fare in the Economics Curriculum; (12) Round-table on the presumed May 1991 encyclical, *Centesimo Anno* (?); and, (13) Other (fill in the blank). Thus, as with previous WCSEs and at least some of the (national/regional) ASE programs, this one was left open-ended, the over-riding consideration being inclusion rather than exclusion.

In that spirit, special efforts were made to secure some representation of minorities (e.g., African Americans and Latinos/Mexican-Americans) and women (locally/nationally) at the Congress. Most unfortunately, these were essentially in vain. At the same time, an attempt was made to see that all constituencies of the ASE and/or former CEA were apprised and made welcome. Finally, a special invitation was sent out to the participants of the fourth and fifth WCSEs and those of the ISINI First International Congress (Paris, Aug. 1990), as the names and addresses appeared on the respective lists. To the proposed topics/themes of the 'response letter' enclosed, this letter (of February 7, 1991) attempted to correct for the "significant omission [of] the area of medical care and health insurance."

The quest for our two featured speakers succeeded when Archbishop John Roach and Father William Byron were secured via the good offices of Archbishop

Daniel E. Sheehan of Omaha, who honored us with his presence as his schedule permitted. The timely topics and wise words of Roach and Byron appear below. Henry Briefs, of the ASE/CEA "older (but not 'oldest') guard," was successfully prevailed upon to entertain and/or enlighten us with a "down memory lane" luncheon presentation, the special event accorded to our Semicentennial celebration. His memorable reminiscences did both; but, for the nonce at least, will have to remain a part of our "oral tradition"!

For the present writer, organizing this conference was much more a pain than a pleasure, and certainly much more the effectuation of a sense of duty than the application of "skill and dexterity." Pleasurable were the conceptualization, theorizing, matrix-designing, etc.; painful, the implementational and, generally speaking, "practical" aspects; impossible, the pulling it off without the material assistance and moral support of those who know who they are. From the very beginning, this party of the first part was very candid, to all concerned, as to his being the last person who should and wanted to be doing this; but, aside from certain "Thomases," regarding the "could," all agreed it *should* be done. Thus, *some*one had to do it; and, again, really, some*ones*. A further problem here will come with their due and proper recognition.

The organizing, may I say, was fraught from the outset — or at least once past the dreaming and original conceptualization stage — with disappointments and frustrations; but, I do not think anyone could or should say, failures. There were several high points or otherwise "coups" that may be noted. First among these, the present writer would note the enabling of our delightful participant from the Soviet Union, Dr. Elena Mikhailova, to be with us. It was a feat, personal and collegial, of near-epic proportions, much too long and involved to repeat here. Suffice it to say that, without the communicational efforts of Dr. Ina Cohn and her husband Yuri back in Moscow, along with the "material support" forthcoming from our Vice President for Academic Affairs, Dr. William F. Cunningham, we would have been deprived of Dr. Mikhailova's valuable contribution.

The second special accomplishment was both simpler and much easier, as it turned out. On March 20, 1991 a letter was posted to "John Paul II, Vatican City, Rome, ITALY," bringing to his "attention the special 6th WCSE we are holding in Omaha this coming August, commemorating the centennial of *Rerum Novarum* and semicentennial of our ASE, formerly (1941-70) Catholic Economic Association," and covering a copy of the advert that appeared in the *IJSE*. The second paragraph read, if I may quote:

> Our participants will include scholars, clerics, et al. from around the globe. We shall feature individual sessions on such topics as "The Socioeconomic Thought of the Early Church Fathers," "Catholic Social Economy and the Social Question prior to *Rerum Novarum*," "Problems of Minority Workers in the U.S.," "The Condition of Labor &c. in the 'Third World'," "Problems of Social Economy: Islamic Perspectives,"...; and a very special session is envisioned on the

forthcoming Social Encyclical Letter we are all expecting from you, which I suppose might open with the words, *"Centesimo anno expleto"*.

The next paragraph identified our two featured speakers and their topics, mentioning the Pastoral Letter just issued by Archbishop Roach,[13] and our intention to "organize a special panel on our own Pastoral Letter on the Economy of Northeast Nebraska, entitled *Human Development: Abundance and Scarcity,* and issued by Archbishop Daniel E. Sheehan, D.D., of Omaha this past January 13." To make the Holy Father's letter more understandable, the last two paragraphs of ours (mine) are here reproduced.

> I peradventure to enclose, along with our announcement/call, a copy of one of the two papers I will present at our Congress;[14] ...This is merely and purely for your information and consideration.
> Whatever comments you would like to make, greetings and even blessings you might be so gracious as to extend, etc., I would be most happy to convey to our several general assemblies, to our Archbishop who has been very instrumental in our preparations, and the representatives of our two Jesuit Universities. -/-
> Most sincerely, ...; ENCL: 2

There were other special efforts of a somewhat personal nature which resulted in the qualitative as well as quantitative enhancement of our numbers; and, alas, one that failed in the end — age and health finally prevented Dr. Franz Mueller from gracing us with his presence. "Regrets" were received from notable prospective participants both here and abroad. Age and health prevented a professor in the Académie des Sciences Morales et Politiques of the Institut de France from attending; two "regulars" had conflicting commitments in other parts of the globe, and two others were budgetarily precluded.[15]

Also of special note are two surprise phone calls the week of the Congress. The first was an 11th-hour inquiry from Giuseppe Gabburo of the University of Verona who was visiting at Cornell University. Having just chanced on one of our adverts in unboxing his effects there, paper in hand, he asked if there were still time to get on the program. An on-the-spot "re-solution" of "la Grande Matrice" enabled an affirmative answer, and inadvertently switched the present party into a simultaneous-session conflict. (Both presentations were made, bilocation, achieved!). The second was from the local airport on the eve of the Congress. Barry Myers of Carleton University informed of his arrival and desired to know how best to get to the hotel. The significance of the appearance of these two "walk-ons" beyond their participation in the regular sessions is that, in a preannounced and properly "cleared" post-mortem meeting following the closing of the Congress proper, they and I constituted an ad-hoc committee for planning the next two WCSEs. Both pledged their universities as respective cosponsors (with the ASE et al.) and host

❖

institutions, and their services as respective organizers/co-ordinators. Professor Gaburro has subsequently confirmed (17.09.91) and reconfirmed (9.09.92) this in writing, with the hope now of staging the seventh WCSE at his university in Verona in mid-August 1994 — pending, of course, the approval of the principal sponsoring organization(s).

## The Present Volume

This "Introduction" is probably at least borderline "unorthodox." My only defense in this, or — as the case may be — excuse, I suppose, is that there is no precedent on which to go. No *Papers and Proceedings* of any of the five previous Congresses have, *as such,* been published.[16] This, I further presume, permits of some of the liberty and latitude I am taking, be the rest license! I shall not address any of the papers which appear on any sort of an individual basis. I perhaps should apologize, or offer some kind of apology, for the time that it has taken principally, if not exclusively, myself to "get with the program"; and, the "reminders" have not been few and far between! Two explanations only are proffered, viz.: taste and time. For the most part, the other resources — human and otherwise — have been available and forthcoming. As people like Bill Waters, John O'Brien and John Davis may realize, it takes a special constitution as well as aptitude to be an editor — editor-in-chief, whatever. If the present party of the first part thought he was no organizer; by now, I think, he has removed any doubt about his being, or ever again wanting to be, an editor-in-chief, or otherwise.

The "Papers" section opens with the formal welcoming remarks of the respective Deans; i.e., of the College of Business Administration at Creighton and the College of Business Administration at Marquette. These are followed by the presentations of the two featured speakers; viz., the "Opening Address" by Archbishop Roach, and the "Keynote Address" by Father Byron. Next, are the conference papers proper, in the order of their appearance in the *Program.* A fair amount of the papers presented are not published here. As was noted at the Congress, two sets of these would appear elsewhere. Thus, those papers presented in Sessions 11, 15 and 20 — "Essays in Honor of John E. Elliott I, II and III" — are appearing in a special *Festschrift* issue of the *IJSE;*[17] and, others, as also known in advance, were prepared for and now appear in the "Anniversary Issue: Centennial of *Rerum Novarum* and Semicentennial of the Founding of the Association" of the *RSE,* XLIX:4, Winter 1991.[18] In those cases and other individual cases of papers presented but appearing elsewhere, to the extent feasible due note of location will be made in the annotated *Program* in the "Proceedings" section. In all such events — i.e., the symposia noted and certain individual cases — the authors were asked to submit "Abstracts" for inclusion here. In the remainder of the cases, the papers presented simply were not submitted — in revised form or otherwise — for publication herewith.

This is a set of conference papers. They have been reviewed and refereed by the Editorial Board, who take final responsibility for remaining shortcomings as well as some improvements that may be noticed. This has been an experiment; and, it is fully anticipated that the next set of WCSE *P&P* will benefit significantly from this experience. As in the case of subsequent organizational efforts, however, the present party of the first part remains available only on a consultative basis.

## Special Acknowledgments

Most of the key players in the present endeavor have already been more or less duly recognized. Yet, so it not remain implicit or get buried elsewhere, the present writer wants to make explicit here his gratitude for the full support and wise counsel extended at the local level by his department chair, dean and the president of the University. The two deans, Guy Banville at Creighton and Tom Bausch at Marquette, are also to be recognized for agreeing to share any residual financial burden of publishing these *Papers and Proceedings* beyond that defrayed out of the registration fees. Moral support and sage counsel was also forthcoming in generous quantities by the likes of Kishor Thanawala, Bill Waters, John Elliot and John Davis — *inter alios.* Joyce Bunger, Director, and Portia Graves in the College of Business Administration Office of External Affairs here are responsible for the photo-ready copy of our *Program,* and technical assistance in the editing of the conference papers. Shirley Gust has exhibited the patience of a saint and dedication beyond job description in doing the final-typing of the major part that remained. Stacee Milan and Karen Hamilton at our Biomedical Communications Department deserve primary credit for the final copy of the volume. Finally, in case it has not been detected and otherwise recognized, the staging of this event has involved tapping into considerable "overhead" here at Creighton — innumerable long-distance calls, various mailings, stenographic assistance, etc.

## Endnotes

*Professor of Economics, College of Business Administration, Creighton University; and General Editor, these *Papers and Proceedings.*

[1] Idem, *QA, AAS,* XXIII (1931), 189, viz., "Conclusion: R.N. *Magna* socialis ordinis *Charta*"; et ibid., *FGE* (1939), p. 135, §39.

[2] In this present regard, especially given these names/titles, we may note that, while, strictly speaking, the term *"economy"* should designate the praxis of "household management," and "eco*nomics"* the discipline (science, theory) thereof, in the English (as well as the French, etc.) they have been used interchangeably; whence, e.g., J.S. Mill (1836-44) used "social economy" to designate "speculative politics," in contradistinction to the "art thereof." And, of course, the *IJSE* and *FSE* are not particularly devoted to (pure, positive) "science"; the *RSE,* to (pure, normative) art, praxis.

[3] In the autumn of 1836, A.-F. Ozanam wrote to his friends, F. Lallier and L. Janmot, successively as follows: "The question which agitates the world around us

❖

today is neither a question of persons, nor a question of political forms, but a social question" (November 5, 1836); "The question which divides men of our day is no longer a question of political forms; it is a social question, i.e. whether the spirit of egoism or that of sacrifice will prevail" (November 13, 1836). In 1839/40, the Spaniard and "social (non-?) Catholic" A. Flórez Estrada, published in two forms his essay on "The Social question; i.e., the Origin, Latitude and Effects of the Right of Property." Subsequently, his countryman and earlier adversary. R. de la Sagra, published (1848/ 49), first in Belgian and then in Spanish, his *Social Aphorisms,* noting up-front in the latter edition his intention "to treat the great social questions of the present epoch." At the same time (1848/49), the Rev. Wm. Em. von Ketteler first presented (Advent 1848) and then published his six sermons on *The Great Social Questions of the Present Time* (Mainz, 1849); subsequently, Bishop von Ketteler would publish his "Hauptwerk,"*The Labor-question in Christianity* (Mainz 1864). The erstwhile "fiery" Abbot F. Lamennais had anticipated that formula by 16 years with the publication of his *Question du Travail* (Paris 1848); while, the very secular French economist, L. Walras, has appended to the title of his *L'Economie politique et la justice: A Critical Examination of the doctrines of M.P.-J. Proudhon* (Paris 1860) the further fact that it would be "preceded by an Introduction to the Social Question." Finally, Claudio Jannet, in his "The School of LePlay" (in idem et al., *Quatre Ecoles d'Economie Sociale,* Genève 1890), opens that first (of four) lecture(s) at the Swiss Christian Society of Social Economy by positing and defining (p. 4) "the grave problem [confronting] all countries enjoying a certain degree of civilization"; viz., "the question of the relations of the classes among themselves, that *question of the rich and the poor....*" It is to the resolution of "that grave question," our devoted disciple continues, that the master addressed his "capital work," *La Réform sociale* of 1864. Three years later, Jannet's "On French Catholics and the Social Question," following on the heels of *RN,* appeared in the January 1893 issue of the *Quarterly Journal of Economics* (Vol. VII, pp. 135-61). While *RN* itself does not *pose* the "social questions" as such, the *direct reference* is clearly there. Thus, in the opening paragraph, where, in the official Latin (*ASS,* XXIII, 641) the subject-title *de conditione opificum* appears in italics, we are informed that the Holy Father is here urged "to treat the question (*tractare quaestionem,* viz. "The Condition of Labor") expressly and at length" (cf. *FGE,* p. 1, §1); whence, in closing (§45, *FGE,* p. 29), we find the Pontiff completing the circle with a concluding reference to "this most difficult question" (from the official Latin, "caussa perdifficili"; and, the 'authentic' Italian, "si arduo problema"—*ASS,* 670; Antonazzi & de Rosa, p. 203). With *Quadragesimo Anno (QA),* we have at once the official baptism and confirmation as Pius XI eulogizes Leo XIII in his *RN* for having "laid down for all mankind unerring rules for the right solution of the difficult problem of human solidarity, called the social question"; viz., "quod universo humano generi ad arduam de humana consortione causam, quam 'socialem quaestionem' appellant, rite solvendam tutissimas statuerunt normas cum maxime id opportunum atque adeo necessarium erat" (*FGE,* p. 125, §2; *ASS,* XXIII:6, 179, 2d par., ital. sup.).

⁴ Having broached and having most succinctly encoded the question now to be treated with "set purpose and detail," Leo XIII went on to specify it further in emphasizing the arduous nature of that task, to wit: "It is no easy matter to define the relative rights and mutual duties of the rich and of the poor, of Capital and of Labour"

❖

— "Caussa ... Arduum siquidem metiri iura et officia, quibus locupletes et proletarios, eos qui rem, et eos qui operam conferant, inter se oportet contineri" — "Questione ... Difficile, perche ardua cosa egli e segnare nelle relazioni tra proprietarii e proletarii, tra capitale e lavoro, i precisi confini" (Eng. *P&P*, p. 134; Lat. *ASS,* 641; Ital., *Civ.Catt.,* 642 — et cf. Antonazzi's "authentic Italian version," idem et de Rosa, p. 79:50-51, the "proletarii" or "proletarî" is omitted, i.e. we have only the relazioni tra proprietarî, tra capitale e lavoro").

⁵ Recently, Gorbachev (March 9, 1992) has written in this regard as follows: "Now it can be said that everything that took place in Eastern Europe in recent years would have been impossible without the Pope's efforts and the enormous role, including the political role, he played in the world arena."

⁶ As per my *Office Memorandum,* "TO: Whomever It May Concern," Creighton University, 15 March 1988. Actually, as indicated there, this seventh WCSE was submitted as one of the "First Year Activities of [the] Proposed Heinrich Pesch Chair/ Professorship in Social Economics," then under consideration — at my instigation — at Creighton.

⁷ Guy R. Banville, Dean, College of Business Administration; Robert F. Allen, Chairman, Department of Economics and Finance.

⁸ Executive Council meeting in Cincinnati, March 31, 1988; and, by phone, May 18 - July 12, 1988.

⁹ My letters of April 12 and 15, 1989; his of May 2, 1989; and tête-à-tête at the Western Economic Association conference at Lake Tahoe, June 18-22, 1989.

¹⁰ Phone call to Thomas A. Bausch, Dean, College of Business Administration, Marquette University, July 14, 1989.

¹¹ Cf. E.J. O'Boyle (Spring 1990, p. 98; Summer 1991, p. 287) for reportage on these matters to the membership of the ASE.

¹² It was recognized here that, with a proposed chair/professorship in social economics "on hold," the present congress would fit admirably into Creighton University's plan for implementing the NCCB's Pastoral Letter on Catholic Social Teaching and the U.S. Economy, Economic Justice for All, of November 1986.

¹³ Citing his "Pastoral Letter on Social Justice" of January 13, 1991 (Roach 1991).

¹⁴ Viz., draft of mine as submitted to the *FSE* (cf. Nitsch, 1991/1992).

¹⁵ Touchingly, Professor Dr. Czeslaw Mojsiewicz of the Uniwersytet im A. Michiewicza Wdyzial-Nauk Spoiecznych, Instytut-Nauk Politycznych i Dzienniarstwa, Poznan, Poland, responded to one of our special invitations as follows: "Dear Professor Nitsch, / Thank you very much for your letter from February 11, 1991 with information about 6th WCSE in August in USA. All is very interest[ing], problems have very important meaning and scientific [significance].

"You wrote about my possibility to participate in this Congress. / My Dear Collegue! / Now in Poland we have very deep economic crisis. My University [has]

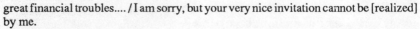

great financial troubles.... / I am sorry, but your very nice invitation cannot be [realized] by me.

"With great attention for you, for my American colleagues, with thanksgiving for your information and invitation — very sincerely, / [Signature, Title]

"P.S. When you will have possibility to come to Poland I invite you to my home [as] private guest. / All the best, [fam.sig.]"

16  At the same time, of course, thanks to the editorial efforts of John O'Brien and publicational auspices of Barry Pettman, selected papers of previous WCSEs have been brought out in the *IJSE*, as, e.g., in the special issues, *Selected Topics in Social Economics*, 9:6/7 (1982), and *Festschrif in Honour of Anghel Rugina: Part I*, 14:3/4/5 (1987).

17  Cf. *FESTSCHRIFT in Honour of John E. Elliott, Parts I and II*, ed. John Conway O'Brien, *IJSE*, 19:7/8/9 and 19:10/11/12 (1992).

18  To these we now add, *The Social Economics of Human Material Need*, ed. J.A. Davis and E.J. O'Boyle, SIU Press, forthcoming.

## References

**Papal Encyclicals (1891-1991)**

Leo XIII. *Rerum Novarum: De Conditione Opificum* (15 May 1891), *Acta Sactae Sedis (ASS)*, XXIII (1890-91), 641-70; and, *Leonis XIII. Pontificis Maximi ACTA*, Vol. XI (Romae: Ex Typographia Vaticana, 1892), 97-144.

_____. "Della Questione Operaia," in *La Civiltà Cattolica*, ser. XIV, vol. X, fasc. 984 (8 giugno 1891), 641-75.

_____. "The Condition of Labor," in *Five Great Encyclicals (FGE)*. New York: The Paulist Press, 1939; 1-30.

_____. "*Rerum Novarum:* The Condition of the Working Classes," in *The Pope and the People (P&P)*. London: Catholic Truth Society 1929; 133-68.

_____. *De Conditione Opificum / Della Questione Operaia*, "Testo Latino" / "Autentica Versione Italiana" — as per Antonazzi and de Rosa, op. cit. infra (1991), pp. 76-207; but, N.B., at p. 79:50-51, the Italian text should read, "...relazioni tra proprietarî e proletarî whence cf. the Latin text opposite (p. 78-52) and Italian text as per *Civ. Catt.* cit. supra, p. 642.

Pius XI. *Quadragesimo Anno: De ordine sociali instaurando et ad evangelicae legis norman perficiendo* (15 May 1931), *Acta Apostolicae Sedis (ASS)*, XXIII:6 (1 Iunii 1931), 177-228.

_____. "Reconstructing the Social Order" (15 May 1931), in *FGE* (1939), 125-67.

John Paul II. *LABOREM EXERCENS:* On Human Work, 14 September 1981. Washington, DC: United States Catholic Conference, 1981.

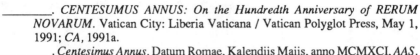

_____. *CENTESUMUS ANNUS: On the Hundredth Anniversary of RERUM NOVARUM.* Vatican City: Liberia Vaticana / Vatican Polyglot Press, May 1, 1991; *CA*, 1991a.

_____. *Centesimus Annus,* Datum Romae, Kalendiis Maiis, anno MCMXCI, *AAS,* LXXXIII:10 (October 9, 1991), 793-867; *CA*, 1991b.

**Other Works**

Antonazzi, Giovanni and de Rosa, Gabriele (eds.). *L'Enciclica RERVM NOVARVM e il suo Tempo.* Roma: Edizioni di Storia e Letteratura, 1991.

Gorbachev, Mikhail S. "My Partner, the Pope," *New York Times,* March 9, 1992; A17.

Gregory, Paul R. and Stuart, Robert C. *Comparative Economic Systems,* 4th ed. Boston et al.: Houghton Mifflin, 1992.

Marx, Karl and Engels, Friedrich. *Marx-Engels Werke,* Erganzungsband, lter Teil. Berlin: Dietz Verlag, 1968ff.

Mikhailova, Elena G. "Peristroika of the Soviet Economy and Help of the USA," paper presented at the Sixth World Congress of Social Economics, Omaha, NE (U.S.A.), 9-11 August 1991.

Nitsch, Thomas O. "Social Catholicism, Marxism and Liberation Theology: From Antithesis to Coexistence, Coalescence and Sythesis," *International Journal of Social Economics,* 13 (1986), 52-74.

_____. "Social Economics: The First 200 Years," in *Social Economics: Retrospect and Prospect,* ed. Mark A. Lutz. Boston/Dordrecht/London: Kluwer, 1990.

_____. *"Centesimo Anno:* The Social Encyclical of May 1991," *Forum for Social Economics, 21* (Fall 1991 / Spring 1992), 1-17.

_____. "Catholic Social Economy and the Social Question: Founders and First-Positors," *Faculty Working Papers,* College of Business Administration, Creighton University, May 1992.

O'Boyle, Edward J. "Minutes of the General membership Meeting, Association for Social Economics, December 28, 1989," *Review of Social Economics, 48* (Spring 1990), 97-100.

_____. "Minutes of the General Membership Meeting, Association for Social Economics, December 28, 1990," *Review of Social Economics, 49* (Summer 1991), 284-87.

Proudhon, P.-J. *Systéme des Contradictions économiques, ou Philosophie de la Misère.* Paris: Guillaumin, 1846.

Roach, Archbishop John. "Reviving the Common Good: A Pastoral Letter," *Origins, 20* (February 14, 1991).

SECRETARIAT OF STATE

FIRST SECTION · GENERAL AFFAIRS                    FROM THE VATICAN, June 17, 1991

No. 285519


Dear Professor Nitsch,

    The Holy Father duly received your kind letter inform-
ing him of the Sixth World Congress of Social Economics to
be held at Creighton University this August.  He appreciates
the devoted sentiments which led you to enclose a copy of
the paper which you will deliver on the occasion.

    His Holiness is pleased that the forthcoming Congress
will commemorate the centenary of Pope Leo XIII's pioneering
social Encyclical <u>Rerum Novarum</u>.  It is his hope that the
Congress will foster a clearer awareness that "the social
message of the Gospel must not be considered a theory, but
above all else a basis and a motivation for action" (<u>Cente-
simus Annus</u>, 57) on behalf of justice and peace, solidarity
and respect for the dignity of all, especially the poor and
the most vulnerable members of society.

    The Holy Father assures you of his prayers and sends
his Apostolic Blessing as a pledge of grace and peace in the
Lord.


                            Sincerely yours,


                            +G. B. Re
                            Substitute



Professor Thomas O. Nitsch
Professor of Economics
Creighton University
California at 24th Street
Omaha, NE   68178-0130

# Papers

---------------------------------- ❖ ----------------------------------

# Welcome to the Sixth World Congress of Social Economics

## *Guy R. Banville\**

On behalf of the faculty, staff and administration of Creighton's College of Business Administration, WELCOME to our midst.

We meet today in Omaha, Nebraska because Dr. Tom Nitsch had the foresight, in the spring of 1989, to approach me and recommend that we collaborate with the International Institute of Social Economics in Hull, England, the Association for Social Economics (formerly Catholic Economic Association) in this country, and Marquette University in hosting and presenting the Sixth World Congress of Social Economics commemorating jointly the centennial of *Rerum Novarum* and the semicentennial of the founding of the ASE (CEA).

Because of the centrality of the great German Jesuit economist Heinrich Pesch — the reputed "commentator on *Rerum Novarum*" and "sourcebook of *Quadragesimo Anno*" forty years later — in the development of modern Catholic social economics and of his disciples in the formation and development of the CEA/ASE, it is as well most fitting that our two Jesuit universities here in the Midwest join in the sponsorship of this special Congress.\*\*

As Jesuit institutions we are proud of our contributions to American education for more than 200 years. One of our missions is to assist young men and women to develop an understanding of the social and economic order, and to inculcate a humanistic value system into the problem-solving needs of each.

Dr. Nitsch informed Pope John Paul II of this upcoming Congress. The Secretary of State of the Vatican responded, and I quote: "His Holiness is pleased that the forthcoming Congress will commemorate the centenary of Pope Leo the XIII's pioneering social encyclical *Rerum Novarum*. It is his hope that the Congress will foster a clearer awareness that the social message of the Gospel must not be considered a theory, but above all else a basis and a motivation for action (*Centesimus Annus*, 57) on behalf of justice and peace, solidarity and respect for the dignity of all, especially the poor and the most vulnerable members of society."

❖

"The Holy Father assures you of his prayers and sends his Apostolic Blessing as a pledge of grace and peace in the Lord."

With this, ladies and gentlemen, I wish you a pleasant sojourn and a stimulating educational experience. God bless!

*Dean, Eugene C. Eppley College of Business Administration, Creighton University, Omaha, NE 68178 USA. Remarks delivered at the opening Plenary Session, Friday, 9 May 1991.

**The CEA/ASE owes its origin to the efforts of two Jesuit economists, both of Marquette University, viz.: Thomas F. Divine, "The convenor of the committee ... who established the Association in New York in 1941"; and, Bernard W. Dempsey, "a student of the work of Heinrich Pesch, [whose] vision was essentially that of the 1931 social ecncyclical, *Quadragesimo Anno,* which in turn came from the thought of Heinrich Pesch" (Wm.R. Waters, "Evolution of Social Economics in America," in M.A. Lutz, ed., *Social Economics: Retrospect and Prospect,* Kluwer Academic Publishers, 1990). (TN, ed.)

---------------------------------- ❖ ----------------------------------

# Welcoming Remarks

## *Thomas A. Bausch\**

The Marquette University College of Business Administration is pleased to be a co-sponsor of the Sixth World Congress of Social Economics commemorating the 100th anniversary of *Rerum Novarum*. I certainly desire to be with you, and am with you in spirit, but, despite many years with the Jesuits, I have yet to learn to bilocate and, therefore, an unmovable obligation draws me elsewhere.

As I think about the work of this conference, four images come to my mind, one from Gerard Manley Hopkins, S.J., two from St. Mark's gospel, and one from a friend thinking through the spirituality of our environmental concerns.

Hopkins sums up what drew me to Catholic social thinking in the first place in his poem, "As Kingfishers Catch Fire, Dragonflies Draw Flame:"

> As kingfishers catch fire, dragonflies draw flame;
> As tumbled over rim in roundy wells
> Stones ring; like each tucked string tells, each hung bell's
> Bow sung finds tongue to fling out loud its name;
> Each mortal thing does one thing and the same:
> Deals out that being indoors each one dwells;
> Selves-goes itself; Myself it speaks and spells,
> Crying what I do is me: For that I came.
>
> I say more: the just man justices;
> Keeps grace: that keeps all his goings graces;
> Acts, in God's eye what in God's eye he is—
> Christ—for Christ plays in 10,000 places,
> Lovely in limbs, and lovely in eyes not his
> To the Father, through the features of men's faces.

For me the dominant theme in all of Catholic social thinking has been the primacy and dignity of the person. As John Paul wrote, "The subject of work is the

❖

person." Each person on the face of this globe is unique and of inestimable value. Our work as scholars is to think through the theoretical and technical foundations of economic and social policy that will foster the dignity of all persons.

My second two images that underly the work of this conference are found in Mark's gospel 6:30-44, the first feeding of the multitudes. In telling the story Mark says, "so as he stepped ashore he saw a large crowd; and he took pity on them because they were like sheep without a shepherd...." This captures, in my opinion, the key element of Catholic social thinking, of the bishops' letter on the economy, the option for the poor. Christ took pity on them. But there is another element to this — "sheep without a shepherd." There is little real leadership in today's world. Our work as scholars is to do the analysis necessary for intelligent leadership to act to help the poor. Realistic options must be present for those people of good will and intelligence who desire to take on the burdens of the issue as we attempt to solve the problems of the poor in our society. "Option for the poor" is a pious statement without intelligent policy.

My third image, the second from this story, is the feeding of the multitude itself. I do not as much see this as some sort of magic multiplication of the loaves as I see it as a miracle of sharing. A sharing that takes place because of the formation of community by Christ. The development of effective tools and policies for the sharing of wealth on a global basis, for that is community today, as well as on the local level, and for the effective formation of community, is another great task facing us as scholars. We as social scientists must do the data-gathering, technical analysis, and hypotheses-development necessary if public policy is to be positive and have a lasting impact.

My final image is that of Brother Rock. As a friend of mine and I were walking recently, we stopped to look at a big rock. He said to me, "Tom, do you think of that rock as Brother Rock?" I thought, "John, you are off of your rocker." But his point soon grabbed me. That rock, as permanent as we may think it is, has a relatively short history, closer to mine than to that of the full history of the universe. Catholic social thinking, social economics, that is not solidly grounded in a firm concern for and analysis of environmental issues is far from the mark. The great theme of private property that is embedded in early Catholic economic thought needs to be reinterpreted and restated in the light of our interconnectedness with all of nature, which is at the heart of the environmental issue.

In conclusion, I think the essence of social economics, of Catholic economic thought, in this era is grounded in four concepts requiring extensive analysis by very competent and professional economists and other social scientists. In an era where technology, social systems, and politics tend to degrade the individual, it is our work to stress the primacy and dignity of the person. Second, underlying all of the work that we do and the policies that we suggest must be a concern for the well-being of the poor. Third, the highest priority must be given in our research and our work to discover the effective technology and social means necessary to foster the sharing of our resources among all. Fourth, any social economics of the last decade of the 20th century not grounded in the solid realities of our environmental issues starts as a bankrupt analysis.

The work of this conference is acutely important. As scholars we seek for the meaning of values and study how they are formed and articulated. As economists we have the tools to do analysis leading to more appropriate public policy. Our work is immense.

*Dean, College of Business Administration, Marquette University, Milwaukee, WI 53233 USA.

---- ❖ ----

# Social Responsibility and the Common Good

## *John R. Roach, D.D.* *

I am pleased to accept the invitation to be a part of the Sixth World Congress on Social Economics which is taking the 100th Anniversary of *Rerum Novarum (RN)* as its theme. I am impressed by the breadth of geographic and academic backgrounds of the participants. Please keep in mind that I am not a member of the academic community. Rather, I will speak from the perspective of a pastor, someone who has lived long enough to have lived as a youth through the Great Depression, one who has had a fairly privileged position of observing both the best and the worst of the human condition, a person who has watched the political processes in this country for a long time and yet has not become cynical, one who has had the privilege of working with the churches of other countries as an officer of our own Catholic Conference of Bishops, and finally, as a critic of the way we in this country do business from time to time; but in my heart, a real optimist and a person of enormous gratitude to Almighty God for my faith and my country. Finally, by way of introduction, I have to tell you that I will be speaking from my own perspective of church and from the context of the social teaching of the Roman Catholic Church, since that is the one I know and the one I am a part of.

I will be addressing the question of the common good as it relates to social justice. I do not mean to exaggerate this picture, but part of my thesis is that one of the reasons we as an American society are losing confidence in the political process, and as a result, are withdrawing from any active participation in it, is that people tend to equate politics with the pursuit of narrow interests and the glorification of self interest. Any notion of a society's common concern for its members is in the eyes of many potential voters lost in tactics and rhetoric which seem mostly self-serving. We need a dose of the old common good philosophy and of the theology which addresses the dignity and worth of the person not as the rugged individualist, but as the social person. I suggest that the key to the renewal of public life is to re-orient the whole enterprise to better affect basic national values in the search for the common good. If not, it will continue to be an arena for partisan posturing, a search

❖

for power for its own sake, interest group conflict, and what that is going to do is create more and more dropouts from any kind of active participation in our political process. Pope John Paul II praised democratic values in his last encyclical *Centesimus Annus,* but he said, "There is a crisis within democracies which seems at times to have lost the ability to make decisions aimed at the common good." The Pope says, "With time, such distortions of political conduct create distress and apathy, with the consequent decline in the political participation and civic spirit of the general population, which feels abused and disillusioned." He then deplores the "growing inability to situate particular interests within the framework of a coherent vision of the common good which demands a correct understanding of the dignity and the rights of the person."

That is what I want to talk about. The Pope says that there are times when our society does not examine the judgments to be made in the light of the criteria of justice and morality, but rather on the basis of the electoral or financial power of the groups promoting particular issues.

There are many in this audience who could trace the genesis of this problem a lot better than I. I know, however, that we are a part of a world which has put a heavy prize on rugged individualism, survival of the fittest, particularly in the market place, and we have found a language to make all of that respectable. We have seen the Christian theory of communality-solidarity as something to be acknowledged and respected, but not taken very seriously as we have gone about the business of pursuing economic theory. The continuing challenge of rooting democracy in our society in human rights and seeking the common good in the midst of many competing interests are not abstract issues for us, but are a responsibility for people committed to justice. We are a nation richly blessed with freedom, resources and strength.

We have accomplished much in our economic, social and political life. However, we are a nation which increasingly must make choices and I should like to hold up the theory of the common good as a rich part of the mix which we must use in addressing those questions.

Let me list just some of the issues that I think we have to begin to look at with a wider prism than we are currently using.

How do we as a nation respond to the haunting needs of vulnerable children in our midst? How do we look at children in poverty? We destroy 1.5 million unborn children a year through legalized abortion. One out of four preschool aged children grows up in poverty. We are a part of a world where thousands of children die every day from hunger and the diseases associated with malnutrition.

I live in a city with a very low rate of unemployment and yet the incidence of homelessness is increasing. As a nation we are looking at such questions as immigration and refugees from an almost totally self-serving perspective.

Prejudice and discrimination are alive and healthy. Racism and sexism are breeding hatred and a terrible kind of pain in the hearts of many.

We really have not processed what happened to us in the Persian Gulf. We needed to celebrate a victory and we needed to celebrate the heroism of people in the armed forces, and we did that, and that is good. However, the more radical questions I am afraid we have smothered in the euphoria of parades.

As we look at these questions and questions like them, for that certainly is not an exhaustive list, we are going to have to ask ourselves how the solutions to the questions touches the human person and whether it enhances or diminishes human life, human dignity and human rights. The Church needs to be a part of that great public debate from which will come the decisions affecting the public order and the public good. We believe that Jesus' commandment to love one's neighbor must look beyond individual relationships to infuse and transform all human relations from the family to the entire human community. When Jesus came to bring glad tidings to the poor, to proclaim liberty to captives and recovery of sight to the blind, and to let the oppressed go free, when He called us to feed the hungry, clothe the naked, care for the sick and the afflicted, and comfort the victims of injustice, He, indeed, spoke to us as individuals, but He also spoke to us as a society. That mandate involves institutions and structures of society. The heart of the social teaching of the Church is that every person is not only sacred, but also social.

Human life is life in community. So, the dignity of the individual is inherently connected to the good of society. In a pastoral letter I wrote in January on this topic, I stated that, "Human dignity can only be realized and protected in community and true community is found only when human dignity is respected." I said in my thesis that everyone has an obligation to contribute to the good of the whole society and to the common good.

Now let me look at this issue of the common good through the eyes of a Benedictine Monk, Father Virgil Michel, who in the late 1920's and throughout the 1930's was the most prolific writer and lecturer in this country in the areas of liturgical theory and social reform. Recall that this was 30 years before Vatican II when we were struggling to cope with the Great Depression. His total accent was on life. In an age where much of liturgical theory and at least some of the teaching on social theory was static, he argued that vitality was essential for growth and that dynamism was liberating. He argued that society could only be freed from an individualism which was destroying it if it could open itself to a vision of a common life flowing from the spirit. The theology of the Mystical Body of Christ was at the heart of most of his vision. While Virgil Michel is probably best known for his liturgical theory, the last few years of his life were devoted more and more to social and economic theory. The image of the members and the interrelationship of people in Christ's body was the wellspring from which came the richness of his writing and lecturing. I want to push this a little bit because I am personally more and more convinced that in our understandable ecclesiology of the people of God principle since Vatican II, we have done a disservice to our teaching on the Mystical Body of Christ and to our sense of community. That theory is not new with me, as you

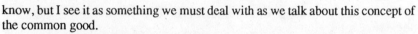

know, but I see it as something we must deal with as we talk about this concept of the common good.

In Virgil Michel's case the more he moved toward seeing liturgy as the very basis of living, the closer and closer he came to understand that liturgical renewal would always be incomplete without what he called social regeneration - which simply means a genuine commitment to justice. Virgil Michel was a tireless worker and at a very young age in 1930 had what at the time was described as a nervous breakdown but was probably closer to what we would define as burnout. He lost his sight for a time and in a decision that I have never quite understood, the Abbot at St. John's sent him to the Red Lake Indian Reservation in Northern Minnesota as a chaplain.

Up to that point in his life Michel was writing almost exclusively about liturgical renewal and reform. He had gradually come to see the Mystical Body as the driving force behind that theory, and so he was almost the first in this country to begin to push for things such as concelebration, the altar facing the people, vernacular in the liturgy, etc..., many years before Vatican II addressed these questions. Now for the first time at Red Lake he saw social depravation and injustice and he began to apply to a social setting the same theological principles that he had been applying to liturgical theory. It changed his life and became the basis for almost a new career in now addressing social teaching. He was on the reservation for three years. His health was pretty much restored and his sight was restored and he went back to St. John's to teach and to write. He died five years later at a very early age, but now wrote with a new kind of enthusiasm and understanding about living life in communion.

Michel used to go out to small rural communities from St. John's in Collegeville, Minnesota and meet especially with young people and talk to them about how you lived out a eucharistic spirituality. He would talk about the unity which comes from Eucharist being the basis for things like cooperatives and guilds. He talked about outreach to one's neighbor as being essential to life in Christ. In an article in 1937 he wrote, "The Christian will find it necessary to live out in his daily life the putting in action of his worship at the altar of God. His participation in the sacrifice of the Mystical Body leads to the sublime school of social service."

When *we* talk about the basic principles that are central to the Church's social teaching — human dignity, the call to community and the common good, the rights and responsibility of the person, the dignity of work and the rights of workers, the option for the poor and vulnerable and principles such as solidarity — we are really talking about exactly the same things that Michel saw flowing from the image of the Mystical Body.

In a June, 1930 article in *Commonweal* Michel wrote, "In the Church, as opposed to the exaggerated individualism of the past and present, all members are spiritually welded together into one living organism and find their full life in promoting the life of the whole. It is opposed to the exaggerated socialism of present and future; each member retains his individuality, has personal responsibility for promotion of the life of Christ in himself and in present and prospective fellow members." I find that statement to be exactly the prescription we need today as we look at our role as Christians, as citizens and as individuals.

At the beginning of this talk I said that I had to speak out of the perspective of Church and the statement of Virgil Michel I just read expresses that in almost a unique fashion for me. For him it was clear that if sisters and brothers were nourished by the one, holy Word of God and were fed by the one Body and Blood of Christ and were united in a common act of worship - if they share in these blessings together, then each bore a responsibility one to another. To people who share the mystery of membership in the Body of Christ, things like discrimination, insensitivity to the marginalized and any other form of injustice must be foreign and unthinkable.

I have spoken of Virgil Michel at such length because to me, at a time when it was not very popular to do so, he saw individualism destroying society and he prescribed the antidote of community. The more I have read of Father Michel, the more it is clear to me that the common good was at the very center of his social and liturgical theory, and that his theory of the common good rested squarely on the theological principle of the Mystical Body of Christ. For you and me as we take a look at what moves our economic and social thought, it is helpful to be reminded that reform is the work of the Spirit who moves among us and moves our hearts. An appreciation of the common good is a constant reminder that people are not islands apart from one another. We are social beings and we do not mature unless we are a part of a people also maturing.

As I look back over the significant social and economic teaching which has looked to our Christian tradition for its orientation, I am more and more comfortable with using the principle of the common good as my measuring stick. Whether we as a society are talking about hunger, peace, civil rights, arms control, capital punishment, the right to education, euthanasia, health care, food distribution, abortion, immigration, or any of the great issues with which we are dealing, I suggest that we do have a tradition of teaching which will assist us in addressing these issues and that woven through that teaching is the notion of the common good.

It is good for us to celebrate that tradition, but also to recognize that it is a living tradition and that each generation has a responsibility to nourish it and to add to it.

*Archbishop of Saint Paul and Minneapolis.

# The Social Question:
# Who Asks? Who Answers?

## William J. Byron, S.J.

Catholic social teaching always speaks to what the Church likes to call "the social question." Good pedagogy begins with good questions. Good social theory emerges when clear thinking engages itself with truly significant social problems.

At issue whenever the Church involves itself with the development of social doctrine is the ability to identify the genuinely significant social problem. Put another way, this points to the ability or inability to ask the right social question.

One of the welcome by-products of our 1991 centennial celebration of *Rerum Novarum (RN)* in books, articles, colloquia, seminars, and, of course, in the publication of the commemorative encyclical *Centesimus Annus (CA),* is the return to currency of that special term "the social question." It is now time, looking to the years beyond 1991, to pose three related questions; who asks? who answers? and what qualifies as the truly significant social question or questions to which the thinking Church ought to be addressing itself in the immediate future?

A curious preference for the singular, rather than specification in the plural, characterizes our employment over the past century of the term "the social question." Often the "question" is stated in quite broad, even ambiguous terms in the teaching documents that followed *RN*. This provides a rubric or canopy wide enough to cover a host of issues, but it also results in a loss of precision, and hence of impact, in relating Catholic social doctrine to contemporary social problems.

For *RN*, the social question focused on "The Condition of Labor," on the right of workers to form associations, to organize themselves into unions and other protective arrangements, against assaults on their human dignity from the new industrialization and the threat of socialism. The social concern of Pope Leo XIII was worldwide, but his preoccupation with and articulation of the social question was more narrow—centered on the nation state of Italy and mindful of the growing influence of socialism there. Not until 1971 did Catholic social doctrine explicitly acknowledge, in the words of Pope Paul VI, "Today the principal fact that we must

❖

all recognize is that the social question has become worldwide" (*Populorum Progressio [PP]*, §3).

It is a frustrating exercise, for minds that work the way mine does, to attempt to match up with the title of every major document in the body of Catholic social doctrine, the precise social question to which the document offers a response. The question is always general; so is the response. Whatever the question, the answer is usually framed in a few general principles accompanied by several general guidelines for programs consistent with the principles. For a universal teaching church, this is the way it should be, I suppose. Moreover, it would require considerable historical and textual analysis to attempt the after-the-fact match-up of question-and-answer that my more practically–and pedagogically-oriented mind would like to have.

When it comes, however, to the future of Catholic social teaching, I cannot help but wonder whether the times might not require more precision of the Church and its teachers, if Catholic social thought is to have greater, even decisive impact. I have in mind precision in the statement of the question and articulation of the principles, not in the outline of specific social programs. Clear questions and sharp principles will, I believe, generate effective programs the teachers would never think of themselves. Programs will be the work of well-informed practitioners in the political, economic, and social spheres.

Who then is to ask the social question? Who will answer? And what are the significant social questions of our time?

In the matter of Catholic social teaching, the Church asks, the Church answers, and the Church identifies the significant problems around which the questions turn. But the Church is a people on pilgrimage making progress by the light of faith. The people, both tutored and untutored, ordained and unordained, experience "the joys and the hopes, the griefs and the anxieties" referenced by Vatican Council II's *Pastoral Constitution on the Church in the Modern World*. Out of the experience of all and the perception of those whose minds are trained to "see" significant social problems, and out of a faith-based openness to both experience and insight, the Magisterium of the Church can, if it chooses to do so, shape and proclaim its social doctrine in the years ahead.

In a splendid book entitled *That They Be One,* Michael J. Schuck (1991) separates Catholic social thought into the pre-Leonine period (1740-1877), the Leonine period (1878-1958), and the post-Leonine period (1959-1989). Readers are encouraged to trace the application of Catholic social principles to: (a) religious practices, (b) political practices, (c) family practices, (d) economic practices, and (e) cultural practices. These categories suggest that elements of "the" social question at any time, indeed a parcel of specific and significant social questions crying for analysis and commentary, can be drawn by competent observers in the areas of religion, politics, family life, economics, and culture.

A teaching Church, not simply content but committed to listening and learning before it speaks out on social issues, would stimulate great intellectual activity in Catholic circles by inviting Catholic scholars to reflect upon and articulate the significant social questions in the areas of their competence. The invitation to articulate the social question should, like the more recent social encyclicals themselves, go out to all persons of good will. The Church in the modern world can hardly content itself to remain aloof from the best in modern scholarship wherever it originates.

Schuck examines the social teaching of papal encyclicals and ferrets out lines of coherence in the social doctrine they communicate from 1740 to the present. He finds that the "papal letters show serious interest in social relations involving not only economic affairs, but also political, religious, family, and cultural life." (p. 191) The papal letters share what Schuck calls "communitarian recommendations" and "persistent negative judgments." (p. 192) The judgments, of course, are rendered against the negative forces that produced the problems the respective encyclicals address. The "communitarian recommendations" are the popes' principled and positive answers to the social question as they and their advisers chose to frame it. The communitarian theme of the teaching is echoed in the title Schuck put on his book. As pastors and teachers, all the popes have the task of bringing God's people closer to the ideal expressed by Jesus in His prayer to the Father: "that they be one, even as we are one." (John 17:22) How to do this would be one way of stating the social question. Papal social teaching expresses, Schuck emphasizes, a communitarian view of both self and society.

Here are some instances of articulation of the social question at various stages in the history of Catholic social teaching. They can serve to stimulate the formation of social questions as the Church approaches the beginning of the 21st century.

At the most general level, the social question can be stated this way: How can the human community of persons and nations live together in peace secured by justice? The protection of fundamental human dignity requires that the question be asked at all times. The organization of human life requires that it be asked in the context of family, workplace, social interaction, civic, economic, religious, political (ranging from local to international politics), and cultural life.

Particular statements of the question appear in papal social teaching, usually not as questions so much as descriptions of conditions that threaten peace, violate justice, or assault human dignity. Here are some examples.

In *RN*, Pope Leo XIII spoke of the "enormous fortunes of individuals and the poverty of the masses." (§1) He pointed out that "The richer classes have many ways of shielding themselves, and stand less in need of help from the state; whereas the mass of the poor have no resources of their own to fall back upon, and must chiefly depend upon the assistance of the state." (§37) As Joseph Gremillion correctly points out, Leo XIII "recognized that the three key factors...underlying economic life are workers, productive property, and the state. Be also showed that their just and equitable interrelation is the crucial issue of Catholic social teaching" (1976, p. 27).

❖

Pope Pius XI in *Quadragesimo Anno (QA)* noted that "immense power and despotic economic domination is concentrated in the hands of a few." (§105)

Both these popes affirm the right to private property (over against socialism) and specify that workers possess the natural right of private ownership as well as the right to organize.

John XXIII wrote *Mater et Magistra (MM)* "to keep alive the torch lighted by our great predecessors and to exhort all to draw from their writings light and inspiration, if they wish to resolve the social question in ways more in accord with the needs of the present time." (§50) Those needs emerge from changes in the fields of science, technology, and economics, from political innovations, and from worldwide political and economic inter-dependence. Both socialization and intervention by public authorities were noted by Pope John to be on the increase worldwide. This pastoral pope thought it important to note in *MM* that "it is right and necessary for man to cease for a time from labor, not merely to relax his body from daily hard work and likewise to refresh himself with decent recreation, but also to foster family unity, for this requires that all its members preserve a community of life and peaceful harmony." (§250)

In *Pacem in Terris (PT)*, John XXXIX reviewed and reaffirmed the doctrine on economic and political rights while taking special note of the emergence of women in public life. "Since women are becoming ever more conscious of their human dignity, they will not tolerate being treated as inanimate objects or mere instruments, but claim, in domestic and in public life, the rights and duties that befit a human person." (§41)

Not surprisingly, and not a moment too soon, this 1963 papal letter opens up the question of disarmament. "Justice, right reason and humanity...urgently demand that the arms race should cease; that the stockpiles which exist in various countries should be reduced equally and simultaneously by the parties concerned; that nuclear weapons should be banned; and that a general agreement should eventually be reached about progressive disarmament and an effective method of control." (§112) In order to do this and to deal with other urgent problems of global proportions, Pope John suggests: "A public authority, having worldwide power and endowed with the proper means for the efficacious pursuit of its objective, which is the universal common good in concrete form, must be set up by common accord and not imposed by force." (§138)

When Pope Paul VI remarked in *PP* that the social question had become "worldwide," (§3) he was simply stating the obvious. Accordingly, Catholic social thought turned to the problems of economic development in the poorest parts of the world. "Today the peoples in hunger are making a dramatic appeal to the peoples blessed with abundance. The Church shudders at this cry of anguish and calls each one to give a loving response of charity to this brother's cry for help." (§3) Catholic social doctrine would soon frame this response in terms of justice and eventually liberation. "Development" would be widely accepted as the "new word for peace."

It is interesting to note Pope John Paul II's comment in *Laborem Exercens (LE)* that "human work is a key, perhaps the essential key, to the whole social question." (§3) But what specifically is that question? It must somehow relate to the protection of individual autonomy and dignity within a large complex society. Human work relates to dignity, provides an avenue of participation, generates income and thus economic security for the individual and the family, and in the process contributes to healthy psychological development. Viewed in that light, work may indeed be the "essential key" in unlocking the answer to the social question. It is worth noting that Pope John Paul II expressed this idea in an encyclical written to commemorate the 90th anniversary of the publication of *RN*.

In 1987, this same pontiff celebrated the 30th anniversary of *PP* by issuing an encyclical *On Social Concern (SS)* in which he suggests, not explicitly but the thought is there nonetheless, that the moral category of "solidarity" might well be the key to the social question. Solidarity—true inter-relatedness and inter-dependence among and between both persons and nations—is this pope's word for peace. "In a world divided and beset by every type of conflict, the conviction is growing of a radical interdependence and consequently of the need for a solidarity which will take up interdependence and transfer it to the moral plane." (§26)

All of this is just a sampling, not a complete inventory of statements of the social question over the years. Nothing has been drawn from *Humanae Vitae,* with its stress on family values, nor from the Second Vatican Council's document of "The Church in the Modern World" where much can be found to formulate fresh expressions of the social question. Similarly, various Synod documents would be useful in articulating the social question, as indeed would be statements of national bishops conferences, not least among them our own bishops' pastorals on peace and the economy. My intention is just to complete this sampler with some excerpts from *CA*, Pope John Paul II's century-after review "of new things" in the spirit of *RN*, and then move on to speculate about new and timely expressions of the social question.

"The United Nations... has not yet succeeded in establishing as alternatives to war effective means for the resolution of international conflicts," notes John Paul II in *CA*. He immediately adds: "This seems to be the most urgent problem which the international community has yet to resolve." (§21) Several paragraphs later he states: "What is needed are concrete steps to create or consolidate international structures capable of intervening through appropriate arbitration in the conflicts which arise between nations, so that each nation can uphold its own rights and reach a just agreement and peaceful settlement vis-a-vis the rights of others." (§27) This sounds very much like a formulation of the social question for our times, one hundred years after *RN*.

Returning to the five categories mentioned earlier, I want now to put them under the perennial or "canopy" statement of the social question, and then insert in each a formulation of a correspondingly significant social question for our time. The over-arching social question will, in my view, always be: *how can the human community of persons and nations live together in peace secured by justice?* The question rests on an unwavering commitment to and concern for the protection of human dignity. The question is at once personal and communitarian, national and international. It subdivides readily and applies easily to religious concerns, political life, family life, economic activities, and cultural life. Within each of these categories a genuine social question calls out for an answer. Simply listing the categories in this fashion serves to remind that the social question, and hence the Church's social doctrine, is not restricted to the economic dimension of human activity.

In the world of religion, I would frame the social question in terms of violence. Freedom of expression, and movement, and choice within a hierarchically structured religious body that respects freedom of conscience but restricts other freedoms for religious purposes would, I know, be identified by many as a more significant social question. I would disagree. I think religious misunderstanding lies at the root of much of the violence in our world. I also think religion's failure to communicate effectively a moral vision of respect for life results in widespread toleration of violence in countless forms among persons who claim to have strong religious commitments.

In the political arena there is always the question of participation—denied in totalitarian states, willfully neglected in democracies. But the pressing social question, I believe, is the one targeted by Pope John Paul II in *CA*, namely, the need to find an effective international device for the settlement of international differences.

In family life, the question, as I see it, is how to shore up the interpersonal commitments that make marriages permanent and thus create an environment of stability for family life, the bedrock of societal stability. Socially accented changes in household definitions and "relationships" must not be accepted as changes in the definition of family. The Church knows better and should never hesitate to say so in its social teaching.

The economic category, central to any discussion of social concerns, is a particularly challenging one when it comes to formulating the social question. Gaps between rich and poor around the world and around the corner cry out for remedy. There is an overemphasis on economic success in industrialized societies (a religious issue perhaps) and with it an excessive individualism that creates mischief not only in economic relationships, but family life as well. Compensation policies and practices are out of control in advanced countries; they remain remarkably free of meaningful links to productivity. As economic life grows more complex, the danger of damage to individual fulfillment and dignity rises accordingly. Both the economic organization and the task it exacts can stifle human initiative. Grinding poverty remains the basic cause of hunger in the world. There are economic culprits behind the environmental crisis. Full employment remains the best hope for economic security and social welfare in modern society. And all of this must be analyzed within historical currents that invite market-oriented mechanisms, balanced by appropriate state activity, to provide the solutions.

My formulation of the social question in the economic area would ask how we might contain the virus of materialism in the world community and in all of its separate political and familial parts. I raise the question at a time when we are losing, here in the United States, our sense of community, both national and conjugal. The materialism, not the "magic," of the marketplace is accelerating this loss of the sense of community and driving us in the direction of surrender to "forces" we cannot control.

Finally, the cultural category calls for an expression of the social question. I view culture not in Matthew Arnold's narrow sense of "the acquainting ourselves with the best that has been known and said in the world, and thus with the history of the human spirit." I prefer Bernard Lonergan's definition: "A culture is a set of meanings and values informing a common way of life, and there are as many cultures as there are distinct sets of meanings and values."

The dominant cultural value in the United States (and in much of the world) is an emphasis on material possessions to the exclusion of serious attachment to the immaterial domain where commitments and convictions reside, where spiritual realities like love, justice, and knowledge are rooted and grow. But I identified materialism as the social question in the economic sphere. In the cultural arena, I would attempt to phrase the social question in terms of the rights and dignity of women in contemporary society. I do not pretend to be able to pinpoint the right question, but neither do I think the attempt to state the question should not be made. Many persons, notably women, should be working now to get the question right so that the target is set for a timely response from Catholic social doctrine. To repeat a point I made at the outset: good social theory emerges when clear thinking engages itself with truly significant social questions. The women's question is of true and timely social significance. It must be phrased correctly, not in the sense of "political correctness," but with social, anthropological, historical, and theological sensitivity.

I noted in passing that Pope John XXIII made special mention of women in *PT* and remarked that women "will not tolerate being treated as inanimate objects or mere instruments, but claim, in domestic and public life, the rights and duties that befit a human person."

Recall that a culture is defined by a shared set of meanings and values. In the category of culture, therefore, the social question centering on women might be assembled from a set of questions like these: What is the meaning of woman in any society? Why is the value of woman an issue in contemporary society? Where is the balance for today's woman in asserting rights and assuming duties "that befit a human person?"

The issues raised by this line of inquiry spill over into all the other categories and touch the "canopy" question of peace and justice that will concern the Church in all ages. The women's question should be phrased properly and answered directly, even if not definitively, without delay.

I bring these reflections to a close with wise words from an unlikely source. Robert M. Pirsig, in *Zen and the Art of Motorcycle Maintenance* wrote:

I think that if we are going to reform the world and make it a better place to live in, the way to do it is not with talk about relationships of a political nature, which are inevitably dualistic, full of subjects and objects and their relationship to one another; or with programs full of things for people to do. I think that kind of approach starts it at the end and presumes the end is the beginning. Programs of a political nature are important end products of social quality that can be effective only if the individual values are right. The place to improve the world is first in one's own heart and head and hands, and then work outward from there. Other people can talk about how to expand the destiny of mankind. I just want to talk about how to fix a motorcycle. I think that what I have to say has more lasting value (1974, pp. 290-91).

Everyone in the Catholic faith community, whether they fix motorcycles, repair fractures, teach classes, write books, raise families, drive trucks, farm the land, run the parishes, or preside over corporations, has something to say at both the formulation and response end of the social question. Prompted by all the rest of us, the Magisterium will eventually ask; and assisted by those who can stake a claim on the attention of the teaching Church by virtue of the quality of what they contribute to asking and answering the social question, the Magisterium will eventually answer. Meanwhile, all of us—teachers and taught in the Church—can get on with the task of making sure our personal values are right, that we keep the commitments we make, that we respect life in all its forms, and that the territory between our ears and beneath our feet can, so far as it is in our power to choose, be marked by the reign of peace and justice.

*President of Catholic University of America, Washington, D.C., USA.

# References

Gremillion, Joseph. *The Gospel of Peace and Justice,* Maryknoll, NY: Orbis Books, 1976.

Pirsig, Robert M. *Zen and the Art of Motorcycle Maintenance,* NY: Morrow, 1974.

Schuck, Michael J. *That they Be One,* Washington, D.C.: Georgetown University Press, 1991.

---
❖
---

# Rich, Poor and Slave in the Socioeconomic Thought of the Later Church Fathers

## *Barry Gordon* *

In the early post-apostolic Church, the almost exclusive focus for socioeconomic thought and action by Christians was the local faith-community. As far as the wider society was concerned, its affairs were matters for the non-Christian powers-that-be.[1] Many patristic writings of the first three centuries A.D. display a belief in the existence of a wide gulf, even an opposition, between Christ and Culture.[2] The works of Tertullian, in particular, provide vehment expressions of that belief.

Attitudes were obliged to change, however, after the accession of the Emperor Constantine, and his Edict of Milan in A.D. 313. Now legitimised within the framework of Empire, many Christians rose quickly to positions of power and prominence. Church Fathers of the fourth and fifth centuries, some of whom had direct access to the powerful and prominent, felt the need to address social issues on a scale which their predecessors had found impossible, if not unthinkable. In the Eastern Empire, the leading figures in this respect are St. Basil the Great (330-379) and St. John Chrysostom (344-407). In the West, St. Ambrose of Milan (339-397) and St. Augustine of Hippo (354-430) are the most significant. The impact of Augustine, in particular, on Western thought over the succeeding centuries was especially profound.[3]

## I. Economic Decline and Monastic Growth

To appreciate the social and economic doctrines of these four writers it is necessary to recognise that in their day the long decline of the Roman economy was continuing apace. In addition, there was a measure of political disintegration in the West. Productive activities were progressively starved of capital, and there was a lack of innovation. Population numbers decreased, as did the mobility of labour. On the other hand, the burden of taxation in support of central government increased,

❖

together with the degree of concentration of ownership of land. The middle class was being squeezed to near extinction.[4] The beneficiaries of these trends were, a tiny elite which accumulated vast tracts of land; bureaucrats (both civilian and military); and, in all probability, slaves.[5] Freemen, of various ranks, were the losers.

Another trend of signal importance was the growth of the monastic ideal. Basil the Great brought monasticism out of the Desert into co-existence with the civilised structures of Empire. Such co-existence, it should be emphasised, did not mean integration. Monasticism was now in the Empire, but was definitely not of it.[6] Nevertheless, monasticism offered an accessible, alternate communal life-style, and a model of economic and social organisation that differed markedly from the traditional.

One of the Fathers, Chrysostom, promoted the monastic model as a vehicle for social reform. The others, however, did not regard it as a blueprint for institutional change. Augustine, for example, regarded the social life of the monasteries as a prefiguration of the life of the City of God that would be manifest only at the end of time.[7] That social life could not be expected to pertain generally inside time, since any human society was necessarily a conflict-ridden admixture of citizens belonging to either the earthly or the heavenly city.[8] For Augustine and the others, social improvement was to be achieved through greater attachment by individuals to Christ-inspired behaviour in their communal engagements. Here, the exemplary lives of Christian monks might play a social role in that they influenced the behaviour of other Christians.

Eschewing any direct assault on existing social structures, the Fathers sought social betterment through the extension to the wider society of the practice of local Christian communities since apostolic days. The key here was charity, in the sense of voluntary giving by individuals. Almsgiving, especially, was seen as the central element of a Christian response to economic problems. State action was not a serious option.[9]

## II. The Economic Problem

The Fathers were keenly aware of, and concerned with, the fact that grinding poverty was the lot of the many for most of the time. Yet, they saw no necessary reason why this should be so. Nature, they argued, is usually bountiful.[10] God gives material things abundantly, and God originally bestowed those things in common to humankind. St. Ambrose writes:

> Nature has poured forth all things for the common use of all men. And God has ordained that all things should be produced that there might be food in common for all, and that the earth should be the common possession of all. (*De officiis,* i, 132).

Production of what is needful for life is not a serious problem, and St. Basil assures his contemporaries, as follows:

❖

He who provided pasture for horses and cattle, thought of your riches
and pleasure.... He who feeds your cattle, will provide for all the needs
of your life. (*Hexameron*, V, 40D).

It follows that if society is experiencing scarcity and want, the sources of
these must lie in consumption and distribution. Scarcity is, generally, a man-made
phenomenon. The economic problem is essentially a moral problem rather than a
technical one, as the modern discipline of Economics would have it. Avarice is at
the root (cf. MacQueen, 1973). The exceptions are the occasional episodes of
famine and allied deprevation which are providential testings, trials, or exercises of
His people by God. Augustine argues:

Who could love us more than God does? Yet, He continually teaches
us sweetly, as well as frightens us for our good. Often adding the most
stinging medicine of trouble to the gentle remedies with which He
comforts us. He tries the patriarchs, even good and devout ones, by
famine... (*Letter* 93, to Vincent).[11]

Against this background, the Fathers analyse the circumstances of the two
economic classes of ancient society: the rich and the poor. Both of these groups
experience the pressures of scarcity, but the causes of those pressures differ
radically as between the two. In the case of the rich, scarcity is engendered by:
increasingly expanding consumption horizons, the desire to accumulate material
assets, the hoarding of money against future expected wants, and the drive for status
through wealth. Basil confronts his fellow, affluent Christians, as follows:

You say you are poor, and I agree with you; for anyone who needs a
great many things is poor, and you have a great many needs because
your desires are many and insatiable.... When they ought to rejoice and
give thanks that they are wealthier than so many others, they are
troubled and sad because some one is richer than they. When they have
equalled his wealth at once they try to reach the fortune of one still
richer (*In Divites*, 56C-57B).

Hence, the rich can solve their problem by purely personal means such as
moderation of consumption, and, above all, by ceasing to be covetous and
avaricious.
    The poor have no such options. The problem of scarcity has been thrust upon
them by institutionalised economic inequality. Such inequality is due to the
existence of the institution of private property, the covetousness of fallen humankind, and the misallocation of productive labour to activities which merely cater for
the superfluities of the rich.

❖

Given the predicament of the poor, the most obvious way of alleviating it is by voluntary transfer on the part of the rich of the surplus they enjoy. Basil asserts:

> For if each one after having taken from his wealth whatever would satisfy his personal needs, left what was superfluous to him who lacks every necessity, there would be neither rich nor poor (*In Illud Lucae*, 49D).

The rich must give alms, if the economic problem of the poor is to be eased, and the rich are to be freed from their self-imposed woes.

## III. Issues in Almsgiving

There are a number of arguments employed to urge almsgiving. The chief argument concerns the spiritual benefits which accrue to the rich.[12] Through almsgiving the rich can hope for salvation, and failure to perform adequately in this respect almost certainly ensures individual damnation. Augustine, for example, counsels:

> A life is not a happy one unless it is true, and it is not true unless it is eternal. We can clearly see that the rich do not yet possess this eternal life, through any delights whatever; hence they are counselled to lay hold on it through almsgiving, in order that they may at length hear: 'Come, blessed of my Father, take possession of the kingdom which has been prepared for you from the beginning of the world; for I was hungry and you gave me to eat' [Matt. 25: 34-5] (Sermon, 346).

Some of the Fathers add that the habit of almsgiving will be conducive to a happier life, in that it reduces attachment to consuming and hoarding. The imperative to give is also seen as according with a Christian notion of stewardship in respect of property rights. Chrysostom affirms:

> For you are steward of your own possessions, not less than he who dispenses the alms of the church. As then he has not a right to squander at random and at hazard the things given by you for the poor, since they were given for the maintenance of the poor; even so neither may you squander your own. For even though you have received an inheritance from your father, and have in this way all you possess; even thus, all are God's (*In Matthaeum*, 74, 4).

It is acknowledged further, although with less emphasis, that the fact that the poor benefit materially from alms is something of a consideration. Occasionally, a macroeconomic argument is employed, namely, that society as a whole will benefit materially from the transfer of surplus. Ambrose reasons:

How unprofitable for their city that so large a number should perish, who were wont to be helpful either in paying contributions or in carrying on business. Another's hunger is profitable to no man, nor to put off the day of help as long as possible and to do nothing to check the want. Nay more, when so many of the cultivators of the soil are gone, when so many labourers are dying, the corn supplies will fail for the future (*De officiis*, iii, 7).

This latter line of argument is only rarely encountered, although Basil employs it also. His context is positive, in economic terms. Basil writes:

As a great river flows by a thousand channels through fertile country so let your wealth run through many conduits to the homes of the poor. Wells that are drawn from flow the better; left unused, they go foul. So money kept standing still is worthless; moving and changing hands, it helps the community and brings increase (*In Illud Dictum Evangelii*, 3).[13]

The emphasis on almsgiving gives rise to a number of problems for the economic behaviour of rich Christians. A major issue is the question of how much should be given. The general answer to this is, all above the ordinary needs of life. Such an answer evokes the further question of whether those "ordinary needs" can be specified in an objective fashion or should be regarded as varying from person to person. The Fathers, generally, allow for variability, taking into account custom, upbringing, and social status. Augustine states:

Let the rich use what their infirmity has accustomed them to; but let them be sorry that they are not able to do otherwise. For it would be better for them if they could. If then the poor be not puffed up for his poverty, why shouldst thou for thine infirmity? Use then choice and costly meats, because thou art so accustomed, because thou canst not do otherwise, because if thou dost change thy custom thou art made ill. I grant thee this, make use of superfluities, but give to the poor inexpensive food (*Sermones*, 61, 12).

Augustine is even prepared to extend this principle of variability of the monastic life (see Letter 211, to the consecrated virgins; et cf. Zumkeller, 1986, p. 151). Chrysostom too advises flexibility, although his references are to the consumption of "pulse" as against "garden herbs", or (for the really weak) "flesh in moderation" (*In Epistolam II ad Corinthios*, 19, 3).

Appropriate consumption patterns represent only one aspect of the problem of almsgiving. Even more pertinent is the question of assets. To what extent should rich persons liquidate assets such as lands, houses, and slaves for conversion into

❖

alms? With the Greek Fathers and Ambrose it is difficult to make any clear assessment of their position.[14] However, Augustine is less opaque on this. Augustine is firmly attached to the principle of economic self-reliance, whether the institution concerned be a monastery or a family household. Hence, almsgiving should not be taken to the point where the maintenance of the working capital of the institution is threatened. Augustine writes:

> But when he [St. Paul the Apostle] spoke of almsgiving itself he said: 'Not that others should be eased and you burdened' [2 Cor. 8.13]. Therefore you should have regulated what treasure is to be laid up in heaven and what is to be left as a means of support for yourselves, your dependents and your son, so that other men be not eased and you burdened (*Letter* 262, to Ecdicia).

He returns to this point concerning maintenance of capital on numerous occasions (see, e.g., *On the Psalms*, ps. 147, 13; *Letter* 130, to Proba; *Letter* 220, to Boniface). An obvious influence here is the economics of the epistles of St. Paul. Augustine's own straightened and non-aristocratic social origins may also have played a part in his forming this view.[15]

On and beyond the question of how much to give in alms is the question of how discriminating one should be in giving. In general, each of the Fathers can be said to allow some measure of discrimination, although emphases vary (cf. Grant, 1978, p. 131). Of the four, it is Augustine who is the most explicit on the need for care. He reasons:

> When He [Jesus] says: 'Give to everyone who asks' He does not say: 'Give him everything he asks'; for you are to give in accordance with propriety and justice.... You are to give whatever will not be injurious to you or to someone else, insofar as that can be humanly forseen or conjectured (*Commentary on the Sermon on the Mount*, 1, 20, 67).

Augustine also draws a distinction between persons who should be sought out as objects of charity, and persons who approach potential donors for alms. In the first case, the relevant dictum is: "Let your alms sweat in your hand until you find a righteous man to whom to give." In the second case, it is "Give to everyone who asks of you." Charitable responsibility varies as between the two (See, *On the Psalms*, ps. 147, 13).

## IV. The Communistic Alternative

St. John Chrysostom is a staunch advocate of almsgiving as a practical response to the situation of the poor, given the prevailing social framework.[16] However, he does not rest at this point. Chrysostom believes that a fundamental

❖

solution can be achieved through communal ownership of property by Christians. What can be brought forward in support of this radical change?

In the first place, the change appears to be in accord with the *Book of Genesis* where God is depicted as bestowing resources in common to humankind. This latter is a patristic commonplace. "The world", Chrysostom observes, "is meant to be like a household wherein all the servants receive equal allowances, for all men are equal, since they are brothers" (*On II Cor.*, xii). Further, reorganisation of Christian society in such terms is commended by the economic behaviour of the primitive church in Jerusalem, as reported by Luke in *Acts*. Flying in the face of the evidence of the Pauline epistles, Chrysostom affirms that the Jerusalem Christians fared well materially. He asserts (*In Acta*, 11, 3) that, "by selling their possessions they did not come to be in need."

Also favouring communal ownership was the contention that this would eliminate the spiritual dangers to individuals associated with the private possession of property. Further, society as a whole would benefit by a reduction in the degree of internal conflict. "People", Chrystom observes, "do not quarrel about what is common to all" (*On II Cor.*, xii). Again, communism would reduce the real per capita cost of living.[17]

Speculation apart, Chrysostom pointed to the great practical exemplar of monasticism as proof of the benefits of communal ownership. For him, the material as well as the spiritual benefits of adopting the monastic model were obvious. He affirms:

> The dwellers in the monasteries live just as the faithful did then [i.e., in Jerusalem]; now did ever any of these die in hunger? Was ever any of them not provided for with plenty of everything? (*In Acta*, 11, 3)

The combination of Scriptural direction and current evidence concerning the economic rationality of the monastic pattern led Chrysostom to urge his urban congregations to institutional reform along the lines indicated.[18]

Other prominent Fathers do not share Chrysostom's enthusiasm. There were a number of arguments (some of which were enunciated by Chrysostom himself) to tell against his, or any other type of, restructuring of existing social arrangements. Inequality, and hence poverty, it could be claimed, was providential, i.e., allowed to persist by God who turns temporal evils to good results. A most eloquent exposition of this claim was undertaken by Chrysostom. He asserted:

> For if with a fitting knowledge and with well considered reflection, you were willing to examine this point too, even if there were nothing else which confirms the providence of God, riches and poverty would evince this most clearly. For if you take away poverty you would take away the whole basis of life, and you would destroy our [manner] of life, neither will there be sailor, nor pilot, nor farmer, nor mason, nor

❖

weaver, nor shoemaker,... nor any other of these workers; and if these did not exist, all things would perish for us. For now, like the best kind of mistress, the compulsion of poverty, sits on each of these, and drives them to work even against their will (*De Anna*, 5, 3).

Further, the existence of the poor was providential in that it provided the opportunity for almsgiving, leading to salvation for the rich. Augustine preaches:

The poor to whom we give alms! With regard to us, what else are they but porters through whom we transfer our goods from earth to heaven? Give away your treasure. Give it to a porter. He will bear to heaven what you give him on earth (*Sermon*, 60).

Again, poverty was seen as conducive to salvation for the poor. Their situation compelled them to work, thus freeing them from the host of temptations associated with idleness.

Private property ownership, itself, could be regarded as part of the providential ordering of society. In Augustine's view, the acquisition of property relates to what is natural to man, but the right to continue to hold the property acquired relates to the power of kings.[19] This power has been bestowed providentially and is not to be questioned.[20] Augustine writes:

It is, however, by human right that someone says, this estate is mine, this house is mine, this servant is mine. Human right, therefore, means the right of the emperors. Why so? Because God has distributed these very rights to mankind through the emperors and kings of this world.... It is by rights derived from kings that possessions are enjoyed (*In Iohan. ev. tr.* 6, 1, 25-6).

Kings then, bestow civil rights. One of the most important of these is individual property ownership. Thus, private possession is bound up with God's providential care for fallen humankind. Ambrose too finds Providence at work.[21]

## V. The Institution of Slavery

Nothing is better illustrative of the Fathers' attitude to social reform than their writings and activities with respect to slavery. With the possible exception of St. Gregory of Nyssa, the brother of Basil, none of them contend that slavery is wrong in principle.[22] In this respect, the teaching of St. Paul the Apostle was influential, as were the household codes of the epistles of the New Testament.

Some of the Fathers put forward arguments in support of slavery as an institution. On the other hand, there are instances of advocacy of emancipation as a thoroughly Christian act. There is also evidence of practical steps being taken to secure the release of slaves, or to prevent free persons being reduced to that condition.

Ambrose is one author who is prepared to justify the continuation of the institution. He argued, as did the Stoics, that a person's legal status is a secondary consideration with respect to true freedom. It is the person who is wise and good that is free. Ambrose also observes that it is probably better for weak characters to be slaves. He adds that the condition of slavery is conducive to the development of certain personal virtues (Dudden, 1935, pp. 544-45).

Augustine locates the bases for slavery in sin, as with the biblical Ham, or in adversity, as with the biblical Joseph. Slavery can be justly imposed on sinners, and it can be to their benefit. This status is not proper to the nature of humankind as originally created. There are no persons who are slaves by nature, as Aristotle and some of the other ancients claimed. Nevertheless, slavery is encompassed in God's providence.[23]

For Augustine, the ownership of slaves is a matter of civil rights. Just as in the case of property rights in general, it is a question of the king's authority and his laws. Slavery is a useful social institution which helps ensure the preservation of order in human society where chaos is an ever-present threat (See, e.g., *De civ. dei,* XIX, 15). God's providence brings good, namely, a measure of earthly peace, out of the evil of slavery.[24]

Against such sentiments, Gregory of Nyssa may be interpreted as coming out in a full frontal attack on slavery as an institution. In his fourth homily on *Ecclesiastes,* Gregory declares that, according to divine precept, no person can own another. He states:

> For you have subjected one who was made precisely to be lord of the earth, and whom the Creator intended to be a ruler, to the yoke of slavery, in resistance to and rejection of His divine precept.... Your rulership has been limited to the extent, namely, that you may only have ownership over brute animals (*Fourth Homily on Ecclesiastes;* P. G. 44, 665-7).

That slavery as an institution is at question here can be contested. Perhaps he is referring only to the attempt to master the soul of another. Gregory does not explicitly ask slave owners to engage in emancipation.[25]

## VI. Initiatives for Emancipation

One Father to call for emancipation is John Chrysostom. He shocked his congregation by advocating (*On I Corinthians,* 40, 6) that Christians should provide an education in a craft for their slaves, and then free them. However this does not amount to an attack on the institution of slavery as being repugnant in principle. Chrysostom is not averse to Christian masters retaining one or two

❖

domestic slaves, but he urges them divest themselves of excessive numbers. His chief concern is to urge the masters to a simpler life-style more conducive to their salvation.

For Chrysostom then, the freeing of a slave is not an issue in social justice. Rather, it is an act of piety or charity. Slaves are capital, and to shed this wealth voluntarily is a praiseworthy ascetical practice.[26]

In the case of Augustine, there is evidence that he took practical steps to free slaves, and used church money to redeem them.[27] As the economic situation in Numidia worsened, he was very active in trying to prevent free persons being sold to the slave traders (see, e.2., V.H.C. Frend 1983b, p. 500). He thoroughly detested these latter, classifying them with usurers (see, *On the Psalms*, pp. 127, 11). Augustine also encouraged released slaves to enter the monastic life, and his *Rule* for that life requires such persons to be treated in just the same way as freemen. Such equality is mandatory for a communal organisation which prefigures the City of God. It is not mandatory for the ordinary life of Empire.

## VII. Socioeconomic Reform

With the exception of Chrysostom, the Fathers did not put any great weight on the direct restructuring of existing institutional frameworks to promote a greater measure of social justice. In this sense, social reform played little part in the patristic agenda.[28] Such reform appears to be either outside their scope of vision or deemed no part of Christ-inspired social action. Rather, they fostered monasticism as an alternate communal life-style and urged almsgiving as the major means of response to economic inequities. Further, in urging almsgiving, and as in the case of the release of slaves, the Fathers' chief emphasis is on the spiritual benefits accruing to the individual who undertakes such action. The effect on the recipient of the benefit is a minor matter by comparison.

Were the leading Fathers totally insensitive to institutional reform to improve the lot of the disadvantaged? Certainly, to a man they were vehement in their opposition to the institution of lending at interest, which Roman law continued to sanction (cf. R. P. Maloney 1973; et idem, 1972). Again, some concern is displayed on the subject of taxation. Basil affirms the principle of ability to pay as a basis for such levies and he also seeks tax exemption for charitable institutions (see Reilly 1945, pp. 96 and 109). In a letter to one Romulus (*Letter* 247), Augustine protests at a case of double taxation of the poor. Further, a passage in the *City of God* (Bk. V, 17) might be interpreted as a general call for a progressive taxation system (cf. Chadwick, 1987, p. 156).

Such isolated instances aside, there would seem to be general scholarly agreement with the judgement of Gerhart Ladner (1959, p. 463) that, "St. Augustine did not envisage a reform of the socioeconomic order as such. In fact, since the Christianization of the Roman Empire not one of the Fathers ... expect a universal change of economic and social conditions to result from the preaching of Christian

❖

morality." Chrysostom, as we have seen, might be accounted something of an exception here. In his view, "separate monasteries should exist now, in order that one day the whole world might become like a monastery (Florovsky, 1957, p. 149)."

It can be claimed, however, that, in the West, certain of Augustine's conceptions concerning creation, history, and the relationships of the spiritual and material contributed significantly to the eventual emergence of the idea of reform. Ladner (1954, p. 873) observes that, "the Augustinian impulse had abiding and recurrent strength. It was not to a small part thanks to it, that by the end of the Middle Ages the west had achieved a considerably greater measure of integration of personal-spiritual and sociative-institutional reform than the Christian east."[29] It may also be claimed that the type of outlook on social issues adopted by Augustine retains a certain modern relevance. James Schall (1984, p. 48) writes:

> St. Augustine provides certain basic correctives that are necessary if the kind of 'development' possible to man and professed by modern politicians and thinkers in fact is to take place. To put it another way, the major causes of continued underdevelopment are the ideologies that promise a this-worldly, perfect human society. St. Augustine's sense of the possible, the awareness of the real condition of men, prevents the kind of absolutism that has often gained dominance over ethical development theory, usually in the name of correcting real evils.

Augustine places the development of individual persons at the centre of any process of socio-economic betterment. His observation — "a people is an assemblage of reasonable beings bound together by common agreement as to the objects of their love.... It will be a superior people in proportion as it is bound together by higher interests, inferior in proportion as it is bound together by lower" (*De civ. dei*, XIX, 24) — remains as true in the contemporary world as in his own.

## Endnotes

*University of Newcastle, New South Wales, Australia.

[1] "We have, I think, great difficulty in imagining the degree to which these early Christians were cut off from most of the social and political life of the world which surrounded them, and, as a result, the extent to which they lived their lives within the confines of their own fellowship of Christian believers, the *ecclesia*, . . . They had to develop their own independent institutions for resolving disputes, for education, and for carrying on such welfare functions as the care of widows, orphans, the poor, and the sick" (Deane, 1973, pp. 420-21.)

❖

² "There was no direct road from the Early Church to social action and what would now be called 'contemporary relevance'" (Davies, in Ellis and Wilcox 1969, p. 40; cf. also Florovsky, 1957, esp. pp. 134-137).

³ "If Whitehead exaggerated only pardonably little in describing Western philosophy as a series of footnotes to Plato, one could point to similar relationship between Christian thought and Augustine" (McEvoy, 1984, p. 574).

⁴ A very comprehensive study of these trends is Jones (1964). See also, Jones (1974) and Cochrane (1957), esp. pp. 141-352.

⁵ On the improvement in the position of the slave class, see, Corcoran (1984), pp. 1-16, 19-36. Corcoran points out that the improvement had little to do with Christianity.

⁶ "The monastic movement represents a way of preserving the earlier sense of alienation from the outward world, only now through an inward, spiritual exodus that does not bring the monk into political confrontation with the reigning social (or ecclesiastical) order" (Rosemary R. Ruether, 1975, p. 257). See also, Florovsky (1957), p. 146.

⁷ ". . . the monastery becomes a symbolic abolition of the antagonism between the different classes of men, and an anticipation of the eternal Sabbath when all injustice will disappear, and all human lordship is annihilated and God is all in all" (Corcoran, 1985, p. 51). See also, Zumkeller (1986), p. 191.

⁸ "Augustine argues that many of the social structures within which we live — indeed all of those that are external, institutional, and coercive rather than spontaneous and communal — are what we deserve because of our own sinful tendencies . . ." (Tesselle, 1974, p. 33). On the implications of this view for the idea of social reform, see, O'Connell (1954), pp. 297-309.

⁹ With the Fathers: "The role of the state in comparison with the vision offered by the classical Greek thinkers has been sharply reduced . . . no longer is it [the state] directly concerned with promoting the good life for its citizens or the highest values of morality and civilization" (Deane, 1973, p. 425).

¹⁰ "One finds in nature alone or in nature aided by art all that is required for one's survival and nuture. [See, *De civitate Dei*, XXII, 24]. If nature were stingy and failed to supply material goods in sufficient abundance, human beings would necessarily be drawn into a life and death struggle for their possession, war and crime would become inevitable, and the goal of virtue would prove illusory. But then one could no longer be blamed for one's wicked deeds and God's wisdom and goodness would be shown to be at fault" (Fortin, 1984, p. 1990).

¹¹ Basil argued in similar fashion during the great drought of 368 in Asia Minor. Cf., Fox (1939), pp. 7-10.

¹² Almsgiving, "is characterized less as a work whose motivation is the alleviation of social ills than as a profoundly spiritual exercise. So it is that its thrust is rather heavily donor-centered. . . . There are very few sympathetic depictions of the underprivileged, portraying them as human beings with particular needs and desires of their own, as

persons in their own right . . ." (Ramsey, 1982, pp. 252-3). An attempt at a reply to this assessment is, Fitzgerald (1989), pp. 445-60. In favour of Ramsey's assessment, it can be remarked that the attitude to the poor which he notes asserted itself quite early in post-apostolic literature. See, Vasey (1986).

[13] Asterius of Amasea, on the basis of practical legal experience, finds that poverty is anti-social in the wider sense in that it contributes to the incidence of crime. See, Vasey (1986).

[14] With Ambrose, for example, there is, "all the old Roman respect for a landed estate inherited from one's fore-fathers. Such property is almost a part of the family, and to dispose of it lightly or to sell it for money seems to him a kind of sacrilege" (Dudden, 1935, p. 549).

[15] Robert M. Grant (1978, p. 113) notes the contrast in the attitude of St. Augustine and that of the Greek Fathers. He writes: "Only Augustine, who had more respect for private property, was the son of a poor freeman. Augustine's philosophical quest led him to Academic Skepticism indeed, but never to the Cynicism affected by Gregory of Nazianzus. . . . The attitude of these [Greek] fathers toward private property was based on Christian asceticism, pagan rhetoric, and upper-class disdain for mere wealth."

[16] With Chrysostom, "fasting takes the last place in the hierarchy of virtues. The greatest are charity and equity and almsgiving — these hit a higher mark even than the virtue of virginity" (Musurillo, 1956, p. 9). Chrysostom followed the example of Basil in establishing a variety of charitable organizations. See Constantelos (1968), pp. 155-56.

[17] As a standard of living for all Christians, Chrysostom wanted, "decent poverty — something that then, as now, was looked on as a special way of life for monks and ascetics, whereas it really is the ideal that Christ's gospel recommends to all" (Attwater, 1959, p. 67).

[18] "While for St. Basil the thought that man cannot be saved if he does not work for his neighbor's salvation had become the great justification of the coenobitical as against the hermitical ideal of monasticism, St. John Chrysostom Church . . . apart from the privilege of marriage, the Christian who lived in the world had the same obligations as the monk" (Ladner, 1959, pp. 126-27).

[19] Note, however, that Augustine also employs a "right use" theory of property rights, at times. On this, see MacQueen (1972).

[20] ". . . the Christian as resident and citizen of the earthly city is obliged to respect civil authority, even the tyrant and the persecutor since 'power and dominion are not given to such men', Nero for example, 'save by the providence of the most high God' [C. D, V, 19]" (Lavere, 1983, pp. 7-8).

[21] For Ambrose, property "became a remedy for concupiscence, a brake on cupidity. It is a means of satisfying needs and remedying, moderating and regulating fallen man's disorderly desires" (Vasey, 1982, p. 113).

❖

[22] "Modern scholars are almost unanimous in minimizing the effect of Christianity on the decline of slavery in the Roman Empire. The real causes of this decline turn out to be political, social and economic rather than religious or moral" (Corcoran, 1984, pp. 1-2).

[23] ". . . though it is but a by-product, the institution of slavery was not introduced independently of the providence of God. Everyone who is a slave, is justly a slave" (Corcoran, 1985, p. 71). See also, Markus (1965), pp. 71-76.

[24] Te Selle (1988, pp. 92-93) comments that here, Augustine's "vision is like that of modern Malthusians or Social Darwinists or champions of market capitalism who are able to contemplate individual catastrophe with equanimity, precisely out of appreciation for the smooth and productive functioning of the system as a whole."

[25] C.f., Corcoran (1984), pp. 8-9. Corcoran adds that: "The institution of slavery had given ascetics and monks a clear model on which to build their lives" (p. 32). Cf. also, Dennis (1982), pp. 1065-72; and, Maxwell (1975), pp. 30-44. Fox (1939, p. 46) observes with respect to Gregory's brother that, "St. Basil's parents had many slaves working on their large estate and that the Saint himself owned slaves . . . . On the whole, we find surprisingly few references to slavery in the works of St. Basil. We may assume that the Saint accepted it as an established institution."

[26] The Fathers in general "saw the manumission of slaves as an act of charity or even more as an act of asceticism, which was performed for the good of the master rather than for that of the slave" (Corcoran, 1985, p. 47).

[27] The purchase and release of slaves was also a practice in the East. See, Attwater (1959), p. 71.

[28] "Reform of society, even as a sign of preparation for the Coming, proved to be beyond the imagination of the time. To Augustine, the powers that be were 'the most authorized' (ordinatissimae) by God, and to desire a change in the status quo was the hallmark of the heretic. For him to think that his Lord had shown that the Kingdom would be established by destroying many of the moulds accepted by society would have seem altogether fanciful" (Frend, 1983, p. 71). On the failure of the Eastern fathers to promote reform, see Constantelos (1968), p. 284.

[29] Amongst the features of Augustine's thought which may be relevant in the above respect are his promotion of a linear conception of history, his emphasis on the role of work in Christian life, and his appreciation of the place of "the arts" in the enhancement of both economy and society.

## References

Attwater, Donald. *St. John Chrysostom, Pastor and Preacher,* London: Harvill Press, 1959.

Chadwick, Henry. "Providence and the Problem of Evil in Augustine," *Congresso Internazionale Su S. Agostino Nel XVI Centenario Della Conversione,* 1987, *I,* 153-62.

Cochrane, Charles Norris. *Christianity and Classical Culture*, New York: Oxford University Press, 1957.

Constantelos, D.J. *Byzantine Philanthropy and Social Welfare*, Rutgers University Press, 1968.

Corcoran, Gervase. "The Christian Attitude to Slavery in the Early Church," *Milltown Studies*, 1984, *13-14*, 1-16; 19-36.

_____. *Saint Augustine on Slavery*, Rome: Institutum Patristicum Augustinianum, 1985.

Davies, W.D. "The Relevance of the Moral Teaching of the Early Church," in E. Earle Ellis and Max Wilcox eds., *Neotestamentica et Semitica*, Edinburgh: Clark, 1969, 30-49.

Deane, Herbert A. "Classical and Christian Political Thought," *Political Theory*, 1973, *1*, 415-25.

Dennis, T.J. "The Relationship Between Gregory of Nyssa's Attack on Slavery in his Fourth Homily on Ecclesiastes and his Treatise De Hominis Opificio," *Studia Patristica*, 1982, *XVII*, Part 3, 1065-72.

Dudden, F. Homes. *The Life and Times of St. Ambrose*, Oxford: Clarendon Press, 1935, *II*.

Fitzgerald, Allan. "Almsgiving in the works of Saint Augustine," in Adolar Zumkeller ed., *Signum Pietatis*, Wurzburg: Augustinus-Verlag, 1989, 445-60.

Florovsky, Georges. "Empire and Desert: Antinomies of Christian History," *Greek Orthodox Theological Review*, 1957, *3*, 133-59.

Fortin, Ernest. "Augustine, the Arts, and Human Progress," in Carl Mitcham and Jim Grote eds., *Theology and Technology*, Lanham: University Press of America, 1984, 193-208.

Fox, Margaret Mary. *The Life and Times of St. Basil the Great as Revealed in His Works*, Washington: Catholic University of America Press, 1939.

Frend, W.H.C. "Early Christianity and Society," *Harvard Theological Review*, 1983a, *76*, 53-71.

_____. "The Divjak Letters," *Journal of Ecclesiastical History*, 1983b, *34*, 497-512.

Grant, Robert M. *Early Christianity and Society*, London: Collins, 1978.

Jones, A.H.M. *The Later Roman Empire*, 284-602, Oxford: Blackwell, 1964, *3*.

_____. *The Roman Economy*, Oxford: Blackwell, 1974.

Ladner, Gerhart B. "St. Augustine's Conception of the Reformation of Man to the Image of God," in *Augustinus Magister; Congres International Augustinien*, Paris: Etudes Augustiniennes, 1954, 867-78.

_____. *The Idea of Reform*, Cambridge, Mass.: Harvard University Press, 1959.

Lavere, George J. "The Problem of the Common Good in Saint Augustine's Civitas Terrena," *Augustinian Studies*, 1983, *14*, 1-10.

Maloney, R.P. "Early Conciliar Legislation on Usury," *Recherches De Théologie Ancienne et Médiévale*, 1972, *39*, 145-57.

_____. "The Teaching of the Fathers on Usury," *Vigilae Christianne*, 1973, *27*, 241-65.

Markus, R.A. "Two Conceptions of Political Authority," *Journal of Theological Studies*, 1965, *17*, 68-100.

Maxwell, John F. *Slavery and the Catholic Church*, Chichester and London: Barry Rose Publishers, 1975.

McEvoy, James. "St. Augustine's Account of Time and Wittgenstein's Criticisms," *The Review of Metaphysics*, 1984), *37*, 547-78.

MacQueen, D.J. "St. Augustine's Concept of Property Ownership," *Recherches Augustiniennes*, 1972, *8*, 187-229.

_____. "Contemptus Dei: St Augustine on the Disorder of Pride in Society, and its Remedies," *Recherches Augustiniennes*, 1973, *9*, 227-93.

Musurillo, Herbert. "The Problem of Ascetical Fasting in the Greek Patristic Writers," *Traditio*, 1956, *12*, 1-64.

O'Connell, James. "The Social Philosophy of St. Augustine," *Irish Ecclesiastical Record*, 1954, *82*, 297-309.

Osiek, C. "Wealth and Poverty in the Shepherd of Hermas," *Studia Patristica*, 1982, *XVII*, 2, 725-30.

Ramsey, Boniface. "Almsgiving in the Latin Church: the Late Fourth and Early Fifth Centuries," *Theological Studies*, 1982), *43*, 226-59.

Reilly, Gerald F. *Imperium and Sacerdotium According to St. Basil the Great*, Washington: Catholic University of America Press, 1945.

Ruether, Rosemary R. "Augustine and Christian Political Theology," *Interpretation*, 1975, *29*, 252-65.

Schall, James V. *The Politics of Heaven and Hell*, Lanham: University of America Press, 1984.

Te Selle, Eugene. *Augustine's Strategy as an Apologist*, Villanova University Press, 1974.

_____. "Towards an Augustinian Politics," *Journal of Religious Ethics*, 1988, *16*, 87-108.

Vasey, Vincent R. *The Social Ideas in the Works of St. Ambrose*, Rome: Institutum Patristicum Augustinianum, 1982.

_____. "The Social Ideas of Asterius of Amasea," *Augustinianum*, 1986, *26*, 413-436.

Zumkeller, Adolar. *Augustine's Ideal of the Religious Life,* New York: Fordham University Press, 1986.

# The Bishops' Pastoral Letter and the Poverty Problem: Early vs. Contemporary Concerns and Doctrines (Abstract)

*Bruce J. Malina and Thomas O. Nitsch\**

In their Pastoral Letter on Catholic Social Teaching and the U.S. Economy (NCCB, *Economic Justice for All*, 1986) the Catholic bishops of the U.S.A. drew upon biblical and early-church sources and themes in arguing the essential immorality of the poverty condition in this country. In other words, they sought in those earlier contexts and formulas the bases — doctrines, principles, etc. — for condemning the current situation and founding the exigency of its amelioration. Yet, when one examines carefully the relevant texts of the past, including secular-philosophical and popular writings, one finds the following themes to be the more salient: (1) the axiomatic wickedness of the rich, and consequently their difficulty in gaining "the Kingdom," or being happy; and, (2) the fact that, apart from natural disasters and wars impoverishing whole tribes, individuals as such would not suffer permanently injurious poverty, deprivation, etc. as we know it — i.e., God or nature would always provide sufficient for an adequately human subsistence.

Poverty in the U.S. is perceived and assessed in terms of a free-standing social institution called economics, and is focused through "the economy." What we call today economic activity and economics in those times and places was embedded in the two free-standing and dominant institutions of polity and kinship. The orphan, widow and stranger in the land were without these "social safety nets," axiomatically. Our poor are generic, cutting across such categories, and (according to some social analysts) forming their own "subculture." In addressing this problem in terms of the societal paradigm we employ, the Bishops draw on their influence to persuade (primarily) those in the polity to exercise their power in coercing necessary, remedial changes in the economy or "wealth" institution. Their primary

❖

focus is the sinfulness of the structures which give rise to the socially scandalous situation they address. The Bible, early Church Fathers, et al., on the other hand, pointed to the inherent wickedness or sinfulness of the rich as persons. It is one thing to condemn institutions, quite another to — in effect — pronounce damnation on individuals.

A conclusion reached earlier by Malina (1985) is repeated:

> So long as even one rich person is judged to be 'good,' and so long as even a single person dies of starvation, then we do not share the social scenarios that invest our biblical texts with the meaning they have.... Given the perception of limited good and an embedded economy, the Gospel injunction to give one's goods to the poor is not about self-impoverishment, but about redistribution of wealth; and motives for giving to the poor are not rooted in self-satisfying charity, but in God-ordained, socially required restitution.

*The authors are, respectively, Professor of Theology and Professor of Economics, Creighton University. An earlier version of the present paper was presented at the Fourth World Congress of Social Economics, Toronto, ON (Canada), August 13-15, 1986. A published version appears in *Humanomics*, 7: 2 (1991), pp. 40-70.

# Christian Anthropology as a Foundation for a New Economics

## Giuseppe Gaburro*

In this paper I will discuss the evolution of economic thought concerning the relation between ethics and economics. I will try to introduce the meaning of Christian anthropology as a foundation for a new economics. The uneasy relationship between ethics and economics is not new, not something limited to our own time, but is rooted in man's earliest reflections on economic matters.

## I. From Classicism to Modernism: Aristotle – Adam Smith

With the term "ethos," the Greeks underscored the abode of the spirit in man, and from that time every human action came to be submitted to the judgment of what is good or evil for man. The notion that there exists an intimate connection between ethics and economics prevailed until the beginning of the modern period, when there was a rupture between the two disciplines. From this point on, there was an attempt to separate economic action from ethical judgment.

The triumph of the ethical vision of economics came about with the development of Scholastic thought. An actual expression of this vision is the concept of "justice in price," derived from the principle of "trade exchange" and the need to impede illicit enrichment at the expense of the weakest. The principal difference between the Scholastic view and the subsequent individualistic view resides in the criterion by which to establish what is right and what is wrong. While in the Middle Ages the "just price" had satisfied human needs according to a social point of view (that is, the "communis aestimatio"), in the "laissez faire" concept, such a satisfaction comes about according to an individualistic point of view creating a need for fairness in the system. In this way, what is right arises from the free play of market forces.

With Nicolò Machiavelli and Jean Bodin, politics became secularized; that is, it became detached from theology and was provided with its own rules of play. According to these new rules, man's behavior is guided by necessity rather than by virtue. What happens to politics is also true for economics, because it fell under

❖

politics until Adam Smith; in both areas, religion has been relegated to a narrower and narrower sphere (Giovanni Tondini 1990, pp. 509-10). Thus, the Scholastic vision, an organic vision based on the hierarchy of values, was shattered.

Notwithstanding several attempts to introduce ethical elements, economic thought remains substantially resistant to religion, and businessmen increasingly bow to the principle that "business is business," with no pretext whatsoever of being inspired or guided by religious principles or rules of good conscience (R. Tawney 1967, p. 26).

All this was possible thanks to the different vision of man that emerged with the Renaissance and which asserted itself in the following centuries. If the Saint was the model that inspired every man in the Middle Ages, after the Renaissance man was inspired by Prometheus. The Saint is a man who spends his life for a greater purpose: he considers perfection as the unity of all human elements in God. Prometheus, on the other hand, is the prototype of the man who considers personal success to be an absolute value to be followed. He looks for his own gain, moved by self-interest; and, even if he sometimes looks for honor and glory, these are only a medieval vestige. The secularization of the aspiration of man's heart is thereby realized (Tondini 1990, p. 511).

If this is possible, it could be accomplished, according to the pre-Enlightenment scholar, Pierre Bayle, by a society of atheists, i.e. a society that needs neither proper virtues nor religion to subsist. This fact overturns Pascal on the possibility that a society not based on love, and therefore intrinsically guilty, could function well without retaining the idea of the hand of Divine Providence. The English transposition of this line of thought came about with Adam Smith, whose "invisible hand" attempts to explain, in terms of economic theory, the fundamental idea that the balance of egoism can generate a nonexistent ethical life. In essence, this theory offers the benefit of a virtuous existence, without any moral-philosophical intention aside from a purely utilitarian one. "It is not from the benevolence of the butcher, the brewer, or the baker that we expect our dinner, but from their regard to their own interest" (Smith 1937, p. 14).

In Aristotelian thought, the natural-harmonious vision of the complexity of interest is seen as a hierarchy that can change according to times and circumstances. According to St. Thomas, in addition to the inclination for self-preservation, there are in man other fundamental inspirations; viz., toward preservation of the species, toward social and political solidarity, toward truth, and thus toward knowledge of the ultimate cause of all things, that is, toward God (Thomas Aquinas 1975, pp. 1-4). In this vision, the real problem of utilitarianism is a problem of hierarchy among inclinations or, rather, among possible goods. The exact opposite of the vision of natural law lies in the antinomies which may be summarized in the expression "mors tua vita mea"; i.e., "Your death, my life."

We have here pointed out that the harmony of interests, so convincingly rationalized by Smith (1937, p. 423), is the result of that automatic and natural mechanism which is the competitive market, alias the "invisible hand." The

❖

necessary condition for a good performance of the market is that the subjects adhere to a precise ethical code of behavior, the so-called mercantile morality, characterized by values such as honesty (maintaining commitments) and trust (believing that others are honest) (Stefano Zamagni 1988, p. 3).

While this cultural operation may give the impression of freeing man from morality, it simultaneously betrays the futility of efforts to separate our two disciplines; for, economics already contains, at the level of embryo, a form of ethic: the "utilitarian" ethic.

In fact, economic action, moved by self-interest, is oriented to good, so it is no longer necessary to make selfishness submit to higher ends.

## II. Efforts to Reach the Dominant Approach

The reactions to the classical and neoclassical approach, which results in the clear separation of ethics and economics, have been articulated across two centuries of the development of Catholic social economics (Th. O. Nitsch, 1991).

Giuseppe Toniolo, an Italian economist of late 19th-early 20th century, and one of the most accomplished exponents of the Christian/Roman Catholic social school, points out the existence of extrinsic and intrinsic bonds between ethics and economics (Nitsch 1990, pp. 63-66). After having shown that ethics involves a hierarchical subordination of economic facts to morality, in the moment in which these are practically realized, ethics appears as an intrinsic link, based on the fact that "in the heart of man exists impulses and tendencies which, in harmony with the Supreme Moral Law, drives him to recognize it, believe it and translate it into action." Economic laws regard human behavior in the natural order as "the result of a bundle of forces, where self-utility acts under the modifying influence of all the other causes, from which it does not remove itself except for a perversion of conscience" (Toniolo 1874, p. 33).

From this situation, Toniolo concludes that economics is intrinsically linked to ethics because the subject is not wealth, but man, who lives and works in society. The result is a complex of individuals whose mind seems linked by a tacit bond, forming a homogeneous whole. According to Toniolo, laws of social sciences cannot be assimilated to physical ones because their importance goes beyond the pure observation of facts. In the world of social facts the observer sees only the sign of another order of laws essentially rooted in the nature of man.

While there was an evolution toward logical and positivist positions, bringing an increasing presence of mathematics into economics, many authors, among them Myrdal, tried to demonstrate the logical impossibility of a neutral social science. In fact, when the scholar poses "meaningful" question before analyzing the facts from which he draws answers, he inevitably evokes value judgments which, in turn, depend on their own concept of reality (Tondini 1990, pp. 519f).

Francesco Vito, another Italian economist of our century, was approaching the same conclusion several decades before, attempting a synthesis between the neoclassical position and the Historical school in the old dispute on method (the

❖

"Methodenstreit"). Facing the problem of the moral dimension of economic matters, Vito (1957, p. 164) began from the concept that "the unbreakable unity of the human act, by its free and responsible nature, prevents the considerations of sectors of activity as existing outside the moral order."

What in conventional (though rather inappropriate) language we call an economic act, which is connected in some way with the use of scarce resources, is always a human act that involves the subject's responsibility and moral evaluations. Vito shows that, far from abandoning an ethical approach to the society, the different schools of thought always return to a very precise morality: utilitarianism for the classical school, hedonism for the first Austrian school, materialism for Karl Marx and individualism for the neoclassical school (Tondini 1990, p. 521).

The various criticisms of the dominant paradigm concerning the relationship between ethics and economics have begun to break the rock of positivistic solidity, arousing a lively debate from which emerges the conviction that goals placed on economic activity ought to be defined through a process in which ideological orientations interact with positive knowledge.

Today we have a crisis of the paradigm that affirms the possibility of obtaining what one wants doing what he wants.

In the years of rapid economic growth since World War II, there was a tendency to affirm the need to marry growth with equity, as John Rawls and Amartya Sen maintain in their works (Sen 1987, p. 66). Rawls proposes a division based on justice, especially on primary goods: fundamental liberties and the possibility of accessing different functions and positions. Besides this principle of initial fair distribution of all social values, he advances another fundamental principle, according to which, once liberty is guaranteed for all, inequality can be accepted, on condition that the well-being of the most disadvantaged persons is advanced (L. Baeck 1988, p. 38).

## III. Basis for a Different Anthropology

In the first part I have recalled the origins of the separation between ethics and economics, due to the overturning of the vision that man had of himself and of his reality, to the development that such an approach has brought, and to the attempts to construct an alternative to the dominant model. Now I shall point out the contribution of the Church's social doctrine, tending to found a different anthropology (cf. John Paul II 1991, #13) and to elaborate on, at the same time, some fundamental principles on which to base an organization of the socioeconomic system compatible with man's happiness.

Siro Lumbardini (1986, p. 5) wrote that every economic theory is conceived in a particular philosophical context, and is based on a particular anthropological concept. The validity of the theory is conditioned by the validity of the anthropological concept. The hinges on which rests the whole social doctrine of the Church are:

1) the centrality of Christ who, revealing to man the truth about God, also reveals the truth about man.
2) the dignity of man, seen as unique and unrepeatable, being in relation with God and with others.

Man becomes conscious of himself only when he opens up to a connection with someone else. From this encounter, he also perceives his limits. The encounter with the Absolute only becomes the ultimate and definitive one. Hence, the Christian view: Christ is this absolute and proper Person because He is God revealing to man the fullness of His personal being. Such a fullness is the foundation of his dignity.

Man also has an objective direction, under which he is subjugated to laws of nature. Nevertheless, the human being cannot be split into two parts, a part as subject and a part as object. This is why it is wrong to study the individual using the method adopted from the natural sciences; for example, the abstraction of *homo oeconomicus*. Such a method is useful in the field of natural sciences because it corresponds to their nature. Applied to the social science, it hinders the study of all human aspects and actions.

This unitary approach is possible only by surpassing human personality; that is, by beginning from an anthropology that reflects aspects that make a person really human.

It is necessary to note that all the attempts to make social sciences comprehend that human situation have assumed the opposition between one person and another as the indisputable point of departure tending to deny the personality of the other. To escape this logic, it is necessary to return to an anthropology on the basis of which the realization of the dignity of a person can come about only in the encounter with someone else, *together with, and never against,* the other (Guido Menegazzi 1970, p. 183).

The father-son dialectic is the kind of human relation in which the affirmation of one's own dignity passes through the affirmation of the other's dignity. The father is what he is because the son exists, and the son is a son only because the father exists. Such a relation comes out of the archetype of all human relations (Tondini 1990, pp. 525f).

As a result of these mere sketches of the foundations of Christian anthropology, we see that this is presented as a serious reflection about the human being, indicating the theories that ought to guide her/his actions. Now we have to cultivate the vast field of forms and categories that give rise to a new economics (R. Cattaneo 1989, p. 67).

## IV. Conclusion and Foreword

Besides Toniolo and Vito, other scholars of our century, from Jacques Maritain to François Perroux, from Father Lebret to Ezio Vanoni, from Gino Barbieri to Menegazzi, have gone in the present direction. For an examination of some of their contributions, I take the liberty of submitting this essay to the Acta of the Congress "For an Economy at the Service of Man." Now I would like to turn to the second part of the presentation, the part regarding the new situation a century after *Rerum Novarum:* the challenges of the twenty-first century.

The reality of the Church is never the result of praxis only, but is also the result of the reciprocal relation between theory and lived experience in community. The year of Christian social doctrine proclaimed by John Paul II, a century after *Rerum Novarum,* cannot be reduced to the study and elaboration of the social "Magisterium" of the Church during these years. Social doctrine is always related to the living context of the whole tradition of Church, in relation to the variety of "new things" experienced in life and to the force of historical circumstances and of the gifts of the Spirit, on the perennial foundation of Christian principles. The first of all these principles is the centrality of responsibility of each human being, who can accept or refuse the gift of the truth that "shall make you free" (Raimondo Spiazzi 1987, pp. LIV-1740; John,8:32)

With the explosion of modern industrialization, new and unforeseen possibilities and problems arose, with immediate responses from the Popes and the charitable works of many Christian communities. Every pronouncement of the Church has a link with these living responses to every "res nova" and has also to face the clash of great ideologies that were competing for the leadership in modern economic and social processes; namely, classical liberalism and socialism.

The concept of man, according liberalism and socialism, absolutizes either theoretical preconceptions or praxis, without the linkage between theory and praxis that is necessary in the real world. Furthermore, they are far from concentrating every civil, economic and political procedure on the responsibility of every individual, who can accept or refuse it. Such a mortal, in reality, can never be completely foreseeable, theorizable and programmable. Outside of reality, every messianism, as well as every system, is only an illusion; and Christianity, which has neither a utopian nor a fatalist bent, purports to propose or endorse no particular system. "The Church has no models to present" (John Paul II 1991, #43). So Christianity lives and works apart from any system, dialoguing with the responsibility or irresponsibility of every person who, however conditioned and limited, transcends every system by the roots of his own tradition.

This is the typical and perennial voice of Christianity, to support liberation from slavery, in the sense of every lived experience aiming at full respect for the rights of every individual, of every person.

It is possible to theorize, as neocapitalism does today, that, using market competition as the only governing principle of obligations, it can be more fruitful than the socialist system in the northern part of the world; that, in fact it produces good fortune, while Communism has produced only misery. But capitalism does not respond to the needs of human solidarity; and, above all, does not conduce to economic justice between North and South. This is the great challenge remaining after forty years of Cold War between East and West (Giuseppe Gaburro 1991, pp. 46-47).

It is possible to hold that the courageous teaching of John Paul II, who contributed to the collapse of the socialist system and its non-violent evolution, started in Poland, to obtain democratic liberties and respect for the individual, even though the mechanism of the marketplace, the focus of everyone's day-to-day activity, marginalized the contribution of the official Church in securing a more just socioeconomic relationship between North and South. The illusion that only neocapitalism can be the driving force of modern development for the whole world is an absurd claim. The response to this new situation that John Paul II offers (1 May 1991) a century after *Rerum Novarum* represents a challenge and an offer for collaboration with the lay world. This challenge ought to be a good opportunity for a lay discussion, without doing it in an instrumental way (Michael Schuck 1991).

After the ruinous experiences in South America, to maintain the capacity of solving the relation with the South, especially with Islam, on the basis of technical and economic relations is really an "adventure without return." This supremacist approach, besides, presages danger of total war (nuclear or bacteriological), and also forecasts dramatic invasions from the South to the North (Herve Carrier, 1985).

Following the example of Christ, Catholics never look to one's ideological origin, but to the destination of same. Until the Council, Catholics believed themselves to be beyond the modern and the anti-modern. But they cannot accept the theory that the only driving force of development, as neocapitalism theorizes, is the exploitative system of unbridled market competition, without any place for solidarity. The Church's social doctrine has always prophetically rejected the notion that the man of competition could suddenly become *homo solidaristicus,* once the ownership of the means of production was violently seized by the state and collectivized.

## V. The Point of Disagreement

"Oh happy fault, that gained for us so great a Redeemer!" This is the dogma or Gospel of original sin, which all modern currents of thought reject as a lack of confidence in the autonomous capacity of man. This generally accepted truth of faith was a safeguard against any illusion that man is capable of salvation, of justice, of love, of community with other men by merely changing the material historical-social conditions. Each man can come to the point of seeing the Good because He is the only way, can even go as far as accepting and desiring Him, only to end up dramatically doing the evil that He says not to covet. Who can free man from this bondage? Historically, he reaches the point of grasping the necessity of a divine redemption or liberation that is different from that which man can offer, a salvation in any condition, in any economic and political system, in any civil context.

This salvation exists and is also recognizable when man frees himself from prejudices. It can always be responsibly accepted or irresponsibly refused, whence every acceptance is free; that is, it can only be an act of love: only the civilization of love is of worth to man.

❖

We can say now that the Christian message which is beyond every earthly messianism, that is beyond every system, is a message that can be accepted by everyone living under any political regime, even the most persecutory one. In fact, the Christian message can cause a cultural and social evolution toward the common recognition of natural law without using violent means. Christianity is never an alternative system to liberalism or socialism, can never become western or eastern, but condemns and militates against systems wanting to be strictly autonomous and tending to degenerate into violent, dictatorial forms in which man is considered as an object and instrument rather than a subject and end.

## VI. The New Situation

Communist ideology is certainly in crisis, and laissez faire, or other neo-capitalist share-holding forms, seem to prevail everywhere, being more fruitful for economic development than socialism is. Laissez faire produces more welfare (above all for the middle class), but it has already led to a continuous struggle in the relations between North and South. This is the true "res nova," that is, the new situation that the Christian community has to face. This is the great challenge of the coming years that the new social encyclical of John Paul II has to face.

## VII. The New Evangelization

For a global evangelization, Christians ought to become real protagonists on the historical scene, at least with the influence of the Christian way of life in ecclesial communities, even if they are a minority, with a substantial link between the ecclesial activity and social teaching.

Western ideologies and contemporary European culture are essentially impotent about the creation of a new order between West and South, and "in primis" between the West and Islam. How can a Europe of merchants, difficult to build as it is, whose only aim or value is exclusively to stabilize the market, whose only controlling reason is that of technical supremacy, create any sort of an international order different from a hegemony based on reason of force rather than force of reason? We cannot describe such a situation as an order, but as bullying or violence.

Only a Europe that also bases the freedom of the market on the Christian roots of the common good for every human being, without distinction between East and West, between North and South, can develop an interdependence of solidarity and justice among the three or four "worlds." Among the principal challenges for the future (North-South demographic imbalances and immigration problems; management of nature and of technical progress, to avoid turning this progress into social regression; reconversion of military industries; construction of a Europe "from the Atlantic to the Urals"; and, finally, the challenge, that is most feared, of bringing the Third World out of misery and underdevelopment) we know very well that the simple interaction of demand and supply — the "invisible hand" of "free and universal competition" even — is totally inadequate to the task.

In fact, the market economy, left to itself, has never succeeded either in regulating production related to needs — that is, in avoiding crises — nor in confronting important global challenges such as environmental protection and the development of the Third World. Until now, only state intervention has succeeded, for better or worse, in making use of "social shock-absorbers" to make internal and external equilibrium more or less enduring. The need for regulation derives from the free play of a competition less and less perfect and more and more dominated and directed by huge international economic and financial groups, operating exclusively in the service of their own interests.

The offensive launched for several years now by some groups and the interests represented by them, to reduce state intervention and promote economic and social deregulation, enhances their own profits, while inevitably aggravating social inequality and rendering nations more and more vulnerable in confronting future challenges.

The future of market economies and their capacity for auto-regulation actually presupposes the organization of balanced forces to oppose the dominating and ever more exclusive power of the international groups, i.e. transnational corporations. The decision maker, according to François Perroux (1967), should be induced to dialogue and to divide the decision-making power with the other subjects who can determine the functioning of society; viz. the state and the workers, whether in their capacity as producers in the enterprise or in their capacity as consumers and savers in society. The state must not, however, carry its economic and social intervention to the point of excessive rules and regulations, overly bureaucratizing the economy and thereby compromising its efficiency. The essential question is the participation of all actors involved in the economy in the working up of decisions on which depend not only the future of the economy, but also the future of the entire society. In this view, the function of the state is not that of governing or intervening directly, but rather that of representing the General Interest, i.e. the Common Good.

As to the workers, they are at the same time producers, consumers and savers. Their participation in decisions involving these functions will oblige unions to expand their own sphere of action to take into account the other two aspects of the worker's life: consumption and saving. To the other two roles, of representation and defense of dissent that, till now, have belonged to unions, a third will be added, viz. that of participation in management in all phases of economic, financial and social life.

The entrepreneur will continue to represent capital, but the participation of the three subjects in the decision process will induce him to broaden his conception of business interests, and to consider, beyond the interest of capital in a narrow sense, those of the other two subjects, that is in short, the interest of society.

Production today, in fact, is no longer merely the choice to create goods and services as a function of price in internal and external markets only, because imbalances in the distribution of wealth and social exclusion caused by crisis cannot be extended beyond the more "solvent demand" for the whole needs of the population (cf. John Paul II 1991, #34). The conquest of new markets, in the industrialized countries as in the rest of the world, necessarily ought to take into account "the insolvent demand" (John Paul II 1991, #34).

The real challenge is to make this demand solvent, using politics adequate to exploit material and human resources; that is, policies securing less imbalance in the distribution of income and wealth. The real question is an economic problem which opens the debate about mechanisms of distribution of income, as no longer a simple social question. In fact, it is necessary to escape "the economics of greed" and to go, at least in the 21st century, into the "economics of Man and of all Men" (Gian Guzzetti 1987, p. 9).

This is possible if all the economic and social partners — businessmen, workers, and the state, guardian of the common good — actually divide the responsibility for economic and social decision-making. Only on this condition will the three subjects consider themselves individually and mutually responsible for each decision, being directly involved in the successes and failures, equally resolved to enhance the former and avoid the latter. This is the way to obtain the "fair distribution" that will regulate more adequately the market economies. In the moment in which not only Europe "from the Atlantic to the Urals," but even the Third World, seem to wish to "convert" to a market economy, the most important challenge for this system is to give full responsibility to all the social partners (Gabburo 1991, pp. 23-37). The economies that succeed in this operation will have the greatest possibilities of success at the dawn of the twenty-first century.

*Il Direttoré, Istituto di Scienze Economiche, Universitá di Verona, Italy.

## References

Baeck, L. "Pour un nouveau paradigme en economié", *Notes et Documents, 38* (1988).

Calvez, Jean-Yves. "Economic Policy Issues in Roman Catholic Social Teaching: An International Perspective," in Thomas M. Gannon, ed., *The Catholic Challenge to the American Economy: Reflections on the U.S. Bishops' Pastoral Letter on Catholic Social Teaching and the U.S. Economy.* New York: Macmillan, 1988.

Carrier, Hervé. "Understanding Culture: The Ultimate Challenge of the World Church?" in Joseph Gremillion, ed., *The Church and Culture Since Vatican II: The Experience of North and Latin America.* Notre Dame, IN: University of Notre Dame Press, 1985, pp. 13-30.

Cattaneo, R. " A Proposito di economia ed etica: serve un codice deontologico o una nuova antropologia?," *Note e Riflessioni, 2* (April 1989).

Gaburro, Giuseppe. *Economia della solidarietà* Verona: Università degli studi di Verona, 1991.

Guzzetti, Gian Battista. *Cristianesimo ed economia*. Milano: Massimo, 1987.

Hirschmann, A.O. *L'economia politica come scienza morale e sociale*. Napoli: Liguori, 1987.

John Paul II. *Centesimus Annus: On the Hundredth Anniversary of Rerum Novarum*. Rome: St. Peter's, 1 May 1991.

Lombardini, Siro. "Economia ed etica. Osservazioni in margine alla lettera dei vescovi americani," Milano: mimeo. Università Cattolica del S. Cuore, 1986.

Menegazzi, Guido. *Il piano dello sviluppo dei popoli*. Milano: Giuffrè, 1970.

Nitsch, Thomas O. "Social Economics: The First 200 Years," in Mark A. Lutz, ed., *Social Economics: Retrospect and Prospect*. Boston: Kluwer Academic Publishers, 1990.

_____, "Catholic Social Economy and the Social Question: Founders and Firstporitors," pap. pres. Sixth World Congress of Social Economics, Omaha, NE (USA), 9-11 Aug. 1991.

Perroux, François. "Populorum Progressio: l'encyclizue de la résurrection," in Y.M.J. Congar and M. Peuchmaurd, eds., *L'église dans le monde de ce temps*. Paris: Les éditions du Cerf, 1967, Vol. I, pp. 201-12.

Schuck, Michael J. *That They May Be One*. Washington, DC: Georgetown University Press, 1991.

Sen, A. *Etica ed economia,* trad. S. Maddaloni. Bari: Laterza, 1988.

Smith, Adam. *An Inquiry into the Nature and Causes of the Wealth of Nations* (1776-89). New York: Modern Library, 1937.

Spiazzi, Raimondo (ed.). *I documenti sociali della Chiesa. Da Pio IX a Giovanni Paolo II (1864-1982)*, 2nd ed. Milano: Massimo, 1987.

Tawney, R. *La religione e la genesi del capitalismo*. Milano: Feltrinelli, 1967.

Thomas Acquinas. *Summa Contra Gentiles, Book One: God,* trans. A. C. Pegis. Notre Dame, IN: University of Notre Dame Press, 1975.

Tondini, Giovanni. "I rapporti tra politica ed economia, le ragioni di una visione unitaria," in G. Gaburro, Romano Milesti, and Giovani Zalin, eds., *Economia, Stato, Societa*. Pisa: Ipem Edizioni, 1990.

Toniolo, Giuseppe. *Dell'elemento etico quale fattore intrinseco delle leggi economiche*. Padova: Sachhetto, 1974.

Vito, Francesco. "Vita economica ed ordine morale," in *Atti della XXIX Settima Sociale dei Cattolici d'Italia,* Berganco 23-30 Sept. 1956 (Roma: I.C.A.S., 1957), as reprinted in idem, *Gli aspetti etico-sociali dello svillupo economico*, ed. F. Duchini. Milano: Vita e Pesiero, 1989.

Zamagni, Stefano. *Efficienza e qiustizia nella società*. Milano: Istra, 1988.

# The Old Capitalism and Recent U.S. Antitrust Policy

## *Robert F. Allen\**

Pope John Paul II's encyclical *Centesimus Annus (CA)* offers a qualified endorsement of competitive capitalism as a social system for promoting the wealth of nations and the dignity and freedom of the individual. Market mechanisms are central to such a system. Private property, individual ownership of the means of production, the law of contracts, the primacy of consumer preferences, and business profits are all embraced by John Paul as the legitimate and indispensable mechanisms of what he prefers to call "...a 'business economy', 'market economy', or simply 'free economy'" (1991, §42).

In an early commentary on the encyclical, Richard John Nuehaus (1991) described John Paul's vision of the market economy as an affirmation of a "new capitalism.' In truth, as regards the workings of a market economy, the responsibilities of the state vis-a-vis the market, and the essential link between the market and human freedom, there is little here that is new. Indeed, the capitalism of *CA* bears a striking resemblance to the "old capitalism" envisioned by political economists from Adam Smith to Henry C. Simons, as is shown in Section I of this paper. An essential element of the Old Capitalism is the responsibility of the state for the maintenance of competitive forces in a market economy. Its sine qua non is a vigilant antitrust policy. Section II of the paper highlights recent changes in U.S. antitrust policy. This policy departs significantly from the prescriptions of the Old Capitalism. It is grounded in a novel and expansive view of economic efficiency. Section III concludes the paper with summary observations on the changing concept of economic efficiency.

## I. The Old Capitalism and *Centesimus Annus*

In the 1945 essay which serves as the introduction to the collected writings of Henry C. Simons (1948) we have a rather complete statement of an intellectual tradition which runs through the works of political economists from Adam Smith and John Stuart Mill to Frank Fetter and Frank H. Knight. These economists were part of an intellectual tradition whose "...distinctive feature ... is emphasis upon liberty as both a requisite and a measure of progress" (Simons 1948, p. 1). Their embrace of market economies was rooted in a belief that "...effective competition is [a] requisite to real freedom of association—and to real power dispersion" (Simons 1948, p. 4).

Property rights in "instruments of production" and "labor or personal capacities" are central to this tradition (Simons 1948, p. 27) as are the right to voluntary associations—as consumer, investor or worker (Simons 1948, pp. 3-4), the embrace of democracy (Simons 1948, p. 8), the appreciation of competition as a means of proper resource allocation (Simons 1948, pp. 46-51), and the insistence on "an elaborate, stable, confining structure of law" (Simons 1948, pp. 3-4).

Above all, the Old Capitalism abhorred monopoly power. "All monopolies, and all very large organizations of sellers(or buyers)," says Simons, " are impairment of that freedom" (1948, p. 4). Thus, for Simons, "It is an obvious responsibility of the state to maintain the kind of legal and institutional framework within which competition can function effectively as an agency of control" (1948, p. 42).

Though more subdued in its argument, *CA* presents a similarly broad orientation with an emphasis on human freedom. Can capitalism, asks John Paul, be offered as the model for emulation by others? Perhaps, but only if "...by 'capitalism' is meant a system in which freedom in the economic sector is...circumscribed within a strong juridical framework which places it at the service of human freedom in its totality, and which sees it as a particular aspect of that freedom,...." (1991, §42). Beyond this sensitivity to individual liberty we find, in *CA*, strong statements pertaining to the market as an allocative mechanism, the condemnation of monopoly, and the need for strong oversight of the economic sector by the state.

John Paul's praise for the efficiency of a market economy is unqualified. "It would appear," he remarks, "that on the level of individual nations and international relations, *the free market* is the most efficient instrument for utilizing resources and effectively responding to needs" (1991, §34, italics in original). "The mechanisms of the market," observes John Paul, "help to utilize resources better; they promote the exchange of products; above all they give central place to the person's desires and preferences, which, in a contract, meet the desires and preferences of another person" (1991, §40).

The manipulation of market forces by the narrow interests of speculators and would be monopolists is condemned. "Ownership of the means of production," writes John Paul, "becomes illegitimate, however, when it is not utilized or when it serves to impede the work of others, in an effort to gain a profit which is not the result of overall expansion of work and the wealth of society...." (1991, §43).

The pope looks to the state for the regulation of unchecked market forces. "The State has the further right to intervene when particular monopolies create delays or obstacles to development" (1991, §48) and to stop "the spread of improper sources of growing rich and of easy profits deriving from illegal or purely speculative activities" (1991, §48).

More broadly, "The State has the task of determining the juridical framework within which economic affairs are to be conducted, and thus of safeguarding the prerequisites of a free economy," writes John Paul (1991, §15).

The antitrust laws of the United States are part of this juridical framework. They were designed to nurture and protect free markets. The administration of these laws by the executive and judicial branches of government changed dramatically in the 1980's. These changes bear closer scrutiny as part of John Paul's invitation to "'look around' at the 'new things' which surround us and in which we find ourselves caught up,...." (1991, §3)

## II. Recent Changes in U.S. Antitrust Policy

### A. The Antitrust Laws

The basic policy in support of competitive markets is contained in the 1890 Sherman Antitrust Act (Sherman Act) and the 1914 Clayton Antitrust Act (Clayton Act). Section 1 of the Sherman Act makes trade restraints among nominally independent businesses illegal. And Section 2 prohibits monopolization and attempts to monopolize. The Clayton Act supplements these general prohibitions by declaring specific types of market behavior illegal. Examples of the latter are exclusive dealing (Section 3), price discrimination (Section 2), and mergers and stock acquisitions where the effect may be to substantially lessen competition or tend toward monopoly (Section 7).

The enforcement of the antitrust laws of the United States is shared among the Antitrust Division of the Department of Justice (the Division), the Federal Trade Commission, the state attorneys general and private parties "...injured in [their] business or property by reason of anything forbidden in the antitrust laws." The latter may recover three times their actual damages plus litigation costs, including reasonable attorney fees.

Table 1 details the history of antitrust litigation initiated by the U.S. Government and private parties since 1940. Private litigation has historically accounted for more than 2 of every 3 antitrust cases filed with the courts. Throughout the 1960's and 1970's, private filings accounted for more than 90 percent of all litigation commenced under the antitrust laws. The total number of antitrust cases filed has roughly doubled every ten years from 1941 to 1980. Since 1980 the total number of antitrust cases commenced has nearly halved and is now running at a rate reminiscent of the 1960's

As shown in Table 1, the reduced level of court filings is due solely to a reduction in private antitrust litigation. After expanding significantly throughout the 1960's and 1970's, private litigation has fallen sharply since 1980. In 1989, 638 private antitrust cases were filed compared to 1457 in 1980. The ratio of private to

❖

public antitrust cases is currently less than 7 to 1 compared to almost 20 to 1 in the late 1970's.

## Table 1
### Antitrust Cases Filed in District Courts During Fiscal Years Ending June 30, 1941 to 1989
### Cases Filed Per Year by

| Fiscal Year | Total Cases | U.S. Government | Private Parties | Ratio of Private Cases to Government Cases |
|---|---|---|---|---|
| 1941 - 1945 | 95.6 | 36.2 | 59.4 | 1.64 |
| 1946 - 1950 | 157.0 | 51.2 | 105.8 | 2.07 |
| 1951 - 1955 | 248.4 | 39.4 | 209.0 | 5.30 |
| 1956 - 1960 | 296.0 | 63.4 | 232.6 | 3.67 |
| 1961 - 1965 | 787.8 | 69.2 | 718.6 | 10.38 |
| 1966 - 1970 | 763.2 | 55.0 | 708.2 | 12.88 |
| 1971 - 1975 | 1373.2 | 78.4 | 1294.8 | 16.51 |
| 1976 - 1980 | 1523.4 | 75.2 | 1448.2 | 19.26 |
| 1981 - 1985 | 1242.4 | 107.8 | 1134.6 | 10.52 |
| 1986 | 922 | 84 | 838 | 9.98 |
| 1987 | 858 | 100 | 758 | 7.58 |
| 1988 | 752 | 98 | 654 | 6.67 |
| 1989 | 737 | 99 | 638 | 6.44 |

Sources: Steven C. Salop and Lawrence J. White, "Private Antitrust Litigation: An Introduction and Framework," *Private Antitrust Litigation* Cambridge: MIT Press, 1988; United States General Accounting Office, *Justice Department: Changes in Antitrust Enforcement Policies and Activities,* October 1990.

## B. Restricting the Scope of the Sherman Act

The reasons for this private sector chill are not difficult to pin down. They are tied to the economic incentives that arise in the antitrust litigation system. The incentive to sue turns on the plaintiff's calculation of the net expected value of the suit. The chief elements of this calculation are litigation costs, the damages award, and the probability of winning (Salop and White 1988, pp. 16-37).

Data bearing on the costs and awards of private antitrust litigation are available from the recently completed Georgetown Project (Teplitz 1988). This Project involved the collection of extensive data on over 2000 private antitrust cases filed between 1973 and 1983 in the five federal districts of Atlanta, Chicago, Kansas City, New York, and San Fransisco. Analysis of this data suggests that the litigation costs of the typical antitrust case are of modest proportions and relatively stable in real terms. For example, Steven Salop and Lawrence White (1988, p. 15) and Kenneth G. Elzinga and William C. Wood (1988, p. 142) separately estimate total legal costs for a "typical" private antitrust case (for both sides combined) to be from $200,000 to $250,000 during the mid 1980's. A single plaintiff's part of this cost is about $75,000 per case according to Salop and White (1988, p. 15). Adjusted for inflation, these costs are reported to be stable over the period 1973 to 1983 (Salop and White 1988, p. 15).

Data on damage awards and/or settlements from the Georgetown Project identify average payments to plaintiffs on the order of $465,000 to $1.6 million per case. The latter statistic is an average of the payments made in 337 cases underlying 12 large multidistrict litigations (Salop and White 1988, p. 12). These values are a considerable multiple of the "typical" litigation costs that emerge from this data.

The expected damage recovery for a given plaintiff may be viewed as (Elzinga and Wood 1988, p. 140):

$$E(R) = pkMD$$

where D is the amount of damages, M is the multiple of damages allowed under the antitrust laws (currently three), k is the probability of the court finding a practice illegal, and p is the probability of establishing the existence of the practice.

Changes in antitrust policy and the case law bear most directly on the parameters p and k. Narrowing the scope of the per se rule of illegality will directly lower the value of k, for example, while raising evidential requirements will lower the value of p. The incentive for private suits will fall accordingly.

As it turned out, the Reagan administration proved unusually adept at lowering the values of k and p in private net benefit calculations. This was achieved, for the most part, through an aggressive amicus program initiated in 1981 by former Assistant Attorney General William Baxter. From mid 1981 through mid 1985 the Division filed 64 amicus briefs with the U.S. Supreme Court and the courts of appeals. This was nearly triple the number filed for the comparable period in the 1970's (United States General Accounting Office(GAO) 1990, pp. 54-62).

The admitted intent of these filings was to persuade the courts to narrow the application and/or interpretation of the antitrust laws. Baxter was especially anxious to see the Supreme Court abandon the rule of per se illegality in cases involving vertical trade restraints (GAO 1990, p. 56). The latter rule embraces such business practices as resale price maintenance, tying arrangements, exclusive dealing, and refusals to deal. Collectively, these practices were found to be the primary illegalities alleged in 43 percent of the cases examined in the Georgetown Project (GAO 1990, p. 69).

The Division was on the winning side in Supreme Court movements away from the per se rule in private litigation involving group boycotts, *Northwest Wholesalers Stationers v. Pacific Stationery & Printing Co.*, 472 U.S. 284 (1985), tie-ins, *Jefferson Parish Hospital District No. 2 v. Hyde*, 466 U.S. 2 (1984), and even garden variety price fixing, *National Collegiate Athletic Association v. Board of Regents of the University of Oklahoma*, 468 U.S. 85 (1984).

The Division was also successful in persuading the Court to raise the level of evidence required of plaintiffs in civil cases alleging trade restraints. The general thrust of the Division's argument was that civil cases should not proceed to trial in the absence of evidence sufficient to contravene any theory of rational independent action. The Supreme Court adopted this position in *Matsushita Electric Industrial Co., Ltd. v. Zenith Radio Corp.*, 475 U.S. 574 (1986) and *Monsanto Co. v. Spray-Rite Service Corp.*, 465 U.S. 752 (1984). According to John DeQ. Briggs (1988, p. 250), the latter case has given "...tremendous backbone to the district courts, motivating them to dismiss at a relatively early stage many types of nonprice vertical restraint cases."

More generally, in a review of 47 cases decided by the Supreme Court between the fiscal years 1980 and 1989, the General Accounting Office found the Division's position adopted in 38, or 80 percent, of the cases (GAO 1990, p. 59). The Division's success rate was only slightly less, 74 percent, for amicus briefs filed with courts of appeals.

It is perhaps too generous to attribute changing court positions during the 1980's solely to the hostility of the Reagan administration to private actions alleging trade restraints. As the noted legal theorist Judge Richard A. Posner has observed (1990), 1981 saw, in addition to the appointment of William Baxter to the Antitrust Division of the Justice Department, the beginnings of numerous appointments of conservative judges to all levels of the federal judiciary, himself included. This judiciary has worked actively to curtail the scope of the anti-trust laws.

Justice Sandra Day O'Connor's concurring opinion in *Jefferson Parish* is illustrative of the way in which judicial and administration thought was coalescing during the 1980's. This case involved the requirement that patients at East Jefferson Hospital use the anesthesiological services of Roux & Associates, the only group authorized to administer anesthesia in the hospital. The court of appeals found this to be an illegal tie between general hospital services and the sale of anesthesiologist's services. While the Supreme Court disposed of this case by treating it as a reasonable exclusive contract, as urged by the Division, Justice O'Connor took this opportunity to argue that tying arrangements should be disposed of under a rule of reason. In her view, the Court should

❖

...abandon the 'per se' label and refocus the inquiry on the adverse
economic effects, and the potential economic benefits, that the tie may
have. The law of tie-ins will thus be brought into accord with the law
applicable to all other allegedly anticompetitive economic arrangements, except those few horizontal or quasi-horizontal restraints that
can be said to have no economic justification whatsoever. (*Jefferson
Parish*, 466 U.S. at 35).

In short, Section 1 of the Sherman Act should be applicable to price fixers, period.

## C. The New Merger Guidelines

At the same time the Division and the courts were moving to restrict the reach
of the Sherman Act, the Division took steps to curtail the use of the Clayton Act to
inhibit merger activity. This was largely accomplished by revising the *Merger
Guidelines* the Division uses to decide if a proposed merger should be challenged.

The new *Merger Guidelines* were issued in 1982 and departed significantly
from the original *Merger Guidelines* published by the Division in 1968. The new
guidelines raise market concentration levels necessary to trigger an investigation
of horizontal mergers(firms supplying the same product), establish market entry
criteria that virtually eliminate challenges to vertical mergers (firms at different
stages of the production- distribution chain), and disregard, as a matter of competitive concern, conglomerate mergers (firms in different product and/or geographical
markets). In 1984, the *Merger Guidelines* were further modified to require
consideration of possible efficiencies before challenging a proposed merger.

The impact of these revisions can be seen in the Division's merger statistics.
Between 1970 and 1980, an average of 12 merger cases per year were filed by the
Division. This dropped by 50 percent to 6 per year between 1981 and 1989.(GAO
1990, p. 44). By 1988-89 the Division was investigating fewer than 3 percent of the
mergers brought to its attention under the pre-notification provisions of the Hart-
Scott-Rodino Amendments to the Clayton Act.

The low merger investigation rate reflects the confluence of three events
between 1979 and 1989: the number of merger pre-notifications filed with the
Division rose from 859 to 2,883, a 336 percent increase, the Division's budget was
cut 29 percent in real terms, and the full-time staff assigned to the Division's merger
review program was reduced by more than 40 percent (GAO 1990, pp. 34, 36, 48).

That some anticompetitive acquisitions would slip through the cracks in such
an environment is hardly surprising. Just how wide these cracks had become can
be seen in Continental Baking's attempt to acquire a significant competitor in mid-
1986.

On May 30, 1986 Ralston Purina and Borden filed pre-merger notices with
the Division (and the Federal Trade Commission) concerning the proposed acquisition by Ralston Purina's Continental Baking Co. of the Drake bakery division of

❖

Borden. The Antitrust Division (and the Federal Trade Commission) expressed no objection to the proposed horizontal merger and the merger was consummated on July 12, 1986. Subsequently, the Tasty Baking Company was able to enjoin the merger by showing in district court the probable lessening of competition proscribed by Section 7 of the Clayton Act. *Tasty Baking Company and Tastykake, Inc. v. Ralston Purina, Inc. and Continental Baking Co.*, 653 F.Supp. 1250 (E.D. Penn. 1987).

The court followed the Division's *Merger Guidelines* in reaching its decision in *Tasty Baking*. The *Merger Guidelines* employ the Herfindahl-Hirschman Index of Market Concentration to set out general standards governing federal intervention in proposed mergers. According to the *Merger Guidelines*, when the post-merger concentration index "substantially exceeds" 1800 and the merger raises the index by more than 100 points "...only in extraordinary cases will [other] factors establish that the merger is not likely substantially to lessen competition" (Breit and Elzinga 1989, p. 447).

The data presented in *Tasty Baking* showed post-merger concentration indexes that ranged from a low of 3005 to a high of 6420, depending on the geographic market and sales data source referenced. The merger's impact on the concentration index varied from market to market with increases ranging from 163 points to 3033 points. These index values are one and one-half to thirty times the values required by the *Merger Guidelines* to establish a compelling case for federal intervention. Unlike the Antitrust Division, the district court had no difficulty seeing the probable anticompetitive effect of this acquisition.

In summary, through an aggressive amicus program and a permissive merger policy, the federal government has severely restricted the reach of the antitrust laws in the United States during the last ten years. The antitrust laws now embrace little more than blatant price fixing and flagrantly anticompetitive horizontal mergers.

This is precisely the result called for by President Reagan's first Council of Economic Advisors. In the view of the Council, a more restricted role for the antitrust laws was desirable to "...make them more consistent with the promotion of economic efficiency" (Economic Report of the President 1982, p. 43). In line with this thinking, Reagan's first antitrust chief insisted that economic efficiency was the only proper goal of antitrust. If the pursuit of such efficiency undermined the structure of a competitive market economy, Congress was advised to find alternative mechanisms to deal with the problem (William R. Baxter, 1982).

## III. Conclusion

Antitrust economics espousing the Old Capitalism was focused on the structure of the market as an important factor in determining the degree of competition prevailing in markets. Mergers and/or contractual relationships which altered the structure of markets and/or increased the pricing discretion of firms were viewed as anticompetitive. Efficiency was defined in terms of the costs of providing goods and the correspondence of prices with marginal production costs. The various components of efficiency (i.e.costs) were thought to be measurable by competent and energetic investigators the likes of Joe S. Bain (1956), George J. Stigler (1958) and F. M. Scherer, et al (1975), among others. The resulting empirical evidence cast considerable doubt on the efficiency claims underlying mergers and other economic arrangements which promised to alter market environments in significant ways. Against this backdrop, public policy favored a vigorous antitrust policy which encouraged internal growth by firms and fragmented markets.

Under the "new capitalism," efficiency has replaced market structure as the focus of antitrust. Unfortunately, efficiency has become little more than a tautological construct. This new view, aptly summarized by Walter Adams, James W. Brock, and Norman P. Obst (1991, p. 11), allows that "whatever consumers choose is 'efficient,' and whatever firms produce maximizes 'consumer welfare.' If this were not so, different choices would be made. The fact that different choices are not made 'proves' that the actual choices reflect a 'voluntary,' non-coerced,'[sic] 'consensus' optimum of 'consumer welfare;'it 'proves' that the current allocation of resources reflects the maximum systemic 'efficiency.'

The widespread embrace of such circular reasoning in recent years is symptomatic of the very market "idolatry" (1991, #40) or "radical capitalist ideology" (1991, #42) that John Paul cautions against in *CA*. The pope's "market economy," on the other hand, is decidedly closer to that found in the intellectual tradition of the Old Capitalism.


## Endnotes

*Professor of Economics, Creighton University, Omaha, NE 68178, USA. The author wishes to acknowledge the preliminary discussions with Dr. Thomas O. Nitsch which contributed to the formulation of this paper.

[1]  The qualifications are many and include questions of macro-economic stability (§48), income distribution (§34), consumerism (§36), environmental externalities (§§37-39) and monopoly (§43), among others.

[2]  26 Stat. 209, 15 U.S.C. Sec. 1-7 (1890).

[3]  38 Stat. 730, 15 U.S.C. Sec. 12-27 (1914).

[4]  Ibid., Sec. 4.

[5]  Ibid.

[6]  The typical case is defined in terms of the central tendencies of the data collected in the Georgetown Project. As described by Elzinga and Wood (1988, p. 142), such a case would involve 68 docket entries, five depositions and just over two years from the filing of the complaint to the final docket entry.

❖

[7] See Department of Justice Release, May 30, 1968, reprinted on p. 360, *Antitrust and Trade Regulation Report*, p. 1 et seq. (June 4, 1968); *Justice Department Merger Guidelines,* June 14, 1984, in *Special Supplement, Antitrust and Trade Regulation Report,* S-1-s-16 (June 14, 1984). The major provisions are reprinted in Breit and Elzinga. (1989, pp. 438-454) For discussions of the more significant changes in the guidelines, see GAO (1990, pp. 50-51) and Waldman (1986, pp. 123-128).

[8] The index is the sum of the squares of the market shares of all firms in the market. The index approaches a value of zero for highly fragmented markets and equals 10,000 for a market with a single seller.

# References

Adams, Walter, Brock, James W. and Obst, Norman P. "Pareto Optimality and Antitrust Policy: The Old Chicago and the New Learning," *Southern Economic Journal,* July 1991, 58, 1-14.

Bain, Joe S. *Barriers to New Competition,* Cambridge: Harvard University Press, 1956.

Baxter, William F. "Interview", *Wall Street Journal,* March 4, 1982, at 28, col.3.

Breit, William and Elzinga, Kenneth G. *The Antitrust Casebook: Milestones in Economic Regulation,* 2nd ed., New York: The Dryden Press, 1989.

Briggs, John DeQ. "Comments on the Operation of the Antitrust System", *Private Antitrust Litigation,* Cambridge: MIT Press, 1988.

*Economic Report of the President.* 1982.

Elzinga, Kenneth G. and Wood, William C. "The Costs of the Legal System in Private Antitrust Enforcement", *Private Antitrust Litigation,* Cambridge: MIT Press, 1988.

John Paul II. *Centesimus Annus,* May 1,1991, Vatican City: Libreria Editrice Vaticana, 1991.

Nuehaus, Richard John. "The Pope Affirms the 'New Capitalism'", *Wall Street Journal,* May 2, 1991, at A16, col.4.

Posner, Richard A. "100 Years of Antitrust", *Wall Street Journal,* June 29, 1990, at A12, col.4.

Salop, Steven C. and White, Lawrence J. "Private Antitrust Litigation: An Introduction and Framework", *Private Antitrust Litigation,* Cambridge: MIT Press, 1988.

Scherer, F. M., Beckenstein, Alan, Kaufer, Erich, and Murphy, R. D. *The Economics of Multi-Plant Operations: An International Comparisons Study,* Cambridge: Harvard University Press, 1975.

Simons, Henry C. *Economic Policy for a Free Society,* Chicago: University of Chicago Press, 1948.

Stigler, George J. "The Economies of Scale", *Journal of Law and Economics*, October 1958, *1*, 54-71.

Teplitz, Paul V. "The Georgetown Project: An Overview of the Data Set and Its Collection", *Private Antitrust Litigation*, Cambridge: MIT Press, 1988.

United States General Accounting Office. *Justice Department: Changes in Antitrust Enforcement Policies and Activities*, October, 1990.

Waldman, Don E. *The Economics of Antitrust: Cases and Analysis*, Boston: Little Brown and Co., 1986.

# Deregulation in the Transportation Sector of the United States Economy and Its Effects on Labor

## Edward L. Fitzsimmons*

In its attempt to define the ideal economic system, Catholic social teaching has endorsed neither free market capitalism nor centralized state-planned socialism. The system it has proposed lies somewhere between these two extremes. The parameters of this ideal, never fully specified, have changed as conditions in society have changed. Yet pope after pope have made two aspects of this model economy very clear, the rights of individual employees in the workplace are to be protected and the collective role of labor in society is to be respected.

It was to defend the rights of labor from the dehumanizing outcomes of nineteenth century free market captialism that Pope Leo XIII wrote his encyclical *Rerum Novarum*. And more recently the National Conference of Catholic Bishops (1986, pp. 73-76, 147-152) expressed its concerns about competition in economic systems when they wrote their pastoral letter *Economic Justice for All*. Thus, it is not surprising that commentators on Catholic social teaching like Helen Ginsburg (1987) have questioned the impact on labor of policies of deregulation which have enjoyed considerable political support in the United States during the last ten or fifteen years.

While Ginsburg focused her criticism on the macroeconomic policies of the Reagan era, some attention should be given to the effects on labor of the microeconomic deregulation which also occurred during this period. Whatever these effects may have been, they should be investigated because deregulation touched the lives of millions of workers in a wide range of industries including banking, energy, communications, and transportation. The diversity of these industries, however, suggests the need for industry-specific study; and so one of them, transportation, has been selected for attention here.

❖

This examination of the effects of deregulation upon employees in the transportation industry will proceed in three steps. First, to provide a context for the rest of the analysis, the rationale and scope of deregulation will be outlined. Second, some of the reasons for expecting deregulation to have an adverse effect on workers in the industry will be discussed. Finally, the actual effects on those workers in the first ten years of the deregulation era will be described, giving attention to wages, fringe benefits, health and safety, unemployement, and union membership.

## I. Rationale and Scope of Deregulation

In the United States regulation of private industry by government has taken two forms, economic and social. Economic regulation can be described as direct government control over prices and output. Social regulation may have indirect effects on prices and output, but its primary concern has been protection of civil rights, health, safety, and the environment. Both types of regulation have been performed by all levels of government, local, state, and federal. In 1976 the federal government began a revision of legislation governing the economic regulation of the transportation industry which resulted in significant changes in the structure of the industry and in the conduct of the firms in it. To better understand how these changes affected workers in the industry some understanding of the nature of federal economic regulation of transportation and the changes which occurred is required.

In 1976 economic regulation of the transportation industry was conducted by four federal agencies. The Interstate Commerce commission regulated railroads, trucklines, buslines, oil pipelines, water carriers operating on inland and coastal waterways, freight forwarders, and other transportation intermediaries. The Federal Maritime Commission oversaw the operations of off-shore waterborne foreign and interstate commerce. The Civil Aeronautics Board controlled interstate and international air service. Finally, the Federal Power Commission watched over natural gas pipelines.

According to Roy J. Sampson, et al. (1990, pp. 284-288) federal economic regulation of transportation shared three common features: control of entry and exit; control of rates and earnings; and control of service. These features, originally intended to insure that the public received needed transport services at reasonable, non discriminatory rates and that transportation companies earned adequate profits, appeared by the early 1970's to be the source of significant resource misallocation and operating inefficiency in three segments of the transportation industry: railroads, intercity trucking, and domestic airlines. According to Theodore E. Keeler (1983, pp. 19-42) restrictions on exit and ratemaking flexibility forced railroads to provide noncompensatory services resulting in financial losses which reached critical proportions with the bankruptcy of the Penn Central and several other major rail carriers. The situation in intercity trucking was just the opposite. According to Clifford Winston et al. (1990, pp. 1-6) rates and profits in the trucking industry, especially that portion of the industry handling small shipments, were unusually high because of restrictions on entry and legally sanctioned collective rate making. But Sampson et al. (pp. 290-91) also noted restrictions imposed by regulators on services resulting in empty backhauls and circuitous routings which raised concerns about efficient use of energy and unnecessary environmental pollution. Elizabeth R. Bailey et al. (1985, pp. 11-26) reported that airline industry profits were erratic inspite of the attention given by the Civil Aeronautics Board (CAB) to the financial health of the industry. Moreover, consumer interest groups became upset about high fares when it was found that unregulated intrastate carriers operating in Texas and California operated profitably while charging lower fares than regulated carriers.

As these economic concerns gained political credence, deregulation began. Congress made its first attempt to reform the regulation of railroads in 1976. Deregulation of domestic air transportation began in 1977 and continued in stages until 1985 when the CAB was abolished. Trucking was deregulated in 1980. Continued financial problems in the railroad industry prompted a second and more substantial reduction of regulation in 1980. Intercity buslines were deregulated in 1982. Finally, in 1986, regulation of freight forwarders was eliminated, ending Congressional deregulation efforts in the transportation industry and leaving only regulation of international air transport, pipelines, and water carriers intact.

While, with the exception of freight forwarders, some degree of federal economic regulation remains in all segments of the transportation industry, government controls in each of the three common areas of regulation were relaxed. Relaxation of restrictions on entry and exit has brought about significant changes in industry structure. Relaxation of controls on rates narrowed the scope of legally sanctioned collective rate making and increased opportunities for setting rates independently. These changes in regulation of pricing combined with new freedom to introduce or withdraw services independently of governmental review have substantially increased competitive conduct with beneficial results for users of transportation.

Among railroads, trucking, and airlines, the most notable change in structure has been an increase in the number of firms. In the railroad industry, Jon H. Mielke (1988) reports that between 1980 and 1987 over 190 new short line and regional railroads were organized as existing Class I carriers used their new found freedoms to discontinue operation of marginal routes. In trucking and air transportation, lowering of barriers to entry previously posed by regulation attracted new firms to start up operations and existing firms to expand operations along profitable routes. Comparison of Interstate Commerce Commission (1980, 1986) annual reports found an increase of almost 19,000 regulated motor carriers between 1980 and 1986. Sampson et al. (p. 313) reported that the number of noncommuter airlines increased from 29 in 1978 to 93 in 1987.

These increases in the number of firms combined with new latitude to adjust prices and services independently of regulatory oversight brought about increases

❖

in price and service competition putting downward pressure on profits and costs which did not exist prior to deregulation. Michael W. Babcock et al. (1985) and Stephen Fuller et al. (1987) found that competition among railroads resulted in reduced freight rates for shippers of agricultural commodities. Looking across a broad spectrum of rail-transported commodities, Winston et al. (pp. 27-29) found little change in freight rates but considerable improvement in rail service while costs of providing rail service were reduced. Winston et al. (pp. 21-24) also examined the effects of deregulation on shippers using truck transportation. Here they found that competitive pressures brought about major reductions in truck rates for small shipments and minor reductions for truckload shipments. Among airlines too, Bailey et al. ( pp. 91-110) found the development, at least in the first years of deregulation, of intense competition steming largely from the emergence of low-cost air carriers using smaller crews and smaller planes than used by the previously regulated carriers.

## II. Expected Effects of Deregulation on Labor

While there has been ample evidence that most users of rail, motor, and air transportation benefited from the increases in competition which occurred during the first years following deregulation, increased competition has had adverse effects on transportation workers. Adverse effects were expected because, other things being equal, both product prices and wages should be higher in product markets which are less competitive than in product markets which are more competitive. Thus, given the increased competition in the transportation industry which followed deregulation, one would expect the wages of workers to fall along with the prices of transportation products. This argument will now be discussed in more detail.

Economists like Ingrid H. Rima (1981, pp. 145-66) and Donald Tomaskovic-Devy (1988, p. 108) have argued that the level of wages paid to employees in an industry is related to the market power of firms in the industry and the bargaining power of unions representing those employees. It is argued that firms with market power will tend, other things being equal, to set higher prices than firms in competitive industries. But if the bargaining power of the unions representing employees of the noncompeting firms is great enough and if the goal of the union is to maximize the wages of its members, wages will rise above wages paid in competitive industries as employees demand their share of the higher prices.

Research by Leonard Weiss (1966) provides some support for this hypothesis as a general proposition although he found that concentration was a more important determinant of wages than union power. Ronald G. Ehrenberg (1979, pp. 10-11) applied this hypothesis to rail, air, and truck transportation arguing that regulation of entry and pricing in these industries limited competition, thereby giving firms the opportunity to charge higher prices and employees the opportunity to demand higher wages than those paid in more competitive settings. Moreover, he found some empirical support for his view noting studies by Wallace Hendricks (1977), who found wages higher in trucking and airlines than in more competitive industries and Thomas G. Moore (1978), who reached similar conclusions but limited his research to regulated motor carriers.

The role of labor unions in securing high wages in the regulated transportation industry was discussed by Robert C. Lieb (1974, p. 17-47) and more critically by Walter Adams and James W. Brock (1983-84). The study by Lieb of the organization of labor in the transportation industry during the early 1970's found union bargaining power to be great. He noted that in 1971 the Teamsters represented 87 percent of the drivers employed by regulated trucking companies and wielded considerable power in national bargaining with an employer's association which represented virtually all regulated trucking firms. Lieb also reported that mergers of some of the many craft unions in the railroad industry, where about 80 percent of all employees were union members, resulted in new unions with considerable bargaining clout. The United Transportation Union, formed in 1969 and the Brotherhood of Railway and Airline Clerks, strengthened by merger in the same year, were instrumental, several years later, in securing generous wage increases inspite of the Nixon wage-price controls in effect at that time. Adams and Brock, based on their studies of commerical aviation, common carrier trucking, and other industries, described those industries as bilateral monopolies. Given the instability inherent to this market structure, they argued that the only rational way for labor and industry monopolists to protect their individual interests was to enter into vertical combinations or conspiracies to maintain mutually agreeable high prices and wages.

But deregulation weakened the market power of both transportation companies and their unions. The companies restricted from setting prices in rate bureaus formerly sanctioned by regulation or before the disbanded CAB and confronted by a flood of new competitors were forced to lower prices or improve services — which is another way to lower the price of the service to the user. But, at the same time, organized transportation labor lost its control of the labor supply and thus much of its bargaining power. It lost its control of the labor supply because the flood of new competitors generally employed non union workers. It lost its bargaining power because, as economists like Morgan O. Reynolds (1984, pp. 31-55) and Emerson P. Schmidt (1973, pp. 19-25) maintain, the key to union power is its control of the supply of workers. Thus wages would be expected to fall along with prices. And fall they did.

## III. Effects of Deregulation on Labor

Winston et al. (pp. 39-40) in their study of the effects of deregulation on surface transportation, reported declines in wages among rail workers and truckers. In a study which focused on the effects of deregulation on labor relations, Ellen F. Curtis and Michael R. Crum (1988) reported wage concessions had been forced on rail, trucking, and airline unions. Average wage levels in these industries also fell as newly organized nonunion companies began operations and existing previously

❖

unionized companies abrogated labor contracts by declaring bankruptcy, setting up nonunion subsidiaries, or outsourcing maintenance and repair work to nonunion contractors. Thus, there seems to be ample evidence that transportation workers received lower wages as a result of deregulation.

Although secular economists focus their attention on wages, John Paul II (1982, pp. 46-49) reminds us that while wages are important there are other dimensions to employment which must be considered. Respect for the rights of workers requires, in addition to adequate wages, sufficient health care, pension, and related benefits, a safe and healthy work environment, protection from the risks of unemployment, and opportunities for membership in labor organizations with sufficient power to protect the rights of their members and to be an influence in society for the good of all. To investigate the effects of deregulation on these other dimensions of employment in the transportation industry, data were collected for employee compensation, wages, occupational illness and injuries, unemployment rates, and union membership. Data from pre- and post-deregulation eras were then compared to obtain an indication of the effects of deregulation.

Trend analysis was used to compare pre- and post-deregulation data for wages, fringe benefits, occupational safety and health, and unemployment. Insufficient data prevented trend analysis of union membership, but comparison was made with the data available. It would have been desirable to collect data only for workers in those components of the industry deregulated. But industry component detail was not available; so data applicable to all transportation industry workers as a group were used.[1]

To separate the effects of deregulation from the effects of other events influencing the various dimensions of employment of interest here, transportation workers were compared to workers in the service industry.[2] Transportation is a service; and so both transportation and service industry employees should be influenced by many of the same economic and social factors. The service industry, however, has not experienced changes in structure and conduct comparable to those changes attributed to deregulation in the transportation industry. Thus, changes in transportation employment data relative to service employment data should be at least a partial measure of the effects of de-regulation.

Since deregulation of various components of the industry occured at various times between 1976 and 1986, timing of the effects of deregulation on industry-wide data should be cumulative, making identification of pre- and post-deregulation eras difficult. Use of quadratic trend analysis avoids this problem by allowing the data themselves to detect the timing of effects if there is evidence of any. A quadratic trend equation contains two terms besides the intercept, a linear term and a quadratic term. If neither term is statistically significant, then there is no evidence of effect, only evidence of random or cyclical variation from a mean unchanged throughout pre- and post-deregulation eras. If only the linear term is statistically significant, there is still no evidence of effect, only evidence of a trend in the data which began before deregulation and persists, without change in direction, after

❖

deregulation. But if the quadratic term is statistically significant, then there is evidence of curvature, a change in direction of the trend, suggesting that deregulation had an effect on transportation workers.

## A. Effects of Deregulation on Labor – Wages

Since the negative effect of deregulation on wages in the transportation industry has been documented by several authors, the analytical procedure just described can be tested by applying it to wage data. Data on wages and salaries per full-time-equivalent employee in transportation and in services for the years 1968 through 1989 were collected from publications of the Department of Commerce.[3] To adjust for the effects of changes in wages brought about by events other than deregulation, the ratio of the two wage series was computed using the transportation data series as the numerator so that any negative effects of deregulation should appear as a decline in the ratio. The results of the trend analysis, shown in Table 1, provide evidence of a trend changing direction since the quadratic term is statistically significant. Figure 1, indicates the timing of the turning point in both the trend and in the actual data. The trend reaches a peak in 1975. The actual data reach a peak in 1978. Relative wages were clearly rising before deregulation and falling thereafter, a pattern consistent with research cited earlier in this paper.

**Table 1.**

**Trend Analysis: Wage Ratio – 1968 through 1989\***

| | | | |
|---|---|---|---|
| Intercept: | 1.5350 | Two-tail Significance Level: | 0.000 |
| Linear Term: | -0.0133 | Two-tail Significance Level: | 0.000 |
| Quadratic Term: | -0.0020 | Two-tail Significance Level: | 0.000 |
| R-square: | 0.945 | Durbin-Watson Statistic: | 0.789 |

\*Intercept located between 1978 and 1979.

❖

**Figure 1.**

**Ratio of Annual Wages: Transportation to Service – 1968 to 1989**

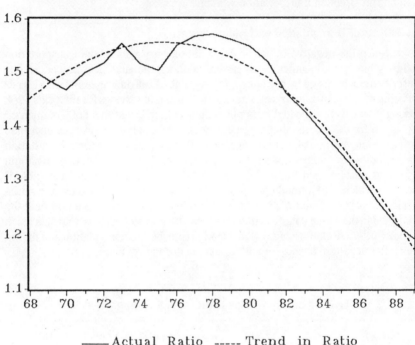

———— Actual Ratio ----- Trend in Ratio

## B. Effects of Deregulation on Labor – Fringe Benefits

In addition to wages and salaries, employer contributions to social security, health care, pension, and related benefits are important sources of compensation for the services of labor. Since benefits are costs to employers much like wages, the same arguments advanced to explain why deregulation should depress wages might be expected to apply to these other forms of compensation. However, use of the same method of trend analysis applied to wages and salaries did not find evidence that deregulation depressed benefit payments.

To measure benefits paid to workers in transportation and services, wages and salaries per full-time-equivalent employee were subtracted from compensation per full-time-equivalent employee computed from Commerce Department data.[4] The trend in the ratio of benefits paid transportation workers to benefits paid service workers is described by the equation in Table 2 and illustrated in Figure 2. Since only the linear term of the equation is statistically significant, there is no evidence of curvature, only evidence of a downward trend in the relative benefit's ratio that began before deregulation and continued afterwards without change in direction.

## Figure 2.

### Ratio of Annual Benefits: Transportation to Service – 1968 to 1989

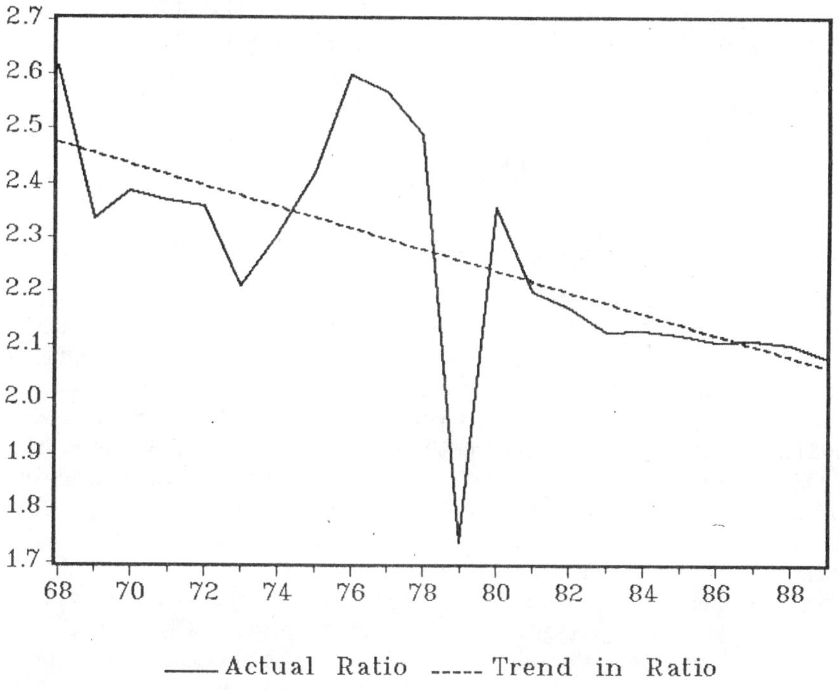

———— Actual Ratio ----- Trend in Ratio

Thus, there is no evidence that deregulation depressed benefits of transportation workers in the same way wages were depressed. In fact there is other evidence that benefit increases were traded for wage concessions. Grant M. Davis et al. (1987), one source of this evidence, noted the increased use of employee stock ownership programs in the trucking industry. Another source, Curtis and Crum, reported growth in stock ownership and profit sharing programs as well as new provisions for employee participation in company decision making. The trade off between wages and stock ownership or profit sharing may be one explanation why deregulation does not appear to have had an adverse effect on fringe benefits overall. Expansion of these types of benefits, long recommended in Catholic teaching as a means of protecting labor's rights, may prove advantageous to transportation workers in the long run. Monetary gains in benefits of this type, however, did not offset wage losses; for trend analysis of ratios of total employee compensation reveals a pattern similar to Figure 1.

❖

Table 2.

Trend Analysis: Fringe Benefits Ratio – 1968 through 1989*

| | | | |
|---|---|---|---|
| Intercept: | 2.2730 | Two-tail Significance Level: | 0.000 |
| Linear Term: | -0.0197 | Two-tail Significance Level: | 0.003 |
| Quadratic Term: | -0.0002 | Two-tail Significance Level: | 0.862 |
| R-square: | 0.380 | Durbin-Watson Statistic: | 1.997 |

*Intercept located between 1978 and 1979.

## C. Effects of Deregulation on Labor – Health and Safety

A safe and healthy work environment is also important to workers, especially to workers in the transportation industry where the incidence of occupational injury and illness is higher than in private industry as a whole. Increased competition resulting from deregulation was expected by some to be a cause of increased accidents as transportation companies tried to cut costs by deferring maintenance and neglecting safe operating practices. Thomas M. Corsi et al. (1988) wrote that a major concern with respect to deregulation of trucking was that competitive pressures would lead to increased accident rates as drivers, forced to work excessive hours, succumbed to fatigue or as equipment failed because of curtail- ment of vehicle inspection and maintenance. Thomas M. Corsi and Philip Fanara, Jr. (1988) noted another concern; namely, that newly organized firms would experience higher accident rates because of lack of experience. Clinton V. Oster, Jr. and C. Kurt Zorn (1987) reported similar concerns associated with airline deregulation. Evidence to date; however, suggests these concerns were largely unfounded. Accident rates of motor carriers and air carriers operating before deregulation were found to be no higher after deregulation. New entrants were found to have higher accident rates than existing carriers, but data compiled by the Bureau of Labor statistics show that overall occupational injury and illness rates have declined in trucking and have changed little in air transportation.[5]

In fact when government data on occupational injury and illness for the entire transportation industry are analyzed using the same procedures used to analyze data on wages and benefits, it appears that the transportation industry was, relatively speaking, actually a safer, healthier place to work after deregulation than before. Table 3 shows the result of the trend analysis of the ratio of occupational injury and illness rates of workers in transportation to occupational injury and illness rates of workers in the service industry. The statistical significance of the quadratic term indicates a change in the direction of the trend. Figure 3 illustrates that the trend in occupational injury and illness rates peaked in 1979 while the actual data peaked in 1978, suggesting that the safety and health of transportation workers actually improved after deregulation.

❖

## Table 3

### Trend Analysis: Illness & Injury Ratio – 1973 through 1989*

| | | | | |
|---|---|---|---|---|
| Intercept: | 2.3820 | Two-tail Significance Level: | 0.000 |
| Linear Term: | -0.0136 | Two-tail Significance Level: | 0.014 |
| Quadratic Term: | -0.0040 | Two-tail Significance Level: | 0.003 |
| R-square: | 0.598 | Durbin-Watson Statistic: | 2.318 |

*Intercept located in 1981.

### Figure 3.

### Ratio of Occupational Injury & Illness Rates: Transport to Service '73-'79

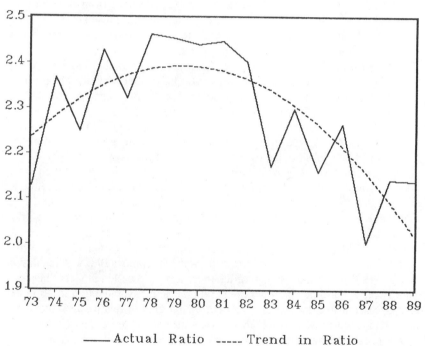

———— Actual Ratio  ----- Trend  in  Ratio

Several reasons for this improvement are plausible and should be investigated further than is possible here. Spurred by concerns expressed about deregulation's adverse effect on safety, the government regulatory agencies responsible for monitoring safety in the transportation industry may have intensified their efforts with salutary effect.[6] But it is also possible that increased competition played a role, for accidents harming transportation workers may also cause service delays or worse harm to transportation customers; thus transportation firms, subject to increased competition, may have increased their efforts to avoid accidents.

## D. Effects of Deregulation on Labor – Unemployment

In addition to the risks of occupational illness or injury, labor also faces the risk of unemployment, and unemployment was expected to result from deregulation. B. Starr McMullen (1986) notes that airline deregulation was expected to have adverse effects on airline employees because increased competition was expected to make it more likely that individual companies would experience financial difficulties. For this reason the Airline Deregulation Act contained provisions to protect displaced employees. Lieb (1985, pp. 376-78) describes congressional efforts to protect railroad workers from the job losses resulting from the consolidations and downsizing which Winston (p. 40) found to be the result of a long-term trend but which deregulation was expected to accelerate because of provisions easing government restraints on mergers and abandonments.

There is no doubt that thousands of transportation workers lost their jobs as transportation companies merged, downsized or failed after deregulation occurred. But the extent to which the unemployment that occurred can be attributed to deregulation has been a matter of considerable dispute; for as noted by McMullen deregulation occurred simultaneously with the fuel crisis of 1979 and the recessions of 1980 and 1982. Moreover, deregulation's negative impact was muted by the thousands of new jobs offered by the entry of new firms into the industry.

Trend analysis of the ratio of the unemployment rate in transportation to the unemployment rate in services, illustrated in Table 4 and Figure 4, does little to separate the effects of recession, fuel price increases, and deregulation, but it does make it clear that relative unemployment rates in transportation were rising prior to deregulation as the recession of 1969-70 was followed by the more severe recession of 1973-75, suggesting that the ratio responds to the severity of the recession. Thus, it is difficult to attribute the peak of the ratio in 1982 to deregulation because 1982 marked the trough of the most severe recession in recent history.[7] Shortly after that time, the trend in the ratio became favorable to transportation employees; but, inspite of seven years of economic growth, relative unemployment rates in the industry were still higher in 1989 than before deregulation suggesting that deregulation has increased the risks of unemployment for transportation workers.

❖

## Table 4.

### Trend Analysis: Unemployment Rate Ratio – 1968 through 1989*

| Intercept: | 1.0353 | Two-tail Significance Level: | 0.000 |
| Linear Term: | 0.0154 | Two-tail Significance Level: | 0.001 |
| Quadratic Term: | -0.0014 | Two-tail Significance Level: | 0.055 |
| R-square: | 0.521 | Durbin-Watson Statistic: | 1.487 |

*Intercept located between 1978 and 1979.

## Figure 4.

### Ratio of Unemployment Rates: Transportation to Service – 1968 to 1989

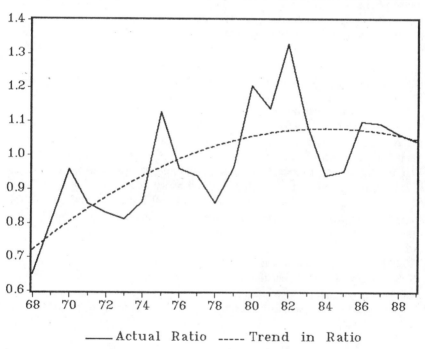

———— Actual Ratio ----- Trend in Ratio

## E. Effects of Deregulation on Labor – Union Membership

Curtis and Crum and Lieb (1984) have noted that unions have suffered declines in membership and bargaining power as a result of deregulation. Unfortunately the methods used to collect data on union membership today were not used prior to deregulation; so there is no timeseries available for trend analysis. Such data as are available suggest that the effect may have been large. The Bureau of Labor

❖

Statistics (1979) reported that in May 1977, near the beginning of the era of deregulation, 1,529,000 employees in the transportation industry were union members, about 50 percent of all employees in the industry. By 1983, after deregulation was well underway, the Bureau (1985) was reporting that the number of union members had fallen to 1,152,000, about 42 percent of industry employment. And by 1989, the Bureau (1990) was reporting that membership had declined to 1,047,000, a number which accounted for only about 30 percent of employment.

Yet, as documented by Larry T. Adams (1985), large declines in union membership and share of labor force represented have occurred not just in transportation but throughout the private sector of the economy. Thus, it seems likely that union losses would have occurred in the transportation industry even if deregulation had not taken place, though it is probably true that deregulation magnified those losses by allowing the entry of so many new firms into the transportation industry.

While it is extremely difficult to evaluate the costs and benefits of the loss of union influence in the transportation industry, the loss of that influence may well be the most significant impact of deregulation to date. This contention rests on two points. First, transportation workers still have good jobs. Second, Catholic social teaching places a premium on a vigorous labor movement as a means to a just society.

The first point can be demonstrated by a quick review of the Figures 1 through 4 and some tributary data. Using the year 1989 as a benchmark, Figure 1 indicates that annual wages of transportation workers were about 1.2 times greater than the annual wages of service industry workers or $28,000 and $23,000, respectively. Figure 2 indicates that annual fringe benefits of transportation workers were worth about twice as much as the benefits received by service workers or $6,000 and $3,000, respectively. Figure 3 indicates that actual illness and injury rates of transportation industry workers were about 2.1 times greater than those of service employees, a ratio as low as any since the Occupational Health and Safety Administration began publishing data for the entire transportation industry in 1973.[8] Finally Figure 4 shows that by 1989 unemployment rates for transportation workers were slightly higher than service workers, 5.0 percent and 4.8 percent, respectively. An unemployment rate of 5 percent, however, is relatively low by recent standards. Thus, when these four dimensions of employment are considered, it appears that transportation workers, inspite of their wage losses, still hold relatively desirable jobs.

But the loss of labor union influence, while not due soley to deregulation, cannot be discounted in this way. Echoing the words of current and previous popes, the National Conference of Catholic Bishops (1986, pp. 147-152) calls for a stronger not a weaker role for organized labor and other institutions structured to protect the livelihood of working people. The bishops see a need for greater institutional protection of the rights of labor in the face of intensified competition and encourage labor to work creatively in partnership with management to

❖

surmount the challenges of competition. But they note that partnership implies that labor has the power to influence decisions. The bishops also see needs in society which touch the workplace but extend beyond it, like discrimination and poverty, which demand organized and cooperative input from workers if those needs are to be justly accommodated. In short, the vision of society idealized in Catholic social teaching has an important role for labor to play. But organized labor weakened by deregulation and other changes in the American economic system will have difficulty playing that role well.

## IV. Summary and Conclusions

Modern Catholic social teaching has staunchly defended the rights of labor and emphasized that maintenance of social justice requires that organized labor play an active and influential role. Yet in the mid 1970's the American political economy consciously chose to follow a policy of deregulation, a policy expected to have at least some adverse effects on workers in industries in which it was applied. The transportation industry was one of those industries.

This paper, having organized information from a number of authors, attempted to provide a unified analysis of the effects of deregulation on transportation workers in three steps. First, the rationale and scope of deregulation were outlined to provide an indication of the timing, reasons for, and beneficiaries of deregulation. Second, the theoretical and empirical bases for expecting deregulation to have an adverse effect on workers in the industry were discussed. Finally, the actual effects on those workers in the first ten years of the deregulation era were described with attention to wages, fringe benefits, occupational health and safety, unemployment, and union membership. Evidence was found that health and safety conditions may have improved. Evidence was found that fringe benefits were not affected but that unemployment rates increased. Wages were clearly reduced. Union membership also declined, both absolutely and relatively, suggesting a decline in influence of organized labor, which decline, given the importance attached to a vigorous labor movement by Catholic social teaching, may prove, in the long run, to be the greatest cost of deregulation not only to workers as a group but also to society as a whole.

## Endnotes

*Assistant Professor of Economics, College of Business Administration, Creighton University, Omaha, NE 68178 USA.

[1] The most detailed data on employment published by the Department of Labor is found in the annual bulletin *Occupational Injuries and Illnesses in the United States by Industry*. For 1983 average annual employment in the transportation industry was reported to be 2,738,800. Estimates of employment in segments of the industry then

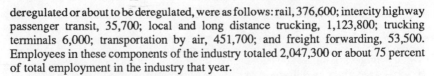

deregulated or about to be deregulated, were as follows: rail, 376,600; intercity highway passenger transit, 35,700; local and long distance trucking, 1,123,800; trucking terminals 6,000; transportation by air, 451,700; and freight forwarding, 53,500. Employees in these components of the industry totaled 2,047,300 or about 75 percent of total employment in the industry that year.

[2] The service industry is comprised of the following components: hotels and other lodging places, personal services, business services, auto repair services and garages, miscellaneous repair services, motion pictures, amusement and recreation services, social services and membership organizations, miscellaneous professional services, and private household services.

[3] Wage and salary data were taken from Table 6.8B of the National Income and Product Accounts published in *The National Income and Product Accounts, 1929 - 82* and *The Survey of Current Business,* July, 1987 and July 1990.

[4] Data on compensation of employees and number of full-time-equivalent employees were taken from Tables 6.4B and 6.7B of the sources mentioned in Note #3.

[5] Using data from the same Department of Labor source mentioned in Note #1, the average injury and illness incidence rate in the trucking industry was 16.6 in the period 1973-1975 and 13.2 in 1987-1989. For airlines the average illness and incidence was 13.7 in 1973-1975 and 13.8 in 1987-1989.

[6] Federal agencies responsible for enforcing safety regulations in the transportation industry include the Federal Railroad Administration, the Federal Aviation Administration, and the Federal Highway Administration.

[7] Using the civilian unemployment rate for the overall economy as a measure of the severity of recession, the unemployment rate in 1970 was 4.9%; in 1975, 8.5%; in 1980, 7.1%; and in 1982, 9.7%.

[8] Injury and illness incidence rates for railroads were not published in the source referenced in Note #1 prior to 1973.

## References

Adams, L.T. "Changing Employment Patterns of Organized Workers," *Monthly Labor Review,* February 1985, *108,* 25-31.

Adams, W. and J.W. Brock. "Countervailing or Coalescing Power? The Problem of Labor/Management Coalitions," *Journal of Post Keynesian Economics,* Winter 1983-84, *6,* 180-97.

Babcock, M.W., L.O. Sorensen, M.H. Chow, and K. Klindworth. "Impact of the Staggers Rail Act on Agriculture: A Kansas Case Study," *Proceedings-Transportation Research Forum,* 1985, *26,* 364-72.

Bailey, E.R., D.R. Graham, and D.P. Kaplan. *Deregulating the Airlines,* Cambridge, MA: MIT Press, 1985.

Corsi, T.M., P. Fanara, Jr., and J.L. Jarrell. "Safety Performance of Pre-MCA Motor Carriers: 1977 Versus 1984," *Transportation Journal*, Spring 1988, *29*, 30-36.

Corsi, T.M. and P. Fanara, Jr. "Deregulation, New Entrants and the Safety Learning Curve," *Journal of the Transportation Research Forum*, 1988, *29* No. (1), 3-8.

Curtis, E.F. and M.R. Crum. "Transportation Labor Relations: Contemporary Developments, Challenges, and Stategies," *Transportation Quarterly*, July 1988, *42*, 359-75.

Davis, G.M., N. Weintraub, and W.H. Holley. "Employee Stock Ownership Programs and Their Use in Trucking: Capital Formation, Employee Participation, or Survival?" *Logistics and Transportation Review*, 1987, *23* (3), 243-63.

Ehrenberg, R.G. The Regulatory Process and Labor Earnings, New York, NY: Academic Press, 1979.

Fuller, S., D. Bessler, J. MacDonald, and M. Wohlgenant. "Effect of Deregulation in Export-Grain Rail Rates in the Plains and Corn Belt," *Journal of the Transportation Research Forum*, 1987, *28* (1), 160-67.

Ginsburg, H. "Teachings of John Paul II on Work and the Rights of Workers," *Social Thought*, Spring/Summer 1987, *13*, 46-59.

Hendricks, W. "Regulation and Labor Earnings," *Bell Journal of Economics*, August 1977, *8*, 483-96.

John Paul II. "Laborem Exercens," In *On Human Work: A Resource Book,* Washington, DC: United States Catholic Conference, 1982.

Keeler, T.E. *Railroads, Freight, and Public Policy*, Washington, DC: Brookings Institution, 1983.

Leo XIII. "Rerum Novarum," 1891. In H. Ginsburg (Ed.), *Poverty, Economics and Society,* Lanham, MD: University Press of America, 1981.

Lieb, Robert C. *Labor in the Transportation Industries.* New, York, NY: Praeger, 1974.
_____. "The Changing Nature of Labor Management Relations in Transportation." *Transportation Journal,* Spring 1984, 23, 4-14.

_____. *Transportation*. Reston, VA: Reston Publishing, 1985.

McMullen, B.S. "Employee Protection After Airline Deregulation," *Transportation Journal*, Spring 1986, *25*, 20-34.

Mielke, J.H. "Short Line Railroad Creations: Terms of Sale, Impacts on Viability and Public Policy Implications," *Journal of the Transportation Research Forum*, 1988, *29* (1), 138-148.

Moore, T.G. "The Beneficiaries of Trucking Regulation," *The Journal of Law and Economics*, October 1978, *21*, 327-43.

Oster, C.V., Jr. and C.K. Zorn. "Deregulation's Impact on Airline Safety," *Journal of the Transportation Research Forum*, 1987, *28* (1), 3-12.

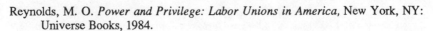

Reynolds, M. O. *Power and Privilege: Labor Unions in America*, New York, NY: Universe Books, 1984.

Rima, I. H. *Labor Markets, Wages, and Employment*, New York NY: W. W. Norton, 1981.

Sampson, R. J., M. T. Farris, and D. L. Schrock. *Domestic Transportation*, Boston, MA: Houghton Mifflin, 1990.

Schmidt, E. P. *Union Power and the Public Interest*, Caroline House Publishers, 1973.

Tomaskovic-Devey, Donald. "Industrial Structure, Relative Labor Power and Poverty Rates." In D. Tomaskovic-Devey (Ed.) *Poverty and Social Welfare in the United States*, Boulder, CO: Westview Press, 1988.

Winston, Clifford, T. M. Corsi, C. M. Grimm, and C. A. Evans. *The Economic Effects of Surface Freight Deregulation*, Washington, DC: Brookings Institution, 1990.

Weiss, Leonard "Concentration and Labor Earnings," *American Economic Review*, March 1966, *56*, 96-117.

Bureau of Labor Statistics. *Earnings and Other Characteristics of Organized Workers, May 1977*, BLS Report #556, 1979.

_____. *Employment and Earnings*, January 1985, 32, 209.

_____. *Employment and Earnings*, January 1990, 37, 232.

Department of Commerce. *The National Income and Product Accounts of the United States, 1929-82*, Washington, DC: U.S. Government Printing Office, 1986.

Department of Labor. *Occupational Injuries and Illnesses in the United States by Industry*. Annual Bulletins for the years 1973 through 1989. Washington, DC: U. S. Government Printing Office, 1975 through 1991.

Interstate Commerce Commission. *Annual Report*, Washington, DC: U.S. Government Printing Office, 1980.

_____. *Annual Report*, Washington, DC: U.S. Government Printing Office, 1986.

National Conference of Catholic Bishops. *Economic Justice for All: Pastoral Letter on Catholic Social Teaching and the U.S. Economy*, Washington, DC: United States Catholic Conference, 1986.

# Sickness Absence in the Welfare State

## Carl P. Kaiser*

The concept of the welfare state connotes the production and distribution of social well-being. To accomplish this, almost all industrialized capitalist countries have created programs that provide sickness absence, pension, unemployment, and retirement benefits to their citizens. However, the emphasis on welfare varies greatly across states. The degree to which the extension of social rights, in contrast to property rights, permits people to maintain their standards of living independent of pure market forces is observed over a wide range among countries. In states in which the emphasis on social well-being is very high, benefits are granted on the basis of citizenship, not on the basis of performance or one's value as a labor commodity, in contrast to what occurs in states that provide only minimal benefits and in which a stigma is attached to the receipt of benefits. States that exemplify the former orientation include the Netherlands and the Scandinavian states, while the U.S., Canada and Australia exemplify the latter.[1]

This paper deals with the economic incentives created by sickness absence in the welfare state. Cross-national comparisons of absence behavior reveal large differences among the frequencies, durations, and patterns of sickness absence. As recently reviewed by Rienk Prins (1990), most of the cross-national absence comparisons indicate that absence rates are highest in nations that most strongly emphasize social rights vis-à-vis property rights and that accordingly adhere closely to the principle of providing social benefits primarily on the basis of citizenship as opposed to other more stringent eligibility requirements.

This philosophy has led most welfare states (except the US) to institutionalize national sickness benefit programs that provide generous payments to absent workers; indeed, in most European countries sickness benefits are equal to normal earnings. Moreover, although the specific features of the programs vary from state to state, the financing of sickness benefits is typically not structured on the basis of actuarial principles that would guide the design of a social insurance program. Rather, sickness benefit programs are conceptually viewed as social security such

❖

that the sickness benefit tax payments that are made by a given firm are not tightly related to the sickness benefits that are collected by the firm's employees. The structure of financing is typically defined such that the tax system entails a low degree of experience rating—the degree to which an employer's tax is determined by the employer's recent experience with sickness absence.

Defining the tax structure in this way is likely to influence absence behavior, thus it is a useful exercise to investigate the economic incentives created by sickness benefit programs. The purposes of this paper are to summarize an economic model of absence behavior[2] that facilitates identification of the mechanisms through which sickness benefit programs influence absence rates and employment levels and to discuss the implications and conclusions that can be drawn from the analysis.

## I. Overview of a Market Model of Absence Behavior

The model summarized in this section addresses the firm's demand for labor proceeding from the assumption that time absent from work and sickness benefits received when absent provide the average employee with utility. The firm anticipates that the average employee will be absent at times during the firm's relevant planning period, for example, during the course of one year. Therefore the firm is assumed to retain a stock of employees, some of whom it expects to be absent on any given day during the planning period.

If the labor market is competitive, the set of job characteristics offered by the employer must yield as high a level of utility as the worker could obtain elsewhere. Accordingly, a competitive labor market will result in that combination of employment, absences, and wage and sickness benefit income that maximizes the utility of workers subject to the economic constraints imposed by product demand, production, the cost of capital, and the benefit and tax arrangements inherent in the structure of the sickness benefit program.

Given these initial perceptions, it has been assumed that the utility received by the average employee is a function of the employee's expected income, which must include both expected wage income and expected sickness benefit income, and the nonpecuniary value that the employee places on time away from work. The other key feature required in a model that analyzes the economic incentives of a sickness benefit program is proper representation of the circumstances that constrain the employer's choices. Accordingly, it has been assumed that the employer's total revenue, as dictated by competition, will be completely exhausted by the firm's costs. These costs include the cost of capital services, the firm's total wage bill, the costs of disrupted production caused by absent workers, and the firm's sickness benefits tax bill. For the purposes of the analysis, the key parameters reflected in this constraint on the employer are the daily sickness benefit amount, $b$, and the fraction of the current benefits paid to the firm's employees that is covered by the firm's tax payments, $e$, which measures the degree of experience rating of the employer's sickness benefits tax.

❖

Given that the employer accepts and may even benefit from employee absence, the choice variables for the model become the number of workers employed on a given day, $N_e$, and the number of employees at work on a given day, $N_w$. Therefore, the solution to the model was obtained by maximizing the utility of the average worker with respect $N_e$, and $N_w$ subject to the employer's cost constraint. Under competition, maximization of the utility of the representative worker yields the quantities of $N_e$ and $N_w$ that are optimal from the standpoint of the firm's desire to maximize profits. The model's solution then permits analysis of the impacts of the parameters of the sickness benefit financing structure on the economic incentives that influence absence behavior.

The solution to model yields the usual choice conditions for the profit maximizing rate of use of labor services; the value of marginal product of labor must equal the marginal cost of labor. As indicated above, in this model the optimal stocks of two concepts of the quantity of labor must be chosen on any given day during the relevant planning period. Therefore, the solution of the model permits the determination of the values of marginal product for the last employee who works on a given day ($VMP_{Nw}$), and the last employee retained by the firm on a given day ($VMP_{Ne}$). Since $N_e$-$N_w$ is the number of employees who are absent, the benefits and costs of absence drive a wedge between the optimal values of the stock of employees and the number of employees who attend work on a given day.

These results bring into sharp focus the impacts of the parameters of the sickness benefit program on absence decisions. The model implies that the firm receives a net sickness benefit subsidy defined as the value of the excess of the net marginal sickness benefits received by the last absent employee over the net marginal cost of the sickness benefit tax. If the subsidy is greater than zero then the firm's labor cost is subsidized by the sickness benefit program. In this case the number of absences is greater than it would be without the subsidy since the subsidy decreases the optimal number of employees who attend work and increases the optimal number of employees retained by the firm.

## II. Absence and Employment Effects of Sickness Benefit Program Parameters

The objective of this section is to establish and indicate how the two key parameters of a sickness benefit program, the daily benefit amount, b, and the degree of experience rating of the sickness benefits tax, e, influence the incentives for employee absence. This involves, first, summarizing the comparative static effects of changes in these two parameters on the optimal values of the choice variables, $N_e$ and $N_w$, the number of daily absences, and the size of the net sickness benefit subsidy received by the employer, and second, drawing some conclusions about the importance of the subsidy given the values of b and e that are typically observed in modern welfare states.

The model unambiguously implies that a decrease in the degree of experience rating of the sickness benefits tax will increase the number employees retained by the employer, decrease the number of employees working on a given day, and hence, increase the number of workers who are absent on a given day. In other words, the weaker the linkage between the firm's sickness absence tax bill and its recent experience with sickness absences (i.e., the lower the value of e), the greater will be subsidy received by the firm and the more it will be inclined to encourage absence.

The effects of the sickness benefit amount, b, are a little more complex, but nonetheless, easily interpreted. The impact of b on the choice variables depends upon the degree of experience rating of the sickness benefits tax. However, the structure of the sickness benefit programs as observed in most modern welfare states suggests that the fraction of the marginal cost of sickness absence that is borne by the employer is typically and substantially less than one; typical values e, which measures the degree of experience rating, are quite low. Adopting this order of magnitude for e allows for an unambiguous interpretation of the impact of a change in b on the firm's choice variables; an increase of the daily benefit amount will increase the number of employees retained by the firm, decrease the number who work on a given day, and hence, increase the number of workers who are absent on a given day. Moreover, these outcomes occur because a greater benefit increases the size of subsidy received by the firm.

## III. Summary and Conclusions

The analysis summarized in this paper assumes that employees maximize utility and employers maximize profits. Employees gain utility from wage income, sickness benefit income, and the relative value of time absent from work. In a competitive environment the employer's total revenue will be fully absorbed by the cost of capital, total wage costs, the disruptive costs of absence, and sickness benefit tax payments. In the analysis, the firm's tax payment has been decomposed into a part that is determined as a function of the sickness benefits received by its employees and a part that is independent of the amount of sickness benefit payments received by its employees. Therefore, to investigate the effects of the sickness benefit program on absence behavior, the two key variables are the degree of experience rating of the sickness benefits tax, e, defined as the fraction of current benefit payments received by a firm's employees that is covered by its sickness benefit tax bill, and the daily benefit amount received by an absent employee, b.

In most welfare states the value of e is substantially less than one, and b is typically equal or close to normal daily earnings. Taking these order-of-magnitude values of e and b as typical, the analysis implies the presence of strong economic incentives that encourage absence. When the degree of experience rating of the employer's tax payment is low, the marginal cost of absence will be very low, and consequently, the firm's labor costs will be subsidized because the last employee taking absence is generously compensated for absence at little cost to the firm. Hence, because neither employers nor employees incur a large share of the

❖

marginal costs of absence, the system simultaneously creates a work disincentive for employees and a wage subsidy for employers. The sickness benefit system creates strong incentives for employees to choose higher absence rates and for employers to encourage or condone higher absence rates.

This result begs the question of whether or not a sickness benefit system that encourages absence is socially optimal? The answer is not clear and, in fact, depends upon social values and norms regarding absence behavior, work, and other economic outcomes. For example, in societies that are highly individualistic such as the U.S., there is a stigma associated with frequent absences; one who is absent frequently appears to be shirking responsibility and seems to exhibit low commitment to the employer. On the other hand, in countries such as the Netherlands in which individual material success is not highly valued but where modesty, rewarding personal relationships and individual well-being are considered very important, a stigma associated sickness absence is not likely to be present because absence is looked upon as a necessary step in regaining one's full capacity to work productively.

In countries that respect the positive aspects of absence, social values will stimulate higher absence rates in at least two ways. First, at the individual level, when one experiences an episode of "perceived" work incapacity, three decisions must be made regarding absence behavior. First, the sickness role threshold defines the point at which the individual considers his/her symptoms "serious enough" to conclude that he/she is sick. Second, the absence tolerance threshold defines when the individual decides that he/she is "sick enough" to be absent from work. Third, is the work resumption threshold, which defines the point at which the individual concludes that he or she is "well enough" to return to work.[3] The typical degree of work incapacity at which an individual passes through each of these thresholds will be different among societies across which social values and norms vary significantly. On these grounds, for example, all other things equal, absence rates will be higher in the Netherlands than they are in the U.S.

The second way in which such social values and norms will affect absence behavior is that they will influence the structure of the sickness benefit program. Since the philosophy of the welfare state entails much greater concern for individual welfare than for holding individual recipients of social security benefits fully liable for the costs incurred by the state for providing those benefits, social security programs (such as sickness benefits) will be deliberately structured with very weak experience rating. To sum up, as compared to countries that adhere to very individualistic values, absenteeism is more acceptable in "complete" welfare states, and because it is seen as having positive value, a sickness benefit program that provides further and relatively strong economic incentives for absence is likely to be implemented.

A sickness benefit program that heavily subsidizes employers for permitting high absence rates and that offers generous sickness benefits, as explained in this paper, entails strong work disincentives. This begs the further question: What does

❖

society get in return for the costs of a sickness benefit program that itself stimulates absence behavior?

The analysis summarized in this paper sheds some light on this issue. Under the assumed typical conditions of a low degree of experience rating of the sickness benefits tax, and benefits that approximately fully replace wage income, a larger sickness benefit subsidy increases absence rates, in part, by increasing the optimal level of employment chosen by the firm. Therefore, the sickness absence program allows the firm to use sickness absence as a means of worksharing; over some (annual) planning period the subsidy implies that a greater number of workers will be employed to achieve a given rate of output. Also it provides a means of hoarding skilled labor through periods of relatively weak demand. Moreover, if the sickness benefit system is structured such that most firms in an economy receive a sickness benefit subsidy, then the scope of the program would go well beyond simply insuring workers against the risk of income loss due to sickness. Under these arrangements the aggregate demand for labor would be greater than otherwise, hence, more workers would be employed. Assuming a given aggregate product demand, the sickness benefit program would constitute a *de facto* macroeconomic policy initiative to combat unemployment.

In a world of generally weak aggregate product demand, a sickness benefit program could be used to substitute absence for unemployment. Weighed against the costs of greater absence are the substantial benefits that accrue from maintaining over the long run an unemployment rate that is lower than would have otherwise been possible. In addition to the lower unemployment benefit costs, at least part of the depreciation of human capital experienced by individuals who endure long spells of unemployment would be eliminated—an outcome that would substantially reduce the long run costs of persistently weak aggregate product demand. Whether or not a sickness absence program that encourages absence is socially beneficial depends first upon our ability to empirically estimate the costs and benefits of such a program, and second, upon a society's interpretation of the estimated benefits and costs as guided by social values and norms.

## Endnotes

*Department of Economics, School of Commerce, Economics, and Politics, Washington and Lee University, Lexington, VA 24450 USA.

[1] See Gosta Esping-Andersen (1990) for a systematic and comprehensive analysis of welfare states in modern capitalist economies.

[2] The complete mathematical development of the model is available from the author upon request.

[3] See Rienk Prins' (1990, pp. 122-123) model of sickness absence behavior.

# References

Allen, Steven G., "Compensation, Safety, and Absenteeism: Evidence from the Paper Industry," *Industrial and Labor\Relations Review*, January 1981a, *34*, 208-18.

_____, "An Empirical Model of Work Attendance," *Review of Economics and Statistics*, February 1981b, *63*, 77-87.

Chadwick-Jones, J.K., Nicholson, Nigel and Brown, Colin, *Social Psychology of Absenteeism*, New York: Praeger, 1982.

Chelius, James R., "Understanding Absenteeism: The Potential Contribution of Economic Theory," *Journal of Business Research*, 1981, *9*, 409-18.

Dunn, L.F., "An Empirical Study of Labor Market Equilibrium Under Working Hours constraints," *Review of Economics and Statistics*, May 1990, *72*, 250-58.

Dunn, L.F. and Youngblood, Stuart A., "Absenteeism as a Mechanism for Approaching an Optimal Labor Market Equilibrium," *Review of Economics and Statistics*, November 1986, *68*, 668-74.

Esping-Andersen, Gosta, *The Three Worlds of Welfare Capitalism*, Princeton: Princeton University Press, 1990.

Hofstede, Geert, *Cultures Consequences: International Differences in Work-Related Values*, London: Sage, 1980.

Jacobson, Stephen L., "The Effects of Pay Incentives on Teacher Absenteeism," *Journal of Human Resources*, Spring 1989, *24*, 280-86.

Kaiser, Carl P., "A Process Model of Work Group Absence Rates," Washington and Lee University, submitted for publication, 1990.

Kopelman, Richard E., "Alternative Work Schedules and Productivity: A Review of the Evidence," *National Productivity Review*, Spring 1986, *5*, 150-65.

Leigh, Paul J., "The Effects of Unemployment and Business Cycle on Absenteeism," *Journal of Economics and Business*, May 1985, *37*, 159-70.

Prins, Rienk, *Sickness Absence in Belgium, Germany (FR), and the Netherlands*, Amsterdam: Netherlands Institute for Working Conditions, 1990.

Reza, Ali M., "Labour Supply and Demand, Absenteeism, and Union Behaviour," *Review of Economic Studies*, April 1975, *42*, 237-47.

Rosen, Sherwin S., "Hedonic Prices and Implicit Markets," *Journal of Political Economy*, January-February 1974, *82*, 34-55.

Steers, Richard M. and Rhodes, Susan, "Major Influences on Employee Attendance: A Process Model," *Journal of Applied Psychology*, August 1978, *63*, 391-407.

U.S. Department of Health and Human Services, *Social Security Programs Throughout the World (1989)*, Washington, D.C.: U.S. Government Printing Office, 1990.

---------------------------------- ❖ ----------------------------------

# Creativity, Entrepreneurship, and Consumer Policy

## Auke R. Leen*

### I. "New Things" of Centesimus Annus Ask for Creativity and Entrepreneurship

With his ninth encyclical *Centesimus Annus (CA)* Pope John Paul II pays homage to the hundredth anniversary of *Rerum Novarum (RN)*. In *CA* John Paul II extends the thoughts over the market economy of his predecessor Pope Leo XIII to the "new things" of our time. A central feature of modern time is the growing importance of human beings in production processes. In early times natural fertility of land was the most important production factor. Later capital, i.e., machines, took over this role. In our time human beings are central, their creativity and entrepreneurship are paramount in production processes (John Paul II 1991, pp. 26-27). Not all people, however, do have the means to participate effectively and in a way worthy to their humanity in modern production processes. Consequently, John Paul II makes a plea for more creativity and entrepreneurship at all levels, especially the lower levels, within a firm.

If more creativity and entrepreneurship is demanded of human beings in their capacity as wage-recipients (producers) there is no reason to deny this to them in their capacity as wage-spenders (consumers). Are there not, as John Paul II in *CA* stresses, other new things of our advanced society: the rise of a consumption mentality and problems in choosing new needs and new ways of satisfying them (John Paul II 1991, p. 30)? Consumer decisions are central in modern society. Besides, consumption and production are not words pointing to a classification of real living human beings. Consumption and production are analytical categories of action. A human being is no split personality; he is one and indivisible; he is a consumer in the same way as he is a producer. So the questions arise (1) how does capitalism allow for the creativity and entrepreneurship of the consumers? And (2) can consumer policy enhance or does it, just the opposite, only stifle consumer's creativity and entrepreneurship?

❖

## II. The Capitalistic Market Economy Is Detrimental to Creativity and Entrepreneurship

In his book *The Joyless Economy, An Inquiry Into Human Satisfaction and Consumer Dissatisfaction,* Tibor Scitovsky argues that capitalism is detrimental to the creativity and entrepreneurship of the consumers. Of course it can be maintained that if people want variety, capitalism can supply it. Is not the market but a huge voting-machine in which the dollars spent by the consumer can be counted as votes? This may be true, and is captured in the notion of consumer sovereignty, but mass production also entails the notion that "almost nothing gets produced that cannot be produced in the thousands" (Scitovsky 1976, p. 7).

The essence of capitalism is mass-production. The division of labor in a capitalistic market economy makes possible an enormous increase of productivity. Economics of scale imply that commodities can be more cheaply produced for many people than for few. In order to make a profit sellers will try to cater to desires which everybody shares. These desires are the more simple ones. The tastes of the crowd are imposed on the whole society, which leads to standardized and homogeneous products. "The monotony of mass-production work is fully matched by the monotony of its product" (Scitovsky 1976, p. 249).

Following Scitovsky, it appears that not only the market economy but also market theory plays down the consumers yearning for novelty. Economic theory is built on a one-sided psychological image of man. Psychologists postulate an optimum level of arousal (level of excitement) caused by stimulation. Deviations from the optimum level in an upward direction cause feelings of tension, fatigue and oppression. Deviations from the optimum level in a downward direction cause feelings of emptiness and boredom. Deviations lead to attempts to restore the optimum level of stimulation.

Arousal reduction has become less problematic in a rich, capitalistic society. There is a lot of what Scitovsky calls comfort: specific needs which are satisfied. Economists have restricted their theoretical approach to arousal reduction caused by feelings of pain, hunger, thirst, coldness, and heat. "[T]he economist's model of consumer behavior . . . comes closest to that half of the psychologist's theory" (Scotovsky 1976, p. 30). But the capitalistic society still has a much more general lack of novelty and stimulation. This second important motive of human behavior with respect to consumption, i.e. the longing for new things, for stimulation and variety, is neglected. The fact that the mass market does not stimulate the consumer has serious consequences. "The yearning for new things and ideas is the source of all progress, all civilization; to ignore it as a source of satisfaction is surely wrong" (Scitovsky 1976, p. 11).

## III. Consumer Policy Emphasizes Maximization

If, as Scitovsky mantains, the capitalistic market economy fails in stimulating creativity and entrepreneurship, what role does consumer policy play in enhancing creativity and entrepreneurship? What are the roots and essence of consumer policy?

## A. The Roots

Since the early beginnings of economic science the welfare of the consumer takes a central position. Economic processes start and end with consumers. Consumption is, according to Adam Smith, the sole end of all production. The interest of the producer ought to be attended to only so far as it may be necessary for promoting that of the consumer. Policies to strengthen the functioning of the market, however, did concern the consumer only indirectly or, if directly, on an ad hoc, temporary base. We may think of rationing devices in situations of extreme scarcity or the prescription of certain product qualities, e.g. food quality, in the case of dangerous products. From the 1960s onward, however, the aim of consumer policy is a systematic and direct improvement of the position of the consumer in the market.

The motivation for consumer policy is based on either one or both of the following reasons. First, consumer sovereignty is absent in present-day society. The will of the consumers is no longer fundamental for production decisions. Second, in choosing, consumers are confronted with a highly complicated, nontransparent market. The consumer faces a situation of information shortage as well as one of information overload (Imkamp 1986, p. 235).

The first reason goes along the following lines. Full sovereignty of the consumer implies a complete servitude of the producer to the consumer. The consumer king, however, is capricious and unpredictable in his behaviour. To secure their capital investments, producers try to plan production and distribution. Through all kinds of sales effort the producer tries to secure its existence. The consumer feels his impotence. He feels himself played upon by the producer. Consumer sovereignty becomes an empty word.

The second reason emphasizes that the consumer also feels a certain discomfort in choosing from all the available, constantly growing and changing, products and services. The present-day consumer is confronted with a rich but, by its magnitude and variation, nontransparent assortment of goods. Product information is mainly given by the producers and is, consequently, one-sided. In choosing the consumer is stifled by information dependence. The market for consumer goods is highly nontransparent.

Consumer policy tries to answer these feelings of impotence and discomfort. The first reason, lack of consumer sovereignty, gives rise to a top-bottom motivation of consumer policy. Aims are deduced from certain basic values or needs of the consumer (Kuhlmann 1990, p. 60). Consumer policy becomes the protection of individual rights in the economic context. Taken from President Kennedy's presidential address of 1962, these rights are (1) the right to safety, (2) the right to be informed, (3) the right to choose, and (4) the right to be heard. The implementation of these rights must restore the equality in the producer-consumer relationship.

The second reason, consumer feelings of discomfort, gives rise to a bottom-top motivation of consumer policy. Inductive methods show consumer complaints. In aggregated form they build up the aims of consumer policy. One of the purposes of the inductively formed aims is to restore the market transparency of the consumers. Consumer policy tries "to insure that all consumers obtain what they really want (were they fully informed), subject to the limitation of their income" (Maynes 1979, p. 97).

## B. The Essence

What measures are taken to strengthen the position of the consumer on the market? Some measures are primarily aimed at changing the behavior of the producer, others at changing the behavior of the consumer. In both fields measures try to protect or inform the consumer. The overall aim of the measures is to secure that no unreasonable physical and economic risks fall on the consumer.

For physical safety, protection means bans on certain dangerous products and, for other less dangerous products, technical standards specifying acceptable safety standards. For economic safety, protection means, e.g., regulation of the information content of advertising, or regulation of one-sided producer formulated standard contracts. Furthermore, there are subsidies for comparative testing, mandatory informative labelling, and quality certification (Thorelli and Thorelli 1974, p. 2). All these measures aim at better consumer information: they try to increase the market transparency for the consumer.

The common denominator of all measures is that somehow the ends-means relationship is supposed to be already known to consumers and government officials. The essence of consumer policy is (1) to increase the efficiency of the known (household) production process, and (2), in cases of conflict between certain ends from an individual or social perspective, to influence the ends of the consumer household. But given a socially accepted hierarchy of ends these latter policies are in a certain sense also only trying to ensure the efficiency of the household production process (Kuhlmann 1990, pp. 5-6).

Consumer policy tries to reduce the known transaction costs of a consumer transaction in terms of physical and economic risk.

The government claims to know which products are unequivocally dangerous and ought to be banned and what the minimally acceptable safety standards are. The government also claims to know the standard price, standard quality, standard contract terms, the relevant product characteristics in comparative testing, and the relevant product characteristics for the product labels.

The theoretical motivation behind consumer policy is taken from the predominant, standard neoclassical market model. In neoclassical theory the consumer is a maximizer: action follows from an optimal choice in a given and known ends-means relationship. Maximization includes situations of measurable uncertainty that can be reduced with search. Because, in reality, the consumer is confronted with an information gap as well as, just the opposite, an information overload, the essence of consumer policy is to direct or restrict the choices of the consumers. Prices per standard quantity and comparative testing, for instance, increase the market transparency for the consumer and direct the choices of the consumers. Laws putting limits to interests rates or prescribing standard rules, on the other hand, restrict the choices of the consumers.

In other words, consumer policy tries to realize the conditions of the neoclassical market model in terms of full knowledge, market transparency, and the homogeneity of goods. It is captured within a given and known ends-means relationship.

## IV. Erring People Depend on Creativity and Entrepreneurship

Next to the well-known neoclassical market model there is the far less-known Austrian market model. At the centre of this market model is the process of conceiving the ends-means relationship. The consumer and producer are more than mere calculators, they are venturing, innovating, exploring, and searching for new means and new ends.

The essential difference between the neoclassical and Austrian market model is the different understanding of the concept of error and the role of error itself in a market economy. Contrary to the neoclassical market model, consumer problems are not always to be attributed to inadequate resources or to a faulty institutional structure. There is also the possibility of sheer error: opportunities costlessly available are overlooked. Let us take a closer look at older and modern Austrian economics to see how the concept of an erring individual has developed.

### A. Austrianism: a Geographical and Pejorative Label

In the 1880s German professors attached the epithet 'Austrian' to the economic theories of Menger, Bohm-Bawerk, and Wieser. It was a pejorative epithet bestowed by disdainful German economists. Why was it a pejorative epithet, and what was the reason for their disdain?

As far as the epithet Austrian relates to a geographical area it is justified because of the historic fact it was founded and first elaborated by three Austrians, holding chairs at the universities of Vienna, Innsbruck, and Prague. In 1871 Carl Menger published his *Grundsätze der Volkswirtschaftslehre* (Principles of Economics). Until the end of the seventies, however, there was no Austrian School: there was only Carl Menger. Later on Menger was joined by two younger economists, brothers-in-law, Eugen von Bohm-Bawerk and Friedrich Wieser. They became the enthusiastic supporters of the new ideas put forward in Menger's book.

❖

The pejorative overtone of the predicate Austrian was the result of another historic fact: never before had any new mode of thinking originated in Austria. "For people who were not familiar with economics, the predicate 'Austrian' as applied to a doctrine carried strong overtones of the dark days of the Counter-Reformation and of Metternich. To an Austrian intellectual, nothing could appear more disastrous than a relapse of his country into the spiritual inanity of the good old days" (Mises 1969, p. 14).

The German economists attached the smear to Menger and his followers because for them Austrian economics meant backwardness. Both the Germans and the Austrians attacked classical economics. The Germans were appealing for an alleged modern historical approach. Menger, on the contrary, although he wanted to rebuild the foundations of economic science too, retained the abstract, theoretical character of economics. The clash over methods is known as the *Methodenstreit*.

## B. Older Austrians

Menger's theory turned the value theory of the classicals upside down. The classical Ricardian theory held that the normal value of consumption goods was determined by their cost of production. Menger's theory, on the contrary, held that the cost of production itself is ultimately determined by the value of consumption goods. Labor is not the source of value, but is a means to value. Value was no longer to be seen as governed by past resource costs but as expressing judgements concerning future usefulness in meeting consumer wants (Kirzner 1987, p. 146). In making these judgements, Menger, according to William Jaffé, describes man not as a "lightning calculator" but as a "bumbling, erring, ill-informed creature, plagued with uncertainty, forever, hovering between alluring hopes and haunting fears, and congenitally incapable of making finely calibrated decisions in pursuit of satisfactions" (Jaffé 1976, p. 521). Menger's theory came to be known as the subjective theory of value.

The classical objective value theory was a second best solution to the problem of how prices are determined. Classical economists "were fully aware of the fact that prices are not a product of the activities of a special group of people, but the result of an interplay of all members of the market society" (Mises 1966, p. 62). But because of the problems encountered in the famous value paradox they considered the activities of the producer only.

According to the Austrians, value is in the mind of individual man, who chooses and maximizes, for whatever reason, his profit or utility. From the interaction of the valuations of the consumers flows the market demand. The market supply of the producers is determined by the expected demand. The interaction of demand and supply determines the market price. By offering a more satisfactory theory of demand, the subjective or marginal theory of value was more comprehensive than the classical theory, which last theory emphasized the activities of the producer only.

## C. Modern Austrians

In modern Austrianism, the post-World War II continuation of the Austrian tradition, the two central figures are Ludwig von Mises and Friedrich Hayek. Israel Kirzner (1986 p. 134 and 152) describes modern Austrianism as an authentic extension of Menger's older static subjectivism: a consequent dynamic subjectivism. Mises and Hayek focus in their theories on market adjustment processes. For Kirzner, building his theory along the lines of Mises and Hayek, one of the greatest failures of neoclassical equilibrium analysis is it takes for granted that an equilibrium is actually brought about. For instance, in a disequilibrium would be buyers who have returned home empty handed should learn that it is necessary to outbid other buyers, and buyers who have paid high prices should discover that they could have obtained the same goods at lower prices (Kirzner 1973, p. 14). The real problem is to describe the possible realization of an equilibrium as the result of "the systematic way in which plan revisions are made as a consequence of the disappointment of earlier plans" (Kirzner 1962, p. 81).

Neoclassical equilibrium theory cannot describe endogenous changes in the end-means framework: its maximization scheme is not fit for the task to generate systematic modifications of choices. The allocation model suffers from a discontinuity in the succession of decisions. Only an exogenous change in the data, e.g., in tastes, in technology, or in information, can generate a new decision, a decision unexplainable in terms of the original framework. Without exogenous changes there is no 'choice-theoretic' explanation why yesterday's plans are replaced by today's.

Mises and Hayek made it possible to describe the adjustment process as a systematic sequence of decisions. Mises' extension of subjectivism was to describe the individual decision unit not only as maximizing but also as finding out the relevant ends-means relationship. This opens the way for incorporating learning into the understanding of market processes. Hayek's extension of subjectivism was precisely to describe the market process as one of learning by discovery (Kirzner 1986, p. 47; cf. Kirzner 1985, p. 26).

Endogenous change in the ends-means relationship is possible with the entrepreneurial element in each individual market participant: alertness (Kirzner 1967, pp. 793-794 and 1973, pp. 70-72). Alertness is the propensity of knowing where to look for information (Kirzner 1973, p. 68), "the propensity... toward fresh goals and the discovery of hitherto unknown resources" (Kirzner 1973, p. 34). A disequilibrium situation points to a situation of market ignorance. From the ignorance emerge profitable opportunities. Entrepreneurial alertness exploits (Kirzner 1979, p. 30). Alertness gives a more realistic image of human action and makes possible the description of the market as a unified discovery process.

"[The] 'alertness' view of the entrepreneurial role rejects the thesis that if we attribute genuine novelty to the entrepreneur, we must necessarily treat entrepreneurially generated market events as not related to earlier market events in any systematic way. The genuine novelty ... attribute[d] to the entrepreneur consists in his spontaneous discovery of the opportunities marked out by earlier market conditions (or by future market conditions as they would be in the absence of his own actions)" (Kirzner 1985, p. 11). "[These] entrepreneurial discoveries are the steps through which any possible tendency toward market equilibrium must proceed" (Kirzner 1985, pp. 11-12).

## V.  Austrians and Neoclassicals Compared

It is well known that there are two other contributors to the marginal subjective value theory: Leon Walras and William Stanley Jevons. In the modern Austrian perspective there are insights to be found in embryonic form in Menger's writings which are not absorbed in, or came to be lost from, mainstream neoclassical Walrasian and Jevonsian (Marshallian) economics (Kirzner 1989a, p. 232).

The differences refer to (1) the subject of, (2) the place of process analysis in, and (3) the epistemological character of economic theory.

### A.  The Equilibrium Situation or The Equilibrating Process

According to modern Austrians, the main difference between the neoclassical and Austrian market model is that in the modern Austrian market model adjustment processes and not market equilibria occupy a central position. In adjustment processes dispersed knowledge and lack of knowledge are of fundamental importance. Correct foresight, full knowledge, is not a precondition for the attainment of equilibrium but the defining characteristic of the state of equilibrium. "The statement that, if people know everything, they are in equilibrium, is true simply because that is how we define equilibrium" (Hayek 1949, p. 46).

In the modern Austrian market model, action does not primarily follow from an optimal choice in a given ends-means relation, as is mostly the case in the neoclassical market model. At the centre of the modern Austrian market model one finds the process of conceiving the ends-means relationship. The change in market model contains a change "from a 'mechanical' Robbinsian [after Lord Robbins] neoclassical economizer to Mises's [modern Austrian] *homo agens*" (Kirzner 1973, p. 72). "[*Homo agens*] is not merely engaged in computing the patterns of means allocation that will most faithfully reflect the hierarchy of given ends [like Robbins' calculating agents]. *Homo agens* is actively seeking out the best course of action, he is venturing, innovating, exploring, searching" (Kirzner 1967, p. 792).

The discontinuity in the succession of decisions in the neoclassical market model indicates that the neoclassical maximizer does not choose at all. "[T]he replacement of one set of given ends by a second set occurs *before* (or at least *outside*) ... [neoclassical] choice itself" (Kirzner 1986, p. 142). "The very circumstance that the 'chosen' course of action is seen as already inexorably implied in the given configuration of preferences and constraints, of ends and means, makes the choice 'mechanical' or 'automatic' - and thus not a true choice at all. True choice surely requires the realistic possibility of more than one alternative" (Kirzner 1986,

p. 139). Choices are not only concerned with merely selecting the highest out of an array of given and ranked alternatives, but also embrace the perception and evaluation of the alternatives identified as relevant (Kirzner 1989b, p. 18).

To discover what are the relevant means and ends must be distinguished sharply from neoclassical search theory. In neoclassical search "[t]he searcher knows what he is looking for, and he knows where to look for it. . . . [In the case of discovery, on the other hand,] the discoverer discovers something he did not know existed, or something, the ready availability of which he had not realized" (Kirzner 1989b, p. 27). Search is concerned with wiping out known ignorance. Discovery is concerned with wiping out utter ignorance: one does not know that one does not know.

The process of discovery is not completely unpredictable. For modern Austrians there is the possibility that the outcome "may emerge as a result of the alert grasping of a hitherto unnoticed opportunity." In neoclassical equilibrium theory, on the contrary, the outcome is "*either* the fully expected result of deliberate plans, *or* the fortuitous expression of pure luck" (Kirzner 1989b, p. ix and p. 30).

## B. Processes: The Start or The End of The Analysis

The neoclassical core of economic theory is the simplified static model. Processes can be studied as the outgrowth of some higher order of, mostly, technical sophistication. For modern Austrians, however, the distinction between process and situation can not be characterized as one of a choice between two, independent subject matters of economics. For modern Austrians the process elements "are central and essential for understanding markets and not merely refinements to our knowledge" (Kirzner 1989a, p. 234) or matters of embarrassment. Process, discovery, and uncertainty are essential for everyday economics. "It is not that markets work in spite of the open-ended uncertainty surrounding human action, but rather that they work *precisely* because of this quality of human action. The open-ended uncertainty of the environment itself provides the scope and possibility for an entrepreneurial process of competitive discovery" (Kirzner 1989a, p. 234).

## C. Methodology

Subjectivism not only characterizes the substance but also the method of Austrian economics. The subjectivistic method, first explicitly written down by Mises and to a lesser extent by Hayek, is called praxeology. A name, the logic of action, introduced by Mises as characterizing the verbal axiomatic-deductive methodology of Austrian economics (Lachmann 1976, p. 56). The ideas for this method Mises found in the writings of some classical economists and older Austrians (Rothbard 1980, p. 29). It is claimed that the praxeological method was the implicit method of the economics profession till the 1950s (Hoppe 1988, p. 9 and p. 11).

❖

Praxeology starts from the fundamental, self-evident axiom that men act by virtue of their being human. Human beings try to exchange a less for a more preferred situation. Mises, as a Kantian, describes the fundamental axiom as a priori to all experience. It is a part of "the essential and necessary character of the logical structure of the human mind" (Mises 1966, p. 34). For Murray Rothbard, as an Aristotelian, on the other hand, the fundamental axiom is "so broadly based in common human experience that once enunciated . . . [it becomes] self-evident and hence does not meet the fashionable criterion of 'falsifiability'", (Rothbard 1976, p. 25). Praxeology consists in the verbal elaboration of the logical implications of the fundamental axiom of human action. There are a few subsidiary axioms. The most important of these broadly empirical axioms are, that individuals vary in tastes and abilities, that human beings regard leisure as a valuable good, and that people learn from experience. We deduce, except for logical errors in the deductive process, true conclusions from a true axiom. "Our science considers only the essential. It views action.... as [a] formal construction" (Mises 1976, p. 13). In this respect, praxeology models sciences like logic and geometry.

The subsidiary axiom that people learn from experience is of fundamental importance to the description of the market as a systematic sequence of economic states. Its 'broadly empirical' character is based on the general propensity of man to be alert to opportunities. "The process by which facts are hammered into human consciousness is not wholly ungoverned by the logic of human action" (Kirzner 1979, p. 30). After recognizing that people do err, we assume at least a tendency for man to notice those facts that constitute possible opportunities for gainful action. "The market process emerges as the necessary implication of the circumstance that people act, and that in their action they err, discover their errors, and tend to revise their actions in a direction likely to be less erroneous than before" (Kirzner 1979, p. 30).

## VI. The Forgotten Consumer

The consumer was central to Menger, no doubt about that (cf. Menger 1923), but the consumer is not central for modern Austrian economics. Somewhere in the trajectory between Menger's contribution to Austrian economics, the way in which all value in economics springs off from the final valuation of the consumer, and the modern Austrian contribution, the process through which consumer valuations are being translated in production decisions, the consumer got lost.

I think the main reason for the oblivion of the consumer is that the Austrian discovery insight is discussed by way of the methodological makeshift of an entrepreneurial producer and a non-entrepreneurial consumer (Mises 1966, p. 253; Kirzner 1973, p. 41). But when is this methodological makeshift (Mises 1966, p. 253) raised? Though alertness is in principle present in every action, in their elaborations the modern Austrians ascribe it to the producer (cf. Rothbard 1985, p. 282; Ekelund & Saurman 1988, p. xx; Pasour 1989, p. 95). Accordingly, alertness is called the entrepreneurial element. Consumers are passive, non-alert, Robbinsian maximizers. For instance, one of the functions of advertising is 'getting the Robbinsians [the potential consumers] to see the availability of ... opportunities' (Kirzner 1973, p. 148). Advertising differs from changing the consumer's taste or providing information (non-entrepreneurial knowledge) to him. Advertising (an entrepreneurial device) makes the consumer aware of available opportunities, regardless of the level of his alertness.

So we get the following paradoxical situation. For Austrian economists, classical economists were at fault because they were able to explain only the actions of the businessman. Classical economists completely neglected the rationality on the part of the consumer. It was precisely this limitation of classical economics, explaining only the actions of the businessman, that the Austrian subjective theory of value was able to overcome (Mises 1976, p. 147 and p. 175). To a certain extent, however, modern Austrian economics, just as the classical economists before them, has lost sight of the consumer, too. The consumer is absent in the elucidation of the market as a dynamic process of entrepreneurial discovery.

The oblivion of the consumer in modern Austrian economics is, as we saw, fully matched by the analysis of creativity and entrepreneurship in *CA. CA*, too, asks for entrepreneurship of human beings in their capacity as wage-receivers, only.

Jozef Solterer, in an article from 1950 "The entrepreneur in economic theory" and a bookreview of Mises' book *Human Action* from the same year (1950b), describes economics, just like the modern Austrians, as the science of human choice and human action (Solterer 1950a, pp. 14-15). Solterer distinguishes three classes of choice. The first class is to buy or sell and is studied in the theory of pure competition. The class corresponds to what the Austrians call the act of maximizing inside a given ends-means relationship. The second class is to choose to build a structure. A structure that would not exist without the acting person. Solterer and the Austrians call the second class the entrepreneurial aspect of choice. Solterer also distinguishes a third class of choice: the task to assign the total product without remainder to the agents who helped produce it. To each of these types of choices Solterer attaches "the name of a virtuous procedure: the first, honesty [commutative justice]; the second, responsibility [social justice]; the third, fairness [distributive justice]" (Solterer 1950a, p. 19). To pursue explicitly the concept of virtuous action distinguishes Solterer's from Mises' conception of economics (Solterer 1950a, p. 15). But Solterer, too, applies the concept of entrepreneurship explicitly to the producer only and not to the consumer (Solterer 1950a, p. 19).

To sum up, Austrian economics sees man as an erring individual, who has the propensity of entrepreneurship: the propensity to notice the implications of earlier errors. With the propensity of entrepreneurship endogenous corrections of earlier errors and market processes can be described. Capitalism, seen as a dynamic process and populated with erring individuals, depends on creativity and entrepreneurship. If error correction is the essence of the market process then people are necessarily endowed with entrepreneurship. Consequently, in Austrian economics, in contrast to Scitovsky's analysis, stimulation and novelty are of the essence of the market process. But, just like *CA* and Solterer, the concept of entrepreneurship is worked out for the producer only.

## VII.  Consumer Policy Is Detrimental to Creativity and Entrepreneurship

How does the Austrian vision of the market process relate to consumer policy? To be more specific: What is the impact of consumer policy upon the perception by consumers and producers of the available array of opportunities? Consumer policy "may effect what it is that decision makers *discover* to be the situation in which they act" (Kirzner 1985, p. 94). It is these consequences that must be taken account of, in terms of costs, in each assessment of the likely consequences of consumer policy.

To describe the ways in which discovery problems may hamper consumer policy I use the same four headings as Kirzner (Kirzner 1985, p. 137).

### A.  The Undiscovered Discovery Process

A consumer problem does not necessarily point to the necessity of government intervention. The market is a discovery process: genuine inefficiencies can be relied upon in the future to generate market processes for their own correction. But the systematic tendency for imperfect knowledge to be spontaneously improved upon is not an instantaneous one. In Austrian economics time is not the problem but part of the solution.

What are, for instance, the market responses to the information asymmetry between producers and consumers? Of course sellers, as specialized producers, know more about their services than non-specialized buyers possibly can. Also, sellers, by knowing more about the quality of their service than consumers, are able to manipulate consumers. This led George Akerlof to his prediction that in equilibrium in the market for used cars, only 'lemons' will be offered for sale (Akerlof 1970, p. 490). The government's answer to the problem of how to protect the public health or safety is often in the form of occupational license or governmental organizations of certification.

But there are also many free market responses to the alleged market failures: producer supplied guarantees, private information services, producer provided quality screening services, and all forms of non-governmental organization of certification. Besides, there are many information surrogates that keep consumers adequately informed: repeatedly purchasing certain services, drawing on the experience of friends, relatives, and neighbors, or inferences drawn from the length of life of firms offering services. To conclude: "if consumers are able to check the veracity of suppliers in any manner, laissez-faire market equilibrium can support [contrary to Akerlof's assertion] high quality" (Young 1987, p. 18). Besides, consumers who prefer lower-priced, lower-quality service will be worse off with licensing, because such suppliers will not be permitted to practice and in this way the poor subsidize the lower information search costs of the rich (Young 1987, p. 21).

In this respect one must notice that even in a nontransparent market like the illegal drugs market there arise institutions which lower the transaction costs of both producer and consumer. A drugs supplier faces high selling costs. It is not easy for him to make selling efforts; there is certainly no room for direct advertising. And, if caught, he runs into high costs in terms of imprisonment and income forgone. For the consumer, too, there are high buying costs. He faces high search costs, high costs in the form of uncertainty over the quality of the goods, and in cases of fraud, there is no law to protect him.

In this disequilibrium situation coordination between buyers and sellers and transaction volume are low. One can expect that some entrepreneurial people try to make some profit as middleman in creating an information market. "We need not," as Kirzner also says, "wait for evidence on the way information comes to spread through a society. We can, instead, employ our logic of choice to identify, within disequilibrium markets, the opportunities for gain that disequilibrium conditions themselves create. Postulating a tendency for such opportunities to be discovered and exploited, we can then explain the way such gradual discovery of opportunities in turn gradually alters the pattern of opportunities presented in the market as the process unfolds" (Kirzner 1979, p. 33). We can be sure of that element in human decision making which Kirzner calls the entrepreneurial propensity in human action: alertness. Alertness is "the propensity . . . toward fresh goals and the discovery of hitherto unknown resources" (Kirzner 1979, p. 34).

As Harald Kunz demonstrates the middleman tries to reduce the high costs for both producer and consumer. He offers information the consumer of drugs needs, and the drugs supplier likes to be spread. For the producer, the middleman separates the market of drugs supply from the market of drugs selling. For a fee, he creates an information market which lowers the selling costs of the supplier. Because he is no drugs supplier, the middleman himself does not face high imprisonment costs. At the same time, he lowers the search costs for the consumer. Both supplier and consumer value the middleman, as he reduces the transaction costs for both of them (Kunz 1985, pp. 93-103).

The self interest of all parties concerned ensures that such a market can exist. The middleman will not share his information about where to buy drugs with too many people. Otherwise the drugs supplier can be sold out when a buyer arrives. The information will be exclusive. If the middleman wants to stay in the market he must be reliable not only in his information on where to buy but also on product quality. The more reliable the middleman is, the more he can charge his customers. The other way around, the supplier has to be truthful about quantity and quality of his drugs to his middleman, otherwise he will loose business. Better quality

❖

commands a higher price for the supplier and a higher fee for the middleman. The result will be that (1) the market will be more coordinated and the transaction volume will be higher than otherwise would be the case; (2) an experience good becomes more or less a search good; and(3) quality does not deteriorate; there is even a stimulus to increase quality.

Clarence Ayres, in a book review of Mises' *Epistemological Problems in Economics*, opposed Mises' condemnation of the mixed economy. Ayres denied the "automaticity" of the self-regulating purely capitalistic economy (Ayres 1961, p. 200; cp. Solterer 1950b, p. 128). As the drugs example showed, by spelling out more clearly the concept of human choice, as the modern Austrians do, part of Ayres critique can be met. "To commence an analysis of choice after a particular ends-means framework has been declared known and relevant, is [indeed] to deal with choice in a manner that renders it completely mechanical. The *creativity* of choice, the element that makes action human, has been left out" (Kirzner 1979, p. 148). The market process, however, depends on creativity, entrepreneurship, and the discovery of hitherto unknown ends and means. An activity that lies between pure luck and rational calculation.

## B. The Unsimulated Discovery Process

How do government officials know what prices to set or qualities to require? In the absence of the pure profit incentive, market opportunities which present themselves in the form of potential profit opportunities are not likely to be discovered by the regulators. "It is doubtful in the extreme if ideals such as benevolence or patriotism can be relied upon, in general, to enable a potential discoverer to identify his own personal interest with that of the discovery of an opportunity for a reallocation of resources desirable for society" (Kirzner 1985, p. 33). The discovery process of the market cannot be simulated by regulatory activity.

Because in consumption the consumer always captures the profit himself, at first sight it looks as if the consumer's alertness is stimulated irrespective of the market form. The relevant information will always be of benefit to the potential discoverer. In a regulated market, however, things are a bit more complicated.

Regulators and consumers in a regulated economy focus on the efficiency of the given and known household production process for which traditional incentives, e.g., lowering the search costs are of help. Consumers in a non-regulated economy, however, are next to the efficiency of the transformation process alert to the discovery of genuine errors: to expect the unexpected. Government regulation of producer decisions, however, takes possible surprises out of the open-ended surroundings of the consumer. Consequently, it is to be expected that a consumer in a regulated market (government takes care of me) is less alert to new ends and new means than the consumer in an unregulated market. Profit inspired diversity in consumer goods and services stimulates the consumer. The consumer's alertness is switched on by the fact that there may be something lurking around the corner. Something he is hopeful or something he is fearful of.

❖

## C. The Stifled Discovery Process

Government regulation, e.g., price and quality restraints, tends to bar entry by potential new competitors. A price restraint does not merely block the upper reaches of a given supply curve but also may inhibit the discovery of as yet unsuspected sources of supply. Next to the discoordination generated by imposed prices in markets for existing goods there is the effect that such ceilings may inhibit the discovery of as yet wholly unknown new products (Kirzner 1985, p. 143). To stick to the example of the drugs market. Think of such 'undiscovered' uses of marijuana as paper, fuel, building materials, clothing, animal food, and a protein source for humans.

At this point one must remember that competition is a two-sided process taking place between producers and consumers and within each group. The likelihood that regulation may discourage, hamper, and even completely stifle the discovery process of the unregulated market counts for producers as well as for consumers.

The Austrian methodological makeshift of a Misesian entrepreneurial producer and a Robbinsian non-entrepreneurial consumer, used for the elucidation of the market process, is at this point of no help and leads to wrong policy conclusions. If the methodological makeshift is not removed then the Austrians do not have valid arguments against those forms of consumer policy which try to increase the market transparency of the consumer. For then there are no valid arguments against passing on to the consumer comparable and relevant product characteristics for the existing supply of products. When the methodological makeshift is not removed, it is possible from an Austrian perspective to make a plea for quality certification as a form of collective (public) good (Hayek 1982, III, p. 44). It is also possible to defend the subsidization by the government of comparative testing by consumer organizations (Kaufmann 1985, p. 24).

From the Austrian vision, however, on the functioning of the market in general, these policies can only be rejected. The question is, what are the relevant product characteristics, and how are these characteristics changed over time (cf. Rothbard 1970, pp. 43-47; O'Driscoll & Rizzo 1985, p. 105 and p. 236)? The consumer, too, discovers new unexpected ends (new forms of utility) to old and new means. It is not always the case that the role of the producer "consists in relieving the consumer of the necessity to be his own entrepreneur" (Kirzner 1973, p. 136). The situation can also be the other way around. The producer hires a trendwatcher. Someone who looks out for what a trendy consumer discovers.

## D. The Wholly Superfluous Discovery Process

Measures taken by government officials to protect the consumers are likely to open up new avenues for entrepreneurial gain: they introduce a different disequilibrium situation. This new disequilibrium situation will generate its own

❖

discovery process with its own wholly unexpected and even undesired final outcomes, e.g. enterprising bribery and corruption of the regulators.

To sum up, I presented a less obvious drawback of policies to protect the consumer. The Austrian understanding of the market economy provides a novel angle for a critique of the regulated consumer. Regulatory restrictions interfere with the spontaneous discovery process that the unregulated market tends to generate. In order to give a full appreciation of the market as a competitive-entrepreneurial discovery process it was necessary to emphasize the entrepreneurial role of the consumer.

For modern Austrians consumer policy stifles the profit or utility incentive that converts a socially desirable opportunity (an opportunity that transcends an existing framework of perceived opportunities) into a personally gainful one. These 'conversions' are the steps of the discovery process through which any possible tendency toward market equilibrium must proceed. So, we end up with about the opposite of what consumer policy intends. Is not the ultimate aim of consumer policy to better the possibilities to satisfy needs by means of consumption? To asses the results of consumer policy as a social policy it is necessary to look at the entrepreneurial behavior of the consumer and the producer.

## VIII. Conclusion

What picture does the capitalistic market economy give us if we extend some of the "new things" pointed at in *CA* from the producer to the consumer? What does creativity and entrepreneurship entail for the consumer in a capitalistic market economy?

For Scitovsky not only economic analysis but the capitalistic market economy, too, has no room for entrepreneurship, for the yearning for novelty by the consumer. Economic analysis is based on a psychological model of man which emphasizes arousal reduction in cases of depreviation. Arousal stimulation in cases of lack of novelty is forgotten. The capitalistic mass market is detrimental to novelty, it leads to homogenized and standardized products. Only the rich can buy variety. Consumer policy, framed within a given ends-means relationship, is of no help either. It tries to realize the conditions of the neoclassical market model and only looks for error correction inside a given and known ends-means relationship.

Austrian economics extends the concept of error and error correction. Error is no longer confined to maximizing decisions inside a given ends-means relationship, but is extended to the creative, entrepreneurial process of conceiving the ends-means relationship. In that way, it makes room for creativity and entrepreneurship.

Consequently, what *CA* asks of the modern market economy, and Scitovsky could not find in it, is spelled out in modern Austrian economics. It is the entrepreneurial element in human decision making. Error correction is the result, not only, of new information purposefully searched for, or, just the opposite, sheer luck but can also be the result of alertness: creativity and entrepreneurship. What the capitalistic market process depends on, is nothing but, entrepreneurship. For Austrians neoclassical inspired consumer policy is detrimental to the entrepreneurship of the consumer.

\*Assistant Professor, Department of General Economics, Wageningen Agricultural University, The Netherlands.

## References

Akerlof, George A., "The Market for 'Lemons': Qualitative Uncertainty and the Market Mechanism," *Quarterly Journal of Economics*, 1970, *84*, 488-500.

Ayres, Clarence E., "Epistemological problems of economics," *Southern Economic Journal*, 1961, *28*, 199-202.

Ekelund, Robert B. and Saurman David S., *Advertising and the Market Process*, San Francisco: Pacific Research Institute for Public Policy, 1988.

Hayek, Friedrich A., *Individualism and Economic Order*, London: Routledge & Kegan Paul, 1949.

_____. *Law, Legislation and Liberty*, London: Routledge & Kegan Paul, 1982.

Hoppe, Hans-Hermann, *Praxeology and Economic Science*, Auburn Alabama: Luwig von Mises Institute, 1988.

Imkamp, Heiner, "Zur Operationalisierung des individuellen Informationsdefizits von Verbrauchern," *Hauswirtschaft*. Wiss., 1986, *34*, 232-235.

Jaffé, William, "Menger, Jevons and Walras De-Homogenized," *Economic Inquiry*, 1976, *14*, 511-24.

John Paul II, *Centesimus Annus* (Dutch edition), Utrecht: Secretariaat R.K. Kerkgenootschap, 1991.

Kaufmann, Peter J., *Passing off and Misappropriation in the Law of Unfair Competition*, Weinheim: V.C.H. Verlag Gesellschaft, 1985.

Kirzner, Israel M., "Rational Action and Economic Theory," *Journal of Political Economy*, August 1962, *70*, 380-85.

_____. "Methodological Individualsm, Market Equilibrium and Market Process," *Il Politico*, 1967, 32, 787-798.

_____. *Competition and Entrepreneurship*, Chicago: University of Chicago Press, 1973.

_____. *Perception, Opportunity, and Profit. Studies in the Theory of Entrepreneurship*, Chicago: University of Chicago Press, 1979.

❖

_____. "Comment: X-Inefficiency, Error, and the Scope for Entrepreneurship", in M.J. Rizzo (ed.), *Time, Uncertainty, and Disequilibrium*, Lexington: Lexington Books, 1979.

_____. in I.M. Kirzner (ed.), *Method, Process, and Austrian Economics: Essays in Honor of Ludwig von Mises*, Lexington, Mass.: Lexington Books, 1982.

_____. *Discovery and the Capitalist Process*, Chicago: University of Chicago Press, 1985.

_____. "Ludwig von Mises and Friedrich von Hayek: The modern Extension of Austrian Subjectivism," in N. Leser (ed.), *Die Wiener Schule der Nationalökonomie*, Vienna: Bohlau, 1986.

_____. "Austrian Economics," in: *The New Palgrave, A Dictionary of Economics*, ed. by Eatwell, J. Milgate, M. Newman, P., London: Macmillen, 1987.

_____. "The Use of Labels in Doctrinal History: Comment on Baird," *Cato Journal*, 1989a, *9(1)*, 231-35.

_____. *Discovery, Capitalism, and Distributive Justice*, New York: Basil Blackwell, 1989b.

Kuhlmann, Eberhard, *Verbraucherpolitik, Grundzuge ihrer Theorie und Praxis*, München: Franz Vahlen, 1990.

Kunz, Harald, *Marktsystem und Information*, Tubingen: J.B.C. Mohr, 1985.

Lachmann, Ludwig M. "From Mises to Shackle: An Essay on Austrian Economics and the Kaleidic Society," *Journal of Economic Literature*, 1976, *14*, 54-62.

Maynes, Scott E. "Consumer Protection: The Issues," *Journal of Consumer Policy*, 1979, *3*, 97-109.

Menger, Carl, *Grundsätze der Volkswirtschaftslehre*, Vienna: Wilhelm Braumuller, 1871. Translated by J. Dingwall and B.F. Hoselitz as *Principles of Economics*, Glencoe, Ill.: Free Press, 1950.

_____. *Grundsätze der Volkswirtschaftslehre*, 2 ed. Vienna: Holder-Pichler-Tempsky, 1923.

Mises, Ludwig von, *Human Action*, Chicago: Contemporary Books, [1949], 1966, 3rd Edition.

_____. *The Historical Setting of the Austrian School of Economics*, New Rochelle, N.Y.: Arlington House, 1969.

_____. *Epistemological Problems of Economics*, Princeton: New York, 1976.

O'Driscoll, Gerald P. and Rizzo, Mario J., *The Economics of Time & Ignorance*, New York: Basil Blackwell, 1985.

Pasour, E.C., "The Effient-Markets Hypothesis and Entrepreneuship," *The Review of Austrian Economics*, 1989, *3*, 95-107.

Rothbard, Murray N., *Power and Market*, Kansas City: Sheed Andrews and McMeel, 1970.

_____. "Praxeology: The Methodology of Austrian Economics," in E.G. Dolan (ed), *The Foundations of Modern Austrian Economics*, Kansas City: Sheed & Ward, 1976.

_____. *The Essential Ludwig von Mises*, Auburn, Alabama: Ludwig Mises Institute, 1980.

_____. "Professor Hebert on Entrepreneurship," *Journal of Libertarian Studies*, 1985, *7(2)*, 281-86.

Scitovsky, Tibor, *The Joyless Economy*, Oxford: Oxford University Press, 1976.

Solterer, Josef. "The entrepreneur in economic theory," *Review of Social Economy*, 1950a, *8*, 10-19.

_____. "Bookreview of Ludwig von Mises' Human Action," *Review of Social Economy*, 1950b, *8*, 123-33.

Thorelli, Hans. B. and Thorelli, Sarah V., *Consumer Information Handbook: Europe and North America*, New York: Praeger, 1974.

Young, David S., *The Rule of Experts*, Washington: Cato Institute, 1987.

# The Person and the Social Economy: Needs, Values and Principles — A Comment

## Kishor Thanawala*

Please permit me to note that I have received and read the introduction by John Davis and the chapter by Peter Danner. I have not had the opportunity to see or read the other chapters of the forthcoming book.**

Peter Danner's chapter is the first in the book and is titled "The Person and the Social Economy: Needs, Values and Principles." A person has individual needs arising from his/her physical, spiritual and emotional requirements. In addition, arising out of our personal, political and economic relations to others, each person has social needs. The values of each person largely determine how the different dimensions of life find expression in and are ordered or arranged in one's economic life. Three social values dominating contemporary social thinking are investigated: liberty, equality and fraternity. These three fundamental values are the basis of the three major principles in economic life: competitive self-interest, government intervention and involvement and cooperative collaboration. In this way, harmonies and conflicts in the value structure of the society are brought out. The dilemmas faced by persons and by groups of persons arising from these conflicts are discussed.

This brief outline of Danner's chapter does not reflect the richness of his discussion. The chapter deals with some difficult material but is lucidly written.

It is said that two groups of people have no questions: those who understand everything and those who understand nothing. I do not belong to the first category. I do have some questions. But I shall let you judge based on the nature of my questions whether I do belong to the second category!

My basic question is: what is meant by needs? I pose this question because it would appear from John Davis' introduction that needs are different from wants. The popular definition or explanation of needs and wants (as given, for example, by Webster's Dictionary) would seem to indicate that there is no, or no significant,

❖

difference between the two. Neither Danner nor Davis attempts a formal definition of needs or wants. I also seem to get the impression that Davis and Danner interpret needs in different ways. There is nothing wrong about this. But I would be interested in hearing both Davis and Danner giving us their interpretations or definitions of needs and how they would differentiate needs from wants. I realize that perhaps exact definitions are not feasible: like, for example, demand as desire backed by purchasing power.

I must admit that my lack of understanding about this basic difference between needs and wants as perceived by Danner has adversely impacted my understanding of all the implications of his discussion. Human being is a complex animal. How he/she manages to have values like equality at the same time as feeling the need to be better and how he/she manages to want cooperation and competition at the same time, as Danner explains, is fascinating. I wish I could understand this in a kind of a formula: $x\%$ of cooperation and $y\%$ of competition in a given situation. But Danner would argue, probably correctly, that the very fact that I express this type of wish disqualifies me from being a questioner on this chapter!

In conclusion, let me say I admire Danner's effort at trying to discuss some difficult questions. But just as a child needs to walk before it can run, perhaps this reader needs to understand what "need" means before he can understand Danner's Social Matrix.

*Professor of Economics, Villanova University
**The Social Economics of Human Needs, ed. John B. Davis and Edward J. Boyle, SIU Press, forthcoming.

# Human Physical Need:
# A Concept that at Once Is
# Absolute and Relative
# (Abstract)

## Edward J. O'Boyle*

*Edward J. O'Boyle**

Need is a requirement for human existence that derives from human materiality. A want is a thing that is desired, whether it is materially needed or not. Conventional economics takes wants and needs, along with whims, fads, cravings, addictions, and the like, and reduces them to wants which are satisfied through a market economy wherein the consumer is represented as *homo economicus*. By adding the "invisible hand" to individualism, conventional economics argues that the well-being of everyone is served best when each individual singlemindedly pursues his/her own self-interest. Further, conventional economics construes resource (re-) allocation in terms of relative prices thereby slipping away from the unmet need of resource holders that attends changes in relative prices.

Social economics rejects this ordering of priorities. The needy are seen as persons, not as objects, and economic systems are established ultimately to meet human material need so that humans are not diminished as persons by their unmet physical need. Market economies use the threat of unmet physical need to (re-) allocate resources in the sense that, whenever a resource holder assigns a price that is too high, the resource becomes idle and no longer produces income. The central dysfunction of the market economy and the dilemma of social economics is how to continue to (re-)allocate resources on the basis of unmet physical need without diminishing the person of those whom the market renders redundant.

Social economics replaces *homo economicus* with *homo socio-economicus* and substitutes personalism and humanism for the individualism and libertarianism of mainstream economics. Social economics and the social economy begin with and center principally on *unmet* human material need. In addition, there is no authentic social economics of unmet human material need without the principle of subsidiarity because without that principle the needy who are helped are seen as instruments or threats and thereby are diminished as persons.

The remainder of the paper defines unmet human physical need as both absolute and relative reflecting the individuality and sociality of human nature and measures unmet need using three major criteria that are applied to two data sets from the Current Population Survey.

*Associate Professor of Economics, Louisiana Tech University, USA.

# Workers' Participation and Democracy in the Workplace — One Hundred Years of Catholic Social Teaching

## Rev. Vincent P. Mainelli*

Two current cases pose the problem of more democracy in the workplace and why Catholic social teaching since Leo XIII in 1891 has been seen by some as utopian. General Motors created a new model automobile, Saturn, and a new model of how to produce it. General Motors and the union agreed to a special labor contract featuring no time clocks, no restrictive work rules and pay linked to profitability. Managers did not have special perks like reserved parking spaces. Everyone was allowed to talk to one another without permission. But more significantly, all workers were expected to participate in business decisions such as those involving production, scheduling and marketing strategy. One writer noted history may judge Saturn's influence not by the sales, but by how much impact this division has on other parts of General Motors (Levin, 1991, p. E4).

The second case involves an Omaha-based corporation, Peter Kiewit Sons' Inc. Since October 1, 1987, some 240 coal miners have been on strike at a large coal mine near Sheridan, Wyoming, owned by Decker Coal Co., and another 40 miners have been on strike at another nearby mine owned by Big Horn Coal Co. Peter Kiewit Sons' Inc. co-owns Decker Coal and wholly owns Big Horn. The local union and Kiewit have been in and out of court and are still at loggerheads.

One case shows a promising development in workers' participation, and the second case shows a typical confrontation between capital and labor reminiscent of the early part of this century in the United States.

Workers are achieving participation by more democratic business structure in certain nations, especially Western Europe. The movement is growing in the U.S. "Ten years ago, worker participation was largely a utopian ideal shared by a relatively few believers," wrote John Hoerr (1990, p. 157) only a year ago. "Today," he continued,

❖

it is a bona fide movement with a large grass-roots following and a real
potential for improving worker commitment, quality and productivity
in the workplace. Even so, the movement has grown more slowly over
the past decade than the potential justifies, partly because it has lacked
ideological backing by conservative business and militant labor groups.
Now, however, that is changing in both camps.

When Catholic social teaching from Leo XIII in 1891 until John Paul II in
1991 upheld a broad humanistic vision of workers' participation and ownership,
many critics called it utopian and socialistic. The first part of this paper will review
a century of official Catholic social teaching relevant to workers' participation and
rights and then briefly note some of the current study and research on the topic in
the U.S. — and, indeed, how feasible the visionary teaching of the church has
proven to be. Or, as an article in the *Harvard Business Review* answered the
question, "How Well is Employee Ownership Working?":

> The lessons for management are clear. Give employees an opportunity
> to acquire a significant share of the company and develop opportuni-
> ties for them to participate as owners. This course is remarkably
> effective, remarkably exciting, and remarkably different from the one
> the vast majority of American companies travel (Rosen and Quarry,
> 1987, p. 126).

In 1891, in an age of great social and economic turmoil which saw the rise of
Marxism and socialism and the worst excesses of capitalism, Pope Leo XIII wrote
in *Rerum Novarum (RN)* about the importance of private property and workers
sharing in ownership:

> But if the productive activity of the multitude can be stimulated by the
> hope of acquiring some property in land, it will gradually come to pass
> that, with the difference between extreme wealth and extreme poverty
> removed, one class will become neighbor to another (*RN*, §66).

He saw the motivating power of ownership. "For when men know they are working
on what belongs to them, they work with far greater eagerness and diligence."
Pope Leo placed great emphasis on what he called "associations of workers."

> In summary, let this be laid down as a general and constant law:
> Workers' associations ought to be so constituted and so governed as to
> furnish the most suitable and most convenient means to attain the
> object proposed, which consists in this, that the individual members of
> the association secure so far as possible, an increase in the goods of
> body, of soul, and of prosperity (*RN*, §76).

❖

In 1919 the United States Catholic Bishops adopted Pope Leo XIII's vision to our country. Their teaching was prophetic for a country wrestling with the issues of legalizing unions, child labor, twelve-hour workdays, massive immigration and urban slums. The bishops wrote:

> Nevertheless, the full responsibilities of increased production will not be realized so long as the majority of the workers remain mere wage earners. The majority must somehow become owners, or at least in part, of the instruments of production. They can be enabled to reach this stage gradually through cooperative productive societies and copartnership arrangements. In the former, the workers own and manage the industries themselves; in the latter they own a substantial part of the corporate stock and exercise a reasonable share in the management. However slow the attainments of these ends, they will have to be reached before we can have a thoroughly efficient system of production, or an industrial and social order that will be secure from the danger of revolution. It is to be noted that this particular modification of the existing order, though far-reaching and involving to a great extent the abolition of the wage system, would not mean the abolition of private ownership. The instruments of production would still be owned by individuals, not by the state (U.S. Catholic Bishops, 1919, para. 36).

In 1931 Pope Pius XI celebrated the fortieth anniversary of *RN* with an encyclical of his own, *Quadragesimo Anno (QA),* and developed many of the same themes: the dignity of labor and the rights of workers to organize and even to participate to some degree in ownership, management and profit. Pope Pius XI faced head on the challenge of communist and socialist economic philosophies. Pius XI wrote that the work-contract should be modified by a partnership-contract, so that workers and other employees could become sharers in ownership or management and participate in the profits received (*QA,* §65).

A renewed emphasis on these same themes developed in the writings of Pope John XXIII. Pope John reemphasized this broader view of work relations, when in his encyclical *Mater et Magistra (MM),* he reaffirmed what Pius XI had said, but went on to develop this theme more fully. "Furthermore, as did our predecessors, we regard as justifiable the desire of employees to be partners in enterprises with which they are associated and wherein they work" (*MM,* §91). He admitted this would vary from situation to situation, but stated emphatically there:

> We do not doubt that employees should have an active part in the affairs of the enterprise wherein they work, whether these be private or public. But it is of the utmost importance that productive enterprises

❖

assure the character of true human fellowship whose spirit suffuses the dealings, activities and standing of all its members.

The Second Vatican Council (Vatican II 1965, §68) emphasized the same points:

Therefore, taking account of the prerogatives of each—owner or employee, management or labor—and without doing harm to the necessary unity of management, the active sharing of all the administration and profits of these enterprises in ways to be properly determined should be promoted.

In 1967 Pope Paul VI broadened and continued the evolution of this view of economic development in his encyclical, *On the Development of Peoples*. He laid stress on integral development, the good of every man and the whole man, as opposed to a narrow view that limits development to mere economic growth.

Pope Paul VI in a public letter to Cardinal Maurice Roy, President of the Pontifical Commission of Justice and Peace, on the occasion of the eightieth anniversary of *RN*, acknowledged that great progress had been made in labor relations, but he also felt that:

in this immense field much needs to be done. Further reflection, research and experimentation must be actively pursued, unless one is to be late in meeting the legitimate aspirations of the workers—aspirations which are increasingly asserted according to their education and their consciousness of their dignity, and as the strength of their organizations increases (Paul VI, 1971, §15).

In very recent years Pope John Paul II and the U.S. Catholic Bishops have continued to advance these themes of workers' participation and democracy in the workplace. Pope John Paul II advanced these ideas in his encyclicals, *On Human Work* in 1981 and *Centesimus Annus (CA)* in 1991. A hundred years later, he echoed Leo XIII when he wrote:

This teaching also recognizes the legitimacy of workers' efforts to obtain full respect for their dignity and to gain broader areas of participation in the life of industrial enterprises so that, while cooperating with others and under the direction of others, they can in a certain sense 'work for themselves' through the exercise of their intelligence and freedom (*CA*, §42).

To conclude the survey of Church teaching, we should note a major contribution of the U.S. Catholic Bishops in 1986, when they strongly continued the ideas of their predecessors in 1919, as well as the papal and conciliar teaching. When the bishops in their 1986 pastoral letter, *Economic Justice for All (EJA)*, called for a "new experiment in bringing democratic ideals to economic life," they envisioned new patterns of partnerships among those working in various enterprises: profit-sharing, employees as stockholders, greater employee participation in workplace policy-making, cooperative ownership, and greater opportunities for more citizens to become shareholders in successful corporations (*EJA*, §§298-299).

Is such Catholic social teaching "utopian?" As we saw above, John Hoerr said ten years ago it was considered so when it was advanced in business circles by other proponents, but today it is a bona fide movement. Ronald Mason (1982) concluded it was unclear whether the United States would keep pace with other nations in the movement toward workplace democracy.

A more recent study by Blinder (1990) is more promising. The research originally focused on increasing productivity growth in the future by changing the way workers are paid. The studies found an unexpected theme directly related to our concerns: Worker participation apparently helps make alternative compensation plans like profit sharing, gain sharing, and ESOPs work better — and also has beneficial effects of its own. Blinder concluded:

> that changing the way workers are treated may boost productivity more than the way they are paid, although profit sharing or employee stock ownership combined with worker participation may be the best system of all (p. 13).

There has been a consistent one-hundred-year development of teaching from Leo XIII to John Paul II of the themes of workers' participation and democracy in the workplace. What was seen by some in the United States as "utopian" economics may well yet be proven to be not only good economics, but also good ethical behavior.

*Pastor, St. Cecilia's Cathedral, Omaha, NE 68131 USA.

## References

Blinder, Alan S. (ed.). *Paying for Productivity*, Washington,D.C.: The Brookings Institution, 1990.

Byers, David. (ed.). *Justice in the Marketplace*, Washington, D.C.: U.S. Catholic Conference, 1985.

Hoerr, John. "The Strange Bedfellows Backing Workplace Reform," *Business Week*, April 30, 1990, 57.

John XXIII. *Mater et Magistra*, May 15, 1961; as in Byers, ed.

❖

John Paul II. *On the Hundredth Anniversary of Rerum Novarum*, Washington, D.C.: U.S. Catholic Conference, 1991.

Leo XIII. *Rerum Novarum*, May 15, 1891; as in Byers, ed.

Levin, Doron P. "Saturn: An Outpost of Change in G.M.'s Steadfast Universe," *The New York Time*, March 17, 1991.

Mason, Ronald A. *Participatory and Workplace Democracy*, Carbondale, IL: Southern Illinois University Press, 1982.

National Conference of Catholic Bishops (NCCB). *Economic Justice for All: Pastoral Letter on Catholic Social Teaching and the U.S. Economy*, Washington, D.C.: U.S. Catholic Conference, November, 1986.

Paul VI. *Octogesima Advenieus: A Call to Action*, May 15, 1971; as in Byers, ed.

Pius XI. *Quadragesimo Anno: On Reconstructing the Social Order*, May 15, 1931; as in Byers, ed.

Rosen, Corey and Quarry, Michael. "How Well is Employee Ownership Working?," *Harvard Business Review*, September-October, 1987, 126-29.

U.S. Catholic Bishops. "Program of Social Reconstruction," February 12, 1919; as in Byers, ed.

Vatican II. *Pastoral Constitution on the Church in the Modern World*, December 1965; as in Byers, ed.

# Practical Applications of Workers Participation in Papal Social Thought

## Michael J. Naughton*

Worker participation in North America has significantly increased in the last ten years. Through programs such as work-teams, quality circles, and job enrichment, employee and employer have sought to tap the full potentialities of their organization as a social entity. With this development of worker participation, however, a debate has arisen over whether worker participation is a moral imperative based on the dignity of the human person, or a financial preference based on the productivity and profitability of particular participatory programs. (See Sashkin, 1984 and 1986) This question has fundamental significance in the organizational world. If the validity of worker participation resides ultimately in a financial framework, its implementation in the organization as well as its underlying philosophy is determined by extrinsic factors such as efficiency, productivity, or profitability. If, however, worker participation is perceived as an inherent human need, reference to the intrinsic considerations such as the psychological, moral, and spiritual development of the human person becomes a moral imperative. The papal social tradition has much to contribute to this debate.

The purpose of this paper is to review Pius XI, Pius XII, John XXIII, and John Paul II's understanding of participation on the plant or organization level. In light of this papal review, the paper discusses a contemporary participative program called work-teams. While papal social teaching on worker participation does not provide specific details on how participation programs should be implemented, papal teaching does provide a moral and religious framework that can supply a specific direction for work-teams.

## I. Pius XI: The Partnership Contract

Pius XI is the first pope to treat explicitly, although briefly, the nature of the workers' role in a firm's actual production process. He explains that workers should

❖

be treated as partners and share in the responsibility and management of the firm. The structure of the workplace should reflect a more personal and social character by recasting the existing wage contract into a contract of partnership. Pius XI refuses to condemn the wage contract, but clearly prefers the partnership contract. In *Quadragesimo Anno (QA)* he states:

> In the present state of human society, however, We deem it advisable that the wage-contract should, when possible, be modified by a contract of partnership, as is already being tried in various ways to the no small gain both of the wage-earners and of the employers. In this way wage-earners are made sharers in some sort in the ownership, or the management, or the profits. (*QA*, §65)

Pius XI, however, does not base the partnership contract on the personal and social nature of the person as Leo XIII did with his statements on associations. Pius XI bases the argument for partnership on charity and expediency. The partnership contract is better than the wage contract, but it does not undermine the moral legitimacy of the wage contract. Consequently, he does not de facto mandate the partnership contract in all cases, or in any particular cases for that matter. He merely suggests it. Endorsing the partnership contract does not concede to workers a right to participate in management. It is a pastoral exhortation, not a demand. It would be an act of charity, not of justice, on the part of the employer.

## II . Pius XII: The Codetermination Debate

### A. Background to the Debate

Pius XI's recommendation of a partnership contract initiated a controversy over the nature of the workplace and whether workers have a *natural right* to participate in the management and ownership of the firm. The debate reached its height in the late 1940s and early 1950s in the context of West Germany's 1951 codetermination laws. Codetermination is synonymous with employee participation in the management, ownership, and profit distribution. It extends from the day-to-day affairs of the production process to the determination of the economic affairs of the enterprise. It became a particular source of controversy with Pius XII when the National Catholic Convention (*Katholikentag*) held in Bochum, West Germany (1949) drafted the following resolution:

> Catholic workers and employers agree that the right of co-determination for workers in **"social, personal and economic"** matters [codetermination] of common concern is a natural right according to the order laid down by God, and corresponding to the collective responsibility of all. We demand its legal establishment. Following the example given by progressive firms, it should be put into practice everywhere from now on. (Newman, 1954, p. 3; emphasis added.)

❖

One of the primary purposes of this *Katholikentag* was to discuss the post-war reconstruction of West Germany's socio-economic life. The authors of the codetermination resolution perceived it as an application of Pius XI's idea of modifying the wage contract into a contract of partnership. However, nine months latter, Pius XII attempted to clarify the debate. He condemned the right of "economic" participation or codetermination as contrary to Pius XI's partnership contract. (He did not include social and personal participation in his condemnation.) Furthermore, he insisted that the rights of private property supercede the right of workers to economic determination. For Pius XII (1950), the nature of the wage contract and the nature of the organization do not establish a natural right to economic participation. He explains (ibid.) that as long as the wage contract respects the personal and social nature of the person, "there is nothing in the private-law relationship as governed by the simple wage-contract," to violate the dignity of the worker. The primacy of the person can be achieved on the basis of a wage contract, making it unnecessary by the virtue of justice for the wage contract to be modified by a partnership contract.

## B. Types of Participation

John Coleman S.J., (1986, p. 174) has described Pius XII as "cool" to worker participation. It would be more correct, however, to assert that he is "cool" to economic participation or codetermination, and not to personal or social participation. Although Pius XII never explicitly distinguishes among personal, social, and economic participation, still, he implies the distinction. To understand clearly Pius XII's position on worker participation, it is important to distinguish the three types of participation.

Distinctions between personal, social, and economic participation are difficult to maintain absolutely, since the different types of participation often overlap with each other. However, each form of participation has its own primary area of application. Personal participation encompasses such decisions as hiring and firing, layoffs, promotion, and change of jobs. Social participation concerns hours, working conditions, wages, vacation schedules, worker safety, pension funds, racial justice, industrial relations, vocational training, job design, social services, and welfare functions within the plant. (Rooney, 1963, p.174.) Economic participation is concerned with investments, markets, capital depreciation, product determination, profits, board representation, plant closings, mergers, basic changes in purpose of the enterprise, introduction of new methods of production, and so forth.[1]

Pius XII neither confirms nor rejects personal and social participation as natural rights. Many commentators argued that he holds them as natural rights by omission. For example, in his address to the International Congress of Social Studies, Pius XII, in an apparent response to the Bochum resolution, uses some of the same language articulated in the 1949 Bochum declaration, when he specifi-

❖

cally condemns (Sept. 9, 1956) the natural right of economic participation but not social or personal. In an address to the International Association of Economic Science, he states that:

> Except his personal and social responsibilities be recognized, the human person cannot develop his full potentialities. . . . It is necessary to look beyond man's physical needs and their demands, to see the truly free activity, both personal and communal, of him for whom the economy exists.

For Pius XII, then, a productive enterprise has a special obligation to develop the workers' personal and social nature. This is particularly true of large organizational units, where the danger of depersonalization is more common. Since many forms of personal and social participation have a strong bearing on the person's dignity, all workers have a right to participate in their process and outcome. And if employers fail to guarantee dignity for workers in the production process, government has an obligation to intervene. Unfortunately, while this train of logic concerning the right of personal and social participation is implied in Pius XII's thought, it is never made explicit.

But Pius XII is adamant that a natural right to economic participation violates owners' rights to private property by taking away their right to control their property. He argues (May 7, 1949) that workers should not be prohibited from economic participation in the enterprise, but that economic participation by the worker is limited by the fact that "the owner of the means of production . . . must remain master of his economic decisions." For Pius XII, the social nature of property can never eradicate the individual nature of property. If the owner permits workers to participate in the economic domain of the organization all the better, but workers do not have a natural right to demand this form of participation unless they own the organization themselves. Pius XII has no difficulty with the practice of economic participation of employees. He even encourages and perceives its development as a healthy sign of a Christian workplace. Pius XII did, however, have difficulties with those who argued that economic participation in the management of the firm is a natural right, and, hence, a necessary activity in the workplace. Certain proponents of this argument, such as those advocates of the Bochum resolution, inferred their conclusion from Pius XI's call to modify the wage contract by a partnership contract. Pius XII (Jan. 31, 1952) argues that this is a distortion of *QA*, because it infringes upon the individual's control of property.

For Pius XII, a return to small and medium size enterprises is the solution to the debate over participation. In an address to the International Congress of Catholic Associations for Small and Medium Sized Businesses, he states (Oct. 8, 1956):

> The economic and social function to which every man aspires requires that control over the way in which he acts be not completely subjected

❖

to the will of another. . . . It is he who anticipates, arranges, directs, and takes responsibility for the consequences of his decisions. His natural gifts . . . find employment in his directing function and become the main means by which his personality and creative urge are satisfied.

Here, capital and labor can examine more clearly the cooperative nature of their activity. Large industries, although unavoidable in certain instances, can replace human relationships between capital and labor with an impersonal bureaucracy. This creates anonymity between the two classes. Within large industries, the possibility for people to experience depersonalization increases. This constitutes a violation of personal rights and stifles the personal and social nature of the individual. Pius XII insists that if organizations built plants of a manageable size, the opportunity for worker participation would increase.

### III. John XXIII: *Mater et Magistra*

John XXIII wanted to reopen the discussion of worker participation on a positive, creative, and more open plane than Pius XII's distinctions allowed. Since he perceived a distinct socio-economic change in society, the debate over worker participation and its distinctions were no longer warranted. Another approach to worker participation would be more effective than the technical debates of Pius XII. In *Mater et Magistra (MM)*, John XXIII avoids the complications of worker participation and the codetermination debate of Pius XII by employing three tactics in his encyclical: (1) He avoided any direct reference to the codetermination debate. He does not distinguish, for example, the different types of participation (personal, social, economic) on which the debate rests, nor does he make an effort, as Pius XII did in that debate, to define the specific economic nature of the organization or enterprise. (2) John XXIII gave the partnership contract a prominent role in his summary of Pius XI's social thought. Unlike Pius XII who qualified Pius XI's call for partnership contract (almost every time he mentioned it as a suggestive and secondary character), John XXIII retains Pius XI's text with no qualification and completely affirms the partnership contract. *(MM*, §32). (3) John XXIII wanted workers to own the means of production, which would give them a strict right to economic as well as personal and social participation of their firm. Worker ownership avoids the whole debate as well as makes unnecessary the various distinctions between economic and political society, personal, social, and eco- nomic participation, and whether worker participation as a natural right infringes on the owner's right to property. While these distinctions still hold, worker ownership avoids their use by making the worker the owner.

John XXIII's teaching on worker participation has developed both because he explicitly bases worker participation on human nature and dignity, and his consideration of the economic and social changes in society. Hence, he justifies worker participation on two levels *(MM*, §93): (1) Natural Law: Worker participa- tion is justified on the basis of the person's human nature as well as the nature of

❖

the enterprise as a true human community. For John XXIII, a participatory nature exists in each person which needs to be exercised in order to fulfill the human personality. (2) Changing Social Conditions: The social and economic change calls for worker participation both on a moral level and on an efficiency level. The increasing socialization which has caused or was caused by the increasing scientific and technical workplace has made a hierarchical dominated workplace no longer humane nor efficient. By arguing on these two levels to justify and promote the development of worker participation, John XXIII makes a significant contribution and development to worker participation in the Catholic social tradition.

## A. Natural Law

John XXIII legitimizes worker participation by rooting it in human nature. He places great emphasis on workers as partners in the process of production, who partly perfect and fulfill their humanity through that process. If the dignity of the human person is held seriously, work must allow the opportunity for workers to develop their talents and potentialities in the production process. Whereas Pius XI and Pius XII perceived the partnership contract as optional, John XXIII extends the application of its use by closely associating it with human nature.

John XXIII states (*MM*, §82) that workers should participate in more important functions in the company. This would enable them to actualize more of their talents, since every person has, "of his very nature, a need to express himself in his work and thereby to perfect his own being." For John XXIII, worker participation springs from human nature and is therefore a matter of justice and rights. He argues (ibid.) that: "Justice is to be observed not only in the distribution of wealth, but also in regard to the conditions in which men are engaged in producing wealth." Prior to John XXIII, the rights and justice question in Catholic social thought rested primarily on ownership or use of capital goods, working conditions, and wage remuneration, and less on the actual production process. John XXIII maintains that worker participation is an essential means to the unfolding and development of the individual's personality, and consequently must be considered a matter of justice and rights.

Participation for John XXIII is an essential part of the process of developing and fulfilling the human relations for those people within the firm. Worker participation is not merely an organizational technique to improve efficiency and productivity among workers. It has a real effect on the determination of the person's being and cannot be seen as anything less. Worker participation leads to the personalization of the worker as well as to the humanization of the workplace. The reasons for John XXIII's advocacy of participation, then, is primarily based on the development of the human personality and consequently on the respect of human dignity. John XXIII does not state, however, whether the basis for participation is economic, personal, or social. His purpose is to raise participation to a general right of the worker with specific limitations, rather that divide participation into three distinct areas as was done by Pius XII concerning codetermination.

John XXIII (*MM*, §51) takes seriously the idea that if workers are not able to act for themselves, that is, to have some sense of personal initiative, then they would not be able to develop their personalities fully. He places great emphasis on personal initiative in all areas of life, particularly in the economic order. When people initiate things they begin to exercise their freedom and develop their personalities in a more wholesome and complete way than if they are simply told and directed by higher authorities.

Personal initiative, while important and necessary for the organization, must never lapse into anarchy. John XXIII (*MM*, §92) explains that in order for the dignity of workers to be developed the firm must "maintain a necessary and efficient unity of direction." Personal initiative and responsibility in the firm must fall within the bounds and limits of the firm, otherwise it wanders into oblivion. The economic nature of the enterprise cannot afford unlimited creativity and initiative. There are limits. Yet, John XXIII (ibid.) goes on to assert that the "unity of direction" of the firm also has its limits. The firm

> must not treat those employees who spend their days in service with the firm as though they were mere cogs in the machinery, denying them any opportunity of expressing their wishes or bringing their experience to bear on the work in hand, and keeping them entirely passive in regard to decisions that regulate their activity.

Management has the right to direction and determination, but they do not have the right to keep the worker passive and inactive.

This is the only place in *MM* that John XXIII mentions the employers right of direction, echoing the codetermination debate of Pius XII. However, even here that debate is overshadowed by John XXIII's insistence on the workers' dignity. Although Pius XII also mentioned these principles, he never emphasized them as strongly as John XXIII. Nevertheless, both John XXIII and Pius XII ultimately hold the same positions: economic participation ultimately rests with the owners, and social and personal participation are natural rights. However, the way the two arrive at these positions are different. Whereas Pius XII is primarily concerned with the violation of the economic determination of property rights, John XXIII is primarily concerned with the violation of human dignity in a non-participatory workplace. Because John XXIII's focus is on the person, the thrust of his discussion on participation is placed on a level of justice. For Pius XII, the focus is on property rights, hence, the thrust of his discussion on worker participation in an organization owned by others is placed on a level of charity. (*MM*, §§82-85)

## B. Changing Social Conditions

Although John XXIII places (*MM*, §93) primary importance on participation as a fulfillment of human nature and personal dignity, he also argues that worker

❖

participation is efficacious in light of the changes and progress in economic, social, and political areas. As the world becomes more complicated and interdependent, all workers will be expected to function by increasing their knowledge. For example, the modernization and automation of production and service systems demand higher qualifications in technical matters as well better of communication skills. If the more technical and interdependent production and service systems are to run smoothly and efficiently, they must be coupled with a more educated and communicative workforce. (*MM*, §94.) This type of argument serves as empirical support for what he states about human nature.

John XXIII (*MM*, §§47-48) is extremely optimistic about the modernization of the workforce. As the technical and scientific advancements occur in the workplace, the organization will become more efficient; and the professional qualifications and the technical skill of workers willingness. Due to this scientific and technological progress, workers will have to spend more time to complete their vocational and professional training. John XXIII (*MM*, §94) believes that this training will lead to further opportunities for "cultural, moral and religious education." This educational advancement can remove the stigma among workers as incompetent, which is often a major reason why many argue against worker participation. Further, as workers become more educated, John XXIII (*MM*, §96) asserts they will want "to assume greater responsibility in their own sphere of employment." He contends that as the level of education increases, the more people will want to become involved in the decisions of their work, largely because they have more to offer with a higher education.

John XXIII maintains that as an expression of the person, the dignity of work grows more out of workers' professional skills than out of the capital goods they attain from work. Without lessening the importance of capital and private property, John XXIII ranks work above capital and property. Labor is intrinsic to workers. It comes from their personhood. He maintains that as the immediate expression of the worker, labor "must always be rated higher than the possession of external goods which of their very nature are merely instrumental." (*MM*, §108, §242.) If labor is developed into further skills and expertise, it always stays with the person, and should have a positive effect on the person's being, civilization, and the production process. This is due to the decrease of monotonous and back-breaking work such as assembly-line work and pure physical toil, and the increase in technical, intellectual, and artistic skills which manifest the faculties of the whole human person. Commenting on *MM*, Matthew Habiger (1990, p. 227) explains that

> The quality of our person is determined, not by what material goods we have or own, but by the richness of our truly human faculties: gifts of mind, will, spirit, heart. To rest one's security in the exercise of their higher gifts, rather than in external material goods, is real progress for our race.

❖

This not only gives more dignity to workers by professionalizing their work (i.e., responsibility, skill, moral standards, etc.), it also provides better economic security for the worker. This professionalization can take place by furthering the education of the worker and by restructuring the workplace to incorporate the "whole" worker. Education and skills are a form of private property which has more worth than capital, because it expresses the human personality in a more perfect way. (*MM*, §106.)

## IV. John Paul II: Co-Creators and Participants

### A. Co-Creation

One of the deficiencies of papal social thought prior to John Paul II is that it did not provide a systematic account of a scriptural understanding of work. This is corrected by John Paul II's *Laborem Exercens (LE)*. In the area of worker participation, John Paul II insists that work is a personal activity which participates in God's ongoing creation. That is, in the work process, people are co-creators with God. Their participation in the work process has profound religious significance. This particular idea is heavily influenced by *Gaudium et Spes (GS)*. In part I chapter III of *Gaudium et Spes,* the bishops discuss the meaning of human activity in light of God's revelation. They discuss (§34) human activity in light of Genesis 1:27-28, focusing on how labor unfolds "the creator's work." John Paul II develops this "co-creation" theme more specifically in his section on the spirituality of work. (*LE*, §24) Although the theme of co-creation can be found both in *GS*, and in Leo XIII and Pius XII, no pope has developed the idea of co-creation in relation to work as thoroughly as John Paul II.

Although John Paul II never uses the term, the idea that people are "co-creators" is ever present in the encyclical (*LE*, §§13 &25). The basis for understanding what he means by co-creation and co-creator is to grasp that creation is not a one-time event. It is a continuing process, sustained through God's power and love, in cooperation with people. He explains (§25) that people continue to develop and perfect creation in collaboration with God by participating in God's continual creative activity. They provide further form and order to what has been given in nature's raw materials. John Paul II maintains that people participate in God's creative activity by carrying out God's command to subdue and have dominion. In this way, they reflect "the very action of the creator" (*LE*, §4). He asserts (§9) that God has given people the command to subdue the earth, and God has provided work as the means to attain this dominion. This command to subdue the earth is an invitation to participate in God's creative activity. Commenting on this theme of co-creation in *LE*, Romano Rossi (1980, pp. 31-32) points out:

> Being endowed with manifold faculties to act on and within the cosmos, and in accordance with the biblical precept (GN 1:28) [subdue

❖

and have dominion], man is called to participate in the remaking of a more perfect creation, while by transforming and dominating the world, he, in a sense, becomes 'partner' with God. Through his work he regains his true greatness as God's collaborator . . . and ensure the continuation of the divine creative action. . . . Thus, the worker becomes the means in order that the whole of creation will be subjected to the dignity of the human being and son of God.

For John Paul II, an inherent and intrinsic unity, then, exists between God as creator, and person as worker. As David Hollenbach notes (1982, pp. 60-61), the relationship is not related as the sacred to the profane, rather, the person's work is related as a participation in God's continuous creation. As stated in *LE* (§25):

The word of God's revelation is profoundly marked by the fundamental truth that man, created in the image of God, shares by his work in the activity of the creator and that, within the limits of his own human capabilities, man in a sense continues to develop that activity and perfects it as he advances further and further in the discovery of the resources and values contained in the whole of creation.

John Paul II explains how the fact that God's creative activity is described as work places Genesis as the first "gospel of work," establishing work as a dignified activity. ("And on the seventh day God finished his work which he had done, and he rested on the seventh day from all his work which he had done" Gen. 2.2; see Psalm 8:4-7.) As God's image, people ought to imitate God's work, since God presents God's own creative activity as work. (*LE*, §25.)

John Paul II perceives the relationship of the workers' activity with God's creative activity as extremely personal. There is an intimate calling and invitation to participate and carry on God's work every day in the workplace. Quoting *GS*, John Paul II (*LE*, §25; *GS*, §34) explains that "'by their labour they [workers] are unfolding the creator's work, consulting the advantages of their brothers and sisters, and contributing by their personal industry to the realization in history of the divine plan.'" [*LE*,§25] quoted from [*GS*, §34] John Paul II's spirituality of work is not a retreat from the world; rather, it is an immersion into the world, so as to fulfill the world within the Creator's order. Again, using *GS* (§34), he points out (*LE*,§25) that humanity's talent and progress which emanate from their work is not in competition or in opposition with God's creation; rather, "'the triumphs of the human race are a sign of God's greatness and the flowering of his own mysterious design.'" For John Paul II, Christians are called to build up the kingdom, that is, to perfect creation, through their work as co-creators within the Creator's order and design. Work as co-creation entails a personal vocation to build the world not only in a technological and scientific way, but primarily in a moral way—as partners in establishing God's kingdom of peace, love, and justice. As a co-creator, the worker has been given a religious reason to participate in the upbuilding of creation. This elevation fulfilled through Christ's grace makes work not only good but holy.

John Paul II's vision of workers as co-creators raises the importance of the work process to a theological level, highlighting the religious structure of the worker's place in the production process. He explains that the capacity for creativity, self-reflection, invention, and innovation in people constitute in part their likeness or image of God as well as the means to further perfect creation. If people are created in God's image and if God's first act is creation, then the characteristics of creativity on the part of workers has an important role to play in their work. Their creativity is an image of divinity that ought to be expressed in the workplace. The whole person should be involved—the physical, the intellectual, the emotional, and the spiritual . Work ought to be designed to use the whole person and not merely one part, as for example, in certain types of assembly-line and bureaucratic structures. Although John Paul II does not offer specific or obligatory models for the workplace, he perceives a moral obligation on the part of employers and experts in the field of organizational behavior and resource management to search for ways of incorporating the full person into the production and service process. For him, the key to utilizing the full person is to recognize the participatory character of each person.

## B. Participation

John Paul II maintains that the priority of labor over capital is sustained in the workplace if workers have a participatory role in the direction of their work. He explains that the worker "must be able to take part in the very work process as a sharer in responsibility and creativity at the work-bench to which he applies himself." (*LE*, §15) For John Paul II, only through the exercise of personal responsibility will the worker truly be able to participate in self-determination, and overcome the traditional hostility between workers and employers. For the worker to become the subject of the production process (the logical outcome of the priority of labor principle), a workplace must be organized to maximize personhood and optimize profits. John Paul II maintains that the means of production are merely instruments for the development and fulfillment of the human personality. Any organization based solely on maximizing profits, efficiency, and productivity reverses the priority of labor over capital, even though they may claim this priority of capital serves the best interest of labor. Such economic values must never be allowed to solely determine the structure of work. Work is a human activity, not merely an economic activity. The workplace should be structured primarily to actuate the development of the worker. John Paul II rejects the old capitalistic adage that the key to successful organizations is the control of production decisions by owners of capital, and by the mangers who represent them. This organizational philosophy stifles the exercise of human faculties.

Because of the formative dimension of work, participation in the organization is extremely important to John Paul II. He, more than any pope before him, has

❖

a systematic understanding of the meaning of participation (Wojtyla, 1979). As a philosopher, John Paul II (Karol Wojtyla)'s fundamental criterion concerning the fulfillment of human acts (which includes the act of work) is whether they are conducive to the participatory structure of the human person. He asks (Wojtyla, 1977):

> do they [acts] create conditions for the development of participation, do they make it easier for a human being to experience a human being and other human beings as the 'other I,' and, through that, allow also a fuller experience of one's own humanity, or do they, on the contrary, impede it, destroying that basic fabric of human existence and activity?

This criterion of participation is important for John Paul II's social teaching on work. Since human acts are self-determining, and since work is a human act, the workplace must be structured in light of the personal formation of the worker. This is the argument on which the priority of labor rests. Those who structure the production process have an obligation of justice to respect the participatory structure of the human person. Just as Leo XIII argued that the wage structure must conform to the needs of the person, that is, wages must be living wages, so John Paul II argues that the production process must conform to the formative dimension of the person. Only through participation can the personal nature of the individual be fulfilled. The work process not only enables the worker *to have more* but also *to be more*.

More specifically, John Paul II relates worker participation to the virtue of industriousness. He points out that virtue "is something whereby man becomes good as man" (*LE*, §9). Hence, if the practice of virtue makes people more human, then work, practiced as industriousness, makes workers more human. Workers need the freedom to practice the virtues that are appropriate to work such as industriousness. John Paul II furthers the idea of virtue in relation to process of work in his new encyclical, *Centesimus Annus* (*CA*, §32). There he includes industriousness but expands the list to include

> diligence, ... prudence in undertaking reasonable risks, reliability and fidelity in interpersonal relationships, as well as courage in carrying out decisions which are difficult and painful but necessary, both for the overall working of a business and in meeting possible set-backs.

John Paul II points out the "principle resource" throughout the production process is the person. The ingenuity, creativity, and intelligence of workers in collaboration with other employees establish "'working communities' which can be relied upon to transform man's natural and human environments." (Ibid.) John Paul II perceives work as a process that transforms not only nature, but also transforms the person to become more of a human being.

## V. Practical Applications of Papal Social Thought: Work-Teams

In the papal social tradition, work has a formative dimension that demands a moral responsibility to develop those participatory programs which increase worker creativity, community, and autonomy, and decrease whatever structures that might stifle worker initiative and ingenuity. The popes maintain that such goals are an inalienably moral aspect of organizing people. Organizational policy that respects the formative dimension of the worker must create an environment that allows participation of the individual workers in creating and using the objects of production.

The present status of worker participation in the U.S. has improved dramatically in last ten years, but it has still a long way to go. One study (Ghilarducci, 1989, p. 6) projected that approximately 60% to 70% of all workers participate little if at all in the decision making of their workplaces. Even though many companies may have some form of worker participation, often only a few employees are involved. For example, the U.S. General Accounting Office reported that 70% of 476 large companies they surveyed had some form of participative management; however, 70% of those companies studied had less than half of the employees involved in those programs (Hoerr, 1989, p. 58). These statistics point to a significant moral question. If the activities of individual workers are important as pointed out throughout this paper, how ought organizations structure themselves to respect this reality? Work is not merely an activity where people put in their time in order to receive a paycheck. People cannot help being who they are, given what they do with most of their days. By virtue of the work they do, people create part of their existence. If it is good work, they can express and expand their own dignity. Hence, the question of how the worker produces the product—with what material and equipment, how fast, how slow, in what environment, how much individual input— is fundamentally an ethical question. One program that attempts to implement and foster worker participation is work-teams.

### A. Work-teams

Work-teams fundamentally redesign work by creating permanent group structures in the organization. Work-teams place the traditional managerial functions of planning and organizing of work in the control of employees. Employees become an integral part of the work process in the day-to-day affairs of the company, since they become part of decision making once reserved solely for management through established production teams. Many organizational theorists maintain that work-teams represent a dominant future trend in work design, since it meets two fundamental requirements of the workplace: sociality and productivity. As Lee Hardy (1990) points out, this "socio-technical approach [to work-teams] is the wave of the future because it best comports with new market demands for flexibility, rapid response, creative problem-solving, and direct client [and employee] relationships." In the U.S., the team-work concept is sometimes implemented as part of the Quality of Work Life program (QWL), which GM introduced in the early 1970's. The concept behind work-teams under QWL is to improve efficiency by creating cooperative work teams rather than individual units on the production line. For example, GM's Pontiac division has 150 teams, each with 8 to 12 workers. The team deals not only with management but with schedulers, maintenance, quality staff, and suppliers. As a group, they decide how to place the tools, machines, and robots to make the job easier and more productive. (Cavanagh and McGovern, 1988, p. 42.) The teams have direct input on how the job is done as well as how to improve it. With work-teams in place, GM's Pontiac plant has seen a 12% improvement in production, and a better cooperative attitude among labor and management. Management has realized that a lack of responsibility among workers breeds apathy and daydreaming which in turn produces inefficiency and shoddy quality. And workers have recognized that cooperation with the company makes work more enjoyable and fulfilling.

The six major characteristics of work-teams are:

1) Membership: It is usually mandatory that everyone in a production area be included.

2) Work area coverage: Workers are responsible for a large enough area, where there is clear input/output delineation.

3) Meetings: Work-teams meet often to determine their schedule and deal with the difficulties of their assignment.

4) Supervision: The leader of the group, who is ultimately responsible to upper-management, is often elected from within the group.

5) Decision making responsibility: Depending on the level of autonomy given by management, decision making within work-teams varies from establishing production goals, quality control, and determining work methods, to hiring, firing, determining pay rates, and managing inventory.

6) Size: Teams often range from 7 to 15 members, but this can vary from team to team. (Lawler, 1986, pp. 103-108.)

Along with these six characteristics are four major goals of work-teams that combine both psychological and financial elements. The goals are to: (1) increase productivity per worker; (2) enhance worker satisfaction; (3) establish long-term job security; and (4) provide a sense of community at work.

An important characteristic of the work-team approach is its decentralization. Pius XII, John XXIII, and John Paul II encourage decentralization based on the principle of subsidiarity. They believe that subsidiarity is an important organizational principle in the ordering of the production process. Subsidiarity, according to the Catholic social tradition, is a principle that guides all social life, and is not merely meant to limit state authority. It places limits on any authority that attempts to deny persons or associations their ability to exercise their faculties and develop their personalities. This includes the employer. If workers can make the decisions and contribute to the welfare of the organization, they should. They have a right to. Workers, according to the principle of subsidiarity, should perform their work in an autonomous environment unless they either cannot or will not perform competently. This is why John Paul II maintains that the workplace should be organized in ways that strives to decentralize authority. This will make more people responsible as well as accountable for what they do. In *CA*, John Paul II (§43) explains that this decentralization in the firm will weaken "consolidated power structures" which will not only contribute to the integral development of the worker but also enhance the long-term productivity and efficiency of the firm. In keeping with the principle of subsidiarity, organizational design in recent years has been reducing levels of management, and allowing workers, largely through work teams, to participate in production decisions. That is, organizations are increasingly allowing lesser associations (work-teams) to perform the task that higher associations (management) once performed. At a General Motors Delco plant, the management/worker ratio was reduced to 1/100 from 1/10, because of restructuring, which allowed workers to manage themselves through their own teams. At Scott Paper, the plant operates on off-shifts with no management supervision. (Lawler, pp. 110-113). Through their work-teams, workers are able to assume much of their own supervision.

Work-teams have given workers a sense of responsibility for, accountability to, and completion of their own labor. Furthermore, by the social interaction among group members, workers have felt pride in the quality of their work, have increased their problem solving skills, and have developed new ideas for the product. Through this process of work-teams, many workers have regained a sense of craftsmanship by acquiring cross-training in each of the jobs done by team members. Team workers are no longer restricted to performing one repetitious act eight hours a day, but participate in the whole work process. Workers develop a sense of accomplishment as well as commitment, knowing that their contribution is an asset to the organization. With work-teams, managers function more as a support-staff than as authority figures. In their book *Workplace 2000,* Joseph Boyett and Henry Conn (1990, p. 225) argue that "No longer does the supervisor make all the decisions and solve all the problems." Employees in work-teams are required to "seek out information the group requires, to make decisions without the supervisor's input, and to initiate action to change policies, procedures, methods of performing day-to-day activities" (ibid., pp. 241-273). Work-teams have been able to concretize John XXIII's hope that workers would become more skilled and educated as well as John Paul II's concern in *CA* (§§31-32) that "the possession of know-how, technology and skill" are key to participation both in the work process as well as to appropriate remuneration. Work-teams encourage the ongoing updating of such know-how and skills, which establish economic stability and the development of the human personality.

For example, at Hallmark's greeting card plant, artists have increased production 15% because of such a team approach. Under the prior system, an artist would work on one particular card, then send it off to an editorial worker who, after

❖

some additions, would send it off to marketing who would determine whether the card would sell or not. This wasted a tremendous amount of time, particularly when the card was rejected by one or another person on the line up to marketing. There was also a psychological impact on the card's creator. Under the new approach, artists, editors, and marketing personnel work as a team. They begin to understand the logic and concerns of the various functions necessary to produce the product. This has reduced the rejection rate, the amount of wasted time, and the psychological stress on all concerned. (Saporito, 1987, pp. 27-28.) It also has a tendency to build solidarity and community among those involved.

Although work-teams, and programs like them have not been proven as a cure for all organizational problems, their presence has been cited as a factor in lowering psychological strain, creating a more skilled work force, increasing feelings of responsibility, instilling more positive attitudes toward work, and increasing production and quality. These programs provide the opportunity for workers to actualize the possibilities of their human potential and dignity, while at the same time address problems of productivity and product quality.

Work-teams are not without their problems, however. Some in management have been threatened by the loss of control and power of work-teams. Instead of using work-teams as a vehicle to increase worker participation, sometimes management employs them merely as techniques to improve production by pitting in, competition one work-team against another. Rather than creating worker solidarity, they destroy it. This is a result when work-teams are perceived merely as productivity techniques, valued solely for their financial benefits. If work-teams are to claim success, success must be based both on human and financial terms.

## VI. Conclusion

Anyone charged with the responsibility of organizing a workplace who also wants to take the principles of Catholic social thought seriously, cannot ignore the concerns of what happens to the person through the process of work. Unfortunately, some theorists and managers advocate or use participative programs not because they are humane and good for the worker, but solely because they are efficient and practical. What usually lurks behind a statement such as this is that the only fiduciary relationship management has is an economic one to owners. What is lost, however, is the personal and social fiduciary relationship management has to employees as well as to themselves by the nature of work. Financial concerns are necessities in the organizational world, but they are not the only factors in running an organization if one maintains, as the papal social tradition does, that work is not only an economic activity. As John Paul II explains in *CA* (§35) "Profit is a regulator of the life of a business but it is not the only one; other human factors must also be considered which, in long term, are at least equally important for the life of a business."

Worker participation occurs within an organization with a human end that entails a personal, social, and economic purpose. Because of its economic purpose,

❖

worker participation will be limited by employee inexperience and lack of skill as well as other factors. Yet, the organization also serves a personal and social purpose which impose on both the employer and employee the responsibility to remove those obstacles which would prevent worker participation and human development.

The papal social tradition affirms worker participation for two primary reasons: (1) The work process is a human activity that has a formative effect on the person. It is a self-determinative activity that not only effects the financial dimension of the person but also the psychological, moral, and spiritual dimensions. (2) The work process is also a participation in the Creator's ongoing activity. Recognizing this human and religious meaning of work, the papal social tradition provides a direction in the organization of work. It never prescribes one solution to the problems of organizing work. Rather, it provides a general direction, and states that the present reality of work is in need of redesign, and that some new solutions are necessary. The direction the popes offer is a workplace that entails partnerships, participation, cooperation, development of personal skills, long-term thinking, accountability, virtue, competence, and a religious meaning that is directed toward a moral order of creation. All of these characteristics are to enhance the dignity of each and every worker.

Fortunately, some in the corporate world have recognized this formative and moral dimension of work. The president of Honeywell, James Renier, expressed the essence of worker participation well when he was asked why he had advocated participation for ten years before gaining any support from his fellow managers:

> If we help people develop into the best they can become, and if we enable people to make their maximum contribution on the job, we will get the innovation and productivity we need. But I suggest to you that even if it I did not get more productivity or make the company more secure, or improve profits, it would still be worth doing. It would be worth doing simply because it is the right thing to do. . . . Think of it [participation] as an ethical undertaking. That will insure that programs like . . . quality work life help our people achieve their objectives and do not degenerate to mere manipulation. (O'Toole, 1985, p. 133.)

Renier realizes that the reason for participation in the workplace is not finally a financial one, but a moral one. As John XXIII and John Paul II have pointed out, participation is a moral principle that stems from belief in the dignity of the worker. That is, workers are not mere extensions of capital. Their labor, their ideas, creativity, ingenuity, as well as their physical energy, have a formative influence on their personal development. Participation in the long run will probably be the best financial strategy, but as a principle, the basis is moral and religious rather than financial.

❖

# Endnotes

\*University of St. Thomas.

[1] Ibid. Distinctions between personal, social, and economic participation are difficult to maintain absolutely, since the different types of participation often overlap with each other. For example, it is difficult to maintain a strict separation between personal and social participation, and economic participation in the case of plant closings. Plant closing is an economic decision for an organization which should have the freedom to do so; however, plant closings also have personal and social costs which employees have a right lesson. Pius XII, unfortunately, does not provide specific guidelines on how to resolve such conflicts of participation.

# References

Boyett, Joseph H., and Henry P. Conn. *Workplace 2000*, New York: A Dutton Book, 1990.

Cavanagh, Gerald F., and Arthur F. McGovern. *Ethical Dilemmas in the Modern Corporation*, New Jersey: Prentice Hall, 1988.

Coleman, John. "Development of Church Social Teaching." In *Official Catholic Social Teaching*, eds. Charles E. Curran and Richard A. McCormick, New York: Paulist Press, 1986, 169-187.

Ghilarducci, Teresa. "John Paul II and American Workers in the Emerging Fourth World." Paper presented at the "The Center of Ethics and Religious Values in Business," Notre Dame, IN, April 24-26, 1989.

Habiger, Matthew. *Papal Teaching on Private Property 1891-1991*, Lanham: University of America Press, 1990.

Hardy, Lee. *The Fabric of This World*, Grand Rapids: William B. Eerdmans Publishing Company, 1990.

Hoerr, John. "The Payoff From Teamwork," *Business Week*, 10 July 1989, 56-62.

Hollenbach, David. "Human Work and the Story of Creation: Theology and Ethics in *Laborem Exercens*," in *Co-Creation and Capitalism*, John W. Houck and Oliver F. Williams eds. Lanham: University Press of America, 1983.

John XIII, Pope. *Mater et Magistra*, in *Proclaiming Justice and Peace*, Michael Walsh and Brian Davies, eds., Mystic: Twenty-Third Publications, 1984, 1-44.

John Paul II, Pope. *Centesimus Annus*, Vatican City: Libreria Editrice Vaticana, 1991.

_____. *Laborem Exercens* (1981), In *Proclaiming Justice and Peace*, Michael Walsh and Brian Davies, eds. Mystic: Twenty-Third Publications, 1984, 271-311.

Lawler, Edward E. *High-Involvement Management,* San Francisco: Jossey-Bass Publishers, 1986.

Newman, Jeremiah. *Co-responsibility in Industry: Social Justice in Labour-Management Relations,* Cork: Cork University Press, 1954.

O'Toole, James. *Vanguard Management: Redesigning the Corporate Future,* New York: Doubleday, 1985.

Pius XI, Pope. *Quadragesimo Anno* (1931), Boston: St. Paul Editions, n.d.

Pius XII, Pope. "Address to the Ninth International Congress of the International Union of Catholic Employers," (7 May 1949), in *Catholic Mind,* July 1949, 446-448.

_____. "Address to the Catholic International Congresses for Social Study," 3 June 1950, in *Catholic Mind,* August 1956, 507-510.

_____. "Address to the Italian Catholic Association of Employers," 31 January 1952, in *Catholic Mind,* September 1952, 569-572.

_____. "Address to the Catholic Association of Small and Medium-sized Businesses," 8 October 1956, in *The Pope Speaks,* Spring 1957, 405-409.

Rooney, Gerald J. "The Right of Workers to Share in Ownership, Management, and Profits," *Catholic Theological Society of America Proceedings,* 18 June 1963, 131-149.

Rossi, Romano. *Human Labour,* The Social Teaching of John Paul II Series, Vatican City: Pontifical Commission Institia et Pax, 1980.

Saporito, Bill. "Cutting Costs Without People," *Fortune,* 25 May 1987, 26-32.

Sashkin Marshall. "Participative Management Is an Ethical Imperative," *Organizational Dynamics,* Spring 1984, 5-22.

_____. "Participative Management Remains an Ethical Imperative," *Organizational Dynamics,* Spring 1986, 62-75.

Wojtyla, Karol. *The Acting Person,* Analecta Husserliana Series, ed. Anna-Teresa Tymieniecka, vol. 10, Boston: D. Reidel Publishing Co., 1979.

_____. "Participation and Alienation," in *The Self and The Other,* Analecta Husserliana Series, ed. Anna-Teresa Tymieiecka, vol. 6. Boston: D. Riedel Publishing Co., 1977, 61-73.

# Catholic Social Teaching and Human Resource Policy: Implications for Equity Investors

## Gerald Jensen, Robert R. Johnson, and Joseph M. Phillips*

Beginning with *Rerum Novarum (RN)*, modern Catholic social teaching has focused attention on the proper treatment of workers by employers. Work and working conditions should reflect the "dignity of the worker" and the "dignity of work" (*Centesiums Annus (CA)*, §6). From this follows certain responsibilities for holders of capital, or shareholders in the case of a publicly traded corporation, in terms of how their firms treat employees.

In *CA* John Paul II directly addresses this point with the following passage:

> The Church acknowledges the legitimate *role of profit* as an indication that a business is functioning well. When a firm makes a profit this means that productive factors have been properly employed and corresponding human needs have been duly satisfied. But profitability is not the only indicator of a firm's condition. It is possible for the financial accounts to be in order, and yet for the people — who make up the firm's most valuable asset — to be humiliated and their dignity offended. Besides being morally inadmissable, this will eventually have negative repercussions on the firm's economic efficiency. (§35)

Thus the Pope enjoins shareholders to be concerned not only with profitability, but also with how workers are treated, and hints that the two are not necessarily incompatible. Indeed, there is growing sensitivity to this issue on the part of investors. Particularly in the United States, Socially Responsible Investing (SRI) is becoming increasingly popular. According to the Social Investment Forum, investments made after consideration of social criteria such as environmental, ethical or political concerns have grown from $40 billion in 1984 to over $625

---

❖

---

billion in 1991 (Scanlan 1991, E1). One form of SRI focuses on supporting companies which follow progressive human resource (HR) policies.[1]

SRI is an effort by investors to weigh principles and values in portfolio decisions. As such, it is very much in the spirit of Catholic social teaching in terms of the overlap of ethics and economics. SRI is of three basic forms. One form involves avoiding firms engaged in objectionable practices, such as maintaining a presence in South Africa. A second approach is for an investor to support a firm on the basis of some positive activity, such as an environmentally conscious outlook. Finally, it may involve taking an equity position in a firm in an effort to seek change in a company's policies. This third form may involve seeking to halt objectionable activities or the initiation of desirable activities. The last strategy is the most radical and typically takes the form of shareholder proposals.

In the present case of an investor wishing to support progressive HR policies, the investor may hold stock in a company that creates a work environment enhancing the dignity of workers, presumably to encourage such policies. Yet some might ask if the investor sacrifices return with such a strategy by limiting the universe of potential equities in the portfolio of the investor? Or, as *CA* suggests, might the investor gain because such policies boost productivity and the value of the firm?

Theory does not provide an answer. Hence, this study attempts to answer this question empirically by analyzing equity investment results of the publicly traded firms listed in *The 100 Best Companies to Work for in America* (Levering, Moskowitz, and Katz, 1984). *100 Best* attempted to identify the most desirable companies to work for from the viewpoint of the employee. The results show that investors using the *100 Best* to screen equity investment would not have sacrificed return, but neither would they have enjoyed statistically significant excess returns on investment. There would have been no penalty to investors pursuing the guidelines of Catholic social teaching for treatment of employees.

Section One of this paper explores Catholic social doctrine in the area of employee relations. Section Two discusses how *100 Best* identified employers using progressive HR policies. Section Three describes other evidence of how HR policies may affect firm performance. Section Four describes the data and methodology of this study. Section Five presents the results of this study, and the final section provides conclusions.

## I. Catholic Social Teaching and Human Resource Policy

While the social encyclicals do not provide a precise outline of how employers should treat employees, one can piece ideas together to make a case that what today is considered to be a progressive HR policy would comply with Catholic social teaching. And these progressive policies were what *100 Best* looked for in its search for desirable employers.

What does Catholic social doctrine, beginning with *RN*, tell us about the responsibilities of employers for employees? First, perhaps the most significant theme in the encyclicals is the necessity of adequate remuneration for employees. But what is "adequate?" Several considerations have been offered in this regard. The level of compensation must, in the words of Leo XIII, "be enough to support the wage earner in reasonable and frugal comfort" (*RN*, §34). There is also the theme that compensation must not just meet basic needs, but that through thrift, the worker should be able to accumulate property (wealth) so as to be freed from the hand-to-mouth uncertainty that can characterize a wage earner (*Quadragesimo Anno (QA)*, §61). This is also explicitly stated by John Paul in *CA* when he writes, "Furthermore, society and the State must ensure wage levels adequate for the maintenance of the worker and his family, including a certain amount for savings" (*CA*, §15). In addition, Catholic social teaching has introduced the idea of the "family wage," whereby the wage is sufficient to support a family with only one spouse working (*Laborem Exercens (LE)* §19; *QA*, §71).

In addition to adequate compensation, employee benefits have also been addressed. Such issues as health and disability insurance and provision for retirement have been addressed repeatedly. And in *CA* (§34) John Paul has written of the necessity of providing training and education to workers so their skills may be upgraded.

It would seem that employee participation in decision making would also be endorsed by Catholic social teaching. This is implicit in statements pointing out how work contributes to the dignity of the worker and that employment should enhance human dignity: "Man's life is built up every day from work, from work it derives its specific dignity" (LE, §1). Participation would seem necessary if work was to affirm dignity in an economic system where increasingly the key input is man himself (human capital) (CA, §32). The endorsement of a participatory workplace is also contained in specific references, for example in CA (§43) John Paul says:

> This (social) teaching also recognizes the legitimacy of workers' efforts to obtain full respect for their dignity and to gain broader areas of participation in the life of industrial enterprises so that, while cooperating with others and under the direction of others, they can in a certain sense "work for themselves" through the exercise of their intelligence and freedom.

Finally, it would seem Catholic social teaching would look favorably upon profit sharing arrangements or employee ownership. Both would tie employee compensation directly to firm performance. It would explicitly recognize the fact that a firm is a "society of persons," "a *community of persons* who in various ways are endeavoring to satisfy their basic needs, and who form a particular group at the service of the whole of society" *(CA*, §35). Indeed, in *LE* (§14) John Paul makes favorable mention of such arrangements, pointing out their earlier endorsement in *Gaudium et Spes* (*GS*, §68) and *QA* (§65).

❖

This brief review of Catholic social teaching has revealed several ways in which the dignity of workers can be affirmed by employers. Now let us turn to a review of the criteria used by *100 Best* in locating desirable employers and see how those criteria match up with the view of Catholic social teaching.

## II. How the *100 Best Companies* Were Chosen

*100 Best* attempted to identify the most desirable companies to work for from the viewpoint of the employee. The general criteria used were in the areas of pay, benefits, job security, upward mobility in the firm, and "ambience," a term used to refer to organization culture and climate. In general, *100 Best* attempted to find companies where employee-management relations were not adversarial and where human resource policies were not manipulative.

The authors of *100 Best* first identified 350 potential companies through informal consultation with a number of contacts. This list was narrowed to 135 firms on the basis of a survey distributed to the 350 firms. Of the 135, 114 firms were visited by the authors; and their employees were interviewed, with the list then being narrowed to 100. Firms selected tended to have the following characteristics:

- Encouraged team work
- Encouraged open communication
- Promoted from within
- Stressed quality
- Had a profit sharing plan
- Had relatively narrow distinctions in the firm hierarchy
- Fostered a comfortable workplace environment
- Encouraged community service
- Encouraged employee saving with a matching plan
- Avoided layoffs
- Provided exercise and medical programs
- Supported training and education

Each of these characteristics would seem to affirm human dignity and to be consistent with Catholic social teaching.[2]

The authors accurately describe their methodology as "journalistic rather than scientific." Using ad hoc criteria they created a list of attractive employers based on their collective wisdom. Yet, in the world of SRI, this type of ad hoc list creation is commonplace. In principle, it appears easy to decide not to invest in companies, say, doing business in South Africa or manufacturing nuclear weapons, or to decide to invest in companies actively promoting women and minorities, but implementing these ideas is a very imprecise art. Lists of companies operating in South Africa are likely to differ significantly from one another. Using the *100 Best* list may appear ad hoc, but in reality it mimics the manner in which SRI is done.

❖

## III.  Human Resource Policies and Firm Performance

Is there any evidence to suggest that HR policies stressed by the *100 Best* will improve employee productivity and firm performance? Economists, industrial psychologists and human resource specialists have studied closely how organization climate affects firm performance. There is some evidence to suggest that HR policies identified by *100 Best* such as building teamwork, open communication, profit sharing, leveling,[3] and avoiding layoffs may boost productivity and firm performance, thus increasing shareholder wealth.

Pay systems in particular have received much attention from researchers, especially in the 1980's when U.S. firms, struggling to boost productivity in the face of stronger domestic and foreign competition, began to experiment with pay systems as a means to motivate workers. Variable pay plans of different types have been employed in an effort to control costs or to encourage innovation in reaching performance targets. There has been a move away from "paying for time spent on the job" (straight salary or wage), to using such strategies as profit sharing, gain sharing, bonuses, individual incentives, small group incentives, pay for knowledge, and earned time off.

Most analyses of these alternative compensation measures have concluded that they succeed in boosting productivity. Schuster (1986) concludes that gainsharing led to productivity improvements, mostly in the form of a one-time shift upon implementation, as well as non-quantifiable benefits such as facilitating cultural change. Weitzman and Kruse (1990) surveyed many different types of evidence bearing on the issue and concluded there is consistent weak support that profit sharing improves productivity, but Blinder (1990) wondered whether such plans pay for themselves. Nalbantian (1987) concluded that financial incentives for employees, whether group or individual, will on average result in improved performance; but there was substantial variation such that inadequately designed plans failed to boost productivity. Voss (1987) found managers of unionized firms felt gainsharing and profit sharing plans boosted productivity. Still, Ehrenberg and Milkovich (1987) cautioned that we know little about the relationship between compensation policy and economic performance, primarily because of the complexity of compensation policies and the difficulty of adequately testing the issue. They also said pay-for-performance practices are poorly implemented, failing to offer pay increases meaningful to employees and neglecting to establish a clear relationship between performance and pay.

Employee participation and communication was another area considered by *100 Best* that has also received the attention of researchers (as well as Catholic social teaching). Employee participation can take such forms as quality circles, team-group suggestions, labor-management consultation, employee board representatives, small problem solving groups, cross functional employee task forces, or autonomous work teams. Several studies reported positive effects for employee participation on worker productivity (Marks, et al. (1986); Cornell (1984); Rosenberg and Rosenstein (1980)). Voos found managers believed that participation programs also boosted productivity. Carson (1985) found firms with participatory management had higher Value Line ratings and better labor relations. On the other hand, an earlier study by Locke and Schweiger (1979) concluded, after an extensive literature review, that employee participation had no positive effect on productivity. Gershenfeld (1987) noted it is difficult to evaluate participation programs because so many are new and the necessary data are largely unavailable. In a survey of the topic, he found many individual cases of productivity improvements from employee participation, but these results are present in less than half of the studies considered. He noted participation programs often do not last, but believed their longevity will increase in the future. It may be that whether participation allows for improved productivity depends on how participation is structured and how it fits into a firm's HR philosophy.

Weitzman and Kruse found worker participation was important in order for profit sharing to boost productivity. Levine and Tyson (1990) found employee participation more likely to have a positive effect when decisions related to the daily work of the employee, involved substantive decision making rights rather than consultation, and occurred in an environment characterized by a high degree of employee commitment and employee-management trust. This would capture much of the organization culture and climate considered in *100 Best* and certainly would result in an environment enhancing human dignity. In general, Levine and Tyson concluded that participation must be part of a package and that package must include gain sharing, team building, no layoffs, leveling, guaranteed rights to build trust, and participation that goes beyond mere consultation. This reflects much of what *100 Best* considered important and would also be consistent with Catholic social teaching. Blinder summarized this whole issue by stating that changing the way people are treated may boost productivity more than changing the way they are paid.

Results of the studies described above are based on methods different from those employed in this paper, where improved performance is measured by increased shareholder wealth. There have been other studies using similar methods, but they have focused on how shareholder wealth might be affected by effects associated with organized labor such as new collective bargaining agreements (Abowd, 1989; Liberty and Zimmerman, 1986), strikes (Becker and Olsen, 1986; Tracy, 1987), union organizing (Ruback and Zimmerman, 1984; Olsen and Becker, 1990), or concession bargaining (Becker, 1987). These event-studies examined shareholder wealth changes as the result of a singular event. The focus of the present research is more encompassing and relates to both union and non-union employees. Of more relevance to this paper is a recent event-study by Abowd, Milkovich, and Hannon (1990) that looked at a range of issues such as general HR system changes, compensation and benefits changes, staffing changes, relocations, and shutdowns to determine how they affect investor returns. The authors concluded there was

❖

little predictable market reaction to such changes. They did find, however, increased variations of abnormal returns in response to announcements of permanent staff reductions, shutdowns, and relocations. Thus, announcements of this type influenced stock prices.

This overview of research on HR policy suggests a SRI policy of investing in firms with progressive HR policies may not necessarily sacrifice return for the sake of principles. It may well be that as *CA* suggests companies following such policies will experience improved performance that will be reflected in increased shareholder wealth. There is no reason to assume a priori that returns to such shareholders will be lower, although the mixed evidence available does not strongly confirm returns will be higher. The following section discusses our empirical investigation of the issue.

## IV. Data and Methodology

Empirical tests described below involve estimating abnormal equity market returns to firms with progressive HR policies. We use the market model technique to estimate abnormal returns. Monthly stock return data were obtained from the Center for Research in Security Prices (CRSP) tape. As a proxy for the market index, we used the CRSP equally weighted index.

Not all of the firms listed in *100 Best* are analyzed in our study. To be included in the sample, the firm had to be publicly traded and report return information on the CRSP tape for the period studied and five years prior to the periods analyzed. As a result, our sample size is not constant over the entire time period. The fewest number of firms appearing in the sample in any one year was 51 in 1989, and the most was 56 in 1981 and 1983. A complete listing of the *100 Best* firms is provided in Appendix A, along with an indication of appearance in the sample for any one year.

The study examines annual returns over ten one-year periods from 1980 through 1989, as well as the entire ten-year period. *100 Best* was first published in February 1984, so we examine returns for four years prior to publication, the year of publication, and five years following publication. Since this is not an event-study, we are not concerned with shareholder returns near the date of publication. The purpose of this study is to ascertain whether shareholders either sacrifice or realize higher risk-adjusted returns by investing in firms practicing progressive HR policies. It is assumed, therefore, these policies were followed for the four years prior to the publication of the book and continued to be followed in the five years following publication.

To assess the return to a shareholder investing in firms with progressive HR policies, we selected a market model procedure. The market model approach adjusts security returns according to the security's systematic (beta) risk and has been extensively employed in the finance literature (Brown and Warner, 1980; Fama, 1976).

❖

We assume monthly stock returns are normally distributed jointly with monthly market index returns. Therefore, for each stock j, there are constants $\alpha_j$ and $\beta_j$, such that

$$R_{jt} = \alpha_j + \beta_j R_{mt} + e_{jt}, \tag{1}$$

and where $E(e_{jt}) = 0$. We also assume that for a given firm j the $e_{jt}$ are homoskedastic and serially uncorrelated at all lags.

The parameters $\alpha_j$ and $\beta_j$ were estimated by ordinary least squares regression using the 60 monthly returns pairs $(R_{jt}, R_{mt})$ over the 60 month interval prior to the event year. We examine a ten-year period, hence the parameters change annually. Using the least squares estimates, $\alpha_j$ and $\beta_j$, (1) generates a conditional forecasting model for firm j's stock returns. The forecast error,

$$\mu_{jt} = R_{jt} - \alpha_j - \beta_j R_{mt}, \tag{2}$$

provides an estimate of the (statistically) abnormal component of stock j's return over the t th monthly interval.

We examine the mean annual forecast error as a measure of excess returns. The annual excess return for stock j in year n is calculated as follows.

$$\Phi_{jt} = \sum_{t=1}^{12} \mu_{jt} \tag{3}$$

The crossectional mean excess return for each year n is derived by averaging the annual excess returns over the J firms in each year, as shown below.

$$\overline{\Phi}_n = \sum_{j=1}^{J} \Phi_{jn}/J \tag{4}$$

The null hypothesis for the existence of statistically significant excess returns is tested using the following t-test and cumulative t-test.

$$t = \overline{\Phi}_n /(S_n/J^5) \tag{5}$$

$$ct = \sum_{n=1}^{10} \overline{\Phi}_n / [\sum_{n=1}^{10} S_n]^{5} \tag{6}$$

❖

where,

$$S_n = [\, (\, \sum_{j=1}^{J} \,(\Phi_{jn} - \overline{\Phi}_n)^2\,) / (j\text{-}1)\, ]^5 \qquad (7)$$

The t-statistic determines the statistical significance of the excess return in each of the years, while the cumulative t-statistic tests for significance over the ten year period. The test statistics will determine the effects on shareholders of investing in firms with progressive HR policies. The results are discussed below.

## V. Results

Table One presents mean annual excess returns accruing to shareholders of the *100 Best* firms. Also provided are standard errors of the mean, t-statistics, and the number of firms appearing in the sample for each year.

**Table 1:**

**Average Annual Excess Returns for Shareholders of 100 Best Firms for Years 1980 through 1989.**

| Year | Mean Annual Excess Return | Standard Error of the Mean | t-statistic | Number of Firms |
|------|------|------|------|------|
| 1980 | 0.098 | 0.036 | 2.75** | 53 |
| 1981 | 0.027 | 0.063 | 0.44 | 56 |
| 1982 | 0.180 | 0.046 | 3.87** | 55 |
| 1983 | -0.094 | 0.039 | -2.43* | 56 |
| 1984 | -0.021 | 0.031 | -0.66 | 55 |
| 1985 | 0.031 | 0.036 | 0.87 | 53 |
| 1986 | 0.044 | 0.032 | 1.35 | 52 |
| 1987 | 0.045 | 0.040 | 1.12 | 52 |
| 1988 | -0.076 | 0.039 | -1.95 | 53 |
| 1989 | -0.028 | 0.031 | -0.89 | 51 |

**Statistically significant at the 1% level.
* Statistically significant at the 5% level.

❖

The cumulative excess return for the ten year period was 2.070% annually with a cumulative t-statistic of 0.22. As is shown, annual excess returns are generally positive, yet statistically insignificant. The cumulative excess return is also positive, yet statistically insignificant. The cumulative excess risk adjusted return of 2.070% annually translates into an excess return of 22.74% over the ten years studied. To ensure that these results are not attributable to a concentration of the sample in particular industries, a breakdown of the sample by SIC code is provided in Appendix B.[4] As can be seen, with the exception of the Business Equipment sector, industry concentration does not appear to be a problem. At a minimum, these results suggest that an investor does not have to sacrifice return by investing in companies practicing progressive HR policies, policies consistent with Catholic social teaching on the treatment of employees.

## VI. Conclusions

Catholic social teaching has stressed that investors should be concerned with more than just profit making. One other concern should be how the human dignity of their employees is enhanced. *CA* even suggests that these may be compatible objectives. This study has examined this issue from the viewpoint of investors seeking to follow a SRI policy of equity investment in firms with progressive HR policies.

The empirical analysis provided evidence that, at the very least, suggests an investor need not sacrifice return when purchasing equities in firms practicing progressive HR policies. It appears that an investor can make investment decisions consistent with Catholic social teaching on the treatment of employees without negatively impacting portfolio returns. At the same time, neither will investors gain from such a strategy. Humane treatment of employees is its own reward. Moreover, there is no evidence contradicting John Paul's statement that labor policies that do not promote human dignity will, in the long run, have an adverse effect on firm performance.

## Endnotes

*Assistant Professor of Finance, Northern Illinois University, Dekalb, IL, USA, Assistant Professor of Finance, Creighton University, and Associate Professor of Economics, Creighton University, Omaha, NE 68178 USA respectively.

[1] For example, Shearson Lehman Hutton has a socially responsible investment management program that screens firms for "...companies that are known for fostering and encouraging fair and beneficial relations with their employees." The Calvert Social Investment Fund seeks to invest in firms which (among other goals) "...are managed with participation throughout the organization in defining and achieving objectives"; and "negotiate fairly with workers, create an environment supportive of their wellness, do not discriminate on the basis of race, religion, age, disability or sexual orientation,

do not consistently violate regulations of the Equal Employment Opportunity Commission, and provide opportunities for women, disadvantaged minorities and others for whom equal opportunities have been denied." Prudential Securities provides a benchmark screen of AFL-CIO boycott targets as part of its Prudential Securities Social Investment Research Service series of socially screened portfolios.

[2] Of course, this is not to deny that other practices of the firm may not be consistent with Catholic social teaching. For example, a firm may be dependent on production of nuclear weaponry or engage in excessive pollution of the environment.

[3] Leveling involves reducing the distinctions of rank between the top management and those in entry-level jobs.

[4] The categorization of SIC codes is the same as employed by Fama and French (1986) and DeFusco, Johnson, and Zorn (1991).

❖

# Appendix A

List from *100 Best Companies to Work for in America*

(An asterisk indicates that the firm appeared in the sample for at least one year).

| | | |
|---|---|---|
| Advanced Micro Devices | Goldman Sachs | Odetics* |
| Analog Devices* | Gore | Olga |
| Anheuser-Busch* | Hallmark Cards | J.C. Penney* |
| Apple Computer | H.J. Heinz* | People Express Airline |
| Armstrong World Ind.* | Hewitt Associates | Phillip Morris* |
| Atlantic Richfield* | Hewlett-Packard* | Physio-Control |
| Baxter Travenol | Hospital Corp | Pitney Bowes* of America* |
| Bell Laboratories | Inland Steel* | Polaroid* |
| Borg-Warner* | Intel | Preston Trucking |
| Leo Burnett | IBM* | Procter & Gamble* |
| Celestial Seasonings | Johnson & Johnson* | Publix |
| Citicorp* | Johnson Wax | Quad/Graphics |
| Control Data* | Knight-Ridder* | Rainer National Bank |
| Trammel Crow* | Kollmorgen* | Ralston Purina* |
| CRS/Sirrine* | Levi Strauss* | Random House |
| Cummins Engine* | Liebert | Raychem* |
| Dana* | Linnton Plywood | Reader's Digest |
| Dayton Hudson* | Los Angeles Dodgers | ROLM* |
| Deere* | Lowe's* | Ryder* |
| Delta Air Lines* | Marion Labs | Saga* |
| Digital Equipment* | Mary Kay Cos.* | Security Pac. Bank* |
| Walt Disney* | Maytag* | Shell Oil* |
| Donnelly Mirrors | McCormick | Southern CA Edison* |
| Doyle Dane | Bernbach Merck* | Springs* |
| Du Pont* | Merle Norman Cos.* | Tandem Computer* |
| Eastman Kodak* | Herman Miller | Tandy* |
| A.G. Edwards* | 3M* | Tektronix* |
| Electro Scientific | Moog* | Tenneco* |
| Erie Insurance | J.P. Morgan* | Time, Inc. |
| Exxon* | Nissan | Viking Freight |
| H.B. Fuller | Nordstrom | Wal-Mart Stores* |
| General Electric* | NW Mutual Life* | Westin Hotels |
| General Mills* | Nucor* | Weyerhauser* |
| | | Worthington Ind. |

# Appendix B

**Sample Breakdown by Standard Industry Classification Code**

| Industry | # of firms in sample | SIC Codes |
|---|---|---|
| Food | 4 | 100-299, 2000-2099, 5140, 5191 |
| Apparel | 2 | 2200-2399, 3140-3149, 5130-5139 |
| Drugs | 5 | 2100-2199, 2830-2849, 5122, 5194 |
| Retail | 4 | 5230-5999 |
| Durables | 5 | 2500-2599, 3000-3099, 3172, 3630-3669, 3860-3949, 3960-3969, 5020-5029, 5040-5049, 5064, 5094-5099 |
| Autos | 1 | 3710-3719, 3792, 5010-5019 |
| Construction | 2 | 1500-1799, 2400-2499, 2850-2859, 2952, 3200-3299, 3420- 3439, 5030-5039, 5070-5075, 5198, 5211 |
| Finance | 7 | 6000-6999 |
| Utilities | 0 | 4900-4999 |
| Transportation | 3 | 3720-3789, 3790, 3799, 4000-4799 |
| Business Equipment | 13 | 3500-3629, 3670-3699, 3800-3859, 3950-3959, 5060-5069, 5078-5089 |
| Chemicals | 1 | 2800-2829, 2860-2899, 5160-5169 |
| Metal Products | 0 | 3410-3419, 3440-3449, 5080-5089 |
| Metal Industries | 2 | 3300-3399 |
| Mining | 0 | 1000-1299, 1400-1499, 5050-5059 |
| Oil | 3 | 1300-1399, 2910-2919, 5170-5179 |
| Miscellaneous | 8 | 2600-2799, 2990-2999, 3110-3119, 3190-3199, 3980-3999, 4800-4899, 5090, 5093, 5110-5119, 5199, 7000-8999, 9910, 9999 |

# References

Abowd, John. "The Effect of Wage Bargains on the Stock Market Value of the Firm," *American Economic Review*, September 1989, *79*, 774-800.

Abowd, John, Milkovich, George and Hannon, John. "The Effects of Human Resource Management Decisions on Stockholder Value," *Industrial and Labor Relations Review*, February 1990, *43*, 203-236.

Becker, Brian. "Concession Bargaining: The Impact of Shareholder's Equity," *Industrial and Labor Relations Review*, February 1987, *40*, 268-279.

Becker, Brian, and Olsen, Greg. "The Consequences of Strikes for Shareholder Equity," *Industrial and Labor Relations Review*, April 1986, *39*, 425-438.

Becker, Brian, and Olsen, Greg. "Labor Relations and Firm Performance," in Kleiner, Morris, et al., eds. *Human Resources and the Performance of the Firm,* Madison, WI: Industrial Relations Research Association, 1987, 43-85.

Blinder, Alan. "Introduction," in Blinder, Alan, ed., *Paying for Productivity*, Washington, DC: The Brookings Institute, 1990, 1-13.

Brown, Steven, and Warner, Jerold. "Measuring Security Price Performance," *Journal of Financial Economics*, September 1980, *8*, 206-258.

Carson, S. Andrew. "Participatory Management Beefs Up the Bottom Line," *Personnel*, July 1985, *62*, 45-48.

Cornell, Paul. "Variables Influencing QWL and Job Performance in an Encoding Task," in Hendrick, H. and O. Brown, eds. *Human Factors in Organization Design and Management*, Amsterdam: Elsevier Science Publishers, 1984, 373-377.

DeFusco, Richard A., Zorn, Thomas S., and Johnson, Robert R. "The Association Between Executive Stock Option Plan Changes and Managerial Decision Making," *Financial Management*, Spring 1991, *20*, 36-43.

Ehrenberg, Ronald and Milkovich, George. "Compensation and Firm Performance," in Kleiner, Morris, et al., eds. *Human Resources and the Performance of the Firm*, Madison, WI: Industrial Relations Research Association, 1987, 87-123.

Fama, Eugene F. *Foundations of Finance*, New York: Basic Books, Inc., 1976.

Fama, Eugene F., and French, Kenneth R. "Common Factors in the Serial Correlations of Stock Returns," CRSP Working Paper No. 200, 1986.

Gershenfeld, Walter. "Employee Participation in Firm Decisions," in Kleiner, Morris, et al., eds. *Human Resources and the Performance of the Firm*, Madison, WI: Industrial Relations Research Association, 1987, 124-158.

Grossman, Blake R., and Sharpe, William F. "Financial Implications of South African Divestment," *Financial Analysts Journal*, July/August 1986, *42*, 15-29.

John Paul II. *Centesimus Annus* (May 1, 1991), Vatican City: Libreria Editrice Vaticana, 1991.

John Paul II. *Laborem Exercens* (September 14, 1981), Washington, DC: United States Catholic Conference, 1981.

Leo XIII. *Rerum Noverum* (May 15, 1891), New York: Paulist Press, 1962.

Levering, Robert, Moskowitz, Milton, and Katz, Michael. *The 100 Best Companies to Work For in America,* Reading, MA: Addison-Wesley, 1984.

Levine, David, and Tyson, Laura D'Andrea. "Participation, Productivity, and the Firm's Environment," in Blinder, Alan, ed. *Paying for Productivity,* Washington, DC: The Brookings Institute, 1990, 183-237.

Liberty, Susan, and Zimmerman, Jerold. "Labor Union Contract Negotiations and Accounting Choices," *Accounting Review,* October 1986, *61,* 692-712.

Locke, Edwin, and Schweiger, David. "Participation in Decision-Making: One More Look," in Staw, Barry, ed. *Research in Organizational Behavior,* Vol. 1. Greenwich, CT: JAI Press, 1979, 265-339.

Marks, Mitchell, Mirvis, Phillip, Hackett, Edward, and Grady, James. "Employee Participation in a Quality Circle Program: Impact on Quality of Work Life, Productivity, and Absenteeism," *Journal of Applied Psychology,* February 1986, *71,* 61-69.

Nalbantian, Haig. "Incentive Compensation in Perspective," in Nalbantian, Haig, ed. *Incentives, Cooperation, and Risk Sharing: Economic and Psychological Perspectives on Employment Contracts,* Totowa, NJ: Rowman and Littlefield, 1987, 3-43.

Neumann, George. "The Predictability of Strikes: Evidence From the Stock Market," *Industrial and Labor Relations Review,* July 1980, *33,* 525-35.

O'Dell, Carol, and McAdams, Jerry. *People, Performance, and Pay,* Houston, TX: American Productivity Center, 1987.

Olsen, Craig and Becker, Brian. "The Effects of the NLRA on Stockholder Wealth in the 1930's," *Industrial and Labor Relations Review,* October 1990, *44,* 116-129.

Pius XI. *Quadragesimo Anno* (May 15, 1931), New York: Paulist Press, 1962.

Rosenberg, Richard, and Rosenstein, Eliezer. "Participation and Productivity: An Empirical Study," *Industrial and Labor Relations Review,* 1980, *33,* 355-367.

Ruback, Richard, and Zimmerman, Martin. "Unionization and Profitability: Evidence From the Capital Markets," *Journal of Political Economy,* March 1984, *92,* 1134-1157.

Scanlan, Christopher. "Protests? Sit-ins? Say It With Investments," *San Jose Mercury News,* June 30, 1991, E1-E8.

❖

Schuster, Michael. "Gainsharing: The State of the Art," *Compensation Benefits Management,* Summer 1986, 285-290.

Second Vatican Council. *Gaudium et Spes* (December 7, 1965), Washington, DC: National Catholic Welfare Conference, n.d..

Tracy, Joseph. "An Empirical Test of an Asymmetrical Information Model of Strikes," *Journal of Labor Economics,* 1987, *5,* 149-173.

Voos, Paula. "Managerial Perceptions of the Economic Impact of Labor Relations Programs," *Industrial and Labor Relations Review,* January 1987, *40,* 94-208.

Weitzman, Martin, and Kruse, Douglas. "Profit Sharing and Productivity," in Blinder, Alan, ed. *Paying For Productivity,* Washington, DC: The Brookings Institute, 1990, 95-139.

# Economic Democracy, Employee-Ownership, and Pay Equity: A Pattern of Convergence

## Dennis A. O'Connor*

The popular press reports that women are making progress in various facets of contemporary labor markets. Reports suggest that women are gaining entrance into previously male-dominated occupations, are filling positions of power and prestige in corporate board rooms across the country, or are experiencing significant gains in matters of remuneration for labor force participation. The alternative press even quips, "There is good news and bad news on the narrowing wage gap issue between males and females. The good news is that females make 64 cents for every dollar of earnings for men. The bad news, females earn only 64 cents for every dollar of earnings for men."[1]

The issue in the equal pay debate has been termed comparable worth. Basically, the concept is one of equal pay for similar or equal work. Comparable worth has developed in reaction to the reality of occupational segregation, and is considered by proponents to be a quick method for ending associated wage discrimination. It is recognized that various jobs within an organization (or cross-organizationally) are of comparable significance, therefore, deserving of comparable pay (Aaron and Lougy 1986 and Gold 1983). Measuring comparability, however, is a difficult task. One may measure the worth of distinct jobs by assigning points to such aspects as knowledge or skill requirements, mental or physical demands, accountability, and the nature of working conditions. Jobs with similar point values are to be paid similar wages regardless of the sex of the individual holding the position.

Comparable worth is not the only issue impinging upon employment relationships. A similar, yet seemingly unrelated, issue is that of workplace or economic democracy, or the search for new organizational structures with some sense of equality among and participation by workers (Carnoy and Shearer 1980).

❖

Workplace democracy comprises many forms and embraces various degrees of employee involvement. For any of these forms of economic democracy to be successful, two elements are crucial. First, participation is essential, which requires the opening of decision-making channels to all employees. Second, a democratic structure is necessary which allows all an opportunity to influence the decision-making process (Bernstein 1980).

A variety of workplace democracy schemes have been implemented within the United States over the past few decades.[2] For our purposes, only employee-ownership, as a form of economic democracy, will be considered. The degree of worker participation in decision-making is circumscribed by the form of ownership plan established. In cooperative situations, organizations are generally established as one worker, one vote. In other ownership arrangements, the degree of decision-making authority is determined by the extent of ownership rights. Authority in decision-making, generally, will be determined by the number of shares of stock distributed to the employees and the extent of associated voting privileges of those shares. Of particular significance here is the employee stock ownership plan (ESOP) that is becoming widely accepted, for disparate reasons, throughout American industry (Hunnius, Garson and Case 1973).

So, what is the significance and the connection of pay equity and employee-ownership, and what is its relevance for the 1990s and beyond? More women are now participating in the labor force, the number of female headed households is increasing, women's wages lag significantly behind men's wages, and females are comprising an ever larger percentage of the poverty class in the U.S., thus examining a structure that may bring pay equity is warranted (Sidel 1987). Comparable worth proponents seek alternatives for increasing pay for those traditional female jobs with their associated low wages. The workplace democracy issue, on the other hand, has surfaced in response to the degrading, alienating nature of modern production activity, and as a grassroots effort to establish some semblance of control over people's working lives. Workers believe that they should be allowed the opportunity to influence the decision-making process because it directly impacts the quality of their lives (Gunn 1984). If we assume that workers are (a) concerned about low wages and perceived inequities in wages, (b) concerned about the ability to influence decisions at work, and (c) if the structure of ownership is altered with concomitant alterations in the decision making process, then, will employee owned (EO) firms pursue or promote pay equity, for whatever reasons?

In approaching this question, this paper does not repeat the arguments for and against pay equity. There is a vast literature available (including Biblical passages[3]) that addresses the issue, and the intent here is not to add to the discussion or the debate on comparable worth. The approach of this paper is as follows: first, there is a discussion of economic democracy, in general, and employee-ownership, specifically. Second, after outlining the research design of this project, the compensable factors for wage determination in the internal labor markets of EO firms is discussed. Third, the results of this investigation on employment, managerial and board of director structures, level of unionization, and the longevity of EO firms are reviewed. Finally, wage differentials for men and women in EO firms are compared to those in conventionally owned firms, and some final conclusions on pay equity in EO firms are discussed.

## I. Economic Democracy and Employee-Ownership

A number of factors point to the need for new strategies in workplace relationships. Perhaps one of the most influential characteristics of this period of exploration in political economy is the change in the social fabric of life (Greensberg 1986, Katzell 1979, and Mason 1982). A period of prosperity allows working people the resources and the time to pursue a variety of interests and activities. It also offers previously suppressed groups the possibility to participate in the political economic system. Any change in attitudes and perspectives of the workforce, whether they emerge from our working life or from aspects of our non-working life, tend to spill over into other realms of our existence (Kochan, Katz and McKersie 1986). Workers are demanding changes in the production process that call for control of their own labor. Given the business expansion through the late 1980s, workers are seeking alterations in both how the economic pie is sliced and who handles the knife (Wells 1987).

A number of internal characteristics in the modern corporation must be dealt with by management and labor. The internal environment consists of management's organizational characteristics, a union's organizational characteristics, and the employees' characteristics. The first component of the internal environment (management's) includes the planning and control systems utilized; technology, its alterations, and associated production changes; the management structure, policies and attitudes; and the organization's size and location. The union's component includes the frequency of elections and meetings; the militancy expressed through the membership's participation in union affairs and on bargaining committees; and the degree of centralization within the union. The employees' characteristics that influence workplace relationships include age, sex, race, skill, experience, education, and attitudes (Lewin 1981). These internal characteristics are influenced by, and in turn influence, the external environment.

The external environment is beyond the control of any particular firm, and includes such considerations as the present economic, political, legal, and social climate of the local environment or of the nation. The transformation process brings together all the inputs, internal and external, to produce the goods and services requested for everyday life. As these internal and external inputs change, obviously associated outputs will change. It is well known that over the past few decades, changes have occurred in workers' attitudes toward work and in the composition of the labor force. Studies indicate that the average American worker is involved with her/his job to the extent that there is a desire for a job that offers "material amenities and personal gratification" (Katzell 1979). This is especially true for the younger, educated members of the labor force.

❖

One study has identified seven critical issues on which to focus the discussion of continuing trends in the workplace: pay, employee benefits, job security, alternative work schedules, occupational stress, participation, and democracy.[4] Lack of attention to such issues has been manifested in the reality of declining performance on the job, as measured by declining labor productivity, and the increasing resistance to authoritarianism in the workplace. At management's insistence, both labor and management are exploring alternative solutions to this productivity crisis.

Internal policies to accommodate changing worker attitudes, and to reverse the dire productivity performance of the past few years, have begun to focus upon worker participation schemes in the decision-making process. Participation programs are not the exclusive domain of domestic capitalists, it is also being explored by managers throughout the world. In fact, it was the success of participation programs in Japan, West Germany, and Sweden that caught the attention of American managers. For example, in Sweden recent legislation provides for employee representation on corporate boards of directors, and is expected to result in partial reconciliation of the diverse interests of employers vis-a-vis employees.

It is important at this point to differentiate the various forms of workplace democracy, since the general theme is so bandied about that it has become both confused and confusing. J. R. P. French, Jr. was a pioneer in the field of participation and defines it as "a process in which two or more parties influence each other in making certain plans, policies, and decisions. It is restricted to decisions that have further effects on all those making the decisions and on those represented by them." (French et al. 1960, p. 3)

The derivatives of this larger theme, known as workplace democracy, vary tremendously in perspective and in amount of democracy the workers may obtain over their working lives. This structure calls for those affected by decisions to participate in that decision-making process. In the industrial sphere it would call for relinking the conceptual component and the execution component of particular tasks. Allowing workers to participate, with management, in the decision-making process is the essence of this approach. One objective is to replace the confrontation and alienation that surfaces in existing management methods, with cooperation from participation. Recall, for a successful participatory program, that participation and democratic structure, are essential.

Changes have been demanded by distinct groups in the workplace that are motivated, not by principle, but by pragmatic reasoning. Philosophical and ideological values need not be the driving force behind workplace changes. Workers may be seeking means of continued employment, a more meaningful and egalitarian work environment, or increased control over their working lives. It should be noted that democracy does not imply control over the entire production process, nor does it mean that workers vote on or participate in all matters of corporate policy. Worker input into the decision-making process is circumscribed by the particular form of change implemented within an enterprise. The implementation, participa-

❖

tion, and control will vary depending upon the peculiarities of the specific enterprise, industry, and plan.

Economic democracy may be achieved by employee-ownership through an employee stock ownership plan (ESOP). Under an ESOP, employees acquire control either by purchasing the company's stock from the current owners, or perhaps the stock is given to the employees through benevolence, or it is acquired in some collectively bargained arrangement. The stock is then placed in an ESOP trust account as collateral against any outstanding debts or loans. As debts and loans are retired, the stock is distributed to the employees based, primarily, on salary and seniority. Surprisingly, the employees may never gain control of the company they own. In some instances a board of directors and hired managers retain control over the long-term direction of the company and in its daily operations. In other cases, given stock distribution schemes, workers never acquire the needed leverage to gain influence or control over their working lives. Even if stock were to be distributed equitably, differences between workers regarding values, perceptions, and desires may be a barrier to any collective action.

Numerous case studies suggest that changes in the methods of managing labor, with worker participation in decision-making, will lead to increases in productivity, improvements in product quality, and decreases in absenteeism and labor turnover. Although we do not wish to review these results, we do wish to ask if the above changes will translate into higher wages or an equalization of wages between men and women in EO firms as compared to conventionally owned firms? Next we shall briefly describe the research design, then explore the results of this effort.

## II. Survey Data

### A. Research Design

This research was conducted through a mail questionnaire to some 437 majority employee-owned firms across the U.S. Respondents covered 28 distinct standard industrial classification codes (SIC codes) at the four digit level. The survey instrument comprised two separate components. The first asked questions regarding the number of male and female employees, gender-associated rates of pay, and asked questions on the nature of the hierarchical structure of the organization. The second component asked questions on the factors to be considered when determining company-wide remuneration rates. The data collected allowed us to construct an original data set on employment, wages, unionization, length of employee ownership, and factors determining wage rates.

### B. Compensable Factors in EO Firms

Wage determination for an individual firm is the result of a number of factors. First, the external labor market will impact wages in a given geographical location through the forces of the supply of and demand for labor. This data may be acquired through community wage surveys conducted by various governmental agencies, or through casual observation by the firm in its respective community. Second, a specific productivity level is associated with any given job in the production process. That is, the wage is not so much the result of worker productivity as it is that of job productivity through engineered production standards. If a particular worker is unable to keep up with the demands of the employment situation, then that worker will be replaced by another that can. Finally, a job evaluation of each worker may be conducted to assess how well each worker performs (Meade 1986). These subjective evaluations are intended to determine if the worker is reliable, dependable, and exhibits good work habits. When the assessment is positive, it generally results in rewards for the worker.

It was asked of each EO firm in our survey to consider which factors were considered to be most important in determining compensation for its employees. The firms were asked to rank various factors from the most important to the least important element. For wage determination in general, points are assigned to each factor and each point acquired is worth a particular stipend. The following is simply a ranking, by EO firms, as to what they consider to be important elements for determining internal wage rates.

The most highly regarded aspect of completing the tasks before the workers in EO firms is initiative and ingenuity. This is followed by decision-making, problem solving, and supervisory authority. Also of importance is the complexity of a particular job, contact with other individuals (whether they are employees or not), the amount of freedom associated with the position, and the effects of one's errors upon the operations. Some of the more obvious considerations, yet not ranked as highly as those listed above, include experience, mental and physical health, previous work history, specific vocational training and education. Of lesser significance are such items as seniority, health hazards, level of discomfort in working conditions, prestige associated with the position, mobility, and age.

These factors are weighted, along with community wages and plant-wide wages, to determine the differential in payments for workers within EO firms. Later we shall offer the wage disparities in EO firms, compared to conventionally owned firms, to determine if greater pay equity is prevalent in the former or the latter. The assumption that we are making is that any firm, regardless of the form of ownership, will consider factors similar to those provided above in making decisions on wages.

## C. The Employment Situation in EO Firms.

For those responding to the questionnaire, employment totaled 23,536 workers throughout all ranks in the hierarchy in 1989. The range of employment was from 6 employees to 7,949 workers. Of the total number of employees, 36 percent are females and 64 percent are males. Females per organization ranged from one to 4,812 with an average of 206. Employed males within these worker-owned firms ranged from one to 7,330 with an average of 1,190 per organization.

❖

This contrasts with the 1989 national averages of approximately 44 percent of the labor force being female and 56 percent male, as reported by the Bureau of Labor Statistics.[5]

Included in this total employment figure we found that nearly 12 percent of the individuals employed held managerial positions. Approximately 26 percent of all employees nationally are classified as managerial. Females held nearly 30 percent of these managerial positions, while 70 percent were held by their male counterpart. According to the Bureau of Labor Statistics, females accounted for approximately 45 percent of all employed managerial positions and males held the other 55 percent of the positions in 1989. Interestingly, one firm reported that no managerial positions existed within its framework. Of all employees in EO firms, only three percent are female managers, while over eight percent of all employees are male managers.

The above suggests three factors of interest when considering an assumed narrowing of the wage gap in EO firms: (a) fewer females are employed in EO firms than in conventionally owned firms; (b) fewer managerial positions exist in EO firms; and (c) fewer women hold managerial positions in these firms than they do at the national level. One may expect the wage disparity to be greater in EO firms since fewer females are employed in such firms, and this is further supported by the fact that with fewer female managers, the issue of pay equity would have fewer voices supporting its initiation.

## D. The Decision-Making Situation in EO Firms.

It is presumed that earnings determination belongs in the hands of either some managerial elite or a board of directors. We have examined the distribution of managerial positions relative to overall employment in EO firms above. If the ultimate decisions rests with the board of directors, then what is the distribution of males and females within this particular organization? In total, approximately 70 percent of the individuals on the boards of directors of the enterprises that responded to our survey, are employees of their respective company. This amounts to more than 21 percent of the boards of directors being female worker-owners. Overall, more than 30 percent of the membership on the boards of directors are females. The point of this last exercise is to shed some light on the concept that if females are in decision-making positions within firms, they may pay closer attention to matters of pay equity.

## E. The Union Situation in EO Firms.

We also inquired as to the percentage of employees covered by a collectively bargained agreement through unionization. More than 30 percent of all employees were covered by a union contract. In at least one instance 100 percent of the employees were union members. In addition, where union representation is involved, approximately 83 percent of the employees are members of the union. In

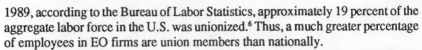

1989, according to the Bureau of Labor Statistics, approximately 19 percent of the aggregate labor force in the U.S. was unionized.[6] Thus, a much greater percentage of employees in EO firms are union members than nationally.

One would expect greater pay equity to result from unionization than from non-union employment situations. Given the high unionization rate in this research, we may tentatively conclude that this is a contributing factor to pay equity between men and women in EO firms. This is an area that warrants further research.

### F. The Longevity Situation in EO Firms.

It also seems appropriate to examine the length of time a firm is employee-owned, since it may lead to greater pay equity the longer the firm is worker-owned. Those responding to our questionnaire indicated that the length of worker-ownership for some was relatively short and for others it has enjoyed more than 40 years of employee-ownership. The average length of worker-ownership was 9.6 years as an employee-owned firm. An area for future research would be to examine length of employee ownership and degree of pay equity.

## III. The Convergence of Pay Equity and Employee-Ownership

The average hourly earnings for all employees in EO firms was $10.20 in 1989. According to the Bureau of Labor Statistics, in the same time period, the median weekly earnings of full-time wage and salary workers was $398.[7] Assuming a 40 hour work week the average hourly pay would be approximately $9.95. Workers in employee-owned enterprises earn slightly higher wages than workers in conventionally owned businesses.

For male employees the average hourly earnings in worker-owned firms was $10.81, with a range of $6.24 to $22.78. According to the Bureau of Labor Statistics, the male average hourly wage is approximately $12.45 in 1989. On average, males in EO firms are paid slightly less than males in conventionally-owned firms. For female workers, we found an average hourly wage of $9.07, with a range of $6.43 to $15.28. The BLS reports that the average wage for female employees was approximately $8.64 in 1989. Females fared slightly better in EO firms than they do under conventional circumstances.

We also asked of earnings disparities when some employees do not share in the ownership rights of the company. The average hourly earnings of non-owner male employees was $7.98; the average hourly earnings of non-owner female employees was $7.93 The difference between male and female earnings is not significant here, but it is interesting to note that non-owner employees earn only 74 percent and 87 percent of their male- and female-owner counterparts respectively. It pays to own a share of the company one works for.

The most significant comparison is found at the national level in 1989. Females earned slightly more than 69 percent of their male counterparts, while in employee-owned firms females earned nearly 84 percent of the earnings of their

❖

male counterparts. At the high end of the distribution, females earned over 67 percent of the male wage and at the low end, females earned 103 percent of male hourly earnings.

This data leads us to a number of implications. First, on average, workers in EO firms earn higher wages than workers in conventionally owned firms. Second, there is greater earnings equality between men and women in EO firms compared to conventional ownership arrangements. The latter point may be explained in one of two ways. First, the higher than average rate of unionization may explain the greater earning capacity of women in worker-owned firms than nationally. Second, and a more acceptable explanation, is that females enjoy greater pay equity in worker-owned firms at the expense of male employees. That is, lower relative male wages subsidize higher relative female wages in EO firms compared to conventionally owned firms.

## IV.  Conclusions

Is greater pay equity in EO firms the result of an intentional policy decision of the worker-owners? If the answer is negative, then our findings would indicate that employee-ownership is an egalitarian method for equal distribution of income. If the answer is positive, then worker-owners concerned with the distribution of income take appropriate action to rectify discrepancies. The longevity of the worker-owned firms would lead one to believe that concern for pay equity does not sacrifice efficiency.

We found that fewer females are employed in worker-owned firms than is true for national employment statistics. This would tend to lend further support to our hypothesis that EO firms exhibit greater pay equity than do conventionally owned firms. Also, male managers out distance female managers by a ratio of seven to three. This would indicate, perhaps, that male chauvinism is not as prevalent in worker owned firms as in conventionally owned firms, or simply that egalitarianism is of concern in EO firms, and the lack of female managers would not tend to bias the outcome of income distribution more than if a more substantial number of female managers were present. Finally, with fewer managers overall, we note that in EO firms there exists less of a need to employ people to watch other people work. Perhaps because of this there is a greater ability to distribute wages in a more equitable fashion.

Obviously, more investigation is called for in terms of employee-owned firms and pay equity. It was never our intention to imply that pay equity, from a philosophical or ideological perspective, was of concern to worker-owned firms. Actually, our hunch was that pay equity would naturally emerge from worker-owned companies because everyone would eventually acquire the belief that each and every job is a vital function in the social process of production, with no one member being "more equal" than another.

The basic question that was before us inquired if employee-owned businesses exhibit a greater propensity toward pay equity between men and women than do conventionally owned firms. The rationale for exploring this question was as follows: if workers enjoy ownership rights in their respective workplaces, participation on various fronts will emerge, and one such line of input will be in decision-making on issues of payment or remuneration for services rendered. If workers are given the opportunity to decide on such matters, will they tend toward pay equity? The answer appears to be yes.

## Endnotes

*Department of Economics, Loras College, Dubuque, Iowa 52001 USA. The author gratefully acknowledges Mr. Donald Dunbar, graduate student at the Univesity of Michigan for his assistance in this research project; and Dr. Kenneth W. Kraus, Academic Dean at Loras College, for his financial and moral support of this research effort.

[1] "Women at Work, Gender and Inequality in the '80s", *Dollars & Sense Anthology*, 1987, p.4. Also, a recent editorial article in the *Des Moines Register*, March 18, 1991, listed the 10 worst jobs in the U. S. for reasons of low wages, degrading conditions, and/or alienating circumstances associated with modern production facilities; Juravich, Tom, "Here are the 10 Worst Jobs in America," *Des Moines Register*, March 18, 1991, p. A-4 .

[2] One may consult a variety of sources on workplace democracy schemes in the domestic or international arenas. Some very accessible reading would include: Christopher Eaton Gunn, *Workers' Self-Management in the United States*, Ithaca: Cornell University Press, 1984; Keith Bradley, and Alan Gelb, *Worker Capitalism: The New Industrial Relations*, Cambridge: The MIT Press, 1985; Thomas A. Kochan, Harry C. Katz, and Robert B. McKersie, *The Transformation of American Industrial Relations*, New York: Basic Books, Inc., 1986; and Donald M. Wells, *Empty Promises: Quality of Working Life Programs and the Labor Movement*, New York: Monthly Review Press, 1987.

[3] The Biblical passage referred to is derived from *Dollars & Sense* (1987), "The Lord said to Moses..."Your valuation of a male...shall be 50 shekels of silver...if the person is a female, your valuation shall be 30 shekels." Leviticus 17:1 - 4. Taking such passages out of context may lead some to believe that the gender based wage gap is the result of divine intervention.

[4] This was compiled from a Special Task Force appointed by the then Secretary of Health, Education, and Welfare, *Work in America*, Cambridge, The MIT Press, 1973.

[5] The data on employment trends are derived from the Bureau of Labor Statistics, *The Employment Situation: January 1989*, Washington, D.C.

[6] Bureau of Labor Statistics, *Union Members in 1990*, Washington, D.C.

[7] Bureau of Labor Statistics, *Usual Weekly Earnings of Wage and Salary Workers: Fourth Quarter 1989*, and *Employment in Perspective: Women in the Labor Force, Fourth Quarter 1989*, Washington, D.C.

# References

Aaron, Henry J., and Lougy, Cameran. *The Comparable Worth Controversy*, Washington, D. C.: The Brookings Institution, 1986.

Bernstein, Paul. *Workplace Democratization: Its Internal Dynamics*, New Brunswick, NJ: Transaction Books, 1980.

Bureau of Labor Statistics. *The Employment Situation: January 1989*, Washington, D.C.

_____. *Union Members in 1990*, Washington, D.C.: U.S. Department of Labor, 1991.

_____. *Usual Weekly Earnings of Wage and Salary Workers: Fourth Quarter 1989*, Washington, D.C.: U.S. Department of Labor, 1990.

_____. *Employment in Perspective: Women in the Labor Force, Fourth Quarter 1989*, Washington, D.C.: U.S. Department of Labor, 1990.

Bradley, Keith and Gelb, Alan. *Worker Capitalism: The New Industrial Relations*, Cambridge: The MIT Press, 1985.

Carnoy, Martin and Shearer, Derek. *Economic Democracy: The Challenge of the 1980s*, White Plains, NY: M. E. Sharpe, Inc., 1980.

French, J. R. P., Jr., Israel, J., and Aas, D. "An Experiment in Particiaption in a Norwegian Factory," *Human Relations, 13*, 1960.

Gold, Michael Evan. *A Dialogue on Comparable Worth*, Ithaca, NY: ILR Press, 1983.

Greensberg, Edward S. *Workplace Democracy: The Political Effects of Participation*, Ithaca: Cornell University Press, 1986.

Gunn, Christopher Eaton. *Workers' Self-Management in the United States*, Ithaca: Cornell University Press, 1984.

Hunnius, Gerry, Garson, G. David and Case, John. *Workers' Control: A Reader on Labor and Social Change*, New York: Vintage Books, 1973.

Juravich, Tom. "Here are the 10 Worst Jobs in America," *Des Moines Register*, March 18, 1991, A-4.

Katzell, Raymond A. "Changing Attitudes Toward Work," in Clark Kerr and Jerome Rosow, eds., *Work in America, The Decade Ahead*, New York: D. Van Nostrand Co., 1979.

Kochan, Thomas A., Katz, Harry C. and McKersie, Robert B., *The Transformation of American Industrial Relations*, New York: Basic Books, Inc., 1986.

Lewin, Davis. "Collective Bargaining and the Quality of Life," *Organization Dynamics*, Autumn, 1981.

Mason, Ronald. *Participatory and Workplace Democracy*, Carbondale and Edwardsville: Southern Illinois Unversity Press, 1982.

Meade, J. E. *Alternative Systems of Business Organization and of Workers' Remuneration*, London: Allen & Unwin, 1986.

Special Task Force To Secretary of Health, Education, and Welfare. *Work in America*, Cambridge: The MIT Press, 1973.

Sidel, Ruth. *Women & Children Last*, New York: Penquin Books, 1987.

Wells, Donald M. *Empty Promises: Quality of Working Life Programs and the Labor Movement*, New York: Monthly Review Press, 1987.

"Women at Work: Gender and Inequality in the '80s," *Dollar & Sense Anthology*, 1987, 4.

---  ❖  ---

# The Choice of Moral Theories in Economic Analysis (Abstract)

## *Monroe Burk**

By declaring itself value- and morals-free, neo-classical economics claimed to be science. In reality, neo-classical economics contains moral premises which cannot be philosophically justified, and are indeed unworthy of a moral civilization. The task of Catholic economics, and of other revisionist economic thought, is to expose the immorality buried in neo-classical economic theory. The re-examination of the moral basis of neo-classical economics reveals not only its ideological character, but its deterministic character, which is basically incompatible with the human capacity to choose or to reject a moral path.

Morality is not to be confused with social norms, which differ from culture to culture and with the passage of time; in hindsight, social norms can be seen to have been immoral. Each person pursues moral enlightment in his own manner, by faith, introspection, science, or by relying on some authority; morality itself contains a rule that each individual shall seek enlightment by valid means.

If morality were merely a code of individual behavior, it would have no or little relevance to social theory, which deals importantly with the behavior of collectivities, such as businesses, labor unions, churches, and governmental units. Moral theory must be broad enough to cover collectivities; thus, it must consist not only of traditional ethics, but of branches of political theory (dealing with the moral behavior of states), economic theory (dealing with the moral behavior of businesses), professional (e.g. medicine, law sciences, engineering, mathematics) behavior, and, indeed, the behavior of all collectivities.

In seeking moral rules, two opposing approaches appear: (1) a goal-seeking framework, and (2) a juridical framework. These opposing approaches can be found in both the Bible and in Greek thought and in philosophic writing to the present day.

The paper is devoted in part to ethical history, and in part to the application of ethical principles to our present circumstances.

*Retired, U.S. Foreign Service, 5449 New Grange Garth, Columbia, MD 21045 USA.

# Trust, Moral Hazards and Social Economics: Incentives and the Organization of Work

## Charles K. Wilber*

A central concern of economics is how an economy allocates its resources—its raw materials, capital, and labor—among competing uses. Economists can often be classified by which of three mechanisms they emphasize in determining this allocation: markets, bureaucratic administration, or moral values. Under a system of allocation by markets, individuals pursue their own self-interest and the market coordinates their decisions, resulting in society's resource allocation. In a bureaucratic control system, individual self-interest is again the motivating force but it is limited to a greater or lesser degree because citizens accept societal constraints, fear the consequences if they do not, or simply have a tradition of acceptance. In a system of allocation by moral values, individual self-interest is limited and cooperation encouraged by a set of widely accepted moral values which in some way transcend the narrow self-interest of one individual.

Free market economists place almost complete reliance on markets, and a central thrust of their policies has been to extend the market allocation mechanism into all possible areas, from school lunches to the environment to civil rights. There are exceptions, of course. The Reagan administration's social agenda of limiting abortion and punishing drug use, for example, generated many bureaucratic interferences in the market that were inconsistent with a libertarian stance. Also in an area like defense, free market advocates accept bureaucratic control as unavoidable. Only at the level of the family is allocation by moral values feasible or desirable. Of course such values are important for the society, but they should be left to charitable impulses of individual decision makers. Efforts to encourage allocation by moral values are seen as self-defeating.

Liberal economists also give markets a central role in resource allocation. However, they find numerous areas in which bureaucratic control is necessary to improve the functioning of markets. Pollution, occupational hazards, and discrimi-

                                    ❖

nation all result if markets operate unfettered, so govenrment must play a role. In addition the political process empowers government to place limits on self-interested behavior and bureaucratic allocation must be used to combat poverty, to prevent corporate wrongdoing, and to provide the many public goods the market will not. They do not place much emphasis on allocation by moral values.

Social economists argue that sole reliance on any one of these mechanisms is misguided, for each has flaws which prevent it from being completely successful in solving our economic problems. The use of markets and and government intervention must be supplemented with the encouragement of moral values.

I argue in this paper that subordination of short-run interests to long-run interests and moral behavior which constrains free riding, in addition to being good in themselves, are essential for the efficient operation of the economy. Traditional economists are wrong when they claim that individual self-interest and bureaucratic controls are sufficient to achieve efficient market outcomes. The next section of the paper outlines the theory underlying this claim. The remainder of the paper applies the theory to the organization of work.

## I. Imperfect Information, Interdependence and Moral Hazards

The importance of this combined approach to creating a better functioning economy and society can be illustrated by recent scholarly work in economics (see Akerlof 1984; Boulding 1973; Hirsch 1978; Hirschman 1970; Schotter 1985; Schmid 1978) that demonstrates that, under conditions of interdependence and imperfect information, rational self-interest frequently leads to socially irrational results. Traditional economic theory assumes independence of economic actors and perfect information. However, the more realistic assumptions that one person's behavior affects another's and that each has less than perfect knowledge of the other's likely behavior, give rise to strategic behavior, or what game theorists call "moral hazards." An example will be helpful.

A classic example of moral hazard, known as "The Parable of Distrust" is the situation where both the employer and worker suspect that the other one can not be trusted to honor their explicit or implicit contract. For example, the employer thinks the worker will take too many coffee breaks, spend too much time talking with other workers, and generally work less than the employer thinks is owed. The worker, on the other hand, thinks the employer will try to speed up the pace of work, fire him unjustly if given the chance, and generally behave arbitrarily. When this is the case the worker will tend to shirk and the employer will increase supervision to stop the expected shirking. If the worker would self-supervise, production costs would be lower. Thus this distrust between employer and worker reduces efficiency.

In this case the pursuit of individual self-interest results in the worker and the employer as individuals and as a group becoming worse off than if they had been able to cooperate,i.e., not shirk and not supervise. The problem is simple and common. The employer and worker are interdependent and do not have perfect knowledge of what the other will do, and the resulting lack of trust leads to behavior that is self-defeating. This outcome is made worse if distrust is accompanied with feelings of injustice. For example, if the worker feels that the contract is unfair( low wages, poor grievance machinery, etc.), the tendency to shirk will be increased.

There are numerous other cases, for example inflation. A labor union fights for a wage increase only to find that others also have done so and thus the wage increase is offset by rising consumer prices. No one union alone can restrain its wage demands and maintain the support of its members. Business firms are caught in the same dilemma. They raise prices to compensate for increased labor and other costs only to discover that costs have increased again. Distrust among unions, among firms, and between unions and firms makes impossible a cooperative agreement on price and wage increases.

The case of recession is similar. As aggregate demand in the economy declines, each company attempts to cope with its resulting cash flow difficulties through employee layoffs. However, if all companies pursue this strategy, aggregate demand will decline further, making more layoffs necessary. Most companies agree that the result is undesirable for each company and for the whole economy, but no one company on its own can maintain its workforce. In effect each company says it will not layoff its employees if all the others also do not layoff their employees. Yet, again, no agreement is concluded.

These cases have two things in common. They all have a group (in these cases, workers and their employers) with a common interest in the outcome of a particular situation. And, second, while each attempts to choose the best available course of action, the result is not what any member of the group desires. In these cases the individual motives lead to undesired social and individual results. Adam Smith's "invisible hand" not only fails to yield the common good, but in fact works malevolently.

Why is it so difficult for the individuals involved to cooperate and make an agreement? The reason is that exit is cheap, but voice is expensive (Hirschman 1970, 1986). Exit means to withdraw from a situation, person, or organization and depends on the availability of choice, competition, and well-functioning markets. It is usually inexpensive and easy to buy or not, sell or not, hire or fire, and quit or shirk on your own. Voice means to communicate explicitly your concern to another individual or organization. The cost to an individual in time and effort to persuade, argue, and negotiate will often exceed any prospective individual benefit.[1]

In addition, the potential success of voice depends on the possibility of all members joining for collective action. But then there arises the "free rider" problem. If someone cannot be excluded from the benefits of collective action, they have no incentive to join the group agreement. Self-interest will tempt people to take the benefits without paying the costs; i.e., watching educational television without becoming a subscriber. This free riding explains why union organizing is next to impossible in states that prohibit union shops (where a majority of the workers voting for a union means all workers must join and pay dues).

❖

The problem is further complicated by the possibility that what started simply as a self-interested or even benevolent relationship will become malevolent. Face-to-face strategic bargaining may irritate the parties involved if the other side is perceived as violating the spirit of fair play. This can result in a response of hatred rather than mere selfishness. Collective action is even more unlikely if the members of the group are hateful and distrustful of one another.

These moral hazards are situations where there is some act under the individual's unilateral control that promises to produce a welfare improvement for that individual that is not consistent with what individuals who share a common preference want to obtain as a long run result. The alternative line of action that would be consistent with the more preferred long run result requires cooperation with others; thus no matter how hard the individual tries, alone she can produce no net benefits or fewer than in the unilateral activity. So the moral hazard exists because the alternative line of action requires some level of trust which can lead all to engage in the process necessary to reach group agreement.

A common consciousness of one's interdependence with others is required for an individual or organization to overcome moral hazards. Collective action requires a degree of mutual trust. If malevolence arises, the moral hazard will be strengthened. In addition, morally constrained behavior is necessary to control free riding. Thus self-interested individualism fails, for moral hazards are ubiquitous in our economy.

Could not a traditional economist construct an "enriched" notion of self-interested behavior that would overcome moral hazards without the need for moral values? I think the answer is a qualified yes. An enriched concept of self-interest could encompass the foregoing of short-run interests for long-run interests, but moral commitment makes this much easier. Furthermore, this would leave the free rider problem unresolved.

The argument might proceed like this. A self-interested person, recognizing the reality of interdependencies and imperfect information, is willing to cooperate with others if it increases his personal welfare. Thus cooperation becomes one more means to maximize one's self-interest.

However, the flaw in the argument is the failure to account for the likelihood of cooperative behavior based only on self-interest to degenerate into individuals cheating on the collective agreement. Free riding must be accounted for. Pushed to its logical extreme, individual self-interest suggests that faced with interdependence and imperfect information, it is usually in the interest of an individual to evade the rules by which other players are guided.

This problem can be illustrated by the case of OPEC. The member countries can be considered to be acting out of enlightened self-interest. They have many fundamental differences— political, economic, religious, geopolitical. At times two of the members— Iran and Iraq— have been in such disagreement as to be in a declared state of war. Nevertheless, OPEC has survived because each member realizes that its own well-being is closely connected with that of the others. OPEC tries to maintain high prices and profit levels by setting production quotas. However, since 1973, their biggest problem has been evasion of the quotas by individual member countries. Enlightened economic actors do cheat. Each member country has an incentive to cheat on the cooperative agreement because, with the production quota holding up prices, if one member expands its output it makes even greater profits. However, if one country violates the agreement, the others usually follow. The result is that the increased output from all the member countries drives down the price and every member is worse off than before. Thus, enlightened self-interest results in a cooperation that is inherently unstable.

Traditional economists could respond with the claim that establishing enforcement mechanisms is the answer to cheating on collective agreements. As an example, OPEC sets up committees to determine production quotas and verification groups to ensure compliance. However, even with a great amount of resources expended on collective enforcement, cheating continues. The recent invasion of Kuwait by Iraq has its origin in the former's production above their quota which had the effect of lowering revenues to Iraq. Not only is cheating a major problem for OPEC, but the costs of policing collective agreements is substantially more than the costs of maintaining those agreements through internalized moral commitments.

How then can we overcome the moral hazards generated by interdependence and imperfect information? The resolution of the problem is not easy, for they are persistent and intractable. There are at least three possibilities: government intervention; group self-regulation; and institutional reinforcement of those moral values that constrain self-interested behavior.

Market failures such as pollution or monopoly have generally been seen as warrants for government intervention. However, there are ubiquitous market failures of the moral hazard variety in everyday economic life. In these cases private economic actors can also benefit from government measures for their protection, because interdependence and imperfect information generate distrust and lead the parties to self-defeating behavior. Certain kinds of government regulation— from truth-in-advertising to food-and-drug laws— can reduce distrust and thus economic inefficiency, providing gains for all concerned. However, government regulation has its limits. Where the regulated have concentrated power (i.e., electric companies), the regulators may end up serving the industry more than the public. In addition, there are clearly situations in which government operates to serve the self-interest of the members of its bureaucratic apparatus. Free market economists would have us believe that such is always the case. This is an exaggeration. Government can serve the common good, but it has clear limits. One major limitation on the ability of government to regulate is the willingness of people to be regulated.

The Kennedy administration's wage-price guidelines were a partially successful attempt to control inflation through public encouragement of labor and management cooperation to limit wage increases to productivity increases. The cooperation broke down because of the growing struggle among social classes and occupational groups for larger shares of GNP. More formal cooperation between labor and management, monitored by government, might reduce the distrust that cripples their relationship. In order to do so government would have to be accepted by all sides as above the fray and willing to encourage agreements that would benefit society. The experience of the 1970's in which government activity delivered less than it promised, and of the 1980's when it was used to serve the agenda of bureaucrats and to facilitate the goals of the powerful, both imply a diminished capacity of government to play this role.

The second way to overcome moral hazards is self-regulation. Sellers could voluntarily discipline themselves not to exploit their superior information. This is the basis of professional ethics. Surgeons, for example, take on the obligation, as a condition for the exercise of their profession, to avoid performing unnecessary operations, placing the interest of the patient first. The danger is that their professional association will end up protecting its members at the expense of others.

This leads us to the final possibility— developing institutions to heighten group consciousness and reinforce moral values that constrain self-interested behavior so that the pursuit of short-run rewards and free riding can be controlled. Is it possible to rebuild institutional mechanisms so that long-run interests and moral values become more important in directing economic behavior? Yes, but we must re-think our view of people as simply self-interested maximizers. Economists have made a major mistake in treating love, benevolence, and particularly public spirit as scarce resources that must be economized lest they be depleted. This is a faulty analogy because, unlike material factors of production, the supply of love, benevolence, and public spirit is not fixed or limited. These are resources whose supply may increase rather than decrease through use. Also they do not remain intact if they stay unused (Hirschman 1986, p. 155). These moral resources respond positively to practice, in a learning-by-doing manner, and negatively to non-practice. Obviously if overused they become ineffective.

A good example is a comparison of the system of blood collection for medical purposes in the United States and in England (Richard M. Titmuss 1970). In the U.S. we gradually replaced donated blood with purchased blood. As the campaigns for donated blood declined, because purchased blood was sufficient, the amount of donations declined. In effect, our internalized benevolence towards those unknown to us, who need blood, began to atrophy from nonuse. In contrast, blood donations remained high in England where each citizen's obligation to others was constantly emphasized.

People learn their values from their families, their religious faith, and from their society. In fact a principal objective of publicly proclaimed laws and regulations is to stigmatize certain types of behavior and to reward others, thereby influencing individual values and behavior codes. Aristotle understood this: "Lawgivers make the citizen good by inculcating habits in them, and this is the aim of every lawgiver; if he does not succeed in doing that, his legislation is a failure.

It is in this that a good constitution differs from a bad one"( Nicomachean Ethics, 1103b).

Habits of benevolence and civic spirit, in addition to heightened group consciousness, can be furthered by bringing groups together to solve common problems. Growth of worker participation in management, consultation between local communities and business firms to negotiate plant closings and relocations, establishment of advisory boards on employment policy that represent labor, business, and the public, all are steps toward a recognition that individual self-interest alone is insufficient, that mutual responsibilities are necessary in a world where interdependence and imperfect information generate distrust and tempt individuals into strategic behavior that, in turn, results in sub-optimal outcomes.

The key point is that competitive situations generate strategic behavior and, in turn, distrust. In an environment of distrust, behavior based on individual self-interest leads to sub-optimal outcomes. Changing the environment from a competitive one to a cooperative one might provide the trust necessary for people to alter their behavior. This is not a call for altruism but is an argument that it is possible to change the environment so that people will realize that their long-term interests require foregoing their short-term interests.

We conclude that no one allocative mechanism can successfully enable our economy to attain the three goals of basic material needs, self-esteem, and freedom. The market, bureaucratic control, and social values all have their advantages and disadvantages as mechanisms for directing society's resources toward those ends. So some combination must be incorporated in any policies that are undertaken to build a new social consensus. In addition, they must be complemented by an environment that encourages cooperative behavior.

## II. The Organization of Work

Distrust between workers and employers leads to inefficient results, if neither side trusts the other to live up to the contract. As a result the worker has an incentive to shirk and the employer has to increase supervision costs to counter the possibility. If somehow workers would self-supervise, i.e. not shirk, productivity would be higher and all could benefit.

Changing the institutional environment from a purely competitive one by adding cooperative mechanisms might enable the trust to grow that is necessary for people to alter their behavior. The most likely approach is encouragement of workers' self-management and worker ownership. Of course, most firms and their managers believe that efficiency and discipline require one absolute center of control over work—their control. Nevertheless, in some cases, managers are exploring ways to change the organization of production to increase their workers' job satisfaction. Quality-control circles and profit sharing are becoming common management responses to encourage employees to make their work contribution through the social group in the factory ( Michael J. Piore 1986, pp. 48-54).

❖

The reason for these new management initiatives is clear—under the old system, many workers expressed their boredom, anger and despair by working as slowly as possible, by appearing at work irregularly, by doing poor quality work, by occasional acts of sabotage, and by frequent job changes. The "efficient" system of authoritarian discipline and minute division of labor has been a contributing factor to lagging productivity in the U.S. economy. These managers see profit sharing and other worker participation devices as a means of establishing the more cooperative relationship with their employees that is necessary to compete in the economic world aborning.

It is useful to look at some ways workers have tried to gain control over their work situations. I summarize a particular form of cooperation, worker management, and two specific instances, the Employee Stock Option Plan (ESOP) at Weirton Steel in the U.S. and the industrial cooperatives of Mondragon in the Basque region of Spain.

## A. Worker Management

Worker-owned and managed firms are relatively new on the national scene in the United States, though some have existed at the local level for many years.[2] They have become important for several reasons. It is becoming clear that profitable plants are being closed, not just unprofitable ones, and this is more common when the plant is a small part of a conglomerate holding company. The plant may be closed because higher profits can be earned if it is moved to a lower wage area, for a tax write-off, or for a variety of other non-production related reasons (Barry Bluestone and Bennett Harrison 1982). In these situations, purchase of the plant by the present employees preserves jobs, which makes it an attractive possibility. In addition, there is now a legal mechanism, Employee Stock Ownership Plan (ESOP), to facilitate employee ownership, and it provides significant tax incentives to firms (U.S. Congress, Joint Economic Committee 1976).

There is increasing evidence that worker-owned firms incorporating employee participation and workplace democracy have rates of productivity at least as high and frequently higher than traditional firms (see Henry M. Levin 1982; R. Oakeshott 1978; K. Friden 1980). Thus worker-owned firms have been used to maintain employment at plants that otherwise would have closed *and* have been used to maintain and improve productivity as well as the quality of work life. In fact, they all appear to be linked. As employees become owners and managers, the old distrust that led to shirking and excessive supervision can often be reduced. The new environment enables workers to see that the short-run advantage of shirking is outweighed by the negative impact on long-run productivity and profits that they share in. Free riding is still possible, of course, if the employees never develop the moral commitments to coalesce as a group (B. Thurston 1980, pp. 19-20).

A 1988 report[3] published in England indicates that stock ownership and profit sharing schemes actually stimulate worker performance. It analyzed the results of 414 companies in the period 1977-1985 and showed that those with such programs

❖

did consistently, and in some cases spectacularly, better than the others. Also, the smaller the firm, the more direct was the impact.

## B. Weirton Steel

An interesting case in the U.S. is Weirton Steel. Since 1984, some 8,400 employees have owned the company under an (ESOP) and have operated the plant profitably. Management and labor attribute this success—under the previous ownership of National Steel the company was on the edge of bankruptcy—to the implementation of the ESOP. In the face of general decline in the steel industry, Weirton has expanded its employment from 7,800 when the ESOP began to 8,400. The company has paid out about one-third of its profits each year—$15-20 million—while reinvesting the remainder in plant modernization. R. Alan Prosswimmer, company Vice-President and chief financial officer, attributes the company's turnaround to the ESOP: "Over $10 million in savings last year alone were attributable to our employee programs." Walter Bish, President of the Independent Steelworkers Union, added that the workers, since becoming owners, "are much more aware of the fact that quality is important." Rank and file workers speak similarly saying that the ESOP has resulted in "a lot of attitude changes," because previously workers "were working for National Steel and the profits went there. Now the profits are staying here" (Pete Sheehan 1987).

## C. Mondragón

Of particular interest as a model for employee-owned and managed firms are the industrial cooperatives of Mondragón in the Basque region of Spain (see Levin 1983a; William Whyte and Kathleen Whyte 1988). Their achievements are quite impressive. The first of the Mondragón cooperatives was established in 1958. Twenty years later the 100 cooperatives together had sales close to $1 billion, one-fifth of which was exported to other countries. Among the many goods produced are refrigerators and other home appliances, heavy machinery, hydraulic presses, steel, semi-conductors, and selenium rectifiers. Among the cooperatives are the largest refrigerator manufacturer in Spain, a bank with over $500 million in assets, a technological research center, a technical high school and engineering college, and an extensive social security system with health clinics and other social services.

The ownership and management structure of the Mondragón cooperatives are of particular interest. Every new member must invest a specified amount in the firm where they are employed. At the end of each year a portion of the firms' surplus or profit is allocated to each worker's capital account in proportion to the number of hours worked and the job rating. The job rating schedule allows for a quite narrow 3:1 ratio between the highest and lowest paid workers. The result is a pay scale quite different from that prevailing in private industry. In comparison lower paid workers earn more in the cooperatives, middle level workers and managers earn the same, and top managers earn considerably less. Each cooperative's board of directors is selected by all the members and, in turn, the board appoints the managers. There is a social council made up of elected representatives of the lowest paid workers which negotiates with the board over worker grievances and other issues of interest.

The purely economic results are impressive. When both capital and labor inputs are accounted for, the Mondragón cooperatives are far more productive in their use of resources than private firms in Spain. One comparison with the 500 largest firms in Spain found that in the 1970s the average cooperative used only 25 percent as much capital equipment per worker but worker productivity reached 80 percent of that in private industry (Levin 1983b).

How might we explain this highly efficient labor force in the Mondragón cooperatives? Clearly worker motivation plays a major part. As workers became owners and participated in management decisions the incentives to shirk were lessened. The structural environment made it easier for trust to develop. Thus strategic behavior declined as workers saw that their short-term individual interests could conflict with their long-term interests. Shirking might benefit them here and now but productivity would benefit them over the long haul.

The free rider problem was controlled by moral commitment to group solidarity. Basque nationalism clearly has been the foundation for this moral commitment, which makes it difficult to transfer the Mondragón experience whole. However, this may be a chicken-egg problem. Must the moral commitment to group solidarity exist first or will the experience of ownership and management help create it? I do not know but the continued deterioration of our industrial structure is creating the conditions for worker buyouts.

Other factors also inhibit the transferability of the Mondragón experiment. Ties with local communities and limited labor mobility appear important to the success of the cooperatives. In the United States, where there is more labor mobility and weaker ties of community, the moral commitment to group solidarity may be more difficult to generate.

Fostering subordination of short-run interests to long-run interests and moral constraints to free riding are our most important challenges. Thus building institutional mechanisms, such as worker management structures, that overcome moral hazards and create trust is essential to provide the necessary incentives.

## Endnotes

*Professor of Economics, University of Notre Dame, Notre Dame, IN 46556 USA.

[1] Exit is more difficult in Japan where the Confucian tradition is much more binding. As a result, with much greater emphasis on harmony and consensus at all levels, voice is more appreciated and cultivated.

[2] The best known and most studied of these firms are the plywood cooperatives in Oregon and Washington. See K. Berman (1967).

[3] The report, *Profit Sharing and Profitability* (1988), was reported on in the *Sunday Times* (1989).

## References

Akerlof, George A. *An Economist's Book of Tales*, Cambridge: Cambridge University Press, 1984.

Berman, K. *Worker-Owned Plywood Companies*, Pullman, WA: Washington State University Press, 1967.

Bluestone, Barry and Harrison, Bennett. *The Deindustrialization of America*, New York: Basic Books, Inc., 1982.

Boulding, Kenneth E. *The Economy of Love and Fear*, Belmont, Calif.: Wadsworth Publishing Co., 1973.

Friden, K. *Workplace Democracy and Productivity*, Washington, D.C.: National Center for Economic Alternatives, 1980.

Hirsch, Fred. *Social Limits to Growth* , Cambridge, MA: Harvard University Press, 1978.

Hirschman, Albert 0. *Exit, Voice, and Loyalty: Responses to Decline in Firms, Organizations, and States*, Cambridge, MA: Harvard University Press, 1970.

_____. *Rival Views of Market Society*, New York: Viking, 1986.

Levin, Henry M. "Issues in Assessing the Comparative Productivity of Worker-Managed and Participatory Firms in Capitalist Societies," in D. Jones and J. Svejnar (eds.), *Participatory and Self-Managed Firms*, Lexington, MA: D.C. Heath, 1982.

_____. (1983a) "The Workplace: Employment and Business Intervention," in E. Seidman (ed.), *Handbook of Social Intervention*, Beverly Hills, CA: Sage Publications, 1983.

_____. (1983b) "Raising Employment and Productivity with Producer Co-operatives," in P. Streeten and H. Maier (eds.), *Human Resources, Employment and Development, Vol. II*, New York: St. Martins's Press, 1983.

Oakeshott, R. *The Case for Workers' Coops*, London: Routledge & Kegan Pual, 1978.

Piore, Michael J. "A Critique of Reagan's Labor Policy," *Challenge*, March/April 1986, (*29*), 48-54.

Schmid, A. Allan. *Property, Power, and Public Choice: An Inquiry into Law and Economics*, New York: Praeger, 1978.

Schotter, Andrew. *Free Market Economics: A Critical Appraisal*, New York: St. Martin's Press, 1985.

Oakeshott, R. *The Case for Workers' Coops,* London: Routledge & Kegan Pual, 1978.

Piore, Michael J. "A Critique of Reagan's Labor Policy," *Challenge,* March/April 1986, (*29*), 48-54.

Schmid, A. Allan. *Property, Power, and Public Choice: An Inquiry into Law and Economics,* New York: Praeger, 1978.

Schotter, Andrew. *Free Market Economics: A Critical Appraisal,* New York: St. Martin's Press, 1985.

Sheehan, Pete. "A New Model of Economic Democracy: The Workers of Weirton Steel," *New Oxford Review,* December 1987, (*54*), 13-17.

Thomas, H. and Logan, C. *Mondragon: An Economic Analysis,* Boston: George Allen & Unwin, 1982.

Thurston, B. "South Bend Lathe, E.S.O.P. on Strike Against Itself?," *Self-Management,* Fall 1980, (*8*), 19-20.

Titmuss, Richard M. *The Gift Relationship,* London: Allen and Unwin, 1970.

Whyte, William and Whyte, Kathleen. *Making Mondragon: The Growth and Dynamics of the Worker Co-operative Complex,* Cornell: ILR Press, 1988.

"Letting Workers in on the Share-Out," *The Sunday Times,* January 22, 1989, E1.

*Profit Sharing and Profitability,* London: Kogan Page/IPM, 1988. U.S. Congress, Joint Economic Committee, Broadening the Ownership of New Capital: ESOPs and other Alternatives, 94th Congress, 2nd session, Washington, D.C.: Government Printing Office, 1976.

# Toward a Just World Economy (Abstract)

## Kishor Thanawala*

*Rerum Novarum* enunciated the position of the Church on social justice, especially in relation to the problems created by the Industrial Revolution. Although the early problems of industrialization in the developed countries may appear to be distant history, many developing countries are still grappling with similar issues. Aspects of economic and social justice within developing countries as well as among various (developed and developing) nations continue to be discussed by economists and philosophers. Several principles have been identified as fundamental to a just economy: respect for human dignity, recognition of the value of human solidarity in the workplace, the opening up of economic activity and decision-making to broader participation and the granting of preferential protection to the poor. There have been several studies on ways to find creative and practical means of implementing these principles within a national economy like the United States. The purpose of the present paper is to examine whether special problems arise in applying the above-mentioned principles to the establishment of a just international economic order.

*Department of Economics, Villanova University, Villanova, PA 19085 USA.
Abstract of an article to be published in the *Review of Social Economy*.

---
❖
---

# Catholic Social Economy and the Social Question: Founders and First-Positors (Abstract)

## Thomas O. Nitsch*

Catholicism contains in its practical consequences the most admirable system of social economy which has ever been given to the earth. (Ch. de Coux, 1832) ... The world is now perched on [a great] abyss, and even the blindest can perceive beyond our political revolutions another and more terrible one, a totally social revolution, because it attacks bodily property itself. (Idem, 1836-40)

The question which agitates our world today is neither a question of persons nor of political forms, but a social question. (A.-F. Ozanam, 1836 ) ... Behind the political revolution we see a social revolution; we see the advent of the thus far insufficiently noticed worker class, from whom the bourgeoisie and their goods have been spared, and for whom the bourgeoisie has done nothing. (Idem, 1848)

Felicité Lamennais (earlier works, 1814-22; *Question du Travail,* 1848), Charles de Coux, and Antoine-Frédéric Ozanam — these were our founders and first-positors, our "sires" and baptizers of Roman-Catholic social economy (alias, *Economie politique chrétienne,* as per A. de Villeneuve-Bargemont, 1834-37) and its focal and all-embracing concern, the "social question" (alias, "Labor Question," etc.). They were followed in due course in the present account by the likes of R. de la Sagra (*Lecciones de Economía Social,* 1840; *Aforismos Sociales: Introducción a la Science Social,* 1848-49) in Spain, whence the great Bishop of Mainz, Wm. Em. von Ketteler, who, as still parish priest, first pronounced and then published his six Advent sermons on "The Great Social Questions of Our Time" (1848-49), and, as Bishop, gave us his more authoritative and influential reflections on *The Labor-*

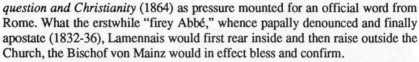

*question and Christianity* (1864) as pressure mounted for an official word from Rome. What the erstwhile "firey Abbé," whence papally denounced and finally apostate (1832-36), Lamennais would first rear inside and then raise outside the Church, the Bischof von Mainz would in effect bless and confirm.

Through this first half-century (1814-64) of development, what has come to be referred to generically as "social Catholicism" addressed that "social question" variously of private property and public poverty, the condition of the working class— the "proletaire" — vs. the power and wealth of the royalty, aristocracy, and the "capitaliste" (de Coux, 1830) or bourgeoisie, and of social revolution, social reform, and social progress. And, more often than not, our analysis shows, this with a perspective which is significantly Marxian. The source of the social unrest is found inside the workshop or "atelier" rather than in the royal chambers; i.e., in the economy rather than in the polity. And, as the universally chosen descriptive "social" (vs. political) indicates, that was overriding and fundamental, as it was to Marx. Again, it was social (vs. political) economy, or otherwise "Christian political economy"; social (or labor) vs. political question, from Ozanam and Lamennais through de la Sagra and von Ketteler; social (vs. political) revolution and reform, and social progress (de la Sagra, 1840; Aug. Ott, *Traité d' Economie sociale*, 1851).

But, obviously, there was a difference. For, with Social Catholicism (R-CSE), the social has always included the political, and private property, and the classes as part and parcel; first, R-C social thought, and subsequently (1891-1991), R-C social doctrine, have always upheld these institutions — and the civil society which comprises them — as fixtures of the natural social order; and, beginning especially with von Ketteler, have pointed to man's "spiritual" or "religious" deficiencies as prime cause and ultimate solution of the social question, condition of labor, etc.

*The author is Professor of Economics, Creighton University. The present abstract is based on a considerably expanded and augmented version of the original paper, which at the time served essentially to set the stage for the more focused concerns of Misner and Brehm (infra).

# Catholic Social Economy and the Social Question in Mid-19th Century Spain: De la Sagra et al.

*Ernst J. Brehm\**

### Introduction: Background and Overview

Spain's political and economic circumstances during the first four decades of the 19th century and its more recent prehistory include the following:

- Enlightened Absolutism under the Bourbon Kings.
- Reforms in agriculture, industry, communication, and commerce.
- Political and social influence of the French Revolution.
- Trafalgar 1805: Destruction of Spanish naval power.
- The War of Independence: 1808-12.
- The Constitution of Cadiz: 1812.
- Return of Ferdinand VII and tyrannical absolutism to 1833.
- The first Carlist War: 1833-40.
- Promulgation of the Royal Statute: 1834.
- The "Desamortizacion": 1835.
- New Constitution: 1837.
- Publication of don Ramón de la Sagra's *Lecciones de Economia Social:* 1840.

Politically, economically, and socially, the 18th century saw Spain on a course of steady progress under the enlightened guidance of three kings and their ministers, who practiced enlightened absolutism during a long period of external and internal peace. The three monarchs concerned sought to maintain a class society, but with equality before the law. The bourgeoisie was favored most and gave support to this policy. Higher learning and high positions in government and administration ceased to be the sole privilege of the aristocracy; an educated middle class penetrated into all branches of government and administration.

❖

Reforms were carried out in communication through extensive construction of roads and canals and in commerce through the abolition of internal customs and tolls, the national standardization of measures and weights, the establishment of model industries, and the so-called *Manufacturas Reales* for the production of textiles, tapestry, silk, porcelain, and glass. Economic liberalism was introduced to oppose the interference of the State and the privileges of guilds and associations. Efforts were made to solve the problems in agriculture, still the main source of the country's wealth. These efforts mostly failed due to considerable obstacles, especially the existence of huge latifundia in the form of Church and private lands held in mortmain. The kings encouraged the formation of "Economic Societies of the Friends of the Country," established by some of the best reform-minded members of the aristocracy, the clergy, and the academic world. Plans for a new land distribution as proposed by Melchor de Jovellanos failed, but they set a precedent and planted seeds in the minds of future proponents of agricultural reform, among them especially Alvaro Flórez Estrada (1766- 1853; op. cit., 1839/ 1970) on the one hand, and Ramón de la Sagra (1798-1871; op. cit., 1840) on the other. The occupation of the Iberian Peninsula by Napoleonic troops and the later-resulting War of Independence (1808-1812) left the country war-torn in every sense of the word: its economy destroyed, its navy and commercial fleet in ruins, and the lifeline to the American possessions cut.

But the enlightened ideas that gave rise to the American and French Revolutions inspired many of the country's leading minds. While the war against the French on Spanish soil was still raging, a constituent assembly or "Cortes Constituyentes," representing the various regions of Spain, formed in Cádiz in 1810 for the purpose of hammering out a Constitution. Two parties had formed: the *Liberales*, who were divided into two groups: a moderate one, seeking reforms on British models, and a more radical one, trying to bring about changes on the French example; and the Royalist party which defended the ideas of an absolute monarchy. The Constitution of Cádiz was finally proclaimed in 1812; among its most important features were the following: (1) Spain was to be a constitutional hereditary monarchy; (2) the national sovereignty was to be rooted in the people, represented by the Cortes, which constituted one single chamber of deputies to be elected without class distinction, one for every 70,000 inhabitants; (3) all males over 25 years of age were to have the right to vote; (4) the legislative power was to be vested in the King and the Cortes while judicial power would correspond to the Tribunals; (5) all privileges of the nobility were to be abolished, (6) the existence of religious orders was regulated, (7) the Inquisition abolished and (8) freedom of the press guaranteed. Finally, (9) King and Church, the traditional authorities until then, were to be placed into a subordinate position in keeping with the more extreme liberal ideas, which was probably the main reason why the majority of the people would not stand behind this constitution.

When King Ferdinand VII returned from his forced exile in France in 1814, he rejected the constitution and exercised a most repressive, absolute power. The intellectual world of Spain, nobles and bourgeoisie alike, rebelled and protested, as did also large sections of the military. The result was persecutions through a net of spies and secret police, arrests, exiles, and executions. Many worthy people fled to France and England. The universities were restricted in their freedom and eventually closed. A military revolt in 1820 led to the reinstatement of the 1812 Constitution, and the king promised to abide by it. The three years that followed proved to be turbulent and coincided with the definite loss of Spain's last great possessions in South and Central America. But the most important monarchies of Europe came to the support of the king. A French army of one hundred thousand men invaded the peninsula and restored Ferdinand to his absolute power.

Shortly after Ferdinand's death in 1833, the first Carlist War broke out, so called after the king's younger brother, Don Carlos. He claimed his right to succession, since Ferdinand had decreed a change in the laws of succession in favor of his minor daughter, Isabel II. Maria Cristina, the queen-mother, became regent, and attempts were made to revive the constitutional monarchy, first with the Royal Statute of 1834, which offered the people some participation in government, and later in the new, more liberal constitution of 1837, which was followed by various others during the later decades.

Under the banner of the Carlist cause a large part of the clergy, the nobility, and the rural population gathered. The outcome was the first civil war which raged for seven years, until 1840. This war did enormous damage to the economy of the country and left vast portions of the people demoralized.

In the midst of this war, precisely in 1835, a radical expropriation of Church lands and also private latifundia and municipal lands held in mortmain was decreed and carried out under the regent's minister, Juan Alvarez Mendizabal, a notable economist of exalted liberal and at the same time anticlerical convictions. This expropriation or "desamortización" comprised all church lands and included the property of all religious orders. The latter were all suppressed except for those dedicated to education and the care of the sick in hospitals. This desamortización was not the first. It had been preceded by several similar measures under the 18th century kings, but they had never been so radical and had not really solved the serious problems of Spain's agriculture. In some areas, especially in Ramon de la Sagra's homeland of Galicia in the northwest corner of the Peninsula, the taxing of tenant farmers, had proven extremely damaging in the 18th century. In years of lean crops and agricultural disaster, peasants, unable to pay the tax, were simply evicted. This gave cause to uprisings.

The problem of landed property and its more manageable, more economical and *just* distribution was foremost on the minds (and works) of Alvaro Flórez Estrada (1839/1970) and later of Don Ramon de la Sagra (1840), as evidenced by his *Lecciones de Economía Social* of 1840. No doubt, one of the major purposes of the desamortizacion was that of making it possible for the peasant who worked but did not own the land to buy a portion of it and thus become a proprietor. However, through corruption, lack of credit, and an underhanded way of selling these

❖

these latifundia, most of the lands ended up in the possession of members of a
wealthy and prosperous liberal-oriented bourgeoisie leaving the peasants in worse
shape than before. They were reduced to underpaid and enslaved day laborers who
soon formed a vast proletariat.

Another result of Mendizabal's action was that the State had to establish
funds for maintaining religious worship and paying the clergy. The Church came
thus under the total financial dependence of the State. Subsequent new reforms and
concordats with Rome brought some changes and returned some property to the
Church and the religious orders. However we are concerned here with the situation
and its antecedents that faced de la Sagra when he delivered his *Lecciones* before
the Ateneo of Madrid, a scientific, literary, and artistic forum founded by Madrid's
"Economic Society" between 1820 and 1823, the short years that the constitution
of 1812 was in force.

### The Lecciones of de la Sagra

I shall now attempt to unfold Don Ramón's ideas and proposals in his *Lessons
on Social Economy*, lessons to be learned from observing the political and social
reality of his time and circumstance. As he pronounced them, civil war was still
raging, for he says (pp. 15-16):

> Concentrating on Spain, we see that the revolution has granted, to the
> classes of property owners and proletarians, political rights which to
> a great extent were desired, as a necessity of the age; others were
> indispensable, although unknown to several classes; and others still
> were neither needed nor called for by the situation of our people. In any
> case, they are now sanctioned, and if they may be of no value for
> hastening the progressive national movement, they will not harm it on
> its march. But right in the middle of gaining possession of political
> participation, a disastrous civil war rendered it almost totally unfruit-
> ful; and the principles of equality, of respect for property, of the free
> exercise of one's physical and intellectual faculties appear rather as
> promise than as realities. Once peace is consolidated, these conditions
> and consequences of the changes performed will become effective; but
> the people will still have to be provided with the enjoyment of the
> material and moral participation it needs and demands in order to be
> happy.

By availing himself of a wide range of demographic, industrial, agricultural,
educational, and penal statistics from a number of European nations, republics,
constitutional and absolute monarchies, and the United States of America, Ramon
de la Sagra examines the presence of misery and wretchedness in their respective
populations and identifies the causes as arising from certain principles and aspects
of human society. Thus he deals with the following:

I.    The problem of inequality of human conditions, caused by and inherent to the right of property (Lecc. 1° and 2°).

II.   The problems inherent to the growth, decrease, and quality of population (Lecc. 3°).

III.  Problems arising from manufacturing (Lecc. 4°).

IV.   Problems afflicting agriculture (Lecc. 5°).

V.    The phenomenon of vice, immorality, ignorance and irreligion in the working classes (Lecc. 6°).

VI.   The causes of these social ills both in the lack and excess of education and the need of concurrent moral formation of society (Lecc. 7° and 8°).

VII.  The role and influence of the wealthy classes and of government and the political and civil institution (Lecc. 9° and 10°).

## I. The Inequality of Human Conditions and the Right of Property

Don Ramón starts (pp. 23-25, 36) with a definition of the concept of social economy:

> It is the goal of the science called social economy to determine the means conducive to the happiness and well-being of nations, of improving their physical, intellectual and moral condition.... Social economy...must occupy itself with the means of improving the material and moral situation of the people.... It is the science of social progress.... Social economy belongs to the great category of the politico-moral sciences; and, both because of its goal and because of the auxiliary sciences it uses on its advance, it must take the highest place in the scale of human knowledge. Indeed, ...social economy...must begin its investigations by exposing the causes of the backwardness and malaise of nations; it must look for the remedies and provide the rules for their wise application....

He then asks: What is the social condition of a nation, under any form of government? He states that the population of a country is divided by its social functions into two large categories: (a) those who govern and (b) those who are governed. The governed in turn constitute two classes: (1) those who own property and (2) those who do not, but live on wages. The property owners enjoy a stable income and are safe from the misfortunes and contingencies of life. Those who depend on wages and daily labor are frequently exposed to deprivations and misery.

They experience hardship and suffering. De la Sagra asks again: Is this difference between the two classes based on rules of justice and is it reasonable and proper that this difference continue? At the basis of the problem is the so-called right to property. If this is an unjust right, founded on an irrational principle, it must first be destroyed and then replaced by the common enjoyment of the goods that now constitute property.

Our author now marshalls his arguments in favor of the right to property. Private property has always existed as is evident in the history of all peoples, even in the most primitive social conditions. Quoting a certain Mr. Droz, he says (p. 38) that primitive man owns his arrows and his hut because he has invested his work in them from which results his right to them. The right to property goes back even further: "...no doubt our first properties are the faculties we have received from the Creator.... Man is, at least, the owner of his person."[1] Without the right to property, there is no permanent society, no permanent family, no incentive to work, no social progress. Economists have defined various kinds of property, distinguishing territorial property, manufacturing property, commercial property, and so forth; and they have attributed to these kinds different degrees of importance, placing at the bottom of the scale the principal one: the property of the physical, intellectual, and moral faculties of the individual.

Such economists have then asked which one among the various kinds of property might be the most sacred. J.B. Say contends that some kinds of property can be more inviolable and sacred — for instance those acquired by work, like capital, manufactures, etc. This implies the possibility of denying the origin and purity of many other kinds of property transmitted by inheritance and exchange, especially landed properties. Don Ramón affirms with Droz, "that all property is and must remain equally sacred, equally inviolable before the law and society."[2] In order to reinforce his argument, our author turns to the right to own land. For this purpose, he quotes (p. 42) the opinion of another Spanish economist, his compatriot, contemporary and adversary, Don Alvaro Flórez Estrada. The latter notes in his (1839) "Opuscula" entitled The Social Question or Origin, Scope, and Effects of the Right to Property (pp. 7 and 20) that

> All articles of wealth are the exclusive product of labor; and since the right to property can only apply to wealth, this must by necessity originate in labor; and as man's intervention does not concur in producing the gifts of nature, these can never be the legitimate property of an individual.... All property which is not the product of the labor of its possessor, owes its existence to a civil law; and it would be absurd to affirm that such property comes from a natural law.[3]

Flórez Estrada and other thinkers like him propose, therefore, a plan of usufruct of the lands, which does not permit anyone to hold more land than one family can cultivate.

❖

Don Ramón concedes that such objections are not new. Lycurgos and Agis in ancient Sparta as well as Tiberius Gracchus in times of the Roman Republic proposed equal distribution of land. Some even quote the laws of feudalism, the laws of Moses and the laws of the Incas to support their argument for land distribution.

Saint Simon proposed in 1825 a social system in which a nonelective hierarchy would be responsible for rewarding each individual according to his capacity and his works; and there are many other similar examples. De la Sagra declares (p. 43) that he wants to "demonstrate that landed property is the result of the work of the individual, the same as of all other properties, and that consequently their titles are equally legitimate and sacred."

Adam Smith and J.B. Say had considered material labor and intellectual work the only source of wealth; but, our author notes (p. 44), Villeneuve (p. 249) points out that this truth is much more ancient, because true productive work originated from man's needs and is traced back to "those terrible words of the Creator, offended by his creature: 'Thou shall eat thy bread in the sweat of thy brow.'"

Land becomes property or property in land when man cultivates it, fertilizes and irrigates it and grows crops on it; this land, modified through industry, can only belong to one individual at a time and is thus considered agricultural property. Land ownership is further supported by the consideration that the one who works the land is not, unless he owns the land, as interested in his labor and product as the one who owns it or has rented or leased it for long periods of time which gives him a sense of stability and duration.

In the view of Flórez Estrada, this is not so, but Don Ramón shows, with exemplary statistics from France, England, Scotland, and Ireland how the quality of cultivation varies. The worst is that practiced by the slave, and next to the worst is that of the tenant or renter for short periods, since the tenant depends on a usufructing landowner and often a middleman. Next come the tenants of caring landowners who manage their own agricultural enterprises. But the best degree of cultivation is achieved by the one who owns and works the land; this is true even of the small owner who can make a good profit from his fields with the necessary help of credit, instruction and the proper guidance of political institutions.

The evils pointed out by economists who attack the right to landed property, de la Sagra assures us, do not proceed from the property right itself but rather from the disparity with which property is divided from the disproportion and inequality of conditions such division brings about. But this applies to all kinds of property, in some nations more to industrial and commercial property than to owned land.

But social inequality is one of the conditions of human nature itself, it suggests wealth on the one hand and indigence on the other. As St. Matthew says: "There will always be poor among you." Don Ramón also finds (p. 61) massive support in these words of Alban de Villeneuve-Bargemont (op. cit., p. 249):

❖

Social life is a necessity for the human race, and the right to property, the inequality of fortunes and conditions are its necessary consequences, because without them the social state could obviously not exist. The plans for a society where community of goods and perfect material equality should be present as established, have never been realized, except in the aggregations of human beings united with a religious purpose and who have, with this very same goal, retired from social life; but they are totally impractical in the organization of an extensive society. Thus, by the very force of things, one part of the population is placed in a condition of inferiority: the ones possess power, the distinctiveness, the wealth; the others are reduced to mediocrity, to labor or to indigence.

How do wealth and poverty appear in modern nations? Evidence shows that the general state of a nation can be that of extreme wealth, while a large number of people in it suffer from abject poverty. This is especially so in England and France; less, in countries where there is less accumulation of wealth, as for instance in Switzerland, Russia, and Sweden.

This allows us to conclude that it is not the quantity of wealth of a nation that produces the greatest well-being among its members but rather the distribution of this wealth among them. Then de la Sagra quotes (pp. 64-66) from the Baron de Gerando's work, *De la Bienfaisance publique* (Paris 1839; Vol. I, p. 143), concerning the two laws of wealth and distribution, and he finds that "indigence increases with increasing inequality of conditions."

But, we are told (p. 68), the inequality of fortunes can benefit the lower classes if the upper ones carry out the holy and philanthropic mission with which they are entrusted, for they must distribute wealth with dignity and cooperate in the well-being and happiness of all. Thus they contribute to sustain the steadiness of the worker, allowing his noble and just ambition to rise. The worker will not curse the rich because he will also reap the benefits of the wise use of capital.

However, he counters (pp. 68-69), if the classes endowed with wealth abuse its application, the inequality of conditions directly influences the misery and malaise of the people. It brutalizes the nation, demoralizes the individual, creates mutual hatred and prepares the big catastrophes of popular vengeance. This eternal struggle can only be reconciled through peace and public order by means of a frank and decisive sanction of the above maxims. Quoting Burke, Don Ramón continues (pp. 69-70):

It should be suggested to the poor to show patience, resignation, work, sobriety, and religion; it is equally urgent and necessary to preach to the rich enlightenment, beneficence, and Christian charity.

Concerning the consoling principles of Christianity, de la Sagra (p.71) once more quotes Villeneuve (p. 122):

> ...the religion that tightens and purifies the relations and needs of people, which makes them look at labor and suffering as a necessary test, while each one, however, retains the fullness of his rights and his dignity, is the only one that can soften the bitterness of the evils resulting from social inequality – in the religious order, it shows the most perfect equality; in the temporal order, it indicates how inequality can transform into a source of usefulness and fortune, thus diminishing, to the degree possible, the principle and the consequences of inequality.

## II. Problems inherent in the Growth, Decrease, and Quality of Population

In his third lesson (pp. 72-118), the author shows the effects of population increase on labor and compensation. Work is a social condition and a social necessity; work produces wealth, and a portion of this wealth is invested annually in paying the workers. This share represents the value of the wages, which are subject to variance, (a) according to the number of workers entitled to them and (b) according to the share of wealth destined to compensate the workers.

Now, if both the number of workers and the share of wealth produced by them annually increases or decreases at the same rate, the wages would be perfectly balanced; but for various reasons that does not happen. This is where the topic of population comes in. De la Sagra states that there are two schools of thought regarding the relation between wages and size of population; one, formed by such thinkers as Montesquieu, Necker, Mirabeau, Adam Smith, Everett, Morel de Vinde, and others, simply assumes that the state will grow in strength and wealth with the increase of its population; the other, initiated by Plato and Aristotle and continued by the Venetian monk Ortes and his contemporary, Ricci, then by Franklin, J. Steuart, Arthur-Young, Towesend, Malthus, J.B. Say, Ricardo, Destutt de Tracy, Droz, Duchatel, Blanqui, Sismondi, de Coax, Godwin, examines the effects with greater depth and looks at population increase more or less as a fatal calamity.

The members of the first school point to the wealth and prosperity of the very populated countries, especially England, Belgium, and France, as proof for their assumption. This may hold true when one looks at the prosperity of the nation as a whole without, however, considering the conditions of its classes, especially the working population. The adherents of the second school examine the condition of the people, particularly in Ireland and England, and counsel the limitation or restriction of population increase, observing that while there is misery among the people of the very populous countries, there is well-being in the less populated ones.

Noting that there are three factors that determine the increase or decrease of the population (birth, death, and immigration/emigration), Don Ramón finds the following:

a) If the rate of birth in a nation remains stationary while the mortality rate increases, the total population will diminish.

b) If the birthrate increases and the rate of mortality decreases, the total population will grow. The quality of the growing population, however, depends on the sex and age of the deceased. If these are women, children and very old people, the general increase will be an advantage, because there will be now a greater proportion of virile and strong people of useful age. If the losses occur among people of the most useful ages, the population growth will not so soon result in a growth in wealth because the replacement, even though in greater number than the dead, is too young and therefore nonproductive.

c) Immigration increases (emigration declines), considering that the individuals involved are mostly and usually adults in vigorous condition, will increase the wealth of the receiving (retaining) population and reduce it in the giving one.

Thus, de la Sagra concludes here (pp. 80-81):

The true strength of a population is not constituted by the mere number of individuals, but a physical, sober, industrious people, even if it shows few individuals, is more potent and worth more than a weak, effeminate, and lazy one. The increase a country may receive through immigration of hard-working males will be worth infinitely more than that attained by another country through the increase of births.

But, there are other factors to consider. First of all, population in general is on the increase. Natural and man-made disasters such as floods, earthquakes, volcanic eruptions, epidemics, famine, and wars hamper this growth; but, with advancing civilization, man has learned to make himself less vulnerable to such catastrophes. After presenting demographic statistics of the United States and a number of European nations, de la Sagra finds that the population is growing in all countries. These statistics, however, are not sufficient to show the quality of the population in each case.

In relating these considerations to labor and production, we need to recall that the population of a country can be regarded as composed of two basic groups, producers and nonproducers. The producers can be subdivided into different classes according to the service they provide; namely, the farming class, the industrial or manufacturing class, the commercial class, the class of employees, etc. (p. 90).

When considering the welfare of a country's population, we shall have to look at the wealthy classes, the industrial classes, the proletariat and the unproductive classes, such as beggars, thieves, prostitutes, etc.

The principal facts manifest in modern societies, according to de la Sagra, are the following:

❖

a) There is greater reproductive strength in the classes most exposed to destruction.

b) The farming population increases at a much slower rate than the industrial population.

c) Mortality in the industrial population is higher than in the rural one.

d) Mortality is higher among the poor than among the wealthy.

e) Civilization, philanthropy, and science cooperate in preserving the weak, thereby sustaining the population increase.

Overall, one observes that in an increasing population the most needy classes, in particular, are growing. Various means of controlling this growth have been proposed: Malthus and disciples suggest the limitation of marriages, while others preach abstinence. An English philanthropist shocks his contemporaries by suggesting contraception under the mythological name of Venus sine Lucina (the Roman goddess of childbirth), and a certain Mr. Marcus even goes so far as to recommend the destruction of all children exceeding three per married couple.

In his discussion of production, Don Ramón distinguishes two large categories of products: (1) those necessary for man's nourishment; and (2) those furnishing materials for man's clothing, shelter, comforts, etc. The former are the immediate or mediate products of the land: cereals, vegetables, roots, livestock; the latter also are products of the land but not for man's nourishment and already modified by him, like fibers, timber, skins, minerals, etc. The production of these two classes of materials occupies two distinct branches of labor: agriculture and industry. Agriculture produces nourishment and certain other primary materials destined for industry. Industry produces and manufactures for purposes other than sustenance or food. The laws of population increase must, therefore, be examined in relation or comparison to those of agricultural production. Showing statistical evidence, especially on France and England, de la Sagra concludes that for several years, the population increase has been in inverse proportion to the means of sustenance, which have decreased less for the rich and considerably more for the lower classes. In addition to that, prices for food have risen, while wages have not.

As to the manufacturing industry, it appears limitless in production (a) because it uses raw materials of supreme abundance in the world, which can be divided, combined, and modified in a great number of ways; and (b) industrial production does not only depend on human and animal strength but is largely run by machines. As a stunning example for his time, de la Sagra states that the cotton spinning machines in England are equivalent to the force of four hundred million individuals while the textile machines represent a minimum of 53,000 horses. Conclusion: Population increase is advantageous for a nation's well-being only when its means of sustenance grow concurrently. On this two-fold progress alone depends the real and positive wealth of nations.

## III.  Problems Arising From Manufacturing (Lecc. IV, pp. 119-45)

Having dealt with the demographic aspect and its influence on the people, the author focuses now on two branches of labor and production; namely, agriculture and industry. Production of the manufacturing industry tends to be limitless due to the use of machines powered mainly by steam. This industry has grown enormously in comparison to agricultural output where the use of machines is still rare and where the amount of available land sets a limit to production. Although, in the future, chemical fertilizer and steam-powered agricultural machinery may revolutionize farming, for the time being, the manufacturing industry dominates in production which results in great comfort in the way of life and well-being of the wealthy classes. It is also true that, as a consequence, products have become cheaper and more generally available and that with expanding industry new occupations and jobs have been created. The social consequences have not been so rosy. The increasing use of mechanical power causes serious upheaval in work and wages. New inventions lead to the displacement of large numbers of workers and reduce them and their families to misery for which even newly created jobs do not compensate. Statistics of most European countries reveal that the highest rate of paupers in proportion to the population is evident in England, the Netherlands, and Switzerland. Workers running new machines require more skill and education; reduced wages lead to the labor of women and children; the mingling of the sexes and their close contact at work is conducive to corruption of women, to their prostitution and general degradation. Economists of the English school have considered only the advantages modern industry provides for the factory owners; namely, increased production and lower wages; but Christian economists and philosophers must look at this situation from the moral and social point of view.

The consequences of factory work on the workers' health, particularly on children, has caused inquiries in the British Parliament and, likewise, in France. These inquiries show that working conditions are crowded, there is a lack of ventilation, and workers are exposed to high temperatures and often to noxious fumes. Work on machines requires a cramped, sedentary position, especially disastrous for children; and working hours are extremely long, as the machines stand still only on Sunday. Ramon de la Sagra states that a bill concerning child labor was made law in England in 1833, limiting the number of work hours per week to 48 and to no more than nine per day.

As to the effect of such working conditions on the adults, one notices a high rate of mortality, frequent alcoholism and its disabling consequences such as prostitution and illegitimate births. The author has seen noteworthy and praiseworthy exceptions in America.

If approached wisely and with true social and Christian concern, everybody could benefit from expanding industry. For the time being, however, the economy is still far away from that.

❖

## IV.  Problems Afflicting Agriculture (Lecc. V, pp. 146-63)

The peasant's prospect of ever living on a secure income instead of daily wages and thus passing from the condition of proletarian to that of property owner are indeed very dim. His work and livelihood depend not only on the change of seasons but also on the hazards of the weather, like hurricanes, hail, frost, floods, long periods of drought, and cattle disease. Such catastrophes bring on famine, sickness, and indigence. Yet even if crops are bountiful, the land will not feed a naturally increasing rural population; so those who no longer find work on the land go to the cities and look for employment in industry. Apart from other problems in finding a job, the farmhand, lacking the specialized skills of the factory worker, may become even more destitute than before.

Much can be done to improve the fate of the peasantry and prevent the drain on the rural population: development of new lands for cultivation, introduction of new cultures, elimination of fallow acreage, substitution of meadowlands by cultivation of feed plants, a better forest economy, and the association of branches of agricultural home-industry with purely agrarian chores. All this will increase the number of hands needed in agricultural industry and thus accommodate a large rural population; it will also result in better and more varied products. Such practices are being used in Holland, Prussia, England, and parts of France, with good results. England makes intensive use of its agricultural lands; as to France, not even one fourth of the land available is being cultivated. In England, the great increase in agricultural production is due to the establishment of huge estates and a more enlightened and cheaper way of cultivation; machines have helped reduce the number of laborers. But if most of the land consists of latifundia owned by a very few, the peasant has no chance of ever becoming a landowner; hence the enjoyment of the wealth produced is tainted by extreme inequality.

France presents another extreme. Due to political events and civil legislation, agriculture is practiced mostly by small landowners. These properties are too small to sustain growing families, however, and their fate is not very different from that of day laborers. The extreme subdivision of land is to the disadvantage of animal production, which, in turn, reduces the amount of dung used for fertilizer. At the same time, animal by-products serving as raw material for manufacture are reduced.

But small properties are not bad as long as they are not further subdivided. De la Sagra suggests the possibility of an intermediate system of agriculture which combines the advantages of both large and small properties, without their disadvantages. He refers to it (p. 157) as "a system of *dividing the properties without dividing the land.*"[4]

An even worse condition than small farming is caused by a renter between the landowner and the farmer. Ireland is a case in point. Big absentee landowners leave administrators with permission to sublet the property to another renter who divides the land into small lots of five, ten, or 20 acres, sub-renting them out to

❖

tenant-farmers. They receive no tools, no seed, no animals; they construct a hut and work the land badly, since they have no means to improve their cultivation and little interest to do so because they have no long-term interest security. The tenant must pay an exaggerated rent to satisfy the earnings calculated by the owner and the middlemen; if he cannot pay, he is thrown off the land with his family and has to go begging. There being no other industry to occupy these poor people hunger and starvation are the result. In a population of 8 million people, 2,600,000 are destitute.[5]

## V. Vice, Immorality, Ignorance and Irreligion in the Working Classes (Lecc. VI, pp. 164-87)

More or less common vices to be found among industrial workers are gambling, drinking, promiscuity, and prostitution of young women. Gambling degrades the morality of the worker who has to maintain his family on meager wages and cannot afford to lose even the smallest amount of money. Hoping to win something without working or saving, the only real sources of well-being, he risks victimizing his wife and children. Lotteries are equally harmful, and they become especially seductive when authorized by the government; fortunately, many governments have abolished such lotteries.

Drinking is another vice, with even more disastrous effects. The worker seeks relief from suffering and misery, but he weakens his health and becomes an alcoholic. The phenomenon is more wide-spread among the working classes of northern European countries and of America than among southern European countries. Ill health, delirium tremens, insanity and criminal acts committed under the influence of alcohol take their demoralizing toll.

Prostitution results from the mingling of the sexes in the working place and the promiscuity of men. Vanity and longing for luxuries they cannot afford degrade many young women to the state of prostitution.

Ignorance, i.e. illiteracy, is another fatal cause of the misery among the industrial proletariat, and the situation worsens as machines substitute for men. The handling of machines requires a trained intelligence, hence industrial instruction. An indispensable element of industrial instruction is primary education, but such instruction must go hand in hand with moral and religious education.

Primary instruction among industrial workers is badly lacking in England and France. The situation is less severe in Belgium and Holland. Prussia has done a great deal for primary education, and some American states have even been more successful with public education programs. Without intellectual and moral training, ignorance and misery are perpetuated, leading also to disease and higher mortality. To prevent such perpetuation, Austria, for instance, does not allow any young worker to marry nor will it admit him to a factory job unless he is able to read, write, and count. The result of this policy has been lower crime rates. Statistics in France, England, Switzerland and the United States show increasing numbers of delinquents who can neither read nor write; ignorance also drives people to beg and to prostitution. The working classes must be instructed to compete with the mechanical forces that substitute for their physical strength. They must develop and use their intelligence.

## VI. Causes of These Social Ills: Lack and Excess of Education; Need for a Moral Formation of Society (Lecc. VII and VIII, pp. 188-250)

Modern governments have responded favorably to the advantage and need of providing education for the people, but they have failed to provide the moral education necessary for the benefit of the people. The middle classes have striven to secure higher learning and academic degrees for their children in order to rise thus above their social level.

True talent has blurred many of the old social barriers. A new generation is making its way to wealth and power in industry, commerce, and politics; and the last bastions of aristocracy by birth and privilege are crumbling. A kind of intellectual fever has seized the people. The professional ranks are suddenly swelling with jurists, physicians, and scholars in philology and literature, but there are not enough openings available to allow them to practice their professions and fulfill their hopes for a better life. Secondary schools, academies, libraries, and museums have been established. Chairs for higher sciences have been endowed, new chairs for the natural sciences and the liberal arts have been created, generous scholarships have been founded, but primary education has been abandoned to itself, and the moral education of the people has been forgotten. This evidences a serious lack of provision for and knowledge of the true social interests of the people.

In France, for instance, young, talented persons find all the means and facilities to study national and foreign literatures, law and medicine, mathematics, physics, chemistry, natural history, etc., but there is hardly any promotion for industrial and agronomic instruction; primary education is left to private hands and charitable associations. As de la Sagra writes (p. 209):

Education has subverted the order of rational ideas, exciting vanity, pride, and rivalry; by giving preponderance to the exercise of talent, it has altered the level and regular proportion that must exist between professions and capacities; it has destroyed the preserving principle of inequality of conditions, of an inequality which is necessary and natural, but which becomes violent, forceful and dangerous when it does not correspond to a similar inequality in the intelligences of individuals.

Don Ramón quotes (p. 209) from Mr. Mathon de Fogeres' *Essai d'économie sociale* (Paris: Chamerot, 1839; no loc. cit.):

❖

... this upheaval of positions and intelligences produces a serious malaise in societies. In the men who have thus lost their true career, one does not see the firm and secure step ... of someone who is in his own sphere, knows his duties and has the necessary talent to carry them out.

It has been shown that the vices of society result in greater numbers of poor and criminals. It is also evident that with the progress of civilization in modern societies, there is a growing number of mentally ill. The nations whose inhabitants exercise most their mental faculties, in imagination and in commercial and industrial speculation and calculation also have a higher incidence of mental illness. While this is not noticeable in less developed nations such as Persia, Turkey, Hindustan, and is infrequent in Russia, it appears on the increase in nations of the European south such as Spain, Portugal and Italy. It is growing in France and Prussia and rises to the point of grave concern in Scotland and England.

Much has been said about the beneficial influence of education as a means of improving the customs and habits of a people. Unfortunately, this supposition is false, for the tendency to crime in the civilized nations seems to follow permanent laws of constant regularity. However, French statistics, for instance, indicate an increase in crimes against persons versus a decline of those against property.

De la Sagra now (Lecc. VIII, pp. 212-50) looks into the relationship between the criminality of people and their respective level of education in general and between the morality of the delinquents and their intellectual advance in particular. He states that it is erroneous to attribute a priori consequences to literacy instruction. The illusion prevailed that instruction was a preventive measure against immorality and crime. As literary instruction was a means of progress in virtue, it followed that the knowledge of the most brilliant minds should be spread among all classes to raise coming generations to higher levels of virtue and morality. Criminal statistics of several governments reveal that literate delinquency is on the rise, that crime among the illiterate or poorly educated does not rise at the same high rate, and that crimes against persons are more frequently committed by educated felons. These findings are supported by the Baron de Morogues in the French parliamentary session of July 5th, 1836.

Primary education is necessary for all classes for their existence and advancement, but moral education alone is capable of improving their morality and of directing them on the path of virtue. Superior instruction is good for societies, but it must be reserved for those individuals who can use it and only in the number corresponding to the needs of the nation. Superior instruction, if not united with a corresponding degree of higher moral and religious education, does not provide individuals with the intellectual benefits it tends to promote. Irreligion supposes lack of faith, hope, and charity. It destroys the seeds of the good. It is harmful in the wealthy classes but still more destructive among the poor.

Following de Gerando again, de la Sagra writes (p. 248): "Religion embraces the whole system of human faculties and the entire course of life simultaneously; it is the torch that illuminates intelligence, the law that regulates customs, the power that dominates the soil, and the motive that presides all man's actions." At the same time, he agrees with Alban de Villeneuve (op. cit., Vol I, p. 431) that

> the worker, in order to avoid indigence and to preserve his family from it, must be educated, hard-working, modest and economical. Who will give him these qualities? ... English political economy answers that the incentive to work, through the attraction of the material pleasures, is sufficient to move the worker to acquire the conditions of his comfort and of his good fortune and that an industrial education is sufficient for him. Christian political economy, however, finds such conditions only in a religious education.

Ramón de la Sagra concludes that the lack of moral and religious formation is the most powerful and active cause of the misery of the working classes, of the vices of modern societies, and of the crimes that populate the prisons. It is safe to assume that a vicious criminal is irreligious. Instruction must not be separated from moral and religious education.

## VII. The Wealthy Classes, Government, and Political & Civil Institutions vis-à-vis Public Poverty and Misfortune (Lecc. IX, pp. 251-70)

The simple aspect of comfort and well-being constitutes an incitement of passions in the poor who look at the apparently carefree possession of wealth, the security of existence it provides, the whims it satisfies, and the honors and considerations it obtains. When on the part of the wealthy there is no merit, no work nor virtue to accredit such privileges, all this is difficult to deny as contradictory and unjust compared to the physical and social deprivations that always accompany poverty and mediocrity. Should the wealthy show disdain and contempt for suffering, hardness and insensitivity, egoism and pride, vice and immorality, then wealth becomes odious. It excites just indignation, engenders vindictive envy and actually approves of the degradation and perverseness of the classes it humiliates and vilifies.

If such immoral behavior is shown by individuals endowed with authority and power, i.e. in the government, the evil produced by a vicious social and political regime continues through many generations. An undeniable truth, the author observes (p. 254), can be derived from all this: the people follow the good or bad example set by the great ones. This principle, the product of experience, leads to another one, presented by the economist of the Christian school de Gerando, in *De la Bienfaisance publique,* to wit:

❖

In the general economy of society and in the eyes of Divine Providence, wealth and power are not a favor but a mission, its task is the betterment of the existence of all — being at the center of social relations, the powerful and wealthy are invested with an honorable sponsorship: it is their job to found the great alliance of universal fraternity ... being at the summit of the human family, they are called to exercise ... the beautiful ministry of benevolence (pp. 254-55).

The degradation of power as a result of abuse and neglect leads to another fatal social evil: the contempt for authority. Such contempt is evident in the present generation of European nations where the prestige of supreme authority has disappeared. The idea of freedom is translated as factious independence, laws have no majesty, authority has no force, and morality has no credit. People blame the new institutions for these disorders and compare them to the peace and order under absolutism. But, Don Ramón points out, the laws of the moral world, like those of the physical world, are superior to the dictorial powers of government, and the so-called free governments promote and provide better for the production and distribution of wealth and for needed social reform because the political institution of free states provides for a range of individual initiative which governments do not tolerate.

Government and public administration involve certain interests that only the people can manage effectively, the author notes. Here, intervention by a supreme power is unnecessary and even detrimental. Government cannot provide for the detailed needs of the people; and, if government assumes the duties of the people, they surrender themselves to the care of the tutor, the State. This abdication of responsibility, in turn, results in the people blaming the State for any mismanagement, thus undermining its authority. Thus, political systems can exercise a great influence on the misfortune and malaise of the poor classes; and the administrative institutions especially are not in simple and easy harmony with the principles of freedom.

Free constitutions sanction freedom of thought, the emission of ideas, the right to vote, and political equality, but when it comes to confiding to the people the exercise of administrative rights, they tend to be frugal and obscure. Why is this so? Don Ramón says that the proponents of free constitutions have considered the individuals of a nation in a mass, as a collective body; but when it becomes necessary to consider the action of the political individual so that he, working independently, might cooperate for the common good, they seemed to fear more that he may go astray than to expect good from his zeal and education. The eye of the government wants to be everywhere, but it is unable to do so; it prefers to condemn the individual to inaction.

The existence of modern nations requires a quantity of life and action in their component parts in relation to the great needs of the times with the same freedom and independence with which individuals manage their private interests. The association of individuals must participate in the management of the interests that concern them. Government cannot replace the force of such action. It can only, with enlightenment, direct all the great movements of the different social spheres, but it cannot and must not interfere in those movements.

Municipal institutions form the first vital element of the people's strength, guaranteed by individual freedom. The same principle applies to provincial institutions, but political power in European nations tends to invade the functions of social power.

Civil laws exercise much influence on the misfortune and misery of the people. They affect the poor classes most, marriage laws serving as an example. Marriage among the wealthy tends to accumulate fortunes; among the poor classes the effect is opposite. Imprudent laws for the control of population growth tend to corrupt customs. In some countries, the magistrate is empowered to judge the spouses-to-be as to their spiritual, professional, and financial fitness in order to stop the spread of indigence, but this also encourages promiscuity. More good can come from salutary counsel and tutelary protection. Laws are also defective where unwed mothers are concerned, causing monstrous inequalities and hardship.

Existing property laws hinder the suitable division of inherited property; the law of primogeniture appears unjust and tyrannical, since the younger children are excluded. Don Ramon says here (p. 264): "The laws may interfere for the preservation of landed property when its division is inconvenient, but without depriving the remaining descendants of its usufruct or an equivalent indemnization by the possessor." The author refers not only to landed property but also to industrial property.

The laws concerning commerce and industry can obstruct progress as well as advance the well-being and happiness of all. Customs and tariffs need to be reformed. Taxation and fiscal spending are areas where great harm is done to the people through bad calculations of the national budget and dissipation of public funds. Governments must represent the general interests of the people; but, besides the stated interests of the whole society, there exist other interests originating from the principle of association: material interests, moral interests, and religious interests. While the first are generally disregarded by many governments or abandoned to individual action, the moral and religious interests are confused with political interests.

The principal material interests are the means of communication, credit institutes, organization of industrial work, and guarantees for the exercise of industry and commerce.

Institutes of credit are the soul of agricultural and industrial enterprises. De la Sagra here (pp. 294f.) relies on a contemporary work by C. Pecqueur:[6]

Credit, in its broadest acceptation, is the solid loan to the one who has nothing except honor and attitude. Lending *credit* to a worker means putting him into the conditions of getting the commodity, the knowledge, the freedom, without any cost to anyone, the lender included. It means tying those who have unproductive capital with men capable of making it produce, to the healthy portion of the proletarian classes, through the ties of recognition and of community of interests that consolidate the social body and put into harmony the classes always ready to become jealous and to despise each other; it is ... giving a reward to morality and activity.

As to the organization of industrial work, our author holds (p. 298) that the supreme power of the state is responsible for

regulating the work of the young in manufactures, guaranteeing the associations of workers and industrials, advancing the means for the exercise of industry, organizing national institutions of credit, trans- forming little by little the extreme agricultural, industrial, commercial, and domestic division, combining new economic means of preparation and common consumption, organizing a good health system in the towns etc. etc.

He then declares (p. 299) that the English school of political economy gives exclusive importance to promoting material interests and consequently experi- ences growing problems. In proportion to the absolute increase of national wealth, the share relative to the masses of workers diminishes. Free competition itself can be a principle of life or death, accordingly as it may be well or badly directed. The social power of the state must intervene here in order to assure a distributive justice in the contracts of the strong with the weak. With this, Don Ramón enters the field of the moral interests, which comprise the teaching and education of the people, public beneficence, prevention and punishment of offenses and crimes, and the moral reform of delinquents.

Education includes the physical, intellectual, and moral faculties of the person. Public education is a moral necessity. It must proceed from the government as the knower of needs and directive center of society.

Public beneficence is necessary in support of inevitable misfortune; the state must attempt to foresee individual and public misery. It must prevent vice engendered by misery itself. Public beneficence in support of victims of misfortune must not encourage laziness and sloth; it must not replace charity and pose as legal means because thus it destroys the feeling of public piety, strangles gratitude, and substitutes a right for a virtue. Beneficence is predicated on religion, and whatever separates or tends to separate it from this noble origin will degrade its results.

The punishing of offenses and crimes constitutes moral means of social betterment and as such is a social duty of government. But government must also assist in the rehabilitation of the transgressor.

All these social duties of the state originate and are derived from the conditions of existence and the moral and religious destiny of societies and mankind. Here, the author quotes again from Alban de Villeneuve (op. cit., Vol. I, p. 167):

> Man has a religious destiny and to comply with it, he must tend towards moral progress. Societies are subject to the same laws because societies also have a religious destiny. The social progress towards the end that brings man closer to his religious destiny constitutes the true civilization. This then does not merely consist of refinement in the arts, nor in the highest culture of the sciences, but rather in the civil equality which only Christianity establishes, in the gentleness of the general custom, in the generosity of public and international law, in the diffusion of charity, in the propagation of religious feeling, i.e. of what is good, just, and true.

In practice, religious direction is incumbent on the clergy, but on the general bases it also corresponds to the supreme power of the state. Though independent from political power, religion belongs to the social power which embraces and comprises all departments. The government's efforts in this regard aim at national regeneration.

### Epilogue

This concludes the present exposition of the foremost treatise on Roman-Catholic social economy in Spain in the mid-19th century. Another outstanding example, prominently referred to by de la Sagra, as we have seen, was Alvaro Florez Estrada's opuscule on *The Social Question,* which first appeared at Madrid in 1839. Finally, toward the close of the decade in question, de la Sagra's *Social Aphorisms* would appear, first at Brussels (4a ed., 1848), and then in his native Castilian at Madrid in 1849. With this little volume, the author proposes "to give an idea of his principles and his manner of treating the great social questions of our epoch" ("Prólogo," Nov. 1849). And, therewith, he provides the final epitome of his Roman-Catholic social economy.

## Endnotes

*Professor of Modern Languages, Department of Classics and Modern Languages, Creighton University, Omaha, NE 68178 USA.

[1]  Joseph Droz. Economie Politique: *Principes de la Science des Richesses,* Paris, 1829. (Ed./TN)

❖

[2] Quoting and citing (p. 40, including nn. 1 and 2) Economie Politique Chrétienne, by the Vicomte Alban de Villeneuve-Bargemont, Tome I, p. 413.

[3] Cf. Flórez Estrada (1839/1970), as in "References," p. 217.

[4] The author here cites/quotes from the article "Progrés de la G. Bretagne," *Revue des deux Mondes*, 1.° Nov. 1836, p. 68.

[5] The author here (pp. 159 ff.) relies on a Mr. de Baumont, *L'Irlande social, politique et religieuse*, Paris, 1839.

[6] Viz., *Des ameliorations materielles dans leur rapport avec la liberté*, 1840.

## References

Flórez Estrada, Alvaro. "La cuestión social, o sea, origen, latitud y efectos del derecho de propriedad" (Madrid, 1839), as in *Revista de Trabajo* (Madrid: Ministerio de Trabajo, 1939-), Vol. 31 (1970), 205-18.

Sagra, Ramón de la. *Lecciones de Economía Social*, Madrid: Imprenta de ferrer y Compañia, 1840.

_____. *Aphorismos Sociales: Introducción a la Sciencia Social*, Madrid: Colegio de Sardo-Mudos, 1849.

---------------------------------- ❖ ----------------------------------

# Antecedents of *Rerum Novarum* in European Catholicism

## *Paul Misner\**

The foremost precursor of Catholic social teaching before Pope Leo XIII, the author of the 1891 encyclical, *Rerum Novarum (RN)*, was by common consent Emmanuel von Ketteler (1811-77, bishop of Mainz from 1850). Leo XIII himself called him *"notre grand prédécesseur"* (Franz Mueller, 1984, p. 70). That he was. Ketteler's report to the German bishops' conference in 1869 was a breakthrough document; his 1864 book, *The Labor Problem and Christianity* had called the attention of Catholics to the subject of the future encyclical and prepared the way for it, as had his addresses on questions of poverty and property already in 1848 (in Rupert J. Ederer, 1982, pp. 439-93 for 1869, pp. 307-433 for 1864, and pp. 1-99 for 1848). My purpose here is not to dwell on Ketteler, however, since he is so well known (cf. Roger Aubert in Hubert Jedin, ed. 1981, 8:302-303), but to track some subsequent antecedents between Ketteler and Leo.

When one focusses on the drafting process of the encyclical itself in particular, some surprising antecedents come to light. One who emerges an an indubitable influence is the Jesuit philosopher, Matteo Liberatore (1810-1892). There is of course a significant difference between "antecedents" and actual "influence," with the latter being harder to demonstrate. Clarifying one strand of actual influence, however, will put the matter of other putative influences and antecedents in a new light.

Schematically, after all, two opposed readings of *RN* suggest themselves. (I shall cite by paragraph numbers in the English-language edition of Claudia Carlen, *The Papal Encyclicals*, 1981, 2:241-58.) Taking a cue from the condemnation of the "wretchedness pressing so unjustly on the working class" *(RN*, §3) and from the independence from classical economics shown in suggesting remedies, some have read the encyclical as a *departure* on Leo's part *from* his previously attempted tactical reapprochment with conservative forces in European society. This view would seem to be corroborated by the pope's contemporaneous moves in regard to France—he was starting to persuade French Catholic monarchists to accept the

❖

Third Republic (the *"Ralliement,"* see Jedin, 1981, 9:96-107). In this reading, in sum, the encyclical is to be interpreted as a "progressive" statement, even a "liberal" one.

On the other hand, noting the anti-socialist polemic that dominates the first part of the encyclical *(RN*, §§4-15), one could suppose that the pope was taking a position *aligned with* the "bourgeois" social reform movements of the time and their conservative line in political economy, especially on the matter of private property. (This was Henry George's reading in 1891.) Although the second option is closer to reality than the first, in a rough and ready way, neither interpretation is close enough. Neither one places the encyclical in the great stream of Roman Catholic *resistance to nineteenth-century liberalism,* both political and economic. Even if *RN* was a great departure from previous papal pronouncements on public-policy issues, it came from within that stream.[1] Accordingly, it will not do to seek the roots of RN in the Liberal Catholicism of an Henri Dominique Lacordaire or a Charles de Montalembert, as was the tendency of a Christian Democratic histori-ography after World War II (cf. Jean Marie Mayeur, 1968, p. 41).

## I. Antecedents, but Influences?

Those who are more familiar with nineteenth-century Catholicism in Europe, therefore, look for pronounced anti-liberal champions of the church and the working class as incubators of the papal doctrine in *RN,* a necessary insight. Of course, the "liberalism" in question was not identical with progressivism. It represented in fact the status quo of the late nineteenth-century. In its churchly opponents' eyes, it was the doctrine of sheer individualism and rationalism, and in economics, of laissez faire. It was associated with the new class of property owners, not hereditary landowners but the bourgeois moneyed class. Generally speaking, at least in the Latin countries, "liberal" anticlericalism engendered as great a fear for the future of Christianity as did the growth of socialism.

This being so, the anti-"liberal" social theorists of the arch-Catholic *Union de Fribourg* on an international level, with contacts in Rome (see Paul Misner, 1991, pp. 202-208), seemed to be one of the most likely candidates for Alcide De Gasperi's (1931) category, "the men who prepared *RN.*" They avowed an indebt-edness to Bishop Ketteler, mediated through his Austrian disciple, Karl von Vogelsang (1818-1890). Vogelsang's ambition was to work out a complete and radical alternative to modern capitalism, called "corporatism." In his version, a corporatist organization of the economy would re-associate capital and labor in a given sector through a sort of collective self-administration, sanctioned but not run by the state, of the sector's human and material resources. With a bit of good will, one can see an idea there that surfaced later in Mondragon-style cooperative enterprises—but of course his idea was more grandiose than that and aimed at a thoroughgoing reconstitution of the whole political economy.

At any rate, a French Catholic nobleman and army officer, Rene de La Tour du Pin (1834-1924), took in Vogelsang's theory while he was stationed in Vienna

❖

as a military attache from 1877 to 1881. Subsequently, together with Bishop Gaspard Mermillod (1824-1892), he gathered leading corporatist Catholics together in the aforementioned Fribourg Union. Its studies and reports, discussed at six annual secret meetings in Switzerland and Rome, were communicated to Leo XIII, who let the members know that he was planning a major encyclical on the social question (see Normand Paulhus, 1983, pp. 12-79). This lineage, from Ketteler to Vogelsang to the *"école de La Tour du Pin"* (thus Talmy, 1963), seems so impressive and conspicuous as to be the main channel through which earlier Catholic thought was transmitted to the Vatican drafters of the encyclical. Most historiography of modern Catholicism, until quite recently, has assumed that the pope drew on this school of thought for his ground-breaking encyclical.[2]

What is right about this over-hasty conclusion is the emphasis on Ketteler's role and the realization that he was an opponent of "liberalism." He anticipated all the themes of the encyclical. He criticized the liberal ideology of property while defending private property as a societal good; he focussed on workers' *wages* as the crucial question; he inculcated the role of the *church* in defending and assisting the proletariat; he stressed the mutual duties of employers and employees and the need for *workers' associations* (here he actually endorsed collective bargaining and union strikes to back it up, going further than the encyclical would); and he recognized the necessary, if limited, intervention of the *state* in economic affairs and labor-capital relations (see Misner, 1991, pp. 90-95 and 136-44). But the actual influence supposedly exercised on the making of *RN* by the intermediate links of the chain is unsubstantiated. Leo evidently did *not* come to these views through the mediation of the Fribourg gentlemen, for there is nothing of the distinctive Vogelsangian notions of a "corporative regime" in *RN*.

## II.  Liberatore and the Drafting of *Rerum Novarum*

Matteo Liberatore, it has been known since Giovanni Antonazzi's edition of *RN* in 1957, had a hand in writing and editing the first drafts of the 1891 encyclical. Does this give us any clues as to the antecedents that counted? The way in which the encyclical was worked up seems to indicate that the pope did not cast his net very wide and did not draw the attention of its drafters to the materials furnished by the Fribourg Union. The influences that are traceable proceeded through Matteo Liberatore. On balance, the pope appears to have sought to take a position like those of his socially conscious co-pastors, Ketteler and Henry Edward Manning (Westminster), and perhaps James Gibbons (Baltimore), with a sensitivity as well to other stands already taken by Catholics. The so-called Catholic "schools" on the problem of labor, those of Liege and Angers (Misner, 1991, pp. 190-94 and 208-209), for example, had made the question of state intervention quite controversial among Catholics; the pope wished to step carefully in all such areas, giving each Catholic party its due.

After Antonazzi's publication and analysis of the manuscripts and the discovery of some additional revisions, the redaction history of *RN* can be summed up in four stages (see Camacho, 1986a, p. 221). In the first stage, a Jesuit and a Dominican were requested to write drafts. Matteo Liberatore was the Jesuit and Tommaso Cardinal Zigliara (1833-1893) was the Dominican. The Jesuit's first draft of 5 July 1890 was given to the Dominican, who produced another draft, following Liberatore's organization of the material. At the second stage, the two were merged and translated into Latin. Pope Leo, not satisfied with the overall effect, had his private secretary, Msgr. Gabriele Boccali (1843-1892), reorganize and rewrite the whole letter. This found the pope's approval, but a fourth and final phase did introduce some further revisions in detail, including the famous opening words, *"Rerum novarum semel excitata cupidine . . . ."*

By choosing two Neo-Thomist philosophers to frame his encyclical, and in particular by asking for Liberatore, Leo tapped another "school" of Catholic social thought not much noted in the older historiography, the school of the *Civiltà Cattolica* of the Jesuits in Rome (cf. Aubert in Jedin, 1981, 8:299-300). This periodical had Liberatore on its staff of writers since its founding in 1850 (Droulers, 1962, pp. 133-35). He and other members of the team immediately began drawing out the implications of Thomism for a social philosophy that would prove a better alternative than the prescriptions of either laissezfaire liberalism or collectivist socialism (Misner, 1991, pp. 128-29). In these early issues of the *Civiltà Cattolica* one can find the social-philosophical taproot of *RN*.

## III. Influences on Liberatore

A short time before he was asked to assist with preparation of the encyclical, Liberatore had completed a series of articles in the *Civiltà Cattolica*. The same material was also published in book form and appeared promptly in English translation as *Principles of Political Economy* (1891). As he made clear in the preface, he had written it for the Catholic youth of Italy, in seminaries and in parishes. What he aimed at was a popularization of economic science in the context of a sound moral philosophy. He did not profess to be an expert in economics, but he claimed that he had read "the best professors" of the discipline and made a digest of what they taught, so that young Catholics would not be at a disadvantage in discussing and facing social problems with an economic component or basis.

From this work one can easily determine who passed for authorities in the study of the political economy in his mind. They turn out to be the standard writers that educated, middle-of-the-road Italians would also read. The economic liberalism that pervaded them did not discredit them in Liberatore's eyes *qua* economic teachings, as it did for the Vogelsangians. For example, Liberatore cites Marco Minghetti (1818-86) often and with respect. Minghetti was the leader of *La Destra* (right-wing "liberals") in the Kingdom of Italy before and after the 1870 annexation of the papal states; he had been prominent as a "liberal Catholic" in the papal states themselves; this was during the 1846-47 interlude when it seemed that the papal states might be modernized and declericalized with the blessings of the new pope, Pius IX. His economics, published at Florence in 1858, was explicitly connected

❖

with law *and* morality, which certainly would commend it to Liberatore. As prime minister in 1873-76, he pursued a balanced budget rather too vigorously for his own political longevity.

But Liberatore was not a man of one book in economics. An earlier figure with papal and French connections, whom he cited and critiqued with respect, was Pellegrino Rossi, the lay minister of the papal states who was assassinated on November 15, 1848. Toniolo's teacher, Fedele Lampertico (1833-1906) appears, but not Giuseppe Toniolo himself (1845-1918; cf. Thomas Nitsch, 1990, p. 61)—no doubt because Toniolo had not yet made a name for himself. Of course, behind such Italian writers stood the great names of international economic science. Liberatore displayed a familiarity with some of their works as well, from Adam Smith, Thomas Malthus, and David Ricardo through Jean Simonde de Sismondi and Frederic Bastiat to John Stuart Mill.

In other words, Liberatore discussed mostly the leading figures in the economics of his time, with a slight but noticeable time lag—and without deigning to notice Karl Marx or any other socialist author. Among Catholic authors, two names stand out: those of Charles Perin (1815-1905) of Louvain (especially his *Doctrines économiques depuis un siècle*, 1880), and of Claudio Jannet (1844-1894) in Paris, a conservative social economist (that is, an adept of mitigated economic liberalism; cf. Nitsch, 1990, pp. 56-58) and member of the "Angers" school of social Catholicism. One can conclude that Leo XIII's resident expert had an eclectic but fairly adequate acquaintance with the economic analysis of his time.

Hence what is striking about Liberatore's popularization, in comparison to contemporary Catholic approaches current in Austria, Germany, and France, is the low level of passionate opposition to liberal economics. For a veteran of the struggle against modern liberalism in all its intellectual and social manifestations, this is especially noteworthy. In common with almost all the wings of the French social Catholic movement, he held the French Revolution responsible for forbidding associations of workers. But he tended to follow Perin rather than de La Tour du Pin in holding that industrial capitalism in itself was not the misbegotten product of the demonic Revolution, as was socialism. Industrialization and its attendent capitalistic system of investment incentives, though potentially of positive moral value, were just unfortunately contaminated by a revolutionary, materialistic ideology in practice.

An interesting point bearing on influences is this. Despite the blanket rejection of modern liberalism which the Jesuit authors of the Neo-Thomist revival at the *Civiltà Cattolica* proclaimed, they took some basic modern economic structures for granted (unlike Vogelsang!). Interest on loans, as in capital lent to an enterprise, is one prime example; individual and unentailed ownership of private property is another. It is clear from his book that Liberatore was no more influenced by the Vogelsangian perspective of the Fribourg Union in 1890 than he was in the 1850s. This is reflected in the final text of the encyclical. All the opposition of the corporatist theorists against usury (meaning what others had long called interest), is dismissed in a single throwaway reference (in *RN* #5) to *usura vorax*.

Liberatore thus accepted modern views of money, without ever raising the hoary question of whether all interest paid on loans was not illegitimate. For all this fierceness against the French Revolution, he was not inclined to embrace radical solutions to the problems posed by modern capitalism, as La Tour du Pin and the other theorists of the Fribourg Union were.

Another comparison that turns to Liberatore's advantage emerges most clearly from the appendix to his book, where he presented his main suggestion to cure the ills of the modern economy (pp. 279-95). This was the creation of "Workmen's Associations." (This idea went into his draft for *RN* and survived all the subsequent redactional stages to become the pope's main recommendation to economic agents, *RN*, §§48-61.) There he cited Leon Harmel's (1829-1915) *Corporation chrétienne* as his chief example of how to go about organizing such associations in "industries on a grand scale" (p. 295, as he mistakenly thought Harmel's family firm was). An option was implicitly taken here, probably without reflection, for one of the less paternalistic models of social Catholic action available at that time. Harmel was beginning to see the limits of the approach of *patronage* (which I may define as employer dedication to labor welfare in an anti-emancipatory fashion, encouraging continued dependence on the benevolence of the *patron*; see Misner, 1991, pp. 130-33). Charles Perin, who endorsed the association of workers only in an indissoluble linkage with *patronage*, still represented the standard approach—and of course Frederic Le Play's (1806-82) focus on paternal authority as alone socially salvific went in the same direction. By contrast, Liberatore promoted "workmen's associations" with distinctly unemphatic paternalistic presuppositions, and this carried over into the final version of the encyclical.

## IV. Neo-Thomism, Social Catholicism, and *Rerum Novarum*

I have highlighted the contribution of Matteo Liberatore as the main channel through which influential ideas on economic ethics came to bear on the writing of *RN*, because his role was crucial and is still poorly appreciated. It would be misleading to suggest, however, that the main pillars of Catholic social teaching as expressed in RN rest on him alone. He is rather to be taken as a leading figure in a movement, the Neo Thomistic revival. This was the work of a relatively small band of thinkers, until one of them, Gioacchino Pecci, became Pope Leo XIII. Henceforth (from 1878 to 1903) he occupied a position from which he could and did declare Thomism to be normative for the whole Roman Catholic communion. What Liberatore represented, therefore, was a re-reading of Thomas Aquinas in a context of the ascendancy of nineteenth-century continental liberalism and with an eye to modern problems (cf. Gerald A. McCool, 1989, particularly 145-66 and 226-40). In this connection one should also remember Luigi Taparelli d'Azeglio, S.J. (1793-1862; see Misner, 1991, index s.v.) as well as Salvatore Talamo (1844-1932). The

❖

latter bears looking into as the co-editor with Toniolo of the *Rivista internazionale di scienze sociali* from 1893 to 1927 and philosophy professor at the Apollinare, a pontifical institute in Rome, since 1879.

The reason why these Italian Neo-Thomists were not affected by the romantic economics of Austrian or French provenance seems to lie, paradoxically enough, in the coup de grace of the already moribund scholastic tradition administered by the French Revolution. Like his older colleague, Taparelli, Liberatore was not himself educated in the scholastic tradition; they had to teach themselves scholastic philosophy and rebuild it from scratch. On the matter of private property rights, Thomas Aquinas, whom they cited, was unrepresentative of the prevailing scholastic views before and after him. (But these Neo-Thomists of the first generation had no way of suspecting this and no inclination to do so.) As a rule, the scholastics and other pre-modern teachers held that it was by reason of original sin and the resulting fallen state of humankind that private property, that is the division of goods by individual and family ownership, was justified: it was necessary to prevent still worse evils and disorder due to greed.

Thomas Aquinas came up with another justification, one based in sound human nature apart from sinful inclinations. To him, private property promoted the better care and cultivation of things (it was good for productivity, one might paraphrase). Of course, he did retain the common insistence on the prior destination of all goods of creation for the use and enjoyment of all persons. At any rate, when Taparelli d'Azeglio was faced with the issue of property, he read Thomas in the light of modern arguments, notably John Locke's, and grounded private ownership in a natural-law argument of "liberal" coloration (on all this, see the article, critical in the best sense of the word, by Leon de Sousberghe, 1950, esp. pp. 580 and 594).

Perhaps the most striking contribution of the Neo-Thomist school in *RN* on a clearly economic issue consisted in retrieving the issue of a worker's wages (*RN*, §20, §43) for consideration in the perspective of "that justice that is called *distributive*" (*RN*, §33; the pope continued to see the redistribution of property in other ways than through wages as predominantly a matter of charity, *RN*, §22). The emphasis on the primacy of the person and the personal in economic relations, balanced by the social interdependence intrinsic to existence as persons, was the guiding principle of Neo-Thomistic philosophical anthropology that shaped its entire social teaching and was prominently placed in the encyclical (*RN*, §20, §40). This foundation was laid methodically already in the early years of the *Civiltà Cattolica*. Although not a systematic thinker like these pioneer Neo-Thomist philosophers, Bishop Ketteler, with his ingrained anti-absolutism, found the same center of gravity in his emphasis on human dignity and drew from it similar social-policy implications.

Short of a thoroughgoing archival investigation of possible other influences on Pope Leo XIII and his approach to the social problem of the nineteenth century in *RN*, then, it would seem that the prominent role of the corporatist theorists led by Vogelsang and La Tour du Pin did not have as much to do with the social teaching

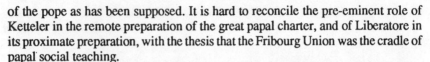

of the pope as has been supposed. It is hard to reconcile the pre-eminent role of Ketteler in the remote preparation of the great papal charter, and of Liberatore in its proximate preparation, with the thesis that the Fribourg Union was the cradle of papal social teaching.

A reconciliation of a different kind might be discernible by hindsight, however. One might interpret *RN* as a convergence of elements in the social thought of liberals and of Catholics in the making. It was not to be apparent to any engaged participant for several decades to come. But when it did become apparent, the social Catholic tradition initially enshrined in *RN* was one of the main avenues of rapprochement between the Roman Catholic Church and the modern world. In this perspective, the present pontiff's "re-reading" of *RN* in his encyclical, *Centesimus Annus*, might be indicative (John Paul II, 1991, §§6-9). The revolutionary "Rights of Man" have become "human rights," and the Roman Catholic hierarchy, in many cases throughout the world, has become their champion. Who could deny that this stands in moral continuity with the urgings of *RN*?

## Endnotes

*Associate Professor, Theology Department, Marquette University, Milwaukee, WI 53233 USA.

[1] The scholar who has emphasized this anti-liberal character of normative Catholicism in the nineteenth century most forcefully is Emile Poulat; see Jean-Marie Mayeur, 1986, pp. 39-45, for an appreciative critique.

[2] The inconsistency of this assumption with the other assumed channel of filiation, Liberal Catholicism, was hardly noted before Poulat's works drew attention to it. Molette and Talmy in the 1960s, for example, like the authoritative Henri Rollet in his article on Albert de Mun (1841-1914) in *Catholicisme*, 9:848, do not doubt the actual influence of the Fribourg Union studies on the papal teaching. By way of contrast, cf. Levillain, 1983.

## References

Antonazzi, Giovanni. *L'Enciclica Rerum novarum: Testo autentico e redazioni preparatorie dai documenti originali,* Rome: Edizioni di Storia e Letteratura, 1957.

Camacho, Ildefonso. (1986a) "La chiesa di fronte al liberalismo e al socialismo: Per una interpretatzione piu completa della 'Rerum Novarum'," *Civiltà Cattolica* (1 February 1986), 137/I, 219-33.

_____. (1986b) "La propiedad privada en la 'Rerum novarum.' Proceso redaccional y texto definitivo de la enciclica," *Miscellanea Augusto Segovia,* Granada: Faculty of Theology, 1986, pp. 303-42.

❖

Carlen, Claudia, ed. *The Papal Encyclicals,* Wilmington NC: McGrath, 1981.

De Gasperi, Alcide. I *tempi e gli uomini che prepararono la "Rerum Novarum",* Milan: Vita e Pensiero, 1984 (originally published under a pseudonym in 1931).

Droulers, Paul. "Question sociale, Etat, Eglise, dans la `Civiltà Cattolica' ¡a ses débuts," *Chiesa e Stato nell'Ottocento: Miscellanea in onore di Pietro Pirri,* 1:123-47, Padua: Antenore, 1962.

Ederer, Rupert J., ed. and tr. *The Social Teachings of Wilhelm Emmanuel von Ketteler,* Lanham, MD: University Press of America, 1981.

George, Henry. (1891) "The Condition of Labor. An Open Letter to Pope Leo XIII," *Complete Works of Henry George, 3,* New York: Doubleday Page, 1906.

Jedin, Hubert, gen. ed. *History of the Church, 8* and *9,* by Roger Aubert, Oskar Kohler et al., New York: Crossroad, 1981.

John Paul II. "*Centesimus Annus,*" Origins, May 1991, *21,* 1-24.

Levillain, Philippe. *Albert de Mun: Catholicisme francais et catholicisme romain du Syllabus au Ralliement,* Rome: Ecole Francaise de Rome, 1983.

Liberatore, Matteo. *Principles of Political Economy,* New York: Benziger, 1891.

Mayeur, Jean-Marie. *Un prête démocrate, l'abbé Lemire (1853-1928),* Paris: Casterman, 1968.

_____. *Catholicisme social et démocratie chrétienne,* Paris: Cerf, 1986.

McCool, Gerald A. *Nineteenth-Century Scholasticism: The Search for a Unitary Method,* New York: Fordham University Press, 1989.

Misner, Paul. *Social Catholicism in Europe: From the Onset of Industrialization to the First World War,* New York: Crossroad, 1991.

Molette, Charles. *Albert de Mun 1872-1890: Exigence doctrinale et préoccupations sociales chez un laic catholique,* Paris: Beauchesne, 1970.

Mueller, Franz H. *The Church and the Social Question,* Washington: American Enterprise Institute, 1984.

Nitsch, Thomas O. "Social Economics: The First 200 Years," *Social Economics: Retrospect and Prospect,* 5-90, ed. by Mark A. Lutz, Boston: Kluwer, 1990.

Paulhus, Normand. "The Theological and Political Ideals of the Fribourg Union," Ph.D. dissertation, Boston College, 1983.

Poulat, Emile. *Eglise contre bourgeoisie: Introduction au devenir du catholicisme actuel,* Paris: Casterman, 1977.

Rollet, Henri. *L'action sociale des catholiques en France (1871-1914),* Paris: Desclee de Brouwers, 1947-58.

❖

Sousberghe, Léon de. "Propriété de `droit naturel': These néo-scolastique et tradition scolastique," *Nouvelle Revue Théologique*, 1950, 72, 480-607.

Talmy, Robert. *Aux sources du Catholicisme social: L'école de La Tour Du Pin*, Tournai: Desclee, 1963.

❖

# Teaching Social Economics in the Principles Course

## *Gerard L. Stockhausen\**

What should a social economist do when teaching a principles course? Teach the principles. In the micro course, this means supply and demand in the product and resource markets, price and output decisions for the firm under various market conditions, and market failure and appropriate government response. In the macro course it means the interrelationship of the economic aggregates, fiscal and monetary policy, unemployment and inflation, and some of the major disputes. This neoclassical synthesis is valuable and powerful. Furthermore, all the other economics courses that students take will assume and build on this material in the principles courses, so it cannot be ignored or treated lightly. Therefore it should be taught well.

I would not call myself a social economist, however, if I did not have serious questions about the neoclassical paradigm. How does this show up in my teaching? What does social economics add to or replace in neoclassical economics? One obvious place to find a definition is in the aims and objectives of the Association for Social Economics. These were defined in 1970 as follows (taken from the 1987 membership directory).[1]

> To foster research and publication centered on the reciprocal relation-
> ship between economic science and broader questions of human
> dignity, ethical values, and social philosophy. The Association strives
> to encourage the efforts of all scholars who are dedicated to exploring
> the ethical and social presuppositions of economic science.

> To consider the personal and social dimension of economic problems
> and to assist with a concern for ethical values in a pluralistic commu-
> nity and the demands of personal dignity.

❖

The *Review of Social Economy,* published by the Association acts as a forceful, critical expression of the centrality of ethical value in economic life and in economic research.

This emphasis on ethics and values suggests strongly that social economics adds an explicitly normative dimension to economics, one that is humanistic and communitarian, and therefore balances the rationalistic and individualistic bias of neoclassical economics.

This leaves the field sufficiently broad that a great deal of non-mainstream material would fall under the rubric of social economics. If social economics were an entirely separate body of material, then I would have to say that teaching social economics has not been a goal of mine. Teaching the basics of neoclassical micro and macro analysis has been a goal. In addition to that, I have had two other goals in teaching principles courses over the last six years. One has been to introduce elements of Roman Catholic social teaching into my courses. The other has been to raise questions about the unrestrained free market approach to economic organization. Unfortunately, I find that the first goal—more commonly described as "covering the material"—often dominates the other two.

In what follows I will first try to describe some of the relevant characteristics of the students I teach, then lay out three approaches that I have used to teach social economics in the principles course, and finally suggest a more integrated approach for future experimentation.

## I. Characteristics of the Student Population

This may seem like a surprising place to start. However, talking about the students reveals some of the obstacles one faces in teaching social economics. Based on my experience I find three student characteristics that I would describe as obstacles.

In the first place, most of my students want practical knowledge; they do not want to "waste" their time learning things for which they cannot imagine a profitable use. This tends to make most of them allergic to economic modeling. They find it difficult to appreciate the role of abstraction and simplifying assumptions, and quickly conclude that "economics is nice in theory, but the real world doesn't work that way." It should be noted that the "real world" is based more often on anecdotal information than on statistical study. Obviously, this makes the teaching of neoclassical economics itself difficult, even if one were not interested in social economics. One result is that more time must be spent teaching the basics, leaving less time for anything else. Another is that students who are not interested in the models themselves will be even less interested in the assumptions that underlie those models.

Secondly, students tend to come in (and usually leave) imbued with American individualism and a strong faith in the Horatio Alger myth of success. They tend to be suspicious of the societal dimension that social economics introduces. Since they intend to work hard (and therefore be successful), they fear that this social ethic will be an attempt to justify redistributing their earnings to the unsuccessful (who are by definition lazy).

Finally, students tend to be subjectivists. By that I mean that for most of them there is no objective truth, no right or wrong, in fields such as philosophy, theology, and especially ethics; it is all a matter of opinion, and, much to the consternation of our colleagues in theology and philosophy, "my opinion is just as good as your opinion." Many students have little stomach for a sustained argument that begins with ethical principles and works its way to conclusions about proper individual action, much less the proper arrangement of the social or economic order.[2] This is clearly bad news for social conomics.

On the positive side, however, there are two qualities that make the task easier. In the first place, students tend to have a strong gut-level sense of fairness. Those who work hard should be rewarded, and those who do not work hard should not.[3]

On the one hand, this makes them angry at welfare cheats, but if they can be convinced that there really are people who work hard but are not rewarded by the economic system, they become equally incensed.

In addition, students starting out in the business college are not yet convinced that "what is good for General Motors is good for America." They can hear criticism without walking away.[4]

Given this background about the students I teach, I will speak about three approaches to introducing social economics in the principles courses. I will begin with the least helpful and move to the more helpful.

## II. Approaches to Teaching Social Economics

I want to make my goals more explicit by way of contrast. In a session on this topic at the 1990 meeting of the Midwest Economic Association, Mark Lutz described how he teaches the neoclassical paradigm and his own approach—which he terms "humanistic economics"—in parallel tracks in the same course. What I attempt is not that ambitious. I insist that they learn the basic tools of neoclassical economics, but I also hope they have some questions about it and know some of its limitations by the time they are finished. In other words, I want them to know that there is more to economics than the neoclassical approach.

## III. Challenging the Neoclassical Theory

As one who is often more at home in the theoretical than the applied world, I am tempted to begin by questioning the presuppositions and criticizing the view of the human person on which the neoclassical paradigm is based. This could involve exploring whether utilitarianism provides a sufficient ethical base for an economic system, trying to distinguish between wants and needs, and questioning

❖

the view of the human person as a self-interest-maximizing rational calculator of utility. It could include the marxist critique of wage labor as exploitation and law, culture, and politics as ideological defenses of the economic system. It could also include the critique of capital made by Chamberlin and Robinson.

While I find all of these topics interesting and important, I think that, for the most part, raising these issues in the principles course is a mistake, or at least counterproductive. (If I do raise them at all, I do so parenthetically.) While I am personally drawn to this sort of critique, I think it is appropriate only after one has come to appreciate the power and usefulness of the neoclassical model. My experience is that trying to call that model into question at the same time that I teach it leads to questions such as: "If you don't think it's right, why do you teach it, and why should we learn it?" or "Why don't you spare us all the theoretical disagreements and just tell us what we need to know?" This is especially true if students see disagreements about presuppositions as simply matters of opinion, and think that one person's opinion is just as good as another's.

Whether or not capital can be measured or labor is exploited or utils exist or "economic man" is an accurate view of the human person, from the students' point of view the tools of economic analysis at the principles level remain much the same. Even raising questions about the limits within which it is appropriate to use the economic model runs the risk of giving students a double message: "I want you to learn this well and be able to use it, but don't learn it so well you want to use it all of the time."

## IV.  Studying Texts that Embody Social Economic Thought

Rather than critiquing the neoclassical model directly at the same time that I am trying to teach it, I find it is often more helpful to have students read and react to statements of church leaders on economic issues.[5]

For example, toward the end of the micro principles course I may have my students read the first half of *Economic Justice for All (EJA)*, with its biblical perspective on and ethical norms for an economy, and write an essay that either critiques the course in the light of the reading or critiques the reading in the light of the course.[6] Similarly, toward the end of the macro principles course I may have them do the same thing with the rest of the letter, with special emphasis on the way it approaches particular issues such as employment, poverty, food and agriculture, and the United States and developing countries.

In the same way, I use encyclicals and other statements by church figures as well as pertinent articles, editorials, and letters to the editor from various publications.

The advantage of using church documents or articles discussing them is that the values tend to be familiar and the ethical/moral norms explicit. This invites students to see that some members—and leading members at that—of the faith community see important connections between religious belief and economic arrangements. Even if they reject the argument, they have to engage it somehow.

A further advantage of this approach is that some of these documents question and critique the economic model and its presuppositions along the lines of the first approach described above. Why do I call that a good thing when I just said it does not work? I find the documents helpful in this area because they are third-party critiques. In other words, I can present the economic model and at the same time challenge the students to understand the pope's critique of it rather than my critique of it. Thus they are exposed to the critique without identifying me as teacher with two contradictory views.

The disadvantage of this approach is that it runs up against the student mindset that sees values and ethical or moral norms as purely subjective, unable to make any claim on them. Ironically, many students react the same way to both Catholic social teaching and the economic model. They say: "These principles are very good in theory, but they are just not practical in the real world."

Whereas I try to avoid the first approach above—the direct critique, I still use this second approach with some regularity despite this drawback for three reasons. First, I am very much at home with these documents, especially those in the Catholic tradition. Second, church documents tend to express their critique in a language that is accessible to students, whether or not they agree. Third, since I teach in a Catholic school, I believe not only that the resources of that tradition are appropriate for classroom use, but that I would be remiss if I did not expose my students to them.

Given students' preference for the practical and concrete, however, these normative statements and documents need to be supplemented with something from the "real world" that will get at some of these same issues. It is to that approach that I now turn.

## V. "Raising Consciousness" by Posing Hard Questions

My frustration with the first approach and the limitations of the second have led me to a third approach. I present the students with concrete situations in which the free market outcome is problematic. Then I ask them to propose and defend a policy response. Given what I said above about students' sense of fairness and embracing the success myth, the best situations for this approach are those in which people experience hardship despite the fact that they work hard and do everything right. My favorite issue here is that of "price-gouging" in the presence of a natural disaster.

The advantage of this approach is that it allows the students to see the power of the neoclassical analysis and the efficiency of scarcity pricing, while it also forces them to ask questions about relative claims of equity and efficiency. It reinforces their learning of the tools of economic analysis at the same time that it raises questions (rather than gives answers) about the free market outcome. It also avoids the theory-vs-real-world split.[7]

The downside of this approach is that "opinion" carries great weight in this setting since many students see no hierarchy of values—all have the same standing.

❖

At least in the second approach students have to wrestle with documents that are explicit about their norms and values. In this third approach, the only values and norms involved are the ones the students recognize. And whereas fairness tends to be an accepted moral norm, care for the poor (much less a preferential option for the poor) is not.

Cases can of course be drawn from the daily press and from publications of the Federal Reserve Banks. In addition many publishers offer collections of cases as supplements to their principles texts. After using a few of these supplements, I tend to favor picking and choosing, partly because of the expense of textbooks and because most supplements have more cases than I can get to in a semester or year, but mainly because I find only a few cases in any one book have the social/ethical issues in the forefront.

## VI. An "Ideal" Treatment of Social Economics

In the best of all possible worlds I would have my own text or at least my own supplement to the standard principles text. It would both highlight the power of economic analysis and demonstrate the limits of that analysis. Until I get my supplement written and published, however, I will have to be satisfied with doing at least some of the following in the principles courses. All of this, of course, must be kept in context of the three approaches described above. While some of these issues can be dealt with directly, an indirect method—presenting students with two sides of an argument or with a concrete situation that illustrates the point—is probably more productive.

## VII. Microeconomics

Most textbooks describe economics as the science concerned with the allocation of limited or scarce resources for the satisfaction of unlimited human wants. It is important to at least raise the question of the difference between wants and needs, and point out that calling everything a want places outlandish luxuries and the bare bones of subsistence on the same level of priority. Even the satisfaction of wants is only the means to a greater end that is something like human happiness or living well. Put in those terms, ethics (how does a human being live well) and values (which things in life are more important and which are less important) clearly need to underlie any discussion of economics.

Another approach to this is to say that economics is a mode of analysis, a powerful tool, whose appropriateness is nevertheless determined by the end it serves. Economics cannot tell me how to choose among ends, or even tell whether a particular means is appropriate to the chosen end. What it can tell is the cost of various means in terms of economic resources. In other words it can choose the most efficient or least costly means to a particular end. But efficiency, the value that economics is built around, is only one value among many.

These points need to be made explicit again when considering demand. Demand for a good, and therefore the monetary value placed on it, is of course dependent on the given distribution of purchasing power. The wants of the wealthy are backed up by more "dollar votes" than the needs of the poor. Therefore the equilibrium price and quantity determined by supply and demand analysis depend crucially on income and wealth distribution, over and above any externalities involved. This means that even if there are no externalities, the equilibrium outcome has no necessary relationship to the outcome that most supports an individual's or a society's values. Despite this, non-equilibrium results are termed "inefficient" or "distorted" even if they lead to a more highly valued outcome than the "efficient" or "non-distorted" result.

More specifically, taxes and other government policy measures such as pollution controls and health and safety regulations are described as having a "distortionary" effect in that they induce something other than the free market equilibrium result. This terminology can suggest that the optimal result is that in which there is no government, no matter the initial distribution of income, wealth, and power. It also ignores the public goods that those taxes pay for, public goods that help to indicate what a society values. This anti-government bias is reinforced by textbooks emphasizing public choice theory, that sees legislators as only self-interested vote-maximizers. This also illustrates "economic imperialism": economists proudly teaching other social scientists to view the human person as a one-dimensional self-interest maximizer.

Of course this basic assumption of the economic model must also be challenged. There is more to the human person than calculating self-interest and maximizing self-gain, and that "more" enters into economic decisions. Otherwise, being rational is equated with choosing what is best for the self, regardless of what may be best for the larger groups of which that self is a part.

This reduction of the human person to one dimension is also present when economics treats human labor as simply one of several inputs into the production process. Students should be encouraged to consider how the workplace produces people as well as products and services, and how laying off workers is qualitatively different from idling machines or leaving intermediate goods and raw materials unused. This is especially true since many of our students see themselves on the success track, more likely making decisions about others rather than being subject to the decisions of others. If the teacher has thick enough skin (given the anti-union bias of most of our students), he or she might even defend unions as "leveling the playing field" rather than "distorting" the equilibrium result in the labor market.

When dealing with international trade, while making the arguments for free trade as opposed to protection, it is important to show the crucial use of the compensation principle. While it may be possible for the winners to pay off the losers and have something left over, unless the losers actually receive compensation, it is not clear that trade makes society better off.

Finally, most students have only fuzzy notions of income distribution and related statistics. Therefore, a survey of the facts is important.

## VIII. Macroeconomics

Most textbooks use the circular flow model to illustrate both national income accounting and the Keynesian system generally. This model shows financial flows going in one direction and real flows going in the other. This can leave the impression that the two flows are similar. But, whereas money is not subject to entropy, real flows are. Thus, scarce resources get used up and waste is produced. The circular flow model also treats human labor as simply one of several economic resources that are hired by firms and so bring income to the household sector.

In microeconomics environmental concerns are considered under the heading of externalities. They may get half of a chapter, but are assumed away from there on. The only mention environmental issues get in macroeconomics is in the GNP accounting (GNP does not measure social welfare) and growth (pollution concerns are not a sufficient reason to be anti-growth) sections, and often the second of these is dropped. Students tend to feel more passion about the environment than I do, so any teaching objectives that can be attached to it should have a good chance of success.

Many students seem to believe unquestioningly the supply-side claims about the disincentive effects of taxes. Couple this with what they learn in micro about the "distortionary" impact of taxes discussed above, and it feeds into the strong anti-tax mood that they pick up at home. Therefore, it is important to lay out the argument for financing public goods by means of taxes based on ability to pay rather than benefits received.

Most texts spend a chapter on unemployment and inflation, usually including some discussion of the costs of each. This is a fine opportunity to make the point that "noneconomic" costs are just as important as "economic" costs, and need to be considered in policy making.

Finally, whereas texts cover the "crowding out" of private investment spending when government spending raises interest rates, they often ignore two things. One is that government capital spending is a socially necessary form of investment; the other is that such government investment can make private investment more productive, and therefore encourage rather than discourage it— a process one of my colleagues refers to as "crowding in."

## IX. Resources

What resources do I find helpful? For documents I use all or parts of recent statements of Catholic social teaching such as *EJA, Sollicitudo Rei Socialis (SS), Laborem Exercens (LE),* and (next time around) *Centesimus Annus (CA).* I keep an

❖

eye on *Origins,* the documentary service of the U.S. Catholic Conference, for other possibilities.

To raise issues, I use controversial columns or editorials in the *Wall Street Journal (WSJ).* These often attract rebuttals in other columns or letters to the editor. Then I have the students read both and write a short essay in which they pick a side and defend it.

The following are some issues (in no particular order) around which discussion could be built in order to bring out some of the points made above: product liability; pollution and acid rain; tobacco, sugar, and other agriculture policy; deregulation; industrial policy and planning; bailouts; social security; comparable worth; mergers; plant closings; parental leave; minimum wage; welfare; budget deficits; protection; LDC debt; illegal drugs; national health care or insurance; sustainability vs. growth; forced conservation; inheritance taxes; progressivity of taxes.

## X. Conclusion

Teaching social economics in the principles course is important because it may be the only exposure most students have to many of these issues. Nevertheless, the focus must remain on the principles themselves lest our students be at a loss in higher-level courses. Given this need to "cover the material", there is not room for massive theoretical detours. What we can do is expose them to some sources of reflection on economics and society. We can also challenge them to think about the real-world implications of what they study in ways that encourage them to keep the human questions in the forefront.

## Endnotes

*Associate Professor of Economics, Department of Economics and Finance, College of Business Administration, Creighton University, Omaha, NE 68178 USA.

[1] See Lutz (1990) for a more lengthy discussion of social economics as distinguished from the more recently defined socioeconomics.

[2] This resistance is perhaps also due to their suspicion that any critique of "the way things are" is calling into question the system by which they have benefitted so far and in which they hope to benefit the rest of their lives.

[3] Any teacher who has tried to explain to a student who claims to have worked hard why s/he got a low grade knows well this attitude.

[4] Thanks to a conversation with Richard Coronado, I apologize for not adding another positive trait of students, namely generosity. This trait gets them involved in service projects that will likely impact their lives and attitudes more powerfully than the best of principles courses.

❖

⁵ Chief among these statements would be those which express Catholic social thought, a body of thought reflected in a set of pronouncements by the Pope or national/ regional assemblies of bishops which deal with social and economic matters. The first of these is commemorated by this conference, and the most recent was issued in May of this year. The documents generally included in this list are: *Rerum Novarum*, 1891; *Quadragesimo Anno*, 1931; *Mater et Magistra*, 1961; *Pacem in Terris*, 1963; *Gaudium et Spes*, 1965; *Populorum Progressio*, 1967; *Medellin Documents*, 1968; *Octogesima Adveniens*, 1971; *Justice in the World*, 1971; *Puebla Document*, 1979; *Laborem Exercens*, 1981; *The Challenge of Peace*, 1983; *Economic Justice for All*, 1986; *Sollicitudo Rei Socialis*, 1988; and *Centesimus Annus*, 1991. Related texts I find useful include *An Ethical Approach to the International Debt Question*, 1987, by the Pontifical Justice and Peace Commission, and *Relieving Third World Debt: A Call to Coresponsibility, Justice, and Solidarity*, 1989, by the United States Catholic Conference Administrative Board.

⁶ Since Creighton has a policy of encouraging "writing across the curriculum" in its undergraduate courses, this approach kills two birds with one stone.

⁷ Perhaps the reason this method is effective is that it allows students to picture themselves on the losing side of an economic situation. This points to a more general strategy—that of enlarging the "we" and "us" by which students view the effects of economic decisions.

## References

Lutz, Mark. "Emphasizing the Social: Social Economics and SocioEconomics." *Review of Social Economy*, 1990, 48, pp. 303-320.

Lutz, Mark and Kenneth Lux. *Humanistic Economics:* The New Challenge. New York, The Bootstrap Press, 1988.

# OIKONOMIA & the Environment/ XPHMATA & the Ozone Layer: Aristotle, Scitovsky, et al. Revisited & Visited (Abstract)

## Thomas O. Nitsch*

Properly understood, translated and interpreted, the original Aristotelian conception of the prudent management or administration of the family household or estate (*oikonomia*) and its *disciplina, oikonomikē*, is exactly what Oscar Lange (art. cit., 1945-46) and Tibor Scitovsky (op. cit., 1951; rev. ed., 1971) have in mind with their definition of economics as a social science concerned with the efficient administration of scarce resources — granted that, in their case, Aristotle's *oikos* would have to be writ much larger, viz. to the human-society level.

For, for Aristotle in his *Nicomachean Ethics* (I.i; VI,viii) and the *Politics* (I), and his pupil Theophrastus of the pseudo-Aristotelian *Oeconomica* I, that *oikonomia* and *oikonomikē* were truly the prudential art and practical or applied science of wealth or riches (*ploutos*), specifically of the necessary acquisition and proper utilization thereof. And the multifarious components of that collectivity were the various *chrēmata*, or useful-things, "choses utiles," i.e. *resources* in our modern parlance. Alternatively, Aristotle (*Pol.* I) and Theophrastus (*Oecon.* I) following him (it) analyzed that household into its constutent parts (*meroi*) of the human members (family, slaves, visitors), livestock, deadstock, the homestead itself and other buildings, inventories and lands; i.e., the human animal, and inanimate resources, assets, property, or — as we might say — *capital*. And, all of these lower forms were to be administered or managed so as to promote the "health and well-being" *(hygieia kai euēmeria)* of the human members. Now, are we not reminded immediately here of A. Marshall's "study of ... individual and social action [aimed at] the attainment and the use of the material requisites of wellbeing" (*Principles*, 8th ed., 1920)?

❖

And, just as Theophrastus might have added — had it not been axiomatic — when he noted (*Oecon.* I, vi) that the homestead should be erected so that it "be airy in the summer and sunny in winter" that — similarly, for the health and well-being of its occupants — its roof be kept in good repair to keep out rain etc., so today were those sages and lovers of wisdom with us they would counsel that we must administer prudently, use wisely, and keep in good repair the ultimate roof of the human *oikos*, viz. the ozone layer. Similar considerations of good economy and sound economics apply to other components of our "natural endowment," "physical environment," etc.; viz., the rain-forests, earth's atmosphere, etc.

But, the problem is that we tend to think of environmental protection, preservation, etc. as the antithesis of economic growth, development, etc.; i.e., of the former as "ecological" and the latter as "economical" concerns. Otherwise, the degradation (depreciation, depletion, despoilation) of our physical environment or natural endowment is regarded as a negative "externality." Our argument is that this is the case only relative to the narrower focus of the market-place; the roof over the family's head is part of the *oikos*, not external to it! From the point of view of the *anthrōpon oikon*, whatever affects the ozone layer is an *internality*; and similarly, for the rain-forests etc. As Scitovsky would also immediately recognize (op.cit., 1971) that ozone layer is a once-free resource now become very scarce, hence to be utilized efficiently (Aristotle: "prudently").

In the ideological sphere of influence, the present Pontiff has recently released two significant pronouncements on the environment (John Paul II, Oct. 1989; 1 Jan. 1990), wherein – unfortunately – the deleterious dichotomy is reinforced; i.e., "the ecological question" is not regarded as a, or put in the context of the, "social question." Earlier (**SRS**, 1986, §34) and later (**CA**, 1991, §§37, 40) this was not the case; good-stewarding of the physical environment is treated in the context of two significant "social encyclicals"; but, even in the latter, *"the ecological question"* is regarded subsidiarily, as attendant to "the problem of consumerism" (§37).

*Professor of Economics, Creighton University.

# Imported Technology and the Return to the Market Economy in the U.S.S.R.

## *Priyatosh Maitra\**

The collapse of so-called socialist economics has raised some fundamental questions, viz.:

(a) Whether a socialist economy could be built in a pre-capitalist society, as in the Russian experiment/experience.

(b) Whether a socialist system could fulfill its aims, social, political and economic, when it is based on technology imported from a capitalist society, recognizing that Russia's socialist development from the start was based on Western capitalist technology.

(c) Both non-Marxist and Marxist schools of Development Economics consider that capitalist transformation of an economy is an essential condition for economic development with the difference that Marxists believe that capitalist transformation is an essential half-way house through to the ultimate socialist development and not by itself the ultimate destination as non-Marxists economists see it. Does the recent collapse of Socialism in the Soviet Union and its return to the market system prove the non-Marxist contention, i.e. capitalist development is the ultimate?

(d) Can a borrowed technology, when it is at its mature, intensive phase, bring about the complete capitalist transformation of a economy? The U.S.S.R. during the New Economic Policy (NEP) period did not show any sign of such transformation—neither does the Indian economy today. (See Tables at the end of my paper "Technology Transfer and the Capitalist Transformation of an Economy" included in this volume).

(e) Is the first country of the capitalist development the first candidate for the real Marxist Socialist Revolution which as a consequence will bring about World Socialist Revolution?

❖

These questions have come to the surface with the recent movement of socialist economies toward market economies. In the limited space of this paper, we have tried to deal with some of these questions using experiences of the socialist development in the U.S.S.R. and its ultimate demise. We will analyze basic features of socialist development in Soviet Russia and the economic reasons for its collapse and attempt to return to a market system. We will also add a brief note on the social-market policy of Gorbachev as against Yeltsin's free-market policy.

## I. The Three Stages in the U.S.S.R.

Three stages have marked the building of the socialist economy in the USSR. These three stages are distinguished by their basic differences in approach. They are: (1) War Communism, (2) Lenin's New Economic Policy and (3) Stalin's "Industry First or Great Leap Forward."

### A. Stage 1: War Communism

The first stage is known as that of War Communism, a temporary policy devised to solve the serious crises caused by the First World War. The policy included nationalization of property and major industries. Because of the prevailing chaotic state of the society, the introduction of a barter economy replaced money exchange. Under War Communism strict labour discipline and the abolition of strikes was decreed in an attempt to create some sort of order. The policy of nationalization of production meant that the Russian government had to bring production and distribution under state control so that resources were properly mobilized, and production and its distribution carried out to meet defense and essential needs of all people. However, former factory owners and managers, as well as many professional bureaucrats from the Tsarist period, were retained in order to keep the economy and society viable. But it was essentially a temporary measure. It should be noted that to save socialism, people all over the country were highly cooperative with the Soviet government, which made the war efforts a great success for a new society born out of the Revolution. This could be interpreted to indicate that the socialist social consciousness that brought about the Socialist Revolution was strong and highly organized, which could have been mobilized and organized into the building of the world's first socialist economy with its own technology to fulfil the aim of Socialism.

According to Marx, the dialectical contradiction between the organized social consciousness and environment is the only factor that determines the nature of technological change in a Society. However, the question that troubled Lenin and other leaders of the Revolution was whether the Russian society was ripe for immediate socialist development, i.e. whether capitalist development in Russia had reached its mature phase as the pre-condition for a complete socialist reconstruction. Lenin wanted to apply the Marxist economic theories in his analysis to Russian society. In his view, the workers were illiterate or poorly educated and could not take over the reigns of government and the economy as Marx envisaged. It is well known that Marx thought that a mature capitalist country like England would have the first socialist revolution. One explanation, following Marx, may be that the capitalist technology evolved from its traditional technology in England as reflected in rapid structural change (i.e. a change in sectoral distribution of the labour force away from agriculture to industry and then to tertiary activities) indicating the complete capitalist transformation of the society (cf. Maitra, "Technology Transfer etc.," infra). Other capitalist countries in Europe gradually attained complete capitalist transformation of their society, even though, unlike countries in the Third World, the former countries imported capitalism from the UK. When the Western European countries began to import technology from the UK, technology in Britain was at its extensive phase of increasing labour absorption, thus generating the forces of capitalist transformation of the economy via structural change. This change was slower in other European countries than in the UK (cf. Maitra, 1980 and 1986, Chs. I and IV). This is evident from Table 1 appended.[1] In the case of the Third World, capitalism in the West reached its mature intensive phase of dispensing with labour as a result of the transformation of competitive capitalism into the monopolistic competition of multinationalism.

## B. Stage II: New Economic Policy

The second stage of the socialist construction is marked by Lenin's NEP (although the concept of NEP was first envisaged by Trotsky). In Soviet Russia at the time of the Socialist Revolution, an overwhelming majority of the population—over 90 percent—were peasants eking out a basic subsistence in the countryside, while the urban proletariat were only a small percentage of Russia's population with about five percent in manufacturing. At the time of the revolution, Russia had had sixty years of imported capitalism from the West since the introduction of Peter the Great's policy of Westernization in the 1860's. We will later take a brief look at the foreign investment in Russia's industrialisation before the revolution of 1917.

Under the circumstances, we cannot say that Russian society at that stage underwent any substantial capitalist transformation. The question whether a society could proceed to socialism without having passed through substantial growth of capitalism was raised by the Russian Village Commune Movement when Marx visited Moscow in 1880 and 1882. The Russian village commune (movement) idea was in Marx's thoughts when he raised a question in 1882; viz., can the Russian 'Obshchina', though greatly undermined, as a form of the primaeval common ownership of land, pass directly to the higher form of communist ownership? Or, on the contrary, must it pass through the same process of dissolution such as constituted the historical evolution of the West (Marx 1948, p.104)? Marx himself responded as follows: "The only answer to that possibility today is this: if the Russian Revolution becomes the signal for a proletarian revolution in the West, so that both complement each other, the present Russian common ownership of

❖

land may serve as the starting point for a communist development" (Marx 1948, p. 104).

However, in no other country in Western Europe has a proletarian revolution taken place even after the 1917 Russian socialist revolution. The rapid increase of markets for Western capital and technology all over the world since the industrial revolution has created an enormous demand for labour relative to its supply in Western capitalist countries bringing affluence to the workers and therefore, a proletarian revolution has no appeal to them. Yet, it is significant to note here that, in *Anti-Dühring* (1947, p. 133), Engels wrote that in the original state of nature, man had held land in common, so that perhaps a communal (*obschina*) seed of socialism has been preserved in the Mir (the village commune). And, a primitive socialist consciousness fostered by the 'Mir' might thusly provide an important spark for a communist revolution in Russia.

It has been concluded by Roy D. Laird and Betty A. Laird (1978) that Bolshevism could never have come to power had not a peasant revolution occurred throughout the countryside. The events of 1917 were surely determined by the inadequacies of the 1861 emancipation; certainly the course became unchangeable when the agrarian reforms of 1906-11 proved to be too little and too late.

The Russian revolution was, unquestionably, a reflection of a high level of communist consciousness which led to the overthrow of the Tsardom and established a socialist state. But the question that remains is about the nature of communist industrialisation that followed after the revolution (Maitra 1986, Chaps. I & IV). It is more or less an accepted view that the NEP was an attempt to introduce capitalism under state control or popularly known as State Capitalism in the Soviet Union. However, Lenin described the NEP as a temporary step backwards allowing private ownership and imports of machinery via concessions. During the NEP, syndicates were allowed to enter directly into trade agreements and also permitted to receive credits from foreign banks and from Soviet institutions. While the Left group within the Bolshevik party led by Trotsky and Preobrazensky strongly advocated a rapid development of domestic machinery in a "trade independent pattern" of industrial growth, the Right group with Bukharin and Shanin wanted an expansion of agriculture and adequate flow of raw materials for use in rapid industrial development with Western capital. NEP has been characterised as a step towards accommodation to reluctant peasants, a temporary measure to utilize the knowledge and experiences of capitalists and a Bolshevik policy to arrest decline.[2]

Lenin introduced as a transitory measure the New Economic Policy of State control of capital goods, industries, infrastructure and large-scale factory production, together with a private sector for agriculture and small manufacturing production. Internal trade was left to the private sector. The NEP, in Lenin's mind, was a short-term strategy in preparing the ground for ultimate socialist development. It may be taken as a step to fulfill the precondition of capitalist development before socialist development. This stage was also necessary to solve problems of food supply, black markets, discontentment among peasants and the overall critical economic situation caused by the World War and civil war. The NEP was regarded then by many as a policy to pacify the peasants and to ease the food shortages.

But the NEP allowed some private enterprise. These sectors required small capital investments which peasants and small artisans could finance. Lenin did not regard the NEP as a long-run strategy nor as a step towards the beginning of the transition to socialism. One of the first measures was known as 'Prodnalog', i.e. a "tax in kind" on the peasants which replaced the practice of requisitioning produce for war. According to Lenin, the key to creating a socialist system was state control of the "commanding heights" of the economy, which included major industries, transport, banking and foreign trade. With this, money exchange was reintroduced and the currency was established. As the trade and private industry began to expand, the need for credit and banks grew. It was a mixed-economy policy with which we are very much familiar. Similarly, as a result of the NEP in the USSR, there took place a fast growth of the private sector as the following data from Weicznski (1976-78, p. 184) indicate: private ownership, 75%; state-owned, 15%; cooperative, 10%.

In 1923 less than ten percent of all industrial enterprises were owned and operated by the State, but they employed about 85% of all industrial workers. Small industrial units were leased to private citizens (often to the former owners) or became cooperative enterprises. Although private enterprise produced as much as 25% of industrial output in 1925-27, private industry was not encouraged. "Foreign concession firms" increased to 68 in 1928, which produced less than 1 percent of all industrial output, from 13 in 1924-25. However, foreign trade remained a state monopoly, as it was to serve as a significant source of Western capital and technology in the rebuilding of the post-war economy and subsequent development of the socialist economy. Imports included machinery, various metals, yard goods and food products contrasted with the mainly primary product exports of caviar, manganese, sugar and cotton.

The economy remained under government supervision with important industries under the control of the Supreme Council of the National Economy (i.e. Vesenkha), although the 'Gosplan' was established shortly before the adoption of the NEP in 1921 with the responsibility of setting up a general state plan and the methods of implementing it. However, there was no concerted direction nor any overall strategy for the economy to follow. There was never any discussion of the three stages of Soviet economic development mentioned above as to the approaches to be followed regarding the development of a technology to suit the aims and objectives of production of a socialist society. Presumably, increased productivity and growth remained the main target of economic development of the Soviet Socialist System with imported capital and technology to be used to overtake capitalist systems. This was the basis of technological change. But this had to be achieved under Socialist ownership and management, which was the only differ-

❖

ence from a mixed economy approach in a Third World economy like that of India. The NEP approach as indicated earlier was closer to the state planning of the mixed economy in India—with the difference only in the degree of state control of production, consumption and distribution and not in kind (i.e. not in terms of generating technology to suit the aims of Socialism). That is, there had been no attempt or any plan to develop human resources to fulfill the objectives of socialist economic development, which would seem a fundamental difference from those of a capitalist system. Socialist economic development was essentially social-being orientated and not material-production and consumerism orientated. The use of imported capital and technology at its intensive phase as has evolved in a capitalist society cannot be efficient, in the sense we understand it in a capitalist system, if these are not market and consumer orientated. We will return to this aspect later after an examination of Stalin's "great leap forward", the third stage in Socialist development.

Unfortunately, Lenin did not live long enough to formulate any schema for long-term socialist economic development. In particular, the question of techno-logical change in building a socialist economy never troubled him nor any other leaders for that matter. The main assumption behind all approaches was that the socialist economy was to be built on capital-intensive technology imported from the capitalist West for the obvious reason of achieving rapid growth. However, this had to be undertaken under the strict socialist principle of state ownership of means of production and distribution so that evils of capitalism such as unemployment, inflation and dualistic development were avoided and at the same time high economic growth was assured. Before we move on to Stage III, it would be helpful if we take a brief look at Lenin's "civilized cooperatives" which were set up during NEP. It may help us understand the nature of organisational and technological change introduced during that time.

## C. The "Civilized Coops"

Earlier forms of Lenin's civilian cooperation in the 1920's are identified by many Russian writers today with socialism; and, in their view, those could have been possible alternatives to collective forms. According to Lenin, as per Karin and Naumov (1990, p. 85), cooperation is "all that is necessary to build a complete socialist society." However, he left a note of caution: "It is still not the building of socialist society, but it is all that is necessary and sufficient for it." Lenin defines the socialist nature of cooperative ventures; viz., they were socialist if they had been set up on land owned by the state and utilized the means of production belonging to the state, i.e. to the working class. In Lenin's view, cooperatives could also develop as closed alliances of small private business in which case they were to be denied state assistance. It has been noted (Kurin and Naumov 1990, p. 85) that the cooperative movement, even in its most rudimentary state-capitalism farms, not only had allowed control of the peasants' private interest, but was an important source of financing the industrialization program without disrupting the normal functioning of the economy. Had this process continued, a firm linkage between agriculture and industry might have been established in the near term, making for an integrated process of socialist development. However, there is one missing link in that scenario. The program for the gradual adaptation of the NEP to the tasks of socialist reconstruction provided for the involvement of peasants in production cooperatives on a scale that was realistic for that time. According to the present evaluation of the NEP in Soviet Russia, the programme was a step by step and balanced approach to setting the pace of industrialisation with an eye to strengthening the alliance of town and countryside and preserving the individual peasant farms as a basis for the development of agriculture for a long time.

The future of such a scheme depends on the source of equipment and machinery for agriculture and industrial development. In support of Lenin's above approach, it may be noted that imported technology at that stage of the intensive phase was still not as labour-dispensing as it has been since the 1960's, while the Western economy in those days was far from the onset of the phase of mass consumption (i.e. consumerism as we known it) of the 1960's — the phase that results from and in the growing need for markets to make profitable use of technology and capital intensive producers and consumer goods.

Yet growth under Lenin's schema, though the main aim of socialist development in the USSR, was much slower for obvious reasons than it was under Stalin's regime. The tempo in the rate of growth of imported technology and the degree of centralization of production and distribution of economic activities and output will account for it.

### D.  Stage III: Demise of the NEP and Rise of Industry; Stalin's 'Great Leap Forward.'

Lenin did not play a major role in the formulation of the Soviet Socialist development policy. Bukharin was the strongest supporter of the NEP and he wanted it to continue for another generation so that Russia's agriculture could improve and thus act as a source of smooth industrial development. The "Get Rich" slogan was introduced by him to encourage the peasantry to increase production. Trotsky wanted the termination of the NEP while Stalin remained noncommittal at first but later in 1925 decried the 'Get Rich' slogan (Weiczynski 1976-78, p. 185).

The decline of the NEP was gradual. The "scissors crisis" brought a serious challenge to the NEP with industrial prices rising sharply and agricultural prices falling. By October, 1923, industrial prices were three times higher in relationship to agricultural prices than their pre-war levels. The peasant, who maintained for so long an increase in agricultural production, lost the incentive and initiative to produce more food or to sell agricultural production. "Smychka" or the ideal of cooperation or collaboration encouraged by Lenin under the NEP between workers and peasants was in danger. Kulaks and poor and middle peasants withdrew a large

❖

proportion of their output from the market while collectivized and state farming contributed more than half of their produce to markets.

Kulaks produced 13 percent of total grains output while marketing only 20 percent of it, middle and poor peasants produced 85 percent and marketed 11 percent, while collectivised and State farms produced 1.7 percent and marketed over fifty percent of it (Weiczynski 1976-78). This indicated that the spread of collectivisation replacing private farms was the only solution for the problems of supplying food to a growing urban market.

The 1928-29 grain shortages facilitated the campaign of collectivization which had been started in 1919. By 1931 over fifty percent of the peasants were on collectivized farms, and by 1936 over 90 percent were on collective or state farms.

This development was the death knell of the NEP. The "Industry First" approach and the introduction of planning and rapid industrial growth under state control in 1929 brought it to an end in 1929. By 1930 private enterprise accounted for less than six percent of industrial production, and in 1931 concessions to private industry ended. There was no enthusiasm to build the economy on a partially capitalist base, although up until 1929-30 there had been a remarkable growth of private farms and small scale private industries.

However, this approach was not very helpful towards the rapid development of socialist industrialization and increased productivity. "Rapid growth" has all along been the target of socialist development in the USSR in order to "take over" and to defend the system from the onslaught of capitalism.

To fulfill the above objective, rapid industrial development demanded a concerted strategy of state control over the mobilization of resources, production and its distribution. This strategy included the need to control all facets of the economy. The need would be greater when socialist development relies on borrowed capital intensive technology. In a free-enterprise and uncontrolled market economy, or in a mixed economy like that of India, efforts towards rapid growth would invariably require foreign capital and technology; and, would inevitably result in dualistic development (co-existence of a limited sophisticated sector and ever-expanding/labour-surplus subsistence sector), problems of unemployment and disguised unemployment and growing economic inequality. These problems are too familiar to need any explanation.

At the same time, any effort towards building a socialist economy using imported technology and capital cannot be successful if the system remains a mixed economy or partially deregulated market economy. Such an attempt would ultimately result in strengthening the private sector, economic inequality and surplus-labour problems; and side-by-side with them, a high rate of economic growth. Therefore, to build socialism to fulfill its objective of rapid growth with economic equality, full employment and no inflation, strict state control of the mobilization of resources and/or production and its distribution is an essential condition to avoid the dualism that generates the above problems.

❖

Since the days of planning under Stalin, growth with rapid capital accumulation accompanied by a lower level of consumption made the former possible, and helped maintenance of full employment of labour not related to the efficient use of the growing capital intensity of technology. Technology in its intensive phase by definition needs not less but more efficient labour, which the Russian economy during the pre or post Revolution period never produced. The development of the extensive phase of using labour more productively through organizational change prepared the ground for the intensive phase of technological change based on science when the economy began to face the problem of shortage of labour relative to its need. The entire process, in terms of factor use and technological change, is known as the capitalist transformation of a society. Whether it takes place under socialist or capitalist systems does not matter. But when this technological change is based on borrowed technology and capital at the intensive phase as occurred in Soviet Russia, socialist management and control helped to avoid dualism, inflation, unemployment and economic inequality. But in reality this approach resulted in disguised unemployment and inefficiency (Maitra 1989).

At the same time, this kind of socialist development makes imperative the need for development of the market and a deregulated economy, and this in turn brings about the ultimate demise of socialism. There are three basic economic reasons for such an unfortunate calamity overtaking a socialist development based on imported technology, to wit:
(1) rapid introduction of imported technology at its intensive phase to realize the socialist ideal of full employment invariably creates problems of disguised unemployment and inefficiency in the use of human resources;
(2) productive utilization of imported capital-intensive technology and a low level of income and consumption, controlled by the socialist state to fulfill its aim of rapid capital accumulation, would again result in efficient use of technology and capital;
(3) an inefficiency resulting from the above makes its products uncompetitive in the world market.

All these inefficiencies need expanding markets and a higher level of consumption or consumerism which, for its effective operation, requires income inequality to generate demand for products and choice of goods — the life-blood of technological change that has evolved with the introduction of science in production in capitalist economies.

## II. Western Capital and Technology in Soviet Development

In Russia the capital investment from the West began in 1860 and France, Germany and Belgium provided nearly half of the total capital investment in the 1890's. During the Tsar Nicholas II regime, foreigners owned 70 percent of the capital. We will here look at:

❖

## A. The Revolution

With the 1917 Revolution, the arbitrary and uncontrolled process of direct foreign investment was terminated and converted into concessions. Under this arrangement, foreign firms were allowed to exploit commercial opportunities in the USSR with the latest technology. Foreigners began to pay royalties to Soviets and lost property rights. They compromised with mixed or joint stock companies where Soviets had 51 percent of the shares or had a controlling vote (Apostolakis 1987, p. 589).

## B. Lenin and the NEP (1921-28)

The second period of technology transfer took place during the NEP (1921-28). Lenin's strategy of development with trade was expressed in his dictum of "learning from the enemy as quickly as possible" (which sowed the seed of the Soviet's ultimate conversion into the enemy's system under Perestroika). The volume of trade grew rapidly from 8 percent of the pre-war level in 1918, to 44 percent in 1928 (Kasir 1969). At the end of the NEP, there were only 59 foreign concessions which accounted for less than one percent of the output of state industry (Gregory and Stuart 1986, p. 112).

## C. Stalin and the First Five Year Plan (1928-32)

With Stalin, major efforts for industrialization via technology transfer occurred during the First Five Year Plan (1928-32). In 1931, Stalin (1942, p. 200) declared his "Industrialization First" policy which in his view would end the backwardness of Russia's society. "We are fifty or a hundred years behind the advanced countries. We must make this good in ten years. Either we do it or they crush us."

Soviet policy was to attain economic self-sufficiency (as indicated under the Soviet Constitution), whence, imports of machinery began to assume greater importance. (But the Soviet authorities did not realize that the economics of technology transfer even under a socialist system made the borrowing country less and less self-sufficient, as the subsequent development in the USSR indicated. In the case of capitalist economies, dependence on technology transfer between themselves is a matter of course.)

In 1930, Levine et al. not (1976, pp. 37-38), imports of machinery and equipment rose to a level of more than half of the total imports of the USSR. Imports of certain types of machines—turbines, generators, tools, boilers, metal-cutting machines—accounted for between 50 and 90 percent of the growth in supply of these machines. On the whole, imports of capital goods amounted to almost 15 percent of gross investment in the USSR, 1928-32.

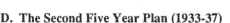

## D. The Second Five Year Plan (1933-37)

Due to the 1930's depression in the capitalist world and the Soviet policy of import substitution to achieve the aim of nondependence in building a socialist economy, Soviet imports in 1933-34 were drastically reduced. On the other hand, domestic expenditure on research and capital investment in science to develop technology on its own was based on Western technology already in use. Some economists might take this approach as one of developing Soviet Russia's indigenous technology. That is a very mistaken idea. The efforts may be likened to the work of translation from another language. Indigenous technology evolves from using labour more productively through organizational change, and the use of traditional technology. The guiding force behind this process is the organized social consciousness depending on the economic systems, Capitalist or Socialist, etc.... When, in this process of economic growth, the demand for labour exceeds the supply of labour, science is used in production. The direction of which, again, is determined by the economic systems. According to Marx, the socialist economy would invariably take place and be successful in Britain. The economy of that country had passed through those two stages of technological change and as a consequence the conversion from capitalist transformation of the society and economy was ripe and the force of the antithesis to capitalism was thought to be mature enough to bring about the Socialist Revolution. We may add here also the countries of imported industrialization of the late 19th century (France or Germany, for example) which borrowed technology from the UK when it was at its late extensive phase of using labour and thus, in due course, complete capitalist transformation of the society had been achieved. Imported capitalism in the later period, when capitalist technological change had reached its intensive phase of labour dispensing, cannot bring about capitalist transformation of a society. I have added at the end of this paper some important indicators of capitalist transformation of a society. This is the reason for the failure of socialist development to continue for long. Socialist development in the USSR from the beginning has been based on technology from the West when the Western technology had reached its intensive phase. Another point to be noted here is that Russian industrial development, from the Tsarist period onwards, has been based on imported technology, not from the UK—the only country in the world generating indigenous industrial technology via the industrial revolution from its own traditional proto-technology—but from countries which themselves used borrowed technology from the UK in the earlier period. History, which we tend to ignore or misinterpret, has a lot to offer in the analysis of a dynamic factor like technological change in economic development. By 1936-37, imported capital goods constituted only about 2 percent of gross investment and fewer than 10 percent of all installed machinery came from abroad (Levine et al. 1976).

However, the use of advanced foreign technology played a significant role in the Soviet Union during the Second Five Year Plan period (1933-37) which, according to one study (Carrick 1978), brought about the tremendous success in developing the industrial base in the USSR.

## E. Post World War II

The reconstruction of the Soviet economy after the Second World War was largely based on Western contributions through Lend-Lease. After World War II, the Soviet policy of self-sufficiency was re-emphasized and reliance on foreign resources was reduced. According to one author, the accelerating growth of capital stock was approaching a rate close to that of investment. During the 1950's investment was increasing at an annual rate of 11.5 percent, while the capital stock, which grew at an average rate of 9 percent, had escalated to 11 percent by the end of the decade (Carrick 1976).

## F. The 1960s/'80s

Again between 1961-65, Soviet imports of machinery and transportation equipment increased by 28 percent. During the 1960s the "technical revolution" in the West which made technology increasingly sophisticated and knowledge-intensive promoted the "internationalization of knowledge" in the USSR. We must note here that the growth of knowledge-intensive technology was the result of developed capitalist economies' fight for markets for their ever-expanding products with very low labour but high capital content. The Soviet economy in its efforts to build socialism began to import the technology and proved their approach to be likened to a round peg in a square hole. The nineteen-eighties reflected these peculiar circumstances in all aspects of Soviet life (Ofer 1987, pp. 1770-75; Maitra 1989).

## III. The Return to a Market Economy: An Inevitable Consequence

Market economy begets and survives on the class system and income inequality. Free market economy and competition cannot survive if there is no income inequality and a changing propensity to consume with changing income distribution. In the Soviet socialist system, most emphasis was laid on productivity growth with consumption limited to essentials. A socialist egalitarian system with market and competition are a contradiction in terms. The use of price incentives, the eventual increase in the price level, factor-substitution elasticities, inequality in income distribution as the source of capital accumulation, and speeding up of consumerism are all part of the dynamic makeup of the market economy. Any system described as efficient is so only under a given income distribution. In particular, the market system can be efficient only in terms of how well it meets the effective demand of those with income; for a given aggregate income level, we would expect the composition of output consistent with efficiency to vary as the income distribution might change. If the distribution were egalitarian, so-called

❖

wage-goods would predominate, whence capital accumulation and investment in the health and education of the people would be thwarted.

In the socialist system, it is expected that investment is geared to raise the level of living of the masses as a whole. Obviously, under this arrangement, consumerism of the Western level, for the whole society, is an impossible aim to achieve. The capitalist-developed economies have been able to achieve a high level of consumption because of income inequality that stimulated the changing propensity to consume among higher income groups, followed by lower income groups as a result of demonstration effects. Diffusion of demand in this process led to fuller utilization of capacity of both the investment-goods and consumer-durables-producing industries. But the main factor behind this development has been the expanding markets of products of a handful of developed economies throughout the world. This stimulated technological change and a higher level of productivity of the working population. Together with income inequality, this made it possible for these economies to reach the mass consumption stage. Since the 1980s, therefore, the neoclassical market economy policy has been the indispensable approach to enable these economies to be increasingly competitive via achieving increasing efficiency through technological change and gaining a greater share of markets world-wide through propagation of consumerism. This is the only way these economies could maintain their high growth rate and fuller utilization of high-technology intensive capital investment.

We may cite here the case of Postwar Japanese industrial growth as an example. During 1955-61 the growth pattern was highly investment or heavy industry oriented. In machinery, the growth rate was 28.6 percent; in iron and steel, it was 19.3 percent; and in chemicals 14.9 percent, but in textiles only 9.1 percent, because of the essential nature of the product here, and the low income-elasticity of demand for it. The 1946-51 period in Japan was one of a proportionate high-pitched growth, while the 1955-61 period was one of a disproportionate high-pitched growth. The former period was so because production increases in every industry were made impossible by a rapid rise in the rate of capacity utilization and because of expanding markets overseas for producer goods. A high level of investment and productivity needs mass production. The growth pattern in the latter was disproportionate because excess demand and the full utilization of capacity coexisted. This is the period marked by an extra-ordinary expansion of consumer durables e.g. television sets, refrigerators etc., later followed by rapid growth of electronic goods, computers etc. Mass production of passenger cars began from this period (Cf. Shinohara 1972, pp. 281-83).

In the Western capitalist economies today, the free-market approach has created a tremendous problem of unemployment and economic inequality which could have been much less had Third World economies been able to achieve take-off using technology supplied by the Western economies. Socialist economies turned market economies will inevitably face this problem tomorrow.

❖

In the Soviet Union, the huge investment in capital and producer goods created tremendous productivity on the one hand and on the other hand, the aim of full employment of the labour force and limited consumption resulted in a disproportionate use of factors of production. With demand of population kept far below the productive capacity, a huge capacity was used for defence production. Under the circumstances, productivity in each hour increases because of the rising capital-intensity of production which should result in a reduction in employment in a capitalist system, but in a socialist economy full employment being the goal, labour engaged is not fully utilized. That is, disguised unemployment emerges. In a capitalist economy, with increasing capital accumulation, hours worked per labourer is reduced which results in unemployment. In a socialist system this development is expected to result in reduction of hours of work to maintain full employment but if the market in the capitalist world becomes the target, the socialist system cannot afford to preserve its socialist ideal of full employment. To be competitive in the international market, the socialist system must transform itself into a market economy. On the other hand, to use fully the huge productive capacity built up through increased capital investment, diversification of and raising the level of consumption become inevitable in a market- and class-based economy. The socialist goals of income equality and full employment policy act as a built-in constraint in such an eventuality as noted earlier.

Another factor behind the need for markets in the Soviet Socialist system is to produce for external markets so that technology and other sophisticated inputs could be imported. Obviously, to export products in the world market, mainly to the developed economies, the Soviet economy has to be cost conscious. Low income with disguised unemployment, limited consumption and limited domestic market makes the unit-cost of production based on capital intensive methods high compared to a developed capitalist economy which has the advantage of large domestic and external markets as well as high labour productivity. Workers in this society are employed and paid on the basis of their marginal product, while in Soviet Russia full employment of the workforce, irrespective of their contribution, is a socialist norm. Export markets of primary goods are limited these days and therefore Soviet Russia would have to be very efficient; and, cost of production is kept to a minimum by—inter alia—reducing labour content as is done in developed capitalist economies. In the Soviet Union, by maintaining the socialist goal of full employment, it would not be possible to reduce costs sufficiently. Again, full employment with low wages, as is the practice now, would result in disguised unemployment, inefficiency and high per unit costs. This will make Soviet products less competitive. The way out is to introduce wage payments determined by market forces which is now being attempted.

Expanding the domestic market is another way of reducing costs via the economies-of-scale effect. In a socialist system with no competitive market system, that objective cannot be achieved. In a socialist system cost is social cost borne by the entire community. If a product is highly expensive but it is regarded as essential and of immediate necessity to the welfare and development of the entire society, and the society has the ability (in terms of skills, education and resources) to produce, then it must be produced by diverting resources from the least important product to the former. Cost is essentially a social cost that matters in a socialist system.

## IV. Conclusion

We have examined the nature of technological change that has taken place in the USSR under socialist ownership and management of resources. Socialist planners in the U.S.S.R. since the 1917 Revolution have been engaged in introducing and developing technology domestically by importing it from Western capitalist economies. The inevitable result has been the inefficiency which has beset the Soviet economy from the very beginning. This mounting inefficiency became visible not only in production centers but also in social and political life in terms of tensions of various forms because of rising personal aspirations and a growing consumerism as the by-product of introduced technology. Attempts to continue socialist management with capitalist production forces or 'technology' are unscientific and counter historical and cannot fulfill the purpose of a socialist production system.

Socialist distribution of income led to the expansion and rise of wages and salaries, and their purchasing power. This came about because of this policy of increasing productivity with capital-intensive technology, with the main emphasis on heavy industries, and at the expense of essential consumer-good industries. The government had to try an indirect measure of taxation upon the majority of consumer goods in an attempt to absorb as much of the population's excess purchasing power as possible. Increasing contact with the West's capitalist standard of living and consumption patterns as a result of technology transfer from the West and trade with them began to create dissension among higher wage and salary earners, who were seeking a higher level of consumption. That is, the demand for production according to private or group need rather than social need began to be louder. This demand has been articulated in the Party Congress:

> As the country advances towards communism, personal needs will be increasingly met...the output of consumer goods must meet the growing consumer need in full and must conform to its changes.... Soviet domestic trade will be further developed as a necessary condition to meet the growing requirements of the people. Good shopping facilities will be made available throughout the country and progressive facilities in terms of trading will be widely applied. The material and technical bases of Soviet trade, the network of shops, warehouse, refrigerators (communal freeze-lockers) and vegetables will be extended (Flenner 1966, p.34).

Kruschev (1964) wrote: "When we have a strong industry and the defense of the country is suitably prepared for, the Party proposes a much faster development of branches providing consumer goods." To achieve economies of scale of production or greater efficiency from the kind of technological change that has been introduced in the U.S.S.R., product differentiation in consumer goods (e.g. durables) is inevitable. This requires a much larger market for achieving efficiency. Therefore, a marketing concept with emphasis on consumption goods, including consumer durables, gets the main emphasis. This is also the result of the pattern of technological change introduced as mentioned earlier, as well as increasing contact with the Western world and its affluent standard of living, where demand pushes supply. Stalin affirmed in his Report to the Party Congress in 1930 that "as a result of advantages of socialism the increment in effectiveness in the Soviet Union always exceeds the increment in production, pushing it forward..." (United Nations 1959, p. 24).

In other words, the socialist principle of "from each according to his abilities and each according to his needs" has been ignored. Present-day supply and demand planning in the U.S.S.R. has strengthened this attitude as reflected in Gorbachev's "Perestroika" and "Glasnosts". Soviet policy was to mobilize huge human resources through social prerogatives and combine them with more advanced instruments of production coming from mature capitalist economies with fundamentally different motives of production. Had the technological change in Soviet Russia evolved by way of utilizing its human resources to develop its traditional technology, the initial level of this technology would have been determined by the organized social consciousness that made socialist revolution possible. Under this condition, productive forces (i.e., technology) could have emerged in such a way as to meet the needs of consumers and/or productivity growth determined by socialist consciousness, i.e., production would have been carried out according to social need. Imported technology, evolved in capitalist economies to meet the combined aim of market-oriented productivity and consumption growth, would inevitably fail to fulfil the aims of production and consumption in a socialist system, the aim of which is collective enrichment of human resources intellectually, culturally and physically. Imported technology from the capitalist society cannot fulfill this role. The motive of production in capitalist society is to achieve profit and efficiency to meet private needs at the cost of social needs through a consumer-product-differentiation policy, which entirely depends on the expected rate of return from the investment of capitalist class. If the rate of return is not up to the expectation of the capitalist class, the capitalist owners would not hesitate to lay off capital and labour for any indefinite period, its social costs notwithstanding. This kind of technology needs a free and expanding market and profit-oriented efficient management. Long use of such technology in a socialist framework and management is obviously failing to achieve efficiency of the level of a developed capitalist economy. Hence, the need for freeing economic management and the introduction of a freer market system which began to be felt after Stalin's death, and which then

❖

took concrete shape under Gorbachev in the form of an organized policy. Soviet policy of industrial growth has been to give priority to heavy and basic industries (energy, steel and machine tools) over consumer-goods-producing industries which can be characterized as capitalist ones. Lenin stressed the point in his *The Development of Capitalism* (1960) that the development of consumers' goods industries might be completely halted while heavy industries forge continuously ahead. In Volume II of *Capital* (1956, pp. 77-78, 414-15), Marx characterised this process as typical of capitalism. Using the Marxian model of simple and enlarged production, the growth limits of the economy are set by the excess of the producers' goods over replacement needs.

Lenin (1960) concluded that the basic contradiction of capitalism lies precisely in the urge to "limitless expansion of production and limited consumption." Soviet industrial development policy has been to use the capitalist approach as a tool in a socialist frame work. Therefore, Stalin hailed the tendency in the economy for demand to outrun supply as a theory of the desirability of excess demand to draw forth supply. This is a capitalist market approach to the development of economic activities. Therefore, the communist dictum of "from each according to one's ability and to each according to one's need" has been replaced by "to each according to his works." Gorbachev's freer market and consumer's private right approach was an inevitable culmination of the approaches based on foreign technology.

That private demand and not social needs has become the guide to production and consumption planning in the U.S.S.R. is evident from a study by Belchuk (1961), which states that the Soviets are aware today that advancements in demand estimation are necessary and can be achieved by more widespread use of coefficients of elasticity indicating a change in demand in relation to changes in the income per family member within the social groups and to changes in price levels per individual commodity group. This same approach is followed in free market-oriented economics. Obviously, to plan production according to demand, a more decentralized approach would be needed. Gorbachev already has that point in this reconstruction plan.

I would like to end our conclusion with a brief note on the controversy over the Social Market policy of Gorbachev versus that of the Free Market of Yeltsin. It is now certain that Yeltsin's policy will dominate economic reforms in Soviet Russia. Gorbachev's policy of a Social Market can be likened to a state-intervention mechanism of the Welfare-State variety as followed in most developed capitalist economies, where it is at present being dismantled. The main aim of the Welfare State policy is to maintain equilibrium between aggregate demand and aggregate supply so that the capitalist economy could grow without any disequilibrium between the two sides of the economy causing unemployment, inflation and recession. This policy helped recovery from depression in the 1930's and the achieving of more than a decade of prosperity with 'full employment' in the 1960's. But a Welfare-State cannot survive in today's world of severe international capitalist competition as its policy results in interest and wage rates which are not determined by market forces. All these effects adversely affect the competitiveness of those economies dominated by big oligopolies and the international conglomerates. Highly intensive technology has turned the organization and marketing of production international. Without the support of internationally organized production and marketing of products, present-day technology is uneconomical. Thus, the Welfare State makes labour and capital expensive as the need for deficit financing to meet welfare measures, unemployment benefits, etc...makes interest rates high, labour costly and the economy vulnerable to inflation. Unhindered operation of market forces results in the availability of workers at a low wage-level, and the absence of deficit financing, reduced rates of interest, and inflation at a very low level, thereby enabling the national economy to be successful in the international economy. This, however, is achieved at a very high social cost, as attested by the growing number of unemployed, increasing supply of food stamps (in U.S.), starvation, increasing poverty, increasing number of school drop outs and suicides as evidenced in all highly developed capitalist economies of today.

As the U.S.S.R. converts to the market economy, with its program of opening it to the direct foreign investment to help its reconstruction, of which the free-market policy is the guiding force, the social-market economy of Gorbachev is rendered completely unworkable. Therefore, to be a viable member of the international community, which is the aim of Gorbachev's Perestroika, Yeltsin's free market approach is the only alternative for the U.S.S.R.

## Endnotes

*Associate Professor, Department of Economics, University of Otago, P.O. Box 56, Dunedin, New Zealand.

[1] The tables in the Appendix indicate the Western-resources contents of Soviet technological development and the rapid rate of penetration of Western technology into Soviet industry.

[2] Maurice Dobb (1966) has presented an in-depth analysis of Soviet industrization during the NEP.

❖

# APPENDIX

### Table 1

### Soviet Aggregrate Imports (in Millions) and Investment (in Billions) of Current Rubles; Selected Estimates

| Year | Imports | Investment | Machinery Imports/Total Imports (Percentage) |
|------|---------|------------|----------------------------------------------|
| 1946 | 692 | 12.33 | - |
| 1950 | 1310 | 17.76 | - |
| 1955 | 2755 | 26.81 | 38.0 |
| 1960 | 5066 | 34.80 | 38.3 |
| 1965 | 7253 | 50.08 | 33.4 |
| 1970 | 10559 | 84.07 | 35.0 |
| 1975 | 26671 | 98.09 | 25.4 |
| 1980 | 44463 | 105.46 | 22.5 |
| 1985 | 67234 | 124.75 | 18.4 |

Source: For Imports: U.N., *Yearbook of International Trade Statistics;* for Investment: U.N., *Statistical Yearbook.*

### Table 2

### Industrial Western Countries' Exports to the Soviet Russia, 1970-81

| Year | 1970 | 1979 | 1981 |
|------|------|------|------|
| Total Trade ($ million) | 2,490.8 | 18,114.3 | 20,854.3 |
| High Technology ($ million) | 402.9 | 2,371.3 | 1,735.5 |
| Manufactures ($ million) | 2,212.4 | 13,642.4 | 14,435.0 |
| High Technology as a percentage of Total Trade Manufactures | 16.2 18.2 | 13.1 17.4 | 8.3 12.0 |

Source: John A. Martens, *Qualification of Western Exports of High Technology Products to Communist Countries,* Washington D.C., Commerce Department, March, 1983.

Table 3

USSR Imports – Share of Commodity Group Machinery and
Equipment and Annual Growth Rate

| Year | Share of Imports/ Total Imports of Machinery | | Growth Rate of Imports of Machinery |
|---|---|---|---|
| | Total | Machinery Equipment | |
| 1961-65 | 100 | 32.9 | 9.4 |
| 1966-70 | 100 | 35.0 | 8.7 |
| 1971-75 | 100 | 33.8 | 19.3 |
| 1976 | 100 | 36.3 | 15.4 |
| 1978 | 100 | 42.0 | 26.6 |
| 1979 | 100 | 38.0 | 0.9 |
| 1980 | -- | 33.9 | 4.8 |

Source: *Comcon Statistics*, pp. 384-385.

Table 4

Foreign Trade, USSR
Imports – Machinery and Equipment (m. rubles)

| | |
|---|---|
| 1913 | 796.8 |
| 1920 | 15.1 |
| 1925/26 | 542.1 |
| 1930. | 1726.6 |
| 1935 | 198.1 |
| 1940 | 353.6 |
| 1950 | 282.0 |
| 1960 | 1508.0 |
| 1965 | 2423.0 |
| 1970 | 3706.0 |

Source: R.C. Clark, *Soviet Economic Facts 1917-1970*, London: Macmillan, 1972, p. 48.

[N.B. Table 5 (here omitted) indicates – inter alia – that, for the 31-year period 1955-85, the ratio of Soviet machinery imports to total imports from the West averaged some 29.32%, with a slight (but statistically insignificant) down-trend for the overall period. Broken in two, the period yielded averages of 34% for the first eighteen years (1955-72) and 23% for the last thirteen (1973-85). / TN, ed.]

# References

Apostolakis, B.E. "The Role of Technology Transfer in Soviet Development," *Review of Radical Political Economy*, 1987, 29, 589.

Belchuk, V. "Economcheskie Namki," translated in *Problems in Economics*, 1961, 5.

Carrick, Roger. *East-West Technology Transfer in Perspective*, Berkeley: University of California, 1978.

Dobb, M. *Soviet Economic Development since 1917*, London: Routledge and Kegan Paul, 1966.

Engels, F. *Anti-Duehring*, Moscow: Foreign Languages Publishing House, 1947.

Flenner, J. *Soviet Economic Controversies*, Cambridge, MA: M.I.T. Press, 1966.

Gregory, P. and Stuart, R. *Soviet Economic Structure and Performance*, New York: Harper and Row, 1986.

Kasir, M. " A Volume Index of Soviet Trade," *Soviet Studies, 20,* 1969.

Kruschev, N. *Izvestia*, October 2, 1964 in Flenner (1966).

Kurin, Lenoid N. and Naumov, Valdimir. *Pages of History*, Moscow: Novosti Press, 1990, 85.

Laird, Roy D. and Betty A. "Soviet Communism and Agrarian Revolution," in D. Mcquarrie, ed., *Marx: Sociology, Social Change and Capitalism*, London: Quartet Books, 1978.

Lenin, V.I. *The Development of Capitalism*, Moscow, 1960.

Levine, H. et.al. "Transfer of U.S. Technology to the Soviet Union," Stanford Research Institute, 1976.

Maitra, P. *The Mainspring of Economic Development*, London and New York: Mehrtens, 1980.

_____. *Population, Technology and Development*, Aldershot: Gower, 1986.

_____. "Technological Change and the Soviet Economic, Development," *Society and Change, 4,* 1989.

Marx, K. *Capital*, Vol. II, Moscow; Progress Publishers, 1956ff.

_____."Preface to the Russian Edition" of the *Communist Manefesto, in Socialist Landmark: A New Appreiation*, London: George Allen and Unwin, 1948.

Ofer, G. "Soviet Economic Growth, 1828-85", *Journal of Economic Literature*, December 1987, 25.

Shinohara, M. "Patterns and Some Structural Changes in Japan's Post-War Industrial Growth," in E. Klein et al. eds., *Economic Growth: The Japanese Experience since the Meiji Era*, New Haven: Yale University Press, 1972.

❖

Sweezy, Paul M. *The Theory of Capitalist Development,* 1942; reprinted ed., New York/London: Modern Reader Paperbacks, 1968.

United Nations. *Economic Survey of Europe,* Geneva: United Nations, 1959.

Weiczynski, J. "New Economic Policy," *Modern Encyclopaedia of Russian and Soviet History,* Florida: Academic International Press, 1976-78.

# Peristroika of the Soviet Economy and Help of the USA

*Elena G. Mikhailova**

The sharpest question posed by peristroika of the economy in the USSR is how to change to a market economy. The degree and speed of solving social and economic problems, the extent and harshness of the consequences for the population, together with the magnitude of the inevitable rise in prices and unemployment, and the implications of the transformation for the condition of labor in general all depend on the manner in which the conversion is accomplished.

The USSR does not have the requisite infrastructure, and there are practically no specialists capable of working well under market conditions. It is here that help from the United States — the country with the most highly developed market economy — is needed. Addressing the Moscow State Institute of International Affairs during his visit to Moscow in July 1991, President Bush promised that the US is ready to support this new revolution in the USSR now under way.

Many Soviet people pinned their hopes on western investments following the (recent) meeting of the Group of Seven ("G-7") in London. But our difficulties have remained, and are not something someone can manage for us. As British Prime Minister, John Major, host of the meeting on behalf of the G-7, confessed: "Soviet problems must be solved by the Soviet people themselves."

Western leaders do not consider Soviet economic reforms to be sufficiently radical and promising, feeling that the Soviet Union has not become mature (sophisticated) enough to get (effectively utilize) western material assistance and to take part in international, financial and economic operations on a full-rights basis. But there is another point of view which has its supporters in the US. Taking into account the difficulties of (securing) foreign investments in the USSR, this position holds that now is the most crucial moment for the USSR, that it is now that the strongest impulse is needed to overcome the inertia.

This writer supports the position of President Bush; viz, when the union is completed and the reforms are firmly in place, then one may speak about full-rights membership of the USSR in the international-financial and economic organizations.

❖

It is not that in London anyone was seeking to shy away from cooperation with the USSR. Everyone took it seriously that technical cooperation (assistance) in the case of energy, the system of food-stuffs distribution, nuclear security and protection of the environment will create favorable conditions for further capital investments. It was remarked in London that one American company wanted to invest $1 million in the USSR but has not been able to do so, because the question of the union treaty has not been resolved. The firm is not sure with whom to deal. When this question is resolved, 100 such companies investing $100 million would noticeably enhance the living conditions of the Soviet people.

People in our country are not free, and have never been free — I mean that inner freedom which is the foremost human form. They have no confidence in their collective forces, and have no faith in self-reliance. But, it is people who are the moving force of economic reforms.

Technicians capable of performing proficiently in a market system, and a populace who are used to relying on collective action and their own individual initiative — these may be thought of as parts of the human infrastructure currently lacking in the Soviet Union (TN).

(Thus,) the USSR will not be able to move a step without people with new (market-oriented) skills, and with a new, modern, western way of thinking. The jump from the kingdom of Marxist freedom to the kingdom of rational necessity**, which we are going to undertake, has no analogue (precedent). It surpasses the majority of reforms in the history of Russia and may be compared with only two landmarks: the Christianization of Russia and Petrov's reforms.

The US may undertake a great mission of creation of a "new people" for the USSR. Here, one may distinguish four main kinds of American assistance: technical aid, economic education, political reform, and medicine.

Of these, economic education is the most important. Great expenditure is required. It is a matter of educating at least 50,000 people from the USSR in the US and western Europe. These people are the golden fund of reform.

The first experience of Soviet-American cooperation in the sphere of economic reforms is Javlinsky's and Harvard's group programme, containing, to my mind, a number of contradictions. The contradictions in the programme concern such key questions as currency, tax and customs policies. For example, the programme envisions an increase in the share of foreign currency receipts which remain at the disposal of an enterprise; while, at the same time, the using of foreign currencies in contracts concluded inside of the country is forbidden. In increasing the access of enterprises to foreign currency, one must forget about the convertibility (exchange-rate) of the rouble. Otherwise, an extremely inefficient distribution of currency in the domestic economy will occur, along with the alienation of domestic prices from the world process, and isolation of the rouble from the general currency circulation.

What will happen in the sphere of taxation is not quite clear. On the one side, balancing of the government's budget is achieved by decreasing expenditures and increasing taxes. On the other side, a new revenue measure foresees a low-limit rate of taxation.

It would not be so dangerous if the drawbacks of the programme were limited to internal logical contradictions. Much worse is the wish to pass off the desirable for what is actually attainable. Ideally, Javlinsky would have helped his American colleagues to better understand the realities of the Soviet economy; and, the members of the Harvard group would have inserted into the programme their understanding of the feasibility of various forms of Westernization. Unfortunately, neither of these happened. Rather, they enumerated the amounts and deadlines for the extension of credits to the USSR by the International Monetary Fund and World Bank, and the Chapter on "Perspectives on the Economic Support of Soviet Reforms" proceeds in terms of standard descriptions of functions (operations) of international organizations applying to any other country in general, rather than to the unique needs of the USSR (TN).

Finally, when there is no middle class in the USSR, one can hardly envisage significant changes. A middle class can only appear when there is private property. And, who is going to invest money in the Soviet economy when there is no private property? Economic behavior is not that irrational.

*Cheboksary Branch, Moscow Co-operative Institute, 24, Gorky Ave., Cheboksary, 428 017 U.S.S.R. The editor (TN) has taken the liberty of rewording parts of the present paper. Alternative expressions where meaning or intent is involved are inserted parenthetically. Other editorial interjections are initialed (TN).

**This is an obvious play on Marx's "Realm of Freedom" ("das Reich der Freiheit") vs. that of "physical necessity" ("Naturnotwendigkeit") as found in sec. III, Chap. XLVIII, Vol. III of *Capital* (Moscow: Progress, 1959, p. 820; *Das Kapital,* Berlin: Dietz, 1949, p. 828). There, Marx speaks of "the socialised man (der vergesellschaftete Mensch), the associated producers, rationally regulating their interchange with Nature (diesen ihrer Stoffwechsel mit der Natur rationell regeln)." (TN)

# Marx on Man's Sociality by Nature: An Inexplicable Omission? (Abstract)

## Thomas O. Nitsch*

No one took more for granted or was more emphatic about "man's" natural sociality (or, otherwise, communality) than Karl Marx. Thus, in *Das Kapital* (1867; 3d ed. 1883), *sub* Kooperation," he stipulates "dass der Mensch *von Natur* ... ein gesellschaftliches Thier ist"; i.e., "that man *by nature* is a social animal" (our emphasis). Yet, with the exception of the lone and relatively obscure translation of the Pauls (1930; 1972), all the prominent English editions of *Capital* (1887, 1906, 1952, 1954; 1976) curiously omit the "by nature" qualification, which is retained in both of the French, both of the Russian, and the Italian and Spanish versions examined. After fully documenting and briefly noting the specific context of Marx's postulation, the significance thereof and possible reasons for this critical and somewhat mysterious omission are more carefully explored.

Since both the "Western" or Anglo-American editions (London, 1887; Chicago et al., 1906 et seq.) and the "official" / Moscow (Progress Publishers, 1954) — as well as the completely new New Left Review (Penguin Books, 1976) — versions are all "guilty," the "conspiracy hypothesis" is precluded. Rather, the best explanation seems to be the singular effort of his English translators — perhaps accepting the decision of Engels himself, who edited the original English edition which appeared four years after Marx's death in 1883, to make the deletion — to "protect" Marx from any static conception of human nature. Yet, anyone who knows the Aristotelian that Marx was, will know that human nature is what human beings are to be when that long-going evolutionary process of becoming is completed, when "Communism B," "the Realm of Freedom," etc. are achieved. It is interesting that, in the passage in question, only Aristotle is allowed to say what *der Mensch* is by nature (viz., "a town-citizen"); the same qualification — again — made by Marx in his own right, and that attributed there by him to Benjamin Franklin (viz. "man [being] *von Natur* a tool-maker"), is deleted.

❖

Why Marx, who personally revised entirely the original and more prominent French edition (1872-75), whence his Russian, Italian and Spanish translators, saw no such need for protection remains the puzzlement.

*The author is Professor of Economics, Creighton University. The published version of the paper presented appears in the *FESTSCHRIFT in Honour of John E. Elliott, Part I*, ed. John Conway O'Brien, *International Journal of Social Economics*, 19:7/8/9 (1992), pp. 108-20.

# Inter-firm and Supra-firm Cooperation in the Workplace and the Marketplace (Abstract)

## Edward J. O'Boyle

Neoclassical economics rests firmly on the proposition that competition is sufficient to activate a market economy. When buyers and sellers compete freely in the marketplace, resources are allocated where they are needed and income is distributed according to the contribution that each person makes to economic activity. The more efficient one's use of resources and the more substantial one's contribution to the economic process, the greater the personal gain. Neoclassical economics denies economic dysfunction or argues that the cure for the problem is more competition.

Social economics sees competition as insufficient to deal adequately with economic dysfunction and argues that a second activating principle — cooperation — is necessary to address the problem. This paper examines cooperation at the inter-firm level and the supra-firm level, leaving aside intra-firm cooperation.

By means of a voluntary agreement on the responsibilities of the various members of a group, inter-firm and supra-firm cooperation direct the individual members to address through collective action the dysfunction in both the workplace and the marketplace which they are unable to resolve through individual action. The individual members are functionally related to one another through some dysfunction in production, distribution, exchange, or consumption.

Cooperation activates those four economic processes by means of a disposition on the part of the individual to undertake certain tasks through collective action. This type of action is not the equivalent of cartel behavior because cartels produce zero-sum outcomes whereas cooperation yields positive-sum results.

This paper examines intra-firm and supra-firm cooperation both in principle and in practice. Five cases are presented as examples of inter-firm or supra-firm cooperation in the workplace or the marketplace. The five derive from the author's field work in St. Louis in 1984 and from site visits in Louisiana over a six-year period starting in 1984.

---------------------------------❖---------------------------------

# Models of Papal Social Thought:
# Leo XIII, John XXIII, John Paul II

## Charles D. Skok*

There is no doubt that *Rerum Novarum (RN)* is a landmark document. It is hailed as the beginning of modern Catholic social thought.[1] Because of this centenary year, I am presenting an extended treatment of the background of *RN*. Then, to show the development, continuity, and discontinuity of models of papal social teaching, I am treating Pope John XXIII's *Mater et Magistra (On Christianity and Social Progress) (MM)* and Pope John Paul II's *Sollicitudo Rei Socialis (The Social Concern of the Church) (SS)*, but in a less extended way. I use the same structural analysis for each of the encyclicals: (1) the primary catalysts; (2) unacceptable solutions; (3) acceptable solutions; (4) theological and ecclesial model; and (5) expected praxis in social and economic justice.

## I. Pope Leo XIII and *Rerum Novarum* (1891)

*RN* has become historically the most noteworthy encyclical of Leo XIII. *The Papal Encyclicals 1878-1903*, edited by Claudia Carlen, lists 136 commentaries on it (1981). Yet, if one were to ask what Leo XIII considered his most important encyclical, *RN* likely would not be high on his list.

### A. The Major Pre-*Rerum Novarum* Issues Confronting Pope Leo XIII

During Leo XIII's lifetime, Bernard O'Reilly prepared a biography which was published under the title of *Life of Leo XIII: From an Authentic Memoir Furnished by His Order*. In the dedication of the work to Leo XIII, O'Reilly states that the Pope "called me, by His formal Order, to come from Dublin to Rome, to undertake His Biography" (1903, no page number). James Gibbons, Cardinal Archbishop of Baltimore, in his introduction to the book, praised *RN* as providing "the greatest service...in the establishment of harmonious relations between large employers and the toiling classes, thus laying the foundation for a new temple of peace" (O'Reilly 1903, no page number). But in the 758 pages of authorized memoirs, *RN* is not mentioned. Apparently in the mind of Leo XIII and his biographer, *other* issues were of greater importance. It is against the background of those issues that the direction and significance of *RN* can be delineated.

What were those troubling issues and events? Shortly after Leo XIII became pope, he wrote his first of some 87 encyclicals entitled *On The Evils of Society (Inscrutabili Dei Consilio) (IDC)*, April 21, 1878. In the Enlightenment, the rise of secular states and the demise of the Papal States, he saw not a neutrality but a bitter hostility "to religion and the Church of Christ" (*IDC*, §5). He stepped forward to defend the religious authority, now "despised and set aside" which "in God's name rules mankind, upholding and defending all lawful authority" (*IDC*, §3). "The enemies of public order," he wrote, "...have thought nothing better suited to destroy the foundations of society than to make an unflagging attack upon the Church of God...by spreading infamous calumnies and accusing her of being opposed to genuine progress" (*IDC*, §3).

Leo XIII's first encyclical saw the breakdown of religion and the attacks upon religious authority as the source of the many evils of society. His second encyclical followed soon after. It was *On Socialism (Quod Apostolici Muneris) (QAM)*, Dec. 28, 1878. Its purpose was to confront dangerous new doctrines:

> We speak of that sect of men who, under various and almost barbarous names, are called socialists, communists, or nihilists, and who, spread over all the world, and bound together by the closest ties in a wicked confederacy, no longer seek the shelter of secret meetings, but, openly and boldly marching forth in the light of day, strive to bring to a head what they have long been planning—the overthrow of all civil society whatsoever (*QAM*, §1).

The major cause of "those poisonous doctrines" was the abandonment of religion. He wrote:

> States have been constituted without any count at all of God or of the order established by him; it has been given out that public authority neither derives its principles, nor its majesty, nor its power of governing from God, but rather from the multitude...The supernatural truths of faith having been assailed and cast out as though hostile to reason, the very Author and Redeemer of the human race has been slowly and little by little banished... (*QAM*, §2).

There is no doubt about Leo XIII's persistent opposition to the socialism of his time. In a letter to the Archbishop of Cologne (Feb. 24, 1880) he wrote of "the pest of Socialism" because it "so deeply perverts the sense of our populations" (O'Reilly 1903, p. 481).

Leo XIII's third encyclical, *On the Restoration of Christian Philosophy (Aeterni Patris) (AP)*, Aug. 4, 1879, marked a significant change in his approach. His writing became much more positive in tone. He continues to see that the "fruitful cause of the evils which afflict us" are the "false conclusions concerning divine and human things, which originated in the schools of philosophy...and have been accepted by the common consent of the masses" (*AP* §2), but now he recognizes that false philosophical conclusions must be countered by true ones. He recounts with praise the great contributions to society made by Christian philosophers from the period of the Fathers of the church to the present time. He singles out Thomas Aquinas as the greatest of them: "Domestic and civil society...would certainly enjoy a far more peaceful and secure existence if a more wholesome doctrine were taught...such as is contained in the works of Thomas Aquinas" (*AP*, §28). The philosophy of Thomas Aquinas becomes one of the foundations stones of Leo XIII's thought.

The assassination of the Russian Emperor, Alexander II, a liberally minded sovereign and a social reformer, on March 13, 1881, by a group of nihilists, was one factor which prompted the writing *On the Origin of Civil Power (Diuturnum), (D)* June 29, 1881. Leo XIII wrote:

A society can neither exist nor be conceived in which there is no one to govern the wills of individuals, in such a way as to make...one will out of many, and to impel them rightly and orderly to the common good...This power [to rule] resides solely in God, the Creator and Legislator of all things; and it is necessary that those who exercise it should do it as having received it from God (*D*, §11).

The exercise of civil power requires those in authority to remember that "political power was not created for the advantage of any private individual" (*D*, §16) but for the common good of citizens.

Leo XIII does not treat specific forms of government. His major concern was stability of government built upon the foundation that those governing recognize that the authority they exercise is from God and that citizens be subject to just governments as coming from God. Leo XIII was not a revolutionary.

These pre-*RN* social encyclicals reveal a pope reluctant to give up the past, especially the ideal of Christendom with civil and religious authorities working together hand-in-glove. At the same time, they reveal a pope, unlike his predecessor, Pope Pius IX, poised to come to grips with the realities of modernity. Through these earlier encyclicals Leo XIII used the power of his writing to vindicate what he saw as the clear and unassailable rights of the religious authority vested in him not only to influence society but to offer directives for it. *RN* is rooted firmly in that conservative tradition of those first years of Leo XIII's papal ministry, yet historically it has turned out to be a truly revolutionary document.

❖

## B. The Primary Catalysts for the Encyclical

The more immediate catalysts for the writing of *RN* were the effects of the industrial revolution—a revolution in production, transportation, and communication. Coupled with the industrial revolution in Europe was a rapid expansion of population which provided the human resources to service the new industrial technology and machinery. Joseph N. Moody, writing on Leo XIII, noted that "the mass movement to the factory towns had shattered customary social patterns and left the recruits isolated in an environment that offered bad housing, marginal subsistence, and periodic unemployment" (1961, p. 66).

Commentators point out three specific influences which likely spurred Leo XIII on to the action he took in *RN*. First there was the Knights of Labor controversy. In 1885 the Archbishop of Quebec, with the support of the Canadian hierarchy, had gone to Rome to seek authorization for their censure. In 1886 the Archbishop of Quebec issued a solemn condemnation of the Knights of Labor by name in a pastoral letter (O'Reilly 1903, p. 674; Raymond Corrigan 1938, p. 263). James Gibbons, Cardinal Archbishop of Baltimore, viewed the Knights of Labor in a different light. He was well aware that large numbers of Catholics were members of the Knights. With only two of twelve bishops opposed, he wrote an impassioned letter to the Holy See December 20, 1887, to challenge their condemnation. He wrote: "That there are with us...public injustices and a threatening social evil...is a truth which no one will dare deny" (T'Serclais 1903, p. 221). He told of monopolies, controlled by individuals and corporations, with "heartless avarice, for the sake of profit" who were "pitilessly oppressing...workingmen...women and even young children" (T'Serclais 1903, p. 222). He flatly stated that "it is the right of laborers to protect themselves" and that "the entire people is under obligation to aid them" (T'Serclais1903, p. 222). "Association," he wrote, "is practically the only method of gaining the attention of the public, of giving force to even the most legitimate resistance, and with to even the most just demands" (T'Serclais 1903, p. 222).

Gibbons called for the church to be "the friend of the people" and he cited England's Cardinal Manning that first in our preoccupations must be "the moral state and the domestic condition of the working population" (T'Serclais 1903, p. 224). His final argument was that the condemnation of the Knights of Labor would cause great irritation, would be unjust, and would not be accepted by Catholics in the United States.

Contrary to its earlier condemnation of the Knights of Labor as requested by the Canadian Bishops, the Roman Congregation responded August 29, 1888: "The society of the Knights of Labor may for the moment be tolerated," but local union regulations, the Congregation admonished, must modify anything which might "smack of socialism and of communism" or which would go against the right to acquire property by legitimate means or which would not respect the rights and the property of every one (T'Serclais 1903, p. 225).

The contemporaneous interventions of Cardinal Gibbons in behalf of the Knights of Labor and of Cardinal Manning in behalf of the dock strikers certainly made an impression on Leo XIII, and must be counted among the incentives to write the encyclical.

Perhaps of greater importance was a succession of French worker pilgrimages to Rome with 1,400 workers coming in 1887 and 10,000 in 1889. These pilgrimages, organized by Leon Harmel and Cardinal Langenieux, met with the Pope in their working clothes. The Pope received them as graciously as he would receive royalty. The effect of these events made a world-wide impression (Moody 1961, pp. 74-75). His address to the workers October 20, 1889, spoke of labor as "the natural condition of man on earth" and to evade it is "at once to be a coward and to betray a sacred duty." As for capital, God prescribes "the right use of temporal wealth," especially "in the presence of misfortune and poverty" (T'Serclais 1903, p. 226). He spoke of the need for capital and labor to be established in a "religious and indissoluble bond" so that the "inevitable inequality of human conditions" could "secure to every man a tolerable existence" (T'Serclais 1903, p. 226). His solution, at that time, was to revive in substance the guilds of the arts and crafts to secure the material and religious wants of workers, facilitate their work, care for their savings, protect their rights, and support their legitimate complaints (T'Serclais 1903, p. 226). He warned the workers against agitators bent on the destruction of civil society and of the right to property; he admonished rich and poor alike against a longing for riches, luxury and pleasure. He won over the workers by calling for regulations to guarantee the interests of the workers, to protect youth, to secure the "domestic mission" of women, and to provide for rest on Sunday (T'Serclais 1903, p. 227).

Those events preceding the writing of *RN* certainly influenced the issuing of the encyclical and the shape it took.

## C. The Unacceptable Solutions

The first unacceptable solution is socialism which he had already roundly condemned in his encyclical *QAM* twelve years before. Socialism denies the right to private property. The very reason for working, he argues, beyond making a living, is to be able to save some money, to buy some land, to own some property, to have a "little estate" (*RN*, §5).

His arguments against socialism are primarily philosophical, with a reliance upon the thought of St. Thomas Aquinas. They are based upon an agrarian model of society. Every person "has by nature the right to own property" (*RN*, §6). The owning of property brings about a stability and a security. It enables a person to provide for the future. Following the teaching of Ambrose of Milan (d. 397) and reaffirmed by Thomas Aquinas, Leo XIII asserts that God has given the earth for the use and enjoyment of the whole human race (*RN*, §8), but that in no way militates against private property because the apportionment of the earth among private owners is the very way the earth ministers to the needs of all. The conclusion is definite: "It is clear that the main tenet of socialism, community of goods, must be utterly rejected" (*RN*, §15).

❖

The second unacceptable solution is to resort to "class warfare," as if one class is naturally hostile to another class and as if the wealthy and the working class "are intended by nature to live in mutual conflict" (*RN*, §19). Again, consistent with earlier encyclicals, the Marxist solution of revolution is tersely ruled out.

A third unacceptable solution is to allow the forces of the economy regarding capital and labor to run their course. Leo XIII was wary of too much state intervention. "The State," he said, "must not absorb the individual or the family" *(RN*, §35), but a policy of non-intervention on the part of civil government would allow the continuation of the very causes of the problem to the detriment of the welfare of citizens and the common good (*RN*, §36).

## D.  Acceptable Solutions

The first acceptable solution is to return to the indispensable role of the church in proclaiming the teachings of the Gospel and the upholding of the principles of right conduct. "No practical solution of this question will be found apart from the intervention of religion and of the Church" *(RN*, §16).

The results of such teaching will lead to a realistic assessment of the differences and inequalities of society and the amelioration of utopian ideas for society here on earth. More importantly, workers will be led to carry out their work agreements with respect for their employers and without resort to violence and disorder; employers will come to respect the dignity of the laborers and not look upon them as slaves or muscle or means in the pursuit of wealth. Time will be provided for religious practice, home and family. Employers will not overwork their laborers or give them work unsuitable by reason of age, sex or strength. Wages will not be reduced by force or fraud. Usurious profit will disappear (*RN*, §20).

The teachings of the church will restrain the rich by stern admonition. It is the proper role of the church to relieve the poor through the organization of the works of charity, but the church is allowed to work in cooperation with other agencies and, in limited ways, with the state in the works of charity (*RN*, §§28-31). The "welfare state" had not yet been envisioned.

The second of the acceptable solutions is to preserve the inviolability of private property. There are ethical limitations upon the use of property and money, but these limitations do not restrict the right of ownership; they demand the proper use of money to provide a person and family with a "becoming" living with any surplus going to the poor from an obligation of charity. Leo XIII retains his "other-worldly" spirituality with a reminder that owning property is no guarantee of salvation, nor is poverty a disgrace (*RN*, §22).

The third acceptable solution is the proper intervention of the state. The government, "conformable in its institutions to right reason and natural law," must make possible the realization of both "public well-being and private prosperity" (*RN*, §32). Leo XIII calls for civil authority to promote an atmosphere of morality, a well-regulated family life, respect for religion, moderate and fair taxation, and the viability of the arts, trades and agriculture.

❖

But the major intervention of the government must be in behalf of the working classes who must be held "in the highest estimation" because "society cannot exist or be conceived of without them" (*RN*, §§33-34). Leo XIII wrote:

> Justice demands that the interests of the working classes should be carefully watched over by the administration, so that they who contribute so largely to the advantage of the community may themselves share in the benefits which they create—that being housed, clothed, and bodily fit, they may find their life less hard and more endurable (*RN*, §34).

The final acceptable solution comes under the heading of workers' rights, the section of the encyclical where Leo XIII uses his most forceful language: reasonable working hours and working conditions, no inappropriate work for women and children, and, most important, just wages. Labor is both personal and necessary. Each person has "a natural right to procure what is required in order to live" (*RN*, §44). Just wages include not only what enable workers comfortably to support themselves and their families, but also, by living modestly, to have savings and to be able to own productive property (*RN*, §§46-47). In complete consistency with earlier teachings, Leo XIII extends the right to own property far beyond only those in the "propertied" class!

How would the rights of workers be secured? The then startling answer was: workers' associations or unions.

The first draft of the encyclical offered the solution of "corporatism." Corporatism would call for unions of employers and workers together in a single body under the guidance of the church. Initiatives would come primarily from the employers who would enjoy a privileged status in public law, but workers would be included in their deliberations. It would be a "family" approach bringing together employers, workers, and even workers' families in a new "social Christian order." These unions would be supported by dues from the members and contributions from the wealthy. They would provide for the needy in times of unemployment, sickness or other needs (Moody 1961, pp. 76-77).

Another draft of the encyclical spoke of associations "consisting either of workmen alone, or of workmen and employers together" (qtd. in Moody 1961, p. 77). It is impossible to trace exactly what influences moved Leo XIII from corporatism to strictly workers' unions. Cardinal Manning? Cardinal Gibbons? A realization of economic realities? A major breakthrough had occurred, but there is no definitive answer as to what brought it about (Moody 1961, pp. 77-78).

The final draft did offer praise for the corporatist approach, but it also insisted that workers have the natural right to organize *as workers* and that the State has an obligation to protect that natural right (*RN*, §51). Catholics, with due regard for their religious obligations, should take an active part in promoting and guiding unions in the securing of workers' rights (*RN*, §§55-59).

❖

The major step had been taken. The "pressing question of the hour" was being addressed: "the condition of the working classes" (*RN*, §60). Workers would have some ground for hope. Some workers, Leo XIII mused, may return to the practice of their faith.

## E. Ecclesial and Theological Models

The model of church underlying the thought of Leo XIII in *RN* is definitely hierarchical and institutional. He views the church as a "perfect society" in the spiritual realm just as the State is a "perfect society" in the temporal realm. True authority in both realms comes from God. The answers to the problems of the day should therefore come from both religious and temporal authorities in harmony with one another. Peoples are divided into rulers and subjects. The hierarchy of the church has the mission to teach, to rule, and to sanctify; the laity have the obligation to be taught, to be ruled, to be sanctified. Church authority not only cares for its own flock, but can also offer, because of divine guidance, much assistance to society at large. Such a model of church enables those in authority to teach and to give directions with self-assurance and confidence. Leo XIII certainly did.

The theological model is akin to the ecclesial model. God is the source of all that is. All history develops under the guiding and providential hand of God. God's revelation in Scripture is a chief source of discovering the will of God; the guidance of the Holy Spirit, promised to the hierarchical authority, inspires trust in the church's teaching authority; and God-given reason is aided in coming to proper decisions and conclusions not only by the power of reason itself but also by reason aided by grace, giving such decisions and conclusions a more urgent and compelling value. This theological anthropology recognizes that all women and men are children of God, but does not hesitate to give greater worth to those individuals called to higher positions. It accepts an inequality among people as a fact in the order of an organic society. It is my conclusion that Leo XIII wrote out of this revelation-from-above model. Those in authority have the obligation to care for those in their charge by mediating the message of God to them for the welfare of their lives and for their salvation. The "sheep" are the recipients of, not the direct participants in, the teaching, governing, and sanctifying ministry of the "shepherds." They are to believe and to obey what is presented to them. This theological model presents doctrine with clearness and moral conduct with decisiveness. There is no doubt as to what is taught as faith or morals. But it also contributes to an indifference to the content of doctrine and a passivity in response to it.

## F. Expected Praxis in Social and Economic Justice

The praxis flowing from the ecclesial and theological models described above depends upon the readers and the hearers taking to heart the message of the teacher. Faithful Catholics, looking upon the Pope as the supreme teacher of the church, listen to the message and begin to devise ways to put it into practice. Some will listen to the message for its reasonableness and good sense. Other will sense the sincere good will of the message and be inspired to do something about the now recognized "misery and wretchedness" of the lives of workers.

The non-reception of the message is also a problem. As a matter of fact, the vindication of the right to property against socialistic teaching encouraged many wealthy property owners to insist upon their right to their property and the power and privilege it gave them, as granted to them from God. The strong condemnation of socialism instilled into many people that the very mention of the word was mortally sinful, regardless of what nuanced form a particular socialism might take. Its categorical condemnation kept many Catholics from becoming involved in anything that even smacked of socialist tendencies. In some countries, the hierarchies, to whom the encyclical was addressed, did not see fit to disseminate it.[2]

But the major effect of the encyclical is that, by its very issuance, the social question became for the Catholic church a religious and a moral question. Leo XIII, perhaps going against some of his deepest patrician instincts, boldly returned the Church, after a long absence, into the mainstream of social justice involvement, more deeply than he perhaps realized. An "other-worldly" church became immersed in "this-worldly" concerns, above all, the concerns of the lives of the poor and the oppressed and the disadvantaged.

## II. Pope John XXIII and *MATER ET MAGISTRA* (1961)

When Angelo Roncalli was elected Pope on October 28, 1958, he was already seventy-seven years old. A few years later, in his own journal, perhaps with subtle humor, he wrote:

> Everyone was convinced that I would be a provisional and transitional pope. Yet here I am...with an immense programme of work in front of me to be carried out before the eyes of the whole world, which is watching and waiting (*John XXIII* 1964, p. 303).

John XXIII was hardly a transitional pope. In the short years between his election in 1958 and his death June 3, 1963, he changed the face of the Catholic Church, particularly through the Second Vatican Council—an Ecumenical Council he announced January 25, 1959, convoked December 25, 1961, and convened October 11, 1962. In his unassuming and humble way, he wanted an *aggiornamento* for the Church; he wanted to bring the Church into the second half of the twentieth century; he wanted the Church to be a vital force in a modern and changing world—and, with very little fanfare, he set about to do it.

### A. The Primary Catalysts for *Mater et Magistra*

The seventieth anniversary of *RN* was not just an excuse to write an encyclical on social justice, much as John XXIII admired Leo XIII. In the first part of *MM*, he

❖

reviews the accomplishments of *RN*, particularly its effect upon the upholding the human dignity of workers and the role of the state to realize the common good of all. He calls *RN* the "*Magna Charta* of social and economic reconstruction" (*MM*, §26). Then he reviews the achievements flowing from *Quadragesimo Anno (QA)* of Pope Pius XI, particularly his teaching of the principle of subsidiarity and his call for workers to participate in ownership and management so that in some way they would be able to share in profits. He makes a brief mention of Pope Pius XII reaffirming *RN's* teaching on private property and the rights of workers.

In the post-World War II world, John XXIII noted a "radical transformation" of the economic scene both within nations and among nations; tremendous scientific and technological advances in nuclear energy, chemistry, communications, transportation, space exploration, and automation of industry and agriculture; sociological developments in social security systems, education, distribution of essential commodities, and awareness of major social and economic problems; and political changes in the independence of former colonial nations and in all classes of citizens demanding a participation in the public life of their nations. The changing aspects of society are the background for the encyclical.

## B. The Unacceptable Solutions

In the second part of the encyclical, "Explanation and Development of the Teaching of *RN*," he reiterates the teaching of Leo XIII, and, in that sense, is again condemning laissez faire economics made possible by the lack of state intervention for the common good; socialism; unjust remuneration for work; inequitable structures in business and industry; and the denial of the right to private property. The unacceptable solutions of Leo XIII remain unacceptable to John XXIII. Socialism is not the answer, nor is unrestrained capitalism. The former denies many rights, including the right to own property; the latter does not have a sufficient social conscience to uphold the basic human rights of all people without discrimination or to prevent their exploitation. Total state control over the economy is not the answer, nor is abdication of responsibility on the part of the state. The development of Leo XIII's thought, however, is such that it becomes distinctively John XXIII's.

## C. Acceptable Solutions

For John XXIII, "the economic order is the creation of the personal initiative of private citizens working either as individuals or in association with each other in various ways for the furtherance of common interests" (*MM*, §51). There is nothing mystical about economics. The economic order is formed by people for people's interests. That is why he says flatly: "The civil power must also have a hand in the economy. It has to promote production in a way best calculated to achieve social progress and the well-being of citizens" (*MM*, §52).

But civil power must keep in mind Pius XI's "principle of subsidiary function" which makes it wrong to withdraw from the individual and commit to the

❖

state what private enterprise and industry can accomplish; larger and higher associations must never arrogate to themselves functions which can be performed efficiently and well by smaller and lower entities (*MM*, §53). Small is "beautiful" wherever small is possible. He is not afraid of state intervention, but he calls for a balance: too much state intervention stifles private initiate and leads to a demand for freedom; too little intervention allows private exploitation and leads to a demand for regulation.

Leo XIII and Pius XI issued vigorous condemnations of socialism. John XIII writes of "socialization" rather than of socialism. He said:

> The recognition of common interests on an ever-increasing scale has led to the introduction of many and varied forms of social planning in the lives and activities of citizens (*MM*, §59).

He looks upon the process of socialization as a fact:

> It is...the result and the expression of a natural, wellnigh irresistible urge in man to combine with his fellows for the attainment of aims and objectives which are beyond the means or the capabilities of single individuals (*MM*, §60).

Socialization can make it possible for individuals to exercise many of their personal rights, especially their social and economic rights. It can give people access to human events the world over. A negative effect of socialization is the possible narrowing of the sphere of a person's freedom of action with the corresponding limiting of a person's initiative and responsibility, but that does not have to be its effect. Again, he insists:

> A balance must be struck between the autonomous and active collabo-ration of individuals and groups, and the timely co-ordination and direction of public enterprise by the State (*MM*, §66).

Within the proper framework of moral and ethical principles, socialization of its nature is not dangerous or detrimental to the individual (*MM*, §67).

Remuneration for work,the just wage, is always a sticky social justice issue. John XXIII does not think in terms of inflexible principles. He states:

> Remuneration for work is not something that can be left to the laws of the market; nor ought it to be fixed arbitrarily. It must be determined in accordance with justice and equity (*MM*, §71).

The "floor" for wages must allow for living in a worthy manner, but, beyond that, the following factors must be included: the effective contribution of the worker to

❖

the enterprise; the financial state of the enterprise; the general standard of living in a country; and the common good of the universal family of the human race *(MM,* #71). These factors allow for many variables, but within bounds. He acknowledges a relationship between wages paid in developing countries and developed countries. There is a call for a certain equity in wage differentials to avoid unfair competition. There must also be an equilibrium between wages and prices.

The justice of an economic system is to be judged not by productivity or wealth or even distribution of wealth; it is to be judged by what it does to people, by how it affects the human dignity of people, by how it affects their sense of responsibility and their freedom of action *(MM,* §83). The effective participation of all involved in the enterprise is the ideal. The safeguarding of smaller enterprises offers the best opportunity for participation, but efforts must be made for greater participation even in the largest enterprises.

True to his predecessors, John XXIII upholds the right to private property, the right to the ownership of goods, including productive goods, as a natural right of "permanent validity." He insists that this right must be extended to all classes of people, if it truly means anything. He does not deny the right of the state for public ownership of productive property, particularly when such ownership, quoting *QA,* carries with it a power too great to be left to private individuals, a power which could become injurious to the community at large.

Productive property can be owned both by individuals (or corporations) and by the state. To counter the increased ownership by the state, he insists upon the principle of subsidiarity. To move away from any hint of laissez faire capitalism, he insists very strongly on the social function of ownership as a teaching consistent with the long tradition of Christianity. The right to own property is upheld but the right to use property is limited by the common good *(MM,* §§119-121).

Perhaps because of his experiences as a child in a peasant farm family, John XXIII took a special interest in agricultural issues. He notes in *MM* the phenomenon of the migration of rural populations to cities. He says that farming has become a "depressed occupation." Productive efficiency of farms has not kept pace with that of industry and services, and agricultural standards of living do not approximate those enjoyed by urban people.

His first call is for the suitable development of essential public services in rural areas "to check or control the drift of population from the land" *(MM,* §127). Farmers should have access to good roads, public transportation, means of communication, potable water, good housing, health services, education, recreation, religious activities—all the things associated with urban life.

He calls for a balance between the industrial and agricultural sectors for the mutual benefit of both. He maintains that the balance cannot happen unless there are sound policies for equitable taxation, access to credit, social insurance and social security, and a certain price protection to safeguard farm income and wages for farm laborers *(MM,* §128-140).

❖

His primary concern is the family farm. To safeguard the family farm, there must be a "community of persons working together for the advancement of their mutual interests" (*MM*, §142). His solution to the problem takes the shape of farmers banding together in cooperatives and forming associations or unions where they would take the initiative in solidarity for their "own economic advancement, social progress, and cultural betterment" (*MM*, §§144-148). Public authority should be a friend in encouraging the private enterprise of farming in economic development (*MM*, §§150-152).

The universality of John XXIII's thought becomes clear when he calls for nations all over the world to facilitate the movement of goods, capital, and people from one country to another. This free movement would help to balance out surplus and scarcity, advanced methods of farming and primitive methods, and plentiful arable land and scarce arable land (*MM*, §§153-156).

He cites efforts being made to alleviate some of the gross imbalances. But he does not want short range answers to problems. Developed nations should not be exporting the products of technology but their scientific, technical and professional training. Aid to underdeveloped nation must respect the dignity and individuality of the country being aided, and the aid should be "disinterested aid," aid which is not just cleverly disguised colonialism. The basic principle underlying his thought is: as each nation seeks its own common good, it must also seek the common good of all nations.

When it comes to population increases and the demands these increasing populations will have upon the resources of the earth, he remains optimistic: "The resources which God in His goodness and wisdom has implanted in Nature are wellnigh inexhaustible" (*MM*, §189). The problems are real, but the resources of human intelligence are also real, and they open what he terms "limitless horizons." There is need for worldwide cooperation among all peoples. He upholds the sacredness of human life, the dignity of the transmission of human life, and the worth of marriage and the family. His approach is to bring to bear scientific and technological resources for the upholding and enhancement of human life in all countries—not for providing "instruments of ruin and death" (*MM*, §§185-199).

To achieve the economic and social betterment of the peoples of the earth, there must first come the breakdown of the mutual distrusts (referring globally to the "cold war"), the acknowledgement of the foundations of justice and morality, and upbuilding of mutual cooperation and trust. Nothing is more harmful to the achievement of that goal than reliance upon incomplete and false ideologies. The social justice teaching of the church can be a valuable ally in the continual reconstruction of the social order.

## D. Ecclesial and Theological Models

The model of church underlying the social doctrine of John XXIII is much less hierarchical and institutional than what is found in Leo XIII (or his successors).

Here the model is the church as People of God presided over by, but not dominated by, the pope and bishops. The church is a people in the midst of the people of the society of the world at large. The people in the church have a solidarity with the people of the world. There will be a constant interchange. In this model there is much less dogmatic presiding, much more thoughtful admonishing. There is a hesitancy in condemning, lest the good be condemned with the bad. John XXIII insisted, as did his predecessors:

> When the Hierarchy has made a decision on any point Catholics are bound to obey their directives. The Church has the right and obligation not merely to guard ethical and religious principles, but also to declare its authoritative judgment in the matter of putting these principles into practice (*MM*, §239).

But at the same time he insists that they show themselves "animated by a spirit of understanding and unselfishness, ready to co-operate loyally in achieving objects which are good in themselves, or can be turned into good" *(MM*, §239) when they are with people who do not share their views.

His model of church as People of God or Community of the Faithful allows him to teach with approachability and persuasiveness. Hales observed: "Part of the charm of Pope John was his refusal to pontificate on public affairs; one feels he is only giving advice; ...not...laying down the law" (1965, p. 28). There is a sense of inclusiveness and a sense of personal worth engendered in this model. It is a community of people presided over not by a domineering father but by a caring elder brother.

Papal encyclicals traditionally have been addressed to the bishops of the Church. *MM* was addressed simply to "Venerable Brethren and Dearest Sons." John XXIII's final encyclical, *Pacem in Terris (Peace on Earth)*, April 29, 1963, not only was addressed to the bishops of the world, but also, the first for a papal encyclical, "to the Clergy and Faithful of the Whole World and to All Men of Good Will"—the "all of good will" is a final reminder to the world of John XXIII's theological anthropology.

### E.  Expected Praxis in Social and Economic Justice

Because social teaching at a universal level will necessarily be more general than specific, it is difficult to assign expected results or to measure results once they have been achieved. The style of John XXIII tended to be inclusive. It was a new style, with new spirit and new themes (Jean-Yves Calvez 1964, p. x). This new style attracted people; it drew people in. Although he used, for example, the traditional term, "social justice," as did his predecessors, he was much more apt to use terms such as "justice and equity" or "justice and humanity" to give a note of universality (Calvez 1964, pp. 94-99). *MM* offered inspiration for many commentaries and articles in a broad variety of journals. Claudia Carlen's (1981) edition of papal encyclicals list one hundred and five of them.

The encyclical itself brings about praxis only when it becomes disseminated and when its ideas percolate down to those concerned about and involved in working for social justice and economic development. The papal approach of John XXIII made *MM* readily accessible and acceptable to those in need of social and economic improvement and also to those able to effect it.

The lasting achievement of *MM* can best be illustrated by an immediate effect, the Second Vatican Council document, *Gaudium et Spes (Pastoral Constitution on the Church of the World Today)* promulgated December 7, 1965. When the preparatory work for the Second Vatican Council was underway, such a Council document was not yet envisioned. Before the fourth and final session of the Council began, many doubted that the social legacy of John XXIII would last. One commentator said: "The bishops loved him, but they ignored him" (Hales 1965, p. 196). It seemed that John XXIII did not succeed in turning the bishops' minds to the world at large and that he was unsuccessful in insisting that the Council "was to provide the world with a light to lead her towards unity, peace, and justice" (Hales 1965, p. 196). However, the last document to be approved by the Second Vatican Council was the one for which John XXIII had opened the door with MM. Now his papal social teaching, perhaps not as completely as he would have desired, was given the weight of the highest teaching authority of the Catholic Church, the magisterial teaching of pope and bishops gathered in ecumenical council.[3]

## III. Pope John Paul II and *Sollicitudo Rei Socialis* (1987)

### A. The Primary Catalysts for *Sollicitudo Rei Socialis* (1987)

Pope Paul VI's encyclical *Populorum Progressio (On the Development of Peoples) (PP)* had been issued March 26, 1967, twenty years before. John Paul II wanted "to pay homage to this historic document"(*Sollicitudo Rei Socialis (SRS,* §3), which treated the major themes of "development" and "solidarity." A second purpose was "to reaffirm the *continuity* of the social doctrine [of the Church] as well as its constant *renewal*" (*SRS,* §3). A third reason for the encyclical was to make "an *appeal to conscience*" to the people of today (*SRS,* §4). Paul VI's *PP* appeared less than two years after the close of Vatican II. John Paul II sees in that fact an immediate attempt to apply the social teachings of the Council's document, *The Church in the Modern World* (1965).

John Paul II heartily affirms Paul VI's treatment of the issues at hand: the poverty and underdevelopment of so many peoples of the world; the incumbent obligation of developed nations to help the developing nations; the legitimacy and necessity of the church, a "religious institution," to be involved in development; the fact of the worldwide dimensions of the "social question"; the unequal distribution of means of subsistence with little concern for the solidarity of the human family;

and the need for development and the demand for justice as an instrument of peace (*SRS*, §§5-10).

The hopes of Paul VI for development, in the time span of twenty years, had not been realized. Vast numbers of peoples are still suffering under the intolerable burden of poverty (*SRS*, §13). The gap between developed nations of the North and the developing nations of the South has widened, not narrowed, not because there has not been progress but because the pace of progress differs. The very terms, First World, Second World, Third World, and Fourth World are a good indication of the problem (*SRS*, §14).

There must be added a contemporary list of concerns: illiteracy; various forms of exploitation; many forms of oppression—economic, social, political and religious; racial discrimination; suppression of economic initiative; and the denial of human rights. These evils, confronted by Paul VI, are still widely present in the world. But, more characteristic of John Paul II's thought, economic underdevelopment is but one *aspect* of a broader ethico-moral malaise. The interdependence of all nations is a fact. All nations must participate in development (*SRS*, §§15-17).

## B.  The Unacceptable Solutions

John Paul II experienced many years of his life in Marxist-Communist Poland. He shows a distinct preference for the freedom of Western societies as opposed to the lack of freedom in Communist countries, but he is not an ardent supporter of *liberal* capitalism. He sees it as a system susceptible to producing materialism, secularism, and consumerism as well as gross inequities between the wealthy and the poor. He sees in it an "all-consuming desire for profit" (*SRS*, §37). He also sees it as spiritually deficient. Liberal capitalism in itself is not an acceptable solution.

Nor is Marxist communism a solution. He shows an unyielding opposition to it. He looks upon it more as a cause of the problem than as any solution.

Nor does he propose a "third way" between the two. The solutions to the problem must be created. The social doctrine of the church does not propose concrete solutions "in economic and political systems" nor does the church "show preference for one or the other" (*SRS*, §41), but the church does propose the basic principles upon which the solutions can be founded.

## C.  The Acceptable Solutions

The first acceptable solution is the proper ordering of the economic development of peoples. That begins with an acceptance of the dignity of human persons and an awareness of human rights. There must also be the recognition of human solidarity in inter-dependence. There must be respect for human life. There must be an awareness of the limits of resources and an ecological concern for the environment. The mere accumulation of goods and services in consumerism must

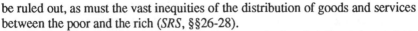

be ruled out, as must the vast inequities of the distribution of goods and services between the poor and the rich (*SRS*, §§26-28).

A second acceptable solution is a return to the interior dimensions of the human person which acknowledge not only affinity with God's creation but also with God, which recognize the human person in the image of God and subject to God, and which see the transcendent reality of the human being. This transcendent reality fosters an optimistic vision of history and an authentic evaluation of human achievements in their relationship to the redemption of Christ and their eternal destiny (*SRS*, §§29-31).

A third acceptable solution is the collaboration of individuals, churches, peoples, and nations in the development of "the whole person" in the fullest dimensions of the human being, including the moral, the religious, and the transcendent. This can happen only in the framework of solidarity and freedom *(SRS*, §§32-34).

John Paul II places the solution to the problems of the development of peoples in a directly theological perspective. The problems are the results of "*essentially moral decisions*" (*SRS*, §35). They are the results of "sin" and "structures of sin." It is important to identify the moral evil and the many sins which lead to the sinful structures and institutions to find the "*the path to be followed* in order *to overcome [them]*" (*SRS*, §§36-37).

The final acceptable solution is an awareness of and an appeal to *human solidarity* among persons within each society and in all societies throughout the world (*SRS*, §§38-40).

The solutions of John Paul II to the social and economic problems of development in the world lean heavily on the moral, the spiritual, and the transcendent. He expresses hope for human social and economic development, but, based on his reading of realties in the world at large, he does not tend to be optimistic.

## D. Ecclesial and Theological Models

John Paul II's model of church does not forget the church as People of God or as a community of believers, but it tends toward a church strongly hierarchical and institutional. If the model of church as family is used, John Paul II is without a doubt the head of the household. He came from a country that lived under a highly centralized and authoritarian rule. Democracy was not a lived experience. Any sharing in decision-making was limited in its extension. His model of church seems to reflect some of those experiences. His model of church does not generate the enthusiasm and the vitality of John XXIII's where people not only sensed that they were welcome to become involved but also that their very involvement was welcomed. John Paul II wants things under hierarchical control.

He looks upon himself as "pastor of the world." He reveals in his addresses and homilies that he sometimes looks upon his people as a "wayward flock,"

❖

particularly in areas of sexual morality but also in their pleasure-seeking material-ism and consumerism. When *SRS* appeared, Roland J. Faley, the executive director of the Conference of Superiors of Men, observed: "Christians are called to greater simplicity in their choices and life styles" (1988). In John Paul II's model of church, there is much more emphasis on individuals being called to conversion, and much less emphasis on communities as communities being called to conversion. In this respect, there is a strong element of the model of church as the proclaimer of the gospel. John Paul II himself names the church a "community of disciples" (*Redemptor Hominis*, §21). Discipleship comes about only through *metanoia*, repentance, conversion.

John XXIII and especially Paul VI saw the church as a community of believers living within the larger community of the people of the world. This believing community was to be servant to that larger community, to make the reign of God more apparent and more effective in their lives through the overcoming of the situations of oppression and poverty. John Paul II's hope is the same, but his model of church is much more directed toward moral and spiritual renewal than toward programs of social and economic development.

His theological model follows his ecclesial model. The keystone is "the dignity of the human person as enunciated in the revealed plan of God" (Faley). People are not to be "cogs in the wheel of state determination or profit-determined goals that submerge the individual" (Faley). His fear of liberation theology was perhaps not so much that it liberated, as it should, but that it might not liberate the human person totally, in all the person's dimensions, including the person's transcendence. His theological anthropology requires that social and economic ills be addressed not "soley by social remedies," but by "authentic conversion." Greed, avarice, ruthless grasping for power and inherent selfishness create the structures of sin. The structures of sin cannot be demolished without addressing the causes (Faley).

John Paul II speaks of the church "as an expert in humanity" (*SRS*, §41). In *SRS* he reintroduces the term of "social doctrine." It refers to "a body of teaching built up by the Papal Magisterium of the Catholic Church over about a hundred years" (Kiliroor 1988).

The concept of "social doctrine" tends to view such doctrine as a constant which needs only to be applied in changing social and economic situations. Matthew Kiliroor concludes: "It is not difficult to see the difference between *development* and *adaptation*" (1988). It takes away from local communities the active role of *"drawing* principles of reflection, norms of judgment, and directives for action" (*Octogesina Adveniens*, §4). The final result:

> This does not favour an ecclesiology of *communio*, nor does it help to encourage the mission and the vocation of the laity in the Church and the world (Kiliroor).

John Paul II's theological model is consistent with his ecclesial model.

❖

### E. Expected Praxis in Social and Economic Justice

The teaching of Paul VI commemorated in this encyclical moved people to action. Base Christian communities were formed in Latin America. It is as if Paul VI had said: "We have talked enough. It is time to act. We are not sure where some of those actions will lead."

John Paul II's encyclical is not so much a call to action as a call to conversion. If that call to conversion is heeded at all levels of individuals and of society, he foresees that there will be social and economic development; he foresees that there will develop a respect for the God-given dignity and rights of individuals as persons and in society; and he foresees that there will be some move toward world peace.

I see a much closer affinity of John Paul II with Leo XIII than with John XXIII and Paul VI. But I also see that the church through its papal leaders will always be involved in the world-wide "social question," because social and economic justice are at base moral issues.

### Endnotes

*Associate Professor of Religious Studies, Gonzaga University, Spokane, WA 99258 USA.

[1]  As examples, David Hollenbach's essay (1977), Donal Dorr's book, *Option for the Poor* (1983), and John A. Coleman's *One Hundred Years of Catholic Social Thought* (1991) all use Leo XIII as the beginning point of their works on modern Catholic social thought.

[2]  One example came from a conversation with two Argentinean priest graduate students in Rome at the time of the issuance of John XXIII's *Mater et Magistra* on May 15, 1961. They reported that *Rerum Novarum* had not been published in their country, and that they were not allowed to have copies of it in their seminary.

[3]  A treatment of the development of social thought in the Second Vatican Council by this author can be found in "The Social Economics of *Gaudium et Spes* The Constitution of the Church in the Modern World," *International Journal of Social Economics*, 1986, *13*(9), 25-44, or in *International Review of Economics and Ethics*, *1986, 1*(3), 25-44.

### References

Calvez, Jean-Yves. *The Social Thought of John XXIII*, Trans. George J.M. McKenzie, Chicago: Henry Regnery, 1964.

Carlen, Claudia, ed. *The Papal Encyclicals 1878-1903*, Raleigh, NC: McGrath Publishing, 1981.

Carlen, Claudia, ed. *The Papal Encyclicals 1903-1939*, Raleigh, NC: McGrath Publishing, 1981.

Carlen, Claudia, ed. *The Papal Encyclcials 1958-1981*, Raleigh, NC: McGrath Publishing, 1981.

Coleman, John A., ed. *One Hundred Years of Catholic Social Thought*, Maryknoll: NY, Orbis, 1991.

Dorr, Donal. *Option for the Poor: A Hundred Years of Vatican Social Teaching*, Maryknoll, NY: Orbis, 1983.

Faley, Roland J. "Pope as Prophet: The New Social Encyclical," *America*, April 30, 1988, *158*, 447-450,462.

Hales, E.E.Y. *Pope John and His Revolution*, New York, Doubleday, 1965.

Hollenbach, David "Modern Catholic Teachings Concerning Justice," in John C. Haughey, ed., *The Faith That Does Justice*, New York: Paulist, 1977, 207-31.

John XXIII. *Journal of a Soul*, New York: McGraw-Hill, 1964.

John Paul II. *Redemptor Hominus*, Washington, DC: USCC, 1979.

John Paul II. *Sollicitudo Rei Socialis*, Nairobi: St. Paul Publications, 1988.

Kiliroor, Matthew. "'Social Doctrinein' in *Solicitudo Rei Socialis*," *The Month*, June 1988, *249*, 711-14.

Moody, Joseph N. "Leo XIII and the Social Crisis," *Leo XIII and the Modern World*, Edward T.Gargan, (Ed.), New York: Sheed and Ward, 1961, 63-86.

O'Reilly, Bernard, *The Life of Pope Leo XIII: From an Authentic Memoir Furnished by His Order*, City Unknown: John C. Winston Co., 1903.

T'Serclais, Charles de. *The Life and Labors of Pope Leo XIII*, Maurice Francis Egan (Trans.), New York: Rand, McNally, 1903.

---  ❖  ---

# Mechanist Justice: An Historical Variant of Institutions with Some Force of Natural Law

## *Ralph Austin Powell, O.P.* *

This paper tries to prove two conclusions: 1) The doubling of GNP over a lifetime is a partially free mechanical cause of justice. 2) A free mechanical cause of justice is a historical variant of institutions with something of the force of natural law.

*By partly free mechanical causes* I mean: social mechanisms whose causality is partly free social causality. This concept of *partly free causality* within mechanical causes is very different from the familiar term "free markets," which denotes *freedom from government interference*. This latter term is usually understood to mean social mechanisms which, when free from government interference, are natural mechanisms like the solar system, utterly *devoid of free human causality* (cf. Coase 1988: 34-36; Demsetz 1988: chs. 9, 17, 18).

This partially free causality with mechanical causes is an assumption that needs proof. In *the first (economic) part of the paper,* I argue from a fact of experience. The fact alleged is that consumer demand in retail markets depends on the differentiated demand of socio-cultural groups; that the public fact of socio-cultural group demand is the sign of social solidarity within individual preference; that group solidarity is then a sign of free obedience or disobedience within individual preference. In the second (philosophical) part of the paper, I argue from causality to prove partly free causality in social mechanisms.

This paper will be divided as follows:

I.   What I mean by mechanist social justice.
II.  Preliminary answers to objections against mechanist justice or injustice of the US political economic system.
III. Mechanist justice is a uniquely modern historical variant of institutions with much of the force of natural law.

❖

IV.   Appendix. Natural Law efficacy within mechanist justive institutions,
      contrasted with political liberalism and political conservatism.

## I.   What I Mean by "Mechanist Social Justice"

By "mechanist social justice" I mean: 1) payment by the total political-
economic partially free mechanism; 2) to the retiring working poor; 3) of income
above the then poverty line; 4) as transaction cost of economic growth over that
generation of their working lives.

I explain the four parts of this definition.

**Point 1:** *Payment by the total political-economic free mechanism*

Economists agree that markets are information mechanisms. Now information mechanisms are sign mechanisms that appeal to people's beliefs as, for
example, traffic lights appeal to the beliefs of law abiding citizens. Some market
sign mechanisms appeal to consumers beliefs in different parts of the public. For
these beliefs differ among the rich, the middle-class and the poor; among teens,
young adults, the middle-aged, and the old; they differ in different regions of the
country and according to the seasons of the year. Now the common beliefs of the
different groups are *signs of the power of the group identity to mold their members
into these common beliefs.* The market offers many rival products, each claiming
to conform better to the demand of a given group. For example, how great is the
power in this country of current women's fashions; how great is the power of the
public of current rock music; how great is the power of the public that knows which
are the best restaurants in town!

Producers strive to fashion their products to conform to the public demand of
such groups. Producers do not strive to conform to individuals' physically determined brain states, as economic determinism held according to the axiom: *Mann
ist was er ist.* For these brain events fall under the *inscrutable privacy* of private
experience. Producers strive to conform to the *public economic power* of groups.
Moreover, producers sometimes change the beliefs of the public. Really new
products even create new publics: the automobile created the automobile public and
eventually the vast social change constituted by the American suburbs. In this way
the automobile industry and the suburbs acquired power to define success for those
publics.

Nevertheless, markets are social *mechanisms that determine prices imper-
sonally,* because no individual or institution can control them completely. Yet
impersonal consumer markets are also where consumers and producers make their
power felt. Effective power, however, is a sign of human freedom, since those who
obey always have the option of disobedience. For example, in the chain of cars
speeding on the Interstate Highway, some may disobey the law. Hence consumers'
markets are partially free social mechanisms. The oligopoly structure of today's

❖

economy is plainly an impersonal market touched with the freedom of major corporations and of government.

Now partial freedom of a consumers' market consists in two things. First, the market as a sign mechanism signifies *its public and social parts: it cannot signify the private thoughts, desires, or intentions of individuals.* Secondly, the power of the differing beliefs that binds each of the several groups together does not constitute the partial freedom of the market either. For each of these groups, the power of the belief that binds them together is a *mere mind-dependent symbol.* And because they are mere public symbols, like the flag or the "Star Spangled Banner," they are incapable of producing real effects in the physical world. *Rather, it is the proportion of each group that obeys the power of its group that belongs to the consumer market mechanism itself.* And that input of free obedience to their respective groups *constitutes the partial freedom of the market.*

By the same method, democratic elections can also be shown to be partially free sign mechanisms, *indicating the winner.* Since the basics of political polling are well known, I can restrict myself to an *argument from analogy:* namely, the analogy between the group authorities in an election and the group authorities in markets (proving that elections are also partially free sign mechanisms).

First of all, elections are *mechanisms*, because from pre-election day samples of 2000 citizens, the voting behavior of 190 million voters is regularly predicted within a margin of error of 2 percent.

Secondly, the predictive power of *representative* samples manifests the mechanism as a *sign mechanism* signifying the majority and minority parties as partisan authority groups. The plurality of the majority party is a public real sign effect indicating the majority party as winner. Hence the election causes a public nationally discriminating real effect. Now that effect is *a free effect.* For a free effect is nothing but a *real rationally discriminating effect indicating "this" and not "that."* The traffic light blinks its signals through the night, whether or not anyone is there to be affected by it. But the election mechanism *causes a free effect* that cannot exist without the voters being affected by it.

Now the full free sign effect of the election mechanism is to change partisan authority blocks into mutually cooperative parts of the government, as *the foreseen promise* of a free election. That is a *just effect.* For it is the *fulfillment of the promise of the election.* That just effect is the *moral authority* of the free election mechanism. Hence the power of the election mechanism is a moral power. That is very different from the power of women's fashions, the authority of the public of rock music and the power of the public that knows the best restaurants in town. Those powers' domains concern "artistic" taste of various sorts. By producing public just effects, *the electoral mechanism is a moral authority.*

In our mixed economy, political and economic mechanisms are one inter-locking total mechanism. And that total mechanism is *partially free* in its central institutions: the consumer's markets and the elections. Point 1 of what I mean by "Mechanist Social Justice" is thus initially explained. It reads: "Payment by the

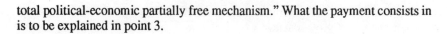

total political-economic partially free mechanism." What the payment consists in is to be explained in point 3.

### Point 2: *to the retiring working poor.*

The retiring working poor are those retiring after some 50 years of a working life. By "working poor" I mean those *regularly employed whose income still falls below the poverty line.* They have short spells of unemployment, but basically they are employed all their working lives. But the working poor do not constitute a distinct social class in US society. They live in working class neighborhoods where regular employment and normal family life are the expected and existing realities for people. Yet they sometimes suffer unemployment and slip further into poverty. *But they never lose their identity with the working class neighborhood where they live.* They do not constitute a social class or a social body distinct from the rest of the working class. These are the people about whom Daniel Patrick Moynihan wrote a memorandum to then President Nixon saying that the Negative Income Tax ("NIT") proposal would abolish the poverty of the working poor from the land. Now NIT is a transfer program. But the definition of "working poor" contained in the NIT was endorsed by the economics profession as a whole when it endorsed the NIT. The working poor, as *those full time employed workers whose income falls beneath the poverty line,* is an *accepted economic definition.*

The *Underclass,* on the contrary, is a distinct social class in the US. It consists of concrete neighborhoods where female headed households, welfare dependency, and joblessness are normal (Sawhill 1986, p.229; Wilson 1987, pp. 56-57).

### Point 3: *of income above the poverty line:*

*More fully articulated,* point 3 is: Income above their retiring year's poverty line equal to middle class income a generation ago, because GNP has meantime doubled.

An *important characteristic of our industrial economies in the last hundred years is that they grew at the rate of 2% annually.* Hence, GNP roughly doubled every 50 years (Gould 1972, p.33; North 1981, p.158). Historians understand this sustained secular growth as characteristic of the Industrial Revolution.

I look at data on the working class at the beginning of a generation as compared with the same working class at retirement, *showing whether their retirement income is within what had been middle class income when they entered the work force in youth.*

Data on the working poor concerns principally *their percent of household budget spent on food.* For the official poverty line takes 1/3 of household budgets spent on food as the line that distinguishes the poor from the nonpoor (Samuelson and Nordhaus, p.105). These authors point out that this 33 per cent of U.S. poverty line incomes budgeted for food is more than 10 times the biological minimum for life support (Samuelson and Nordhaus, p.805 and note 26). That does not prove that

❖

it is "generous," since the Federal Bureau of Labor Statistics found the official poverty line of 1975, $5500 for a family of four, way below the $8588 it considered "austere" (Wilson, p. 171). But the official poverty line is nevertheless tied to the state of the US economy, since as Samuelson and Nordhaus write a bit facetiously, it would "please an Indian maharajah" (p. 805).

In his *Morality of Spending* (pp. 173-175), Daniel Horowitz published the results of hundreds of surveys of working class and middle class budgets based on data collected by the Massachusetts Bureau of Statistics in 1875. These surveys take as a basic item the percent of budgets spent on food. Horowitz considers these surveys "relatively rigorous." I cite only his surveys of 1875 and 1918-1919 which cover 44 years, approximately a generation. I cite only the variation of percent of food budgeted from the poorest working class families to the most solid middle class families. For 1918-1919 at the end of that generation Horowitz has more reliable statistics than he offers for 1875. They are the first reliable statistics of the federal government on the working poor. Horowitz himself points out that the outstanding contrast between the 1875 and 1919 data is the drop in percent of food budgeted by the working class. Now the price index varied greatly between 1875 and 1919, namely from 137 in 1875 to 180 in 1919 (ibid., pp. 20-21). But since the contrast in percent of food budgeted by working class and middle class families would be equally or nearly equally affected by variation of price indices, this fact seems negligible.

For 1875, Horowitz' data are from the Massachusetts Bureau of Labor Statistics. They give percent of food budgeted by five levels of family income (p. 174). Horowitz points out that the data themselves highlighted the drama of "these families as they struggled against enormous odds to make ends meet...(and) illness and unemployment were the principal specters that haunted people." Therefore, since all these families in 1875 were struggling to make ends meet, in fear of illness and unemployment, we can be sure that the lowest level of income was that of the working poor,namely those with yearly incomes between $300 and $450. They spent 64 percent of their budget on food. Now the best-off families in the survey with incomes over $1200 were surely middle class, according to Horowitz. They spent 51 percent of their budget for food.

For 1918-1919, Horowitz' data are from the Federal Bureau of Labor Statistics. In that year the poorest category of families had incomes less than $900, and they spent 44.1 percent of their budget for food. Assuming that the young poor of 1875 remained stuck in the lowest income category when they retired in 1919, their percent of budget spent on food dropped from 64 percent in 1875 to 44.1 percent in 1919. That was 6.9 percent less than the 51 percent budgeted by the middle class families in 1875.

For the generation 1930's-1980's, from the depression low of 1935 to the post-recession year 1984, that first post-recession year will not yet have much effect on the working poor since they are the last to experience the recovery. Comparing the poorest quintile's share of all families' income in the 1930's and their then

❖

retiring share in the 1980's shows their passage *into what had been the middle class income of their youth.*

The 1935 poorest quintile's share of all families' personal income was 4.1 percent (*Historical Statistics,* 1960). The 1984 poorest quintile share of family income was between 6.7 percent and 7.3 percent depending on how to count it (Levy 1987, p. 195). Now assuming GNP doubled in the 50 years between 1935 and 1984. Hence *the retiring* poorest quintile share *in terms of 1935 GNP was twice 7 percent,* or 14 percent. Now 14 percent of the 1935-1935 all families income would have given them 0.1 percent short of *the third quintile's minimum percent of 14.1 percent.* Hence, working poor who entered the work force in 1935 *retired in 1984 in the solid middle class by the standards of 1935-1936.*

In fact GNP more than quadrupled. Samuelson and Nordhaus (1989, pp. 808-809)show the growth of the poorest quintile's share of all families' income from 1929 until the mid 1980's, *in constant 1988 dollars.* The lowest quintile's share in 1929 was about $1900 of post transfer income. Its post transfer share in the mid 1980's, also in constant 1988 dollars, was about $8300. So their retirement income at 73 (at an age perhaps typical of the working poor) 57 years after beginning work at age 16, was *more than quadruple of what it was when they began working.*

Now the higher quintiles benefit more from a rising economy than the lower quintiles. Hence in the time between 1929 depicted by the Samuelson and Nordhaus graph and the data given by the *Historical Statistics in the United States* for 1935-1936, the distance between the lowest quintile share and that of the second and third lowest quintiles probably increased somewhat. Hence we can take the 1935-1936 distance between the lowest and the next two quintiles above it as somewhat greater than it had been in 1929. In 1935-1936, the lowest quintile got 4.1 percent; the second, 9.2 percent; the third, 14.1 percent. Hence we can take these figures as somewhat overstating the gap between the lowest quintile and the next two quintiles above in 1929. Since our graph shows a sharp rise in income for the lowest quintile from $1900 to about $3500 in 1935-1936, we must assume that the second lowest and the third lowest increased their incomes even faster in constant 1988 dollars. Hence when we take the lowest quintile's share in 1929 as 4.1 percent, and that of the next lowest two as 9.2 and 14.1 percent respectively, we take a minimal estimate of what the graphs were. Finally, we conclude that on retiring the lowest quintile had more than 4 times the 4.1 percent (i.e., 16.4 percent) of the 1929 family distribution of income in constant 1988 dollars. That put them in the third quintile distribution of 1929 which began at 14.1 percent. Hence the working poor retired as solid middle class. That confirms the previous conclusion drawn from Frank Levy.

**Point 4:   as transaction cost of economic growth over that generation of their working lives *is mechanist social justice.***

The working poor will retire in middle class status if the economy doubles in that generation. But the doubling of GNP in any generation *does not automatically occur,* because the economy is *a partially free mechanism.* Moreover, the economy consists of two great sectors *that differ vastly by their input of causal freedom into the economy:* namely *the market sector and the transaction sector.*

Before explaining the difference between the market and the transaction sectors, I must first explain the difference between "free causality" and "free competition." Freedom in ordinary language means free action, e.g., "people are free to do or make whatever they please in their leisure time." But, in economics, "free competition" means the opposite of that: it means not being able to make prices whatever one pleases. It means exclusion of freedom to affect market prices. This economic meaning of freedom seems to go back to late medieval and early modern revolt against Church and State restraints on economic activity. Early apologetes for capitalism argued that, without these restraints, a new dynamism would be introduced into economic life that would be very beneficial (Douglass, 1987, p.27). Hence, *historically*, "free competition" meant *independence* of the market from regulations by Church or State. This concept of freedom as *independence* is found in the statement: "The Revolutionary War made the US free from Great Britain." But this concept of freedom states nothing about freely making what one pleases by those who gain independence: e.g., "The Soviet revolution of 1917 set the Russian people free from Tsarist government."

Now the market sector is sharply differentiated from the transaction sector by the predominance of free competition that prevents firms from fixing their prices as they please. That is *very different* from a transaction institution *such as government* which can run its costs into huge deficits when it so pleases, and do so for years on end. Nevertheless some industries do have firms *that have free but limited power over their market prices.*

First, there are a few cases of *natural monopoly*, where a single firm supplying the entire market is the most efficient economic organization. The usual kind of natural monopoly is that of local public utilities; electricity and local telephones. These industries are regulated by law. Public commissioners customarily require prices where the demand curve intersects with average cost. That is far below what the unregulated monopolist would do. Even so the public utility's average cost is still well above its marginal revenue. But, under perfect competition, its price *would be* where marginal cost and average cost are equal and intersect the industry demand at the same point (Samuelson and Nordhaus, 1989, pp. 583, 589, 610). Hence the regulated public utility has the free legal and effective power to set its price well above what perfect competition would determine.

*Oligopoly* is a market structure such that one firm controls 60% to 80% of a market. That is the situation of IBM, Xerox, and General Motors. In oligopoly the dominant firm sets its price at MC=MR. But that point is far above where it would be under perfect competition, since MC and AC would be equal *and intersect* the firm's demand curve at a far lower point. Hence the dominant firm has effective freedom to set its price above where it would be under perfect competition. The dominant firm in oligopoly sets its price where marginal revenue equals marginal cost and does it freely. But Samuelson and Nordhaus (1989, p.610) point out that

❖

its price is higher and its quantity produced lower than under perfect competition. Hence natural monopoly and oligopoly have this in common that they *freely set* their *prices higher* with *less production* and address *a lower market demand* than would be possible under perfect competition, which sets price at marginal cost equals marginal utility of demand (Samuelson and Nordhaus 1989, p.968).

Ultimately, demand derives from retail markets where consumers purchase. Retail markets consist of millions of small stores selling the same things, for example, 140,000 gas stations, according to Samuelson and Nordhaus (1989, p. 612). But each small firm sells to a special public with a peculiar need, e.g., a gas station serves customers that usually pass it. Thus, retail stores conform to the vast sociocultural diversity of neighborhoods, ethnic groups, religious groups, racial groups, economic and social classes, sex and age publics. By conforming to these idiosyncracies of society, firms obtain a small monopolistic control of price, e.g., two or three cents on the price of gasoline. Since none of these firms satisfies more than a tiny fraction of the total retail market, the retail market is called one of monopolistic competition. But since each firm has a small control over the price of its wares, it enjoys that much free causality in its market. On the other hand, various social publics by the solidarity of their demand have a small amount of free causality over what is sold to them.

I find now in Douglas North a distinction between transacting costs and market determined costs. In a 1983 article with John Joseph Wallis, North distinguishes transaction institutions from transformation industries (Wallis and North 1986). Transaction institutions are defined *in general* as "costs of exchanging property rights," or "costs of enforcing contracts," or "costs of capturing the gains from the specialization and division of labor" (Wallis and North, pp. 95-161). But Wallis and North *count only transaction costs which are observable by economists.* These are transaction costs which *can be measured because they result in marketed goods or services* (Wallis and North, p. 99). Such transaction costs they call transaction services. Adding up the transaction services in both the private and public sectors, they find that in 1970 *between 54.71 percent and 46.66 percent of GNP was in the transaction sector of the economy* (Wallis and North, p. 121).

The transaction sector consists of institutions and parts of institutions indispensable to transformation industries such as steel, automobiles, electronics, etc. Transaction institutions sell their services to transformation industries, so the cost of their services passes into market prices. But transaction institutions have a structure incompatible with market structure. Transaction institutions have hierarchical authority under which personnel voluntarily cooperate according to contracts enforceable by law. Hence they consist of the perfectly legal "inside trading" which is legally forbidden to competitors in the market. Hence transaction institutions have causal freedom like that of drivers on an interstate voluntarily cooperating under the rules of law. By contrast, free causality in the markets comes from institutions having some power over the market, not from market competition itself. Hence, transaction institutions have more free causality than markets. On the structure of transaction institutions, I have consulted Professor Henry Briefs, 1986, p. 75-79; John Joseph Wallis and Douglas C. North, 1986; R. H. Coase, 1988; Harold Demsetz, 1988; and Peter F. Drucker, 1989.

Now the greater freedom of the transaction sector makes it the principal cause of free causality in the economy as a whole. Outside the transaction sector, the only other source of free causality in the economy as a whole is the very limited freedom in the sociocultural diversity of non-hierarchical social groups. They determine what products are sold to them by the solidarity of their demand on retail stores. But these sociocultural and economic groups pay firms a small monopolistic higher price for their free control of demand.

In determining the responsibility of the transaction sector's free causality for social justice, it is crucial to know what percent of GNP belongs to this sector. In finding this percent, I follow closely the above cited article by Wallis and North (1986).

First of all, the State is the most important part of the transaction sector. For the State precisely specifies and effectively enforces property rights. Without those transaction services by the State, modern impersonal price determining markets would never have replaced the personal haggling markets of prehistoric times (North 1981, pp. 17-18, 42). Other transactions institutions sell transaction services in the market. Thus all institutions that transfer property rights serve to identify who has legally enforceable property right over what things; and that is a transaction service without which markets could not exist. Now Wallis and North identify *some whole industries as doing so*, and name them "transaction industries." Examples are finance, insurance, real estate, wholesale and retail trade (Wallis and North, p. 121). In non-transaction industries, Wallis and North measure the percent of transaction institutions they employ by the total incomes transaction type occupations are paid (Wallis and North, p. 108; itemized at 126-127). The *total private* transaction sector of the economy amounted to 40.8 percent of GNP in 1970 (Wallis and North, p. 121). In that year, 10 percent of GNP was paid to transaction type occupations in nontransaction industries (Wallis and North, p. 109). Hence private sector transaction industries accounted for 30.8 percent of GNP in 1970.

The government in 1970 accounted for 33 percent of GNP. But Wallis and North only consider 11 percent of GNP as transactive services by the State (Wallis and North, p. 116). Those services were those that secured property rights and promoted trade: national defense, postal services, police, air and water transportation and financial administration (Wallis and North, p. 114). *Notably, they excluded transfers* (Wallis and North, p. 114).

Why transfers are to be excluded from mechanist justice is explained in my Conclusion, paragraph 3C. Government transaction services totalled between 5.86 percent and 13.90 percent of GNP in 1970 according to different ways of estimating these services (p. 121). Finally, the 40.8 percent in the private sector and the 5.86 percent or 13.90 percent in the State sector add up to either 46.66 percent or 54.71 percent of GNP in 1970 (Wallis and North, p. 121). Now, striking the mean figure between these grand totals, I conclude that circa *50 percent of GNP belonged to the transaction sector of the economy in 1970*.

Just as a free social mechanism exists among the mutually adjusting cars on an interstate, so in the typical transaction institution we find a free social mechanism. On the interstate, the law is observed *without anyone being in charge* of the chain of cars. Likewise, the free causality of the typical transaction institution is *not a hierarchy of command* and control (Drucker, 1989, pp. 208-14; H. Briefs, 1986, pp. 75-79). Transaction institutions are typically structures where the hierarchy in top management is sensitive to the collegial input from lower levels of experts knowledgeable about results. Therefore the causal freedom of transaction institutions is usually a process of *mutually adjusting* top management's expectations to collegial inputs on results. That involves the institution as a whole. Hence *the whole institution is a free mechanical cause*.

Since the transaction sector is circa *50 percent of GNP*, and since almost *all free causality to control prices lies in that sector*, GNP *cannot be doubled in 50 years without a great input of free causality from that sector*. But if GNP does not double in 50 years, the working poor will not retire in middle class status. But if GNP does double, it doubles as a partially free mechanism *that distributes middle class status to the working poor*. Now, doubling in 50 years has been the expected effect of our historical growth economy for the past hundred years. *It does not matter* that the free economic growth mechanism never intended to do social justice to the working poor. The intention of doing justice belongs to social justice as *a final cause. Free mechanical causality only requires that the publicly predicted effect of doubled GNP, which effects social justice for the working poor, be effected*.

It is noteworthy that this definition of mechanist social justice resembles the definition of the law by Oliver Wendell Holmes, the founder of the School of Legal Realism. In his "The Vaguer Sanction of Justice" (1920, p. 171) Holmes wrote:

> If you want to know the law and nothing else, *you must look at it as a bad man who cares only for the material consequences which such knowledge enables him to predict*, not as a good one, who finds reasons for conduct, whether inside the law or outside of it [italics added].

Likewise, *mechanist social justice consists in freely effected predicted effects on social status*.

So I conclude my explanation of mechanist social justice proposed on page 3. As the revised points 3 and 4 now read: for the working poor to retire above the poverty line, in what had been middle class income before GNP doubled over that generation of their working lives, is *mechanist social justice*.

## II. Preliminary Answers to Objections against Mechanist Justice or Injustice of the US Political-economic System

The preceding argument shows that twice in the previous one hundred years doubling of GNP made the working poor retire in the middle class status of their youth. Radical critics of the US system will however object that this success was at cost of injustice to the US Underclass and to the Third World poor. Without some philosophical argument these objections cannot be fully met. However, the following preliminary answers can be given within the limits of historical experience.

*Objection:*

Neither the US underclass nor the Third World poor share in US middle class standards of life. But the US must owe social justice to its own underclass citizens. Likewise, since the US certainly depends heavily on Third World labor for its high standard of life, it also owes social justice to the Third World poor for their labor. Therefore the US cannot raise its working poor to US middle class status without doing the same for its own underclass and for the Third World poor, *if it is to do social justice.* But if the US did those two things, its vaunted middle class standard of life would be siphoned away.

*Answer:*

This argument ignores the historical *time* required and the great *transaction costs needed* for building *free causality into social mechanisms.* The US political-economic mechanism does not have the degree of freedom of the young St. Francis of Assisi, who fled nude from his father's wealth into the street!

Mechanist justice is the free effect of a historical mechanism. And a historical mechanism is a product of history. But in a free historical mechanism, freedom is restricted to what would be the *12th act of the mind* in a perfectly virtuous person like St. Francis of Assisi: namely, it is restricted to the *act of command.* In the act of *command* all the concrete ends and means have already been determined, and all that remains for freedom is execution. Aquinas shows that twelve acts of the mind are required for a free act of choice (*Summa Theologiae* I-II, q. 11-17); but in a free social mechanism, the first eleven acts of the mind are already determined by history, either wholly as in many tribal societies, or partially as in national states. In national states, anything that impedes free functioning of the free mechanism obstructs the free causality of social justice. When some part of the national state is not quite firmly enough integrated into the mainstream, the political-economic mechanism has enough free causality to integrate that part into the mechanist justice of middle class income. That happened for the US working poor in this century. But the mechanist connections with the US underclass and with the Third World poor are far too obstructed to be integrated into the US free causality of social justice.

The US Underclass is not strongly enough integrated because it consists of inner city neighborhoods in metropolitan areas with a total population of about 2,500,000 people. This population is characterized by female headed households having children out of wedlock, male joblessness, high school dropouts, and flagrant lawlessness (Sawhill 1988, p. 229; Wilson 1987, p. 58). Hence obviously the underclass neighborhoods are not strongly enough integrated into our historical political-economic mechanism to share its very limited freedom to raise the poor to middle class status. As long as the underclass's insufficient connection to the political-economic system endures, mechanist justice will concern only the metro- politan areas whose central cities are threatened by the social disorders of the underclass neighborhoods. For metropolitan areas are where free causality indus- tries (banking, insurance and real estate) need protection if economic growth is to be maintained. The historical time and the great transaction costs required might indirectly make the underclass into part of the working poor and thus sufficiently integrated into the mainstream. For mechanist justice can only effectuate justice to the free parts of its own mechanism or to other free mechanisms of foreign states.

As regards the Third World poor, the free US political economic mechanism is connected to them *only through their own governments and ruling elites.* The US political and economic elites have very *little capacity to understand Third World societies* that are so far removed from US historical institutions. Obviously the Third World poor are not sufficiently integrated into the historical US institutions to share in their very limited freedom to raise the poor to middle class status. This integration would concern four billion people who have had no historical experi- ence of Enlightenment mechanist justice into which they are supposed to be integrated. That integration *would first require adapting US Enlightenment mecha- nist justice to religious and family orders,* which are the only social structures historically experienced under the regimes of the Third World. In Part III, I shall try to show how mechanist justice belongs to the natural law orders of family and religion.

Indeed, this answer to the claims of the underclass and of the Third World poor seems too harsh for an advocate of social justice to the working poor. Yet this is not a final "No" to mechanist justice for them. But I must show first how mechanist justice is part of natural law.

## III. Mechanist Justice is a modern form of *ius gentium:* i.e., mechanist justice is natural law in history

### A. The upward mobility of the retiring working poor is the mechanist justice of a customary American institution.

The working poor, by retiring in the middle class status of their youth, have been lifted from marginal poor into mainstream America. Such upward mobility of the working poor has occurred during the past hundred years as the customary effect of growth of GNP, and so it is a customary institution. Moreover, that much upward mobility by the working poor in the US is objectively proportionate only to a lifetime of hard work, because it makes them pass from the marginalized poor into mainstream America. Now their retiring income is a distributive effect of the growth of GNP. That distributive effect proportionate to a lifetime's work is *objective mechanist justice.* For it is impossible for the working poor to have achieved that much upward mobility except as the free effect of the customary doubling of GNP over the past century. Therefore this objective mechanist justice to the retiring working poor *is a customary American institution*. Every year, another group of retiring oldsters from the working poor receive mechanist justice from this customary American institution, if all has gone well with the growth of the GNP in recent years. Long periods of depression or recession will impede this customary mechanism of social justice to the retiring working poor. Not all depressions or recessions are due to abuse of free causality by the transaction sector. The OPEC cartel of 1973, for example, caused an economic slowdown independently of the free causality of the industrial democracies. In the measure that these interruptions in customary growth are due to free causality, it is an injustice to the working poor who retire in those periods. But the customary institution of growth has so far proved strong enough to recover and renew customary growth after every recession and depression. At some point in future history, that customary growth may cease, and perhaps that cessation will not have resulted from free human causality. At that time, social justice to the working poor will not result from customary free growth of GNP.

**B.  Mechanist Justice as Natural Law in History: A Philosophical Analysis.**

For St. Thomas, *ius gentium belongs to positive law* (S.Th. I-II, q. 95, a. 2; cf. Ramirez, 1953, p. 77). *Nevertheless, it also belongs to natural law, because it consists of conclusions of natural law*, that everyone can see (S. Th., I-II, q. 100, aa. 1, 3, 11). Consequently, *ius gentium* is part of the *positive law of* all *nations* because every normal person in every nation perceives it to be true (S. Th., II-II, q. 57, a. 3; *Commentary on Aristotle's Ethics*, Book V, lesson §1019 and 1023). *Ius gentium* is *positive law with some of the force of natural law* (S. Th., I-II, q. 95, a. 2 ). The precepts of the Decalogue which pertain to the Creator do not belong to the *ius gentium* because proof of the existence of the Creator lies beyond the untutored rational capacity of the average person. Indeed the average person sees that the order of the world manifests some first cause. But some identify the first cause with the elements of matter; some identify it with the heavenly bodies; and some identify it with their political leaders (*Contra Gentes*, Book III, Chapter 38). In S. Th., II-II, q.2, a. 4, St. Thomas writes (my translation):

> Many would be deprived of the knowledge of God unless it were proposed to them by divine faith, either because of feebleness of intellect, or because of practical needs of earning a living prevented them from the study of science, or because of laziness, . . . Hence people must receive knowledge even of the existence of God by faith.

The existence of God must be known by faith precisely because it *cannot be easily known to everyone by reason. Now ius gentium consists of what can be easily known of natural law by everyone— hence easily known by reason. Hence the existence of the true God does not belong to ius gentium according to St. Thomas.*

———————————————— ❖ ————————————————

But the remaining seven decalogue precepts do belong to *ius gentium,* because they are easy conclusions of natural law evident to everyone (S. Th., I-II, q. 100, a. 2; q. 95, a. 2). So also belong to ius gentium the sanctity of treaties and the safety of ambassadors (*Commentary on Aristotle's Ethics,* Book V, lesson 12, §§1019 and 1024). *Ius gentium* consists of justice so elementary that society cannot exist without repressing violations of it: e.g., it cannot exist without repressing murder, theft, adultery, and false witness, as in the last 7 precepts of the Decalogue ( S. Th., I-II, q.95, a.4). Since society cannot exist except by repressing such elementary injustice, people in every nation see *ius gentium* positive laws as implied in their most elementary apprehension of justice (S. Th., I-II q. 94, a.2). So *ius gentium* is at *a twofold remove* from natural law in its origin. First of all, it consists of positive law with *only some of the force of natural law,* so it is not natural law in the strict sense. Secondly, this positive law is seen by people of every nation as implied by natural law, yet it is not natural law itself, in the strict sense.

Natural law in the strict sense is something that people naturally apprehend as just: for example, not harming the people with whom one lives (S. Th., I-II q. 94, a.2 and q. 100, a.3). What is apprehended as strict natural law justice is action objectively measured as *adequate* to another in a *concrete relationship.* For example, a man who gets a woman pregnant is naturally apprehended as owing what is objectively measured adequate for the upkeep of their child (S. Th., II-II q. 57, a.3). Natural law in the strict sense is the concrete reality of justice in relationships.

Jacques Maritain chaired the UNESCO commission of philosophers of violently opposed traditions that prepared the UN Declaration of Human Rights. He reports that at one meeting a philosopher expressed astonishment that people of such opposed ideologies could agree on a list of human rights. But the others replied: "Yes, *we agree about the rights,* but on the condition that *no one asks why.*" So the philosophers could agree about *justice in the concrete,* but could not agree about philosophical explanation of the concrete (Maritain, 1949). Just as *ius gentium* is what the ordinary person apprehends in the concrete positive law of their own society, so natural law in the strict sense is what ordinary people apprehend as just in concrete relationships.

Now, *ius gentium* concerns *justice only.* For as regards one's own action that *does not affect others,* it seems to ordinary persons that they can *do as they please.* The ordinary person *must learn from wise men that acts other than those of justice are moral duties.* Thus they *must be taught* that acts of prudence, fortitude, temperance are moral duties ( S. Th., I-II, q.100, a.5 ad 1; II-II q. 122, a.1).

St. Thomas explains *this difference between justice and the other virtues* in S. Th., II-II q.57, a.1. Ius is the object that specifies justice, for *ius* is *what is just.* And what is *just* is the term of an action of justice, *even without considering how it is done by the agent.* The other virtues perfect one only in what concerns oneself. In the other virtues, *nothing is right except it be done in a certain manner by the agent.* Since *ordinary people feel they can do as they please if it does not* affect others, they feel *no moral obligation to the objects of the other virtues.* St. Thomas' *Commentary on the Politics of Aristotle,* (I, l. 1, §§32-37) brings out the disastrous consequences of this moral blindness in societies in which these other virtues cannot be acquired. His commentary shows that everyone has a natural instinct to acquire virtue *because civil society is the natural end of natural households and natural villages.* Now the acquisition of *justice* and the *virtues* is the *proper effect of civil society,* and cannot be achieved by ordinary people except in civil society. Therefore everyone has a natural desire of the virtues because their natural *non virtuous households and non virtuous villages have civil society as their natural end* (§40-§41). Only those have no instinct for civil society who are incapable of civil life, either because their nature is corrupted or because their virtue is so superior to civil life, like St. Anthony the Hermit (§35). For before the first civil societies were founded, due to the moral impossibility of acquiring virtue, the great powers of human nature were used as weapons for inflicting harm. Instead of the virtue of *prudence,* men were astute in concocting frauds. Instead of the virtue of fortitude, men were savage and cruel. Instead of the virtue of temperance, men pursued the pleasures of sex and food without limit (§41). So, *without life in civil society, life according to virtue is morally impossible for the average person,* according to St. Thomas.

Hence, for St. Thomas, the moral tragedy of village life is that *the vast natural potential for moral freedom that people have lies unusable due to the absence of civil institutions.* For *virtue alone adds that extra ordering of one's powers that makes possible achievement of the maximum of human freedom* ( S.Th.,I-II, q.56, a. 3). And that *added efficacy to one's moral freedom can only be acquired in civil society.* It cannot be acquired in village society except by rare saints like St. Anthony the Hermit (§35). St. Thomas' view is the *opposite* of the view that man is naturally morally good and that civilization corrupts him.

However, one should not be deceived by these derogatory remarks about households and villages that are not parts of civil society. For his whole *argument for civil society* as a *natural community* is that households and villages are *natural communities,* and that since civil society is *their natural end,* it too is a natural community. Moreover, he expressly states that justice and injustice are naturally known in the *household,* the most *primitive of all national communities* (§37). Furthermore, it is necessary to point out that in the derogatory remarks about nonvirtuous households and nonvirtuous villages, he does not deny that they *practice either justice or injustice.* Hence nonvirtuous *households* and nonvirtuous villages *are institutions of ius gentium,* because they are regulated by positive law *having something of the force of natural law justice.*

According to this political philosophy, *civil society is supposed to cause the virtues of prudence, justice, fortitude, and temperance.* For in civil society, *only those who have* the virtues of prudence, justice, fortitude and temperance *have the right to rule (Commentary on the Politics,* III, l. 3, §375). Now prudence is the moral

——————————————————————— ❖ ———————————————————————

truth and standard of all the moral virtues (S. Th., I-II, q. 64, a.3). Hence, the moral truth of prudence in the rulers of civil society is the moral standard and truth of the moral virtue of all those citizens in whom civil society causes virtue.

Of course, this philosophy of civil society *stands in stark contrast* to the present interpretation of the US constitution by the Supreme Court. But I believe that this stark contrast *will illumine mechanist justice* as a *ius gentium institution*. For the prudence of the rulers is their personal truth, and according to the Supreme Court, their personal truth is *subordinated* to the *impersonal mechanism of the market of ideas.*

Fortunately, a much heralded recent Supreme Court decision hinges on the subordination of public figures' personal moral truth to free trade in the market of ideas (*Hustler Magazine,* 1988; text in Smolla 1988, pp. 314-21). Smolla was Flynt's lawyer in this case before the Supreme Court. He is Professor of Constitutional Law at William and Mary College. His book *Jerry Falwell v. Larry Flynt; The First Amendment on Trial* (Smolla 1988) is a long commentary on the case. The opinion of the Court was written by Chief Justice Rehnquist and the vote was eight to nothing; the ninth member, Justice Anthony Kennedy, had not been confirmed at the time of the argument in the case.

The opinion of the Chief Justice can be summarized as follows. In *public debate about public figures,* there are no false ideas (Smolla, 1988, pp. 316, 318). The best test of ideas is free trade in the market place of ideas; and hatred honestly believed about public figures, even when false, contributes to the free market of ideas (Smolla 1988, p. 317). Thus, hatred of public figures honestly believed, even when false and the cause of emotional stress, contributes to the free market of ideas. Therefore, *hatred honestly believed about public figures even when false and the cause of emotional stress is constitutionally protected by the First Amendment* (p. 318).

Now the personal ideas of which the Court speaks are those of *government people* and of those who participate in public debate. And the court cites an opinion of Oliver Wendell Holmes, making the *very foundation of people's conduct subordinate to free trade in the market of ideas* (p. 316). But the *foundation of virtuous conduct* is *one's personal idea of a standard of moral truth.* For everyone participating in public debate about public figures, their personal idea of a standard of moral truth is *subordinate* to the impersonal mechanism of *free* trade in the market of ideas. But this subordination of personal moral truth to the market of ideas does not apply to those who cannot influence the political system: *only those who can influence public policy are subjected to the impersonal market of ideas* (pp. 316-318).

Thus, we have shown that the US political-economic system freely causes mechanist justice or injustice to the retiring working poor, according as they retire in the middle class status of their youth, or not. And it is precisely *characteristic of ius gentium* institutions to *cause justice* or injustice *without need of moral truth and virtue,* and *without causing moral truth in their members.* But the mechanist justice

❖

or injustice caused by the US political-economic system to the retiring working poor is *just that* very thing. For the US public debate *subordinates to itself* all personal standards of moral truth and virtue. Hence moral truth and virtue *are not causes of US mechanist justice or injustice, and cannot cause moral truth and virtue among the citizens. Therefore, US mechanist justice is a ius gentium* institution.

In Aristotelian tradition, *ius gentium* is positive law with some of the force of natural law as understood by a given age and people. *Hence mechanist justice is a positive law institution having something of the force of natural law in the historical era of democratic states.* It is positive law with something of the force of natural law. For *it is a free effect independent of any individual person's idea or feelings.* But it nevertheless *manifests a true proportion between a lifetime of hard work and food budgets' percent of income lowered to what were middle class percentages in their youth. Such increase of disposable income constitutes objective upward mobility from poverty into middle class status of their youth which retiring workers could scarcely forget.*

According to Richard McBrien (1987, pp. 29-30), many politically liberal people with little or no religious conviction accepted Reinhold Niebuhr's "frank break" between social justice morality and the religious morality of pure unselfishness, because this latter is politically unworkable. Now that is basically the frank break which I discern *between the morality of ius gentium mechanist justice* and the *morality of personal moral truth and virtue.* Hence this position is that of many politically liberal people, according to McBrien.

Although the political system is indifferent to life according to virtue, nevertheless the Supreme Court holds that state laws enforcing virtue to be allowed by the US Constitution, if that corresponds to the belief of the people of that State. For example, the Supreme Court found that majority opinion in Georgia that sodomy was immoral was sufficient basis for a state law against sodomy. Moreover, 25 states have laws against sodomy (Noonan 1987, p. 273).

Though US political and economic institutions are *ius gentium* institutions, it does not follow either that no civil institutions exist in US society, nor that they can never muster majority vote to get laws *enacted on the basis of what Aristotelian tradition calls moral truth and virtue. But the revolution of modern politics, of which the US is an example,* has *nationalized* the struggle between *ius gentium institutions* and *civil institutions.* Within the US exist churches, synagogues, neighborhoods and families in which leadership is reserved *by the institution itself* for persons possessing moral truth and virtue; where explicit rules or customs deny leadership to those who do not so qualify. But these institutions frequently cause moral truth and virtue in many of their members. These civil institutions effectuate virtue in their members inasmuch as leaders possessing personal moral truth and virtue are institutionalized role models to which the members' roles are freely oriented by extrinsic formal causality. *There is of course no efficient causality of virtue* in its members by civil society. But the lesser causality of extrinsic formal causality whereby social roles are interrelated is explained in the next section.

❖

This modern *revolution in politics changed the state from a civil institution where leadership was reserved to persons possessing moral truth and virtue*, as was then supposed to be the case, *to a ius gentium institution wherein the market of ideas subjected moral truth to market forces*. The ancient system was structured by the military conflict between civilized societies and barbarous nations. The new system substitutes for military conflict *peaceful struggle between ius gentium institutions and civil institutions. Ius gentium* institutions in the political and economic systems have overwhelmingly *superior political* and *economic* power. But the *civil institutions* are *superior in moral truth and virtue*. The modern revolution could be seen as a *purification of civil institutions*.

C. **The Extrinsic Formal Cause: The Cause of Future-destined Motions of Moving Bodies**

Until now we have argued that US mechanist justice or injustice is the free effect of social mechanisms devoid of personal truth and virtue. But unless it is certain that social mechanisms are partially free causes, they cannot be causes of justice or injustice. So far we been obliged to rely for proof merely on public social experience; for example, in the argument from cars on the interstate adjusting to one another according to law and custom. But nothing in science or philosophy is definitively certain *except from the cause that shows it cannot be otherwise*. And so to that causal proof we now turn.

From the point of view of mind-independent reality, *social mechanisms consist of the destined future relative motion of human bodies towards one another*, e.g., a chorus line is such a social mechanism. From the point of view of mind-independent reality social mechanisms follow Newton's First Law of Motion: namely, a moving body is destined to continue in straight line motion, unless acted upon by a new force. In the motion of a nonliving body and in the motion of human bodies within a social mechanism the presently moving body specifically necessitates its future motion to a given direction only *if not acted upon by some new* force. Hence some type of causality necessitates specifically destined future motions of these bodies. *This type of cause is peculiar*. First, the necessitated *effect* is a *future direction* of motion that *does not yet exist*. Other types of causes, like material and formal causes in Aristotle, are simultaneous with their effect. Secondly, the presently moving body which is the cause, specifies the future necessarily destined motion *thanks to the motion which it has happened to have contingently acquired at the present moment, since nothing intrinsic* to a body such as a ball rebounding from a wall determined that it should strike the wall. Without the adventitious motion presently acquired, the rebounding ball would not specify the same necessarily destined future motion. That necessarily destined future motion was what Aristotelian philosophers called a *real relation. It is instantiated in Newton's First Law of Motion*. And the cause proper of real relations they called the *extrinsic formal cause*. They called it a formal cause since it specified real relations, and specifying causes were called "formal" causes among the Aristotelian causes. And they called it *extrinsic* formal cause because the future effect that does not yet exist is manifestly outside the presently moving body (cf. Poinsot 1985, *Index Rerum*, p. 538).

Now a mechanism is a per se order of moving bodies. *A per se order of moving bodies is an order of moving bodies in mutually adjusting relative motions:* e.g. the solar system or the traffic on the interstate. It consists of mutually adjusted future motions of the moving bodies in the per se order.

However, in social mechanisms, human bodies not only move relatively to one another like the relative motion of the planets around the sun, but their movements are coordinated to one another under the influence of cultural symbols such as laws and customs. Hence understanding of social mechanisms requires understanding the influence of cultural symbols.

Symbols are ideas such as beliefs and theories, and they are mental objects which have no more power to coordinate social mechanisms than people's nightmares. Of course, one can maintain that symbols acquire causal power by being encoded in people's brains. And since the encoding in brains throughout the population is correlative, the effect is an organized social mechanism. Now human social mechanisms do resemble a bee hive to a considerable degree. The bee hive has its "queen," its workers and its drones, which are signified to one another by their appropriate biophysically determined signs. Similarly biophysically determined signs appropriate to children, men and women signify to them the appropriate differences between them. And, of course, these biophysically determined signs are encoded in the people's brains.

But we have seen in the case of *Hustler Magazine v. Jerry Falwell* that what directly affects public life is not ideas encoded in people's brains, but free trade in the market of ideas whereby public figures' public images are produced. Those ideas being traded are symbols. Free trade in the market of ideas is the precise way in which encoded symbols in people's brains actually play a partial role in specifying citizens' motions towards the public images of public figures.

Now partial specification of citizens' notions to the public images of public figures cannot be biophysically determined by the market of ideas. For that would make objects of human knowledge and belief independent of the functioning of human brains. For the outcome of the market of ideas is not encoded in the human brains of those in the market before the social mechanism has produced the public image of the public figure in question. Hence individual brains encoding the outcome is not the cause of the outcome but its effect. Now indeed with the extrinsic formal cause we have a cause existing before the existence of its effect. But it is impossible to have an effect existing before its cause exists. The only alternative to admitting nonbiophysically determined causality between social symbols and social mechanisms is to ascribe the repeated apparent causality to chance. But that is absurd.

Proof of freedom of social mechanisms by the extrinsic formal cause that specifies a twofold way is similar to the traditional proof of free choice by analysis of final causality. In the proof by final causality, *the universal good* is *the natural and necessary specifier of all human willing.* Any object of choice is a mere means respecting that ultimate end. The natural specification of the will by the *universal good* is necessary, and so lacks freedom. But the secondary specification by the object of choice is *not necessary,* since it has *inadequate and limited particular goodness* respecting the unlimited goodness which alone can move the will by necessity. So in this argument by the extrinsic formal cause, two kinds of people's motions in social mechanisms are found. The destiny of human bodies' motions to their future motions is necessary, like that of any bodies by Newton's First Law. But their partial specification by the free trade in the market of ideas is free of biophysical determination.

Now mechanist justice or injustice occurs without any individual intending it. It is the effect of a free social mechanism, but not the effect of an individual. Does that make any sense in Biblical religion? Yes! Scripture does not lack examples of sins committed without people intending to commit the sin. John R. McKenzie points to four cases of which I find two of them most striking (1990, p. 1306, §130). These two cases are: (1) Jonathan violated his father's oath of which he did not know; and God later responded that he was guilty (1 Sm, 14:27, 41). (2) Uzzah steadied the Ark of the Covenant lest it tip off a moving cart and, because a layman had no right to touch the Ark, God struck him dead (2 Sm, 6: 6-7). McKenzie interprets these events as characteristic of primitive morality. But I find them characteristic of mechanist justice and similar to the natural law found in the US political and economic institutions. St Thomas' interpretation of Old Testament law generalizes its non-appeal to personal virtue. For him, Old Testament law directed people without virtue to do works of virtue by threats of punishment, and by promises of honor and wealth, which are extrinsic to personal motivation by virtue ( S. Th., I-II, q. 107, a. 1, ad 1). Old Testament people intended to acquire honor and wealth, but, in fact, did works of justice! Oh, how similar that was to US mechanist justice!

## IV.    Appendix — Natural-law Efficacity within Mechanist Justice Institutions Contrasted with Political Liberalism, and Political Conservatism

The foregoing analysis shows that mechanist justice as social justice for the working poor can be achieved without requiring personal moral truth or virtue in our political and economic institutions. That fact in no way challenges the truth of centuries of experience of the virtue of prudence as personal moral truth, and of the virtues of fortitude and temperance as rational training of the passions. But it shows that impersonal mechanist justice is the public institution in which the personal virtues of prudence, fortitude, and temperance are to be acquired, and in which *impersonal mechanist justice* can become *the personal justice of individuals.* For institutions of mechanist justice are objects of public experience having something of the force of natural law. Hence the very impersonal and public character of mechanist justice as having something of the efficacity of natural law *makes its natural law efficacity more evident than any moral efficacity in personal moral experience.* Therefore, *justice only, i.e., impersonal mechanist justice,* having something of the force of natural law, is *the public origin* of *all natural virtue, defined as maximum in one's power.*

1. *The basic beliefs of political liberals.*
   a. *Social justice depends almost exclusively on government transfers to the poor.*
   b. *The time scale* for measuring social justice is either *annual* or *a short span of years.*
   c. *The standard of social justice is liberal values:* such as increasing the income of the lowest quintile, so as to decrease the gap between the lowest quintile and the rest of the nation. A particularly important liberal value is universal health care insurance which covers the lowest quintile.
2. *The basic beliefs of political conservatives.*
   a. Markets are natural mechanisms devoid of free causality: any government interference is destructive of economic prosperity. A more moderate conservative view is: government interference should be restricted to exceptional circumstances and peculiar services (e.g. the postal service).
   b. Private ownership by individuals is the principal economic power in the US.
3. *Natural law efficacity within mechanist justice institutions, contrasted with liberal beliefs.*
   a. Liberal values are *sectarian beliefs by liberals rejected by conservatives* ... That is not how liberals see it and does not denigrate the beauty of liberal values; but it makes the obvious point that liberal values do not belong to the structure of the political economic system, since conservative values are equally legitimate in our system of free trade in the market of ideas. By contrast, the free doubling of GNP is not just a beautiful political value. *It is a real long range tendency in the political-economic system* which occurred between 1875 and 1919, and again between 1935 and the mid 1980's as shown above. But it is not inevitable. Rather, it is a *free probable destiny* due to the wedding of science, technology, and social science with a large 50 percent of free causality from the nonmarket sector of GNP. Moreover, misuse of free bargaining of any of the non market public or private sectors is an injustice to the working poor if it cripples doubling of the national GNP.
   b. The political economic mechanism is a real partially free cause whose real parts include human lifetimes of work. Hence *the measure of*

❖

*social justice cannot be an annual span or even a short span of years;* but a lifetime of work.

c. *Against the liberal view that social justice depends almost exclusively on government transfers to the poor.* Only one-fifth of the free causality in the political-economic mechanism lies in government's 10% of GNP, which is spent on enforcing property rights. Full 40% of GNP lies in the free causality of the transaction industries of the private sector. Hence government cannot be the sole responsible free cause of social justice by its transfers to the poor, as liberals imagine. Government is only *primus inter pares* as cause of social justice or injustice to the poor. Either justice or injustice will result from government's bargaining with the major transaction industries to inject enough free causality into business cycles to limit excessive swings that prevent steady growth of GNP. That system is formalized either in law or custom in several industrialized democracies (Wilenski 1983: p. 52-57, especially, p. 53; Wilson 1987: pp. 155-156; Galbraith 1987: p. 192-193; Drucker 1989: p. 93). Moreover, economists have never been able to disentangle massive government transfers to the poor from decreased growth in GNP (Lenkowski 1986; pp. 188-189; Samuelson and Nordhaus 1989: pp. 810-819).

Now mechanist justice results from generating long GNP growth. Hence, mechanist justice cannot result from massive transfers. In fact, massive transfers are *rather an effect of generation long GNP growth as historically determined by an Enlightenment egalitarianism.*

4. *Against the views of political conservatives.*
   a. *Markets are not devoid of free causality.* One-half of GNP lies in the free causality of the nonmarket economy of either the public or the private sector.
   b. Business *cannot function without government's huge input of 10 percent of GNP in enforcing property rights.* Hence even moderate conservative claims that government interference should be restricted to exceptional circumstances and peculiar services (e.g., postal services) *neglect government's central role in the economy as its political framework and legal structure.*
   c. The principal economic power of private property in the US today lies in *managerial power over stock holders' private ownership.* Private ownership of property has little influence compared to the corporate power of managers.
   d. Conservative values include family and religious values. But if the full causality of the nonmarket sector is not rightly used, modern economic growth can destroy family and religious values. Thus Goetz Briefs

pointed out that early capitalism destroyed precapitalist societies and their ethos patterns (G. Briefs 1983, p. 277).

*Aquines Institute, 97 Waterman Place, St. Louis, MO 63112 USA.

## References

Aquinas, St. Thomas. *Summa Contra Gentes,* Turin: Marietti, 1922.

_____. *In X libros ethicorum Aristotelis ad Nicomachum expositio,* R. Spiazzi, ed., 3rd ed., Turin: Marietti, 1964.

_____. *In libros politicorum Aristotelis expositio,* R. Spiazzi, ed., Turin, Marietti, 1951.

_____, *Summa Theologiae,* Foucher ed., Paris, Lethielleux, 1939, 5 vols.

Briefs, Goetz A. "The Ethos Problem in the Present Pluralistic Society," *Review of Social Economy,* December 1983), *41,* 271-299.

Briefs, Henry. "The Limits of Scripture: Theological Imperatives and Economic Reality" in R. Bruce Douglass, ed. *The Deeper Meaning of Economic Life: Critical Essays on the U. S. Catholic Bishops' Pastoral Letter on the Economy,"* Washington, D.C.: Georgetown University Press, 1986, 57-96.

Coase, R.H. *The Firm, the Market, and the Law,* Chicago: University of Chicago Press, 1988.

Demsetz, Harold. *Ownership, Control and the Firm,* Vol. I. Oxford, Basil Blackwell, 1988.

Douglass, R. Bruce. "First Things First," in *Economic Life: Critical Essays on the US Bishops Pastoral Letter on the Economy,* Washington, D.C.: Georgetown University Press, 1987.

Drucker, Peter F. *The New Realities,* New York: Harper and Row, 1989.

Galbraith, John Kenneth. *Economics in Perspective,* Boston: Houghton Mifflin, 1987.

Gould, John N. *Economic Growth in History,* London: Methuen, 1972.

*Historical Statistics of the United States 1960,* Washington, DC.: U.S. Printing Office, 1960.

Holmes, Oliver Wendell. *Collected Legal Papers,* New York: Harcourt, Brace, 1920.

Horowitz, Daniel. *The Morality of Spending,* Baltimore: John Hopkins Press, 1989.

*Hustler magazine Inc. v. Falwell,* 108, S. Ct. 876 (1988).

Lenkowsky, Leslie. *Politics, Economics and Welfare Reform,* Lanham, MD: University Press of America, 1986.

❖

Levy, Frank. *Dollars and Dreams: The Changing American Income Distribution*, New York: Russell Sage Foundation, 1987.

McBrien, Richard. *Caesar's Coin*, New York, MacMillan 1987.

McKenzie, John R. "Aspects of Old Testament Thought," in R. A. Brown, J. A. Fitzmeyer, R. E. Murphy, eds., *New Jerusalem Biblical Commentary*, Englewood Cliffs, NJ: Prentice-Hall, 1990, 1284-1315.

Maritain, Jacques. "Introduction" in *Human Rights: Comments and Interpretations*, New York: Columbia University Press, 1949.

John Noonan. *The Believer and the Powers That Are*, New York: MacMillan, 1987.

North, Douglas C. *Structure and Change in Economic History*, New York: Norton, 1981.

Poinsot, John. *The Semiotic of John Poinsot*, John Deely and RalphPowell eds., Berkeley: University of California Press, 1985.

Ramirez, Santiago, OP. *El Derecho De Gentes*, Madrid: Studium, 1953.

Samuelson, Paul A. and Nordhaus, William D. *Economics*, 13th edition, New York: McGraw-Hill, 1989.

Sawhill, Isabel V. *Challenge to Leadership: Economic and Social Issues for the Next Decade*, Washington, D.C.: Urban Institute, 1986.

Smolla, Rodney A. Appendix II of: *Jerry Falwell v. Larry Flint: The First Amendment on Trial, 1988*. New York: St. Martin's Press, 1988, 314-321.

Wallis, John Joseph and Douglas C. North. "Measuring the Economy, 1870-1970," in Stanley L. Engerman, and Robert E. Gallman, eds., *Long Time Factors in American Economic Growth*, Chicago: University of Chicago Press, 1986.

Wilenski, Harold L. "Political Legitimacy and Consensus: Missing Variables in Assessment of Social Policy," in Shimon E. Spiro and Ephraim Yuchtman-Yaar, eds., *Evaluating the Welfare State*, New York: Academic Press, 1983.

Wilson, William Julius. *The Truly Disadvantaged*, Chicago: University of Chicago Press, 1987.

# Education and Human Capital (Abstract)

## Frank Brown*

With elementary and secondary school students from the United States generally being outclassed by students from other leading industrial nations in tests on academic subjects essential to modern economic production, and the U.S. economy losing ground to heavy competitive pressure from various established and emerging nations, this paper urges that the U.S. intensify its analysis of the relationship between education and human capital. After reviewing the most generally accepted versions of human capital and defining the relationship between human capital and human resources, the paper considers the institutions that help to shape the person, including family, religion, schooling, and culture. The paper criticizes the concept of public schooling in the U.S., arguing that it is responsible for declining educational achievement in the U.S. The paper concludes by recommending greater recognition that the development of human capital takes place in all institutions, not just the schools. Families should be given greater control over primary and secondary eduction through increased public funding of private schools and expanded school choice.

*Professor of Economics, DePaul University, Chicago, IL 60604 USA.

---
❖
---

# Nonmarket Failure and Apartheid Labor Regulation in South Africa

## Brian Dollery*

A vast research effort has been invested in a debate surrounding the origins, nature and effects of ideological apartheid in South Africa during the post-1948 era. More recently, scholarly interest has focused on the economic underpinnings of apartheid institutions generally, and especially on the impact of racially discriminatory labor legislation. The sheer complexity of apartheid labor regulation has left many interesting questions unanswered (Steenkamp 1983). One such question hinges on the differential incidence of labor apartheid on public and private sector employment patterns in South Africa. To date attempts to explain this empirically well-established phenomenon have relied on assumptions which effectively assert the more rigorous application of discriminatory legislation in the public sector (Adam 1971; Welsh 1974; van der Horst 1976; Nattrass 1981; Bromberger 1982). The present paper seeks to explain a greater incidence of labor apartheid in the South African public sector by employing the theory of nonmarket failure.

The paper itself is sub-divided into five main parts. Section I provides a brief review of the literature on the economics of apartheid. The mechanics of racially discriminatory labor legislation are outlined in Section II, and Section III surveys empirical evidence on the existence of the differential incidence of labor apartheid in the South African public sector. Section IV deals with the application of the theory of nonmarket failure to public sector employment patterns. The paper ends with a short conclusion in Section V.

## I. The Economics of Apartheid

The political economy of apartheid, and particularly labor apartheid, has long attracted the attention of scholars of South African historiography. In consequence, a voluminous literature has arisen around debates concerning the causes, mechanisms and consequences of racial discrimination in South Africa (Kalley 1987). In

❖

the postwar era emphasis has fallen on the relationship between capitalism, as it is manifested historically in the South African milieu, and apartheid. The ensuing debate has been characterized by the development and refinement of two broad schools of thought. In crude terms, an orthodox or "liberal" perspective attempted to provide a coherent account of South African political economy by construing the "irrational" racist policies of apartheid as dysfunctional to the rational forces of South African capitalism (Hutt 1965; O'Dowd 1977; Butler, Elphick and Welsh 1987). As Davenport (1977, p. 371) has argued, "scholars in this tradition are economic liberals who believe the pull of the market would crush ideological racism and its supporting structure of pass laws and colour bars ...". A competing "revisionist" or marxian body of opinion tried to explain the historical evolution of events on the premise that the institutions of apartheid facilitated and enhanced the expropriate power of South African capitalism (Murray 1988). Johnstone (1970), Legassick (1974), Davies (1979) and others, argued that capitalist development and apartheid policies formed a collaborative partnership which maximized the extraction of surplus value from the labor repressive South African economy.

In an effort to investigate the efficiency and equity repercussions of apartheid legislation in post-1947 South Africa, economists operating in the liberal tradition have attempted to formally model the complexities of modern South African political economy. Work in this area has evolved in two broad directions. First, some writers have examined the allocative and distributional consequences of the purported contradictions between apartheid and economic efficiency on the assumption that the edifice of apartheid laws is exogenously determined by political considerations (Enke 1962; Knight 1964; Porter 1978; Lundahl and Ndlela 1980; Lundahl 1982; Findlay and Lundahl 1987; Dollery 1989). And secondly, other economists in the public choice mould have treated the plethora of apartheid regulation as endogenously determined through the complex interplay of apartheid legislation accordingly (Lowenberg 1989; Lipton 1985; Lundahl 1989; Dollery 1990). By attempting to account for the differential impact of apartheid regulation in the public sector of the South African economy on the basis of nonmarket failure, the present paper falls within the second of these two broad approaches to South African political economy.

## II. The Nature of Labor Apartheid

For most of the twentieth century black labor has been subject to a myriad of statutory legislation imposing a mass of restrictive regulations on its use. A useful method of reducing the material complexity of analysing racially discriminatory labor legislation in South Africa is to invoke Lipton's (1986) distinction between vertical discrimination and horizontal discrimination.[1] Vertical discrimination in the labor market sought to preserve various occupations for members of specified racial groups, and has long been an important feature of South African employment patterns. Historically, vertical discrimination has appeared in two different forms. Firstly, direct discrimination embodied in colour bar or job reservation laws which

❖

expressly forbid people of defined racial categories from performing certain functions, like the Mines and Works Act of 1911, which reserve certain types of work for white people. Alternatively, indirect vertical discrimination seeks to limit entry to particular skilled occupations by reducing the access of some population groups to the requisite training programs or by setting minimum educational standards disadvantaged groups find difficult to attain, such as the Apprenticeship Act of 1922. Generally, job reservation laws were employed to "protect" unskilled white workers, whereas indirect vertical discrimination is usually enacted in order to reserve skilled occupations for whites. The economics of both forms of vertical discrimination is straightforward. By artificially restricting entry on the basis of racial characteristics, the legislature effectively transfers wealth from employers and black labor to white workers in the shape of contrived rents.

In contrast to vertical discrimination, horizontally discriminatory labor legislation sought to regulate the stocks and flows of primarily unskilled black labor within and between the various sectors of the economy. Historically, horizontal discrimination has assumed two distinctive forms. Firstly, legislation aimed at controlling the movement of economically active black labor from legally-created tribal homelands to various areas of the South African economy. The statutory mechanism for this kind of discrimination lay in the 1913 Land Act, and the amended 1936 Bantu Land and Trust Act, which defined the land rights of the African people. And secondly, enactments seeking to determine the allocation of non-homeland blacks between different productive sectors, most notably the infamous pass laws.

## III. The Incidence of Labor Apartheid

Given the nature and statutory incidence of the various forms of racially discriminatory labor legislation in South Africa, the question arises as to the economic incidence of labor apartheid. This issue may be examined from at least two different perspectives. First, aggregative welfare losses deriving from both vertical and horizontal impediments to labor mobility can be investigated. A plausible hypothesis might anticipate that the resultant allocative and productive inefficiencies in labor markets would be reflected in terms of an opportunity cost of foregone economic growth. Surprisingly, expectations of this kind fly in the face of conventional wisdom concerning the growth performance of the South African economy in the 1950's and 1960's (Hobart Houghton 1978; Davies 1988). However, new empirical evidence now available indicates that earlier views of South African economic growth rates were misplaced (Moll 1990). The following observations have been persuasively argued:

> The post-war South African economy enjoyed many features which
> suggest that its growth-potential was high. Measured by a range of
> indicators, however, it seems the apartheid economy failed to achieve

❖

its growth-potential. Economic growth after 1948 was only fraction-
ally faster than before, despite highly favorable external economic
conditions. South Africa's comparative output-growth record is poor,
and its record in terms of the growth of manufactured exports and total
factor productivity verges on the disastrous (Moll 1991, p. 19).

Secondly, the sectoral implications of apartheid labor regulation may be
scrutinised. An important question in this latter regard resides in the differential
incidence of discriminatory labor practices between the various sectors of the South
African economy. At least two plausible hypotheses may be pursued. Firstly, it can
be argued that on ideological and other grounds apartheid labor regulation was
more stringently enforced upon public sector employers than their private sector
counterparts. And secondly, even with a given level of cross sectoral enforcement,
the incentive structures confronting private firms are such that it can be anticipated
that their compliance with apartheid regulation would be lower than equivalent
public agencies. In order to sustain these hypotheses empirically it is necessary to
demonstrate that in general, employment patterns differed between private and
public sector employers relative to the aggregative racial composition of occupational skills in South Africa, and in particular, employment patterns were more
biased away from this norm in the public sector. Numerous studies exist which
verify these propositions. For example, Terrington (1974, p. 158) notes that "... in
general, the labor force in the major urban areas has remained strictly segregated
as between Africans and Whites..." after examining occupational trends over the
period 1949 to 1973. In their study of the racial division of labor between 1969 and
1977, Simkins and Hindson (1979, p. 44) conclude as follows:

The size of the occupational classes varies considerably between
sectors. Certain classes are proportionally over-represented or concentrated in one or two sectors....

Moreover, they demonstrate for the period under review races other than
whites are the most underrepresented in the public sector, excluding racial bureau-
cracies in the homelands and elsewhere (Simkins and Hindson 1979, p. 39,
especially table XD). Similarly, Standish (1984) shows that the South African state
has actively favored white over black labor in its employment policies by examining the proportions of black and white labor in various occupational categories
relative to both aggregate proportions and private sectoral proportions. One
outcome of apartheid labor regulation during the post-1948 period was the
emergence and endurance of an excess demand for white labor in the public sector.
With respect to this issue, Standish (1984, p. 231) comments as follows:

The questions which the above raises is why has the State, or at least
a very large section of the State, allowed itself to suffer white labor
shortages since the late 1940's, a period of nearly forty years?

❖

He attempts to answer this question by arguing that the South African public sector saw itself as "... employer of last resort for whites" (Standish 1984, p. 232), and consequently rigorously enforced discriminatory labor legislation. But ideological assertions of this kind do not explain the economic mechanisms involved in maintaining a relative high degree of racial discrimination in public sector employment. And it is to this issue that we now turn our attention.

## IV.  Labor Apartheid and Nonmarket Failure

In a series of pathbreaking publications, Wolfe (1979; 1987; 1988) has sought to construct a conceptual analogue to the familiar notion of market failure under the generic term non-market failure. Although the phenomenon of nonmarket or collective failure was known to classical economists (see, for example, Bentham 1952), Wolfe's analysis nevertheless represents the first comprehensive effort at providing a taxonomy or typology of nonmarket failure, and has already generated a secondary literature (Vining and Weimer 1990). The Wolfe (1979) paradigm is not without its critics. Peacock (1980, p. 34) for instance, attacks Wolfe's deliberate attempt to generate a paretian equivalent of Bator's (1958) anatomy of market failure:

> The use of a paradigm closely allied to Paretian Welfare economics obscures the importance of government actions, often characterized by collective failure, which promote countervailing action within the private sector and the 'spread' of collective failure beyond the confines of government organizations.

Despite this possible shortcoming, the Wolfe framework nonetheless remains a uniquely useful conceptual tool in the analysis of nonmarket failure, and consequently forms the basis of the present examination of apartheid labor regulation in the South African public sector.

In essence, Wolfe (1979; 1987; 1988) argues that market and nonmarket activities may be distinguished by their special demand and supply characteristics. He identifies five major representative features of non-market demand which contribute to the phenomenon of nonmarket failure. All five of these properties of nonmarket demand appear to have been present in the particular historical circumstances of the post-1948 South African public service. In the first instance, Wolfe (1987, p.55) postulates that "...an increased public awareness of market shortcomings" has lead to reduced tolerance of them, and consequently heightened demand for state intervention. It is evident that demands of this kind have long played a prominent role in statutory labor regulation in South Africa. Indeed, a widespread perception amongst the white population that market outcomes were generally integrationist may have resulted in the "Civilized Labor Policy" of 1936, in terms of which all government departments were obliged "...to substitute 'civilized' labor

❖

for 'uncivilized' labor, [where] 'civilized' labor was recognized as white labor..."
(Abedian and Standish 1985, p. 38). Moreover, the relaxation of this policy during
World War Two due to militarily induced shortages in white manpower, and the
attention paid to subsequent black advancement by the Afrikaner National Party in
its watershed 1948 election campaign, appear to have contributed significantly to
its electoral victory (Davenport 1977). In sum, white workers recognized that
unfettered labor markets would produce employment patterns conducive to efficient labor utilization rather than white exclusivity and prosperity, and therefore
demanded state intervention in the form of both vertical and horizontal discriminatory labor regulation.

A second characteristic attributed to the demand for non-market activity
resides in "political organization and enfranchisement" (Wolfe 1988, p. 40). In a
peculiarly South African context this is likely to be especially significant since the
single most important feature of apartheid is the systematically reinforced, racially
segmented, asymmetrical access to political power. With some notable exceptions
prior to the gerrymandered Separate Representation of Voters Bill of 956, all but
white South Africans were excluded from representation in Parliament until the
constitutional reforms of 1984.[2] Moreover, even during periods of representation
from the time of Union in 1910 onwards, the political power of non-white groups
remained severely constricted. Consequently, the nature and purpose of legislation
emanating from the South African Parliament may be largely explained by the
complex interplay of various interest groups drawn from segments of the white
population (Dollery 1990). Given the awareness of the white working class that
market outcomes would threaten rents earned by them, it is clear that the South
African constitutional structure provided an efficient mechanism for the enactment
of apartheid labor regulation since counteractive lobbying by affected black groups
was inherently limited (Benson 1984).

The third and fourth characteristics of the demand for nonmarket activity
postulated by Wolfe (1988) are undoubtedly present in the South African political
milieu but no obvious a priori reasons exist which make them more significant than
in other representative democracies. With some exceptions, historically white
candidates have been elected to national political office by a white electorate, and
enjoy a constitutionally determined maximum period of tenure of five years
between elections. Consequently, although both the "structure of political reward"
and "the high time-discount of political actors" are present as enhancement devices
in the demand for nonmarket interventions, they apparently cannot explain the
unique forms of labor regulation which have appeared in South Africa, nor the
differential incidence of apartheid regulation between the public and private
sectors.

The final attribute of the demand for nonmarket activity identified by Wolfe
(1988, p. 41) resides in "...the decoupling between those who receive the benefits,
and those who pay the costs, of government programmes." Wolfe (1988) argues
that decoupling occurs in two different forms. On the one hand "microdecoupling"

arises where the benefits of collective action accrue to a particular group, whereas the costs of such action are dispersed amongst all groups. On the other hand, "macrodecoupling" occurs where the benefits of collective action are shared by all groups, but the costs of this action are concentrated on some specific group.

Apartheid labor regulation generally, and the incidence of apartheid labor regulation specifically, reflect both forms of decoupling. The primary beneficiaries of apartheid labor regulation in the public sector are clearly white workers directly employed in racially reserved occupations. Secondary beneficiaries include white politicians competing for the support of white workers as well as other white workers who perceive that at some future date they may need protected jobs in the civil service, and consequently regard the continued existence of an artificially generated excess demand for white workers as a form of unemployment insurance (Doxey 1961). The costs of this kind of apartheid labor regulation are dispersed amongst the general population at large insofar as a misallocation of labor reduces income per capita, inefficiencies occur in the public production of goods and services, and public service positions are foregone by black jobseekers. It follows that the extensive nature of apartheid regulation in the public sector can be explained partly by the phenomenon of microdecoupling. Moreover, since private firms would bear significant costs directly should similar labor restrictions have been equally enforced upon them, they possessed powerful incentives to engage in counteractive lobbying to prevent this from occurring (Benson 1984). Consequently, the differential incidence of apartheid labor regulation between public agencies and private firms may also be explained by the use of microdecoupling by the latter group.[3]

Given that the characteristics of nonmarket demand in the particular historical and political circumstances of post-1948 South Africa facilitated the asymmetrical imposition of vertical and horizontal discriminatory labor legislation on the civil service, the question arises as to how this was accommodated by public sector institutions. An explanation may be sought in the general conditions under which public production takes place. Wolfe (1988) identifies four basic attributes of nonmarket supply. Firstly, he argues that "nonmarket outputs are often hard to define in principle, ill-defined in practice, and extremely difficult to measure as to quantity or to evaluate as to quality" (Wolfe 1988, p. 51). Consequently, it has long been customary in South Africa as elsewhere to measure public sector output by means of quantifying inputs employed to produce that output. This provides latitude for X-inefficiency which, in the context of the South African civil service, meant inter alia the employment of relatively inefficient white workers since efficient black workers were excluded from employment. Direct evidence exists which documents the costs of this form of apartheid labor regulation to the fiscus. Standish (1984, p. 193) for instance, notes with respect to the South African Railways that the "... cost of implementing the civilized labor policy became so embarrassing to the Railways that the Railways and Harbour Board minuted the

General Manager of the Railways that he need no longer record the cost of the policy."

Secondly, Wolfe (1988) postulates that nonmarket outputs are generally produced by a single public agency often operating as a legally constituted monopoly. The resultant lack of competition makes any meaningful estimates of economic efficiency difficult, and consequently serves to obscure allocative and productive inefficiencies. In South Africa deliberate government policy extended state production activity far beyond the provision of public goods. Some idea of the size and importance of public sector activity, especially in the form of public corporations, may be gained from the fact that gross domestic fixed investment under public control increased from about 35 per cent in 1950 to around 46 per cent in 1970 (Hobart Houghton 1978, p. 207). Labor apartheid regulation was enforced in most of this sector.

Thirdly, Wolfe (1988, p. 52) argues that "the technology of producing nonmarket outputs is frequently unknown, or if known, is associated with considerable uncertainty and ambiguity," and consequently may be associated with productive inefficiency. Evidence exists which indicates that technological efforts were made to sustain white labor shortages attendant upon apartheid labor regulation in the South African public sector. Standish (1984, p. 204), for example, notes the following:

> [N]owhere is mention made of the pragmatic possibility that blacks should permanently fill white posts. The response was rather to introduce labor saving capital where ever possible, two examples of which are the containerization program of the Railways, and automatic sorting machines of the Post Office, which were introduced during this period [1965-1971].

Finally, Wolfe (1988) proposes that public production activity is characterized by the lack of any "bottom-line" evaluation mechanism equivalent to profit or loss for appraising success. To some extent, this may not be reflective of the parastatal production sector in South Africa, containing public firms like the Iron and Steel Industrial Corporation and the Electricity Supply Commission, which were mandated to produce final accounts before Parliament. However, public production concerned with public goods clearly had no satisfactory evaluation mechanism.

Given the unique constitutional and political circumstances in South Africa in the post-1948 era, the conditions of nonmarket demand and supply facilitated the more stringent application of apartheid labor regulation in the public sector. Conversely, it has been argued that the relative absence of these conditions in the private sector mitigated against a rigid enforcement of horizontal and vertical labor restrictions in private employment. The resultant nonmarket failure can be classified and evaluated in terms of the taxonomy of market failure. Wolfe (1979)

❖

identifies four generic types of nonmarket failure which include "internalities and private goals," "redundant and rising costs," "derived externalities," and "distributional inequalities." The South African public sector exhibits all of these forms of non-market failure to at least some degree. But because of the structure of the South African constitution and the attendant racially asymmetric access to political power, the outcome of nonmarket failure often differs in comparison to comparable western economies. For instance, although the delinkage between revenue and cost characteristics of public production necessarily implies a misallocation of resources and X-inefficiency as elsewhere, in South African labor markets this has in addition led to public sector labor regulation biased toward white workers. It follows that nonmarket activity by the South African state also exhibits distributional inequities in the sense that it has redistributed employment opportunities away from black workers. Moreover, nonmarket failure in the form of derived externalities or "the unanticipated side effects of nonmarket activities..." (Wolfe 1988, p. 77) has occurred in the form of political repression on the part of the authorities and attempts at violent insurrection by elements of the black population, quite apart from aggregative negative derived externalities in the form of reduced economic growth (Moll 1991). Internalities or "the goals that apply within nonmarket organizations to guide, regulate, and evaluate agency performance and the performance of personnel" (Wolfe 1988, p. 67), which typically include budget growth, technological advancement, and the acquisition and control of information may in addition include a racial element in the South African public sector. Noting that virtually all managers in South Africa are white, Knight and McGrath (1977, p. 264) observe that "while the good relationship which often exists between management and workers is likely to be based on rational economic calculation by management, there may be an element of racial sympathy and fellow-feeling."

## V. Conclusion

The preceding analysis attempted to explain the well-established empirical observation that the economic incidence of vertical and horizontal apartheid labor regulation fell more heavily on public sector employers in the post-1948 South Africa than their private sector counterparts, despite an intended uniform statutory incidence, on the basis of the characteristics of nonmarket demand and supply. In essence, it was argued that within the constitutional and political milieu of apartheid South Africa, the structure of institutional incentives embodied in the demand for and supply of public sector outputs facilitated the relatively effective imposition of racist employment criteria. Moreover, the resultant forms of nonmarket failure exhibited characteristics congruent with the racially asymmetrical attributes of South African constitutional arrangements. Whilst the origins of apartheid regulation can be satisfactorily explained as the outcome of rent-seeking behavior (Dollery 1990), their actual incidence is thus further illuminated by invoking the differential nature of public and private sector production.

❖

The present argument diverges from the conventional wisdom surrounding the differential incidence of apartheid labor regulation in post-1948 South Africa. Previous discussion of the same phenomenon relied largely on accounts of the ideological climate of the period and on derivative, but unsubstantiated assumptions simply asserting a more rigorous enforcement of apartheid labor regulation in the public sector. To the extent that the present analysis provides an economic and political mechanism for observed differences in the incidence of apartheid labor regulation, it may represent a superior explanation.

## Endnotes

*Visiting Professor, Department of Economics and Finance, College of Business Administration, Creighton University, Omaha, NE 68178, U.S.A., and Senior Lecturer, Department of Economics, University of New England, Armidale NSW 2351, Australia.

[1] In fact, Lipton (1986) employs a more extended tripartite classification. More specifically she uses the following classification: "A key feature of apartheid was the extensive system of controls over black labor. They can be divided into: (i) controls over movement, or horizontal controls; (ii) controls over the allocation of jobs, or vertical controls; (iii) other measures restricting workers' rights" (Lipton 1986, p. 18).

[2] Until the Separate Representation of Voters Bill of 1956, "coloured" or mixed race voters elected a limited number of white representatives to the South African Parliament. The constitutional reforms of 1984 enfranchised "coloured" and asian voters, and allowed for some parliamentary representatives to be directly appointed by the State President.

[3] Elements of macrodecoupling may also be present. Given the highly unequal distribution of income and wealth amongst the white population of South Africa, the additional tax burden imposed by apartheid labor legislation in the civil service implies a greater proportionate tax incidence on a relatively small number of affluent whites. In effect, a small group of rich whites is thus obliged to subsidize a form of unemployment insurance for the remaining large group of whites.

## References

Abedian, I. and Standish, J. B. "An Economic Inquiry into the Poor White Saga," University of Cape Town, Saldru Working Paper No. 64, 1985.

Adam, H. *Modernizing Racial Domination,* Berkeley: University of California Press, 1971.

Bator, F. M. "The Anatomy of Market Failure," *Quarterly Journal of Economics,* 1958, 72(2), 388-400.

Benson, B. L. "Rent-Seeking from a Property Rights Perspective," *Southern Economic Journal*, 1984, 52(2), 388-400.

Bromberger, N. "Economic Growth and Political Change in South Africa," in L. Schlemmer and E. Webster (Eds.), *Change, Reform, and Economic Growth in South Africa*, Johannesburg: Ravan Press, 1977.

_____. "Government Policies Affecting the Distribution of Income 1940-1980," in R. Schrire (Ed.), *South Africa: Public Policy Perspectives*, Cape Town: Juta, 1982.

Butler, J., Elphick, R. and Welsh, D. (Eds.). *Democratic Liberalism in South Africa: Its History and Prospect*, Cape Town: David Philip, 1987.

Davenport, T. R. H. *South Africa: A Modern History*, London: Macmillan, 1977.

Davies, C. "Apartheid versus Capitalism: The South African Contradiction," Discussion paper in European and International Social Science Research No. 23, Reading University, 1988.

Davies, R. *Capital, State and White Labor in South Africa*, New Jersey: Humanities Press, 1979.

Dollery, B. E., "Capital, Labor and State: A General Equilibrium Perspective on Liberal and Revisionist Approaches to South African Political Economy," *South African Journal of Economics*, 1989, 57(2), 124-136.

_____, "Labor Apartheid in South Africa: A Rent-Seeking Approach to Discriminatory Legislation," *Australian Economic Papers*, 1990, 29(2), 113-127.

Doxey, G. V., *The Industrial Colour Bar in South Africa*, Cape Town: Oxford University Press, 1961.

Enke, S., "South African Growth: A Macroeconomic Analysis," *South African Journal of Economics*, 1962, 30(1), 34-43.

Findlay, R. and Lundahl, M. "Racial Discrimination Dualistic Labor Markets, and Foreign Investment," *Journal of Development Economics*, 1987, 27(1), 139-148.

Hobart Houghton, D. *The South African Economy*, (5th ed.), Cape Town: Oxford University Press, 1978.

Hutt, W. H. *The Economics of the Colour Bar*, London: Deutsch, 1964.

Johnstone, F. A. "White Supremacy and White Prosperity," *African Affairs*, 1970, 69(1), 1-15.

Kalley, J. A. *South African Under Apartheid: A Selected and Annotated Bibliography*, Grahamstown: Rhodes University Institute of Social and Economics Research, 1987.

Knight, J. B. "A Theory of Income Distribution in South Africa," *Oxford Bulletin of Economics and Statistics*, 1964, 27(2), 289-310.

                                    ❖

_____ and McGrath, M. "An Analysis of Racial Wage Discrimination in South Africa," *Oxford Bulletin of Economics and Statistics*, 1977, *40*(3), 245-271.

Legassick, M. "Legislation, Ideology and Economy in Post-1948 South Africa," *Journal of Southern African Studies*, 1974, *1*, 32-41.

Lipton, M. *Capitalism and Apartheid: South Africa 1910-1984*, Claremont: David Philip, 1968.

Lowenberg, A. D. "An Economic Theory of Apartheid," *Economic Enquiry*, 1989, 27(1), 57-74.

Lundahl, M. and Ndlela, D. B. "Land Alienation, Dualism, and Economic Discrimination: South African and Rhodesia," *Economy and History*, 1980, *23*(1), 106-132.

_____. "The Rationale of Apartheid," *American Economic Review*, 1982, *72*(3), 1169-1179.

_____. "Apartheid: Cui Bono," *World Development*, 1989, *17*(6), 825-837.

Moll, T. "Output and Productivity Trends in South Africa: Apartheid and Economic Growth," unpublished doctoral thesis, Cambridge University, 1990.

_____. *Did the Apartheid Economy 'Fail'?*, Centre for African Studies, University of Cape Town, 1991.

Murray, M. "The Triumph of Marxist Approaches in South African Social and Labor History," *Journal of Asian and African Studies*, 1988, *23*(1/2), 70-101.

Nattrass, J. *The South African Economy: Its Growth and Change*, Cape Town: Oxford University Press, 1981.

O'Dowd, M. "The Stages of Economic Growth and the Future of South Africa," in L. Schlemmer and E. Webster (eds.), *Change Reform and Economic Growth in South Africa*, Johannesburg: Ravan Press, 1977.

Peacock, A. "On the Anatomy of Collective Failure," *Public Finance*, 1980, *35*(1), 33-43.

Porter, R. C. "A Model of the Southern African - Type Economy," *American Economic Review*, 1980, *68*(3), 743-755.

Simkins, C. E. W. and Hindson, D. "The Division of Labor in South Africa 1969-1977," Development Studies Research Group Working Paper, No. 7, University of Natal, 1979.

Standish, J. B. "State Employment in South Africa," unpublished masters thesis, University of Cape Town, 1984.

Steenkamp, W. F. J. "Labor Problems and Policies of Half a Century," *South African Journal of Economic*, 1983, *51*(1), 58-87.

Terrington, D. "An Examination of Occupational Wage Structure in Selected Industries Covered by the Wage Board," unpublished masters thesis, University of Cape Town, 1974.

❖

van der Horst, S. T. "Labor Policy in South African 1948-1976: A Sketch," in M. L. Truu (Ed.) *Public Policy and the South African Economy*, Cape Town: Oxford University Press, 1976.

Vining, A. R. and Weimer, D. L. "Government Supply and Government Production Failure: A Framework Based on Contestability," *Journal of Public Policy*, 1990, *10*(1), 1-22.

Welsch, D. "The Political Economy of Afrikaner Nationalism," in A. Leftwich, (Ed.), *South Africa: Economic Growth and Political Change*, London: Allison and Busby, 1974.

Wolfe, C. *Markets or Governments: Choosing Between Imperfect Alternatives*, Cambridge: MIT Press, 1989.

_____. "Market and Nonmarket Failures: Comparison and Assessment," *Journal of Public Policy*, 1987, *6*(1), 43-70.

_____. "A Theory of Nonmarket Failure: Framework for Imple-mentation Analysis," *Journal of Law and Economics*, 1979, 22(1), 107-139.

# A Systems Approach to Manpower Modelling and the Inter-regional Mobility of Labour: The Case of Venda in Southern Africa

## P. N. Palmer*

The provision of education and training must be one of the more important priorities of any government (Halstead 1974). This is clearly true in the case of the nascent State of Venda where government is formally involved in education, manpower assessment and training and planning through its Department of Education and Internal Affairs (Republic of Venda Report 1990).

Venda is currently one of four independent National States bordering on the Republic of South Africa (RSA). This satellite State was created adjacent to the RSA, sharing a common border with both the RSA and Mozambique. Constitutionally, it has evolved from being a nascent, self-governing state to one which currently enjoys the status of a sovereign, independent state in terms of the National States Constitution Act 21 of 1971 (Maasdorp 1990).

However, recent, far-reaching changes to the RSA's political landscape could mean the reincorporation of the hitherto independent national states into the RSA, indicative of a desire for political and economic unification among the current constellation of states bordering on the RSA (KPMG, Aiken and Peat 1990). In view of Venda's immediate geographic proximity to the RSA the dynamics of inter-regional labour mobility has a considerable impact on the quality and supply of labour to and from Venda (Republic of Venda Report 1990). Indeed, since migrant labour and commuters form an integral part of the de jure economically active population of Venda, close cooperation with the RSA regarding education and training is essential. The mechanisms which facilitate this interaction comprise multilateral technical committees consisting of representatives from both countries (Development Bank of Southern Africa 1990).

Given that education is a function of the quality of the supply of manpower to the labour market, it is significant that this derives from three sources, notably:

❖

formal education, informal education, and non-formal education (Halstead 1974). Moreover, it is noteworthy that the quality of labour indigenous to Venda continues to improve, particularly from the point of view of formal education, both in terms of the number of school-going children and the pupil-teacher ratio (Republic of Venda Report). Nevertheless, the quality of this stream of labor stands to be diluted, given the impact of migratory labour from the surrounding regions which form part of the RSA. The most notable example is that of the self-governing state of Lebowa where unemployment is the highest in the RSA while the GDP per capita is the lowest (Development Bank of Southern Africa 1989).

## I.  A Systems Approach to Manpower Modeling for Venda

### A.  Structure and Relationships in a Systems Model

Venda's main supply of manpower continues to be provided by the existing educational and training systems in the country, subject to the effect of inward migration from neighbouring regions. These labour inputs, being both **probable** and **serial** inputs into the labour market, have to be evaluated in terms of their potential output for the regional economy of Venda as determined by the various development scenarios that have been postulated for this developing country (Republic of Venda 1990).

Systemically speaking, a serial input is the result of a previous system with which the focal system (the one in question) is directly related. Serial inputs are also referred to as "direct coupling" or "hooked-in" inputs in the sense that they represent the output of a previous system which now becomes the input to other systems (Schoderbeck et al. 1985).

On the other hand, probable inputs represent potential inputs to a system. The focal system must determine which of the available outputs of the alternative systems or subsystems will become its inputs. Or, otherwise stated, each available output of other systems has a probability of being chosen as an input to the focal system (in this case, the labour market germane to the Venda economy). This probability, which is, of course, less than one for each individual potential input, is determined by the degree of correspondence between the input needs of the focal system and the attributes of the available inputs. The actual selection of the focal system is then based upon this probability distribution and the decision criterion used by the system. Indeed, the study of probable inputs is the study of the decision-making process in a system (Schoderbeck et al. 1985).

Against this backdrop, the supply of and demand for manpower has the potential of being modelled systematically, particularly in the context of potential outputs being produced by a formal education system. Such outputs constitute probable inputs into an indigenous labour market which provides the throughput mechanism for meeting the labour requirements of the regional economy of Venda. Hence it may be postulated that a **symbiotic** relationship exists between this formal source of supply and the regional labour market germane to Venda. However, the reality of inter-regional labour mobility, in so far as it affects the Venda labour market, also provides for a **synergistic** relationship between the various sources of supply and the Venda labour market (Wadsworth and Pissarides 1989).

For the purpose of this paper it may be argued that a synergistic relationship, though not functionally necessary, is nevertheless useful because its presence adds substantially to the systems performance. "Synergy" means "combined action." In systems nomenclature, however, the term means more than just cooperative effort (Schoderbeck et al. 1985). Synergistic relationships are those in which the cooperative action of semi-independent subsystems taken together produces a total output greater than the sum of their outputs taken independently.

By contrast, a symbiotic relationship is one in which the connected systems cannot continue to function alone. In certain cases the symbiotic relationship is unipolar, running in one direction; in other situations the relationship is bipolar, that is, running in both directions (Schoderbeck et al. 1985). This is particularly true in the case of the various sources of labour supply which feed the local labour market in Venda, thereby giving rise to a mutualistic symbiosis (Wadsworth and Pissarides 1989).

Manpower modelling, in this **systemic** context, reflects the effects of a **synergystic** relationship between diverse inputs on the one hand and the throughput process – as typified by the local labour market – on the other hand. The effect of this relationship is to improve the system's (labour market's) performance in terms of the required labour outputs for the regional economy of Venda.

## B. Socio-economic Constraints Focusing the Development of the Model

To the extent that the proposed manpower model divides the population up into groups, or cohorts which then change or flow into other groups as time progresses, it reflects the tenets of a systems approach to manpower modelling, with inputs being constrained by the following parameters:

1.  **Demographic constraints** – reflecting the educational, economic and age profiles of the population. This provides essential input to both the demand and supply models and is intricately linked to both.

2.  **Economic constraints** – indicative of the predicted growth of the economy. This would indicate what the manpower needs of the economy would be if economic growth at an assumed rate were to materialize. The real issue here relates to the required manpower combination to sustain an expected lever of economic growth. It would also indicate the growth in job opportunities that would be available if the economy were to grow at an expected rate.

3.  Whereas economic considerations typify the situation prescribed by economic restrictions, the constraints – epitomized by **social**

❖

needs – reflect a normative or value approach to manpower modelling. According to this parameter, society determines the number of persons needed, particularly in those professions rendering socially important services to that society. It gives an indication of the ideal situation as determined by society (Halstead, 1974).

## II. Manpower Modelling and Planning

### A. Developing a Systems Model into a Useful Planning Tool

Presuppositional to manpower modelling is the concept and practice of **manpower planning or human resources planning** which describes a future-orientated tool and approach that deals with the policies, plans, analyses, **systems** and methods to establish and implement programmes that bring about an effective work force (Burack and Mathys 1980). That is, it is an approach that seeks to reconcile, to the extent possible, the prospective employee's need and desires for the future with those of prospective employers, via an appropriate labour market mechanism.

Therefore, manpower planning is the process of obtaining the right number and kinds of people at the right time in order to fulfill specific organisational or institutional needs. To this end manpower planning comprises forecasting and programming. Forecasting involves generating the numbers, types, and qualities of personnel needed by a prospective employer at some time in the future. Programming is the process and activities by which the forecast is implemented, in this case, with the aid of the systems approach to manpower modelling.

Moreover, because there is a direct connection between internal changes and the external events that affect the policies and strategies of manpower planners, manpower planning provides the critical link between policy information and planning at the macro-level and the specific manpower requirements of focussed economic activities germane to the regional economy of Venda. To this end the following questions are pivotal to manpower modelling in the context of interregional labour mobility (Wadsworth and Pissarides 1989):

1. How is manpower planning related to the economic goals of Venda?

2. How is manpower planning carried out in terms of meeting specific manpower needs in the midst of uncertainty and rapid change?

3. How will manpower planning relate to the specific requirements of a wide range of labour inputs – both indigenous and exogenous – given the profile of skills peculiar to such a potential labour force.

—————————————— ❖ ——————————————

Consequently, three levels of manpower planning are basic to all systems, regardless of the complexity of the manpower model in question (Burack and Mathys, 1980).

## B.  Levels of Manpower Planning

At the *broadest level,* there are general issues to be considered. This includes those elements concerned with the broader concepts, policies and issue's related to manpower planning. *Change* forms a part of top-level, or macro issues because it often determines the urgency and the type of planning that needs to be done. At this juncture in South Africa's socio-economic and political history, the prospect of the independent National States, including Venda, being reincorporated into South Africa both politicially and constitutionally, holds daunting implications for the manpower development strategy for Venda. This is because such a macro-level phenomenon must impact on the relationships between manower planning and the formulation of revised development strategies to take account of this impending change to the current political landscape (McDiarmid 1985).

At the **next level** of manpower planning are those activities that are pivotal to skills recruiting and which are seen as critical to the success of this activity (Burack and Mathys 1980). This calls for practical information on the availability and quality of skills, their potential performance in response to the demand for such skills, and the analysis relating to the demand for and supply of manpower skills, given the inter-regional mobility of labour peculiar to the Venda economy (Wadsworth and Pissarides 1989). These could include the use of the following: the job vacancy survey; the supply lag theory; occupational ratios; expenditure ratios; the social need theory (Halstead 1974). For the sake of brevity these analytical techniques are subject to the following description.

The **job vacancy survey** rests on the popular conception of a labour shortage expressed as the number of jobs exceeding the number of workers available at the prevailing wage. In a free market, such an imbalance usually does not persist over a long period of time because some employers are able to attract additional employees by raising salaries, and employers unable to offer higher wages reorganise their operation in such a manner as to continue with the same number of workers. As a result of higher wages and reorganisation, the supply of workers is increased and the demand reduced. Eventually supply and demand become equal, but more workers are being paid higher wages.

The **supply lag theory** recognises that repeated increases in demand followed by minimal increases in supply will result in a continuing series of temporary labour shortages accompanied by rising wages. In short this means a series of temporary shortages will persist "when the number of workers available (the supply) increases less rapidly than the number demanded at the salaries/wages paid in the recent past." If employers seeking to hire more workers raise wages these wage increases, in turn, may be used as a shortage indicator. It should be noted that

—————————————————— ❖ ——————————————————

part of the supply lag in certain skills categories is due mainly to the extended time required for training and also to imperfect market information and labour immobility.

The hypothesis that underlies the **occupational ratio** method of projecting long-range demand is that statistical relationships between employment in a given occupation and total employment in a given sector can be analysed and utilised in making projections. The soundness of this hypothesis rests upon the degree to which total employment in any given sector has a causal or logical and reasonably stable relationship to employment in any of a number of occupational subcategories. Since each industry has a unique occupational structure, it is reasonable to expect there will be a close relationship between the number of workers in a given occupation and total employment in that industry. The success of the method depends on the accuracy with which this relationship can be projected and, even more basically, on the degree to which an accurate independent projection of total employment in the sector is possible.

Another factor that bears a causal or logical relationship to employment levels is the **amount spent** to purchase goods and services in a given sector or, the monetary value of expenditure and employed manpower. When levels of employment in different occupations are related to total expenditures within the industry, projections of this ratio can be applied to alternative estimates of future expenditures based on expected national and iudustrial growth. The validity of this type of approach rests fundamentally on the accuracy with which total future expenditures in any given sector can be estimated and on the relevancy and stability of employment levels to these expenditures.

Although expenditures in many areas are probably related to the volume of production and manpower requirements, management decisions to increase production depend on a variety of factors difficult to measure and project. Among them are the amount of return on investment expected, attractiveness of alternative allocations of resources, and the impact of competition. Assuming that the problems involved in evaluating these factors are surmounted and that projections of expenditures are derived, it is still necessary to know something of how the funds are to be allocated; specifically the amount to be devoted to facilities, equipment and personnel. Further, if is necessary to know what changes can be anticipated in worker productivity, due to technological changes.

The previous analytical techniques described rely on a free market to ensure optimal resource allocation and to establish equilibrium between manpower supply and demand. The **social need theory** differs from these economic-orientated methodologies in that it is based on a moral or value approach. It proposes that a shortage exists in any occupation whenever fewer persons than ought to be are employed. The theory is based on the premise that certain enterprises, particularly public enterprises providing a public service, require a certain number of staff members if they are to operate effectively and in the best interests of the public and the economy. Thus in the case of a teacher shortage, this would mean from a pedagogically desirable viewpoint too few qualified teachers are teaching too many students. In the case of medical doctors, a shortage, according to the social need theory, occurs whenever there is an insufficient number of physicians to provide adequate and proper medical services for the existing population, which means that some health needs are not met.

Pivotal to our understanding of this notion is that a shortage defined on the basis of social need will not disappear by normal market action because a shortage so identified is based on a value judgement rather than on employer or consumer demand. A shortage based on social need will be alleviated only when public demand is sufficient to bring about an increase in pay and thereby attract an increased supply. Whether or not society will take such action depends on how much value it receives from these services as against the amount received from alternative expenditures.

The most serious limitation of the social need theory lies in the fact that any single group receiving services does not accurately represent all of the multiple populations benefiting from the same services. Whereas the most valid use of this theory is when it is applied to the teaching or health profession, where the base population and desired personnel ratio can be determined without too much controversy, in as much as these occupations independently provide direct services to individuals. Such is not the case, however, for professions that combine with other occupations to produce varied and interrelated services such as attorneys.

Contrary to the two levels of manpower planning already addressed, the **bottom level** deals with the basic functional activities relating to manpower provisioning such as the actual staffing process (Burack and Mathys 1980). This is the result of a distillation process resulting in a narrow manpower planning focus – but which has its origin in the policy and planning dimensions germane to the first and second levels already addressed.

## C. Validation of a Systems Model

Pragmatically speaking, therefore, "manpower planning" refers to the matching of manpower requirements and resources, whether it be for a single enterprise or within a whole economy. It purports to synthesise the interplay of factors, ranging from demographics through to social, political and economic factors. If this interplay of factors is to be monitored, logically understood and used as a predictor of future manpower trends, it is desirable that it be encapsulated in modular form (Wadsworth and Pissarides 1989). The dynamics thereof can be systematically described, as typified by the symbiotic and synergistic relationships between the input throughput and output variables peculiar to such a model. To this end, it purports to represent an overall conceptual model, capable of facilitating the formulation of a national manpower development strategy for Venda.

The validity and consistency of the model is conducive to rigorous empirical testing, as a prelude to a final situation analysis. Such a situation analysis would

❖

address the two cardinal aspects of manpower planning, namely demand and supply, reflecting as it does the underlying demographics indicative of the future educational and training needs of the country.

A situation analysis presupposes the formulation of a mission, objectives and goals for manpower development (Burack and Mathys 1980) given the complexities peculiar to Venda, due primarily to the flux of manpower across the boundary of the country. These migratory patterns invariably impact on the macro-manpower planning process, particularly in so far as future predictions of supply and demand are concerned (Wadsworth and Pissarides 1989). Inasmuch as potential migratory labour inputs represent **probable** inputs into Venda's labour market, the proposed manpower model represents a focal system typifying the reception of alternative inputs and the release of potential outputs into the surrounding environment.

## III. Implications of a Systems Model for Planning

It stands to reason, therefore, that Venda's national manpower development strategy cannot be formulated in isolation. It needs to be formulated in the context of the broader suprasystem pertinent to the manpower model comprising, as it does, a national development policy as well as specific regional development policies and planning frameworks developed for the country as a whole. Inherent in such policy considerations are the stimulation of economic growth, agricultural development and industrial development and the stimulation of concomitant job creation opportunities which impact on the manpower modelling process (Republic of Venda 1990).

Indeed, these variables depend upon and affect the others by means of positive and negative feedback due to the causal relationship between them. It is noteworthy that the model attempts to reflect these sensitivities as well. The model does so by:

1.  highlighting the need to promote a healthy balance between population growth and the increase in opportunities for every citizen to lead a dignified life;

2.  focusing on the need to develop all economic sectors so as to stimulate economic growth, employment creation and higher income generation;

3.  emphasising the development maintenance and optimal utilization of the country's human potential;

4.  implicitly recognising the need for technology improvement within the country, without the detrimental effect thereof on the creation of employment opportunities.

❖

To this end the model purports to be deterministic in that it depicts both the condition and flow of labour in terms of educational and training profiles peculiar to the population characterised by the Venda labour market. This is because the current and future potential of existing education and training systems to deliver trained manpower (probable inputs) at different levels is synthesised in the model. Pivotal to this process is the necessity of taking cognisance of the attrition of existing manpower and the inter-regional mobility of labour as it affects Venda when engaging in manpower or human resources planning for the region.

## IV. Conclusion

In the final instance, Southern Africa's ethnic and geographic configuration accounts for the most striking feature of the dynamics of the model, notably, as a result of the impact of the inter-regional mobility of labor, which manifests itself in the flux of manpower to and fro across the boundary of Venda. To this end it is important to understand the influence of labour on expected regional economic development in Southern Africa. This is because the external environment peculiar to any system (labour market) is an influential factor. In this case, it influences the manpower forecasts for Venda and must be properly accounted for. This can best be done by adopting a holistic, systems approach to manpower modelling, given the dynamics of inter-regional labour mobility in the context of Southern Africa's constellation of national states.

*Professor of Economics, Department of Business Economics, University of South Africa, 0001 Pretoria, South Africa.

## References

Burnack, E. H., and Mathys, N. J. *Human Resource Planning: A Pragmatic Approach to Manpower Staffing and Development,* Brace-Park Press, 1980.

Development Bank of Southern Africa: Centre for Information Analysis. *Economic and Social Memorandum - Region G.,* 1989.

Development Bank of Southern Africa: Centre for Information Analysis: SATBVC Countries: *Statistical Abstracts,* 1989.

Halstead, D. K. *Statewide Planning in Higher Education,* Washington, DC: U.S. Department of Education, 1974.

KPMG Aiken & Peat. *Investment in South Africa,* 1990.

Matthews, J. *South Africa in the World Economy,* New York: McGraw-Hill, 1987.

McDiarmid, O.J. *Unskilled Labour for Development, its Economic Cost,* Washington, D.C.: World Bank, 1985.

❖

Nattrass, J. *The South African Economy: Its growth and change*, Cambridge: Oxford University Press, 1982.

Maasdorp, G., ed. Regional Policy in South Africa, *South African Journal of Economics*, June, 1990.

Report of the Committee for Economic Affairs on *A Strategy for Employment Creation and Labour Intensive Development, President's Council* - RSA, 1987.

Report of the Panel of Experts on the *Evaluation of the Regional Industrial Development Programme as an Element of the Regional Development Policy in Southern Africa*, Development Bank of Southern Africa, January 1989.

Republic of Venda. *National Manpower Development Strategy*, Phase 1 - Report, Situation Analysis, Institute for Labour Economics Reserach, Human Sciences Research Council, April, 1990.

Schoderbeck, P., Schoderbeck, C., and Kefas, A. G. *Management Systems*, Business Publications, 1985.

Smith, A. W. *Management Systems: Analyses and Applications*, Holt-Saunders International Editions, 1982.

Wadsworth, J. and Pissarides, C. P. "Unemployment and the Inter-Regional Mobility of Labour," *The Economic Journal*, September 1989, *99*, 739-55.

---❖---

# Exploitation and International Development (Abstract)

## Kishor Thanawala*

Dymski and Elliott in their 1989 article have discussed the popular as well as technical meanings of exploitation in the context of workers and owners of capital within a country. It is possible to extend (with some variations) their schema to a discussion of exploitation in the international setting. The international dependence model can be, and has been, interpreted as an extension of Marxist theory (where owners of capital dominate the workers as well as the national economy) to the global economy where developed countries and multinational corporations operating therefrom dominate the economies of the developing countries.

*Department of Economics, Villanova University, Villanova, PA 19085. Abstract of an article to be published in the *International Journal of Social Economics*.

❖

# Comments on *Centesimus Annus*

## Gerard L. Stockhausen*

### I. *Centesimus Annus* and Trade

International trade is one of my main areas of interest in economics. There is not much in *Centesimus Annus (CA)* that deals with trade. Nevertheless, I would like to highlight a couple of things. Obviously, trade, like every other element in an economy, should serve the common good (about which I will say a little more below).

The common good can no longer be achieved simply by the internal efforts of each country. Coordination is necessary to achieve a regional and even international common good. Indeed, movements toward peace and supranational bodies that ensure peace between and among nations serve the common good by reducing the amount of resources diverted to weaponry and other uses not related to development.

With regard to LDCs, *CA* sees import substitution approaches as mistaken and encourages integration into the world economy, but notes that

> the chief problem is that of gaining fair access to the international market, based not on the unilateral principle of the exploitation of the natural resources of these countries but on the proper use of human resources (*CA*, §33).

The pope then says:

> It would appear that, on the level of individual nations and of international relations, *the free market* [emphasis in the text] is the most efficient instrument for utilizing resources and effectively responding to needs (§34).

This statement is true, however, only when human needs are met and human dignity is preserved, only "if [the human person's] work and his [or her] very being are not to be reduced to the level of a mere commodity" (§34).

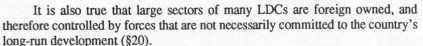

It is also true that large sectors of many LDCs are foreign owned, and therefore controlled by forces that are not necessarily committed to the country's long-run development (§20).

This suggests support for a world of free trade, but a qualified support, since free trade can never occur at the cost of human needs and human dignity. Just as we might question the optimality of free-market outcomes in domestic situations where power is not balanced among market participants, so too in the international arena. "The grave imbalances that exist between the various geographical areas of the world...have shifted the centre of the social question from the national to the international level" (§21).

## II. *Centesimus Annus* and the Common Good

The common good is a major theme of this document. I do not wish to go into detail regarding what *CA* says here; instead, I will mention a few major points, and then approach it from another angle in the third section of my remarks.

The basic thrust of *CA* is that the economy should serve human beings in their various communities and not the other way around. *CA* does not define the common good anew, and it for the most part repeats what was called for by *Rerum Novarum (RN)*. This includes anything that supports the dignity of workers and the dignity of their work, especially private property (so long as it is subject to the universal destination of goods), workers' organizations, just wages, appropriate working conditions, and adequate rest (§§6-11).

The government/state, meanwhile, is secondary to the individual, family, and society, and is meant to see that these have what they need. The state should see to it that the various sectors of society all contribute to the common good. For this to be possible, the state is to maintain the balance of power in the economy between labor and capital and support the weakest at the same time that it promotes economic activity (§15). The state should have special concern for the poor, since they have no other resources to fall back on as do the non-poor.

The ideal description of a society in which the common good is being pursued is given in §19 and described as a democratic society inspired by social justice. This involves free markets, stable currency, harmony of social relations, and economic growth, but under public control that allows people to have jobs, job training, social security, unions, and unemployment assistance—a society in which human labor is not a commodity. As suggested above, the attainment of this ideal has become more and more something that cannot be achieved by any country in isolation, but only by seeking for an international common good (§§21, 27). As the economy becomes more global, global institutions must be created that will preserve the international common good (§57). In sum, the market must be subordinated to society and the state in order to see that human needs are met and human dignity is preserved (§35).

In treating the fall of communism in the fall of 1989, the pope says that the social order must take into account original sin so that the good of the person and the good of society are not in conflict (§23). Human work should be the way that human beings participate in God's work of creation and at the same time contribute to the common good. They should be rewarded for this contribution and encouraged in this participation by being able to hold private property (§§31, 43).

Conversely, an important part of the common good is that all are able to use their resources, especially their personal ones—the term "human capital" is not used in *CA*—to add to the common good. That is why concern for development is so important—so that the untapped resources of the billions of humans in developing areas might be contributed to the common good of all (§33).

The pope also extends the notion of the common good to relations within an individual firm. Since a firm is a community of persons, relations within the firm must be ordered to the common good of all. Clearly, profit is necessary for the life of a firm, but so are these other things that lead to its common good (§36).

An element of the common good that has risen to consciousness in recent times is ecology (§37). This extends from concern for the natural world to concern for the human environment in which we live and especially the family (§38). Concern for ecology, important in its own right, quickly becomes an image useful for discussing the common good. One of the primary ways in which the state contributes to the common good is by preserving both the natural and the human environment.

A necessary part of the common good is the guarantee of human rights. This is possible only where there is a coherent set of social values based on the dignity of the human person. Without such a coherent set of values, the common good is replaced by the outcome of competing power groups (§47). While it is important for the state to have a part in the common good by ensuring both political and economic stability, caring for the environment, and protecting human and economic rights, there is a danger of the state taking over too much of society. Therefore, the principle of subsidiarity must be observed to keep the state from working against the common good (§48).

A proper balance is needed to serve the common good. Neither the state nor the market is an end, but both should serve the common good. Similarly, the common good will not be achieved in a climate of individualism, and such individualism can be overcome only by a commitment to solidarity and charity (§49).

## III. *Centesimus Annus* and Leisure

The word "leisure" is used rarely if at all in *CA*, but as *CA* speaks of the search for the common good and the proper role and reward of human labor, it is clear that leisure is essential to the common good. I am speaking of leisure here in the sense used by Joseph Pieper (1963). Leisure it not the same as rest or recreation, but includes those things that are most humanizing—culture, contemplation, celebration, worship, the liberal arts. Whereas work at its very best is participation in the work of creation, and so is humanizing, participation in the contemplation of the creator who looked on what had been made and saw that it was very good is at the heart of leisure. What leads to wholeness and holiness is leisure. Pieper anticipates *CA* when he says that workers can have real leisure only by the following means: "by giving the wage-earner the opportunity to save and acquire property, by limiting the power of the state, and by overcoming the inner impoverishment of the individual" (p. 51).

Those things mourned by the pope—lack of social harmony, breakup of the family, freedom that becomes license, loss of the dignity of the human person and of human work—are due to a lack of leisure, either because people are forced to work without time for leisure, or because they have time for leisure, but squander it in pursuit of sensations (§39).

The pope argues that authentic freedom can exist only when it is linked to truth and to the rights of others (§17). Thus attempts to defeat Marxism that denied the dignity of others were just as mistaken as the Marxist approach that reduced the individual to but one cog in a social machine (§12). This applies to the national security state that ignores the rights of the individual, and the materialist-consumerist state that tries to defeat communism on the level of production and consumption, without concern for who or what gets lost along the way. Again, in the context of leisure, both attempts will be exposed as false. Noteworthy about the fall of communism in 1989 was its—for the most part—lack of violence and close relationship to the Catholic Church. Poets, playwrights, and churchpeople took leadership roles, resisting violence and seeking to treat their enemies as human beings, inviting them to step down voluntarily rather than demanding their heads.

In the industrialized countries there is the tendency to confuse wants and needs and to want always what is more and better (§36). When one is engaged in leisure—reading, contemplating, conversing, celebrating, pursuing the liberal arts—one is neither producing nor consuming. A society based on economics alone places no value on such activity—or non-activity as it then appears. This is an idolatry of the market, wherein these things that are clearly goods are ignored since they are not marketable (§40).

When treating of ecology, the pope is clear that the basic error is that of taking God's gift—creation—and making it something that humans own and can do whatever they want with. Leisure, with its foundation in the sabbath rest, recognizes that God is the one who creates, and any human dominion over creation is on the order of stewardship rather than ownership and control (§37). As Pieper says, "Leisure is possible only on the premise that [humankind] consents to [its] own true nature and abides in concord with the meaning of the universe" (p. 42).

The encyclical speaks of alienation, which is defined as the confusing of ends and means. Thus production and consumption, that should be means to human happiness, become ends, and human beings, who should be ends in themselves, become means to be manipulated and used in order to bring about more production and consumption. People are treated as things, and things are given the attributes

❖

of human beings. This can be overcome only by the truth, the kind of truth that emerges out of leisure, contemplation, and worship (§41). Pieper argues, "The point and justification of leisure are not that the functionary should function faultlessly and without a breakdown, but that the functionary should continue to be a [human being]" (p. 44).

While the church supports democracy as a way of avoiding totalitarianism, there is a danger that democracy leads to relativism—rule by the majority, but with no transcending principles. Thus the values of the culture and society are crucial to a democracy that is humanizing. Those values will never be developed or articulated in a society that lacks leisure (§46). Without a coherent set of cultural and social values based on the dignity of the human person, democracy is nothing more than competing power groups (§47). Even here, however, it must be said that true leisure is not ordered to an end such as making society better, but is ordered to allowing human beings to be whole, and a better society naturally flows from that.

Ironically, as the industrialized nations pursue production and consumption in a way that indicates that they have no coherent set of social values, they also look down on the cultures that do have a coherent set of values because the latter cannot match them on the level of production and consumption. The world needs the material and spiritual resources of those cultures now at the margins of economic and international life. Leisure, which allows stepping back from the everyday, can make possible the valuing of the gifts of those cultures which the drivenness of economic imperialism cannot find space for (§52).

Many activists in the struggle for economic justice have discovered that they cannot continue for long without some spirituality—without tending to their relationships with other humans and with the transcendent. In a similar way, human society can not reach its common good without leisure that allows for the tending of those same relationships.

*Associate Professor of Economics, Department of Economics and Finance, College of Business Administration, Creighton University, Omaha, NE 68178 USA.

## References

John Paul II, *Centesimus Annus* Encyclical Letter, Vatican City: Liberia Editrice Vaticana, 1991.

Pieper, Joseph, *Leisure, the Basis of Culture,* New York: Random House, 1963.

# Recent Developments in Islamic Economic Thought

## Musa M. Al-Hindi*

The regeneration of the Islamic ethos and the intensified role of Islam in the political processes in the Muslim countries during the past few years has attracted a great deal of scholarly as well as media coverage. Western scholars, journalists and statesmen have come to use various labels to depict and understand this phenomenon of greater politicization of Islam, such as Islamic Resurgence, Islamic Revival, Islamic Fundamentalism or Islamic Militancy. The overall Western response to it has been characterized by confusion and fear. While one man, the late Ayatollah Khomeini, and one event, the Islamic Revolution in Iran, have come to be equated with the reassertion of Islam in Muslim life, in fact, contemporary Islamic resurgence is more than an exercise in political activism. It symbolizes broader fundamental change in the present-day Muslim world: an attempt to move away from the cultural foundations of the Western civilization towards rediscovering Islam as the basis for a new political, social and cultural system. Thus, Islamic resurgence is a broad based, multi-dimensional phenomenon which is still in its formative stage.

Contemporary revival of Islamic thought is a facet of this resurgence. In the last few decades many Arab, Indian, Pakistani and Iranian Muslim scholars have been actively involved in defining and creating a "new" economics based on Islamic axioms and values derived from the Qur'an, tradition and interpretation of Islamic jurisprudence. They maintain that they are in the process of "rediscovering" a paradigm in economics whose components are even older than mercantilism. These Muslim intellectuals are extremely ambitious and strongly believe that Islamic economics, defined as the sum of historical, theoretical and empirical studies that examines the economic problems of a people imbued with the values of Islam, is capable of doing wonders. In the words of a proponent of Islamic economics:

At this time — when the world of business and industry is crying out for ethical safeguards against large scale corruption and the storage of

energy poses a threat to humanity — the moral teachings of Islam can
provide not only the ethical guidelines needed for effective control of
economic behavior but also compelling motivation for international
cooperation in the efforts toward the salvation of humanity (Abdul-
Raut 1979, p. 1).

Although many details of the Islamic economic system are yet to be worked
out, there is a prevailing consensus among Muslim economists that since the
foundations of the desired system are already in place, it is reasonable to foresee
how an Islamic economy would function. The objective of this paper is twofold. On
the one hand, I plan to explain in non-technical language the methodology and
axioms of Islamic economics which constitute the philosophical foundations of this
economic system. On the other hand, I will present a critical examination of this
"new" economics and suggest where its main weaknesses lie.

Many of the principal assumptions and arguments in the Islamic literature are
similar to other economic doctrines, notably the Judaic, Christian, Buddhist, and
Marxist. But, while some of the following criticisms of Islamic economics also
apply to other systems, my goal is neither to offer a comparative critique nor to
address imperfections in existing economic systems. The question here is not
whether existing systems can be improved, but whether Islam advances a viable
economic alternative.

## I. Current Trends in the Development of Islamic Economics

Although Muslim intellectuals have discussed the economic teachings of
Islam as early as the turn of this century, Islamic economics did not appear as a
discipline in its own right until the mid-1960s. Earlier years witnessed the
emergence of some books and articles, most notably the works of Mawlana Abu-
Al'a Al-Mawudi and Sayid Qutub, the most prominent of modern Islamic
thinkers. But these works demonstrated no interest in the economic theories and
tools of analysis developed in recent centuries, notably in Europe and North
America. The Islamic economists who have appeared on the scene recently tend to
be of a different mold: having been familiar with modern currents of thought, they
are more willing to borrow concepts and analytical methods from non-Islamic
writings. Khurshid Ahmad, one of the founders of the contemporary discipline of
Islamic economics, described the major lines of this transition among Muslim
thinkers:

> Initially the emphasis was on explaining the economic teachings of
> Islam and offering Islamic critique of the Western contemporary
> theory and policy. During this phase most of the work was done by the
> *Ulama*, the leftists and Muslim social thinkers and reformers. Gradu-
> ally the Muslim economists and other professionals became involved

❖

in this challenging enterprise. Perhaps the First International Conference on Islamic Economics [held in 1976] represents the watershed in the history of the evolution of Muslim thinking on Economics, representing the transition from "economic teachings of Islam" to the emergence of "Islamic Economics" (Khan 1983, p. 7).

Thus, the more traditional approach focused on the "economic teachings of Islam." There was an attempt to examine the verses of the Qur'an which have economic connotations. This was supported by a parallel collecting of the Traditions of the Prophet Muhammad which have economic implications. This method has as its foundation a vast conglomeration of separate propositions and specific historical cases which were then used to provide the legitimizing proof for particular views. From the perspective of many proponents of this approach, this methodology had the advantage of grounding the presentation in explicitly Islamic sources and axioms. It also highlights the effort to go beyond apologetically attempting to prove that Islamic teachings are compatible with some Western concepts (Esposito and Voll 1990, p. 32).

However, many contemporary Muslim intellectuals found the traditional approach to be problematic for a variety of reasons. It tends to result in an accumulation of discussions rather than a more integrated analysis. Further, this approach involved the researcher in theological arguments of Qur'anic and *Hadith* (sayings of the Prophet Muhammad) analysis. For instance, old arguments about annulment of one *Hadith* by another or by a Qur'anic verse became the necessary starting points of analysis. Such debates were considered of crucial significance in presentations of "the economic teachings of Islam."

Islamic economics, on the other hand, is a more holistic undertaking. Muslim economists are conscious of specific Qur'anic verses and traditions, but they constitute the foundation for their viewpoint rather than the starting point for their analysis. They speak of the broader Qur'anic value-patterns rather than the particular provisions of certain verses and traditions. This, in turn, enables them to advance a more broadly integrated paradigm of Islamic economics rather than a list of Islamic characteristics.

## II. Principles of Islamic Economics

### A. Fundamental Islamic Values

There exists within the tradition of Islam four essential values which guide all aspects of human conduct, including economic conduct. The first of such values is *Tawheed*, which literally means unity. In an absolute sense, unity relates only to God by differentiating between Him and the created, requiring unconditional surrender by all to His will. From a socio-cultural perspective, *Tawheed* refers to the interrelatedness of all that exists. It links the political, economic, social and spiritual aspects of man's life into a homogenous whole. Thus, the concept of Unity

———————————————— ❖ ————————————————

connects the worldly and heavenly life in a way that discourages Muslims from leading a life of otherworldliness. The Qur'an instructs Muslims: "... [A]nd seek the abode of the hereafter in that which God has given you and neglect not your portion of the world" (Qur'an, Sura 28.11). From an economic perspective, *Tawheed* underscores the gist of Islamic economics in that it calls on man to treat his fellow human beings in light of his relationship with God.

The second basic value in Islam is free choice. Free choice refers to the relative freedom of man, within the limits established by Islam, to embrace or refuse whatever is on Earth, to choose between right and evil in each of his activities and thoughts (Naqvi 1981, p. 52). Man in Islam is an individual being in his aspirations, but his individual identity is not separate from his social milieu. While in no circumstances can a person be denied this right to freedom of choice and decision, his welfare is bound up with the welfare of the society (Ahmed 1988, pp. 343-344).

However, the Islamic notion of freedom differs from that proposed by many Western social philosophers who argued that the individual's almost-unlimited privilege to acquire private property is a "natural" right. Islam does not bestow unqualified sanction to an individual's right to own and manage property, because all property belongs to God and man is only His trustee on earth. Ownership is, in other words, stewardship of God's property rather than an absolute right of the individual human (Naqvi, p. 52).

The third essential principle of Islam economics is responsibility. This principle constitutes a counter-balancing constraint on man's behavior by establishing limits on what man is free to do by making him accountable for all that he does (Naqvi, p. 241). Man, being given the power to choose between good and evil, must endure the consequences of his decisions. The Qur'an emphasizes that he who intervenes in a good cause will have the reward thereof, and he who intervenes in an evil cause will bear the consequences for his actions. Furthermore, Muslim theologians stress the obligation of every person to continually improve his own condition and the circumstances of the society in which he lives. The Qur'an points out: "Verily never will God change the condition of a people until they change it themselves" (Sura 13:11).

### B. Economic Implications of Islamic Values

#### 1. Economic Implications of Tawheed

A significant characteristic of modern economic theorizing in the West has been the exclusion of the influence of "exogenous factors," particularly ethical ones, on economics. This is rejected by the Islamic faith, which calls on people to blend the two. Such a fusion has far reaching consequences for economic behavior. First, the character of the "Economic Man" is entirely transformed. His utility-maximizing conduct is subjected not only to whether the commodity demanded is producible, but also to "the allowability constraint," which categorizes certain products as prohibited to be either consumed or produced (Naqvi, p. 63).

Second, the desire of a person to consume goods is not totally "insatiable" with respect to every good, by virtue of the Qur'anic order, "... eat and drink, but do not be wasteful" (Qur'an, Sura 7:31). Thus, the utility-maximizing consumption behavior will be different in an Islamic economic system than in any other system. Professor Zarqa argues that the main difference between "Homo Islamicus" as opposed to "Homo Economicus" is that the consumption behavior of the former is deeply influenced by a consideration of the penalty or reward in the life after death (Zarqa 1976, p. 9).

Third, the synthesis of economics and ethics compels consumers and producers to take into consideration the consumption and production behavior of others in the community. Therefore, contrary to neo-classical utility analysis, man neither can remain "selfish" in his consumption behavior, nor can he produce independently of what others are producing. From an Islamic perspective, the Economic Man must simultaneously be an individual as well as a collective entity (Naqvi, p. 64).

## 2. Institutional Structure and the Principle of Free Choice

Free choice demands that proper institutional arrangements should be made to secure economic freedom for individuals within specific ethical limitations. This is not to say that *laissez faire* approximates the Islamic ideal, for several reasons. First, the Islamic notion of individual freedom is forwarded in a way to make it consistent with a substantial role of the state in an Islamic economy. Second, an explicit recognition of externalities in consumption and production will be sharper in an ethically-oriented society than in societies which claim to be ethically neutral. For example, the opposition will be greater in such a community to the construction of industrial plants which cause grave harm to public health. Thus, the frequency and extent of state intervention in an Islamic state will be greater than in a capitalistic one (Naqvi, p. 67). Direct and unambiguous state intervention limiting individual economic freedom in order to bring production and consumption levels in line with what is socially just is a normal "fact of life" in an Islamic society.

Third, communal rights in Islam take precedence over individual prerogatives. Thus, individual rights are guarded only to the extent that they do not deviate from the overall social needs. For example, Islam acknowledges the individual right to private property only as long as this right does not interfere with societal needs and goals. Moreover, the right to private ownership of property is not absolute since absolute ownership belongs to God alone, while "human ownership must be relative only" (Esposito 1983, p 230). Furthermore, such relative ownership is limited to purposes which are beneficial for the welfare of the Islamic society. The personal right to ownership is also confined to the goods that are the products of human labor. Thus, Islam does not recognize the individual right to ownership of natural resources, since they are not the products of a person's work.

When individual and societal rights prove to be inharmonious, the Islamic authorities must give primacy to the latter. However, when both categories of rights

❖

are compatible, individual rights must be respected and protected, and a delicate balance between the two should be established.

An Islamic state is charged with the responsibility of ensuring the welfare of the Muslim community. Muhammad was quoted as saying: "He whom God has made an administrator over the affairs of Muslims but remains indifferent to their needs and their poverty, God will also be indifferent to his needs and poverty" (Donahue and Esposito 1982, p. 224). He also observed: "The ruler [state] is the supporter of him who has no supporter" (Donohue and Esposito, p. 224).

### 3. Economic Behavior and the Axiom of Responsibility

Since Islam assigns each individual the responsibility to ameliorate the quality of his socio-economic milieu, a person's consumption behavior is not solely a function of his own income. Rather, it must reflect an awareness of the income and consumption levels of others, too. Moreover, the consumption levels of other members of the community do not necessarily have to be proportional to their earnings, since the goal of an Islamic state is to bring individual consumption behavior in line with what is considered socially desirable in an Islamic society. Once again, state intervention becomes necessary to implement this process.[18]

In addition, the principle of responsibility influences an individual's consideration of what is just. "Social justice [in Islam is] the overriding goal of all economic transactions" (Choudhury and Rahman 1986, p. 61). The Qur'an quotes the Prophet Muhammad to have said "[M]y Lord enjoys justice" (Sura 7:29). A.K. Brohi observes that establishing a just order — whether that has reference to economic, political or social order in the community—is Islam's overriding mandate (1975, p. 104). The Qur'an explicitly stresses the importance of those responsibilities when it obliges every Muslim to participate in economically productive activities. Qutub pointed out that ". . . [I]slam is the enemy of idleness in the name of worship and religion. Worship is not an occupation of life. It has but its appointed time" (Esposito, p. 93).

Thus, within an Islamic society, a Muslim producer has to take into account various considerations. First, in estimating the profit returns, wage costs must conform to what is considered to be a socially acceptable minimum in an Islamic state. Therefore, the ceilings of the profit margins are specified, especially since wages must be settled in advance because hiring an individual for an uncertain wage is prohibited (Nasr 1970, p. 70). Second, Islam forbids all arrangements in which the buyer is not always in a position to predict the full financial consequences of a transaction. A classic example is the advance sale of the expected fruits of a tree which has not yet borne fruit. In this case, the buyer cannot be made to suffer if the fruits do not grow (Naqvi, p. 68).

### III. Policy Basis of the Islamic Economic Principles

The above-mentioned axioms of Islamic economics require specific policy instruments in order to translate them into practical application. The three main principles of Islamic economics are mobilized by three key policy instruments. They are (1) the institution of *mudarabah* (profit-risk-sharing); (2) the elimination of *riba* (interest on capital); and (3) the institution of *zakat* (wealth tax).

## A. Institution of *Mudarabah*

The Islamic profit-loss-sharing system is defined as the percentage share of the supplier of capital in the profits of the entrepreneur, or the working partner in the *mudarabah* contract. *Mudarabah* may take many forms: capital-capital, labor-labor, or capital-labor, based on the agreement that the returns of joint endeavors will be shared among the participants on the basis of predetermined proportions determined by the market value of the resource inputs (Choudhury 1989, p. 34). Islamic economists argue that the expectation for high profit rates facilitates the increase in both the amount of enterprises and the rate of investment, which, in turn, will help ". . . raise grass roots entitlement through cooperative participation and wage labor" (Choudhury 1990, p. 48).

## B. Elimination of Riba

Since its onset in Arabia centuries ago, Islam has quite frankly and categorically forbidden the existence of interest in all economic transactions. This stance toward the taking of interest stemmed from the Qur'an: "Those who squander usury will stand as stands one whom the Evil One by his touch has driven to madness. That is because they say: 'trade is like usury,' but God has authorized trade and prohibited usury" (Sura 2:257). The reasons for forbidding *riba* are clear. First, interest reinforces the tendency to concentrate wealth in the hands of a few, while at the same time minimizing man's concern for his fellow man. Second, usury creates an idle class of persons who receive their income from accumulated wealth. Thus, the community is stripped from the labor of such people.

Mawdudi, one of the leading theoreticians of modern Islamic revivalism, has argued that interest leads to a basic imbalance between production and consumption. This occurs when interest on productive loans increases the cost of production, hence the prices of consumption goods. The amount of money taxed away from consumers, in the form of higher prices falls in the hands of a class with a lower than average propensity to consume. Mawdudi argues that such imbalance is the fountain of many evils, including stagnation, monopoly and, ultimately, imperialism (1966, pp. 86-87).

Islamic economists reject the notion that abolishing interest would decrease the propensity to save, thus lowering the level of investment. Quoting Keynes, they point out that savings are primarily the function of income and earning interest is only a secondary motive of savings. In the absence of interest, the possibility of securing profits on common stock or through a *mudarabah* contract will serve the same purpose.

❖

Regarding investment, some modern Muslim revivalists argue that interest holds back investment in production (Mannan 1970, p. 69). Interest thwarts the channeling of capital towards projects with low returns even though they are socially very beneficial (Mawdudi 1966, p. 110). They point out that it is not the rate of interest but the priorities of a modern state and the rates of profit in various sectors of the economy that are decisive so far as allocation of investible funds is concerned (Siddiqi 1970, p. 112).

### C. Institution of *Zakat*

*Zakat*, one of the five immutable pillars of the Islamic faith, refers to an orderly form of social aid in an Islamic polity financed by tax on all kinds of income and wealth surpassing a certain minimum exemption level (Choudhury 1986, p. 15). It is in a way intended as a system of social security for all of those who become destitute in Islamic countries. Through the institution of *zakat*, wealthy Muslims are made accountable for providing for the fundamental needs of all members of the society.

A special economic importance of *zakat* is that it prevents hoarding. According to the tenets of Islam, a person's wealth has to be spent partly on the necessities of living and comfort, in investment, and for the good of Muslims in general. After these, whatever is left standing for a year or more is subject to being taxed. *Zakat* revenue is made of a levy of 2.5 percent on all idle wealth, one-tenth to one-twentieth of all agricultural produce, one-fifth of all mineral wealth, and a duty on the earnings from capital of the state (Choudhury 1986, p. 18).

The method by which *zakat* is to be collected has been a subject of debate among Islamic legal scholars, with the primary point of agreement being what comprises apparent property, on which *zakat* should be collected by governmental agents, as opposed to non-apparent property, on which *zakat* is disbursed directly by the owners. Other legal scholars have contended that, to insure proper distribution among the needy, the state must supervise all *zakat*, with the right to collect it by force when Muslims ignore their obligations (Esposito, p. 29). However, it must be clear that it is only the principle behind *zakat* that is unchangeable in Islam and not the methods of collecting and allocating it.

## IV. Conclusion

The foregoing has been a brief delineation of current aspects of Islamic economic thought. In recent years, many religious-minded Muslim activists, as well as many socially inclined Muslim theologians, have been enthusiastically engaged in developing the principles and methodology of Islamic economics. Not only because of the eagerness of these intellectuals and the creation of numerous institutions devoted to research in Islamic economics, but also because many formerly secular economics departments throughout the Muslim world have been transformed into Islamic ones, will the world witness a great deal more research in Islamic economics.

Nonetheless, for a variety of reasons, it is uncertain that Islamic economics will evolve into a sufficiently established, internally consistent economic system. First, there exists within Islam different sects with rather diverse, and at times opposed, interpretations of Qur'anic verses and *Hadith*. Second, another difficulty stems from the fact that various Muslim intellectuals and activists have different ideological persuasions. For instance, while some find Islam in harmony with capitalism, other Muslims, by adhering to Lenin's theory of imperialism, find Islam more in harmony with Marxian socialism. Third, the absence of a body-theoretic foundation for Islamic economics has hindered it from advancing with the same momentum and vigour of modern conventional economics. What Muslim economists have today are the rudiments of particular behavioral norms and principles of public policy developed centuries ago and worked upon by contemporary intellectuals to give them more analytical dimension. However, these works can hardly be regarded as providing a sufficiently established Islamic economic theory (Choudhury 1986, p. 201).

Islamic economics has still a long way to go to formulate a comprehensive system. The foregoing has been a concise outline of the major axioms of this "new" discipline, the main concern of which is to distribute and utilize societal resources in a manner that will insure a greater degree of social justice than existing capitalist and socialist systems. The principles in this regard stem from the Qur'an and Islamic tradition.

*M.A. candidate, Department of International Relations, Creighton University, Omaha, NE 68178 USA.

# References

Abbasi, Sami M, *et al.* "Islamic Economics: Foundations and Practices," *International Journal of Social Economics,* 1989, *16,* 5-17.

Abdul-Rauf, Muhammad. *The Islamic Doctrine of Economics and Contemporary Economic Thought: Highlight of a Conference on a Theological Inquiry into Capitalism and Socialism,* Washington, D.C.: American Enterprise Institute for Public Policy Research, 1979.

Ahmad, Khurshid. "Islam and the Challenge of Economic Development," in Altaf Gauhar, ed., *The Challenge of Islam,* London: Islamic Council of Europe, 1978.

Ahmed, Akbar S. *Discovering Islam,* New York: Routledge and Kegan Paul, 1988.

Brohi, A.K. *Islam in the Modern World,* 2nd ed. Lahore: Publishers United Limited, 1975.

Chapra, Umar M. "The Islamic Welfare State," in John Donohue and John Esposito, eds., *Islam in Transition: Muslim Perspectives*, New York: Oxford University Press, 1982.

Choudhury, M.A. *Contributions to Islamic Economic Thought: A Study in Social Economics*, New York: St. Martin's Press, 1986.

_____. "The Blending of Religious and Social Orders in Islam," *International Journal Of Social Economics*, 1989, *16*, 13-45.

_____. "Islamic Economics as a Social Science," *International Journal Of Social Economics*, 1990, *17*, 35-59.

_____ and Rahman, A.N.M., "Macroeconomic Relations in them Islamic Economic Order," *International Journal of Social Economics*, 1986, *1*, 60-78.

Esposito, John, ed. *Voices of Resurgent Islam*, New York: Oxford University Press, 1983.

_____. and Voll, John. "Khurshid Ahmad: Muslim Activist-Economist," *The Muslim World*, January 1990, *80*, 24-36.

Haddad, Yvonne. "Sayyid Qutub: Ideologue of Islamic Revival," in John Esposito, ed., *Voices of Resurgent Islam*, New York: Oxford University Press, 1983.

Khan, Akram. *Islamic Economics: Annotated Sources in English and Urdu*, Leicester, England: The Islamic Foundation, 1983.

Mannan, M.A. *Islamic Economics: Theory and Practice*, Lahore: Muhammad Ashraf, 1970.

Mawdudi, Sayyid Abu al-A'ala. *Sud (Interest)*, Lahore: Islamic Publications, 1966.

Naqvi, Syed Nawab Haider. *Ethics and Economics: An Islamic Synthesis*, London: The Islamic Foundation, 1981.

Nasr, S.H. *Science and Civilization in Islam*, New York: New American Library, 1970.

Pryor, Frederic. "The Islamic Economic System," *Journal of Comparative Economics*, 1985, *9*, 197-223.

Qutub, Sayyid. *Al-Adala al-Ijtima'iyah Fi al-Islam (Social Justice in Islam)*, Cairo: Maktabat Misr, 1945.

Siddiqi, Muhammad N. *Some Aspects of Islamic Economy*, Lahore: Islamic Publications, 1970.

Tibi, Bassam. *The Crisis of Modern Islam: A Preindustrial Culture in the Scientific-Technological Age*, Salt Lake City: University of Utah Press, 1988.

Zarqa, M.A. "Social Welfare Function and Consumer Behavior: An Islamic Formulation of Selected Issues," Paper presented at The First International Conference on Islamic Economics, Mecca, 1976.

Ziauddin, Ahmed. "Socio-economic Values of Islam," *Islamic Studies*, 1971, *10*, 343-355.

# An Islamic Theory of Moral Entitlement in Comparative Perspective

*Masudul Alam Choudhury\**

In this paper the concept of entitlement is equatable to property rights but with the singular difference that it is conditioned by the characteristics of the vectors of goods to be owned as against simply the right to own such goods. Thus, this concept of entitlement carries with it the dual and inseparable conditions of the nature of ownership and the responsibility inherent in such ownership. When such a concept of entitlement is invoked it is obvious that mere transfer incomes to target groups under study do not make up the essence of such an entitlement, nor does ownership or antecedental holding of property necessarily legitimize any concept of absolute ownership.

Such a concept of entitlement is at variance with the ones presented in the literature by Amartya Sen (1986) and Robert Nozick (1974).[1] The essential difference arises in terms of the unbridled and unperturbed sanctity that these authors attach to the original endowment of holdings. That initial condition of holding property legitimizes all forms of exchange in the market system. To Sen any form of interruption in such means of entitlement as trade, production, own labour, inheritance and transfer is seen as the cause of economic deprivation. To Nozick such interruption in entitlement based on original holdings is considered as immoral and inefficient. Thus, to Nozick the very idea of redistribution of incomes through taxes and other institutional arrangements is objectionable.

Our concept of entitlement as a conditioned idea of property rights necessarily alters the notion of the market, exchange and, thereby, the nature of the principal socioeconomic activities that take place in the polity-market nexus.[2] The market cannot anymore be viewed as a primordial sway of unbridled freedom enacting the neutral functions of exchange between buyers and sellers of any goods that these deem desirable. It is equally no more the function of the polity to superimpose its predominance over the market in order to give it socialistic essence.[3] The market

❖

continues to exist as a prominent institution of economic activity. But it is now involved in the exchange of goods with special attributes that legitimize this vector within the entitlement due.

The role of the market in concert with the polity in establishing the exchange milieu within the entitlement context, therefore, alters the conjoint functions of consumption, production and distribution. A general-equilibrium system is thus invoked in the entitlement concept just as is the case in the Walrasian general equilibrium-system and its variations in other systems of multimarket version of interactive relationships among these economic activities and between the household, the product market, and the labour market. However, in the Walrasian general-equilibrium system the role of government and institutions in regulating economic activities is nonexistent.[4]

In the present paper we shall, first, develop the concept of moral entitlement in view of the ethicoeconomic/general-equilibrium system it configures.[5] This will be exemplified by an overview of the Islamic general-equilibrium system in light of the Islamic concept of moral entitlement. Next, we examine the Islamic concept of moral entitlement itself and its interactive function in the socioeconomic system. Finally, the contrasts between Islamic and other theories of entitlement are investigated. Here, the intention is to show that there are certain epistemological problems underlying the received theories of entitlement in the literature in respect to well-defining the concept of moral entitlement and its interactive role in the social economy. The theory of moral entitlement in resource allocation here is derived directly from the *Quran* as the principal source.

## I. The Concept of Moral Entitlement and the Polity-Market System

The concept of moral entitlement must necessarily be developed in a polity-market interactive setting. To undertake this construction, one can first note the idea of the antecedental function of the market in received economic theory.[6] This antecedental premise is characterized by the original ownership and endowment of vectors of items that remain at the sole disposal of the sellers and at the sole desire of the buyers. The moral standing of the market in such a perspective is then judged by the consequentialist effects it leaves in the society at large. The consequentialist result, given the unperturbed function of market exchange relying on its antecedentalist legitimacy of holding, is seen as one for which the market itself is not responsible. The responsibility for the nature of the consequentialist effects of the market exchange given original holdings is seen as being vested with the polity. Sen refers to this as an evaluation of the market in different institutional arrangements.[7]

The market system in economic theory is thus morally benign or ethically neutral. Consequently, market exchange is seen as an ethically neutral medium of setting values. What this means is that while there can be moral compunction in the consumption and production of "bads" (e.g. pollution), yet given the neutrality of market exchange to the nature of such "bads," it is solely left to economic exchange to determine the moral standing of the "bads" in that exchange. When the exchange is completed and the activities of consumption and production have taken place, the market system simply reflects the final result of the exchange mechanism. Such a reflection can be a bad one when "bads" rather than "goods" are transacted. But the exchange mechanism by itself is seen to be immune to the sensitivity of this end result.

Such an ethical neutrality of the market system and, consequently, of the exchange mechanism defining consumption, production and socioeconomic value, has pervaded mainstream economic doctrines.[8] The profound difficulty in sensitizing the market system to ethical relevance in exchange emanates from the way market and polity have been treated in the literature. Here we see the institutionally unperturbed vision of the "free" market ruled by atomistic buyers and sellers with no particular inter-group hegemony. Thereby, all agents get swayed by the same preset order of preferences.[9] Even in the case of distortionary treatment of resource allocation in a market setting the Second Best problem of sub-optimality is used.[10]

The real cause of ethical neutrality of the market system can now be seen to reside in the dual picture of the antecedentalist and consequentialist concepts of exchange in mainstream economic reasoning. The antecedentalist idea vests the original holding in the hands of the owner, who can dispose of that holding in any way that he/she desires. The consequentialist idea gives the net result of the exchange for better or for worse. It relieves itself of the responsibility for the exchange mechanism that runs the show. The evaluation of the market is predicated on its consequentialist reflection, not on the antecedentalist one, for the free-market system is seen not to interfere with the original holdings in the first place. Otherwise, as Nozick says, the result will be "moral horrors." This is what western entitlement theory sees as the unwanted effect of institutional intervention in the market-allocative process.[11]

In the concept of moral entitlement the separation between the antecedentalist and consequentialist viewpoints of the market system and market exchange cannot exist. The responsibility to be morally thinking and morally acting is placed on both of these premises of the total market function. There is no exonerating the exchange system and the original ownership of the vectors of goods from the moral responsibility that these entail. Thus, there is neither any concept of separating the market system from polity nor of considering the self-interested preference formation for the consumer and the producer. Economic distribution is determined in the venue of the consumption and production menus that so emanate.

Since primordial ownership loses its unbridled primacy in the moral entitlement concept, the concept of absolute ownership is replaced by the relevant concept of functional ownership.[12] The market system and its element of property rights are now guided by the role of polity in them. Yet, it is not polity that controls the market function. Indeed, the market system continues to be upheld as the supreme allocator of resources. The substantive change now is that the market becomes a morally guided system in the sense that such moral guidance is not enforced but integrated with the preferences of the consumer and the producer. V. Nienhaus (1990) refers to some such distinct view of his own as an "economic theory of morality."[13] The moral standing of the market now integrates with an equitable distribution menu and the precept of socioeconomic value. It is in this sense of moral integration of polity with the market system that the ethically neutral concept of the market is relinquished and is replaced by an ethical set endogenous to the economic system.[14]

One can turn to the entire expanse of western and eastern socioeconomic doctrines to find that political-economic thought has always been swayed singularly by the precept of ethical neutrality and of ethical exogeneity to the socioeconomic system. This comprises the age-long period from the Greeks to modern day public-choice theory in western economic thought; and from the Buddhistic Mahayana and Hinayana, as two levels of man's quest for Nirvana, the "ying" and "yang" (micro- and macro-views of the cosmos) of Confucianism, to present day philosophy of the One and the Many in eastern philosophy.[15] The common epistemological premise of all these ideologies is seen to be based on the separation of their views of reality into a dualistic mould of perception. That perception of reality is seen to be divided between an a priori essence of goodness and a noninteractive, a posteriori element of sense perception.[16] Unfortunately, several of the Islamic thinkers also fell victims to such dualistic ways of thinking as is shown by the works of Avicenna, Averroës, the Ikhwan al-Safa, al-Farabi and Ibn Khaldun.[17] The pursuit of the study of Islamic economics in the neoclassical tradition by Islamic economists today is another example of this dualistic methodology being adopted in Islamic studies.

Yet the argument of this paper is that the singular difference of ethical endogeneity in social-scientific reality lies essentially in the perception of a unified world view of reality. The Quran presents this unified percept, although this view is not the one always pronounced by all Islamic thinkers, perhaps because of their subservience to Islamically extraneous realms of knowledge-seeking.[18] In this perception of reality there are several elements to be noted, all of which together finally establish the Islamic concept of moral entitlement.

In this perception of reality the primordially a priori premise of God's unicity, governance and guidance in the order of things is integrated with the worldly response of its comprehension. The a priori is thus interrelated with the a posteriori in continuous bonds of evolution of the "Tawhidi" percept in the social-scientific reality.[19] Such an integration bestows the primal and evolutionary character of morals in the social-scientific structure. Now, in the context of the Islamic socioeconomic system, the consumption, production and distribution menus are all primordially influenced by the input of the a priori moral premise. But through the integrative function of this moral premise, the a priori becomes one with the a posteriori. The separation between moral polity and "positive" marketplace (ecological system) disappears.[20]

## II. The Islamic Concept of Moral Entitlement

The Islamic concept of moral entitlement is now established. The essential Islamic belief that absolute ownership of all resources lies with God alone relegates all temporal forms of ownership to be of the nature of functional ownership. With this change in the concept of primordial property rights, there remains the margin of essential irrevocability for moral intervention. All property rights are thus limited by the moral conditions of consumption, production and distribution. These conditions are derived in the polity by the transcendence of the moral law, which in Islam is the Shariah. The Islamic Law or Shariah derives its sources from the *Quran*, the traditions of Prophet Muhammad (Sunnah) and Islamic discursive analogy (Ijtehad).[21] The development of Shariah, its extensions over time and the acceptance of such extensions and abrogations or revisions of the extensions are vested on social-consensus formation in the Islamic polity, called the Shura.

Yet it is not the ruling of the Shura on intellectual and policy matters alone that performs the ethically integrative function in the Islamic socioeconomic system. Rather, the most important cycle of integration comes from the side of the market (ecological) feedbacks to the Shura. Such feedbacks signal the attained robustness of the polity-market integration back to the Shura. They enable the Shura, thereby, to continue on the cycles of moral interaction and transformation in concert with the changing preferences in the socioeconomic system. The Shura thus responds to the ethical change that proceeds on in evolutionary cycles of comprehension emanating from the polity-market interactions.[22] Such is the learning-by-doing process that integrates the Shura and the ecological system together. The market is a specific subsystem of the grand ecological order.

## III. The Principle of Ethical Endogeneity in Establishing Moral Entitlement

The Principle of Ethical Endogeneity underlies this Shuratic process of polity-market integrative moral transformation. It can be explained as follows: There is a direct relationship between institutions (Shura) and the formulation of ethical policies. These ethical policies are then made to interact with the market (ecological) environment, leading to a general-equilibrium relationship between consumption, production, and distribution. In each case these activities are influenced by the ethical policies. This results in the generation of social product. This social product then sends feedback signals to the polity in two ways. In the short run, the institutions are influenced to revise their policies and the interactions continue. In the long run, social consensus is formed. This further influences the polity and economy to generate higher levels of interactions between the polity, market and broader-social system. General equilibrium in the market/society set is explained in terms of interactions among the socioeconomic variables. General equilibrium in the polity is explained by social-consensus formation. The integrated general equilibrium in the economy and polity constitutes the Islamic Ethico-Economic General Equilibrium.[23]

❖

## IV. The Islamic Ethico-Economic/General-Equilibrium System in Relation to Moral Entitlement

A brief epistemological explanation of the above concept of Islamic ethico-economic/general equilibrium in the light of the moral-entitlement concept is now presented as follows: A Quranic verse speaks on the topic of production, spending and distribution in the light of the epistemological foundations of the Islamic economic and social order. This verse is in several interrelated parts.[24]

First, reference is made here to the primary and produced goods that are delivered in the market or exchanged as gifts. Here it is shown that production is essentially a technical application to resources that are owned absolutely by God, with man as a trustee of those goods in their primary and produced forms. Thus, the verse brings out the attributes of delivery of produced goods to be based on the honest production and delivery of things of use and benefit, not things that are useless and corrupting. The emphasis in this ethics is placed on the premise that all such deliveries are of goods that are not owned by man absolutely. Therefore, man has no right to misuse those things according to the Islamic Law. This principle is simply the principle of moral entitlement now being established on the production side.

Secondly, the verse goes on to point out the wisdom of market exchange of gifts or in the buying and selling of produced goods. The corrupt and dishonest exchange of useless and harmful items when not characterized by the Godly-set of moral values are disbanded by the Shariah. According to moral characterization, all production, just as all types of spending, must be instilled with the attribute of God-consciousness.

Thirdly, by implication, the question of moral entitlement is extended to the functional ownership of means and items of production. While the attributes of the Godly-set of values are now extended to the production menu, mankind comes to acquire the rights and obligations of appropriate functional ownership, the appropriate use and the dispensations of duties respecting those property rights. A two-way production and exchange mechanism is inevitable in this relational implication. First, while it is the obligation and duty of the producer of primary or produced items to see that the appropriate good is delivered, the appropriate technology used, and the social-justice tenets of distribution maintained, so also it is the producer's right to obtain the appropriate thing in exchange. This exchange can occur in the form of goods or in the form of money-capital. A social-market exchange mechanism in the product and factor markets is thus implied.[25]

The interrelationship among the various sections of the Quranic verse herein mentioned is seen in terms of the epistemological meanings of appropriate production of goods and appropriate technology, in the fair-market exchange of those items that establishes moral entitlement, and in the social control and balance potentially delivered by the production activity. The early seeds of the Islamic theory of production are thus planted in this verse. These involve the role of productive activity in the general/ethico-economic system of Islamic political economy. The social exchange is made to relate to these two by determination of the social control and balance of production and consumption, and the extension of implications of social justice to the factor market.

I have earlier presented briefly the Islamic ethico-economic/general-equilibrium system. It was shown to explain the interactions between the Shura and the ecological order. The social/market system being a subset of this grand ecological order, I have shown that the concept of general equilibrium in it means the determination of social goods under the interrelationships between the three basic activities of the Islamic economy. These are the activities of social consumption, social production and distributive equity (social justice). These three activities then relate with the ethical guidance of the Shura. But such a guidance comes about not through any coercive policing rules of the Shura and its supportive organizations. The freedom for the Shuratic process to be reinforced in the market venue, indeed, reflects the spontaneous response of the acceptance of truth, reason and the fruits of felicity that are naturally generated out of the ethico-economic system. The strength and clarity of such a system is repeatedly shown in the referred-to Quranic verses to be due to the inexorable and impeccable presence of the Godly-set in the order of things. Such a sure prevalence of truth is shown to lie in the essence of the human pursuit for truth in spite of aberrations among some sections of humankind over time. Polity and market in the amoral liberal order are seen to be promoters of a false image of progress and development.[26]

## V. Formalization of the Principle of Ethical Endogeneity in the Islamic Economic System.

The epistemological basis of the interrelationships mentioned in the Quranic verses referred to here now leads to the formalization of the general ethico-economic system in its rudimentary form. Toward developing this we define the set characterizing the social goods (SG),

$$SG = f(CS,PS,DS,z); \text{ wherein,} \tag{1}$$

$PS = f1(CS,z)$, $DS = f2(PS,CS,z)$, and $CS(z) = PS(z) = DS(z)$; and, SG, CS, PS and DS denote, respectively, a bundle of social goods, the demand for social consumption and investment goods, social production and social distribution (distributive equity), while z is the vector of ethical values. Here, $PS = f1(CS,z)$ means that the supply of output responds to the demand for that output in the social market. $DS = f2(PS,CS,z)$ means that distribution in the factor markets depends upon the production characteristics and the market exchange that generates prices, and thereby profits, which are distributively shared between the participants in a profit-sharing environment (mudarabah). The presence of z-vector as the Islamic ethical values in all of these menus shows the role of polity-market interaction necessary for social balance and control in the ethico-economic system. This equilibrium position is shown by $CS(z) = PS(z) = DS(z)$. Note that in the Islamic

———————————— ❖ ————————————

economy the principle of simultaneity between economic efficiency and distributive equity gives primacy to the goal of distribution to the Shura. This in turn determines the consumption-investment menu and the distribution menu in the light of the costs and incomes generated by wages and profit shares.[27]

Additional relations here are formalized as follows: The given functions are invertible in the z-vector. There is a "basis" set of elements of the z-vector that defines the X-set inculcating traits of committment, motivation and justice, all of which are so essential in driving the ethically endogenous system toward social consensus.[28] The basis vector establishes temporary equilibrium (optimality) in the set SG of social goods. Such an equilibrium then regenerates itself over different phases of ethical perfection attained by the evolving Islamic polity-market interactions over time. Since a temporary equilibrium exists in the SG-set over a particular phase of polity-market interactions, an optimal situation is temporarily attained in this set. Hence, there is an equilibrium-optimality for each of its compact subsets — i.e. CS, PS, DS — that simultaneously attain.[29]

Now, while the the Godly-set (G-set) is a topologically compact one over a particular phase of Islamic transformation, the set of equilibria over different phases of Islamization remains unbounded, as there is no limit to the ethical perfection that individuals and society can attain. The supreme example of moral perfection is believed by Muslims to have been completed in the life of Prophet Muhammad (Sunnah). Hence, over different phases of Islamization there exist mappings of the unbounded and open Z*-set comprising all possible sets of equilibrium z*-vectors, onto the corresponding SG*-set. That is, it is mathematically impossible now to define a finite limit point for the Z*-set existing in the SG*-set. The implication of this property of the SG*-set with respect to the Z*-set is that such sets are locally stable but globally unstable.[30] Shura comprehension, priorities, policies and directions are, thus, constantly revised. These changes bring about different configurations on consumption, production and distribution menus. They in turn trigger responses between the polity and market systems.

## VI. The Concepts of Islamic Market and Islamic Economy in Relation to Moral Entitlement

### A. The Islamic Market

The concept of the Islamic market emanates from yet another verse of the *Quran*.[31] In the light of this verse a generalized definition of markets, M, can be provided. Now, $M = M (p,r,qd, qs)(z)$, where p denotes the market price in the immediate sale of the goods and services; r denotes the price for long-run sale of goods and services, and is, therefore, a rate of return; qd and qs denote demand and supply of goods, respectively, immediately transacted in the market, or in the long run. qd is also the demand for capital, I(t), i.e. $qd = I(t)$; qs is also the supply price of capital, P(V), i.e. $qs = P(V)$. The social aspect of these markets is shown by the dependence of all such variables on the Z-set.

Since the z-vector is invertible in the Islamic ethico-economic/general-equilibrium system, the spending set, production set, distribution set and the above-mentioned market variables must be interrelated with each other through the z-vector. For instance, given a Shuratic ethical-policy z-vector by the Shura of the firm, the consumption, production and distributional menus result in a spending regime whose growth rate is governed by a declining interest rate and an increasing profit rate in the process of Islamization as discussed above.consequently, greater mobilization of investment capital into Islamically requisite ventures strengthens the consumption, production and distribution menus of the ethico-economic/general-equilibrium system.

**B. The Islamic Economy**

The Islamic economy denoted by the topological set $E(CS,PS,DS/W, > \sim)$, wherein $> \sim$ stands for indifferent preferences,[32] is essentially an ethico-economic/general-eqilibrium system based on direct and implicit contracts that influence the CS, PS and DS sets in the economy-topological set; more explicitly, in the ethico-economic consumption set, $CS = f1(p,r,qd,ds)$. Here the variables are defined in the static form if immediate delivery of goods in market mechanism is involved; or, as rates of return, investment and present values, when long-term transactions are involved. The following relations are then well-established socially:

$$PS = f1'(CS) = f2'(p,r,qd,qs);$$
$$DS = f3'(CS,PS) = f3'(p,r,qd,qs) \qquad (2)$$

Incorporating the Islamic market with the superstructure of the Islamic economy, we can now extend the definition of the Islamic economy as follows: An Islamic economy is defined as an ethico-economic/market system, EM. Such a concept of economy is characterized by the topology, $E[M(p,r,qd,qs)(z)/W, > \sim]$, where—again—$> \sim$ denotes indifferent preferences. The ethical market system is characterized by the price-quantity vector, $(p,r,qd,qs)(z)$. The interaction between polity and the socioeconomic system is shown by the implied invertibility of these vector functions on each other as sets of values connected by iterated z-values. The "ethicized" market system M defined by these variables is seen to be embodied in the economy E.

Exchange contracts in the EM system take place between individuals, in which case the production menu can assume the form of a household production function.[33] They can also take place between investors and businesses. In either case, the direct contract establishes the full force of the market through which the short-run delivery of fairness and utility of exchange contracts are established for buyers and sellers. In the case of long-term transactions, it is relevant to consider investments. Now the implicit contract is to deliver the appropriate goods and adopt the fairest means according to the attributes of the Z*-set. The net result of all these is both increased material as well as spiritual welfare of the individuals and society at large.

## VII. Islamic Inheritance as Moral Entitlement

Islamic inheritance is an important medium and criterion for establishing moral entitlement in society. The *Quran* gives the formula for distribution of inheritance. But an inheritance that is squandered away cannot be categorized as deserving its entitlement by the recipient. In order to protect the status of moral entitlement in the Islamic society and mobilize it through inheritance, the Shariah provides necessary safeguards that are built into the distribution, socioeconomic mobilization and maintenance of inheritance through the Islamic economy.

That is why the Islamic inheritance system is shown to be embedded in a profit-sharing (i.e. Mudarabah-driven) polity-market interactive process that generates wealth and perpetuates the capital-formation process through household activity. In this type of socioeconomic relationship where both household division of labour, complementarity between men and women as well as economic efficiency and self-reliance are recognized, there must necessarily exist also an ordering among various categories of recipients. The Quranic ranking of shares of inheritance is as follows: sons' share > daughters' share > mother's share > relatives' share > other share.[34]

In the final analysis, however, the mobilization of such shares through the Mudarabah profit-sharing system in the Islamic economy at large, complements the initial differentials in the shares as the rates of return become equalized among all participants through such mobilization of capital. In the aggregate economic sense the initial differential is further reduced as all individuals become beneficiaries in the total volume of inheritance mobilized into social services.

## VIII. Zakat or Wealth-Tax Moral Entitlement

A very important part of moral entitlement in Islam is the institution of wealth tax, known as Zakat. With the addition of Zakat to the Islamic spending vector,[35] the ethical attributes of the Islamic expenditure model show how the worldly felicity derived from the doing of righteous acts emanates from the application of God's Laws in society.

The earlier expenditure function of the Islamic economy which was in terms of consumption expenditure is now extended to include Zakat expenditure. The expenditure set is now augmented by the following Zakat expenditure set:
$$H = U(i=1 \rightarrow 8)Hi \qquad (3)$$
where, Hi are the subsets of Zakat expenditures specified as in the verse, $i = 1$(kin), 2(orphans), 3(needy), ..., 8(ransom of slaves). The Islamic Zakat expenditure is a suitable combination of these subsets of expenditures according to needs and priorities. Thus,
$$\cap \ (i=1 \rightarrow 7)Hi \neq 0.[36] \qquad (4)$$
The functional form of Hi(z) is based on the fact that Zakat expenditure is not forced on people. Rather, it is Taqwa creating (God-consciousness) and therefore,

invokes expenditure out of love for God. By the same token the payment of Zakat in the process model of social-preference transformation in the Islamic society does not mean ostentatious or politically motivated dues accruing to the community or the state. The motivation to pay and collect Zakat must be spontaneous according to the need for forming productive entitlement at the grass roots levels.[37]

The Islamic expenditure model, IEx, is now an augmented one as follows:

$$IEx = CI(Z) \ U \ H(Z) = \{[cI(z) + h(z)], \text{ such that}$$
$$cI(z) \in C^*1 \ U \ C^*2 \ U \ C^*3, h(z) \in H, z \in Z(e1,e2,...,e7)\} \qquad (5)$$

Note now that, since both C and Z depend upon z-values, they must be complementing each other. Because Zakat is a social expenditure variable, complementarity here would mean that, with a given endowment of resources, the $C3^*$ subset of luxuries will be becoming smaller in measure as the H(Z) set increases in measure. Therefore, in the limit, $\lim\{u[H(Z)] \rightarrow \infty.u[C3^*(Z)] = 0\}$, the Islamic social expenditure set, SEx, equals the Islamic individual expenditure set, IEx. u(.) denotes the mathematical mapping on the sets shown within brackets (.).[38] This means further that,

$$IEx = CS(Z) \ U \ H(Z) = \{[cs + h(z)], \text{ such that, } cs \in CS =$$
$$[c(z),z(c)]\} \ \lim\{u[H(Z) \rightarrow \infty.u[C3^*(Z)] = 0\}. \qquad (6)$$

Therefore, $CS(Z) = cI(z)$; and by the invertibility of the CS, cI and h functions on the Z vector,

$$Z(CS) = z(cI). \qquad (7)$$

The above results establish the fact that under the influence of Zakat, individual consumption preferences must be inevitably transformed into social preferences. Also in Islamic social and economic frameworks individual ethics gets to be conformed finally with Islamic social ethics. This is indeed the process of ethical transformation that the Islamic worldview aims at. The invertibility properties on the Z-vector mean that the rational and empirical synthesis of the Islamic moral values with the functions of society are at once primordial and derived from the Islamic social felicity that society attains from moment to moment in its evolution. This process is the same as a social evolution along a dynamic regime of basic needs. This is characterized by bundles of necessaries that rise from simpler forms to highly sophisticated ones. But at every moment of its transformation it preserves its life-sustaining ethical substance.[39]

The principle of simultaneity between economic efficiency and distributive equity is at work again. Higher degrees of distributive equity being entitlement-generating in the Islamic economy must necessarily result in greater production and consumption, bringing along with it higher levels of felicity. If one form of spending in the total category of the Islamic spending set does show signs of misuse and free-ridership, it is followed by a change in the mode and priority of spending. This is particularly true when spending including collection and disbursement of Zakat becomes organized.

## IX. Conclusion

The theory of moral entitlement in Islam is intrinsically linked with the foundation of social and distributive justice as elaborately established by the Shariah. Within this purview all functions of the socioeconomic order revolve, bestowing forms and meaning in an ethico-economic general equilibrium framework. The principle of ethical endogeneity and the essentially unified nature of reality pervades such a system. In this context, the Shuratic process that both endows and reinforces itself over evolutionary phases of Islamization sustains all social and economic relationships with the primacy of the Principle of Tawhid, the Principle of Justice and the Principle of Moral Entitlement. The Islamic precept of social justice becomes the foundation of the precept of moral entitlement.[40]

## Endnotes and References

*Professor of Economics, University College of Cape Breton, Sydney, Nova Scotia, Canada; editor, *Humanomics*.

[1]  A. Sen, *Poverty and Famines: An Essay on Entitlement and Deprivation*, Oxford, England: Clarendon Press, 1986; and, R. Nozick, *Anarchy, State and Utopia*, New York: Basic Books, 1974.

[2]  For another view on the market and the entitlement-formation process see, K. Polanyi, *The Great Transformation*, Boston: Beacon Press, 1944.

[3]  The dual or mixed economy should not be construed as an example of such an ethico-economic system, for such models predicate neoclassical ethical exogeneity and their methodologies are either not independent of neoclassicism or are not significantly well-known. The latter is the case with the historical institutionalists; the former, with the new institutionalists and Gunnar Myrdal. See, S. Tsuru, "Keynote Address: Economics of Institutions or Institutional Economics," in T. Shiraishi S. Tsuru (eds.), *Economic Institutions in a Dynamic Society: Search for a New Frontier*, London: Macmillan Press Ltd., 1989.

[4]  The treatment of applied problems in Walras is of a normative nature. See, J. van Daal and A. Jolink "On the Economics of Walras," paper presented at the First International Conference on the Intercommunication of New Ideas, La Sorbonne, Paris, France, Aug. 1990.

I also refer here to a comment made by Professor Thomas Nitsch during the questions and discussion from the floor following presenation of this paper. His point was that, in the development of his "complete" system of political and social economy, Léon Walras gave effect to the present idea of ethical endogeneity. In this regard, the reader is now referred to Nitsch's "Social Economics: The First 200 Years," in *Social Economics: Retrospect and Prospect*, ed. M.A. Lutz (Kluwer Academic Publishers, 1990), esp. pp. 38-41; and, more recently, his "Preface" to my forthcoming work, *A Theory of Ethico-Economics*, Barmarick Publications, Hull, England.

[5] Details of such theories can be found in M.A. Choudhury and U.A. Malik, *The Foundations of Islamic Political Economy*, London: Macmillan Press Ltd., forthcoming.

[6] A. Gewirth, "Economic Justice: Concepts and Criteria," in K. Kipnis and D.T. Meyers (eds.), *Economic Justice, Private Rights and Public Responsibilities*, Totowa, NJ: Rowman Allanheld, 1985.

[7] A. Sen, "The Moral Standing of the Market," E.F. Paul, F. D. Miller, Jr., and J. Paul, (eds.), *Ethics & Economics*, Oxford, England: Basil Blackwell, 1985, pp. 1-19.

[8] M.A. Choudhury, "A Critique of Developments in Social Economics and Alternative," *International Journal of Social Economics*, 18 (11/12), 1991, pp. 36-61.

[9] For a description of the use of preferences in political associations see, J.L. Coleman, "Market Contractarianism and the Unanimity Rule," in E.F. Paul et al.(eds.), op cit. (1985), pp. 69-114.

[10] J.O. Ledyard, "Market Failure," in J. Eatwell et al. (eds.), *The New Palgrave: Allocation, Information, and Markets*, W.W. Norton, 1989.

[11] R. Nozick, "Foundations of Ethics", in *Philosophical Explanations*, Cambridge, MA: Harvard University Press, 1981, pp. 399-570.

[12] A.H.A. Sulaiyman, "The Theory of the Economics of Islam: The Economics of Tawhid and Brotherhood," *Contemporary Aspects of Economic Thinking in Islam*, Indianapolis: The Association of Muslim Social Scientists, 1980.

[13] V. Nienhaus, "Normative and Positive Knowledge in Political Economy: New Answers to Old Questions?," *Humanomics*, 6, 1990, pp. 32-49.

[14] The principle of ethical endogeneity is derived directly from the *Quran*. See, *Al-Quran*, Chapter XIV, vs. 24-27: Seest thou not how

God sets forth a parable?
A goodly Word
Like a goodly tree,
Whose root is firmly fixed,
And its branches (reach)
To the heavens,...

And the parable
Of an evil Word
Is that of an evil tree:
It is torn up by the root
From the surface of the earth:
It has no stability.

It brings forth its fruit
At all times, by the leave
Of its Lord.
So God sets forth parables
For men, in order that
They may receive admonition.
What He willeth.

God will establish in strength
Those who believe, with the Word
That stands firm, in this world
And in the Hereafter; but God
Will leave, to stray, those
Who do wrong: God doeth

The principle of ethical endogeneity is the keynote of M.A. Choudhury (ed.), *Political-Theoretic Foundation of Ethico-Economics*, Sydney, Nova Scotia: Centre of

❖

Humanomics, 1989. See also, idem, *A Theory of Ethico-Economics*, (forthcoming), Hull, England: Barmarick Publications, 1991.

[15] F. Capra, *The Tao of Physics*, Bantam Books Inc., 1984; L.T. Sun, "Confucianism and the Economic Order of Taiwan," *International Review of Economics and Ethics*, *1*(2), 1986; and, R. Rucker, *Infinity and the Mind*, Bantam Books, Inc., 1983, pp. 60-78.

[16] I. Kant, *Groundwork of the Metaphysics of Morals*, trans. J.J. Paton, New York: Harper and Row Publishers, 1956.

[17] S.H. Nasr, *An Introduction to Islamic Cosmological Doctrines*, Boulder, CO: Shambhala, 1978.

[18] M.A. Choudhury, "The Epistemological Foundations of Islamic Economic, Social and Scientific Order," mimeo., Department of Social Sciences, University College of Cape Breton, 1990.

[19] The understanding of the Tawhidi Field and the Tawhidi Precept are essential elements of an evoluationary epistemology of the Islamic thought processes. Such an approach although being fundamental has not been tried in the Islamic literature. Two other papers on the Tawhidi epistemology are M. al-Fadl, "Contrasting Epistemics: Tawhidi, the Vocationist and Social Theory," *American Journal of Islamic Social Sciences*, 7(1), March 1990, pp. 15-38; and, A. Schleifer, "Ibn Khaldun's Theories of Perception, Logic and Knowledge: An Islamic Phenomenology," ibid. 2(2), December 1985, pp. 225-31.

[20] M.A. Choudhury, "Islamic Economics as a Social Science," *International Journal of Social Economics*, 17(6), 1990, pp. 35-59.

[21] A.R. I. Doi, *Shariah, the Islamic Law*, London, England: Ta Ha Publishers, 1984.

[22] Choudhury and Malik (forthcoming).

[23] M.A. Choudhury, "The Blending of Social and Religious Orders in Islam," *International Journal of Social Economics*, 16(2), 1989, pp.13-45.

[24] *Al-Quran*, Chapter II, verse 267:
O ye who believe!
Give of the good things
Which ye have (honourably) earned,
And of the fruits of the earth
Which We have produced
For you, and do not even aim
At getting anything

Which is bad, in order that
Out of it ye may give away
Something, when ye yourselves
Would not receive it
Except with closed eyes.
And know that God
Is Free of all wants,
And Worthy of all praise.

[25] K.E. Boulding presented a non-neoclassical view of moral exchange in his "Economics as a Moral Science," as in J.F. Glass and J.R. Staude (eds.), *Humanistic Society*, Pacific Palisades, CA: Goodyear Publications, 1972.

[26] W.M. Sullivan, "The Contemporary Crisis of Liberal Society," in H.B. McCullough (ed.), *Political Ideologies and Political Philosophies*, Toronto: Wall and Thompson, 1989.

[27] M.A. Choudhury, *The Principles of Islamic Political Economy: A Methodological Enquiry*, London: Macmillan Press Ltd., forthcoming.

[28] For a formalization of the committment model see, R.H. Frank, *Passions within Reason*, New York: W.W. Norton, 1988.

[29] M.A. Choudhury, "A Study of Ethico-Economics in the General Equilibrium Field," *International Journal of Social Economics*, 14(3/4/5), 1987, pp. 207-18.

[30] For concepts on stability of economic equilibrium see, J. Quirk and R. Saposnik, *Introduction to General Equilibrium Theory and Welfare Economics*, New York: McGraw-Hill, 1968.

[31] *Al-Quran*, Chapter II, vs. 282:
O ye who believe!
When ye deal with each other,
In transactions involving
Future obligations
In a fixed period of time,
Reduce them to writing
Let a scribe write down
Faithfully as between the parties: let not the scribe
Refuse to write: as God
Has taught him,
So let him write . . . .

[32] Cf. G. Debreu, *Theory of Value: An Axiomatic Analysis of Economic Equilibrium*, New York: John Wiley and Sons, 1965.

[33] For a concept of household production function see G.S. Becker, "A Theory of the Allocation of Time," *Economic Journal*, 75, September 1965, pp. 493-517.

[34] *Al-Quran*, S.IV, vs. 11:
God (thus) directs you
As regards your children's
(Inheritance): to the male
A portion equal to that
Of two females: if only
Daughters, two or more,
Their share is two-thirds
Of the inheritance;
If only one, her share
is a half.
For parents, a sixth share
Of the inheritance to each, . . .

[35] The Chapter, "Al-Baqara" ("The Cow") of the *Quran* provides a complete list of elements of the Islamic spending vector.

❖

[36] *Al-Quran*, Chapter II, vs. 177:

| | |
|---|---|
| It is not righteousness | To spend of your substance, |
| That he turn your faces East or West; | Out of love for Him, |
| But it is righteousness — | For your kin, |
| To believe in God | For orphans, |
| And the Last Day, | For the needy, |
| And the Angels, | For the wayfarer, |
| And the Books, | For those who ask, |
| And the Messengers; | And for the ransom of slaves . . . . |

[37] M.A. Choudhury, "Theory and Practice of Islamic-Development Co-operation: Some Asian Cases," mimeo., Department of Social Sciences, University College of Cape Breton, Sydney, Nova Scotia, 1990.

[38] I.J. Maddox, *Elements of Functional Analysis,* Cambridge: Cambridge University Press, 1970.

[39] H. Hosseini, "Islamic Economics — A New Economic or an Old Dogma?" *Forum for Social Economics,* 16(2), Spring 1987, pp. 45-58.

[40] M.A. Choudhury, *The Principles of Islamic Political Economy: A Methodological Inquiry,* (forthcoming).

Here a point of common note can be struck between this paper and the central focus on social justice in the Old Testament brought out in John Elliot's paper at this session of the Sixth World Congress of Social Economics, entitled, "Domination, Exploitation and the Condition of Labor in the Old Testament."

# E. F. Schumacher's Work in the U.S.A.: 1991

## Glen Alexandrin*

The question explored here is: "How sound was the economic thinking of E. F. Schumacher?" It is a personal question to the present writer who is interested in the discipline of economics, who feels that some of the key issues of the past and of the future are economic in nature, and who believes that, after twenty or so years, Schumacher's contribution and legacy are still worthy of examination.

A part of Schumacher's work is to this day seen as a stepping stone to the Ghandian, Buddhist and, perhaps, Humanistic economics. This creates the impression that his work was partial; it neglects the discussion and the overview of his system. Thus, by being given credit for contribution in a narrow field, his work is not assessed from the broader point of view.

In trying to appraise the impact of Schumacher's work on economic thought one might want to read the writings of his followers, those who are the academic economists and those who are the publicists. However, there is a dearth of people in the first category, and this needs some explanation. Also, a complication arises with the writers in the second group. Hazel Henderson (1981), for example, a self-declared pupil of Schumacher, explicitly would do away with the discipline of economics and have something new invented. Wendell Berry (1977) reduces economics to farming and Peter Barnes focuses on the technology of farming.

So, a peculiar impression is created by some self-appointed spokespeople. They use the word economics; they do not discuss it. And they would dump economics – perhaps in favor of some ill-defined, hands-on approach. This is disconcerting to those still intent on using Schumacher's *Small Is Beautiful* (1973) in classes and those who feel that it has messages for the future.

Yet another input into the framing of our answer is the lack of an obvious Schumacherian School of Economics. A multitude of possible answers suggest themselves: one, like Joseph Schumpeter, Schumacher was too broad for anyone to encompass; two, like the Voluntary Economics Society formed by Catherine the Great, the economics investigated has simply to do with technology and belongs

❖

properly to production management, industrial engineering, or such. When assessing Schumacher, we are carried by his sensible prose and feel naturally that the future could be secure and that practical but human-scale efforts are necessary to assure the realization of this future. But this optimism is not the story told by those concerned with competitiveness and productivity or by today's economic advisors. This was not the position taken at G-7 in London in 1991.

To conclude our setting up of the assignment, we attempt to explore these issues from the point of view of the History of Economic Thought and from the point of view of the Economics of Education. We want to look at Schumacher's economics and meta-economics, his theory and policy. We ask: What kind of world did he talk about? Where was his *Republic*? What was his economics?

## I.  The Structure of Schumacher's System

We can present several alternative models of Schumacher's socio-economic and utopian system. Its essence is simplistic – but not necessarily naive. Like Plato, he felt that the best way to provide for the future is by living in small cities and to have small farms and good water supply.

His system can be abstracted as follows:

a)  There is a big "split," in reference to scale or appropriate size, between the city and a village.

b)  It can be measured in terms of population density, income spent, income generated, peoples' intentions, structure of institutions, etc.

c)  City-to-village ratio historically varies: it was high in the period of Roman decline and is high in the U.S. now; it was low in the middle ages. There is an ideal ratio but a computer alone cannot find it.

d)  Some people attach importance to the social implications of this split. Thomas Jefferson, Lev Tolstoy, and Mohandas Gandhi wrote about its maintenance or re-establishment.

e)  This difference is important psychologically. Although Economics is built on the model of the factory, on the assumption of returns to scale, and of linearities, people fall into two categories: the city-lovers who are materialistic maximizers, who plan, design and coordinate; and the land-lovers who are anarchistic minimizers, seeking intimacy and self-reliance.

f)  Schumacher expresses sympathy with village values and hankers for the realization of an ideal ratio rather than for the "economies of scale."

Schumacher's system stands on four basic pillars:

1. *The Individual:* His individual can relate to meta-economics and to economics both on its demand and supply side. These attitudes are incorporated into decision making both on the supply and the demand side.

2. *The Government:* Schumacher recognized that economic policies absorb almost the entire attention of modern government, a government which he sees as being increasingly unable to handle problems of crime, alienation, stress, social

being increasingly unable to handle problems of crime, alienation, stress, social breakdown, mass unemployment and pollution because it is inthralled of the prevailing technology.

3. *The Demand Side:* On the demand side he discusses income and tastes and recognizes the extent of objective rationality. But Schumacher gives demand a new interpretation and his system can be a problem-solving system only to the extent that this redefinition takes place.

Of all the components in his system, this is the most Eastern and organic. His interpretation introduces the logic of interdependence between needs, demand, attitude toward resources and uses of commodities. Demand, for Schumacher, as in Theravada Buddhism, is being mindful and considerate of oneself, of others and of resources. It implicitly contains the deeply seated notion of reincarnation, and thus attentiveness to future generations.

4. *Supply Side:* Schumacher (1973, p. 75) describes the fourth pillar thus:

> We must learn to think in terms of an articulated structure that copes with a multiplying of small-scale units. If economic thinking ... cannot get beyond its vast abstractions, the national income, the rate of growth, capital/output analysis, labor mobility, capital accumulation... and make contact with human realities ... it is useless.

We can also present our conclusions on Schumacher's system in the equation form. These relate to how the world, under Schumacher's conditions, may operate. These are points which need to be fulfilled or satisfied for the operations of the desired economic system to take place. It is a short list of things to be done, and which will be done by sensible people.

*"Equation One"* states the equality of supply and demand. It is reached through the operation of the market forces; exchange takes place and there are no surpluses or deficits.

*"Equation Two"* results in the suitable rural-urban ratio. The city becomes more like the village: there are more parks; cabbages are grown in the abandoned lots. This has beneficial results: more employment; lower rate of inflation. This, conjoined with Voluntary Simplicity, contributes to the stability of GNP growth and certainly to the growth of "Net Economic Welfare."

*"Equation Three"* is MC = MR plus "Other Things." It is implicit in Schumacher's discussion, and it stands as an assurance that all benefits costs will be covered. "Other Things" are the internalized meta-economies. Equation Three suggests that product prices will be lower; employment preference will be in the direction of people rather than machines; use of capital and its cost will be less.

*"Equation Four"* states that religious sentiment is in-grained. This equation is spelled out in Schumacher's three popular works. Schumacher's written works returned economics to its roots in philosophy — political and social. How fortunate we are that he reached the stage where he could write *A Guide for the Perplexed*

(1977), leaving the legacy of his own journey. How lucky we are to have this road-map in addition to his pragmatic works, both written and concrete.

Although the *Guide* does not deal directly with economics, it is a document showing us the model of a true civil servant. Much as *Small Is Beautiful* smacks of Royal Commission Reports, the *Guide* reads like the journal of the experienced government worker: a man with/of civic virtues who has learned that all problems are not amenable to the tools of science; a moral, even religious, man who accepts that the most important problems can be transcended by ethical compromise.

His *Good Work* (1979) dealt directly with the question pivotal to Schumacher's system and to those who were concerned about bringing human moral virtues back into everyday life. With the death of the Protestant Work Ethic and the urge to "do your own thing," this handbook, written by a man in the field, sharpened the reader's view of reality.

Of Schumacher's three books, *Small Is Beautiful* was most popular because it addressed the concerns of the times and said something on a human scale could/should be done about them. The fact that he was a practicing economist gave weight to his words. The fact that he promoted meta-economics spoke to the need to bring values back to the realm of economic discourse.

## II. The Contemporaries of Schumacher

In the late 1960s and early '70s, certain concrete and abstract signs of weaknesses were being seen in the U.S. and its economy. The statistics from many other industrial countries showed smaller increases in per-capita real-income growth or growth in real GNP, sometimes even decreases. There were increases simultaneously in the unemployment and inflation rates, notably in the costs of medical care and education. This led to the conclusion that it should also be part of an economist's job to study zero economic or even negative economic growth. A sense of dissatisfaction within a growing portion of the nation's population also led to a demand for less materialistic goals and more qualitative measures of well-being.

With this recognition, there was an increase in economic literature in categories other than "classical," "Marxian," "Keynesian," and "neo-Keynesian." This literature may be divided into at least three groups.

### A. The "Warm Fuzzies"

The first group, the "Warm Fuzzies," is often characterized by either a lack of historical perspective or a congenital vagueness about their plans for reform. These thinkers may attempt to portray a situation using nothing more than one set of statistics. In surveying their interpretation of the "economic now," it is convenient to summarize their views about current socio-economic problems — their definitions and solutions. It ought to be clear that no sincere intellectual effort should be too briefly summarized, but the following writers can stand here as examples or prototypes of many others.

Ivan Illyich (1973) zeroed in on solutions – education and conviviality. John Kenneth Galbraith (1964) found numerous problems, inflation in particular, and believed that moderate democratic socialism had the answer. Kenneth E. Boulding (1963) believed that inadequate understanding of economic reality could be solved by modernizing national income accounting. Daniel Bell (1976) counted "machine" technology, alienation, and inefficiency as problems to be countered by "intellectual" technology and communal society. Robert L. Heilbroner (1974) found no solution to the problems engendered by capitalism.

What most of these thinkers seemed to be saying was often not much more than that the economic present has its rusty lining and from this we can conclude that the economic future will not be as "glorious" as our recollections of the economy of the recent past.

## B. The "Limits-to-Growthers"

The second group, the "limits-to-growthers," are action-oriented and differ in approach. They had a definite future in mind that would be attainable, they concluded, by redesigning the present. They were often numerical and concrete, using up-to-date economic machinery for defining situations and alternative futures. Or they delineated a transformed system of values to reach their desired future.

The first approach of the "limits-to-growthers" is exemplified by the Club of Rome *Reports* where available statistical information on the unprecedented but now familiar conditions, such as shortage of various commodities (beef, gasoline) and increases in prices, boycotts, strikes, and layoffs, was put into a system of linear equations (a model) and projected by computer to draw futures often more distressing than that prevailing. Of the alternative futures reached through the model's simulation, they labeled one "preferred" – the stationary state or the state of equilibrium in which the change or the rate of change is zero and where variables such as construction, production of goods, etc., would not increase regardless of demand.

For economists, the "pay off" of this methodology was that global equilibrium could be defined numerically and that the numerical criteria were given. Thus we have Jay Forrester and Daniella Meadows et al. (1972) and Walter Leontief et al. (1977) presenting a numerical criterion for a preferred future. Also, Mesarovic and Pestel (1974) and Laszlo (1977).

The other approach of the "limit-to-growthers" was characterized by a discussion of values. Proponents of a "steady state" or less "violent" economy in the future, such as Schumacher and practioners of voluntary simplicity or other alternative lifestyles, proposed a change in values to create and facilitate the necessary transition from the present state (cf. Vanden Broeck, 1978; Thurow, 1971; Commoner, 1976; and Harrington, 1962). They, one could say, wished to change the individual numbers or variables which go into making the economists' data and models.

                              ❖

Schumacher, for example, recognized a category of people who can affect demand to overcome shortages even before they arise! Following the Buddhist Middle Way of voluntary simplicity, he says, is a step towards reaching the equilibrium state of the model builders. Appropriate technology leads to decentralization of growth effort and to a quicker transformation to equilibrium.

## C. The "Anti-Mechanists"

While the "limits-to-growthers" attempted to find a concrete community solution to current and future economic problems, the social philosophers in the third group or the "anti-mechanists" – utopians, romantics, and anarchists – were usually anti-scientific and disliked the method and tools of the professional economist almost as much as they disliked the economic reality. These thinkers may be best exemplified by Robert Reich (1983), Theodore Roszak (1969; 1972) and Murray Bookchin (1976). They sought a less "capitalistic" future, but the transvaluation remains primarily one of individual conscience or of consciousness.

A need for new definitions of economic man also arose from similar dissatisfactions within the ranks of the economics profession (e.g. Nitsch, 1981; 1982). In America this discontent produced many suggestions for further study of data and much limpid thought on the nature, the past, the present and the future of capitalism and the role of man in capitalist society.

## D. Buddhist Economics

Conspicuously absent from most of the economists' list was a study of the motives and values of today's economic man. Schumacher, however, believed that man has many motives and one could construct an economics regardless of the type of man one postulates to analyze. Our state of mind determines our tastes, feelings, decisions and actions. To the extent that the assumptions of "classical" economics are superseded, he said, a new variant of economics or a meta-economics would be created. The global future is in our mind.

A Buddhist Economics, according to Schumacher (1973, p. 62) is a good basis for a study if you are interested in the promotion of spiritual values. It enables you to find "the right path of development." The principles of Buddhist Economics are to be found in the sayings of the Buddha, but Schumacher (1973, p. 52) feels that each major religion holds such notions.

By looking at Burma under U Nu, Schumacher notes, we see that the people and government declared that there was no conflict between religious values and economic programs. This gives rise to a hypothetical Buddhist economist with whom we, as Westerners, hold a conversation throughout Chapter 4 in *Small Is Beautiful*.

The first economic premise is that Buddhist Economics is a door to liberation. Buddha wants the purification of human character. Character is formed by school and work. "The very start of Buddhist economics planning would be a planning for full employment" (1973, p. 57). Given full employment, work should be whole-some and develop the individual as the contributor to social wealth.

Next, Schumacher goes to the demand side and dwells on goods. The idea behind production of goods is to satisfy needs not to enflame cravings and attachments to samsara, which is the chief cause of bondage.[1] Demand is to be suppressed. Goods are to be the result of the optimal pattern of productive effort — they are to come up from the soil people dwell on and from the village organiza-tions. These goods are to be simple, easy to make and traditional: "products in from local resources for local needs is the most rational way of economic life" (1973, p. 59).

At this stage, the question of trade and of natural-resource depletion comes up. The answer is in the Buddhist's view of nonviolence to all sentient beings — on taking care of the total ecosystem. For the buddhist economist and for Schumacher, the use of non-renewable resources is to be minimized and the use of renewable resources is to be carefully managed.

The last two pages (61-62) of that chapter in *Small Is Beautiful* suggest the implications of not following this pattern, the situation which Schumacher and his contemporaries seemed to be addressing. The character of individuals as providers will deteriorate and lead to supply shortages and shoddy goods. The character of consumers will become more avaricious. There will be resource depletion and inevitable pollution. This leads to devolution: a goods-oriented, resource-deplet-ing, lazy and grasping society.

## III. The Greening and the Withering of America

The postwar decades had been marked by an interest in and the achievement of economic growth and an increase in labor productivity and average real incomes. The prevailing public philosophy was that the primary aim of modern society was to provide physical security and promote material well being for its members. As much individual choice as possible was to be encouraged regarding the goals of activity – scientific and technological advancement.

Thus, in the '50s, economics had a more important role than politics. Jan Tinbergen (in Kirschen, 1964) examines the question of rapprochement between mature capitalism and mature socialism – the systems could co-exist – and the techniques of both could be seen to apply in corporate and government planning. Politics became more important as the Cold War intensified. While competition between the USA and the USSR was emphasized during the turn into the 60s (in science, in space), the public good at home was defined as the national harmony achieved through equally sharing the benefits of economic growth. The competi-tive market plus the private economic institutions were the core mechanisms for growth. The government, through administrative intervention, would balance the operations of the market in the interests of economic growth and social harmony. Increasing standard of living, full employment and compassion from government

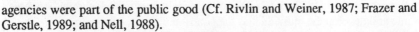

agencies were part of the public good (Cf. Rivlin and Weiner, 1987; Frazer and Gerstle, 1989; and Nell, 1988).

As the 60s turned into the 70s there was already opposition in intellectual and professional circles to future growth. Resistance to growth's companions — environmental damage, congestion, risks of new products and processes — became reflected in the popular writings as well as the "counter culture" which evolved. Problems seemed inherent in the public promotion of growth.

Schumacher's *Small Is Beautiful* was part of the voiced disillusionment in regard to the possibilities, to the prospect of material progress. The four themes of the infeasibility of sustained growth (because of scarcities and the effect on the environment), of a distrust in the measurers of growth, of declining satisfaction from material goods and of technology's dehumanizing threat became common elements of this "adversary" culture's concern.

To some extent, these themes did become propagated and implemented in politics and policies by pressure groups, lobbyists and politicians during the Carter years. Economics was seen as part of this political "war." President Carter (an engineer, not an ideologue) was also the first president to use an essential economic policy, the grain embargo, as part of a lever for political justice: to get the Soviets out of Afghanistan.

But while the heart of the bourgeois government may have been sensible, measured, steady, rational and junctional, the bourgeois society had lost its moral basis and much of its optimism. And the popular (high-culture) style was romantic, tragic, idiosyncratic, instinctual and even amoral.

So, there was a conflict. The government was forcing growth, implementing economic policy and making decisions through its taxing and spending activities which used to be made either privately or controlled by the market. The cultural and political processes became separated from these public policy decisions because neither the leadership nor the public understood the technological or "scientific" effects of this growth-oriented activity.

The lack of reflection of the values of the "popular style" in the "bourgeois government" led some to call the government unjust and morally bankrupt. Others called for new "products" such as a non-polluted environment. Some called for more conscious centralization (more regulations) or more technological and managerial expertise.

The result of all this turmoil, by the '80s, was Reaganomics and David Stockman. No longer would there be Jimmy Carter's attempts at fine-tuning of the economy with government initiative providing the stimulus for economic democracy. The New Federalism would essentially get government out of market management. The main aim of government was seen to be to safeguard peace and security to enable self-reliant individuals (part of society's all-inclusive interest group) to pursue their largely economic aims in freedom. Growth then was necessary as the basis of national defense (Cf. U.S. Presidents, 1980ff).

In short, there was a change from a policy trend where the government should be appropriate, suitable, helpful to people, where economic and political ideologies were seen as decisive, and the country's leaders were to encourage virtue (thrift, conservation, human rights) to a view where, essentially, politics was converted into economics. The economic difficulties of the 70s, instead of bringing economics as if people mattered, brought a regearing of capitalism to a highly competitive and unfriendly means of conducting economic wars.

Whatever the ends of the government during the Reagan and Bush years, the means used have not been Schumacherian, and the economics they have pursued have not been those where the importance of people has mattered.

The visionary advice which Schumacher gave is still sound and needed. But only during a few years, which externally corresponded with the period right before and during the Carter presidency, did there seem to be a matching of Schumacher's meta-economics with the prevailing social and political trends. The growth of the seed depended on the soil and the watering!

The fact that Schumacher was an economist and an activist did make his writings an acceptable and popular voicing of the sixties' desire to make life more "liveable." "Hippies" did "drop out" to "do their own thing" on a human scale. The popularity of *Small Is Beautiful* was reflected at that time by the flowering of references to Schumacher's work in the media.

Schumacher himself believed that it was the fact he was involved in applications of his own economic ideas (e.g., Intermediate Technology) that made his books popular. His concept of intermediate technology, embodied in the Intermediate Technology Development Group in London in 1965, had by 1979 already spread to groups in 20 different countries. Tools and equipment are being deliberately designed to be relatively small, simple, capital-saving and environmentally nonviolent.

In a less concrete and more intellectual way, the E. F. Schumacher Society has also continued to acquaint people with Schumacher's hopeful vision of "a sustainable, decentralized economy nurturing the earth and its inhabitants," with seminars on such subjects as "Tools for Community Economic Transformation," conferences featuring actual case studies of programs and organizations, lectures on bio-regionalism, agriculture, the family as a small society, and the community's role in appropriate technology, and working papers on self-financing techniques, community survival in the age of inflation and what everyone should know about banking and money!

One could say that the "neglect" of Schumacher in the realm of academia (papers presented at economic meetings, inclusion in textbooks or books of readings, and the like) and in political speeches and pronounced policies has been countered by the embedding of his proposals by those with his values in specific areas such as technological change, regional economics and natural resources.[2]

Economists could do well to re-read his work, particularly *The Guide,* for its explicit exposition of the "Christian" values which already underlie his and others'

❖

efforts. Schumacher's meta-economics, his concern for community, freedom, and social justice, his attention to the ethical aspects of economic problems, and his inquiry into the impact of policy on the social order and the common good, clearly make him a "social economist," a stance less than popular with today's politicians.

## IV.  Criteria for Assessing Positive, Normative and Meta-Economics

The discussion of what is 'good' economics or 'viable' economics need not be regarded as an irreverent occupation. The roots of this question stretch back to the Mercantilists, to the time when individual pamphleteers tried to outdo each other in their usefulness.

This question is more often raised by presidents, philosophers, reformers and dictators. In this story, economics is the hand-maiden to politics, statehood, and, sometimes, to the people. In 1991, in London, at G-7, this question confronted Mikhail Gorbachev. President Bush's answer was that good economics is democracy plus the market. Period.

Table 1 lists some criteria which, it is believed, need to be met by economics to make it "good." The source or origin of these criteria is important and needs be identified: some are of our own making (A); some are Peter Drucker's (1981;D); and some are due to Schumacher (S), as we feel his work needs to be judged by his own standards.

**Table 1**
**Criteria for Assessing Economics**

POSITIVE ECONOMICS

Discussion of Motive/Incentive (A)
Criteria for Equilibrium (D)
Theory of Productivity (D)
Theory of Capital Formation (D)
Theory of Credit and Interest (D)
Discussion of Role of Government (D)
Integrated Policy and Analysis (D)
Laws (Principles of Economics) (A)

NORMATIVE ECONOMICS (in addition to those above)

Humanistic Values (S)
Civic Virtues (S)
Moral Laws (A)

Table 1 contains some critera for a "New Economics" as envisioned by Drucker. In his opinion, the fashioner of economics needs to discuss these topics before he states a claim as to the viability of his economics. Few of us would be surprised with Drucker's shopping list and most of us would want to add to it. Some of us would subtract certain items or question their priority.

To Drucker's list we have added the three following critera: motives, laws (principles) in the economic and material realm, and laws in the moral or religious realm.

## A. Motives, Incentives

One of Adam Smith's virtues was isolating the force that drives economic behavior. It is the vigorous competition of rivals in the market place, spurred by the quest for profits among entrepreneurs and for subsistence among workers. The simple animus driving his trucking-bartering-exchanging creatures was their innate self-love (Smith, 1937, bk. I).

Schumacher emphasizes the motives of altruism and rationality, but he does not regard people as being born therewith. Rather they are learned (1979, p. 115).

They are learned in all situations to which children and adults may be exposed. Tradition, folk wisdom, and grandmothers are important learning tools. But schools alone, for Schumacher, do not imbue people with correct motives. The outcome of the true learning process is the will "to do good work for my neighbor as well as for myself" (1979, p. 116).

We have three fields in which our needs express themselves: spiritual, social and personal. They are satisfied, and we feel fulfilled, when we develop concern for values and are value-rich; when we can contribute to the well-being of other people and various sentient beings; and when we develop desire for self-growth. Education gives us the pathway to get to these realizations. It engenders the moral behavior, neighborly attitudes, and ability to use our own gifts.

It is in this way that we grow into the realization of the ultimate motive – the guide which gives us purpose in life – and it is the Kingdom, nirvana, or perfection. Then our lives can be dedicated to getting there and we have assurances that our end will make us happy. This makes our path a happy one. The path is 'good work,' *karma* yoga.

Motives, for Schumacher, then, are 'right things to do.' They are other-reflected. They are organismic in the sense that they are the culmination of the realization of the fact that we are all in the same boat.

What results from this is the acceptance of volunteerism as a natural behavior. Giving it a tad of Teutonic touch, Schumacher feels that these volunteers want to be told how to solve problems.

Whether motives, in the sense discussed here, are economic or psychological or spiritual is not the topic for discussion. It is clear, it seems, that the energy behind good work will have its economic expressions in the fields of production, consumption and leadership.

## B. Criteria for Equilibrium

In our earlier discussion, when we summarized the shape of the Schumacher system, we pointed to his awareness of the 'equilibrium conditions.' They are not of the textbook type nor need they be.

We can note two of his additional criteria or guides to equilibrium and to the restoring of equilibrium in case it is lost. First, the distinction between the renewable and non-renewable resources need be kept in mind if one is thinking about building and maintaining a system in the long run. This system is not natural in the sense that it occurs in nature and all we have to do is to stumble onto it. We have to design it. We do this by thinking and re-thinking (1979, p. 16), by keeping or making the operational units small (1979, p. 20), and by constantly searching out "more organic systems."

Achieving of equilibrium is an on-going process. To continue to maintain it we have to keep constantly changing the technology. By adjusting the mode of production, we eliminate problems before they arise and thus track the equilibrium path.

His discussion of this important criterion, if not the most important, to the economists, may leave something to be desired. One can wish that Schumacher were more explicit and specific. It is unfortunate that Schumacher, an economist, has not assumed this task; for, it is an important aspect of his system.

The other way to approach this point is by saying that there is no need to specify the system fully and that specifications will come up as the experiment rolls on. In an unfolding world, with many possibilities, as Schumacher conceives it to be, it is contrary to the design; it is contrary to the designers' wishes to have it all specified and blue-printed.

## C. Theory of Productivity

This criterion may not be important if one wants to talk about a sustainable society. To some extent, but not quite, this may be Schumacher's view. We operate, he says, under constraints: high unemployment, budget deficits, shortage of loanable funds, reliance on international trade. He is talking about the 1960s, Great Britain and the underdeveloped countries (1979, p. 16). Schumacher teaches by giving examples of the mini-plant for cement production which, he says, with little capital, resulted in high productivity. He seems to use the idea of measuring of productivity in an extended sense to include the unemployed.

If Schumacher pays attention to productivity it is the productivity of the scarcest factor of production that is important to him. Capital assets 'should be' small, simple, cheap, non-violent, and of low capital intensity; in short, structures should be planned as if the economies of scale did not exist. To the natural question, "Who would demand such things?" he gives the Zambian and the life-boat farming examples (1979, pp. 58, 62).

Schumacher does give guides to enhancing productivity: education makes us 'richer'; think 'capital-saving technology'; in decision-making think poor; think import-substitution (1979, pp. 133ff).

**D. Role of Government**

Chapter 5 of Part 5 *Small Is Beautiful* is devoted to the constitution of a company called a "Commonwealth." This requires a specific legislative act including such self-denying ordinances as the following: size is limited to 300 workers; wages are more or less equal; there is job security; there are no shareholders; profits are not to be accumulated; payment of bonuses and charity. The role of government would be to encourage such economic units as part of the change in technology.

**E. Laws, Values and Virtues**

By laws of economics we mean the integration of economics with the natural sciences. Fields like environmental economics, resource economics, even the question of housing in tropical third-world countries are inconceivable without integrating chemistry, physics, engineering and economics. Strong examples of this approach are to be found in the Limits to Growth literature and in Nicholas Georgescu-Roegen's work (1976; et cf. Vacca, 1974).

Most economists are not accustomed to extending the concept of laws to the divine realm. Indian science, however, begins with the laws in the spiritual realm. These are laws of thought; and from them laws of language and then of behavior develop. Physical laws – gravity, health, longevity, proclivities – result from these in turn. From this point of view, then, thought determines matter (Varma, 1973).

What is the use of such a laws? If one understands gravity, one will not jump from the third story. If one knows about the divine, one will try to free oneself from and abandon the material realm. What is necessary then is to know the purpose of human life on earth.

Schumacher tends to ignore 'economic laws' as we usually understand them. But he does believe in the existence of "divine" laws which man can naturally understand. Schumacher details the moral, religious and spiritual attributes of the universe in the epistemology of his *Guide*. Man's understanding and the development of values and virtues, are furthered by education, good work and community. From this basis, Schumacher takes his discussion of economic affairs.

The economic terminology which Schumacher used is "good" economics as colored by this normative foundation. It is these three "values" criteria which make for an "economics as if people mattered." Mere "scientific laws" are not enough.

## V. Conclusion

We end as we began, by affirming Schumacher's general philosophy and resultant economics. His work, taken as a whole, is a guide to the restoration of a modest social economy.

——————————— ❖ ———————————

There is no doubt that we could have had a Presidential Economic Advisor waving a green *Small Is Beautiful*. It did not happen for two groups of reasons: one, involving the form of Schumacher's work; and, the other, the Zeitgeist. Schumacher's written contributions were made when he was an old man. They are in the nature of a lesson plan and not his accomplished work. They express faith in the individual, indicate general directions of socioeconomic development, and provide hope that on a thusly mapped, broad highway into the future we will surmount the obstacles to a more truly human economy. It is a mature hope, if optimistic, and leads us on a long leash.

The road, however, remains to be taken. Schumacher's optimism regarding the abilities and energies of man has exceeded the contemporary realities. Today, "Small is Beautiful" and "Simplicity" are no problem, if they are left to voluntarism. However, we are entering a period of deindustrialization, of lowered educational achievement and decreasing real incomes. Smallness and simplicity may yet become the dictates of historical necessity.

## Endnotes

*Department of Economics, Villanova University, Villanova, PA 19085 USA.

[1]   Cp. the early Catholic-social (Christian-political) economist Alban de Villeneuve-Bargemont (op. cit. 1834/37) as per Nitsch, 1990, esp. p. 19.

[2]   Thus we have the American Green Movement's "Ten Key Values," (ecological wisdom, non-violence, decentralization, community-based economics, post-patriarchal values, respect for diversity, global responsibility and future focus) as per *Creation*, 1989, p. 15; and the bio-regionalism movement headed by its founder, Kirkpatrick Sale. Susan Meeker-Lowry's *Economics As If The Earth Really Mattered* (1988) and George McRobie's *Small Is Possible* (1981) are current expositions on "appropriate" corporations and cooperatives and alternative environmental and ecological groups.

## References

Bell, Daniel. *The Cultural Contradictions of Capitalism*, New York: Basic Books, 1976.

Berry, Wendell. *The Unsettling of America: Culture and Agriculture*, San Francisco: Sierra Club Books, 1977.

Bookchin, Murray. *The Modern Crisis*, Philadelphia: New Society, 1986.

————. *Post-Scarcity Anarchism*, Philadelphia: New Society, 1971.

Boulding, Kenneth E. *The Economy of Love and Fear*, Belmont, CA: Wadsworth, 1973.

E. F. Schumacher's Work in the U.S.A., 1991        381
❖

Commoner, Barry. *The Poverty of Power: Energy and The Economic Crisis,* New York: Knopf, 1976.

Drucker, Peter F. *Toward the Next Economics and Other Essays,* New York: Harper, 1981.

Fraser, Steve and Gerstle, Gary. *The Rise and Fall of The New Deal Order,* Princeton, NJ: Princeton University Press, 1989.

Galbraith, John Kenneth. *Economic Development,* Cambridge: Harvard University Press, 1964.

Georgescu-Roegen, Nicholas. *Energy and Economic Myths: Institutional and Analytical Economic Essays,* New York: Pergamon Press, 1976.

Harrington, Michael. *The Other America: Poverty in the United States,* New York: Macmillan, 1962.

Heilbroner, Robert L. *An Inquiry Into the Human Prospect,* New York: Norton, 1974.

Henderson, Hazel. *The Politics of the Solar Age,* Garden City, New York: Anchor Books, 1981.

Illich, Ivan. *Tools for Conviviality,* New York: Harper & Row, 1973.

Kirschen, E. S. (ed.). *Economic Policy in Our Time,* Vol. I. Amsterdam: North-Holland, 1964.

Laszlo, E. (ed.). *Goals for Mankind,* New York: Pergamon, 1977.

Leontief, Wassily, et al. *The Future of the World Economy,* New York: Orxford University Press, 1977.

Loebl, E. *Humanomics; How We Can Make the Economy Serve Us, Not Destroy Us,* New York: Random House, 1976.

McRobie, George. *Small Is Possible,* New York: Harper, 1981.

Meadows, D. H. (et al.). *The Limits to Growth,* New York: Universe Books, 1972.

Meeker-Lowry, Susan. *Economics As If The Earth Really Mattered,* Philadelphia: New Society, 1988.

Mesarovic, M. and Pestel, E. *Mankind at the Turning Points,* New York: E. P. Dutton, 1974.

Nell, E. *Prosperity and Public Spending; Transformational Growth and the Role of Government,* Boston: Unwin Hyman, 1988.

Nitsch, Thomas O. "Economic Man, Socio-economic Man, and *Homo-economicus Humanus,*" *International Journal of Social Economics,* 9(6/7), (1982), 20-49.

_____. "On Human Nature Presuppositions in Economics: *Homo Oeconomicus and Socioeconomicus,*" *Midsouth Journal of Economics,* 7(1), (May 1983), 13-36.

❖

_____. "Social Ecopnomics: The First 200 Years," in *Social Economics: Retrospect and Prospect*, ed. M.A. Lutz, Boston: Kluwer Academic Publishers, 1990.

Reich, Robert B. *The Next American Frontier*, New York: Times Books, 1983.

Rivlin, Alice and Weiner, Joshua. *Economic Choices: 1987*, Washington, D.C.: Brookings, 1987.

Roszak, Theodore. *Making of a Counter Culture*, Garden City, NJ: Doubleday, 1969.

_____. *Where the Wasteland Ends; Politics and Transcendence in Post-Industrial America*, Garden City, NJ: Doubleday, 1972.

Schumacher, E. F. *A Guide for the Perplexed*, New York: Harper, 1977.

_____. *Good Work*, New York: Harper, 1979.

_____. *Small Is Beautiful; Economics As If People Mattered*, New York: Harper, 1973.

Smith, Adam. *Wealth of Nations*, New York: Modern Library, 1937.

Thurow, Lester C. *Dangerous Currents; The State of Economics*, New York: Random House, 1983.

_____. *The Zero-Sum Society*, New York: Basic Books, 1971.

U.S. President, Reagan and Bush, *Economic Report of the President*, 1980ff.

Vacca, Roberto. *The Coming Dark Age*, New York: Doubleday, 1974.

VandenBroeck, Goldian (ed.). *Less is More; the Art of Voluntary Poverty*, New York: Harper, 1978.

Varma, V. P. *Early Buddhism and Its Origins*, New Delhi: Munshiram Manoharlal, 1973.

Weisskopf, Walter A. *Alienation and Economics*, New York: Dutton, 1971.

❖

# Poverty in the Netherlands

## J.A.C. van Ophem*

When the welfare state emerged in the western and northern parts of Europe (e.g. the Scandinavian and Benelux countries, FRG (Bonn), Austria, Great Britain) it was characterized by an attempt to reconcile conflicting aims: to give the population some minimum livelihood within the framework of a market economy with private means of production and parliamentary democracy. A welfare state implies state intervention and relatively high government expenses as a fraction of GDP. The welfare states, with their inherent control or guidance of market forces, were successful in many ways compared to other economies, for they belonged to the richest nations in the world. Yet they were still characterized by a poverty problem that became more prominent during the 1980's. This paper will focus on this dilemma by examining the experience of the Netherlands.

The Netherlands is one of the richer nations in the world. Labour productivity in the Netherlands is one of the highest in the OECD countries (Visser 1991). Still, the percentage of the workforce experiencing long term unemployment rose during the 1980's. The 1980's also witnessed increased income disparities in the Netherlands. The profit share grew after 1983, as did the salaries and wages in the private enterprise sector (Visser 1991; van Ophem 1988). At the same time the earnings of civil servants grew less as did social security benefits. A substantial part of the Dutch population makes use of the social security system (see Table 1).

A definition of poverty is an essential first step for poverty research. The number and characteristics of the poor will depend on the definition used. It is not the aim of this paper to make an extensive review of various poverty definitions and concepts. Others have done this (Hagenaars, 1986; Townsend 1970 and 1979). One conclusion is that any definition of poverty is relative, depending on place and time.

This paper will use the policy minimum (het beleidsminimum) set by the government of the Netherlands as a poverty line. This line varies according to the type of household (100-90-70 formula)[1]. A household is entitled to have the relevant minimum amount, so that no one has less than the minimum amount[2]. This choice for the policy minimum definition is based on two arguments. Firstly, it is

❖

the norm fixed by Dutch society through the parliamentary process. Secondly, in comparison to other concepts or definitions, it can be used relatively easily for policy objectives. Statistical data are available. We make, therefore, use of an objective and 'absolute' poverty concept. The minimum in the Netherlands may be luxurious for an inhabitant of a Third World country. Without doubt, there will be persons with a household income above the minimum who feel poor and some living on a policy minimum may not feel themselves poor. Still, in Section II we will see that a majority of assistance receivers consider themselves to be poor in the context of Dutch society. But any delineation is arbitrary and subject to controversy.

**Table 1**

**Social security in the Netherlands in 1990**

|  | expenses (in Dfl) | number of persons |
|---|---|---|
| Social Security |  |  |
| - Sickness (ZW) | 7,500 million | 264,000 |
| - Disablement (WAO/AWW) | 26,160 million | 829,000 |
| - Unemployment |  |  |
| WW | 3,700 million | 173,010 |
| RWW | 7,100 million | 384,000 |
| - Old Age (AOW) | 29,300 million | 2,011,400 |
| - Widowhood/Orphanity(AWW) | 4,300 million | 188,500 |
| - National Assistance |  |  |
| (ABW excl. RWW) | 4,000 million | 520,000 |

Source: CBS, Statistical Yearbook 1991
DNB, Annual Report 1990

The aim of this paper is to shed light on four questions. First, we want to answer the question of who are the poor and what are their characteristics (section II). Secondly, how do the poor behave as consumers (section III)? Third, what are the possibilities for income improvement (section IV)? Fourth, what are the policy implications, given the fact that the poor face problems with respect to consumption and income improvement (section V)? As indicated, this paper reviews the situation of the Netherlands. It attempts to place the problem of poverty into a welfare state perspective.

## I. Some Empirical Data on the Composition of the Poor in the Netherlands

Table 2 shows households by type and income. One parent families and one person households show the lowest average incomes. Table 3 gives information on recipients of National Assistance (ABW and RWW) according to type of house-

❖

hold. Singles and one parent families are the dominant types of low income household.

## Table 2

### Household income by type of household in 1986

| Household type average | Households with income | Persons per household | | total income |
|---|---|---|---|---|
| | | total | among whom with income | |
| | X1000 | | | X1000 |
| One-person household | 1,518 | 1 | 1 | 24.2 |
| Multi-person households | 3,969 | 3.2 | 2.0 | 50.1 |
| Non-family households | 289 | 2.0 | 2.0 | 47.8 |
| One-family housholds a – married couples without | 3,519 | 3.2 | 1.9 | 49.8 |
| children | 1,165 | 2.0 | 1.7 | 44.8 |
| – married couples with children | 2,073 | 3.9 | 2.0 | 54.5 |
| – single-parent families | 280 | 2.6 | 1.9 | 36.5 |
| Other one or multi-family households | 161 | 4.3 | 2.8 | 59.3 |
| Total b | 5,488 | 2.6 | 1.7 | 42.9 |

a. Excluding other persons.
b. Including households of which the head has no income or less than 52 weeks income.
Source: CBS, 1990

## Table 3

### Recipients of National Assistance (ABW and RWW) according to type household in 1989 (percentages)

| type of household | frequency | |
|---|---|---|
| singles   m. | 29.6 | 57.2 |
|          f. | 27.6 | |
| one parent  m. | 0.8 | 23.0 |
| family     f. | 22.2 | |
| couples without children | 7.1 | 7.1 |
| couples with children | 11.2 | 11.2 |
| others | 1.5 | 1.5 |
| N (=100) | | 5.499.000 |

Source: CBS, 1991

❖

Table 4 gives information on the duration of the assistance benefit (ABW and RWW). Only 19.5 percent of the ABW-recipients younger than 65 and 27.7 percent of the unemployed with national assistance are of short duration (< 1 year). Of long duration (> 6 years) are 38.8 percent and 28.5 percent respectively of the beneficiaries. These figures are based on crossection data. A substantial part of the assistance receivers do have a long assistance history. There are no panel data of assistance receivers to trace the dynamics of poverty status. However, Van der Aalst and Peters (1991) established that 45 percent of the assistance receivers belong to the hard core (> 3 years).

**Table 4**

**Recipients of National Assistance (ABW and RWW) according to duration of assistance benefits at the end of 1990 (X1,000)**

|  | Type of assistance | | |
| --- | --- | --- | --- |
|  | ABW-sec ≤ 64 yr. | ABW-sec ≥ 65 yr. | RWW |
| Duration of benefits (in months) |  |  |  |
| ≤ 6 | 18.3 | 1.1 | 54.9 |
| > 6 and ≤ 12 | 15.7 | 1.1 | 37.9 |
| > 12 and ≤ 18 | 13.3 | 0.9 | 32.1 |
| > 18 and ≤ 24 | 11.7 | 0.8 | 23.6 |
| > 24 and ≤ 30 | 10.2 | 0.7 | 22.0 |
| > 30 and ≤ 36 | 8.9 | 0.6 | 17.4 |
| > 36 and ≤ 42 | 8.0 | 0.8 | 16.1 |
| > 42 and ≤ 48 | 7.1 | 0.5 | 12.9 |
| > 48 and ≤ 54 | 6.4 | 0.5 | 12.0 |
| > 54 and ≤ 60 | 6.7 | 0.4 | 10.6 |
| > 60 | 67.5 | 3.3 | 95.6 |
| unknown | 0.1 | 0.1 | 0.1 |
| total | 174.0 | 10.8 | 335.2 |

Provisional figures, rounded up to hundreds.
There may be a rounding up bias when adding the figures.
Source: CBS

Table 5 relates recipients of RWW to age and sex. Recipients here are housholds. The younger (<45 year) dominate within the male and female categories. Note that men are the main breadwinner more frequently than women and this becomes more likely with age.

### Table 5
### Recipients (households) of a RWW-benefit according to
### age and gender, end 1989 (X1,000)

| age | gender male | female |
|---|---|---|
| 15-24 | 46.1 | 41.9 |
| 25-34 | 88.4 | 43.5 |
| 35-44 | 55.7 | 22.9 |
| 45-54 | 34.3 | 15.5 |
| 55-64 | 16.6 | 5.2 |
| total | 241.0 | 129.1 |

Source: CBS, 1991

There are no nationwide figures on the education level of assistance recipients. From various surveys in the Netherlands it is known that the lower educated dominate. (Goossens et al. 1990 and Herberigs 1990). The share of long term unemployed (> one year) in total unemployment has risen in the eighties from 22.5% to 53.0% in 1989 (Verhaar 1990).

This review of the data leads to the following conclusions: singles and one parent families are the dominant types of household within the category of assistance receivers. The younger dominate. The majority of benefits is not of short duration. The majority of RWW-recipients are long term unemployed.

## II. Poor households as consumers

In order to learn more about the financial situation of poor households, we can review the responses of 514 poor households to a survey conducted in 1988. Implicit in this reasoning is that households are the best judges of their own financial situation. The sample is stratified by six household types and region[3]. In this sample families with children are probably overrepresented (see Goossens 1990), but due to inaccessible government statistics proper adjustments cannot be made.

The 1988 study can be compared with a 1983 study (van Ophem 1988). The two studies are similar in design, and the results found in both studies mirror those found in other studies of the Netherlands in the 1980's ( e.g. Oude Engberink 1987; Engbersen and Van der Veen 1987; Kroft et al. 1989; De Vos and Hagenaars 1986; Miltenburg and Wolderingh 1990). The 1983 study is more reflective of all income groups, providing an important basis for comparison.

Table 6 gives the opinion of survey respondents on the sufficiency of their household income. For all Dutch households 16 percent in the 1983 survey consider

❖

their household income insufficient against 77 percent for the poor in the 1988 survey. Among poor families, 86 percent felt their income was insufficient.

**Table 6**
**Opinions of respondents on their household income (in percentages)**

|  | 1989 SCP 1989 n=1508 | low income households, 1988 | | |
|  |  | all n=514 | one parent family n=170 | family n=94 |
|---|---|---|---|---|
| insufficient | 16 | 77 | 81 | 86 |
| sufficient nor insufficient | 36 | 11 | 7 | 7 |
| sufficient | 48 | 12 | 12 | 7 |

t < 0.001
Source: SCP (1990) and Goossens et al. (1990)

Table 7 gives additional indicators of the financial situation and management of low income households. Low income households in the 1988 survey evidence a weaker financial position than households in 1983. Although these differences are expected, the extent of these differences is striking, especially with regard to payments in arrears.

**Table 7**
**Financial situation of households, one parent families**
**and families, comparison of 1983 population and low income**
**population in 1988 (in percentages)**

| situation | population 1983 n=275 | low income households, 1988 | | |
|  |  | all n=514 | one parent families n=170 | families n=94 |
|---|---|---|---|---|
| savings | 50 | 31 | 31 | 24 |
| loan by bank | 19 | 33 | 28 | 55 |
| loans by relatives/friends |  | 25 | 35 | 25 |
| being in arrears with payments (bank,relatives, friends,shops) | 8 | 49 | 51 | 59 |

t < 0.001
Source: Van Ophem (1988) and Goossens et al. (1990)

❖

Table 8 reports on household strategies used to cope with inadequate income. When we look at the economizing on expenditures on daily necessities and clothing we get the impression that when confronted with scarcity of income, poor households adopt strategies similar to those used by other households, but they exercise these strategies more intensively. Table 8 shows evidence of rational economic behavior in the face of low household income. One aspect of this is an improvement in purchasing efficiency. This can be attained by showing more cost-conscious behaviour when making purchases, paying more attention to the relation between price and quality, making more inquiries before buying goods and services, and spending more time looking for special offers. On all these points, efficiency can be enhanced; if it is enhanced on at least three points, this will be

**Table 8**

**Household strategies to cope with low/lower income, one parent families and families, comparison of 1983 population with population of 1988 low income households (in percentages)**

| strategies | population 1983 n=275 | low income households 1988 all n=514 | one parent family n=170 | family n=94 |
|---|---|---|---|---|
| buy food and other necessities in cheaper stores | 65 | 61 | 59 | 71 |
| pay more attention to special offers in daily shopping | 54 | 78 | 78 | 90 |
| raise vegetables | 11 | 18 | 8 | 42 |
| buy cheaper food products | 55 | 64 | 70 | 70 |
| buy clothing less frequently | 83 | 83 | 78 | 83 |
| make more clothing yourself | 54 | 43 | 44 | 53 |
| buy cheaper clothing | 48 | 57 | 65 | 79 |
| buy second-hand clothing | 27 | 23 | 28 | 20 |

chi-square n.s.
Source: Van Ophem (1988) and Goossens et al. (1990)

❖

regarded as a strong increase in domestic economic rationality. According to Table 9 this efficiency is less frequent among low income households. A possible explanation might be that the longer one experiences low income circumstances the lesser the possibilities for an increase in efficiency since these strategies may already have been adopted.

**Table 9**

**Households according to increase in domestic economic rationality (one year period) population 1983 compared to low income households, 1988 (in percentages)**

| Increase | population 1983 | low income households, 1988 | | |
|---|---|---|---|---|
| | | all | one parent family | family |
| | n=275 | n=170 | | n=94 |
| no/little | 40 | 56 | 53 | 44 |
| strong | 60 | 44 | 47 | 56 |

t < 0.05
Source: Van Ophem (1988) and Goossens et al. (1990)

Insofar as "regular expenses" (i.e. expenses incurred regularly at short intervals) can be adjusted by individual households, households will try to economize on them. "Incidental expenses" are irregular expenditures and include the purchase of consumer durables. A household's freedom to opt for postponing the purchase of such goods is greater than in the case of regular expenses. Durables will be purchased less frequently when the scarcity of income is greater. In other words, one expects more durable goods of poor quality among low income households than among non-poor households after a period of time.

Table 10 gives information on standard durables considered to be of poor quality by poor respondents according to type of household. "Standard goods" are durables the possession of which can be considered as normal in a Dutch household (Townsend 1979). Standard goods include: refrigerator, vacuum cleaner, washing machine, colour television set and lounge suite. These standard goods are present in a majority of the households, but in 43 percent the purchase of one of these items has been postponed. In 70 percent of the households one or more of the standard goods is a second hand one. It appears that the quality of the stock of durable goods of the poor is less than that of the non poor, although the 1983 survey does not provide sufficient information for ascertaining this.

❖

**Table 10**
**Broken and/or worn-out standard durables for low income households**
**by type (in percentages)**

|  | all<br>n=514 | one parent<br>family<br>n=170 | family<br>n=94 |
|---|---|---|---|
| refrigerator | 11 | 11 | 14 |
| vacuum cleaner | 13 | 15 | 16 |
| washing machine | 32 | 34 | 42 |
| colour TV-set | 20 | 22 | 26 |
| lounge suite | 5 | 6 | 9 |
| one or more broken/<br>worn out | 52 | 52 | 69 |

Source: Goossens et al. 1990

**Table 11**
**Necessary expenses and the sum of fixed expenses and**
**variable expenses according to type of household per month**
**(in Dfl)**

|  | single<br>< 65 yr | single<br>≥ 65 yr | one parent<br>family | couple<br>< 65 yr | couple<br>> 65 yr | family |
|---|---|---|---|---|---|---|
| necessary<br>expenses[a] | 810 | 850 | 1080 | 1100 | 1210 | 1270 |
| sum of<br>fixed and<br>variable<br>expenses[b] | 1030 | 990 | 1350 | 1390 | 1480 | 1610 |
| assistance<br>norm[c] | 1045 | 1103 | 1343 | 1492 | 1492 | 1492 |

[a] Direct housing expenses (rent, gas/electricity, etc.) and expenses on food, clothing, home furnishing and personal care.
[b] Necessary expenses and expenses on communication (newspaper, telephone, TV), insurances, loan payments; expenses on transport, child care, contributions to clubs etc.
[c] Level of full assistance (1-1-1988), holiday and child allowances excluded.
Source: Goossens, et al. 1990

Table 11 gives a general picture of fixed and necessary expenses. In general, one can see that these expenses take up almost the whole of assistance benefits.

There is little left for holidays, entertainment and the like. For families and single
parent families, expenses exceed assistance norms because the norm is not adjusted
for family size. They receive, however, the child allowance.

In this section we have given some insights on the variety of strategies or
tactics of poor households as consumers. Living on a low income has consequences
for daily living: a decrease in the level and quality of the financial and non-financial
wealth, difficulties in paying off loans, and the need for economizing behaviour[4].

## IV. Income improvement possibilities

### A. Extra earnings

More than 90 percent of low income households receive a social security
benefit. They do not have a steady job or an amount of paid labour sufficient enough
to affect their benefit eligibility. This does not automatically mean that they do not
have income from extra earnings. Some amount of earnings is allowed for
beneficiaries. Table 12 gives some characteristics of the income procurement of
low income households. A minority of households sees the potential to raise
household income in the future, and to some extent this is negatively related with
age. Only a very small category reports to have a part-time job. The average monthly

Table 12

**Some elements of the income procurement of low income
households according to type of household (in percentages)**

|  | singles all | singles < 65 | one parent | couples families | families < 65 |
|---|---|---|---|---|---|
| sees possibilities to raise future household income | 32 | 48 | 35 | 27 | 39 |
| does have extra earnings | 21 | 28 | 25 | 14 | 28 |
| average yearly amount of extra earnings[a] (in Dfl.) | 2280 | | 1570 | 2490 | 1830 |
| does have a part-time job[b] | 5 | 2 | 5 | 7 | 9 |

[a] Calculated for the extra earners
[b] Level of earnings are less than the official minima
Source: Goossens et al. 1990

earnings of the part-time jobs are Dfl 440. Officially between 50 to 75 percent of these earnings are deducted from the benefit, but in reality the extra earnings (the average amount is Dfl 145 for the extra earners) are mostly not deducted from the benefit. Either they are not reported to the authorities or they fall below the threshold for deduction (+ Dfl. 200 a month for a couple). Most striking in Table 12 is that a large majority report not having any extra earnings. The extra earnings are mostly derived from activities such as cleaning, house work and taking care of children. Similar results have been found in other studies of low income groups in the Netherlands (Engbersen 1987).

## B. Search and application behaviour

Persons older than 65 are not supposed or obliged to work in the Netherlands. The same is true for one parent families with young dependent children. The rest of the low income population has to search for employment in order to receive benefits. Mostly they are the lower educated. The labour market behaviour of the unemployed in the Netherlands is extensively studied in research funded by the Ministry of Social Affairs and Employment and by some district offices of the Labour Exchange. One such study was done in 1988 for Friesland, a rural province in the north of the Netherlands (Verhaar 1990). A survey of 687 unemployed registered at the Labour Exchange was completed. The sample is weighted due to underrepresentation in the survey of the lowest educated and unemployed living in urban areas. With regard to duration and gender the sample is representative.

One general conclusion regarding job-search and application behaviour of the Frisian unemployed is that they appear to be actively looking for work. They even score a bit better than the national group of unemployed (Verhaar 1990). According to human capital theory the productivity of an individual increases with more and higher education and more training (e.g. on-the-job training). For the demand side of the labour market, the level of completed (formal) education is an important signal of the potential productivity of a job seeker. Therefore, employers select the better educated from the queue of unemployed. The result of this labour market effect is a relatively low share of the higher educated within the group of unemployed compared to the share of higher educated in the group of labour suppliers with a job. But education also has a supply side effect. Besides money costs, education has time costs. The latter leads to less expected lifetime employment activity. Due to the higher price of their time the higher educated will search more intensely and apply for a job more frequently than the less educated. The level of the expenses of an education and the costs of borrowing will only increase this effect. Due to a life-cycle effect, to build up an existence independent of parents, one may expect that younger persons are much more eager to enter the labour force. This implies that a more intensive job search and application behaviour is to be expected within this category of younger people.

Besides education and age, the duration of unemployment also has an influence on labour market behaviour. For the long term unemployed (more than one year unemployed) the probability to stay unemployed is higher than for the short term unemployed. One explanation is the duration effect: long term unemployed have a higher probability to stay so because of the loss of human capital and motivation. Another explanation is the heterogenity effect: the more productive find a new job more easily than the less productive. One may expect that the duration of unemployment does have a negative influence on job search and application behaviour. The longer one stays unemployed, the less active labour market behaviour is expected to be. Also, in this respect a distinction can be made between the demand and supply side. A job seeker becomes less active as the disappointment caused by rejection of one's applications grows. Less motivation can imply a deterioration of human capital. On the demand side, the characteristic of being unemployed for a longer period of time is considered to be a negative feature by potential employers. The productivity of the longer term unemployed is seen to be less because of obsolescence of knowledge and experience and less acquaintance with labour discipline. Also, the fact that a person has not been selected for a job earlier is considered to be a negative signal. One might expect that the longer term unemployed are aware of these signals and are consequently negatively influenced in their job search and application behaviour. This may prolong the duration of unemployment.

An unemployed person may be the major breadwinner in a household. His or her income influences, by definition, the income procurement in the household to a large extent. Unemployment, and especially long term unemployment, implies a decrease in household income. This leads to pressure on the financial situation of the household. The supply of labour of other members of the household will increase as household income earned by the major breadwinner falls (due to unemployment). This is even more true when household members are more or less "perfect" substitutes in the labour market. If a household is characterized by few feasible substitutes for the main breadwinner, for instance in the case of a "traditional family", that pressure will be greater. Due to the less important position of the non-main breadwinner in the income procurement of the household, a less active behaviour is then to be expected.

The amount of unemployment benefits also may influence the search duration. A higher benefit, or a benefit which is more related to the earnings before unemployment, will increase the search duration ("reservation wage"). Besides the formal unemployment benefit and other benefits, household income can be increased by so called "informal incomes" in order to prevent a sharp deterioration in the standard of living of the household. Apart from the feasibility of this alternative for the majority of unemployed, it might also have an effect on search behaviour and the resulting application for a job. The income effect of informal income activities in combination with the decrease in available time to find a new job may lead to an increase of the costs of search. This implies a less active formal labour market search. The amount of the search and application for a job will decrease as the share of informal income in total household income rises. This has been discussed elsewhere (Lancaster 1979; Nickell 1979; Yoon 1981; Ridder 1987; Kooreman and Ridder 1983; and Van den Berg 1990). The above discussion suggests the following hypotheses, namely that the probability of less active search and application behavior is higher when:

4.1 the unemployed are relatively lower educated,
4.2 the unemployed are older,
4.3 the unemployed are longer term unemployed,
4.4 the unemployed are not major breadwinners,
4.5 the unemployed belong to a household with informal income in total household income.

Table 14 gives the results of a regression model which tests the hypotheses for search and application behaviour[5]. Two equations were estimated for the two aspects of search and application behavior. According to the F-values both equations do have statistically significant explanatory power. The R-square is not high, but is satisfactory given the type of data (cross-section).

**Table 14**

**Results of the regression analysis on search and application behaviour for unemployed with household income equal to the minimum benefit**

| Independent variables | Dependent variables | |
| --- | --- | --- |
| | Search-behaviour (Beta) | Application-behaviour (Beta) |
| - Presence of informal income | -0.09* | -0.01 |
| - Duration of unemployment | -0.19** | -0.12* |
| - Level of education | -0.01 | 0.16** |
| - Being major breadwinner | 0.05 | 0.01 |
| - Age | -0.14* | -0.21** |
| Multiple R | 0.27 | 0.33 |
| R square | 0.08 | 0.11 |
| F | 6.00 | 7.35 |
| Sign F | 0.0 | 0.0 |

Unweighted Data
n = 211
* significant at 5%-level      ** significant at 1%-level

─────────────────── ❖ ───────────────────

Since the data is drawn only from people who are still unemployed, there may be a bias introduced because there is no information on individuals with completed spells of unemployment (Bosworth 1992). This also makes it difficult to trace the influence of the expected wage or the acceptance of a job offer on unemployment. Nevertheless, because we are interested in the sign of variables, we can draw the following conclusions from our regression results:

- the relatively higher educated do not search more actively for a job than the relatively lower educated, but they apply for a job more intensely. Hypothesis 4.1 is partially confirmed.
- the younger unemployed do search and apply for jobs more actively than the older unemployed. Hypothesis 4.2 cannot be rejected;
- the longer term unemployed show a less active search as well as application behaviour than the shorter term unemployed. Hypothesis 4.3 is confirmed;
- the unemployed main breadwinners do not show a more active labour market behaviour than non-main breadwinners. Therefore, hypothesis 4.4 is rejected;
- the unemployed for whom informal income is part of the household income do have a less active search behaviour but no less active application behaviour than the unemployed with no informal household income. So, hypothesis 4.5 is partly corroborated.

These findings are in line with a study of Groot and Jehoel-Gijsbers (1989). They also establish that the younger unemployed search and apply for a job more actively and that the higher educated show a more active application behaviour than the lower educated but not a more active search behaviour. From several studies in the Netherlands, using two moments of measurement and large samples, it is known that long duration, low education and older age diminish the chance to leave the unemployed (Jehoel-Gijsbers and Groot 1989; Boin and Van Dijk 1992; Van Dijk and Folmer 1992).

## V. Policy Implications and Issues

In the previous sections we have discussed characteristics of the poor, the poor as consumers, and income improvement possibilities for the poor. We used the policy minimum of the Dutch state as a poverty line. Assistance receivers are the vast majority of the poor. Before we discuss several policy issues we would like to give the main conclusions found thus far:

(1) Singles (one person households) and one parent families are the dominant types of household within the category of assistance receivers.
(2) Younger recipients tend to dominate assistance programs.

(3) The majority of beneficiaries are longterm recipients.
(4) The majority of RWW-recipients are longer term unemployed.
(5) Living on low income has consequences for daily living: a decrease in the level and quality of financial and non-financial wealth, difficulties in paying off loans, and increased economizing behaviour.
(6) A majority of poor households do not have earnings or extra earnings. Moreover, some are pessimistic with regard to any improvement of their household income in the future.
(7) Age, duration of unemployment, and educational level are three important variables in the explanation of search and application behaviour.

In the Dutch social security system, national assistance is the safety-net for events which are not covered by any of the social insurances. The aim is to guarantee poor households a minimum level of income. In general, one can say that a majority of the Dutch population endorses a redistributional role for the state. The outcomes of the market process with regard to income distribution are to be corrected to achieve more social justice. The way and the extent this is done is sometimes a matter of considerable debate.

Most public debates are characterized by a macroeconomic viewpoint and by a non-users' perspective (the costs for the state, society, tax payer, etc.). In these public debates the voices of economists, sociologists, politicians and other policy makers are very loud, in contrast to those of the users. It is not our aim here to review these debates. We will discuss only a few issues. But first, we will give some policy recommandations based on elements discussed in previous sections. In contrast with several other EC countries, the Netherlands has moved from the concept of "family policy" toward the concept of "equal opportunities for all" to enjoy prosperity, welfare and health (Presvelou and de Hoog 1991). When equal opportunities for all is a societal objective, an active policy from various sides is warranted. For poor households this implies the following: to guarantee the continuity of the household and to create the possibilities for households to leave poverty.

For poor households as consumers, efficient second-hand markets on a local level are important. Special assistance should be used more frequently to finance replacement and repair of basic durables such as washing machines.

A high percentage of poor households is indebted. The burden of indebtedness can be rearranged in various ways (extension, arbitration). Budget extension and assistance for lower income groups on a local level can be stimulated.

The creation of local information systems for consumers on price and quality is important for low income groups (Maynes, 1979). This information will not only benefit low income groups. Private initiative in this field may be stimulated through subsidies by local and national governments. Alleviation of some consumer problems can be achieved in this way. Drawing on savings, the purchase of inventory and borrowing money can alleviate current budget constraints, but bear risks for the budget in the long run. Installment and interest payments reduce the available budget later and depletion of financial and non-financial wealth creates its own problems.

The majority of poor households are of the opinion that a higher household income can only be achieved by earnings. To be temporarily poor is different from being permanently poor. The unemployed, one parent families and younger singles are able or considered to be able to leave the poverty situation with some help. Their source of income can be changed: earnings instead of a social benefit. Various types of extra schooling programs, better working of the labour exchange, specific measures (a tailor made approach), and more child care facilities are the most common suggestions for improving their employment prospects. At the end of the 1980's many iniatives and programs were started to prevent the further rise of the share of the long term unemployed among the unemployed. Whether they will be successful is subject to debate. Of course, more jobs are necessary for any program to succeed.

There is no evidence to support the popular belief that people accept living on assistance. Various labour market studies in the Netherlands have established this (Jehoel-Gijsbers and Groot 1989; Kloosterman 1987; Verhaar et al. 1990). But, what are the chances to escape from poverty? We must be aware that living on assistance means bureaucratic control, either from the municipal social service department or from the Labour Exchange. The labour market position of many low income groups is not good (see the previous section), e.g. the elderly or people with low levels of education or job training. Further, a distinction should be made between the regular category of earnings and the irregular category of extra earnings. In the previous section we have seen that some assistance recipients have some extra earnings. They are allowed to receive them to a certain level and for a restricted period. In view of their difficult financial situation, restrictions on the time period for extra earnings should be abandoned. Within the category of assistance receivers a distinction is made between people who have to look for and accept a suitable job (passende arbeid), the RWW-recipients, and people who do not have to look for a job, the ABW-recipients. To the latter category belong the elderly and, especially, the heads of one parent families. The majority of these are female headed (see section II). More striking is the fact that 62 percent of these households belong to the hard core e.g. more than three years living on assistance (van der Aalst and Peters 1991). So, heads of one parent families do not have to look actively for a job, full-time or part-time. Full-time or part-time jobs are not easy to combine with the care of dependent children, due to the shortage and absence and high price of child care facilities. It is doubtful whether having a paid full-time or part-time job has any positive gain for one parent families after deduction of the costs of having a job (expenses on travel, clothing, child care). Perhaps, for single parent families an efficient remarriage market would be more helpful! Contrary to

❖

many feminist beliefs, single parent families are not the worst off category of the low income households, due to the help of friends and relatives (see Goossens et al. 1990).

For most younger singles the positive gain of having a paid job is there. The amelioration can be Dfl 400 net a month for a person 23 years or older in a full-time job. This will be less in a part-time job. Moreover, there are not many jobs with the minimum wage as compensation. In the previous section, we have already seen that the younger unemployed do have more active labour market behaviour than older workers. For the elderly the situation is much more difficult. Although in the future the private pensions of the elderly, as a supplement to the state pensions, will be better, this does not give much relief for the present elderly poor. For some, the fruits may be bitter. They have built up the welfare state in the past by hard work, yet the state pension is unlikely to be raised in the coming years.

In this paper we have only discussed the national assistance systems in the Netherlands. As indicated above, the Netherlands gives minimum benefits under certain conditions. The terms of the unemployment, sickness and disablement acts are, at present, more generous than assistance benefits. These benefits are related to previous earnings as a consequence of the principle of securing the previous level of living. This principal is under attack now in many government proposals. In fact, the Dutch social security system is moving in the direction of giving citizens a guarantee of a minimum level. Along with this, the system is moving from being an insurance system to a tax financed system. In the last tax reform, the social insurance premiums were incorporated into the first tax bracket of 35 percent (38.55 percent in 1992). This means more state control and less influence of employers and employees' organisations. Viewed from the present budget deficit of the Dutch government, limitations in the social security benefit can be expected. This means that more households will have a minimum income in the coming decade. The changes in the Disablement Act, proposed in July 1991, are a good example of this. More people will receive a minimum benefit without much chance to escape from it. Besides that, distrust in the policy making process will spread due to one-sided changes in the terms of social insurance. Premiums or taxes will probably not be lowered. The resulting deterioration in the price-quality ratio of social security may lessen the willingness to pay for it.

An international comparision falls beyond the scope of this paper. Still it should be said that the Dutch system is not as generous as is often believed. The social security system in the Netherlands is frequently called a soft one, in contrast to, for instance, that of Sweden. However, although there have been recent initiatives with respect to schooling and labour exchange, there is reason to doubt that. Fear of increased competition due to the unification of the European markets after 1992 is a motive for some to change the social security system or to propose to do so. Some even think that this is the way to rescue the system. But, fear is a bad adviser. Social security expenses as a percentage of net national income do not

———————————————————— ❖ ————————————————————

differ very much between the richer countries in the European Community. And the richer countries do have some comparative advantages. Despite all its problems, the idea of the welfare state is still attractive for many people and nations, and the idea of an underclass is not.

## Endnotes

*Department of Household and Consumer Studies, Agricultural University Wageningen, P.O. Box 8060, 6700 DA Wageningen, The Netherlands. I would like to thank Peter Kooreman, Lammert Jansma, Kees Verhaar and Kees de Hoog for comments on a earlier version of this paper, and Joseph Phillips for editorial suggestions. Of course, they are not responsible for the contents of this paper.

[1] The social security system in the Netherlands comprises three subsystems: 1) the insurances for employed persons 2) the insurances for all inhabitants 3) the supplementary Benefits Act (TW) and the national assistance act (ABW). The Unemployment Insurance Act (WW) the Disablement Insurance Act (WAO), the Sickness Benefits Act (ZW) and the Health Insurance Act (ZFW) belong to the first category. Benefits according to one of these acts are income related e.g. 70 percent of previous income to a certain level. The General Old Age Pensions Act (AOW), the general Widows and Orphans Act (AWW), the general ruling for exeptional medical expenses (AWBZ) and the General Disablement Benefits Act (AAW) belong to the second category. The benefits of these insurances are a fixed amount, of which the level is mostly linked to the net minimum wage in case of an income replacing regulation (AOW, AWW for the widows, AAW). The third subsystem consists of the two regulations which were already mentioned. Benefits under these regulations are means tested e.g. a household income test and mostly a net wealth test. Supplementary benefits and national assistance are not higher than the relevant national minimum level. This depends on the type of household (100-90-70 formula). Couples receive 100 percent of the poverty line, one parent families with dependent children 90 percent and singles 70 percent. The minimum amount for couples is linked to the net minimum wage for persons 23 years and older. In net amount they are nearly the same. For singles younger than 23 the monthly payment is lower (see table note 1). Households with children are entitled to child allowances. For a majority of low income tenants the individual rent subsidy is also of importance. The tax free income amount depends largely on the marital status. There are three tax brackets with marginal tax rates of 35, 50 and 60 percent. The taxable income of the poor lies within the 35 percent group (38.55 percent in 1992). This 35 percent tax rate comprises also various insurance contributions. Tax deductions related to family and work matters, including unlimited tax-deductibility of mortgage interest, are possible.

## Table 13
## Gross Minimum Monthly Wage 1991

| Age | (in Dfl per month) |
| --- | --- |
| 23 years and older | 2,067.00 |
| 22 | 1,757.00 |
| 21 | 1,489.60 |
| 20 | 1,271.20 |
| 19 | 1,085.20 |
| 18 | 940.50 |
| 17 | 816.50 |
| 16 | 713.10 |
| 15 | 620.10 |

Source: SZW, 1990

[2] Most households with a minimum income receive a social benefit. Only 4.2 percent of the labour force receives a minimum wage and only 2.5 percent of persons between 23 and 64 years old receive the minimum wage (CBS, 1991). For couples the percentage is even lower due to age-income profiles, dual earners etc... One person households with the minimum wage for 23 years and older have more than the national assistance norm. In 1983 about 80 percent of households with a minimum income consisted of assistance receivers (ABW and RWW) and elderly with no extra or insufficient state pension (De Kleyn 1984). Because of a system of the incidental benefit (eenmalige uitkering) the number of households was known at that time, and there is no indication that this composition has fundamentally changed after 1983 (Goossens et al. 1990). At this moment, the fraction of households with minimum income from earnings in all households with a minimum income is unknown. In the middle of the 1980's the percentage was less than 5 percent excluding the self-employed (De Kleyn 1984). Due to the income improvement in the second half of the 1980s for most of the working population and the increased labour market participation of women it is probably lower now.

[3] Of the respondents 283 are living in the countryside and 231 in the city. Six types of households are discerned. Singles younger than 65 (102), singles older than 65(58), one parent families(170), couples younger than 65(56), couples older than 65(34) and families(94). The sample consists of recipients with ABW, RWW or AOW benefits.

[4] There are some studies which by means of qualitative research and sometimes quantative research try to get insight into the perception of poverty by poor households. For the enthusiast who can read Dutch see Kroft et al. 1989; Verhaar et al. 1989; Kullberg et al. 1990. If comparable, the results from these studies are in general in accordance with the results derived from quantative research.

⁵ Search behaviour is an index, with a range from zero to four, made up by the answers (yes or no) on: to look at advertisements, to search on one's own initiative, to search via family and friends, to go to the Employment Exchange on one's own initiative. Application behaviour and being major breadwinner are yes/no variables. The presence of informal income, also a yes/no variable, is a proxy variable for the amount of informal income. The education variable ranges from one (=primary education) to seven (=university education). The duration of unemployment is measured as the number of months of being out of work.

## References

Atkinson, A.B. *The Economics of Inequality,* 2nd edition, NY:Oxford University Press, 1983.

Boin, R. and van Dijk, J. "The Effectiveness of a Local Government Labour Market Policy" in C.H.A. Verhaar et.al. (eds.), *The Mysteries of Unemployment,* fourthcoming, 1992.

Bosworth, D. "Duration of Unemployment: An Analysis of the Labour Force Survey" in C.H.A. Verhaar et.al. (eds.), *The Mysteries Unemployement,* fourthcoming 1992.

Central Bureau of Statistics (CBS). *Statistical Yearbook 1991,* The Hague, 1991.

_____. *Statistical Yearbook 1990,* The Hague, 1990.

De Hoog, C. and van Ophem, J.A.C. "Gezinnen en Armoede" ("Families and Poverty"), *Gezin,* 1990, 2, 144-156.

De Galan, C. and Miltenburg, A.J.M. *Economie van de Arbeid (Economics of Labour),* (2nd edition), Alphen aan den Rijn, Samson 1985.

De Goede, M.P.M. and van Ophem, J.A.C. "Job Search Behaviour of Unemployed in the Frisian Labour Market", in C. Verhaar et.al., *Frisian Long Term Unemployment,* Leeuwarden: Fryske Akademy, 1990, 81-107.

Deleeck, H. and Bergman, G. *Sociale Zekerheid Tussen Droom en Daad (Social security between dream and action),* Antwerp: Van Loghum Slaterus, 1980.

De Nederlandsche Bank (DNB). *Jaarverslag 1990 (Annual Report 1990),* Amsterdam, 1991

De Vos, K. and Hagenaars, A.J.M. *Inkomens, Bestedingen en Schulden (Incomes, Expenditures and Debts),* The Hague, Ministry of Social Affairs and Employment, 1986.

De Kleyn, J.P. "Huishoudens met een Eenmalige Uitkering ("Households With an Incidental Benefit"), in *Economisch Statistische Berichten,* 1984, 69, 1016-1021.

❖

Engbersen, G. and van der Veen, R. *Moderne Armoede (Modern Poverty)*, Leyden/ Antwerp: Stenfert Kroese, 1987.

Goossens, R.C., de Vos, E.L., de Hoog, C. and van Ophem, J.A.C. *De huishouding van Minima. Een Onderzoek Naar de Huishoudvoering van Ontvangers van RWW, ABW en AOW (The Household Activities of Households With a Minimum Income)*, Department of Household and Consumer Studies, Wageningen Agricultural University, 1990.

Groot, W. and Jehoel-Gijsbers, G. *De Invloed van Loon en Uitkering op Arbeidsmarktgedrag (The Influence of Wages and Benefits on Labour Market Behaviour)*, The Hague, Ministry of Social Affairs and Employment, 1989.

Hagenaars, A.J.M. *The Concept of Poverty*, Amsterdam: North-Holland, 1986.

_____. and Wunderink-van Veen, S.R. *Soo Gewonnen Soo Verteert. Economie van de Huishoudelijke Sector (Economics of the Household Sector)*, Leyden/ Antwerpen, Stenfert Kroese, 1990.

Herberigs, H.A.G. "Survey. De Sociaal-Economische Omstandigheden Van Werklozen In Friesland" ("Survey. The Social-economic Situation of Unemployed in Friesland"), In part 1 of: Verhaar, C.H.A., J.A.C. van Ophem and M.P.M. de Goede (eds.), *Research Into the Economic Situation and Labour Market Behaviour of the Long-term Unemployed in Friesland*, Leeuwarden: Fryske Akademy, 1989.

Kapteyn, A., van de Stadt, H. and van de Geer, S.A. "Uitkeringen, Armoede en Welvaart" ("Benefits, Poverty and Welfare"), in *Economisch Statistische Berichten*, 1985, *70*, 384-389.

Kloosterman, R.C. *Achteraan in de rij (At the back of the Queue)*, The Hague, OSA, 1987.

Kroft, H. et al. *Een Tijd Zonder Werk (A Period Without Work)*, Leyden/Antwerp: Stenfert Kroese, 1989.

Kooreman, P. and Ridder, G. "The Effect of Age and Unemployment Percentage on the Duration of Unemployment, "*European Economic Review*, 1983, *20*, 41-57, 1983.

Kullberg, J., Goossens, R. and de Vos, E.L. *Daar Moet ik Alles Mee Doen. Portretten van Mensen met een Minimum-Uitkering (I Have to Live With This. Portraits of People With a Minimum Social Benefit)*, Nederhorst den Berg; Variant, 1990.

Maynes, E.S. "Consumer Protection: The Issues," in *Journal of Consumer Policy*, 1979, *3*, 97-109.

Miltenburg, T. and Woldringh, A. *Langdurige werkloosheid (Long-term Unemployment)*, Nijmegen: ITS, 1990.

Ministry of Finance. *Tax Revisions 1990, Application For Advance Reduction In Wage Tax/Social Insurance Contributions*, The Hague, 1989.

—————————————————— ❖ ——————————————————

Ministry of Social Affairs and Employment (SZW). *Minimum Wage, Minimum Youth Wage, Minimum Holiday Entitlements and Allowances*, The Hague, 1990

Ministry of Social Affairs and Employment (SZW). *A Short Survey of Social Security*, The Hague, 1991.

National Institute for Budget Education (NIBUD). *Budget Handbook 1991*, The Hague, 1991.

Nickell, S.J. "The Effect of Unemployment and Related Benefits on the Duration of Unemployment," *Economic Journal*, 1989, *98*, 34-49.

Oude Engberink, G. *De Belans Drie Jaar Later (The Balance After Three Years)*, Rotterdam, 1987.

Presvelou, C. and de Hoog, C. *Information Grid on the Netherlands*, Wageningen, European Family Policy Observatory, 1991.

Ridder, G. "Life Cycle Patterns in Labor Market Experience," Ph.D. dissertation, Amsterdam, 1987.

Sen, A.K. *On Economic Inequality*, NY: Oxford University Press, 1973

Sen, A.K. "Poverty: An Ordinal Approach to Measurement," *Econometrica*, 1976, *44*, nr. 2, 219-231.

Sociaal Cultureel Planbureau (SCP). *Social Cultural Report*, The Hague: Staatsuitgeverij, 1990

Social Insurance Bank (SVB). *Information on Child Allowances*, Amsterdam; 1991.

Spence, M. *Market Signalling*, Cambridge, MA: Harvard University Press, 1973.

Theeuwes J. "On Equilibrium Unemployment," Paper for The Act of Full Employment Conference, Maastricht, 1989.

Townsend, P. *The Concept of Poverty*, London: Heineman, 1970

Townsend, P. *Poverty in the UK, A Survey of Household Resources and Standards of Living*, Harmondworth: Penguin, 1979

Van den Berg, G.J. "Structural Dynamic Analysis of Individual Labour Market Behaviour," Ph.D. dissertation, Groningen, 1990.

Van der Aalst, M. and Peters, W. *De Harde Kern in de Bijstand* (The Hard Core in Assistance), The Hague: Ministry of Social Affairs and Employment, 1991.

Van Dijk, J. and Former, H. "The Impact of Personal and Regional Employment on Individual Wages in the Netherlands," in C.H.A. Verhaar et al. (ed.), *The Mysteries of Unemployment*, 1992.

Van Ophem, J.A.C. "Huishoudens en Inkomensdaling ("Household and Real Income Decline"), Ph.D. dissertation, Wageningen, 1983.

Verhaar, C.H.A., de Goede, M.P.M., van Ophem, J.A.C. and de Vries, A. *Frisian Long-term Unemployment*, Leeuwarden: Fryske Akademy, 1990

_____. Jansma, L.G., de Goede, M.P.M., van Ophem, J.A.C. and de Vries, A. (eds.), *The Mysteries of Unemployment,* Boston: Kluwer Academic Press, 1992.

Visser, W. "The Politics of Mass Unemployment and Economic Decline," in C.H.A. Verhaar et al. (eds.), *The Mysteries of Unemployment,* 1992.

Vos, K. "Micro-economic Definitions of Poverty," Ph.D. dissertation, Rotterdam, 1991.

Yoon, B.J. "A Model of Unemployment Duration with Variable Search Intensity," *Review of Economics and Statistics,* 1981, *63,* 599-609.

———————————————— ❖ ————————————————

# Catholic Social Teaching and Family Income: Results from across Nine Industrialized Countries

*Jeff A. Ankrom and Joseph M. Phillips\**

*Rerum Novarum (RN)* was a bold critique of the economic systems of its day. The document outlined the conditions for a just economic system, conditions it hoped all societies would aspire to. Among the objectives it set out for an economy is adequate remuneration for workers and support from society for those suffering the "scourge of unemployment." But what is a just and sufficient income level to allow workers to support themselves and their families? And how have the nations of the world performed in meeting these objectives? Certainly the Less Developed Countries (LDCs) have not met these challenges, but how have the industrialized countries fared? This is the thrust of this study, to empirically analyze these important questions.

The study uses data from the Luxembourg Income Study (LIS) for nine western countries. The countries included in this study are Australia, Canada, France, West Germany, Italy, Luxembourg, Norway, Poland, and the United States. This represents a healthy cross section of industrialized countries, including one semi-industrialized country perhaps described by some as an LDC (Poland). The diversity for the industrialized countries ranges from a very free market oriented economy (the U.S.) to one which relied heavily on central planning at the time the data were collected (Poland), with a selection of market oriented countries falling in between these two extremes.

The organization of the paper is as follows. Section one reviews Catholic social doctrine in the area of family income and employment compensation. Section two discusses the data and methods for assessing the adequacy of income. Section three presents the empirical analysis of the question, and the final section presents conclusions.

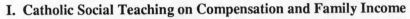

## I. Catholic Social Teaching on Compensation and Family Income

Perhaps one of the most important concerns of Leo XIII in writing *Rerum Novarum (RN)* was the adequacy of remuneration given to workers. Leo speaks of the "personal" and "necessary" characteristics of work (*RN*, §34). The former refers to the use of skills to perform a task for personal gain (where the worker defines and fulfills himself), but the latter refers to the necessity of work in order to preserve life. Therefore, employment must provide sufficient remuneration with which to live:

> The preservation of life is the bounden duty of each and all, and to fail therein is a crime. It follows that each one has a right to procure what is required in order to live; and the poor can procure it in no other way than by work and wages (§34).

This passage suggests that for many *only* through employment will they be able to support themselves and their families; thus the necessity of being able to procure employment. Leo XIII went on to say that "remuneration must be enough to support the wage-earner in reasonable and frugal comfort" (*RN*, §34). Earlier in speaking of employers, the pontiff wrote that their "great and principal obligation is to give to every one that which is just" (*RN*, §17). Employees should receive adequate wages.

But what constitutes just and adequate remuneration? Subsequent encyclicals and documents have expanded on this question. Writing in *Quadragesimo Anno (QA)*, Pius XI introduced two considerations — the "family wage" and savings. By family wage we mean a wage sufficient to support a family with only one spouse working. Thus Pius XI said:

> Intolerable, and to be opposed with all Our strength, is the abuse whereby mothers of families, because of the insufficiency of the father's salary, are forced to engage in gainful occupations outside the domestic walls to the neglect of their own proper cares and duties, ... (*QA*, §71)

This concept of the family wage received further elaboration and support in John Paul II's *Laborem Exercens (LE)*. Here, John Paul introduced the term "family wage":

> Just remuneration for the work of an adult who is responsible for a family means remuneration which will suffice for establishing and properly maintaining a family and for providing security for its future. Such remuneration can be given either through what is called a family wage — that is, a single salary given to the head of the family for his work, sufficient for the needs of the family without the spouse having to take up gainful employment outside the home ... (§19)

It is interesting to note that the concept of the family wage has not been reemphasized in *Centesimus Annus (CA)*, John Paul's latest encyclical written in commemoration of *RN*. That, however, should not be taken to mean that the pontiff is backing away from the idea.

In *QA* Pius XI also introduced the idea that remuneration should be sufficient to allow for the possibility of saving by workers. Thus Pius said:

> Every effort, therefore, must be made that at least in the future a just share only of the fruits of production be permitted to accumulate in the hands of the wealthy, and that an ample sufficiency be supplied to the workingmen. The purpose is not that these become slack at their work, for man is born to labor as the bird to fly, but that by thrift they may increase their possessions and by the prudent management of the same may be enabled to bear the family burden with greater ease and security, being freed from that hand-to-mouth uncertainty which is the lot of the proletarian (§61).

Saving allows for the acquisition of private property, and beginning with *RN* Catholic social teaching has stressed the desirability and right of individuals to be property holders. Thus, in *RN* Leo XIII made a strong statement in support of broad property ownership, saying that "every man has by nature the right to possess private property as his own" (*RN*, §5). He goes on to say that the ability to properly support a family, as outlined above, necessitates the ownership of "profitable property" (*RN*, §10). The pontiff saw three benefits deriving from dispersed property ownership: increased social harmony, increased productivity, and decreased migration (*RN*, §35). All this led Leo to conclude that "the law, therefore, should favor ownership, and its policy should be to induce as many people as possible to become owners" (*RN*, §35). In *CA* the theme of wages sufficient to allow for saving is again underscored when John Paul writes, "Society and the State must ensure wage levels adequate for the maintenance of the worker and his family, including a certain amount of saving" (§15).

*RN* made clear that it is the duty of the state to ensure that workers have adequate remuneration. Thus Leo wrote:

> Justice, therefore, demands that the interests of the poorer population be carefully watched over by the administration, so that they who contribute so largely to the advantage of the community may themselves share in the benefits they create — that being housed, clothed, and enabled to support life, they may find their existence less hard and more endurable.... It cannot but be good for the commonwealth to secure from misery those on whom it so largely depends (§27).

❖

Unemployment, of course, would interrupt the receipt of wages and prevent workers from meeting their needs. So it is that in *CA* John Paul can argue that by protecting the worker from "the nightmare of unemployment," society and the government can perform their proper function and restore dignity to work. In this way we have come to see government as "ensuring in every case the necessary minimum support for the unemployed worker" (§15).

Finally, another consideration with respect to adequate family income is whether Catholic social doctrine would favor a relative standard or would insist upon an absolute standard to be applied across all countries. A relative standard would allow for variation based upon local conditions, customs, and conventions. It would appear that social teaching would want to apply a relative standard, for this possibility has been raised in *Mater et Magistra (MM):*

> It is clear that the standards of judgment (for remuneration of work) set forth above are binding always and everywhere. However, the measure in which they are to be applied in concrete cases cannot be established unless account is taken of the resources at hand. These resources can and in fact do vary in quantity and quality among different peoples, and may even change within the same country with the passing of time (§72).

This review of Catholic social teaching on worker compensation and family income has found that justice argues that employees should receive compensation that allows them to obtain some modest level of living, and that compensation should be sufficient such that with effort saving can be set aside while only one spouse works. It also would appear that the acceptable standard of living will vary across countries so that a relative rather than absolute standard would apply. Catholic social doctrine also suggests that it is the duty of the state to ensure that remuneration for labor is adequate. This involves monitoring the sufficiency of wages but also stepping in to fill the breech in the case of unemployment.

With these views in mind, let us review the adequacy of income across several industrial countries.

## II. Data and Methods

The income concepts used in this study are transformations of variables found in the Luxembourg Income Study (LIS) microdata set for nine different countries. The source and survey year for each country are given in Table I. Since the data set was designed specifically for cross-national comparisons, the sponsors at the Center for Population, Poverty and Policy Studies have gone to great lengths to ensure that income concepts are comparable across countries. The LIS data are the best available for a study of this nature. A detailed description of the data set can be found in Buhmann, et al. (1988).

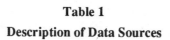

## Table 1
## Description of Data Sources

Australia: 1985-86 Australian Income and Housing Survey

Canada: 1987 Canadian Survey of Consumer Finances

France: 1979 French Survey of Individual Income Tax Returns

West Germany: 1984 German Panel Survey: Wave 2

Italy: 1986 Bank of Italy Income Survey

Luxembourg: 1985 Luxembourg Household Panel Study

Norway: 1979 Survey of Norwegian Tax Files

Poland: 1986 Polish Household Budget Survey

United States: March, 1985 U.S. Current Population Survey

The nine countries used in this study are for the most part industrialized countries located in Europe. Each is considered to be a "high human development" country in the Human Development Index classification of the United Nations Development Programme. Also, with the exception of Poland, each is categorized as a "high income country" by the World Bank.

Table 2 presents some descriptive statistics in this regard, although the reader is cautioned about making comparisons between countries on the basis of per capita GNP. Inclusion of these nine countries in this study is not due to any common characteristics they may have, however, but rather to their availability in the LIS dataset and the ease of estimating the income measures used in this analysis. Table 2 also presents evidence on the location of each country in the business cycle at the time of its survey. The table shows that each economy was growing, although some were expanding much faster than others. The unemployment rate for different countries shows that the employment situation for Luxembourg and Norway was much more favorable at the time of their survey than was the case for the other countries. These economies were doing better at providing employment to citizens, meeting a key concern of Catholic social thought.

❖

## Table 2
### Country Descriptive Statistics

|  | Human Development Index[a] | Real GDP Per Capita (1987 PPP $)[b] | Real GNP Per Capita (1988 US $)[c] | Survey Year Real Output Growth | Unemployment Rate[e] |
|---|---|---|---|---|---|
| Australia | .978 | 11,782 | 12,340 | 2.9% | 7.9% (8.2) |
| Canada | .983 | 16,375 | 16,960 | 4.0 | 8.9 (8.9) |
| France | .974 | 13,961 | 16,090 | 3.2 | 5.9^ (6.1) |
| Germany | .967 | 14,730 | 18,480 | 2.8 | 9.1^ (7.4) |
| Italy | .966 | 10,682 | 13,330 | 2.5 | 11.1^ (7.5) |
| Luxembourg | .934 | 18,550[d] | 22,400 | 3.7 | 1.7 |
| Norway | .983 | 15,940 | 19,990 | 5.1 | 1.4^ |
| Poland | .910 | 4,000 | 1,860 | 4.9 | ____ |
| U.S. | .961 | 17,615 | 19,840 | 3.8 | 7.1 |

[a]   A score greater than .80 indicates "high human development."

[b]   In purchasing power parity dollars.

[c]   "High income countries" have per capita income in excess of 6,000 in 1988 U.S. dollars.

[d]   In 1987 U.S. dollars.

[e]   A "^" indicates the unemployment rate rose from the previous year, otherwise assume the unemployment rate fell. Number in parentheses is unemployment rate using U.S. definition. Sources: *Human Development Report* (1990), *World Development Report* (1990), *Statistical Yearbook* (1985/86 and 1987), 1987 *National Accounts Statistics: Main Aggregates and Related Tables,* and *Statistical Abstract of the U.S.* (1986 and 1989).

It should be noted, however, that official unemployment rates are not strictly comparable across countries because countries use different methodologies and definitions in computing the statistic. Table 2 also presents for some countries their unemployment rate using the methodology of the U.S. Using this common definition the differences in umemployment rates narrow significantly. Table 2 also indicates whether labor market conditions in the different countries were improving or deteriorating at the time of the survey. The unemployment rate was rising in four countries (though the rise was very slight in Norway), while falling in four others. Economic growth and labor market conditions must be kept in mind when making comparisons across countries because adverse conditions should cause deterioration in family incomes, especially for lower income families. If conditions were substantially different across countries, it would make little sense to make cross-country comparisons.

Discussions of family income and compensation in Catholic social thought proceed with the assumption of a nuclear family with both spouses present. This poses a challenge to not only the reality of divorce, separation, and birth out of wedlock, but also to how the LIS data have been collected. Across the nine countries there can be significant differences in how a household is defined. Despite the potential difficulties presented by these cross-country differences, the decision to focus on married couple headed units makes intercountry comparison feasible. The difference in the definition of a household headed by a married couple is not significant across the data sets. Another advantage of focusing on married couple households is that it is consistent with Catholic social teaching's vision of what a family should look like.

In order to assess the questions this study wishes to address, three measures of income are derived for each of the countries. These measures are (1) wage and salary income of the primary earner (PEI), (2) factor income (FI), (3) and disposable personal income (DPI). The derivation of these income concepts is described in Table 3. PEI will be used to assess the success of an economy in providing a family wage. FI will be used to determine how important income from accumulation and secondary worker income are in meeting family needs. Finally, DPI will allow us to examine how the tax and benefits program of a nation contribute to the achievement of an adequate standard of living.

## Table 3
## Description of Income Concepts Used

(1) Primary Earner Wage and Salary Income (PEI)

+ wage and salary income of other family members

+ cash property income

equals (2) Factor Income (FI)

+ unemployment, sick, accident, and disability pay

+ child and maternity allowances

+ state provided and private pensions (including military)

+ food, housing, heating, and medical benefits

+ other cash and near-cash benefits

equals gross income

- payroll taxes

- income taxes

equals (3) Disposable Personal Income (DPI)

Note: All income concepts are adjusted with equivalence scales and normalized around mean family size for each country.

Each income concept was adjusted for family size by using equivalence scales. Buhmann et al. have discussed the role of equivalence scales in comparative studies of poverty and inequality, concluding that it is possible to proxy adequately family well-being (W) using the following expression:

$$W = Y / S^e$$

where Y equals family income, S equals family size, and e is the equivalence elasticity coefficient with $0 \le e \le 1$. If e equals zero then W equals Y, implying that for a given Y any number of persons can live as well as one with the same income.

❖

If e equals one then W equals family income per capita, implying that no joint consumption possibilities exist in family living. Clearly, the "true" e lies between zero and one since the consumption of some goods (e.g. housing) will not double as family size doubles. For this study e was set equal to .55 for all countries, the mean value estimated by Buhmann, et al. based on their analysis of poverty line standards in eight different industrialized countries. All measures of W for each country are normalized around mean family size, making W equal to Y if S equals average family size.

A crucial issue for this study is the determination of what constitutes adequate family income across countries. Ideally, Catholic social teaching would provide a clear definition, but our survey has revealed only the outlines of a standard. One thing that does seem clear is that the standard will vary across countries or, in other words, a relative as opposed to absolute standard is appropriate. In this analysis the standard used is 50% of median disposable personal income (DPI). Using such a standard assumes that the basic needs level in each country is relative to the standard of living in that country. It would be possible to use an absolute benchmark such as the U.S. poverty line and to apply that standard to all countries, however comparing incomes across countries is fraught with difficulties. Such comparisons, as might be made with the data presented in Table 2, must be made with caution. Among the most vexing problems are determining a common unit of measurement (such as an individual country currency or an "international dollar") and differences in relative prices across countries. Attempts to solve these problems have been made by the United Nations International Comparison Project where an internationally comparable scale using purchasing power parities has been developed. An example of these estimates is provided in Table 2. Still, such an approach cannot account for different social customs which influence what a society might consider an acceptable standard of living. For these reasons, this study does not develop a common standard to be used across countries.

## III. Empirical Results

Table 4 provides summary statistics derived for the nine countries examined in this study. Figures are provided for both all households and married couple households only. There it can be seen that family size varies within a relatively narrow range, while there is a much broader range across countries for the number of wage earners per household. The number of earners is notably larger in Canada and the U.S., suggesting that these countries may not do well in providing a family wage and that it is necessary for more than one household member to work in order to maintain an adequate standard of living. However, evaluating the wage of the primary or secondary earner against factor income, the proportion of factor income coming from the primary or the secondary wage earner in Canada and the U.S. is roughly equal to the mean for all countries analyzed. This indicates that households in these two countries do not have an unusually high dependence on second Incomes.

**Table 4**

**Descriptive Statistics For Country Data\***
**(in current domestic currencies**

| Country | Mean Household Size | Mean Household Wage earners | Mean Proportion DI From Primary Earner | Mean Proportion DI From Secondary Earner |
|---|---|---|---|---|
| Australia | 3.29 (2.69) | 1.52 (1.22) | 53.7% (55.7) | 19.1% (15.7) |
| Canada | 3.30 (2.71) | 1.84 (1.50) | 57.4 (59.8) | 22.6 (18.8) |
| France | 3.36 (2.77) | 1.34 (1.11) | 57.7 (58.9) | 17.7 (15.8) |
| Germany | 3.09 (2.37) | 1.30 (1.00) | 61.1 (63.5) | 16.4 (13.3) |
| Italy | 3.48 (3.08) | 1.22 (1.07) | n.a. n.a. | n.a. n.a. |
| Luxembourg | 3.24 (2.70) | 1.23 (1.01) | n.a. n.a. | n.a. n.a. |
| Norway | 3.34 (2.49) | 1.47 (1.10) | 60.8 (64.4) | 20.3 (16.0) |
| Poland | 3.34 (3.21) | 1.14 (1.10) | n.a. n.a. | n.a. n.a. |
| United States | 3.24 (2.64) | 1.74 (1.37) | 57.8 (60.0) | 21.7 (17.4) |

\*For married couple households/families. Statistics for all households appear in parentheses.

Table 5 provides the percentage of married couple households falling below the acceptable standard of income in the nine countries using the three measures of income. This concept of household is analyzed because it both allows for comparing across countries and conforms with Catholic social teaching's vision of family structure. The most striking result is that these relatively affluent countries do a poor job of providing for a family wage. This can be seen by looking at the proportion of households who do not meet the standard with PEI. On average across all nine countries 26.8% of households do not meet the standard. The worst situation was in France where some 35% of households could not meet the standard based upon the salary of one wage earner. Even in the best situation, Norway, some 19% of households could not attain 50% of mean disposable personal income. Undoubtedly, Norway is helped by its low unemployment rate.

**Table 5**

**Proportion of Married Couple Households/Families Falling Below
50 Percent of Equivalent Median DPI for all Households**

|  | PEI | FI | DPI | % Change FI to DPI |
|---|---|---|---|---|
| Australia | 28.4% | 15.8% | 7.2% | -54% |
| Canada | 28.4 | 14.7 | 5.9 | -60 |
| France | 34.9 | 21.1 | 5.9 | -72 |
| Germany | 23.2 | 13.8 | 3.4 | -75 |
| Italy | n.a. | 24.2 | 9.7 | -60 |
| Luxembourg | n.a. | 18.0 | 3.8 | -79 |
| Norway | 19.1 | 9.5 | 1.6 | -83 |
| Poland | n.a. | 16.7 | 5.4 | -68 |
| United States | 26.8 | 13.4 | 6.6 | -51 |
| Mean | 26.8 | 16.4 | 5.5 | -66 |
| Median | 27.6 | 15.8 | 5.9 | -63 |

By observing figures for FI, we see that adding in other salaries and property income significantly improved the situation, reducing the proportion of families with insufficient income by some 40 to 50 percent. The average percentage of households not meeting the standard drops to 16.4%. Again, the best result was found in Norway where slightly less than ten percent of households failed to meet the standard. The worst result was in Italy where over 24% of households were below the standard. Finally, by observing DPI it can be seen that government fiscal programs had a significant impact on household income, causing the proportion of families not meeting the standard to fall between 51 and 83 percent, with an average decline of 67%. The average for the group falls to 5.5%. Generally speaking, these nine countries appear to make a significant societal effort to provide for families through social programs, making up for significant shortcomings in their labor

❖

markets. Thus they are attempting to meet this dimension of their responsibilities as outlined in Catholic social doctrine. The success of the fiscal system in Norway, Germany, and Luxembourg is particularly noteworthy in this regard, while the effect of the fiscal system is weakest in the U.S. In terms of the overall result, Norway turns in the best performance in minimizing the number of households not meeting the income standard, with less than two percent in this category. The worst performance is in Italy where nearly ten percent of households do not meet standard. Clearly, more could be done in some of these countries to ensure adequate income for households.

In addition to seeing how families fair in achieving the income standard, we can also look at how individuals fair. The results would be expected to differ since average family size of poor families is higher than for all families. A revised measure showing the proportion of individuals falling below 50% of median equivalent DPI is shown in Table 6. As expected, with the exception of Germany and Luxembourg, the proportion of individuals not meeting the standard is higher than the proportion of families. The rise is especially high in Poland and the U.S.

### Table 6

### Measures of Poverty

| | Proportion of Individuals Falling Below 50 Percent of Median Equivalent DPI (all households) | DPI Poverty Gap |
|---|---|---|
| Australia | 7.49% | 1.85% |
| Canada | 6.47 | .86 |
| France | 6.45 | 1.02 |
| Germany | 3.43 | .35 |
| Italy | 10.43 | 1.25 |
| Luxembourg | 3.48 | .35 |
| Norway | 1.65 | .45 |
| Poland | 6.21 | .61 |
| United States | 7.74 | 1.04 |
| Mean | 5.93 | .86 |
| Median | 6.45 | .86 |

❖

Thus far this study has focused on the number of families failing to meet the standard for equivalent income. A shortcoming with this approach is that it does not account for the degree of shortfall below the standard. It obviously matters whether a family needs $100 or $1,000 to be brought up to the standard. The sum total of deviations of family income from the poverty line is sometimes referred to in poverty studies as the "poverty gap." In this study we calculate a modified version of this measure defined as the fraction of societal DPI that must be redistributed from families above the line to those below to bring all families up to standard. Poverty Gap DPI is calculated as follows:

$$\text{Poverty Gap DPI} = \frac{(MD - ADB) * PF}{AD * F}$$

where MD is 50% of median equivalent DPI, ADB is average equivalent DPI of families below 50% of median DPI, PF is the number of poor families, AD is average equivalent DPI, and F is the number of families.

Poverty Gap DPI estimates for each country are shown in Table 6. There it can be seen that on average a redistribution of .86% of DPI would be needed to allow all families to meet the standard. The situation is most favorable in Germany, Luxembourg, and Norway, and least favorable in Australia and Italy. In general, it appears that a relatively modest redistribution of income would achieve the desired result.

Finally, it might be interesting to see what, if any, influence Catholic social doctrine has had on the success of these nine countries in providing for families. Although this is a very complicated question, perhaps some suggestive evidence can be gleaned from comparing country performance with the strength of the Catholic church in that country. As a proxy for the strength of the church we use the percentage of the population belonging to the Catholic church. Information for this analysis is presented in Table 7 where the proportion of Catholic population for each country is compared to the proportion of familes with PEI and DPI below standard and the reduction in the proportion not meeting standard in going from FI to DPI (all taken from Table 5). If the Catholic church had any influence on policy, we would expect a large Catholic population to be correlated with low values for the proportion of families with PEI and DPI below standard PEI and DPI and large differences in FI and DPI. Pearson, Kendall, and Spearman correlation coefficients comparing Catholic population to the three variables indicate otherwise, however, showing that Catholic influence is associated with higher values of PEI and DPI and smaller differences between FI and DPI. This suggests that such countries underperform in providing a family income, in minimizing the persistence of inadequate family income, and in designing a fiscal system to alleviate inadequate family income. However, Catholics need not be overly alarmed by these results because for the most part these correlation coefficients are not statistically signifi-cant. Nevertheless, the absence of evidence indicating that Catholic societies do better along these lines may be troubling for some.

**Table 7**

**Catholic Influence on Performance and Policy**

| | Percent Population Catholic | Proportion of Families Below Standard When Family Income is Measured by | | Reducation in Proportion of Families not Meeting Stan-dard after Fiscal Programs |
| --- | --- | --- | --- | --- |
| | | PEI | DPI | |
| Australia | 26.9% | 28.4% | 7.2% | 54% |
| Canada | 45.3 | 28.4 | 5.9 | 60 |
| France | 84.7 | 34.9 | 5.9 | 72 |
| Germany | 46.4 | 23.2 | 3.4 | 75 |
| Italy | 98.0 | n.a. | 9.7 | 60 |
| Luxembourg | 94.0 | n.a. | 3.8 | 79 |
| Norway | 0.4 | 19.1 | 1.6 | 83 |
| Poland | 95.0 | n.a. | 5.4 | 68 |
| United States | 21.8 | 26.8 | 6.6 | 51 |
| Mean | 59.9 | 26.8 | 5.5 | 66.9 |
| Median | 46.4 | 27.6 | 5.9 | 68 |
| Pearson Corr. | | .824* | .381 | .114 |
| Kendall Corr. | | .552 | .141 | .085 |
| Spearman Corr. | | .638 | .218 | .075 |

* Significant at the .05 level.

Source: Various issues of the *Catholic Almanac* and Table 4.

❖

Correlation analysis was also done between PEI, DPI, and the percent difference between FI and DPI and three variables from Table 2 — the Human Development Index, per capita purchasing power parity GDP and per capita GNP. The expected relationship would be that lower values of PEI and DPI and a large difference between FI and DPI would be associated with high values of the variables from Table 2 since more affluent nations would be better positioned to provide adequate income to households. Pearson, Kendall, and Spearman correlation coefficients generally return the expected sign, indicating that more affluent countries generally do better in providing household income. However, these results in most cases also are not statistically significant.

## IV. Summary

The main thrust of this paper has been to evaluate how nine different industrialized countries perform in providing sufficient income for families from the perspective of Catholic social teaching. We find that they have done a poor job in providing a family wage, in other words adequate income for a family based on one working spouse. In many countries the contribution of the income of the second spouse is important to maintaining household living standards, providing roughly 15 to 20% of FI.

While these nine countries do poorly in providing a family wage, their social welfare systems appear to make up for a substantial amount of the deficiencies in their labor markets. As a group these nations substantially reduce the number of families below the standard through their fiscal systems. While problems remained in virtually every case, there is no denying that their redistribution systems had a significant role in raising many household incomes to offset unacceptable outcomes in their economies. Clearly, these nations have recognized some of the obligations laid out for them in Catholic social doctrine.

There was no evidence to support the view that in countries where the Catholic church had more strength that labor market conditions or public policy were influenced by church doctrine. The strength of Catholicism appeared to have no effect on the provision of a family wage or on redistributive efforts to compensate for labor market deficiencies. Perhaps this simply means that all Christians are concerned with human diginity, not just Catholics.

*Department of Economics, Wittenberg University, Springfield, Ohio 45501 USA; and, Department of Economics and Finance, Creighton University, Omaha, Nebraska 68178 USA.

# References

Buhmann, Brigitte, Rainwater, Lee, Schmaus, Guenther, and Smeeding, Timothy "Equivalence Scales, Well-Being, Inequality, and Poverty: Sensitivity Estimates Across Ten Countries Using the Luxembourg Income Study (LIS) Database," *Review of Income and Wealth*, 1988, *34*(2), 115-42.

Foy, Felician A., ed. *Catholic Almanac*, Huntington,IN: Our Sunday Visitor: 1981-89.

John XXIII, *Mater et Magistra* (May 15, 1961), Washington, DC: United State Catholic Conference, 1981.

John Paul II, *Centesimus Annus* (May 1, 1991), Vatican City: Libreria Editrice Vaticana, 1991.

John Paul II, *Laborem Exercens* (September 14, 1991), Washington, DC: United States Catholic Conference, 1981.

Leo XIII, *Rerum Novarum* (May 15, 1891), New York: Paulist Press, 1962.

Pius XI, *Quadragesimo Anno* (May 15, 1931), New York: Paulist Press, 1962.

Second Vatican Council, *Gaudium et Spes* (December 7, 1965), Washington, DC: National Catholic Welfare Conference.

United Nations, *National Accounts Statistics: Main Aggregates and Related Tables: 1987*, NY: United Nations, 1990.

United Nations, *1987 Statistical Yearbook*, NY: United Nations, 1990.

United Nations Development Programme, *Human Development Report 1990*, NY: Oxford Univesity Press, 1990.

U.S. Department of Commerce, *Statistical Abstract of the U.S.*, Washington: Government Printing Office, 1986 and 1989.

World Bank, *World Development Report 1990*, NY: Oxford Univesity Press, 1990.

# Economics of the Golden Mean: A Preliminary Inquiry (Abstract)

## Li-teh Sun*

The importance of the golden mean or moderation in human life has been advocated almost universally by all the great teachers of the world. Ordinary people, though, may not fully know its true meaning, pay lip-service to it, and to some extent follow it. Thus, "All work and no play make Jack a dull boy." Also, everyone certainly can experience the comfort of Spring and Fall, of a 70-degree room temperature, and of a good night's sleep after a hard day's work. The significance of the golden mean seems therefore quite clear for our everyday well-being. In the sphere of economics, however, the validity of it appears to have little recognition. Economic man is supposed to *maximize* utility, profit or income. Economists seem to be either for the free market or government intervention; for private ownership or public ownership.

It is the purpose of this paper to begin a preliminary inquiry as to whether some evidence can be found to support the hypothesis that the golden mean in economics may be as valid as it is in the daily life of every individual human being. Due to the availability of data, the fifty states of the United States are chosen for the study. A total of 13 ideology indicators are selected to classify the states into three groups: conservative, moderate, and liberal. They are:

1. Percentage of vote cast for president, U.S. senators and representatives by Democrats.
2. Percentage of women in state legislature.
3. State and local tax collection per $1,000 state personal income.
4. Per capita state and local government expenditures.
5. State individual income tax collection as a percentage of total state tax collection.

6. State individual income tax rate.

7. State and local government full-time equivalent employment per 10,000 population.

8. Weekly unemployment benefits as a percentage of weekly disposable personal income.

9. Percentage of vote cast for presidential candidate George Wallace.

10. Legal abortions per 1,000 live births.

11. AFDC payment as a percentage of per capita disposable personal income.

12. "Safety nets" for the poor.

13. Business attractiveness.

Then, 19 performance indicators are used to determine whether there are differences among the three groups of states. Performance indicators are:

1. State personal income per capita.

2. Unemployment rate.

3. Average annual percentage change in state gross product.

4. Retail sales increase per household.

5. Wholesale trade increase.

6. Export-related trade as a percentage of total manufacturer shipment value.

7. Federal food-stamp recipients as a percentage of all households.

8. Poverty rate, or percent of persons below the poverty level.

9. Business failures per 10,000 concerns.

10. Commercial banks closed or assisted by FDIC as percent of total banks.

11. Rate of return on assets of FSLIC-insured savings institutions.

12. Net farm income to debt ratio.

13. Female labor-force-participation rate.

14. Per FTE public college student appropriations.

15. Infant mortality rate.

16. Hospital beds per 100,000 population.

17. Physicians per 100,000 population.

18. Total crime rate per 100,000 population.

19. Full-time equivalent employment police protection per 10,000 population.

❖

The result of observing these performance indicators is that the liberal group of states seems to perform better than either the conservative or the moderate group. However, according to the principle of the golden mean, the moderate group should have the best performance. Explanations for this deviation from the golden mean might be that the liberal group, having the smallest sample, is not representative, or that the liberal ideology in the U.S. is really the moderate ideology in a world perspective. That is to say, the finding indeed supports the validity of the golden mean in economics.

*Department of Economics, Moorhead State University, Moorhead, Minnesota 56563 USA.

# Social Encyclicals and Social-market Economics

## Siegfried G. Karsten*

Social-market economics addresses imbalances between economic and ethical norms in the private and public sectors, ideological prejudices about common welfare and a socially caring state, insufficient commitment to the fact that it is in everyone's interest to be concerned about everyone's welfare, and distortions of the principle that "government should govern as little as possible but not do as little as possible."

Walter Eucken, with his paradigm of a functionally competitive social market economy, established the basis for a free market economy which institutionalizes concerns for economic and social justice. Social encyclicals such as *Rerum Novarum, Quadragesimo Anno, Mater et Magistra, Pacem in Terris, Populorum Progressio, Laborem Exercens,* and *Centesimus Annus,* approach the concept of a social and just economy from a Christian moral tradition. Similar to Eucken's conception of a social market economy, the social encyclicals also postulate that the evolution of a just and fair market economy — as the guarantor of freedom, human dignity, and justice — cannot be left to chance but needs to be consciously guided. In essence, these encyclicals call for the integration of economic theories and policies with notions of "fairness" and "justice," advocating a holistic approach in viewing the economic system as an organic whole.

This paper argues that the broad economic guidelines, which the social encyclicals suggest, fall within the framework of a functional market economy, a social market economy, facilitating a moral-economic dialogue.

## I. Encyclicals and Their Principles

Major papal "social encyclicals," issued over the course of a century, from 1891 to 1991, represent links in a chain of pronouncements on economic conditions and policies. The basic proposition in all of these papal circulars to the bishops is that economic policies and religious beliefs are complementary and not adverse in nature.

———————————————— ❖ ————————————————

During the last 100 years, the encyclicals which specifically addressed economic conditions in industrialized countries take Leo XIII's *Rerum Novarum: On the Condition of the Working Classes, (RN)* (1891) as a point of departure. This document proved to be of significant importance in its seminal influence. All subsequent "social encyclicals" celebrated its publication, reemphasized the thoughts expressed therein; and, by taking account of changing socioeconomic and political conditions, further elaborated on it.

In 1931, Pope Pius XI observed the 40th anniversary of RN with *Quadragesimo Anno: On Social Reconstruction (QA)*, calling it the "Magna Charta of the Social Order" (pp. 19-20). This was followed by John XXIII's *Mater et Magistra: Christianity and Social Progress* (1961) and *Pacem in Terris: Peace on Earth* (1963). The former addressed questions with regard to the economic order whereas the latter dealt mostly with political issues. The topic of world-wide economic interdependence was dealt with by Paul VI in *Populorum Progressio: On the Development of Peoples* (1967). John Paul II's *Laborem Exercens: On Human Work* was promulgated in 1981.

In the most recent encyclical in this chain, *Centesimus Annus (CA)* (1991), Pope John Paul II not only commemorates the 100th anniversary of *RN* but also extends his moral authority in support of the free market system and to capitalism if they are constrained by a judicial framework which not only assures competition but also the freedom and dignity of all men.

In 1986 the Catholic Bishops of the United States published the final draft of a significant "Pastoral Letter," *Economic Justice for All*. Although it is neither a papal encyclical nor accepted by the Vatican, it nevertheless is an important document on "Catholic Social Teaching and the U.S. Economy" which cannot be ignored (Earlier drafts 1984, 1985; Karsten 1986).

The basic themes which permeate all of these encyclicals and the Bishops' Pastoral Letter are: (1) Material things have value in so far as they aid in attaining the purposes of life. (2) How well does the socioeconomic system provide access to humanizing work? (3) How well does it care for those who cannot work? For example, the Bishops stipulate that "Every perspective on economic life that is human, moral and Christian must be shaped by three questions: What does the economy do *for* people? What does it do to people? And how do people *participate* in it?" (NCCB 1986, p. 1) (4) Work is made for man and not man for work. (5) Work enhances the dignity of man. To deny someone work is to deny him freedom, cocreation, and to interfere with the divine plan for salvation (Leo XIII 1891, pp. 30-31, 35, 50; John Paul II 1981, pp. 17, 23, 39, 57, 59, 62).

All of these pronouncements essentially emphasize "that work, as a human issue, is at the very center of the 'social question'" it is "probably the essential key to the whole social question" (John Paul II 1981, pp. 7, 10; NCCB, p. 49). They also stress that both "labor and capital are indispensable components of the process of production in any social system" (Leo XIII p. 18; John Paul II 1981, p. 49), to be united in a spirit of solidarity. The substance of all these encyclicals and of the

❖

Bishops' Letter can best be summarized by Ederer's characterization (1983, p. 18) of RN as:

1) an affirmation of the right of private ownership extending also to the material means of production;
2) an invitation to the state to return to an active regulative and sometimes promotional role in economic life;
3) the right of every adult workingman to a just wage to be secured also by the organization of labor unions.

## II. Classical and Neoclassical Views

These major social encyclicals as well as the Bishops' Pastoral Letter call for a reorientation of socioeconomic policies to take account of notions of "fairness" and "justice." In this regard they follow well established precedence.

Adam Smith, more than 200 years ago, concerned himself with similar questions of social justice. "All the members of human society stand in need of each other's assistance" (1966, p. 124). He believed, for example, that it is justice, specifically economic justice, which holds society together. The prevalence of injustice must destroy it (pp. 124-25).

The principle of laissez faire, of perfect competition, or of the free enterprise system, was essentially born out of the concern for people. Classical and neoclassical economists considered unemployment and poverty as primary social problems with potentially destructive consequences and other social ills. Those fully committed to the principles of laissez faire envisioned the solution in a perfectly competitive economy. Exclusive privileges and practices, which interfered with a "free market," were to be prevented or eliminated. Then unrestrained competition would not only assure economic growth to lift everyone up, but would also bring about greater socioeconomic equality.

Some neoclassicists, however, such as Alfred Marshall and Léon Walras, as well as John M. Keynes and Eucken, took the position that unrestrained laissez faire would degenerate into imperfect competition. Hence, economic growth, by itself, would not tend to make the distribution of income and wealth more equal; it may make it more unequal. They concluded that ethical norms and social justice tend to be endangered in an unrestrained market economy — similar observations are made in the encyclicals (Leo XIII, pp. 5-7; Pius XI 1931, pp. 6, 44-45). Hence, they devised theories and models to improve the market system through strengthening the price mechanism and by resolving problems of injustice and poverty (Jensen 1977).

Solutions to imperfect competition were sought in institutional reforms, to protect price competition where it existed and to recreate it where it had vanished. This is also Walter Eucken's approach in his paradigm of a "social market economy," modified by an "economic constitution" which is to assure freedom, justice, and human dignity (Karsten 1985). The objective of "social market

---
❖
---

economics" may best be quoted from Marshall (1966, p. 47): "the wellbeing of the whole people should be the ultimate goal of all private effort and public policy." This is what the "social encyclicals" essentially aim at (Leo XIII, pp. 28-30; Pius XI, pp. 13, 44).

> Economic activity, especially the activity of a market economy, cannot be conducted in an institutional, juridicial or political vacuum. On the contrary, it presupposes sure guarantees of individual freedom and private property, as well as a stable currency and efficient public services (John Paul II 1991, pp. 92-93).

> ... there are many human needs which find no place on the market. It is a strict duty of justice and truth not to allow fundamental human needs to remain unsatisfied, ...(John Paul II, p. 67).

Despite the apparent mutual objectives of Catholic social doctrine, abstracting from those of a purely religious nature, and of the paradigm of a social market economy, the former did not support the latter on the basis of "soulless economic determinism" (Moschel 1989, p. 149). As Oswald von Nell-Breuning discusses (1975), this was the unfortunate result of misconceptions about social market economics. The following sections will detail a high degree of correspondence in socioeconomic principles between these two schools of thought.

## III. Justice and Dignity

For Immanuel Kant "freedom" was the center of his moral universe. Similarly, Eucken considered freedom, justice, and economic security as being central to his economic universe. Both of them treated man as the end, not as the means to an end (Donaldson 1982, p. 301; Miksch 1950, p. 280).

As Marshall had suggested with his "economic chivalry," self-interest should not be viewed merely in terms of profit maximization. The activities of business, labor, and government should be guided by what will improve the socioeconomic setting in general, coupled with concerns for the common good, notions of socially responsible behavior, and the idea of "stewardship" (Walton 1982, p. 273). In the words of John Paul II (1991, p. 83): "A business cannot be considered only as a society of capital goods'; it is also a 'society of persons.'"

The focus of social and economic justice, of the social encyclicals, the Bishops' Pastoral Letter, as well as of a social market economy, is best expressed by Franz Mueller, paraphrasing Gladstone and Pesch: "That what is morally wrong can never be economically right. There can be no conflict between what is economically and ethically true and good" (1977, p. 295).

Similarly, Wilhelm Ropke, one of the leading exponents of the paradigm of social market economics, took the position that economic life does not exist in a moral vacuum. In his perception, the forces of supply and demand, of competition, or of the market, do not create ethical norms or rules; "they presuppose them and consume them." They have to come from outside the market. Reminiscent of Marshall's economic chivalry, Ropke postulated (1960, pp. 124-25):

> Self-discipline, a sense of justice, honesty, fairness, chivalry, modera-
> tion, public spirit, respect for human dignity, firm ethical norms — all
> of these are things which people must possess before they go to market
> and compete with each other. These are the indispensable supports
> which preserve both market and competition from degeneration.
> Family, church, genuine communities, and tradition are their sources.

As John XXIII put it (1961, p. 63), "The cardinal point of this teaching is that individual men are necessarily the foundation, cause, and end of all social institutions." And, in the words of John Paul II (1991, p. 67), "there exists *something which is due to man because he is man,* by reason of his lofty dignity." These observations essentially follow Leo XIII's "No one may with impunity outrage the dignity of man, which God Himself treats with great reverence" (p. 35).

Eucken, in formulating his paradigm of a functionally competitive (social market) economy, essentially accepted Marshall's and Ropke's positions and anticipated Thomas Donaldson's synthesis of William Nozick's and John Rawls' theories of justice. It stipulates that each individual has a right to: (1) have his capacity for positive freedom respected; (2) those goods necessary to develop and sustain himself as a human being; (3) maximal negative liberty; and (4) goods and positions which are the result of his efforts (Donaldson 1982, p. 308).

More specifically, Eucken actually followed similar principles which Rawls had formalized in his theory of justice which holds that "all social primary goods — liberty and opportunity, income and wealth, and the bases of self-respect — *are to be distributed equally unless an unequal distribution of any or all of these goods is to the advantage of the least favored* (1971, p. 303, italics mine). In Rawls' view, a just system needs to concern itself with "fundamental social problems, in particular those of coordination, efficiency, and stability." He defines injustice as "simply inequalities that are not to the benefit of all" (1971, pp. 6-7, 62). As Beauchamp puts it (1982, p. 296),

> ...the difference principle could allow, for instance, extraordinary
> economic rewards to entrepreneurs if the resulting economic stimula-
> tion were to produce improved job opportunities and working condi-
> tions for the least advantaged members of society.

This "difference principle" is reflected in various social encyclicals and the Bishops' Pastoral Letter. For example, Leo XIII observed (p. 16):

———————————————— ❖ ————————————————

Neither the talents, nor the skill, nor the health, nor the capacities of all
are the same, and unequal fortune follows of itself upon necessary
inequality in respect to these endowments. And clearly this condition
of things is adapted to benefit both individuals and the community.

And the NCCB pronounced (p. 15):

The dignity of the human person, realized in community with others,
is the criterion against which all aspects of economic life must be
measured.

Some degree of inequality not only is acceptable, but also may be
considered desirable for economic and social reasons.... However,
unequal distribution should be evaluated in terms of meeting the basic
needs of the poor and the importance of increasing the level of
participation by all members of society in the economic life of the
nation. These norms establish a strong presumption against extreme
inequality ... (John XXIII, p. 92).

## IV. Eucken's Economic Constitution

Many classical, neoclassical, Keynesian, social-market economists, and
others started with "a genuine concern for things as they are, that is with a
socioeconomic problem arising from the inadequacies of the status quo, and
presented alternatives to that status quo" (Cochran, p. 123). Or, as Thomas Nitsch
relates, "every social encyclical is a product of its times" (1991, p. 2).

Leo XIII's *RN* was in response to the growing socialist critique of the existing
socioeconomic conditions and his observation that "eagerness for change would
pass from the political sphere over into the related field of economics" (p. 5). John
Paul II realized that changing "conditions and demands will require a reordering
and adjustment of the structures of the modern economy and of the distribution of
work" (1981, p. 7; 1991, p. 106).

Given a realistic view of man, the validity and meaning of a competitive
market economy depend upon economic laws which originate from the existing
socioeconomic, legal, and institutional structure and the ethical value system.
Eucken in his paradigm of a social market economy sees social problems as being
interconnected with economic, political, and ethical issues and called for a
conscious shaping of an economic system that will provide for human freedom,
justice, economic security, and efficient economic processes to the maximum
extent possible (Eucken 1948, pp. 76-77; 1959, pp. 123-32, 182; Karsten 1985).

The greatest threat to freedom, according to Eucken, originates with problems of economic equity and justice, which raise the threat of state intervention
(Eucken 1948, p. 48; 1959, pp. 10, 21-22, 179, 194; Jöhr 1950, p. 274). In the words
of William Byron, "social systems ... can sustain, enlarge, diminish or destroy

human beings.... It all depends on the quality of private ownership and the quality of private decisions in the free market mechanism" (1982, p. 313).

The paradigm of a social market economy shifts the emphasis from an unrestricted price mechanism to guiding the economy towards socioeconomic goals. As Aba Lerner puts it, it is a change from quantity to quality, to assist policy makers to broaden the middle class, to maintain high employment, to control inflation, to restrict monopolistic power, and to encourage (discourage) socially beneficial (harmful) activities (1969, p. 133). The shift is from the purely laissez-faire economy to a socially responsive free-market economy, to capitalism with a conscience (Hartrich 1980, p. 10).

This is essentially the approach of the paradigm of social market economics as exemplified by Eucken. Like Keynes, he believed that economic forces without the guide of a "functional" institutional framework do not evolve by themselves for the welfare of the people, except for those in positions of dominance. Eucken recognized, as many present-day economists do, that monopoly power and special privileges are sought by the major participants in the economic process. Unrestrained laissez-faire evolves into economic power, concentrated in monopolies and oligopolies, threatening not only freedom but also the efficient allocation of resources. Prices then no longer function as efficient allocation and rationing devices, leading to increasingly greater intervention by the state in the economy. That is, contemporary monopolistic capitalism is not synonymous with a free market economy, as envisioned by the advocates of freedom and democracy. The solution, therefore, was to establish a "functional" market economy (Eucken 1948, pp. 73-74; 1949, pp. 3-7).

Leo XIII called for a "good order" in the interest of private and public welfare (p. 32). Pius XI was more to the point in stating that "Free competition ... cannot be the ruling principle of the economic world.... It is therefore very necessary that economic affairs be ... subjected and governed by a true and effective guiding principle" (p. 44). John XXIII felt that "there cannot be a prosperous and well-ordered society unless both private citizens and public authorities work together in economic affairs" (1961, p. 18). Pope Paul VI pointed out that "without abolishing the competitive market, it should be kept within the limits which make it just and moral, and therefore human" (pp. 36-37).

John Paul II, following *RN,* expresses it best (1991, p. 31) in terms of the framework of a social market economy:

> There is certainly a legitimate sphere of autonomy in economic life which the State should not enter. The State, however, has the task of determining the juridical frame-work within which economic affairs are to be conducted, and thus of safeguarding the prerequisites of a free economy, which presumes a certain equality between the parties, such that one party would not be so powerful as practically to reduce the other to subservience.

As was pointed out above, the exponents of a social market economy take the position that economic forces, without the guidance of a "functional" institutional framework, do not evolve by themselves for the welfare of all men, except for those in positions of dominance. As the Bishops see it, a free market does not automatically generate social and economic justice (Eucken 1959, p. 34; NCCB, p. 48).

For Eucken, and his paradigm of a social market economy, no socioeconomic policy is viable in the long run which does not take into account people's desire for economic security, for a life in dignity, and for protection from economic calamity which is beyond an individual's control. In other words, questions of freedom and welfare are closely interconnected (Eucken 1942, p. 48; 1949, p. 88; 1959, p. 194; Jöhr, p. 274). As Dahrendorf puts it (pp. 103-4), social safety and justice are timeless issues (cf. Eucken 1959, pp. 10, 21-22, 179).

Eucken (also the encyclicals) viewed social problems as being interconnected economic, political, and ethical issues. Therefore, he called for the conscious shaping of an economic system that would provide for human freedom, justice, economic security, and efficient economic processes to the maximum extent possible, combining advantages of competition with concerns for justice and equity — the hallmark of his paradigm of a "social market economy," i.e., a socially responsive free-market economy (Eucken 1948, pp. 76-77, 90; 1959, pp. 123-32, 182; Miksch, p. 280).

According to Eucken, and also implied by the Papal documents, each economic system has to give structure to the economic process and to provide it with a necessary momentum. The objective is to establish "order" or an "economic constitution" for the socioeconomic framework. With Eucken, it is to be found in his concept of a "functional" social market economy, guided by "structural" and "regulating" principles to assure "order" and "justice." His "social market economy" is to facilitate policies which are economically and ethically justifiable and which enhance man's opportunities for a "productive" life (Eucken 1959, pp. 122-23, 182).

> The state has to consciously shape the structures, the institutional framework, the order, in which the economy functions. It has to set the conditions under which a functional and humanly dignified economic order evolves. But it is not to direct the economic process itself ... government planning of the structure, yes. Government planning and directing of economic processes, no. (Eucken 1959, pp. 92-93, my translation; also see NCCB, pp. 59-62).

The paradigm of a social market economy, therefore, advocates a "right order" in economic relationships, in the interrelationship between capital, labor, and government. It is to be achieved through a neutral monetary policy, the elimination and control of monopolistic powers, a functional price mechanism and incomes policy, and stable fiscal and monetary policies. This "order" is to facilitate

❖

solutions which are economically and ethically justifiable and which enhance individuals' opportunities for a "productive" and dignified life.

Eucken defined his "economic constitution" for a competitive social market economy in terms of eight "structural" and five "regulating" principles (1949, pp. 32ff; 1959, pp. 160-77). Underlying his paradigm are five general principles.

The following sections will investigate the correspondence of the pronouncements in the Papal social encyclicals with the tenets of Eucken's model. With regard to the "structural" and "regulating" principles, one needs to keep in mind that the encyclicals are not treatises dealing with specific economic theories and make suggestions for economic policies only in general terms.

## V.  General Principles

Although not formally specified in Eucken's "economic constitution," it is essentially premised on five general principles which in varying degrees are accepted by others as well as "market economists" (Gemper 1983, pp. 10-13). These principles are also reflected in the various social encyclicals.

1. The "*principle of individual responsibility*" stresses the importance of individual initiative and decision making within the framework of moral accountability. Pius XI enunciated this subsidiarity principle in *QA:*

> It is a fundamental principle of social philosophy, fixed and unchangeable, that one should not withdraw from individuals and commit to the community what they can accomplish by their own enterprise and industry. So it is an injustice and at the same time a grave evil and a disturbance of right order, to transfer to the larger and higher collectivity functions which can be performed and provided for by lesser and subordinate bodies (Quoted in John XXIII 1961, p. 17).

John XXIII affirmed that human dignity requires that man is encouraged to freely practice initiative and to act responsibly (1961, p. 17; 1963, p. 13). Similarly, John Paul II (1991, p. 62) observed that in the organization of production and the creation of economic wealth, "disciplined and creative human work" as well as "initiative and entrepreneurial ability" are essential.

2. The "*solidarity principle*" emphasizes the reciprocal relationship not only among individuals but between individuals and society. Adam Smith's invisible-hand argument and Say's Law of the Markets posit a systemic interdependence among persons and groups and universal harmony of private and public interest that render any form of altruism or social consciousness essentially redundant. Heinrich Pesch, in proposing his model of economic solidarity, suggested "social justice" and "social charity" as essential prerequisites. The latter he defined "as an active on-going concern for the common good" (Ederer 1983, pp. 21-22; Pesch 1925, pp. 272-76).

❖

Following similar lines of thought, Leo XIII, addressing the question of class conflict, expressed that: "Each needs the other completely: neither capital can do without labor, nor labor without capital" (p. 18). Pius XI (p. 35) further elaborated on Leo XIII:

> For unless human society forms a truly social and organic body; ... unless, above all, brains, capital and labor combine together for common effort, man's toil cannot produce due fruit.

Popes John XXIII, Paul VI, and John Paul II, leaning on their predecessors, made similar pronouncements (John XXIII 1961, pp. 9, 12, 28; Paul VI, pp. 14-15, 27). In the words of John Paul II (1981, p. 49; 1991, p. 84 – respectively):

> In the final analysis, both of those who work and those who manage the means of production or who own them must in some way be united in this community.

> By means of his work man commits himself, not only for his own sake but also for others and with others. Each person collaborates in the work of others and for their good (John Paul II 1991, p. 84).

3. The *"principle of self help"* underscores the obligation of government to motivate individuals to assume responsibility, to change things which are in their power to change, to practice self-help by supportive legal and regulatory measures as well as by appropriate fiscal policy initiatives. In other words, the paradigm of a "social market economy" makes allowance for both the market and legislation as well as government action to resolve socioeconomic challenges.

Pius XI makes the point that "opportunities for work be provided for those who are willing and able to work" (p. 38), which also found its manifestation in the U.S. Employment Act of 1946. John XXIII (1961, p. 26) recognized that in order to achieve this the state must provide conditions which encourage individuals to assume responsibilities and to engage in productive activities. This is re-emphasized subsequently (idem 1963, p. 21):

> That State activity in the economic field, no matter what its breadth or depth may be, ought not to be exercised in such a way as to curtail an individual's freedom of personal initiative. Rather it should work to expand that freedom as much as possible by the effective protection of the essential personal rights of each man and every individual.

According to John Paul II, "the State must contribute to the achievements of these goals directly and indirectly ... by creating favourable conditions for the free exercise of economic activity, which will lead to abundant opportunities for employment and sources of wealth" (1991, pp. 32-33).

Both the Bishops' Pastoral Letter and the Lay Commission's Letter (the anticipatory conservative opposition criticizing it), stress greater initiatives to strengthen families, local programs of self help and assistance, and greater cooperation between the public and the private sectors. Both letters point to the crucial role of the entrepreneur, private initiative, and the complementarity of capital and labor. Calling attention to the fact that "no economy can be considered truly healthy when so many millions of people are denied jobs by forces outside their control" and that "the nation make a major new commitment to achieve full employment," the Bishops state (NCCB, pp. 77-78) that:

Expanding employment in our nation will require significant steps in both the private and public sectors, as well as joint action between them. Private initiative and entrepreneurship are essential to this task.

Effective action against unemployment will require a careful mix of general economic policies and targeted employment programs.

We recommend that the fiscal and monetary policies of the nation — such as federal spending, tax, and interest rate policies — should be coordinated so as to achieve the goal of full employment.

Similarly, the Lay Commission's Letter posits (p. 66):

One of the best ways to help the poor, and especially to help family life among the poor, is to generate new jobs.

... the creation of wealth is simultaneously a social and a personal good. It helps the creator of wealth; it helps others — and the society as a whole.

4. In terms of Alfred Marshall's redefinition of laissez-faire, the "*principle of common welfare*" encourages government "to do that work which is vital, and which none but government can do effectively." That is, "the function of government is to govern as little as possible; but not to do as little as possible" (Pigou 1966, pp. 336, 363), especially with regard to the social infrastructure, education, health, poverty, the environment, technological developments, etc., which are also greatly elaborated by John XXIII (1961, p. 39; 1963, p. 21). The foregoing is well summarized in Leo XIII's RN (p. 29):

States are made prosperous especially by ... justice, moderate imposition and equitable distribution of public burdens, progressive development of industry and trade, thriving agriculture, and by all other things of this nature, which the more actively they are promoted, the better and happier the life of the citizen is destined to be. The state is bound by the very law of its office to serve the common interest.

5. The *"principle of the socially caring state"* mandates that society helps those who cannot help themselves, i.e., the provision of a "social safety net," to assist individuals in bearing burdens which are beyond the individual's capacity to resolve. This principle permeates all of the social encyclicals and the Bishops' Pastoral Letter. As Leo XIII writes:

> The end of civil society concerns absolutely all members of this society, since the end of civil society is centered in the common good, in which latter, one and all in due proportion have a right to participate (p. 43).

Pius XI asserts that government "must have special regard for the infirm and needy." In the words of John XXIII, "it is necessary that economic undertakings be governed by justice and charity." He further stressed that a social safety net should be made available to all citizens so that "in case of misfortune or increased family responsibilities, no person will be without the necessary means to maintain a decent standard of living." Specific recommendations are made by John Paul II, calling for unemployment insurance, medical insurance, and care for the old and disabled (Pius XI, p. 13; John XXIII 1961, p. 12; 1963, pp. 9, 21; John Paul II 1981, pp. 43-47; 1991, p. 67).

The encyclicals, the Bishops' Pastoral Letter, and the Lay Commission's Letter (p. 5), stress the principle of subsidiarity, which is a fundamental premise of social market economics. Using Ederer's characterization, this principle stands for:

> the common sense notion that all organs of society ... exist to serve the individual person and the family — not vice versa. More comprehensive and higher social bodies come to be established by people as they are needed to do for them what they and their families and other lower, closer-in social units cannot do for them (p. 20).

As the Bishops indicate, "the principle of subsidiarity thus calls for cooperation, collaboration and consensus-building among the diverse agents in our economic life, including government," i.e. for solidarity.

## VI.  Structural Principles

The structural principles consist of:

1. *Commitment towards a competitive social market economy.* The objective of a "competition policy," anchored in law, to prevent its abuses, is to be found in

❖

the protection of economic freedom and in the constraint of monopoly power. Economic efficiency is viewed as a derivative of individual freedom of action in the market system (Moschel, p. 142).

The commitment to (a wholesome) "competition" has been implied in all of the social encyclicals, stressing the importance of initiative, the subsidiarity principle (e.g., John Paul II 1991, p. 32), and the ownership of property. Pope Pius XI calls for a competition constrained by "guiding principles" to prevent its abuses and growing monopoly power (pp. 44-45, 50-52). The most explicit comments on competition, along the lines of a social market economy, are to be found in John Paul II's *CA* (e.g., p. 39). "It would appear", he writes (p. 66), "that ... *the free market* is the most efficient instrument for utilizing resources and effectively responding to needs." Again, however, he adds that "this is true only for those needs which are 'solvent'" (p. 67). The inability of the market mechanism to properly administer *"collective goods"* and provide for needs which are not served by "mere commodities" is also noted (p. 78). Further, the Pontiff also advises (pp. 92-93) that:

> Economic activity, especially the activity of a market economy, cannot be conducted in an institutional, juridical or political vacuum. On the contrary, it presupposes sure guarantees of individual freedom and private property, as well as a stable currency, and efficient public services.

2. *Primacy of monetary policy,* to stabilize the value of money as a necessary condition for a functionally competitive economy.

Some of the social encyclicals make reference to the utilization of monetary and fiscal policies. As could be expected, none of them stress the supremacy of the former over the latter. John Paul II, however, is concerned with the importance of a "stable currency" (1991, pp. 39, 92).

3. *Open competitive markets,* i.e., the elimination of restraints on demand and supply, for both domestically and foreign-produced goods. This implies the control of monopoly power which will be discussed below.

The encyclicals stress the importance of individual economic freedom. However, according to Paul VI, "freedom of trade is fair only if it is subject to the demands of social justice" (pp. 35-37).

4. *Stable and predictable economic policies* which are essential for long-term decisions. "Competition policy" is to be anchored in "a rule of law which, in contrast to political *ad hoc* decisions, has continuity. Protection of competition is impeded if it is determined by political decisions" (Möschel, pp. 152-53).

In essence the social encyclicals take a similar position. For example, John XXIII, following Pius XI, advocates that:

> both within individual countries and among nations there be established a juridical order, with appropriate public and private institu-

tions, inspired by social justice, so that those who are involved in economic activities are enabled to carry out their tasks in conformity with the common good (1961, p. 13).

5. *Private ownership of the means of production.* Social market economists view the ownership of property as a fundamental "condition of a competitive order ... of an economically efficient order of conduct. It links the capacity to take decisions and responsibility" (Möschel, p. 154). Also, they are of the opinion that only a competitive social market economy can effectively control property as a basis of socioeconomic power and, therefore, make it tolerable.

All of the "social encyclicals," following the declarations in *RN*, strongly defend the ownership of private property, although they make a distinction, going back to Aristotle, that ownership should be private but its uses should be in the context of general concerns for the common good, discouraging its abuses. For example, Leo XIII (pp. 8, 40-41) asserts that:

Nature confers on man the right to possess things privately as his own.

The right of private property must be regarded as sacred.... the largest possible number among the masses ... prefer to own property. If this is done, excellent benefits will follow, foremost among which will surely be a more equitable division of goods.

When men know they are working on what belongs to them, they work with far greater eagerness and diligence.

Pius XI re-emphasizes the right to own property as given by nature and the Creator Himself and that the state has no right to abolish it; it may, however, control its uses in the interests of the common welfare. He posits that ownership of property has a "twofold character" — individual and social. That is, owners of property are not to use it "only for their own advantage, but also the common good" (pp. 23-26). The other encyclicals take essentially the same positions, positing that ownership of property is essential for a just order and human dignity (John XXIII 1961, pp. 8, 32-36; 1963, p. 11; John Paul II 1981, pp. 34-37; 1991, pp. 58-59, 84).

6. *Freedom to enter contracts* to increase competition and to restrict its abuses. Contracts which restrain trade abuse the freedom of contract and are detrimental to competition.

The Papal encyclicals essentially take the position that states are more prosperous if they pursue policies which promote industry and trade within the context of maximizing people's well-being and the common good. This implies that governments should pursue policies favorable to responsible competition, within the confines of social justice (Leo XIII, pp. 29-34; Pius XI, pp. 13, 44; John XXIII 1961, p. 45; 1963, p. 21; John Paul II 1991, pp. 22-23, 81-82).

7. *Accountability for actions restricting competition*, which has manifested in the form of antitrust laws in various countries. Observations with regard to the encyclicals made in connection with the preceding principle would also apply in this case. It also concerns the regulation of monopoly power.

8. *Interdependence of all structural principles* — applied in isolation they lose their basic purpose and effectiveness.

## VII. Regulating Principles

The regulating principles address:

1. *Reduction and control of monopoly power*. If the latter cannot be eliminated, the state is obligated to control and supervise monopolistic industries in such a manner that their prices approximate those that would have existed under perfectly competitive conditions.

As with the ownership of private property and with regard to an incomes policy, some encyclicals exhibit a strong position relative to the control of monopoly power and the enhancement of competition. Pius XI warns that the new "syndicated and corporative institution(s)" had their origins in unrestrained competition; "immense power and despotic economic domination is concentrated in the hands of a few," which in turn is detrimental to a "better social order" (Pius XI, pp. 45, 47, 50-51; et cf. John XXIII 1961, p. 12). In the words of John Paul II, "the state has the further right to intervene when particular monopolies create delays or obstacles to development," i.e., to optimal social welfare (Paul VI, p. 16; John Paul II 1991, pp. 69, 88, 93).

2. *Incomes policy*. The operation of a free market does not by itself resolve problems of economic security or equity and justice in the distribution of income and wealth. Therefore, free market rules need to be modified. Specific policies could take the form of tax and regulatory reform to abolish special privileges, which tend to distort market prices. Other measures include social welfare legislation, industrial policies, codetermination between labor and management. All of these are justifiable as long as they increase competitive conditions, make prices more reflective of scarcity, and do not discourage long-term investment.

It was concerns of this type which led Alfred Müller-Armack (1989, p. 83) to define a social market economy "as a regulative policy which aims to combine, on the basis of a competitive economy, free initiative and social progress." The encyclicals, as could be expected, very much stress the necessity of a social safety net. Leo XIII recommends that not only action be taken to assure people work and adequate wages, but also that a mechanism be established (e.g., workers' association) which assists workers when they confront unforeseen circumstances through layoffs, illness, old age, or other misfortunes (pp. 16-19, 22, 28-33, 48-50). Other encyclicals make essentially similar suggestions for a social safety net (Pius XI, pp. 30, 34, 36-37; John XXIII 1961, p. 25; 1963, pp. 11, 21; Paul VI, pp. 13-14, 21, 29-30, 45; John Paul II, 1981, pp. 42-47, 52; 1991, pp. 31, 39, 66-67); addressing basic human dignity, John XXIII (1963, p. 9) writes:

Every man has the right to life, to bodily integrity, and to the means which are suitable for the proper development of life; these are primarily food, clothing, shelter, rest, medical care, and finally the necessary social services. Therefore a human being also has the right to security in cases of sickness, inability to work, widowhood, old age, unemployment, or in any other case in which he is deprived of the means of subsistence through no fault of his own .

The topic of an incomes policy in the Papal encyclicals is not limited to the social safety net. For example, John XXIII calls attention to the necessity of an adequate social infrastructure and education (1961, pp. 11, 28, 39; 1963, pp. 10, 21). John Paul II suggests an industrial policy approach (p. 72). Furthermore, the right for workers to form trade associations is emphasized and worker participation in management decisions is suggested.

3. *Prices are to reflect all costs* of production, to serve as true allocators of scarce resources. This implies that detrimental externalities, which pass some of the costs of production to society as a whole be eliminated. For example, environmental costs, caused by discharging effluents into the air, water, and the ground, are to be borne by the users of the products in question.

The Papal encyclicals stress the importance of a "just wage" as an essential cost factor. Leo XIII reflects that a worker should be provided with "an honorable means of supporting life"; that is, "the wage shall not be less than enough to support a worker who is thrifty and upright" (pp. 18-19, 39). Similar demands are made by Pius XI (pp. 34, 36) and by John Paul II (1991, 17), for example.

4. *An integrated countercyclical policy approach* to reflect the interrelatedness of all problems, e.g., unemployment, inflation, growth, investment, environment, poverty, etc. Pressures from special interest groups to deal with these in isolation are seen as the primary source of socioeconomic instability. This essentially calls for the coordination of fiscal and monetary policies in order to deal with socioeconomic challenges effectively. Neither inflation nor unemployment by themselves are to be the primary objective of public policy; both must be addressed.

Both John XXIII and John Paul II suggest the use of countercyclical policies. For example, the former observed that "developments make it possible to keep fluctuations in the economy within bounds, and to provide effective measures for avoiding mass unemployment" (1961, p. 18; John Paul II 1991, p.93).

5. *Establishment of a monetary numeraire* to depoliticize and to stabilize monetary policy (with the supply of money to be tied to a basket of commodities). Eucken saw the practice of "money creation" through credit extension as the major cause of economic fluctuations. As was pointed out above, John Paul II had expressed his concerns for a stable currency (1991, pp. 39, 92).

It was Eucken's position that the "structural" and "regulating" principles cause of economic fluctuations. As was pointed out above, John Paul II had expressed his concerns for a stable currency (1991, pp. 39, 92).

It was Eucken's position that the "structural" and "regulating" principles complement each other, and, therefore, need to be integrated in a unified approach. He was concerned that if it were not possible to establish a competitive social market economy, as outlined by his "structural" and "regulating" principles, the alternative would be increased state intervention in economic activities, which may result in reduced personal and economic freedom.

## VIII. Socioeconomic Reality

The paradigm of a social market economy takes a holistic approach in treating the economy as an organic whole. It recognizes the individual's claim to a share in society's output, to a life of relative security, and for protection from circumstances beyond one's control. For Eucken and other advocates of this paradigm, as well as for the authors of the social encyclicals and the Catholic Bishops, the central concern is a life in freedom and dignity which allows a person to develop her/his potentials.

The model of a social market economy rests on the premise that social issues cannot be dealt with successfully unless they are tied to an efficient economy. The "general," "structural," and "regulating" principles of Eucken's "economic constitution" are oriented towards establishing an efficient functional market economy.

Individuals are to be encouraged to change things which are in their power to change. However, social action is required to change causal factors which are beyond the individual's reach, justifying a "social safety net." A functional competitive market economy, characterized by a flexible price mechanism and stablizing economic policies, is to protect man not only from economic distress but also from the dangers of a totalitarian system (Eucken 1959, pp. 179-87; Dugger, pp. 308-9).

The pronouncements in the papal encyclicals and in the Bishops' Pastoral Letter as well as the Lay Commission's Letter express similar views. As the latter points out, for example: "The American system is not a free-market system alone, or a free enterprise system alone. The political system has many wholly legitimate and important economic roles, including care for the truly needy" (p. 32). Or, as Paul VI states: "the economy is at the service of man" (p. 17).

An enterprising market economy is characterized by technological development, economic growth, and institutional change — all of which are disruptive. A social market economy takes account of the fact that the market does not necessarily resolve, on its own, conflicting interests or all socioeconomic problems. Eucken's economic constitution provided for a consensus-generating mechanism to avoid self-destructive disequilibria. Hence, social legislation is justified as long as it enhances competitive conditions, makes prices more reflective of scarcity, does not discourage long-term investment, and, therefore, does not inhibit economic growth and a rising standard of living.

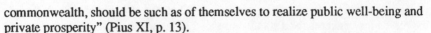

commonwealth, should be such as of themselves to realize public well-being and private prosperity" (Pius XI, p. 13).

In the narrower sense, the papal encyclicals call for social and economic policies to broaden the income base, serving the self-interest of every segment of a population and economy. The better off people are in general, the more prosperous every individual and business is going to be.

In a wider sense, the papal encyclicals represent a reaffirmation of fundamental Judeo-Christian teachings. They express the view that economic growth and greater wealth, for their sake alone, cannot be a lasting condition. Every society also needs to cultivate its state of consciousness. The Bishops (NCCB, p. 3) best express this as follows:

> People shape the economy and in turn are shaped by it.... Serious economic choices go beyond purely technical issues to fundamental questions of value and human purpose.

Pius XI asserted that it is "Our right and duty to deal authoritatively with social and economic problems" (p. 21). It was Müller-Armack who added the word "social" to Eucken's "market economy," to emphasize that a realistic socioeconomic model had to consider not only economic but also social policy objectives (Lenel 1989, p. 262). In the final analysis, it appears that the direction has to be towards a greater emphasis of social consciousness as an integral part of a functional social market economy.

*Professor of Economics, West Georgia College, Carrollton, GA 30118 USA.

# References

Beauchamp, Tom L. "The Ethical Foundations of Economic Justice," *Review of Social Economy*, December 1982, *40*, 291-99.

Byron, William J. "Christianity and Capitalism," *Review of Social Economy*, December 1982, *40*, 311-22.

Cochran, Kendall P. "Why a Social Economics?" *Review of Social Economy*, April 1979, *37*, 121-32.

Dahrendorf, Ralf. *Die Chancen der Krise*, Stuttgart: Deutsche Verlagsgemeinschaft, 1983.

Donaldson, Thomas. "What Justice Demands," *Review of Social Economy*, December 1982, *40*, 301-10.

Dugger, William M. "Social Economics: One Perspective," *Review of Social Economy*, December 1977, *35*, 299-310.

❖

Ederer, Rupert J. "The Papacy and Economics," *Homiletic and Pastoral Review*, March 1983, 17-26.

Eucken, Walter. "Wettbewerb als Grundprinzip der Wirtschafts-verfassung," in *Schriften der Akademie für Deutsches Recht*, Vol. 6, Gunter Schmolders, ed. Berlin: Duncker & Humbolt, 1942, 29-49.

_____. "Das Ordnungspolitische Problem," *Ordo-Jahrbuch für die Ordnung von Wirtschaft und Gesellschaft*, 1948, *1*, 56-90.

_____. "Die Wettbewerbsordnung und ihre Verwirklichung," *Ordo-Jahrbuch für die Ordnung von Wirtschaft und Gesellschaft*, 1949, 2, 1-99.

_____. *Grundsätze der Wirtschaftspolitik*, Edith Eucken Erdsieg and K. Paul Hensel, eds., Hamburg: Rohwolt Verlag, 1959.

Gemper, Bodo B. "The Implications of Ordnungspolitik" (Paper presented at the Third World Congress of Social Economics, Fresno, California, August 17-19, 1983).

Hartrich, Edwin. *The Fourth and Richest Reich*, New York: MacMillan, 1980.

Jensen, Hans E. "Economics as Social Economics," *Review of Social Economy*, December 1977, *35*, 239-57.

John XXIII. *Mater et Magistra*, "Christianity and Social Progress," 15 May 1961, Boston: Daughters of St. Paul.

John XXIII. *Pacem in Terris*, "Peace on Earth," 11 April 1963, Boston: Daughters of St. Paul.

John Paul II. *Laborem Exercens*, "On Human Work," 14 September 1981, Boston: Daughters of St. Paul.

John Paul II. *Centesimus Annus*, May 1, 1991, Vatican City: Libreria Editrice Vaticana.

Jöhr, Walter Adolf. "Walter Eucken's Lebenswerk," *Kyklos*, 1950, *4*, 257-78.

Karsten, Siegfried G. "Eucken's `Social Market Economy' and Its Test in Post-War West Germany," *American Journal of Economics and Sociology*, April 1985, *44*, 169-83.

_____. "Pastoral Economics Within the Framework of a Social Economy," *Forum for Social Economics*, Fall 1986, 45-58.

Lay Commission on Catholic Social Teaching and the U.S. Economy. *Toward the Future* New York: Lay Commission on Catholic Social Teaching and the U.S. Economy, 1984.

Lenel, Hans Otto. "Does Germany Still Have a Social Market Economy?" in *Germany's Social Market Economy: Origins and Evolution*, Alan Peacock and Hans Willgerodt, eds., New York: St. Martin's Press, 1989, 261-72.

Lerner, Aba P. "On Instrumental Analysis," in Robert L. Heilbronner, ed., *Economic Means and Social Ends*, Englewood Cliffs, NJ: Prentice Hall, 1969, 131-36.

Leo XIII. *Rerum Novarum*, "On the Condition of the Working Classes," 15 May 1891, Boston: Daughters of St. Paul.

Marshall, Alfred. *Principles of Economics*, 9th ed., London: MacMillan and Company, 1961.

Miksch, Leonard. "Walter Eucken," *Kyklos*, 1950, *4*, 279-90.

Möschel, Wernhard. "Competition Policy from an Ordo Point of View," in Alan Peacock and Hans Willgerodt, eds., *German Neo-Liberals and the Social Market Economy*, New York: St. Martin's Press, 1989, 142-59.

Mueller, Franz H. "Social Economics: The Perspective of Pesch and Solidarism," *Review of Social Economy*, December 1977, *35*, 293-97.

Müller-Armack, Alfred. "The Meaning of the Social Market Economy," in Alan Peacock and Hans Willgerodt, eds., *Germany's Social Market Economy: Origins and Evolution*, New York: St. Martin's Press, 1989, 82-86.

NCCB (National Conference of Catholic Bishops). *Economic Justice for All*, "Pastoral Letter on Catholic Social Teaching and the U.S. Economy", Washington: United States Catholic Conference, 1986. (Two earlier drafts of this Pastoral Letter were published and circulated in 1984 and 1985).

Nell-Breuning, S.J., v. Oswald. "Können Neoliberalismus und Katholische Soziallehre sich verstandigen?" in Heinz Sauermann und Ernst-Joachim Mestmacker, eds., *Wirtschaftsordnung und Staatsverfassung*, Tubingen: J.C.B. Mohr, 1975, 459-70.

Nitsch, Thomas O. *"Centesimo Anno:* The Social Encyclical of May 1991," draft of a paper to be presented at the Sixth World Congress of Social Economics, Omaha, NE, August 1991.

Paul VI. *Populorum Progressio*, "On the Development of Peoples," 26 May 1967, Boston: Daughters of St. Paul.

Pesch, Heinrich, *Lehrbuch der Nationalökonomie*, Vol. II. Freiburg i.B.: Herder, 1925.

Pigou, A. C. ed., *Memorials of Marshall*, New York: Augustus M. Kelley, 1966.

Pius XI. *Quadragesimo Anno*, "On Social Reconstruction," 15 May 1931, Boston: Daughters of St. Paul, 19-20.

Rawls, John. *A Theory of Justice*, Cambridge, MA: Harvard University Press, 1971.

Röpke, Wilhelm. *A Humane Economy*, South Bend, IN: Gateway Editions, Ltd., 1960.

Smith, Adam. *The Theory of Moral Sentiments*, New York: Augustus M. Kelley, 1966.

Walton, Clarence C. "The Connected Vessels: Economics, Ethics, and Society," *Review of Social Economy*, December 1982, *40*, 251-89.

---
❖
---

# Technology Transfer and
# Capitalist Transformation:
# A Hundred Years Later

## *Priyatosh Maitra\**

In the nineteenth century, in late-comer countries, technology transfer successfully brought about capitalist transformation. In late-comers of the Third World, a hundred years later, it is failing to achieve the same transformation. This paper attempts to analyse the factors responsible for this failure. By capitalist transformation, we mean economic-structural change (in terms of Fisher's and Kuznets-Clark's theories) which include an analysis of demographic transition as a function of the capitalist transformation of a society (A.G.B. Fisher 1939, pp. 17-23; S. Kuznets 1957; idem, 1966, pp. 86-160; and, C. Clark 1951, pp. 595-440).

We will begin with a brief account of the phases of technology transfer since the industrial revolution, which will be followed by a discussion of the indicators of the capitalist transformation, and will conclude with an examination of the need for reinterpretation of the demographic transition theory with special reference to the capitalist transformation of an economy. However, the pattern of demographic transition depends on the nature and source of technological change which, in turn, determines the level of the capitalist transformation of an economy. The demographic and the capitalist-transformation effects of technological change in an economy have been completely different a hundred years later in the Third world countries. In this paper we will re-examine the Demographic Transition Model using the experiences of the capitalist-transformation effects of technological change introduced in the Third World. In this context the two phases of technological change — extensive and intensive — will be analysed with their effects on the demand for labour and the consequent effects on the fertility rate. This will be studied using the cases of:

    (i)   the U.K., where technological change has evolved from the extensive phase to the intensive phase influencing the demographic change patterns; and,

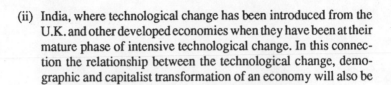

(ii) India, where technological change has been introduced from the U.K. and other developed economies when they have been at their mature phase of intensive technological change. In this connection the relationship between the technological change, demographic and capitalist transformation of an economy will also be examined using the U.K. and India as case studies.

Thus the analysis will involve re-examination of the Demographic Transition Theory in terms of effects of (i) capitalist transformation of an economy; and (ii) two phases of technological change. These two are functionally related as experienced in developed economics. The theory in its original form has ignored these two factors, which have serious effects on demographic change and, consequently, policy implications of the theory for demographic policy for the Third World have been impaired. Two cases, as mentioned earlier, have been chosen, in this study: First, the case of the British economy as the pioneer economy which underwent capitalist transformation and generated modern technological change in two phases with consequent demographic effects. The cases of France, Germany and some other European countries may also be mentioned in this group, however, with some qualifications; secondly, the case of India in the mid 20th century which has achieved substantial industrial growth with the policy of introduced technological change but failed to achieve sufficient capitalist transformation of its economy and thereby solve the enormous demographic problem.

The indicators of capitalist transformation of an economy together with definitions of extensive and intensive phases of technological change vis-à-vis demographic transition and economic growth will be presented in the following section. This will be followed by a study of the interrelationship between the demographic transition, capitalist transformation and technological change using the two contrasting cases of the U.K. and India. The paper attempts to examine whether the demographic effects depend on

(i) the extent of capitalist transformation of an economy and
(ii) nature and level of imported technological change.

The well-known Demographic Transition Theory of W.S.Thompson (1929 and 1944) and F.W. Notestein (1945, 1948, 1950 and 1953) and subsequent discussions on the theory have ignored these two aspects (for example A. P. Thirlwall 1989; Michael Todaro 1989).

We shall begin first with a brief outline of indicators of the capitalist transformation of an economy. The demographic effects of an economy depend on the nature of capitalist transformation of the society, which, in turn, is determined by the nature and sources of technological change, that is, on whether it has been introduced, as occurred in late-comer countries, as a result of technology transfer in the nineteenth and twentieth centuries, or whether it has evolved indigenously,

❖

organising and using its surplus labour with proto-technology into large scale production as was the case in the United Kingdom the only country of the Industrial Revolution (Priyatosh Maitra 1980, pp.14-69, 70-90; idem., 1986, pp.16-45; W.O. Henderson,1954 and 1953). In the cases of introduced capitalism which resulted from a technology transfer from the already developed capitalist countries, the question remains whether the transfer took place when the technology was at its extensive phase or intensive phase. The phase of relatively large-scale organisation based on an increasing division of labour to use labour and proto-technology more productively was the first phase (1760s 1860s) of the Industrial Revolution (E.J. Hobsbawm, p.29; K.E. Boulding 1983, p.3). France and Germany, for example, borrowed technology from the U.K. at the later part of this phase. Rapid capitalist transformation (relative to the present day cases of introduced capitalism via technology transfer from mature capitalist economies) marked the process of development of these countries with concommitant demographic effects (Maitra 1986, pp.30-65).

In the cases of introduced capitalism in the later period via technology transfer from the mature capitalist economies of today, technology has already reached its intensive phase, particularly since the 1950s. The capitalist transformation effects of technology transfer, in terms of economic structural change and consequently, of demographic and social changes, would be basically different from the cases of the Industrial Revolution and those of earlier technology transfer (see Tables 1A - 3a, App. A). The discussion on these effects will follow in the next section on indicators.

## I. Capitalist Transformation of an Economy: Some Basic Indicators

The capitalist transformation of a society is indicated by the following changes:

(1) Dynamic changes in the sectoral distribution of the labour force with labour gradually moving out of the primary sector to the secondary or the industrial sector, and then to the tertiary sector (C. Clark 1957; Kuznets 1966; J. Gould, 1973). These changes are functionally related to technological changes from the extensive to the intensive phases. However, in some Third World countries, the labour force dependence on agriculture has declined at the cost of disguised unemployment in the urban sector in service and family enterprise activities.

(2) With the capitalist transformation of an economy, the disguised unemployment of surplus labour, characteristic of a pre-capitalist economy, is replaced by a cyclical open unemployment. The factor price e.g. wage payment system based on the average product of

❖

labour (i.e. sharing of the output of labour in small scale and family enterprises) of the past is replaced by the marginal product. (Arthur Lewis 1957; Fei and Ranis models 1963)

(3) The capitalist transformation of an economy should have significant demographic effects. That is, with the capitalist transformation, population growth tends to rise in the initial stage, when technological change, at its extensive phase, creates increased demand for labour, and begins to decline with the rise and expansion of the intensive phase of technological change. Both these trends are affected by changes in birth rates; unlike the Third World, population growth in half-baked capitalist economies today is caused by rapidly falling mortality rates.

The above changes in economic structure, demography and the factor-pricing system must take place simultaneously because of the nature of their inter-relatedness in a society that is undergoing capitalist transformation.

Unfortunately, Third-World countries have hardly shown any sign of these changes, despite the rapid growth of modern capitalist enterprises (see above Tables 1 and 3 (App. A) showing the structural changes in different periods with India as an example). The following studies will also show the nature of capitalist transformation in India and other Asian countries despite rapid growth of modern capitalist industries.

The reference to the *Asian Drama*, a basic social study on the continent by Gunnar Myrdal (1968), however, offers a proper starting point for the discussion on the informal sector (i.e. non-capitalist sector) in South Asia. The informal sector characterizes pre industrial and pre-capitalist economic activities. He writes (pp. 112-13):

In South Asia's urban areas, [certain] economic activities are to be found, which are sometimes labelled "informally organized" although they are actually unorganized or very loosely organized. This category embraces a wide range of heterogeneous activities that have only one attribute in common: a set of institutional properties differing from those observed in either the more formally structured westernized units of production or the traditional rural crafts. These "informally organized" activities have in many ways been shaped by Western intervention and the increase in monetized economic activity accompanying it. Some are geared to serve modern demands—at least for those types of goods and services increasingly sought as a result of the expansion of monetized economic activity and import restrictions. Most, however, have tended to perpetuate traditional patterns, such as an emphasis on the family as the central unit of productive organization. The services sector contains perhaps the most conspicuous and

❖

pervasive example of the loosely organized—if not totally unorganized—type of economic activity. In South Asia service occupations
typically account for a far larger proportion of the urban labor force
than do all varieties of urban manufacturing.

The crowded field of retail trade accounts for a substantial share of the tertiary
sector's claim on the labor force. Much retail trade is conducted on a petty basis by
itinerant hawkers and pedlars.
        An Indian economist, B. Dasgupta, (1982, pp. 23-24) presents a very
illuminating account of India's unorganised sector based on his research:

> The presence of a large, elastic informal sector in the bigger urban
> centres is an important feature of urban life in India. According to
> various estimates, the informal sector accounts for between two-fifth
> and half of the earners in the major industrial centres of the country.
> Compared with the size of this sector, its contribution to national
> product is marginal; the vast majority of coolies, domestic servants,
> street pedlars and trades, magicians, car-minders and so on are under-
> taking those activities, not because they are remunerative, but because
> that alternatives to these are unemployment and no income. The
> informal sector is usually dominated by migrants, especially the more
> recent ones who do not see any immediate prospect of a regular job,
> and who, for various reasons, are unwilling to return to their villages.
> The ease of entry, small need of capital and skill, and the flexibility of
> operation attract them to a wide range of informal activities.

Limited capitalist transformation effects can be assessed also from the
following research studies. Conditions described above are getting worse as days
go by because of the failure of industrial growth to create sufficient demand for
labour in organised productive activities. Technological change is becoming
increasingly human-capital intensive, requiring a higher level of human capital.
Quality labour is replacing quantity labour and therefore, the number of disguised
unemployed in all unorganised and family labour based activities: agricultural
service, transport and small industries are growing.
        According to V.M. Dandekar (1978, pp. 179-80) "it is only monopoly capital,
whether state or private, and monopoly labour, that is organized, which can
combine and share common gains. This organized sector comprising about 20
million workers constitutes only one-ninth of the total working population."
        A recent study (I. Levi 1989, p. 194) based on the 1981 Census of Population
shows the following distribution of workers:

1. Pre-Capitalist Class
   Cultivator class
   Agricultural labourers                              73.5%
   Household industry
2. Independent workers in the capitalist sector        8.9%
3. Employees                                             2%
4. White collar employees                              6.8%
5. Blue collar workers                                 9.8%

According to Dandekar like many others, the process of capitalist transformation in India has been checked "because of the rise of the state and private monopoly capital and monopoly of the organized labour". Perfect competition prevailed when technology was simple requiring a relatively small resource commitment and small market. With the development of intensive technology, perfect competition has been transformed into a monopoly and subsequently monopolistic competition as the basic condition, because a large market and an increasingly sophisticated resource base (human capital and more productive energy) requires concentration of resources, markets and a decision making process, in a few monopolistic but competitive organizations to make the technology nationally and gradually internationally competitive. India's industrial growth is based on imported technology from the West when its technology has reached the mature intensive phase. Therefore, monopolistic concentration of resources and control of the market have resulted long before we have traversed the perfect competition stage of early capitalist development. Trade-union monopoly is also an inevitable development in the Western labour short economies and and we have imported this trade union practice with technology as a part of the package of the technology transfer. In the nineteenth century the situation was different as discussed in my works (Maitra 1980, 1986, and 1991). Dandekar and most other economists consider technology as 'neutral' to history, factor endowments and the economic system and its aims of production and hence this confusion.

## II. The Demographic Transition Theory: A Brief Outline

With this background of knowledge of limited effects of capitalist transformation based on imported technology when it is at its intensive phase, we should examine the Demographic Transition Theory.

The Demographic Transition Theory can be traced to works of W.S. Thompson (1929 and 1944) and of F.W. Notestein (1945, 1948, 1950 and 1953). Thompson-Notestein theory seeks to explain the causes of the modern rise of population via the effects of modernisation.

Notestein's 1945 article is important in the sense that it outlines the mechanism by which the demographic transition had occurred and could take place in the future together with the causes of the inferred changes. According to Notestein, "the growth of population came from the decline of mortality" and "so far as we can tell from the available evidence, no substantial part of the modern population growth has come from a rise in fertility" (Notestein 1950, p.39). The fertility rate in all pre-industrial societies was already high and therefore, further substantial acceleration could not occur. The death rate was also equally high and occasionally in those days it rose further. But with the onset of the agricultural and industrial revolution, availability of better food, shelter, sanitation and clothing, the death rate began to decline slowly and later with the development of modern medical technology and health services, it started falling sharply. The birth rate remained high but began to decline with increasing demand for labour in excess of its supply. We have explained this.

Notestein's theory can be summarised here in the form of four propositions:

1. The demographic revolution is initiated by the secular decline of mortality.
2. Mortality decline is caused by the cumulative influences of the agricultural, the industrial and the sanitary revolutions which, respectively, lead to better food supplies, an improvement in the factors of production and the standard of living in general, and improvements in public health.
3. Rapid population growth is the result of the temporal lag between the decline of mortality and that of fertility.
4. Fertility decline eventually occurs because the social and economic supports to high fertility are removed. The materialism and indi-vidualism associated with the urban way of life give impetus to the rational control of fertility by means of contraceptive practices.

In Notestein's theory of demographic transition, three stages are involved: high mortality and high fertility; low mortality and high fertility; low mortality and low fertility. The analysis of demographic effects of technological change and the capitalist transformation of an economy requires reinter-pretation of the Demo-graphic Transition Theory. The theory has ignored these basic factors in influenc-ing the demographic change. Analysis of these two factors will help us in understanding the difficulties in applying this model to explain the demographic trends in the Third World and also the basic factors that brought about the demographic transition in the developed capitalist economics which have been left out in the original model. This present analysis has serious policy implications.

## III. A New Interpretation of the Demographic Transition Theory: Technological Change and the Capitalist Transformation

We now attempt to reinterpret the Demographic Transition (DT) Model and explain the limitations of its applicability to the Third World. When technological

————————————————— ❖ —————————————————

change evolves within an economy from the stage of proto-technology through the extensive to the intensive phases, consequent changes in the economic structure in terms of dynamic changes in the sectoral distribution of the labour force reflect the process of the capitalist transformation of the economy, as has been the case with the U.K. first followed by late-comers of the 19th century (cf. Tables 1 and 2, App. A). This process of transformation creates first a demand for labour in excess of its supply, which then promotes conditions conducive to the decline in population growth. This happens when the need for the intensive phase of technological change emerges when modern science begins to be used in production (1860's). In the Third World, the above conditions favourable to the decline in population growth do not arise because of their faulty technology approach. As noted, the DT theory can be traced to works of W.S. Thompson (1929 and 1944) and F.W. Notestein (1945, 1948, 1950 and 1953). Recent developments of this theory may be summed up as follows:

The First Stage is marked by high birth rates and high death rates. The pre-industrial period in most economies has this demographic characteristic. The beginning of the second stage of demographic transition was initiated during the first quarter of the 19th century when the Industrial revolution in the U.K. was at its extensive phase of technological change. This Second Stage of demographic transition is characterised by slowly falling death rates and the continuation of high birth rates. It is mainly caused by its relatively high demand for labour and thereby making child labour an important source of labour, which had the effect of maintaining the previous trend in the high birth rate. This period was also accompanied by slowly falling death rates, due to better economic conditions and the improvements in medical and sanitation services.

The Third Stage of declining birth rates did not really begin until the intensive phase of technological change had progressed substantially, i.e. until the late 19th century. The intensive phase of technological change was accompanied by the rapid expansion of literacy, primary and secondary education and soon by higher education. Obviously this had an effect on the fertility of the population. The Third Stage was also gradually accompanied by a mass consumption stage which also affected fertility rates. The neoclassical model of family fertility has tended to explain it in its familiar market-mechanism model. The technological explanation has been advanced above. The economic structure at this stage becomes dominated by the Tertiary Sector in which research and development activities in technology, education, information, and communication infrastructure play the dominant role. In the early phase of modern technological change, i.e. from the beginning of the extensive phase until the early intensive phase when demand for labour gradually begins to exceed its supply, economic structural change is indicated by labour moving out of agriculture into the manufacturing sector. Primary or agricultural sectors by then began to shed labour for industry, which in turn started supplying productive inputs for agriculture. (See Tables 2 and 3, App. A.)

The model of microeconomic determinants of family fertility, advanced in recent times to explain rapidly falling birth rates in developed economies today, is shown in the Third Stage of the DT Model ( M. Todaro 1989 and A. P. Thirlwall 1989; E. A. Wrigley 1969). This model is based on the traditional neoclassical framework of household and consumer behaviour in the mass-consumption stage of development of a society and uses the principles of economy and optimisation to explain family size decisions. According to this model demand for children is determined by the given level of income. The costs of having a child (i.e. the difference between "anticipation costs"), are mostly the opportunity cost of a mother's time and benefits, potential child income and old age support, prices of all other goods and the tastes for goods relative to children. Some economists and demographers regard the time element as the most important factor in influencing technological change and thus demographic trends. The technological change from extensive to intensive phase is a result, first, of increasing demand for "quantity" labour followed by demand for "quality" labour when science began to be introduced in production to substitute the former and the need to be competitive in national and international markets. The following changes are intended to use time more productively:

I.   The Extensive Phase Period of Technological Change ( P. Maitra 1986 and 1991). — In this stage, the demand for "quantity" labour was high which stimulated the fertility rate; therefore, this period is marked by a high birth rate (Fig. 1, App. B). This was reflected in the movement of the labour force away from the agricultural to the industrial sector (Table 1, App. A).

II.  The Intensive Phase Period of Technological Change (P. Maitra 1986 and 1991). — This is the period when the demand for labour exceeded its supply, necessitating the introduction of science (i.e. modern technology) in production to substitute "quality" for "quantity" labour. A period of declining birth rate ensued (Fig. I, App. B; Table 1-3, App. A).

These changes had effects first on the structure of the economy which was marked by an increasing proportion of the labour force being absorbed in manufacturing activities in place of agriculture and which then began to bear the burden of increasingly smaller population, and in the development of education from primary to secondary, whence higher education. With the emergence of the intensive phase, the tertiary sector began to absorb the larger proportion of skilled labour and the secondary sector's share declined. Tables 1, 2 and 3 and Figure II (App. A and B) illustrate this.

The First Phase of technological change (i.e. the extensive phase) failed to emerge in the Third World societies. The birth rate remained high until the 1960s, when there was a slight decline due to the modern sector effects on a limited section

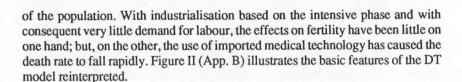

of the population. With industrialisation based on the intensive phase and with consequent very little demand for labour, the effects on fertility have been little on one hand; but, on the other, the use of imported medical technology has caused the death rate to fall rapidly. Figure II (App. B) illustrates the basic features of the DT model reinterpreted.

## IV. Demographic Effects and the Population Question

The basic point about demographic effects is that with the onset of the capitalist transformation of an economy, population growth tends to decline as a result of an increasing demand for labour in productive activities. The main point is about the spontaneous decline of population growth resulting from relatively high economic growth and the sustained demand for labour in excess of its supply. This became evident in the U.K. after the late nineteenth century. Children, hitherto, regarded as assets began to be considered as burdens which had profound demographic effects notably, a declining birthrate. This change in attitude was reinforced by the need for sending children to schools to acquire skills which were in great demand, as skilled jobs in the meantime became competitive. When technology was simpler and at the extensive phase, the supply of quantity labour was adequate and job markets obviously were not competitive. With the technological change from the extensive to intensive phase, the need for skills, with job markets becoming increasingly competitive, made parents conscious of family size. This was the period when the financial responsibility of education of children was borne by parents. When technological change needed "quality" labour the supply of "quantity" labour automatically declined in the process. Family planning, the technique of which was already in the market, began to receive a spontaneous response. With the increased demand for labour, time becomes the most important factor of production. Technological change helps by reducing the need for time per unit of labour and output. And technological change, at this stage, by definition requires quality labour and not quantity labour, which in turn creates the condition for a spontaneous response to family planning. (Technological change at the initial stage needed more labour to bring about improvement in existing proto-technology organized in large scale units at the "manufactory" stage).

Secondly, a sustained demand for labour indicates a relatively high rate of growth and an increasing possibility of jobs for women with or without skills. Thus, the opportunity cost of rearing a larger family became prohibitive. Higher education and/or vocational training led to the delay in marriage and/or reluctance to have a larger family.

Thirdly, when the economy reaches the mass consumption stage (as defined by Rostow 1960), the choice between consumer durables and the number of children one will have, results in a falling birth rate in the circumstances of a capitalist system where consumption demand at the mass consumption stage is greatly influenced by consumerism effects and income-distribution effects. Under these circumstances, people become conscious of the need for family planning which gradually becomes an in-built condition of such a society. High economic growth caused by rapid expansion of foreign trade, the need for constant technological change to be competitive in the local and international markets and later growing consumerism result in a falling birth rate and an increasing supply of human capital of higher level. People become receptive to family planning, a technique which also undergoes improvement all the time with technological change. In other words, a shortage of labour increases the need for skilled and more productive labour to substitute quality labour for quantity labour, and technological change with economic growth is mainly stimulated by the rapid expansion of foreign trade which technological change makes possible. In Marxian terms, stored capital embodied in human capital becomes the main factor of production in the developed or post-industrial economies. These economies are characterised by very low growth of the population because of a falling birthrate to almost 12 per thousand per annum with a death rate of about 14 per thousand. But the rapid technological change and the increasing sophistication of skills are proving more than enough to meet the requirements of labour as a factor of production in these economies. Growing unemployment of human capital has become a disturbing trend in these economies in recent times. Technological change from the extensive through intensive phase to the mature intensive phase of post-industrial stage in developed economies is reflected in their economic structural changes (See Table 2 on U.K. in App. A.).

## V. The Population Question

According to the recent U.N. report on World Population (cf. "The Population Bomb," 1991), India will face a serious population and a consequent resource crisis by the end of this decade. It seems that we do not learn lessons from history. We are very keen on borrowing technology, education, capital and so-called modern things from the West because it is easier to borrow those things than making efforts to think and also to learn from what the history of these labour short economies has to offer as lessons. When an economy creates sustained productive demand for labour in excess of its supply, population growth i.e. the birth rate, spontaneously tends to decline entirely for economic reasons. Family planning then becomes a matter of inbuilt condition of such development. To create effective demand for labour is a function of technological change. Imported technology today, undoubtedly brings about tremendous growth in output and in its diversification, but creates little demand for labour.

Population growth in this kind of technological change is stimulated or at least remains high because of the effects of

(i)   imported medical technology on one hand, and on the other,

(ii)  the lack of demand effects of such imported labour dispensing technology.

❖

Surplus labour, therefore, has to depend on labour-intensive technology which either stimulates the birth rate or makes people indifferent towards family size. The dictum is that the larger the family, the higher is the total income of the family in such labour surplus economies. We have never been taught that population growth and the nature of technological change are functionally related. When population growth results from increased economic demand for labour, it stimulates the fertility rate and thereby induces further economic growth, which in turn creates further demand for labour. When an economy reaches this condition (England in the nineteenth century exemplified this condition), demand for labour was so high that child labour prevailed for a long time and even attending school was discouraged so that the supply of labour to factories was not reduced. This is the first stage. Science is used in production to make more productive use of the existing labour force, in other words, the process of substituting for quantity labour by quality labour (i.e. human resource by human capital) emerges in any economy. This results in an automatic decline in birth rate for entirely economic reasons. (England again supplies the example: the birth rate began to decline in England from the late 19th century.) This development indicates the first criterion of the beginning of the process of capitalist transformation of a society.

Thus population growth patterns (i.e. the period of high population growth as a result of increased economic demand for labour, followed by the period of declining population growth as a result of the excess of economic demand over supply of labour, necessitated the use of science in production and thus technological change and development of education become interrelated in replacing the human resource by human capital or, in other words, quantity labour by quality labour), technological change and development of education are interrelated (see Maitra 1990 and 1991).

The sustained and effective demand for labour is reflected in the economic-structural change indicated by the dynamic sectoral distribution of the labour force away from agriculture to the secondary and later the tertiary sector. All capitalist countries have had to pass through these changes and are still undergoing this process. This indicates the second basic criterion of the capitalist transformation of a society. India, on the other hand, borrows technology from these countries with her stagnant economic structure heavily biased towards agriculture (absorbing nearly 70 percent of the labour force for the last century) indicating the capitalist transformation is confined to only about 12-15 percent of the economy. This type of capitalist transformation lacks the essential quality of capitalism i.e. dynamism, meaning that when capitalism emerges in a society, it gradually and rapidly transforms the entire pre-capitalist economy into a dynamic capitalist one. In the case of an introduced capitalism, the transformation process remains confined to a limited area.

Thus by following a policy of importing technology and pushing family planning, even if an economy becomes successful in reducing population growth and raising output per capita, it would not be able to get rid of its population problem, poverty and underdeveloped economic structure. India's population problem, underdeveloped economic structure and poverty on one hand, and rapidly increasing sophistication of the industrial sector on the other, provide sufficient testimony to this.

The so-called danger of the world's resource depletion in the near future was disputed by many economists on the ground that the history of natural resource use shows that the increasing scarcity of particular resources fosters discovery and the development of alternative resources, not only equal in quality but often superior to those replaced. This is simply because every subsequent stage of the need for newer resources requires increasingly higher levels of human capital, technology, organization and infrastructure. The physical quantity of resources is not known at any point in time, because resources are only sought and found when they are needed and when societies are ready for them.

Energy consumption up to the 19th century was characterised by man's use of renewable energy resources, primarily through the food he consumed but later through the utilisation of beast of burden, wind and falling water. Increasingly, population growth and its pressure on existing resources led to the more productive use of fuels at the initial stage of Industrial Revolution and subsequently, to relatively more productive fossil fuels, first coal and then petroleum. In turning to the future, it seems unlikely that non-renewable fossil fuels will predominate in man's energy use far into the 21st century. Hopefully, human capital, technology and infrastructure would also evolve to be ready to use effectively renewable sources based on backstop technology.

Energy use patterns have always been conditioned by the level of economic development, i.e. by the level of the economic infrastructure and factor endowments. India has a vast but idle human resource base due to the underdeveloped economic structure, i.e an unutilised natural resource. Resource scarcity that we face today is an artificial one caused by our dependence on imported technology with very little local human resource content.

## VI. Conclusion

The capitalist transformation of an economy in terms of demographic change and sectoral distribution of the labour force depends on technological change. With technological change indigenously developed from its traditional proto-technology as in the U.K. at the time of the Industrial Revolution, the transformation automatically takes place; when the technological change takes place in a country as a result of its transfer, the capitalist transformation of its economy depends on the stage of the technological change. If it takes place when it is at its extensive phase (i.e. labour absorbing phase), it creates demand for labour in excess of its supply and thus produces effects of demographic and capitalist transformation of the economy. If the technological change is at its intensive phase, technology transfer fails to create demand for labour and lead to the capitalist transformation of the economy. The problem of overpopulation of an economy and resource

❖

scarcity is essentially a matter of the nature and source of technological change as discussed above. Technology transfer, although once successful in achieving the capitalist transformation of the economy, one hundred years later is proving unsuccessful for reasons stated earlier. The demographic-transition theory, therefore, needs reinterpretation so that its policy implications are put right.

Patterns of population growth, depend on the growth of demand for labour in productive activities, which, in turn, depends on the nature of the source of technological change, indigenous or introduced, and on the phase of the change, i.e. extensive or intensive. The DT model has ignored this aspect. Another more important implication of this study is that imported technology, when it has reached its mature intensive phase, cannot bring about the capitalist transformation of the economy leading to a full fledged and integrated development.

In terms of analyses of both Bourgeois and Marxist economists, the capitalist transformation of an economy is an essential condition of economic development, while according to the former, it is ultimate, and in the latter's view, it is a precondition for ultimate development, i.e. socialism followed by communism. The collapse of the socialist system based on technology borrowed from the capitalist system has thrown a flood of light on this issue (see Maitra, 1992).

Lastly, I would like to refer to a valuable work of Clem Tisdell (1990) which has an excellent summary (Ch. 5) of pessimistic and optimistic views, and predictions about economic growth and natural resource availability. I agree with his conclusion (p. 72) on this aspect.

Few, if any, grounds exist for being complacently optimistic that technological progress will extricate us without fail from the predicament that we may face due to continuing economic growth and careless and profligate use of non renewable resources to satisfy high levels of mass consumption.

That is, the ultimate solution to the resource problem depends on how we would change our present consumption and production patterns. Tisdell's conclusion (pp. 162-63) is worth noting here; viz. that "in the choice of a suitable development path, we cannot be safely guided by individualistic self-interest alone but must pay attention to relationships between human beings and between humans and nature." This view can be translated into a (the) Marxian conception of industrialisation as "the humanisation of nature and naturalisation of human being" (cf. Marx 1975, p. 298; idem., 1954, p. 715). This, however, raises a vital question regarding the nature of the economic system and its aim of production.

*Associate Professor, Department of Economics, University of Otago, P.O. Box 56, Dunedin, New Zealand.

❖

# Appendix A: Tables

## Table 1

**Population Change in India and United Kingdom:
Crude Birth Rate and Crude Death Rate (per 1000)**

A.

| India | CBR | CDR | PGR |
|-------|-----|-----|-----|
| 1965  | 45  | 21  | 24  |
| 1987  | 32  | 11  | 21  |

Source: World Bank Development Report, 1989.

B.

| United Kingdom | CBR | CDR | PGR |
|----------------|------|------|------|
| 1776-1800 | 35.5 | 26.4 | 9.1 |
| 1826-1850 | 36.0 | 22.5 | 13.5 |
| 1851-1875 | 35.8 | 22.2 | 13.6 |
| 1876-1900 | 32.8 | 19.2 | 13.0 |
| 1901-1925 | 24.2 | 14.2 | 10.0 |
| 1926-1950 | 16.6 | 12.2 | 3.9 |
| 1951-1975 | 16.7 | 11.7 | 5.0 |

Source: Mathias, P. and Davis, J. A. (eds) The First Industrial Revolution.
Oxford: Basil Blackwell, 1989, 142.

C.

| United Kingdom | BIRTH RATE | DEATH RATE |
|----------------|------------|------------|
| 1965 | 18 | 12 |
| 1987 | 13 | 12 |

Source: World Bank Development Report, 1989.

continued . . .

❖

D.    **Population of Undivided India**    (In Millions)

| Year | Population | % growth from previous year | Year | Population | % growth from previous year |
|---|---|---|---|---|---|
| 1872 | 255 | | 1921 | 306 | + 0.99 |
| 1881 | 257 | + 0.78 | 1931 | 338 | + 10.46 |
| 1891 | 282 | + 9.73 | 1941 | 389 | + 15.09 |
| 1901 | 285 | + 1.06 | 1951 | 437 | + 12.34 |
| 1911 | 303 | + 6.32 | 1961 | 534 | + 22.20 |

"The main reason for the growth of population by an acceleration since 1931 was the check to the so-called positive checks, eradication of malaria, weakening impact of epidemics, resulting in a stationary birth rate and a declining death rate. But qualitatively the growth has regressiveness in its blood. An economic growth implies a constant transfer of surplus population from village to urban centres of non-agricultural actives (sic), a constant shift from primary to secondary and tertiary sectors. But this process never started. On the contrary, after three plans, the main problem of unemployment is one of a swelling backlog gaining momentum like a snow ball in course of its movement over time towards an avalanche."

Source: D.P. Battacharyya, 1969.

## Table 2

### Broad Occupational Distribution of Labour Force: United Kingdom

| Year | Primary | | Secondary | | Transport and Communications | Service Sector | | | Other | |
|---|---|---|---|---|---|---|---|---|---|---|
| | Agriculture Fishing and Forestry | Mining | Construction | Manufacture, Elec. and Gas | | Commerce and Finance | Profession & Entertainment | Government Services | Private Domestic Services | Short Services |
| 1841 | 23.1 | 3.1 | 5.8 | 36.6 | 3.0 | 5.7 | 2.9 | 1.1 | | 19.1 |
| 1881 | 12.3 | 4.1 | 6.7 | 39.9 | 5.9 | 9.2 | 3.8 | 1.9 | 16.6 | |
| 1901 | 8.7 | 5.9 | 8.0 | 32.5 | 9.8 | 11.0 | 4.4 | 2.5 | 14.3 | 2.0 |
| 1911 | 7.8 | 6.9 | 5.2 | 34.6 | 8.0 | 18.7 | | 4.2 | 9.0 | 5.6 |
| 1921 | 6.7 | 7.3 | 4.1 | 38.7 | 8.1 | 13.2 | 3.7 | 6.4 | 7.0 | 4.5 |
| 1951 | 4.5 | 3.9 | 6.3 | 39.5 | 7.8 | 14.2 | 7.0 | 8.0 | 2.3 | 6.8 |

Source: Colin Clark, The Conditions of Economic Progress, 1957, 515.

Note: This table indicates the pattern of broad occupational distribution of the labour force in a developed economy. This may be compared with Table 3a giving the same information for India for the period 1901-1961.

## Table 3a

### Percentage Distribution of Workers by Industrial Categories, 1901-1961 (India)

| Year | Total population | Total workers | Non-workers | Cultivator | Agricultural labour | Mining, livestock forestry fishing housing etc. | Household industry | Manufacturing, other than household | Construction | Trade and commerce | Transport, storage, communications | Other services |
|---|---|---|---|---|---|---|---|---|---|---|---|---|
| | | | | PRIMARY SECTOR | | | SECONDARY SECTOR | | | TERTIARY OR SERVICE SECTOR | | |
| 1901 | (100) | 100 (46.61) | (53.39) | 50.64 (23.61) | 16.89 (7.87) | 4.33 (2.01) | - | 11.73 (5.47) | 0.78 (0.36) | 6.05 (2.82) | 1.12 (0.53) | 8.46 (3.94) |
| 1911 | (100) | 100 (48.07) | (51.93) | 49.49 (23.94) | 20.57 (9.88) | 4.74 (2.80) | - | 9.93 (4.77) | 0.96 (0.46) | 5.51 (2.65) | 1.12 (0.54) | 7.38 (3.55) |
| 1921 | (100) | 100 (46.92) | (53.08) | 54.39 (25.52) | 17.40 (8.16) | 4.48 (2.10) | - | 9.29 (4.36) | 0.84 (0.40) | 5.79 (2.69) | 0.94 (0.44) | 6.93 (3.25) |
| 1931 | (100) | 100 (43.30) | (56.70) | 45.04 (19.51) | 24.79 (10.73) | 5.18 (2.24) | - | 8.91 (3.86) | 1.04 (0.45) | 5.59 (2.42) | 1.08 (0.44) | 8.42 (3.65) |
| 1951 | (100) | 100 (39.10) | (60.90) | 50.02 (19.56) | 19.72 (7.71) | 2.96 (1.15) | - | 9.00 (3.52) | 1.05 (0.41) | 5.24 (2.05) | 1.53 (0.64) | 10.49 (4.10) |

Source: B.R. Kabra, "A note on the working force Estimate 1901-1961," in Final Population Tables Paper No. 1, 1962.

Note: Figures in brackets indicate percentage distribution of population into workers and non-workers classified by broad occupation.

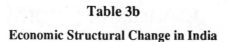

## Table 3b
### Economic Structural Change in India

Labour Force Distribution

| Year | Agriculture | Industry | Service |
|------|-------------|----------|---------|
| 1965 | 74 | 11 | 15 |
| 1983 | 71 | 13 | 16 |

Sectoral Domestic Product

| Year | (A) | (I) | (M) | (S) |
|------|-----|-----|-----|-----|
| 1965 | 47 | 22 | 15 | 31 |
| 1983 | 36 | 26 | 15 | 38 |

Source: World Development Report, 1985.

# Appendix B: Figures

**Demographic Transition Model Reinterpreted**

**Figure I**
**Developed Capitalist Economies: The Case of the U.K.**

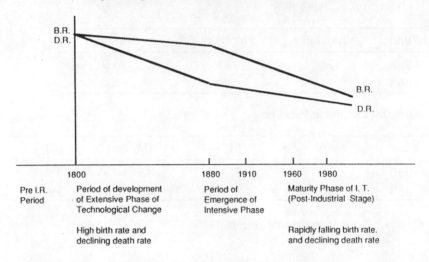

| Pre I.R.
Period | Period of development
of Extensive Phase of
Technological Change | Period of
Emergence of
Intensive Phase | Maturity Phase of I. T.
(Post-Industrial Stage) |

High birth rate and
declining death rate                     Rapidly falling birth rate.
                                          and declining death rate

**Figure II**
**Developing Economies: The Case of India**

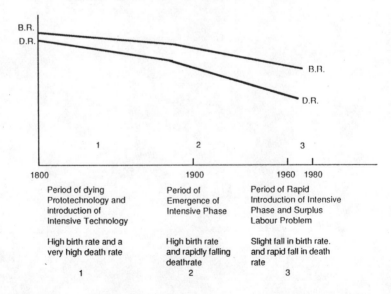

| Period of dying
Prototechnology and
introduction of
Intensive Technology | Period of
Emergence of
Intensive Phase | Period of Rapid
Introduction of Intensive
Phase and Surplus
Labour Problem |

High birth rate and a          High birth rate          Slight fall in birth rate.
very high death rate           and rapidly falling      and rapid fall in death
                               deathrate                rate

1                              2                        3

❖

# References

Armengaud, Andre. "Population in Europe 1700-1914" in C.M. Cipolla, ed., *The Industrial Revolution*, London: The Fontana Economic History of Europe, 1973.

Bhattacharyya, D. P. "Socio-Economic Trends in India," in *Trends of Socio-Economic Change in India 1871-61*, Simla: Indian Institute of Advanced Studies, 1969, 15-41.

Boulding, Kenneth E. "Technology in the Evolutionary Process," in S. Macdonald et al., eds., *The Trouble with Technology*, London: Francis Pinter, 1983.

Clark, Colin. *The Condition of Economic Progress*, London: Macmillan, 1957.

Dandekar, V. M. "Nature of the Class Conflict in the Indian Society," *Artha Vignan, 20*, 1978.

Dasgupta, B. "Migration and Development," Paris: UNESCO Reports and Papers in the Social Sciences, 1982.

Fei, John and Ranis, Gustave. "A Theory of Economic Development," *American Economic Review*, May 1961, 553-565.

Fisher, A.G.B. "Production: Primary, Secondary, and Tertiary," *Economic Record*, March 1939, 17-23.

Gould, John. *Economic Growth in History*, London: Methuen, 1973.

Henderson, W.O. *Britain and Industrialization in Europe*, Liverpool University Press, 1954.

_____. *Britain and the Industrial Revolution*, Liverpool University Press, 1955.

Hobsbawm, E. J. *Industry and Empire*, London: Penguin, 1969.

Kabra, B.R. *Final Population Tables*, 1901-61, Census of India, No.1, 1962.

Kuznets, Simon. "Industrial Distribution of National Products and Labour Force," *Economic Development and Cultural Change*, July 1957, 6, 84-91.

_____. *Modern Economic Growth*, New Haven: Yale University Press, 1966.

Levi, Imre. "Unorganized Unemployment and Organized Employment," *Asian Journal of Economics and Social Studies, 8*, 1989.

Lewis, Arthur. "Development of Labour Surplus Economy," *Manchester School*, 1954, 22, 139-91.

Maitra, Priyatosh. *Population, Technology and Development*, Aldershot: Gower, 1986.

_____. *The Mainspring of Economic Development*, London: Croom Helm and New York: St. Martin's Press, 1980.

_____. "Education, Technological Change and Structural Change," in G. Tortella, ed., *Education and Economic Development since the Industrial Revolution,* Valencia: UIMP, 1990, 185-209.

_____. (1991a) "Education, Technological Change and Economic Development," *Indian Journal of Social Science,* July 1991, 4.

_____. (1991b) *Indian Economic Development, Population Growth and Technological Change,* New Delhi: A.H.P.,1991, 7-23.

_____. "Technological Change in the USSR and Return to a Market Economy," *International Journal of Social Economics,* forthcoming (1992).

Marx, Karl. "Private Property and Communism" (1844), as in Karl Marx and Frederick Engels, *Collected Works,* Vol. 3; New York: International Publishers, 1975, 293-306.

_____. *Capital,* Vol. I; Moscow: Progress Publishers, 1954ff.

Mathias, Peter and Davis, John A. *The First Industrial Revolution,* London: Blackwell, 1989.

Myrdal, Gunnar. *Asian Drama,* Vol. II, London: Hammondsworth, 1968.

Notestein, F. W. "Population: The Long View," in T.W. Schultz, ed., *Food for the World,* Chicago: Chicago University Press, 1945.

_____. "Summary of the Demographic Background of Problems of Underdeveloped Areas," *Milk Bank Memorial Fund Quarterly,* 1948, 26, 249-255.

_____. "The Population of the World in the Year 2000," *Journal of the American Statistical Association,* 1950, 45, 335-45.

_____. "Economic Problems of Population Change," in *Proceedings of the 8th International Conference of Agricultural Economists,* London: Oxford University Press, 1953, 13-31.

O'Brien, Pat and Kuyder, C. *Economic Growth in France and Britain 1780-1914,* London: George Allen and Unwin.

OECD. *Manpower Statistics,* 1950-62, Paris, 1963.

_____. "Population Bomb," editorial, *The Statesman Weekly,* New Dehli and Calcutta, 19 June, 1991.

Rostow, W.W. *The Stages of Economic Growth,* London: Cambridge University Press, 1960.

Teich, M. "Science and Technology in the 20th Century," *4th International Economic History Congress, 1968,* London: Mourton, 1973.

Thirlwall, A.P. *Growth and Development,* London: Macmillan, 1989.

Thompson, W.S. "Population," *American Journal of Sociology,* 1929, 34, 959-75.

❖

_____. *Plenty of People*, Lancaster Pa.: Cattel Press, 1944.

Tisdell, Clem. *Natural Resources, Growth and Development*, New York: Praeger, 1990.

Todaro, Michael. *Economic Development in the Third World*, London: Longman, 1989.

Wrigley, E. A. *Population and History*, London: Weidenfeld and Nicholson, 1969.

The World Bank. *World Development Report*, New York: Oxford University Press, 1985 and 1989.

# The Influence of the Encylicals on the Solidarist Theory of Social Economy

## William R. Waters*

The *Review of Social Economy (RSE)* first published in 1944 was the organ of the Catholic Economic Association (CEA), founded in 1941. The papal encylicals, with their insistence that economies be ethically reconstructed, influenced the establishment of this organization and its review. Of primary inportance were the 1891 encyclical, *Rerum Novarum (RN)* and its 1931 extension, *Quadragesimo Anno (QA)*. To paraphrase and abridge the seven aims and objectives listed in the January, 1944 issue of the *RSE* (January, 1944, pp. 108-111), the CEA had as its purpose to extend and develop economics, particularly that part of the science that treats the relationship of economic to other values, to resolve problems of policy, to clarify the science's relationship with other social disciplines particularly social philosophy, to evaluate its assumptions and methods and to forumlate practical programs all in the light of Christian moral social principles. Such principles were at the heart of *RN* and *QA*. Almost thirty years later, in 1970, the members of the organization changed its name to Association for Social Economics (ASE) in order to broaden its membership and signal a clearer welcome to non-Catholics. New aims and objectives no longer stipulate an exclusively Christian approach but the influence of many of the economists who started the organization remains strong, as does the inspiration of the encylicals.

This paper is a review of contributions to a theory of social economy by writers in the *RSE* from volume one in 1942 to volume 28 in 1970, the first issue of the *RSE* as a publication of the Association of Social Economics instead of the Catholic Economic Association. But first two notes, one on the meaning of "theory of social economy" and the other the best name for the kind of social economic theory that evolved under the influence of the encyclicals. In the 1965 volume of the *RSE* social economic theory was defined as comprising "the principles that shape the economic sector of society" and supply "the means to evaluate policies,

———————————————————— ❖ ————————————————————

welfare models and planning" (Waters 1965, p. 115). Further, it is that body of knowledge that explains the nature of economic reality in a broad (social) sense and evaluates the ethical validity of its institutional structure. The best choice of name for the theory that developed under the influence of the encyclicals is probably solidarist, although no name is completely satisfactory in an area where names (liberal, capitalist, socialist, and so forth) are emotionally charged. Solidarism is most often used to identify the personalist approach pioneered by the German Jesuit social economist and intellectual *grand pere,* Heinrich Pesch (1854-1926), so closely identified with this tradition.

The order of appearance in this paper of the building blocks of the theory is mostly chronological beginning with a contribution by one of the giants of the field, Bernard Dempsey.

## I. On the Validity of the Concept of Equilibrium in Social Economics

In the third article published in the *RSE* titled (very relevantly to our task) "Economics in the Social Encyclicals," Dempsey writes of the economics of *QA* as an institutionalist economics. As such, and unlike "economics taught to Americans [which] has been a lineal descendant of eigthteenth century French 'Liberalism,'" it is an economics of dynamic, social, corporative equilibrium..." (Dempsey 1942, pp. 15, 18).

This claim was not tasty food for thought for some members of the CEA because while they agreed to the dynamic and social aspects of the approach and with the view to corporate, semi-autonomous societies within the economy at large, the suggestion that economics should include equilibrium as one of its heuristic devices was jarring and reactionary. Not surprisingly, then, in a discussion of Dempsey's article, John Shea (1942, p. 20) makes this very point.

> From a methodological point of view, these conclusions (that the economics of th encyclicals is an economics of dynamic, social, corporate equilibrium) are strange bed fellows. Since Institutionalists have little patience with Equilibrium Theorists, it is confusing to have the encyclicals put in both camps.

Dempsey's view that equilibrium belongs as a tool in a sound social economics was convincing but the kind of role he proposed for it was not. Dempsey agreed that the concept of equilibrium came to economics from the social philosophy of the Enlightenment in the eighteenth century when the science was in its very formative stages. Enlightenment philosophy was instrumental in changing the perspective away from the Aristotelian/Xenophonic tradition concerned with managing (as one manages a household, says Xenophon) to one of viewing the economy as operating automatically according to the forces of the natural physical

❖

law. The very name economics from two Greek words for household and to rule reflects this approach. Equilibrium, on the other hand, is part of a later perspective of automaticity, analogous to the working of the solar system described by Newton. The two perspectives are opposites. If accepted fully, automaticity reduces management from a pivotal position in economic life to a law of nature. Moreover, since part of the natural lawfulness viewed by Adam Smith and others is the propensity to behave "rationally" according to one's self-interest, economics built upon this principle leads logically to what many social economists view as destructive policy positions. For example, Social Darwinism, trickle-down effects, and the cruel acceptance of *laissez faire*, all enveloped in what is termed free market economics, were a part of a package generally rejected as false and socially destructive.

Nevertheless, this powerful movement of ideas from the Enlightenment is not without value and should not be summarily rejected, according the Dempsey. The concept of equilibrium is a sound and essential part of the economist's conception of reality. A special early vision of it is Dudley North's concept of homeostasis – the equilibrating quality that economies have to heal themselves when disturbed. This may be a powerful heuristic device in an effective theory of social economy.

On the other hand, one wonders about the value and validity of Dempsey's use of equilibrium. He says that since solidarism is concerned with societies within a larger society, or with groups intermediate between persons and families and the governing body of the state, they must coexist in general (Walrasian-like) equilibrium. In his words,

> Walras boldly and brilliantly undertook the construction of a general equilibrium with the industry as a unit. Both (he and Marshall, however) came to grief when the supply curve as a useful instrument dissolved upon closer scrutiny as Clapham opened the boxes and found them empty....
>
> (If neither the supply curve of Walras or Marshall, nor Chamberlin's firm is unit what choice is there?) There remains, evidently, but one more possibility – within the scheme – a general equilibrium analysis with the industry as unit – but we must find some kind of statistically tenable cost curve to use rather than supply curves. This is the analysis "implicit" *in Quadragesimo Anno*. The *economic orders* are to be in equilibrium. (Dempsey 1942, p. 15, emphasis added.)

This attempt by Dempsey at social architecture is not convincing. By some statistical measure of the cost curve he wishes to calculate the right proportion between wages and prices in the various industries. Economists are to find the empirical data so that the right proportion – the equilibrium – may be judged.

---

...there are ratios between wages and between prices which are correct, and there are others that are not correct. The right ratios are socially just, maximize employment, and represent equilibrium....

If an industry is not putting back into the community what is takes out (without radical alteration of the distribution of income and barring cases of innovation), equilibrium is being upset and social justice will be violated (Dempsey 1942, p.16).

This reconstructive recommendation is not attractive. It gives the government, the apparent user of this information, excessive micro-theoretic power that in addition to being authoritarian may well retard dynamic change. But Dempsey is correct that the concept of equilibrium should be preserved in the attempts to describe economic reality; natural balances are observable. A more persuasive example of equilibrium in the formation of a solidarist social economic theory was suggested by Schumpeter in his talk to Montreal businessmen three years after Dempsey's article in 1945 where he spoke in support of *QA*. He proposed to build upon an equilibrium of solidarity and antagonism found in all well-ordered human arrangements; a balance of cooperation and conflict, he says, coexists within every kind of economic transaction, even within the family. In summary,

it is essential to understand that antagonistic relationships are *not* less necessary to the functioning of a group or an entire society than cooperative relationships....

In a normal group of society, these antagonistic elements are integrated with cooperative elements in a *harmonious manner* with the framework of a common culture and a common faith which prevent the antagonisms from increasing.

The solution to problems of disorganization lies in corporate organization of the type advocated by *Quadragesimo Anno*. Many people would consider it inappropriate for an economist to comment so favorably on the Pope's moral message. However, he could extract economic doctrine from it .... It recognizes all the facts of the modern economy. In addition, by supplying a remedy for present day disorganization, it demonstrates how private initiative can function with a new framework. The corporate principle organizes but does not regiment. It is opposed to all social systems that strive for centralization and to all bureaucratic regimentation; it is indeed, the only means for rendering the latter impossible. (Schumpeter 1945, pp. 3,4,6, italics added.)

❖

Schumpeter's wise observation about an effective social economy being one where there is a stable balance between antagonistic and cooperative elements is a persuasive illustration of the use of equilibrium in the development of a solidarist theory of social economy. There, of course, are many more.

## II. Social Justice – A Key in Solidarist Theory

In an article on "Ability to Pay" Dempsey (1946) (consciously or not it is not clear) leaves the Newtonian perspective of automaticity and returns to the Aristotelian Xenophonic tradition that economics is the study of the management of an economy. The implication is that managing the economic sector of society is a continual process that calls for specific kinds of *just* societal behavior. Dempsey's contribution here emphasizes social or contributive justice – a concept of justice, beyond that of the ancients, developed by medieval and modern solidarists.

> The principle of social, contributive justice furnished the basis for genuine government of economic life....
>
> Until Americans fully recover their sense of community in economic life, and revive the sense of social and contributive justice that underlie town-meeting economics, we are without an adequate principle to lead us out of the economic muddle. (Dempsey 1946, p.13.)

In reviewing earlier forms of justice Dempsey notes that Aristotle was familiar with the two kinds that define proper relations (a) between equals and (b) betweeen the totality of society and its members; these are commutative and distributive justice, respectively.

> Beside commutative, exchange justice and distributive justice, both essential and requisite but insufficient, social justice is absolutely necessary. Distributive justice administered by the State attempts to regulate economic society from without. Exchange justice operates from within but it concerns only the actions of individuals.

Social justice acting from within goes beyond the demands of commutative and distributive justice.

> Man is normally a member of many communities – the family, the town, the province the club, the church. To each of these communities he owes a debt of social justice, also called by Fr. Pesch, very aptly, contributive justice. (Dempsey 1944, p.12.)
>
> Social justice places a positive *responsibility* on every member of a sociey to *contribute positively* to the common good of that society. In

❖

the matter of wages, social justice demands not only that the worker receive the economic value of his work, that is, exchange justice, but that he must receive the *social value of his work*....

[As there are social inadequacies] every person – owner, investor, manager, worker, consumer, supplier, neighbor – may have an obligation to contribute positively to the solution of the probem. Cooperation of every sort may be demanded of all to discover a more efficient method of dealing with the workers, the materials, the processes, the products of that industry so that the economic value of the worker's contribution shall be equal to its social value. (Dempsey 1944, p. 5, emphases added.)

Mueller (1946, p. 37) elaborates by quoting a passage from Pesch's *Lehrbuch*, "Social justice demands the fulfillment of all duties and the realization of all rights which have for their objective the social weal." (1946, p. 37.)

Social justice differs from the other two components of justice, in that while all are obligatory, social justice demands much more. Commutative and distributive kinds of justice require honestly and fairness respectively – passive virtures; social justice is something more active, being the responsibility to reconstruct society so that the economy may be managed more effectively and for the common good. It is the active and sometimes creative response to omnipresent dynamic social change.

## III. The Big Blend

In 1968, the arrangements committee of the Allied Social Sciences Association (ASSA) wanted to know more about the seven charter member organizations of the ASSA. They asked what is the origin of the CEA and what does it do? Cyril Zebot was commissioned by the executive council of the CEA to answer these questions. His statement said that the founders "wished to bring rigorous analysis to bear on the growing body of Catholic social thought that evolved from the social encyclicals of the modern popes" (Zebot 1968, p. 191).[1] The fact is that Zebot's answer was not correct – members hardly ever did this. Cause and effect ran in the opposite direction. The encyclicals were used to critique the prevailing science of economics while at the same time retaining and absorbing what was realistic and valid in it. Apparently, the encyclicals were used by the members of the CEA to do three things: to examine the philosophical premises of the dominant economics paradigm, to present a more acceptable social economic philosophy drawn from the Aristotelian-Thomistic tradition, and to retain and absorb what was valid and realistic about modern economics and market liberalism. These efforts brought forth a social economics that was a blend of Catholic social thought and conventional economics.

From the earliest years of the CEA, writers for the *RSE* debated the compatibility of the science of economics and the Aristotelian-Thomistic tradition of Catholic social thought. *RSE* articles reflect a series of controversies as to what is philosophically and economically sound in conventional economics and what is not. The writers when they dealt with these fundamentals as a central focus (for the *RSE* also published articles on popular issues of the day such as inflation and incomes policy): a) sometimes defended the science as valid and approved of natural physical lawfulness, as Dempsey did in his treatment of equilibrium, and b) sometimes condemned the prevailing science as built upon false premises distorting the nature of the person. What follows is a short enumeration of each; to combine them is to get a social economics that blends Newtonian automaticity and Aristotelian institutionalism.

## A. Regarding the Aristotelian-Thomistic Philosophical Premises

Economics is homocentric according to Pesch (Ederer 1953, p. 86). It is the study of persons and their economic institutions operating to satisfy human material need. It should not be taken to be, as often practiced, a science of money flows. Moreover, it is the personal entrepreneur with a supporting team that is the principal cause of wealth; it is not nature or capital (Mueller 1952, p. 38). The economic unit as social animal is not an independent entity maximizing satisfaction; the economic unit, the person, sometimes acts because duty dictates. The person lives and works in a community, cooperating with fellow employers and employees and participating in economic decision-making processes. This aspect needs incorporation in the science. The result is an alternative to the prevailing economics. The two approachs are different in their very essence.

The social philosophy that sanctified the rational, self-interested individual, and, at the other extreme, the philosophy of centralized collectivism that developed to protect society from him, left a social vacuum between family and state. In the social philosophy of medieval Europe, the space between had been populated with decision-making organizations termed vocational groups. But, this idea of an intermediate structure was destroyed in no small measure by modernist ideas of rationalism, naturalism and individualism. The older conception of a social economy must be reconstructed, says the solidarist teaching of Pesch and the *QA*. The requirement of vocational groups as a decision-making institution on a level intermediate between firms and the state dominated the *RSE* articles that dealt with the encyclicals.[2] An illustration of what it would be like today is a health industry that would combine doctors, nurses, technicians, public health officers, aides, pharmacists, pharmaceutical manufacturers, hospitals and clinics to planning and establishing an adequate health delivery program for the common good.

The idea of industrial councils (a name sometimes used as a synonym for vocational groups) makes good social sense but our country did not respond to this prescription for reconstruction. With the exception of some little known organizing attempts by the construction industries of St. Louis (O'Boyle 1990, pp. 140-41) and Indianapolis (Lohman and Mayer 1984, pp. 330-38), this unique characteristic of

❖

solidarism did not take root. The philosophical principles may have to be applied in other ways.

A function of the vocational group is to thwart the actions of "what Americans call 'pressure groups,' groups that put pressure on the law-makers to make laws for the benefit of their *special interests*" (von Nell-Breuning 1952, p. 115). If contemporaries have no strong desire to establish vocational groups, how can the crucial function of social justice be effected? Nell-Breuning proposed a "true organic pluralism on a macro level," such as the European Economic unity (von Nell-Breuning 1952, p. 116). This solution apparently did not interest the writers of the *RSE*. Solidaristic reconstruction was abandoned in frustration.

Later, an alternative solution was proposed, namely, worker participation in decision making. Its only form in the period under consideration was co-determination, that is, representation of labor on the boards of directors of corporations (Kurth 1953, p. 55). As von Nell-Breuning said, it was specifically a German affair (von Nell-Breuning 1962, p. 104) and, as such, had but limited interest to American writers in the *RSE*.[3]

Another principle that the writers did not abandon is the principle of subsidiarity. According to Franz Mueller, the name was coined by Gustav Gundlach (Mueller 1965, p. 189) the German Jesuit who prepared the first draft of *QA*. It says that organizational decisions must be from the bottom up. Organization of town and vocational groups, says von Nell-Breuning (the second of three German experts who did the spade work for *QA*), is,

> not from the top to the botton, as the universalistic guild theory would have it, but from the bottom to the top by associations on the basis of both proximity of habitation an vocation (von Nell-Breuning 1952, p. 109).

Its importance cannot be overstated. The guiding spirit of solidarist organization according to Mulcahy, is the twofold respect for the principle of subsidiarity and for the importance of the common good (Mulcahy 1957, p. 31).

Responsibility for decision-making in issues of social morality is on the lowest possible institutional level. The government, says Goetz Briefs, was never meant to be an arbiter of things moral; but, this is what has happened. "It goes without saying that in this shift of responsibility from groups to the govenment and back again to the groups, and from one group to another, the basic prinicple of all social order, the principle of subsidiarity has no chance to come into its own (Briefs, p. 630). Such a limited view of government makes solidarism a very liberal social economics.

Another example of philosophy relative to the formulation of a sound social economics is Briefs' principle of marginal ethics. (Briefs was the third expert, who with Gundlach and von Nell-Breuning worked on *QA* prior to its final preparation in Rome.) The principle says that what constitutes a socially ethical life changed

❖

through the years from seeking perfection to achieving minimal (or "marginal") standards of good. As a consequence, the motivation to form the good society was weakened. In Western civilization, the orientation of ethics toward the perfection of the Christian life broke down under the impact of nominalism and secularism. "At best, religion and religious ethics were considered private concerns" (Briefs, p. 50).

> The early stirrings of capitalism in Italy, e.g. in the Florentine woolen industry, had already affected the traditional ethical teaching and the prevailing ethos. [Briefs quotes Schoellgen here and elsewhere regarding his explanation of the evolution of marginal ethics.] The shift became more pronounced between the 16th and 18th centuries. Two radically different ethics fought for survival and recognition within the Church. The great moralists of that time, the casuists, concentrated their efforts on deciding how far legalism began to creep into ethical doctrine; the line had to be drawn between the just tolerable practices and those which a Christian community cannot allow. This approach sharply differed from the past. Instead of emphasizing the perfection of Christian life, casuist ethics determined the minima of the just tolerable ethical behavior: the marginal ethics. (Ibid.)

The upshot of this was, "The common good as the lode star was replaced by the formula of the greatest happiness of the greatest number, or by the sum total of the individual good" (Ibid.) This formula became the normative base for the conventional science of economics. "Justice and charity were reduced to heteronymous standards devoid of meaning and function in the mechanics of economic and political forces" (Ibid.) And so it followed that the popular science of economics was built upon a base of satisfying tastes, however moral or amoral these tastes may be. Bryce Jones (1964, p. 8) criticizes the prevailing science for reducing everything to tastes: "Fundamental equity principles are not in the same category as judgments about the deliciousness of olives."

Briefs' historical appraisal is ominous. But, he repeated several times, the condition is not irreversible (Briefs, pp. 49, 54). Solidaristic reconstruction is still possible.

Another premise driving the encyclical-influenced economists was realism, or the lack of it, in economics. Analytic methods, as evidenced in the publications of the *American Economic Review, Econometrica* and such, were given low grades for realism. The implication is that economists' training should not be reduced to working analytic puzzles and building models based on highly restrictive sets of *ceteris paribus* assumptions contributing little to one's knowledge of the essence of economic reality. Froehlich, for example, pushed for a more realistic conception of the firm manager in economic theory,

❖

....behind some modern theories of the firm and of decision-making lurks the acknowledgement of the businessman (the decision-making person in a social structure) as a human person much more varigated, much more open to all kinds of moral, pseudo-moral, traditional and other influences, and more fully the human being than the pale figure traditional theory has let us surmise (Froehlich 1966, pp. 129-30).

Also, in several articles Boris Ischboldin criticized the popular subdiscipline of econometrics for its lack of realism. (Ischboldin 1960 and 1961)

The condition may be traced to the economics departments of American Ph.D. granting institutions that determine curricula. The prevailing programs emphasize the mathematical and logical consistency of micro and macro models and econometric techniques; there is very little education of a social economic dimension. Realism in research that would explain the essence of the economy is simply not given high priority. Even more persuasive criticism is found recently outside of the *RSE*. According to Colander and Klamer (1987, p. 47), only three per cent of polled economics graduate students say institutional knowledge is very important to getting on the fast track in economics; 68 per cent think it unimportant (Quoted also in Colander 1991, p. 29). Even in the crucial areas of underdeveloped countries, the criticism is sustained. "It may astonish the layman that it is the technical justification (of the analytic and empirical bases) that is most open to question" (Lal 1985, p. 2). The CEA/ASE has been a haven for economists who object to this waste of scholarly resources in the preparation of unrealistic dissertations and review articles.

## B. Regarding What is Sound and Acceptable from Conventional Economics and its Natural Physical Law Heritage

Solidarist economists are forever confronted with the choice of what is automatic about the reality they wish to explain and what is exclusively homocentric and subject to personal decision-making. They criticize conventional economics as extremist in the role it gives to automatically functioning markets. A major question is how much should markets be left unfettered to determine prices, allocate resources and direct production, consumption and distribution. Of course, no consensus developed in the *RSE* to answer this question but a number of interesting tendencies resulted.

Solidarists are extremely supportive of competition and market determination of prices. This is surprising because their acceptance of the role of nature is limited. They generally oppose giving authority to either vocational groups or governments to interfer with the operation of the market to control prices or wages of any kind. Moreover, they contend that the scholastic doctors also supported free markets; they did not favor guild monopoly. Medieval scholastic economic theory was based on a competitive ethos, said medieval scholar, Raymond De Roover (1957, p. 78):

❖

Scholastic economic theory was closer to the competitive ethos of the
classical and neo-classical schools than is commonly assumed.
...As a rule, the scholastic doctors did not favor the guilds any more
than did Adam Smith (De Roover 1957, p. 78).

The solidarist tradition says that fair competition paves the way to fair prices
(Mueller explaining Pesch 1952, p. 75), and "under ordinary conditions we may
assume the competitive price to approximate the just price" (ibid., p. 74).

Having defended the validity of competition, solidarists explain further, in
what to some may seem contradictory and to all would appear at least a paradox,
that solidarists do not subscribe to any mechanistic concept of justice and optimum
welfare (Mueller 1952, p. 74).

[Pesch] considers it unrealistic and, in view of the daily evidence to the
contrary, even preposterous to expect from mere freedom of competition
the right formulation of prices (ibid.).

"Competition in order to regulate prices needs, itself, to be regulated in the first
place" (Mueller 1952, p. 75). The important question is what form should regulation
take.

One form is to thwart "superior forces and interests" from controlling the
market or any other extraordinary conditions that interfere with the normal manner
in which prices are formed. Under such conditions,

the presumption that the market price is the just price, ceases to be
valid. Particularly, wherever the profit motive is paramount, the
prospects for a "harmony of interest" are diminishing rather than
increasing: (Mueller 1952, p. 74.)

This presumably calls for government regulation of markets in a conventional
antitrust and/or economic administrative sense.

That form of social control is not nearly as crucial as a second form of
intervention. It is the kind of market control that is in effect in the U.S. currently,
namely, preconditions to market determination are imposed by means of subsidies,
quotas, land tenure, restrictions of police power and eminent domain, taxes,
industrial policy promotions and similar effects. They are set in place before the
market is permitted free rein. With them all, there is not a product that does not have
its supply and demand importantly affected by government and other social
institutions. Solidarists would retain this structure but insist on an essential
difference, namely, that the preconditions to the market be determined on the basis
of the common good instead of special interests.

Gundlach makes this distinction between determining the formation of the
market in a socially just way and giving the market free rein. Bishop Karl Alter

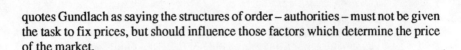

quotes Gundlach as saying the structures of order – authorities – must not be given the task to fix prices, but should influence those factors which determine the price of the market.

It is, therefore, not [society's task] to fix prices and directly interfere with the market. No, its task is to influence a spatially and vocationally differentiated system of order, those factors which determine the formation of markets. (Gundlach quoted by Alter 1952, p. 99.)

The preconditional arrangement applies especially to wage rates. If wage rates are determined in competitive markets, says von Nell-Breuning (1952, p. 93), the workers would be a means, when in effect they are the subjects of the economy. The just wage is more than something determined by the competitive market; it must reflect the person's true social value.

Cooperation of every sort may be demanded of all to discover a more efficient method of dealing with the workers, the material, the processes, and the products, ...so that the economic value of the worker's contribution shall be equal to its social value (Dempsey 1946, p. 5).

Influence from the mainstream of economic science upon solidarist writers of the *RSE* had to do especially with two other topics: the dynamic nature of the economy and the role of banking in the reconstructive process. The work of Joseph Schumpeter stands out most importantly in both of these areas, as does the solidarist writer, Josef Solterer, who drew heavily upon him.

The economy is dynamic. To place so much emphasis upon comparative statics as neoclassical economics does is to distort the essence of economic reality. To solidarist reconstructionists, change is of the essence; the statical scope of prevailing theory is too narrow. A sound social economics is as dynamic as it is institutional.

In speaking of a desired pluralistic society, that is, one in which the plurality is united or integrated, Solterer identifies a double modality of economic action – one statical – repetitive action in the circular flow, past determined, and one dynamic – the innovation action, intending to fashion the future (Solterer 1956, p. 18). One cannot exist without the other. Equilibrium is a useful concept to describe the first mode; the second is disequilibrating. Conventional economics treats the first more than adequately – note the emphasis on allocative and technical efficiency; the second is almost ignored except by Schumpeter and a limited number of solidarists who recognize the economic significance of personal creativity. The second, pertaining to dynamic efficiency, occurs wherever there is creative choice and action, that is, entrepreneurship. The econony becomes pulsating as the development process proceeds. "Entrepreneurship is in some measure exercised sometime by every person – though not always responsibly" (Solterer 1950, p. 19).

❖

Should the action stop, personal creativity ebbs; depersonalization is likely because it thrives in statical conditions.
The entrepreneur is order-forming and the agent for social justice.

> The entrepreneurs or leaders are the makers of a new order; their acts of innovation have a vastly greater significance than do simple acts of exchange; entrepreneurial activity is order-forming. Business leaders are essentially organizers, in whose acts we can see more clearly certain meanings of social justice. (Solterer 1951, p. 16.)

> Social justice does not consist primarily, or even mainly, in the prevention of exploitation, retaining otherwise all the machinery and attitudes which stem from the basic assumption that labor is simply a commodity. A just organization must be founded on a different conception, in which labor is not merely a commodity, but the laborer a member of a cooperative venture called a firm. (Solterer 1951, p. 17.)

> We recognize [entrepreneurship] as the architectonic function, the building function, the function in which responsibility is exercised (Solterer 1950, p. 19).

The dynamic modality of the economy does not consist of innovation alone. It has also to do with its complement, financial capital, needed for the attainment of necessary resources to implement the innovation.
To Solterer (1952), the reconstructive task lies more in establishing an effective financial structure than in promoting innovational activity because the latter is quite automatic. Given the proper financial milieu innovations will occur naturally. He proposed an accounting system for evaluating assets as to their liquidity in addition to how they are presently evaluated as to their utility. If a nation stalls in its development it is because of inadequate liquidity; this twofold acccounting of assets should facilitate the development process.
Other articles on finance were compatible to the idea of the dual nature of the development process and its relation to social justice. Works on credit unions are pertinent (Ryan 1966 and Croteau 1949) because these financial organizations were a valuable support to community development in parts of western Europe and Canada. Also note Ryland Taylor's work showing that when credit unions grow large the revenue motive endangers the solidaristic aspect of financing small businesses.

> The conflict which may appear as the cooperative gets larger presents a problem regarding its economic future and retention of the goals of cooperation. The possibility of self help overcoming self-interest

❖

diminishes as the organization becomes more conflictive. (Taylor 1971, p. 216.)

This recognition of the symbiotic relationship of innovation and fianancial capital is the basis of all reconstruction, and supplies a focus for social economists in recommending policy. It gives new insight into the nature and importance of the present financial crises in the banking and savings and loan industries. The function of financial organizations of properly evaluating project proposals – which means being neither too liberal nor too conservative – may be the most crucial of economic institutions.

## IV.  Conclusion

A theory of social economy does emerge out of the writings of the economists influenced by the encyclicals. As would be expected it is Peschian. But, an important part of Pesch's vision was set aside in frustration; there appeared to be little grass roots desire to reconstruct the economy with vocational groups – to make whole industries cooperative decision-making units.

Solidarists did not give up, however. Community economic development of the future appears to lie in restructuring firms, not industries, along the lines of worker participation and management, with the community network extended beyond the firm to include financial facilities. Mondragon is an illustration that it can be done. But this is another story that would draw upon essays in the *RSE* since 1970, when the journal became a publication of the ASE. There is much to be done, but significant contributions have been made already by O'Boyle, Bruyn, Ellerman, Lutz, Booth and others in the *RSE*.

As the theory has progressed to date, it describes a socially just economy as one populated by persons (instead of rational utility maximizers) who make choices *combining* motives of self interest and duty. At times, these economic units are creative in an always developing (or least always changing) economy. The participating persons have a responsibility (but do not always live up to it) of looking to the common good. This is necessary because solidarists deny that one can rely upon a non-preconditioned, freely operating market to optimize the social weal.

Several policy directives emerge from the solidarist tradition: one is the great principle of subsidiarity that holds decision-making should be from the bottom up. Another is that markets are to be left free to operate but only after preconditions to market determination are made on the basis of the demands of justice: commutative, distributive and, especially for solidarists, social.

## Endnotes

*Professor of Economics Emeritus, DePaul University, 25 E. Jackson Blvd., Chicago, Illinois 60604 USA.

[1] Zebot's full statement is, "The Catholic Economic Association was founded in 1941 in New York by a group of American economists who together with their professional interest in economic analysis shared a personal commitment in Christian principles of social ethics. Proceeding from the realization that welfare economics involved ethical judgments, the founders of the CEA – Father Bernard W. Dempsey, Father Thomas F. Divine, professor Edward H. Chamberlin, professor Josef Solterer and others – wished to bring rigorous economic analysis to bear on the growing body of Catholic social thought that evolved from the social encyclicals of modern popes. During the 25 years of its existence, the Catholic Economic Association, through its national (annual) and regional meetings and its journal *(Review of Social Economy)*, has made significant contributions to the progress of theoretical and practical welfare economics informed by the social principles of Christian ethics."

[2] Even the hierarchy was called to testify. Bishop Karl J. Alter said in the *RSE* of September 1952, p. 98 that, "The Church's program consists, first, in a rejection of the heretofore widely accepted socio-economic priniciples, namely, unrestrained competition, monopoly, dictatorship, and class conflict, (and) secondly, it consists in positive recommendations in favor of a new and higher form of cooperation, based on the reestablishment of organized industries and professions, or, as called sometimes, guilds or vocational groups. The principle or bond of the unity and cooperation is to be found, on the part of both employers and employees, in sharing of a common economic function; and in the mutual objective of promoting the common good."

[3] The only encyclical to address solidaristic reconstruction by worker participation is Pope John Paul's *Laborem Exercens*. For this we had to wait until 1988.

## References

Alter, Bishop Karl J. "The Industry Council System and the Church's Program of Social Order," *Review of Social Economy*, September 1952, *10*.

Briefs, Goetz. "The Ethos Problem in the Present Pluralistic Society," *Review of Social Economy*, March 1957.

Colander, David. *Why Aren't Economists as Important as Garbagemen? Essays on the State of Economics*, Armonk: M. E. Sharpe, 1991.

Colander, David and Klamer, Arjo. "The Making of an Economist," *Journal of Economic Perspectives*, Fall 1987, *1*, 95-111.

Croteau, John T. "The Credit Union: Legal Form Versus Economic Function," *Review of Social Economy*, September 1949, *7*, 10-28.

❖

Dempsey, Bernard W. "Economics 'Implicit' in the Social Encyclicals," *Review of Social Economy*, December 1942, *1*, 12-18.

Dempsey, Bernard W. "Ability to Pay," *Review of Social Economy*, January 1946, *4*, 1-13.

DeRover, Raymond. "Comment: Professor Zebot on the Ethos Patterns in a Competitive Society," March 1957, *15*, 76-79.

Ederer, Rupert J., Review of Richard E. Mulcahy, S.J. *The Economics of Heinrich Pesch, S.J., Review of Social Economy*, March 1953, *24*, 122-131.

Faulhaber, Robert. "Review of Paul Blumberg's Industrial Democracy," *Review of Social Economy*, March 1970, 28, 117-121.

Froehlich, Walter. "The Businessman as a Person: Some Aspects of the New Theory of the Firm," *Review of Social Economy*, September 1966, *24*, 122-131.

Ischboldin, Boris. "A Critique of Econometrics," *Review of Social Economy*, September 1960, *18*, 110-127.

Ischboldin, Boris. "Reply," *Review of Social Economy*, March 1961, *19*, 67-69.

Jones, Bryce. "Comment," *Review of Social Economy*, March 1964, *22*, 7-8.

Kurth, Edmund A. "Co-determination in West Germany," *Review of Social Economy*, March 1953, *11*, 54-69.

Lal, Deepak. *The Poverty of Development Economics*, Cambridge, MA: Harvard University Press, 1985.

Lohman, Jeff and Mayer, Henry C. "Top Notch is More Than a Slogan," *Review of Social Economy*, December 1984, *42*, 330-338.

Mueller, Franz H. "The Principle of Solidarity in the Teaching of Rev. Henry Pesch, S.J.," *Review of Social Economy*, January 1946, *4*, 31-39.

Mueller, Franz H. and Thomasine, Sr. M. O.P. "Comment: The Peschian Value Paradox," *Review of Social Economy*, March 1952, *10*, 169-75.

Mueller, Franz H. Review of Gustav Gundloch, S.J., "Die Ordnung der menschlichen Gesellschaft," *Review of Social Economy*, September 1965, *23*, 188-191.

Mulcahy, Richard. "The Role of Marginal Ethos in the Rise of a Pluralistic Society," *Review of Social Economy*, March 1957, *15*, 26-32.

Nell-Breuning, Oswald von. "The Social Structural Order and European Economic Unity," *Review of Social Economy*, September 1952, *10*, 108-120.

Nell-Breuning, Oswald von. "Some Reflections on Mater and Magistra," *Review of Social Economy*, Fall 1962, *20*, 97-108.

O'Boyle, Edward J. "Catholic Social Economics: A Response to Certain Problems, Errors and Abuses of the Modern Age," in Mark E. Lutz, ed., *Social Economics: Retrospect and Prospect*, Boston: Kluwer Academic Publishers, 1990.

Ryan, William F. "The Influence of the Church in the 'Take-off'; The French Canadian Experience," *Review of Social Economy*, March 1966, *24*, 32-48.

Shea, John L. "Comment on Dempsey," *Review of Social Economy*, December 1942, *1*, 19-22.

Schumpeter, Joseph A. "The Future of Private Enterprise Confronted by Modern Socialism," a presentation to Montreal businessmen November 19, 1945 translated by John H. Niedercorn. Another translation is found in *HOPE*, Fall 1975, 294-298.

Solterer, Josef. "The Entrepreneur in Economic Theory," *Review of Social Economy*, March 1950, *8*, 10-19.

Solterer, Josef. "Quadragesimo Anno: Schumpeter's Alternative to the Omnipotent State," *Review of Social Economy*, March 1951, *9*, 12-23.

Solterer, Josef. "The Pacing of Capitalism," *Review of Social Economy*, September 1952, *10*, 127-137.

Solterer, Josef. "The Structure of a Pluralistic Economy," *Review of Social Economy*, March 1956, *14*, 14-30.

Taylor, Ryland. "The Credit Union as a Cooperative Institution," *Review of Social Economy*, September 1971, *24*, 207-217.

Waters, William R. "On the Theory of Social Economy," *Review of Social Economy*, September 1965, *23*, 115.

Zebot, Cyril. "The Roots of Welfare Economics: A Review Article," *Review of Social Economy*, September, 1968, *26*, 168-175.

# Some Observations Concerning the Institutionalist Approach to Social Economics

## *Lewis E. Hill**

It has long been my conviction that institutional economics and social economics are thoroughly compatible and that both of these heterodox schools of economic thought could be improved if a creatively symbiotic relationship could be established between them. This conviction was first expressed in my essay, "Social and Institutional Economics: Toward a Creative Synthesis," where the following argument was developed:

> The purpose of this paper is to create a synthesis of the goals and objectives of social economics with the philosophy and methodology of institutional economics. It is my belief that social economics is characterized mostly by a unique set of socio-economic goals and objectives, rather than by unique methods. Institutional economics, on the other hand, consists mostly of a unique philosophy and methodology for the economic science. Institutionalism is an open system with respect to any goals and objectives that are consistent with its theory of normative value. (Hill 1978, p. 311).

This major theme can be decomposed into two subsidiary hypotheses: (1) that the philosophy of institutional economics is compatible with social economics; and (2) that the institutionalist epistemology could provide a valid and useful methodology for social economics. The purpose of these observations is to explain and support these subsidiary hypotheses.

Social economics may be defined as the socioeconomic analysis of human behavior within a broad social and political context for the purpose of improving the quality of life and enhancing human welfare. Social economists have always expressed and demonstrated a very special concern for the economically deprived

---
❖
---

people who comprise the have-nots of our society. Most social economists accept the humanistic values of the Judeo-Christian tradition and base their commitment to human welfare on metaphysical preconceptions. All social economists are dedicated to the quest to achieve social justice. Social economics is an applied policy science that is intended to solve the problems of social injustice and economic privation (Hill 1989, p. 156). Institutional economics may be defined as a pragmatic theory of socioeconomic behavior, derived empirically through the application of inductive logic to qualitative and quantitative historical facts, and applied instrumentally to the solution of practical socioeconomic problems (Hill 1989, p. 164-165). This definition suggests that the institutionalist methodology can be induced from the pragmatic philosophy, the empirical epistemology, inductive logic, and instrumental methods of solving practical problems.

## I. Pragmatism

The philosophical basis of institutional economics is instrumental pragmatism. The pragmatic philosophy holds that all reality has practical consequences and that, therefore, the best way to know and to understand reality is through the inductive analysis of practical consequences. According to this philosophy, the reality and the truth of any proposition, belief, or idea can be correctly specified and accurately evaluated only in terms of its practical consequences. Conversely, if any proposition, belief or idea has no practical consequences, then it is not real and, therefore, it cannot be true (Peirce 1965, p. 113-136). Instrumental pragmatism is a variation on pure pragmatism which was developed by William James and John Dewey; it involved an instrumental definition of truth and a heavy emphasis on solving practical problems. Some social economists have contended that instrumental pragmatism is philosophically incompatible with social economics. Mark A. Lutz (1985, p. 169) has expressed this view very succinctly:

> Our critical survey of the mutual compatibility of pragmatism and instrumental value theory, with the image of man underlying social economics, has pointed to what I consider to be irreconcilable differences. It appears to me that such incompatibility resides in the adherence of instrumental value theory to the same radical naturalism and relativism that is the sad hallmark of the modern secularized mind; a mind increasingly alienated from its own spiritual self and source of dignity.

Lutz found no incompatibility between social economics and the philosophy of Charles S. Peirce, who originated pragmatism, because Peirce based his version of the pragmatic philosophy on metaphysical preconceptions and derived his normative values from the Judeo-Christian tradition (Lutz 1985, p. 141-145). Peirce's theory of normative value is drawn from his theory of religion and based on the Christian Doctrine of the Two Ways. According to this doctrine, the Way of Life motivates the creative and benevolent behavior that is compatible with good normative values, and the Way of Death motivates the destructive and malevolent behavior that is compatible with bad normative disvalues (Peirce 1965, p. 354-355).

But Lutz insisted that social economics is philosophically incompatible with the instrumental pragmatism of William James and John Dewey (Lutz 1985). James formulated a functional epistemology, according to which an idea should be considered true only if it is useful to us when we make practical decisions and solve practical problems. True ideas help us to achieve our objectives, but false ideas deceive and mislead us into wrong courses of action and cause failure in our efforts to achieve our objectives. All true ideas are useful, and all useful ideas are true. The truth of an idea is a prediction of its usefulness; the usefulness of an idea is the verification of its truth (James 1925, p. 197-238).

Dewey rejected concepts of absolute value and divinely ordained ends; he formulated his instrumental theory of normative value and his instrumental method of solving practical problems. He believed that ordinary people can learn from their own experience how to make very good normative value judgments and how to use these judgments to help solve their practical problems (Dewey 1939). Lutz believes that James' functional epistemology and Dewey's instrumental theory of normative value are incompatible with social economics.

But James also formulated a pragmatic theory of religion which, in my judgment, can be used to reconcile pragmatism with the religious implications of social economics. He wrote: "On pragmatic principles, we cannot reject any hypothesis if consequences useful to life flow from it" (James 1925, p. 273). Obviously, consequences useful to the lives of many people flow from their religious beliefs; therefore, religious beliefs are true for these "tender-minded" people. But religious beliefs are not true for the "tough-minded" people who find these ideas to be useless (James 1925, p. 273-301). James (1925, p. 301) elaborated his theory of religion in the following quotation:

> But if you are neither tough nor tender in an extreme and radical sense, but mixed as most of us are, it may seem to you that the type of pluralistic and moralistic religion that I have offered is as good a religious synthesis as you are likely to find. Between the two extremes of crude naturalism on the one hand and transcendental absolution on the other, you may find that what I take the liberty of calling the pragmatistic or melioristic type of theism is exactly what you require.

It is my belief that James' "pluralistic and melioristic religion" that represents a compromise between "crude naturalism and transcendental absolutism" is philosophically consistent with both the secularism of instrumental pragmatism and the meta-physical preconceptions of traditional social economics. Therefore, his theory of religion seems to be a reasonable basis for resolving any incompatibility that may exist between the philosophy of institutional economics and social economics.

## II. Institutionalism

The institutionalist school of economic thought was first originated by Thorstein B. Veblen, a radical economic philosopher of the late nineteenth and early twentieth centuries. Veblen conceived man to be a social animal who is driven by opposing instincts or propensities. He found value in the affirmative or benevolent propensities which motivate creative, productive, and useful behavior; he found disvalue in the negative or malevolent propensities which motivate destructive, exploitative, and wasteful behavior (Tool 1977, p. 824-827; Veblen 1950). This dichotomy between the affirmative and negative propensities became the basis of Veblen's theory of normative value, which closely parallels Peirce's value theory. Peirce's Way of Life and Way of Death symbolize Veblen's affirmative and negative propensities, which motivate creative and destructive behavior.

John R. Commons, the second among the originators of institutionalism, combined the empirical epistemology with the historical method to create a nonquantitative historical empiricism, which he utilized to induce his theory of the labor movement from American labor history. Commons and his associates first researched and wrote a definitive history of organized labor in the United States (Commons and Associates 1946). Observations were then drawn from this historical record, and inductive logic was used to generalize the theory of the American labor movement from these observations (Commons and Associates 1946, I: 1-11). Implications from the theory were applied to the formulation of economic policies and to the solution of practical economic problems. Commons' historical empiricism represented a major methodological innovation because it produces inductive theories that are much more empirically relevant to the conditions and problems of the real world than the abstract and irrelevant deductive theories which can be derived from a rationalistic epistemology (Gruchy 1967, p. 135-243).

Wesley C. Mitchell, the third among the originators of institutional economics, pioneered the development of precise scientific methods for the quantitative analysis of empirically observed data. Mitchell applied his quantitatively oriented historical empiricism to the analysis of business fluctuations — a subject on which he became perhaps the world's greatest authority. He derived an empirically relevant inductive theory of the business cycle, and he wrote the definitive book on that subject (Mitchell 1927). Mitchell added a new precisely quantitative dimension to the institutionalist methodology and raised institutionalism to a new and higher level of academic acceptability and scientific respectability (Gruchy 1967, p. 247-333).

## III. The Ayresian Synthesis

Clarence E. Ayres, the last of the originators of institutionalism, integrated and synthesized the philosophical tradition of instrumental pragmatism, which had come from Peirce, through James, to Dewey, with the economic tradition of institutionalism, which had come from Veblen, through Commons, to Mitchell. In the process of integration and synthesis, he made the philosophy of institutionalism compatible with social economics, and he created a valid methodology which is proving to be useful for social economists.

Ayres formulated his theory of normative value by integrating the substantive aspects of the Veblenian dichotomy with the procedural aspects of Dewey's instrumental theory of normative value. Ayres formulated the concept of the technological or instrumental life process to summarize and to symbolize the benevolent propensities and the creative, productive, and useful behavior that constitute the affirmative aspect of the Veblenian dichotomy. This life process is the basis for all true normative value judgments; it is the standard by which all normative value judgments are judged to be true or false (Ayres 1944, p. 205-230). Ayres has written:

> It is in this, the life process of mankind, that values arise. .... When we judge a thing to be good or bad, or an action to be right or wrong, what we mean is that, in our opinion, the thing or act in question will, or will not, serve to advance the life process insofar as we can envision it (Ayres 1961, p. 113).

Ayres based the procedural aspects of his theory on Dewey's instrumental theory of normative value. Like Dewey, Ayres believed that ordinary people are entirely capable of using inductive logic to induce very good normative value judgments from their own past experience and of verifying these judgments by reference to their own subsequent experience. This theory is a secularization of Peirce's metaphysical theory of normative value. Ayres' life process is the secular equivalent of Peirce's Way of Life. It is for these reasons that Ayres' institutionalist-instrumentalist theory of normative value represents a reconciliation of institutional and social economics.

Ayres integrated the empirical epistemology and the inductive logic, which had been developed by the institutionalists, with John Dewey's instrumental method of solving practical problems. This synthesis of institutionalism, with its emphasis on empirical relevance, and pragmatic instrumentalism, with its emphasis on solving practical problems, has created a more valid and more useful methodology, which could be very effectively utilized by social economists. Clarence Ayres' instrumental institutionalism provides a sound basis for a creative synthesis between institutional and social economics.

*Professor of Economics, Texas Tech University, Lubbock, TX 79409-1014 USA.

❖

# References

Ayres, Clarence E. *The Theory of Economic Progress*, Chapel Hill: University of North Carolina Press, 1944.

_____, *Toward A Reasonable Society*, Austin: University of Texas Press, 1961.

Commons, John R., and Associates. *History of Labour in the United States*, Volumes I and II, New York: The Macmillan Company, 1946.

Dewey, John. *Theory of Valuation*, Chicago: University of Chicago Press, 1939.

Gruchy, Allan G. *Modern Economic Thought*, New York: Agustus M. Kelley, 1967.

Hill, Lewis E. "The Institutionalist Approach to Social Economics," in *Social Economics: Retrospect and Prospect*, edited by Mark A. Lutz, Boston: Kluwer Academic Publishers, 1989, p. 155-174.

_____. "Social and Institutional Economics: Toward a Creative Synthesis," *Review of Social Economy*, 36.3, December 1978: 311-323.

James, William. *Pragmatism: A New Name for Some Old Ways of Thinking*, Longmans, Green and Co., 1925.

Lutz, Mark A. "Pragmatism, Instrumental Value Theory and Social Economics," *Review of Social Economy*, 43.2, October 1985: 140-171.

Mitchell, Wesley C. *Business Cycles: The Problem and Its Setting*, New York: The National Bureau of Economic Research, 1927.

Peirce, Charles Sanders. *Selected Writings*, edited by Philip P. Weiner, New York: Dover Publications, Inc., 1965.

Tool, Marc R. "A Social Value Theory in Neoinstitutional Economics," *Journal of Economic Issues*, 11.4, December 1977: 820-842.

Veblen, Thorstein B. *The Portable Veblen*, edited by Max Lerner, New York: The Viking Press, 1950.

---
❖
---

# Catholic Social Economics:
# A Response to Certain Problems,
# Errors, and Abuses of the
# Modern Age
# (Abstract)

## *Edward J. O'Boyle* *

   Catholic social economics is an amalgam of economic science and moral discipline in which economics is perceived as (1) one of several distinct sciences that study human beings and (2) dependent on moral discipline in order to address the problems, errors, and abuses that beset humans in the Modern Age. More specifically, Catholic social economic thought is a response to the problems of capitalism's excessive individualism and socialism's excessive collectivism.

   Excessive individualism means that capitalism uses the threat of economic insecurity to (re-)allocate resources and thereby puts humans at risk of not being able to provision their material needs. Capitalism is unstable because, of necessity, the capitalist economic order makes human beings insecure.

   Excessive collectivism means that socialism seizes complete control of the means of production under the mistaken notion that economic insecurity derives from private property. Socialism is unstable because it denies humans what is rightfully theirs under natural law in order to provision their material needs.

   Catholic social economics asserts that two reforms are need to deal with these two evils. An organizational reform is needed to establish and develop industry councils that are intermediate in the economic order between the smaller, less powerful, private enterprises experiencing economic dysfunction and the larger, more powerful, state. A moral reform is needed to encourage human beings to act according to the demands of justice and charity.

   From the perspective of Catholic social economics, the means of production are privatized under capitalism and nationalized under socialism. What is required is a socialization of human beings wherein they reject the strict individuality of

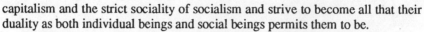

capitalism and the strict sociality of socialism and strive to become all that their duality as both individual beings and social beings permits them to be.

Catholic social economics frequently is criticized for its idealism. However, unless human beings respond affirmatively to the challenge to become all they truly can be, they will remain vulnerable to the insecurity and anarchy of capitalism and to the loss of what is rightfully theirs and the tyranny of socialism.

*Associate Professor of Economics, Louisiana Tech University, USA.

---

❖

---

# Henry George, *Rerum Novarum,* and the Controversy Concerning Private Property in Land

## *Jack Schwartzman\**

### I. Prologue

In 1879, a book was published in New York that was destined to become an all-time "best seller" among economics texts, and which was translated into all the major languages of the world. The title was *Progress and Poverty;* the author was Henry George.

Contending that monopoly of land deprived mankind of access to nature, thereby causing homelessness, unemployment, poverty, depression, and war, George proposed a "remedy" ("single tax," some have called it), by means of which only land values would be taxed, and all other levies would be abolished. Land-value taxation would make impossible the holding (especially for purposes of speculation) of the currently vast natural resources, thus causing land to become available to the public for the continuing production of wealth. Additionally, the removal of the presently prohibitive and crushing taxes on earnings, trade, improvements, and all other personal property, would, in turn, spur human endeavor toward further production of goods and satisfaction of demand. This twofold solution would end economic ills, provide necessary public revenues, restore liberty to mankind, and bring peace to the universe.

However, George warned, no economic solution could be permanently effective unless mankind abide by the precepts of natural law and conform to the principles of moral living. Therefore, economics and ethics must be eternally conjoined.

George became internationally famous. As a prominent speaker and political figure, he twice ran for the office of Mayor of New York (dying a few days before Election Day in his second attempt).

One of his most noted "disciples" was a Roman Catholic priest, Doctor Edward McGlynn, an outstanding orator and much-loved pastor of an affluent

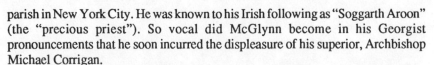

parish in New York City. He was known to his Irish following as "Soggarth Aroon" (the "precious priest"). So vocal did McGlynn become in his Georgist pronouncements that he soon incurred the displeasure of his superior, Archbishop Michael Corrigan.

A modern writer stated that Corrigan was "the lackey of Tammany Hall, the corrupt, vicious, political organization that licensed harlotry, encouraged thievery, and prostituted democracy" (Lissner 1967, p. 1). Corrigan ordered McGlynn to discontinue his support of George. When McGlynn disobeyed, Corrigan suspended him from his priestly duties for two weeks (Bell 1937, p. 38).

Some time later, Corrigan again suspended McGlynn, this time for urging people to read *Progress and Poverty*. The archbishop informed the authorities in Rome that McGlynn was preaching doctrines that were contrary to Catholic belief (Curran 1989, p. 189).

The result was, according to a biographer of McGlynn, that

> Dr. McGlynn had received four summonses to go to Rome, the last of which came from Pope Leo himself and set a limit of forty days for his appearance at the Vatican, under penalty of excommunication if he failed to appear. He not only had not gone, but he had offered no excuse for not going, other than a denial of the right of his Archbishop or other ecclesiastical superiors to order him to Rome to answer...unspecified charges connected with his exercise of the right of an American citizen" (Bell, p. 135).

As a consequence, McGlynn was summarily excommunicated. The official order was issued on July 4, 1887, prompting McGlynn's biographer to observe ironically that the date of the decree was "the One Hundred and Eleventh anniversary of our national independence" (Bell, p. 122).

McGlynn's excommunication only triggered more controversy. Various attempts were made by the New York Church to punish the McGlynn faction, and McGlynn himself was even accused of immorality (Curran, pp. 193, 195).

Undaunted, McGlynn continued to espouse the philosophy of Henry George and to attack the Roman Catholic hierarchy. In one appearance before an enthusiastic audience, he asked rhetorically, "Who is the Pope?" and answered his own question: "A poor old bag of bones, just ready to drop into the grave" (Post 1930, p. 94). Two weeks later, in a sensational address, McGlynn denounced "The Ecclesiastical Machine in American Politics" (ibid.). Another famous speech ended with a ringing defiance: "Take up, then, the cross of the new crusade" (Bell, p. 81).

Seeing that the excommunication of McGlynn only exacerbated the schism within the Church, Corrigan and his cohorts became convinced that punishing McGlynn would not help their cause unless and until the "source" of this upheaval, Henry George, were punished as well.

❖

In October, 1887, Corrigan "formally petitioned the Pope that the Congregation of the Index examine *Progress and Poverty*." Cardinal Gibbons of Baltimore strenuously opposed this petition. "A year and a half later, the Holy Office compromised by condemning George's writings, but it refused to allow any promulgation of the condemnation" (Curran, p. 196).

George, who was a Protestant, never learned of this action by the Vatican, although he always contended, sometimes to skeptical listeners, that the encyclical, *Rerum Novarum (RN)* (of which we shall speak presently), was directed against him personally. He died in ignorance of the conspiracy against him. It is only recently that modern scholarship has unearthed these facts.

"Presumably," stated a biographer of George in the 1950's, "this condemnation ... holds to the present day. At the very lowest estimate, the principles of Archbishop Corrigan's pastoral letter ... were quietly endorsed by the highest authority" (Barker 1955, pp. 489-90).

Since George was the object of papal condemnation, it is to be noted that even though he was a very religious man himself, George, nevertheless, strongly opposed organized ritual. In 1891, the year of *RN,* he wrote to a friend (as per Geiger 1933, pp. 359-60):

> How sad it is to see a church in all its branches offering men stones instead of bread, and thistles instead of figs. From Protestant preachers to the Pope, avowed teachers of Christianity are with few exceptions preaching almsgiving or socialism and ignoring the simple remedy of justice.

(Contrary to popular belief, George was not a socialist, and attacked the doctrine in his writings.)

In another letter, this one to a Catholic priest, George declared (Geiger): "It is very sad to see all clergymen ... avoid the simple principle of justice. As Tolstoi has put it, they are willing to do anything for the poor, except get off their backs."

As will be seen from his *Open Letter (OL)* to the Pope, however, George addressed the pontiff with a great deal of respect. Even while disagreeing with him, George acknowledged that the Pope was "animated by a desire to help the suffering and the oppressed" (Barker, p. 572). And in a comment made after *RN* was published, he admitted: "I have for some time believed Leo XIII to be a very great man" (Barker, p. 576).

This was the situation in 1891 (one hundred years ago), when Pope Leo's encyclical burst upon the world.

## II. Dialogue

### A. The Publications

On May 15, 1891, appeared *RN,* Pope Leo's encyclical, "often...called the Magna Charta of the workingman" (Barker, p. 571). This same biographer of

George indicated that the encyclical represented a desire by the Catholic Church, "in a democratic age to seek popular in place of princely support," and a wish to establish "a new organization of society based upon some conception of equality" (Barker, loc. cit.).

The basic theme of *RN* was that since "the very poor ... were wretched and defenseless," the Pope felt compelled to propose his own solution to the economic problem. While repudiating "socialism" and justifying private property in land, the pontiff advocated the formation of labor unions, in the spirit of the medieval guilds. He also suggested that the State help redress injustice where and when needed (Barker, pp. 571-72).

Henry George reacted to *RN* by immediately claiming that even though the book professed to be a denunciation of "socialism," it was actually an attack on George and his views. Interestingly, his arch enemy, Corrigan, agreed with this contention. "Neither Henry George nor the single tax proposition were specifically named," wrote George's son, "yet Archbishop Corrigan ... hailed the papal letter as the highest sanction of his own opposition to the single tax doctrine as preached by Dr. McGlynn and Henry George." Cardinal Manning also declared "that the Pope's letter aimed at the Henry George's teachings" (Henry George, Jr. 1980, pp. 565-66).

Not everyone agreed with the view that the Pope had George in mind when he wrote the encyclical. George's son commented: "A number of Mr. George's Catholic friends from the first contended that the Pope did not condemn the single tax doctrine" (George Jr., p. 565). A noted biographer of George, usually sympathetic to his views, felt that there was a "suspicion of megalomania in Henry George's hot individual reaction to a document drawn up for universal reading and guidance" (Barker, pp. 572-73).

George would not be swayed from his conviction. He firmly declared (George, pp. 565-66):

> For my part, I regard the encyclical letter as aimed at us, and at us alone, almost. And I feel very much encouraged by the honor.... I think I ought to write something about it. Of course the Pope's letter is very weak; but to reply to him might give an opportunity of explaining our principles to many people who know little or nothing about them.

George decided, therefore, that it was necessary to compose an immediate answer to the Pope's encyclical — and he did. "The reply, which took the form of an open letter to the Pope, grew in his hands... It was not finished until September, and comprised twenty-five thousand words; twice as many as the encyclical, which he printed with it" (George, Jr., p. 566).

George sent this reply, known as *The Condition of Labor: An Open Letter to Pope Leo XIII (OL)*, to the pontiff in September, 1891. "In addition, Leo received into his own hands, from the prefect of the Vatican Library, a handsome copy of the

❖

Italian edition" (Barker, pp. 574-75). This "handsomely printed and bound copy was presented to the Pope, but George never received any acknowledgement of his work from the Holy See" (Geiger, p. 363).

Did the Pope actually read George's reply? One biographer declared: "George learned that he did, more than once" (Barker, p. 574). In 1892, George remarked: "Whether he ever read my letter I cannot tell, but he had been acting as though he had not only read it, but had recognized its force" (Barker, p. 576). A modern scholar, who recently traveled to the Vatican to search the archives for the American and the Italian editions of George's *OL,* could find neither copy, nor any reference to them. (Nuesse 1985, p. 248).

One Catholic writer believed that it would have made no difference in the final outcome whether the Pope read the *OL* or not, since George and the Pope just would not have been able to communicate with each other. The Pope relied on classical Catholic philosophy, which "limited" the right to untold possession of wealth. George, on the other hand, was said to be influenced by the thinking of John Locke, which emphasized the right to possess, without limit, *all* the fruits of one's labor (Benestad 1980, p. 115). (It is amusing to note that *both* the Pope and George, on opposite sides of the argument, called their respective opponents "socialists.")

How did the friends and foes of George regard his OL? George's followers were ecstatic and jubilant; George's detractors were outraged by his "insolence" in daring to lecture the Pope. "The Archbishop and his friends," wrote McGlynn's biographer, "including the bulk of the secular press ... ridiculed the pretentions" of Henry George "to debate these high matters with so great a personality as the Pope" (Bell, p. 208).

It is time to discuss, thematically, the Pope's *Condition of Labor* (otherwise known as *RN)* with George's *Condition of Labor* (otherwise known as *An Open Letter to Pope Leo XIII).* To that topic we now turn.

## B. The Confrontation

The best way to present an analysis of *RN* and the *OL,* and to compare and contrast the main views of Pope Leo XIII and Henry George, is to "set up" a fictitious debate (a philosophical dialectic) wherein the exact words of each man will be used. Since the Pope's encyclical letter appeared first, George, of necessity, has the final word. (As seen above, the Pope never responded to George's *OL.)*

The "confrontation" follows below. (For the purpose of this "dramatic dialogue," all quotation marks at the beginning and end of each paragraph are omitted.)

POPE:      Socialists, working on the poor man's envy of the rich, endeavor to destroy private property.... They are emphatically unjust, because they would rob the lawful possessor (Leo XIII 1982, p. 111).

GEORGE:   Your use ... of the inclusive term "property" or "private property" ... makes your meaning ... ambiguous. But reading it as a whole, there can be no doubt of your intention that private property in land shall be understood when you speak merely of private property (George 1982, p. 24).

Private property in land, no less than property in slaves, is a violation of the true rights of property. They are different forms of the same robbery (George, p. 26).

The essence of slavery is in empowering one man to obtain the labor of another without recompense. Private property in land does this as fully as chattel slavery (George, p. 26).

POPE:       When a man engages in remunerative labor, the very reason and motive of his work is to obtain property, and to hold it as his own private possession.... Thus, if he lives sparingly, saves money, and invests his savings, for greater security, in land, the land in such a case is only his wages in another form; and consequently, a workingman's little estate thus purchased should be as completely at his own disposal as the wages he receives for his labor (Leo XIII, pp. 111-12).

GEORGE:     Purchase and sale cannot give, but can only transfer ownership. Property that in itself has no moral sanction does not obtain moral sanction by passing from seller to buyer.

If right reason does not make the slave the property of the slave-hunter, it does not make him the property of the slave-buyer. Yet your reasoning as to private property in land would as well justify property in slaves (George, pp. 61-62).

POPE:       Man ... not only can possess the fruits of the earth, but also the earth itself.... Nature ... owes to man a storehouse that shall never fail, the daily supply of his daily wants. And this he finds only in the inexhaustible fertility of the earth (Leo XIII, p. 113).

GEORGE:     Man may indeed hold in private ownership the fruits of the earth produced by his labor.... But he cannot so own the earth itself, for that is the reservoir from which must constantly be drawn not only the material with which alone men can produce, but even their very bodies (George, p. 31).

Industry expended on land gives ownership in the fruits of that industry, but not in the land itself, just as industry expended on the ocean would give a right of ownership to the fish taken by it, but not a right of ownership in the ocean (George, p. 37).

POPE:       When a man ... spends the industry of his mind and the strength of his body in procuring the fruits of nature, by that act he makes his own that portion of nature's field which he cultivates—that portion on which he leaves, as it were, the impress of his own personality; and it cannot but be just that he should possess that portion as his own, and should have a right to keep it without molestation (Leo XIII, p. 114).

For the soil which is tilled and cultivated with toil and skill utterly changes its condition; it was wild before, it is now fruitful; it was barren, and now it brings forth in abundance. That which has thus altered and improved it becomes so truly part of itself as to be in great measure indistinguishable and inseparable from it. Is it just that the fruit of a man's sweat and labor should be enjoyed by another (Leo XIII, pp. 114-15)?

GEORGE:     If industry give ownership to land, what are the limits of this ownership? ... Is it on the rights given by the industry of those who first used it for grazing cows or growing potatoes that you would found the title to the land now covered by the city of New York and having a value of thousands of millions of dollars?

There is, indeed, no improvement of land,... that, so long as its usefulness continues, does not have a value distinguishable from the value of the land. For land having such improvement will always sell or rent for more than similar land without them (George, p. 36-38).

POPE:       The common opinion of mankind ... has consecrated by the practice of all ages the principle of private ownership, as being preeminently in conformity with human nature, and as conducing in the most unmistakable manner to the peace and tranquillity of human life (Leo XIII, p. 115).

GEORGE:     Even were it true that the common opinion of mankind has sanctioned private property in land, this would no more prove its justice than the once universal practice of the known world would have proved the justice of slavery.

But it is not true. Examination will show that wherever we can trace them the first perceptions of mankind have always recognized the equality of right to land.

Private property in land as we know it ... has never grown up anywhere save by usurpation of force. Like slavery, it is the result of war (George, pp. 40-41).

As to private property in land having conduced to the peace and tranquillity of human life, it is not necessary more than to allude to the notorious fact that the struggle for land has been the prolific source of wars and of lawsuits, while it is the poverty engendered by private property in land that makes the prison and the workhouse the unfailing attributes of what we call Christian civilization (George, p. 43).

POPE:       The right to possess private property is from nature, not from man; and the State has only the right to regulate its use in the interests of the public good, but by no means to abolish it altogether. The State

 

|  |  |
|---|---|
|  | is therefore unjust and cruel if, in the name of taxation, it deprives the private owner of more than is just (Leo XIII, p. 141). |
| GEORGE: | That private property in the products of labor is from nature is clear, for nature gives such things to labor, and to labor alone. |

GEORGE: (continued)
But who will dare trace the individual ownership of land to any grant from the Maker of land? ... How can ... individual ownership attach to land, which existed before man was, and which continues to exist while the generations of men come and go? So far from there being anything unjust in taking the value of landownership for the use of the community, the real injustice is in leaving it in private hands—an injustice that amounts to robbery and murder (George, pp. 52-53).

POPE:
Whenever the general interest of any particular class suffers, or is threatened with, evils which can in no other way be met, the public authority must step in to meet them.... The limits must be determined by the nature of the occasion which calls for the law's interference (Leo XIII, pp. 133-34).

GEORGE:
I have already referred generally to the defects that attach to all socialistic remedies for the evil condition of labor.

Of these, the widest and strongest are that the State should restrict the hours of labor, the employment of women and children, the unsanitary conditions of workshops, etc. Yet how little may in this way be accomplished.

The greatest difficulty in enforcing such regulations comes from those whom they are intended to benefit. It is not, for instance, the masters who make it difficult to enforce restrictions on child labor in factories, but the mothers, who, prompted by poverty, misrepresent the ages of their children even to the masters, and teach the children to misrepresent.

Nor can the State cure poverty by regulating wages. It is as much beyond the power of the State to regulate wages as it is to regulate the rates of interest (George, pp. 71-73).

POPE:
If a workman's wages be sufficient ... he will not find it difficult ... to put by a little property; nature and reason would urge him to do this....The law, therefore, should favor ownership.

Many excellent results will follow from this; and first of all, property will certainly become more equitably divided.... If working-people can be encouraged to look forward to obtaining a share in the land, the result will be that the gulf between vast wealth and deep poverty will be bridged over (Leo XIII, p. 140).

GEORGE:
The same hopelessness attends your suggestion that working-people should be encouraged by the State in obtaining a share of the land.... Supposing that this can be done even to a considerable

❖

|          |                                                                      |
| -------- | -------------------------------------------------------------------- |
|          | extent, what will be accomplished save to substitute a larger privileged class for a smaller privileged class (George, p. 74)? |
| POPE:    | Most important ... are Workmen's Associations.... History attests what excellent results were effected by the Artificers' Guilds of a former day.... Such associations should be adapted to the requirements of the age in which we live (Leo XIII, p. 141). |
| GEORGE:  | Labor associations can do nothing to raise wages but by force.... They *must* coerce or hold the power to coerce employers; they *must* coerce those among their own members disposed to straggle; they *must* do their best to get into their hands the whole field of labor they seek to occupy and to force other working-men either to join them or to starve. Those who tell you of trades-unions bent on raising wages by moral suasion alone are like those who would tell you of tigers that live on oranges (George, pp. 76-77). |

What I wish to point out is that trades-unionism, while it may be a partial palliative, is not a remedy; that it has not that moral character which could alone justify one in the position of your Holiness in urging it as good in itself. Yet, so long as you insist on private property in land, what better can you do (George, p. 80).

| POPE:    | Every minister of holy Religion must ... cherish ... and try to arouse in others, Charity, the mistress and queen of virtues. For the happy results we all long for must be chiefly brought about by the plenteous outpouring of Charity ... which is always ready to sacrifice itself for others' sake, and which is man's surest antidote against worldly pride and immoderate love of self (Leo XIII, p. 151). |
| GEORGE:  | Charity is indeed a noble and beautiful virtue, grateful to man and approved by God. But charity must be built on justice. It cannot supersede justice. |

What is wrong with the condition of labor through the Christian world is that labor is robbed. And while you justify the continuance of that robbery, it is idle to urge charity.

All that charity can do where injustice exists is here and there to mollify somewhat the effects of injustice. It cannot cure them.

And thus that pseudo-charity that discards and denies justice works evil. On the one side, it demoralizes the recipients.... On the other side, it acts as an anodyne to the consciences of those who are living on the robbery of their fellows (George, pp. 92-93).

Servant of the Servants of God! I call you by the strongest and sweetest of your titles. In your hands more than in those of any living man lies the power to say the words and make the sign that shall end an unnatural divorce, and marry again to religion all that is pure and high in social aspiration (George, p. 104).

---
❖
---

## III. Epilogue

What happened after the publication of *RN* and *OL?* How did the two letters influence the consequent events, especially in New York and in Rome?

"No formal reply was ever made by Pope Leo to Henry George's rejoinder," wrote McGlynn's biographer (Bell, p. 124), "but it was not without its effects in Rome." A year and a half after *RN* appeared, a "most important episode" occurred. Dr. McGlynn was fully reinstated, "not at the instance of Dr. McGlynn himself, but of the Papal authorities." McGlynn drew up his own doctrinal statement. It was reviewed by a committee of four church authorities, who declared that it contained "nothing contrary to Catholic teachings," and on December 23, 1892, "Dr. McGlynn was declared free from ecclesiastical censures, and was restored to the exercise of his priestly functions" (Geiger, pp. 354-56). This restoration was accomplished without even consulting Archbishop Corrigan and his shocked supporters.

George's son wrote about the matter: "Many have thought that the reply that Henry George made to the papal encyclical in 1891 ... had influenced the broad-minded Leo XIII to review the case" (George, Jr., p. 560). In any case, "in June 1893, Father McGlynn visited Rome and was graciously received by the Pope, who gave him his apostolic blessing" (Geiger, p. 356). McGlynn later became pastor of St. Mary's Church in Newburgh, New York, remaining there until his death in 1900.

To the followers of McGlynn and George, McGlynn's victory was a cause of great rejoicing. "It is interesting," wrote a noted Georgist scholar, "that Henry George and Edward McGlynn won the greatest vindication—adoption of their position by the Magisterium, the teaching authority" (Lissner, p. 1). "But Father McGlynn's vindication," the writer noted further (Lissner, p. 3), "was to be even more complete. At the second Vatican Council, the Council Fathers ranged the Church on the side of land reform in the Constitution on the Church in the Modern World."

McGlynn lived to deliver a most impassioned eulogy at the funeral of Henry George, whom he survived by less than three years. He himself is remembered and loved (to this day) by Georgist followers, one of whom paid this tribute to his memory: "There is already a bronze monument to McGlynn, but he has in fact wrought out for himself a monument more lasting than bronze" (O'Regan 1942, p. 11).

What about Henry George? How did he fare after the publications of the Pope's letter and his own in reply?

A prominent Georgist answered the question unequivocally: "Henry George read the Pope a lesson in the history of economic doctrines and in the relations between economics and ethics in his *OL*. The work of George's had a profound influence upon Catholic social thinking in Europe and America" (Lissner, p. 3).

However, a biographer of George remained dubious about George's influence on the Pope:

Recent Catholic scholarship assumes that George's book did have an effect within the Church, and did help to restore McGlynn. This seems the only plausible assumption. Yet if this is true, the outsider's little book helped to establish a very puzzling church situation. For the ... decision appears to contradict utterly the secret condemnation of George's works, by the Inquisition, three years earlier (Barker, p. 577).

A well-known Georgist theorist also had his doubts about George's influence on the Vatican.

There is...no evidence to show that George's letter had any bearing upon Father McGlynn's unsolicited reinstatement. It is probable that this unusual action on the part of the Holy See was instead determined largely on the grounds of general church policy, for Dr. McGlynn's punishment had created a decided schism in the ranks of New York and even of American Catholicism (Geiger, p. 370).

What about Pope Leo's social status after the publication of the encyclical? Mention was already made of RN as the "Magna Charta" of the working man. The Pope's encyclical was of decisive import in Catholic social tradition. *RN,* according to one source,

still stands as the authoritative utterance of Pope Leo XIII. Succeeding Pontiffs and innumerable priests and prelates have quoted from it and endorse it. It still seems to condemn the Georgean land doctrine. Its apparent inconsistency with the judgment of ... the Catholic ... authorities in the McGlynn case puzzled many clergymen and laymen (Bell, p. 298).

In this centenary year of 1991, the case continues to puzzle. The matter remains unresolved.

*Professor of English, English Department, Nassau Community College, State University of New York, Garden City, New York, 11530 USA.

# References

Barker, Charles Albro. *Henry George,* New York: Oxford University Press, 1955.

Bell, Stephen. *Rebel, Priest and Prophet,* New York: The Devin Adair Company, 1937.

Benestad, J. Brian. "Henry George and the Catholic View of Morality and the Common Good, II," *American Journal of Economics and Sociology,* January 1986, *45,* 115-123.

                                    ❖

Curran, Robert Emmet. "The McGlynn Affair and the Shaping of the New Conservatism in American Catholicism, 1886-1894," *The Catholic Historical Review*, April 1980, *66*, 184-204.

Geiger, George Raymond. *The Philosophy of Henry George*, New York: The Macmillan Company, 1933.

George, Henry. *The Condition of Labor: An Open Letter to Pope Leo XIII*, in *The Land Question*, 1-105, New York: Robert Schalkenbach Foundation, 1982.

George, Henry. Jr. *The Life of Henry George*, New York: Robert Schalkenbach Foundation, 1960.

Leo XIII. *The Condition of Labor (Rerum Novarum)*, in *The Land Question*, 107-151, New York: Robert Schalkenbach Foundation, 1982.

Lissner, Will. "Father McGlynn and Catholic Social Doctrine," *The Henry George News*, June 1967.

Nuesse, C. Joseph. "Henry George and 'Rerum Novarum'" *American Journal of Economics and Sociology*, April 1985, *44*, 241-254.

O'Regan, P.J. "A Catholic Layman Looks at George," Henry George School of Social Science, New York, n.d. (Reprinted from *The Catholic World*, December 1942.)

Post, Louis F. *The Prophet of San Francisco*, New York: The Vanguard Press, 1930.

# Rerum Novarum and the American Connection

## L. A. O'Donnell*

It is my thesis that the actions of Cardinal Gibbons of Baltimore and Terence Powderly of Scranton, leader of the Knights of Labor, were a significant factor leading to the issuance of the encyclical whose centennial we are here to commemorate. In the 1880s the efforts of these two men made peace between the Roman Catholic Church and organized labor, resolving a potentially dangerous conflict in a way that had a lasting impact; an impact which played no small role in persuading Pope Leo XIII to issue *Rerum Novarum (RN)*.

## I. Labor in the Post Civil War Period

Let me begin my analysis by sketching the economic and social climate of America in the Post Civil War period in which a labor crisis for the Roman Catholic Church arose. It was a period of vigorous but uneven growth in the economy. Real GNP grew at an annual rate of 3.9 percent and real per capita output at 1.6 percent from 1855 to 1905. But in each of the last three decades of the nineteenth century there were serious recessions. In two of these (the 1870s and 1890s) the unemployment rate averaged ten percent (Lebergott 1984, pp. 61, 497). Much of this instability was attributable to wide swings in railroad investment. Needless to say there was no safety net at this time.

The downturn beginning in 1873 was the most severe and prolonged. A major contributing factor was the bankruptcy of Jay Cooke's Northern Pacific Railroad venture in September of 1873. That collapse was almost assured when Congress refused further aid to the Northern Pacific because of the Credit Mobilier scandal (then current) involved in the building of the Union Pacific Railroad. In short, public outrage at the railroads was building. When, due to the depressed economy, wage cuts were imposed by the railroads in 1877 spontaneous strikes broke out, first against the B&O Line in Martinsburg, West Virginia and then spread rapidly across the country with enormous destruction of railroad property.

In the same period a pioneering union of miners in the anthracite region of Pennsylvania was broken in the long strike of 1875 by the intransigence of Franklin Gowen, president of the Reading Railroad. Gowen wanted no union to interfere with profits he expected from efforts to monopolize transportation of coal to the Philadelphia market. In the aftermath of the failed strike, violence erupted in the region. Attacks on mine operators and destruction of mining property were attributed to a secret society of Irish miners labelled the "Molly Maguires." After trials prosecuted by Gowen himself, twenty Irishmen were hanged in 1877 and 1878. This episode left a heavy residue of uneasiness in the parishes of the anthracite region.

## II. Terence Powderly and James Gibbons

An understanding of the Church and labor crisis will benefit from acquaintance with the careers of the two leading figures in this drama.

Though the Archbishop of Baltimore had no direct contact with the anthracite region, Terence Powderly, the youngest son of a large Catholic family grew up there. He was thoroughly acquainted with the mining industry in which his father had worked for fifteen years and had at one time operated a small mine.

As a youth Terence Powderly was strongly influenced by ideals of the original American Republic which predominated in industrial towns like Carbondale and Scranton, Pennsylvania when Powderly was growing up in these communities. Artisanal Republicanism is a term historians have used to refer to these ideals as they inspired craft workers beginning early in the nineteenth century. In its insistence on the dignity of labor and its concern for the commonweal, Artisanal Republicanism had much in harmony with ideas which appeared in *RN*.

For skilled workmen and small entrepreneurs in this milieu God's earth and human labor were to be used for the benefit of all – for the commonwealth. Work ennobled the individual, enabled him to realize his talents, his humanity. It amounted to participation in God's creation for it produced goods for society's happiness and progress. The worker-citizen must have a voice in making rules for the shop as well as for the governance of society. To be a productive member of both he must be free of tyranny from his employer and his government. An orderly republican form of democracy would make this possible if its members exercised the responsibilities of informed, intelligent citizenship.

Active citizens could assure that human and civil rights were protected. It is essential that citizens exhibit virtue in the form of restraint of individual indulgence or aggrandizement in favor of the common good. The just society need not be classless, but required equality of opportunity and fair reward for thrift and hard work. Such was the nature of what historians have begun to call Artisanal Republicanism.

At age thirteen Terence Powderly entered the world of work as a switchman for a coal hauling railway. Four years later, with his father's help, he was

❖

apprenticed to James Dickson, master mechanic in the Delaware and Hudson Railroad shops.

Terence Powderly's career was bound up with the coming of age of American railroads. In a variety of ways it was linked to the rise of and reaction to railway corporations – its high and low points were connected to dealings with this industry. The railroads which had reached the Mississippi River a few years after he was born in 1849, represented America's first large scale corporations. They were the first enterprises to employ men by the tens of thousands – introducing depersonalized employee relations – a sure cause of worker disaffection. The large administrative structures of railroads required some of the nation's earliest professional managers whose decisions and whims directly affected the livelihood of employees, and inspired employees to an effort to control their destinies through organization – frequently involving the Knights of Labor.

Railroad executives importuned state and federal legislatures for laws favorable to them in regard to charters, tax assessments, or abatements, land grants, loans, and so forth. This was often done by distributing railroad passes, corporate stock at below market prices and straightforward bribery, so that standards of republican government were subverted. These developments stimulated instincts of reform in Powderly and his movement.

Requirements for capital to build the railroads were far larger than for earlier enterprises and led to the institutionalization of investment markets in New York, opening opportunities for financiers, speculators and lawyers which not infrequently were used to manipulate stock prices, engage in insider trading and attempts to create monopoly which offended adherents of republican ideals (Chandler 1965, pp. 9-12).

In view of all this it was hardly unexpected that Congress regulated the railroads in 1887 through passage of the Interstate Commerce Commission Act. Impetus for the law came primarily from farm organizations with abundant support from the general public.

After failure of his mining venture, Terence Powderly's father became an early employee of the fledgling Delaware and Hudson Railway (a feeder line between mines and the D&H Canal). Subsequently he obtained employment for his thirteen year old son and namesake with the same firm in 1862.

Terence Powderly first became a union member on November 2, 1871 when he joined the Machinists and Blacksmith's Union which by that time had a large part of its membership in railroad shops. By February of 1873 he was elected president of a local in Scranton. However, the decisive event in his conversion to an advocate of workers' welfare was his layoff and subsequent blacklisting at the onset of the panic of 1873. The protracted economic downturn affected him deeply. He was rudely apprised of railroad labor policy by Walter Dawson his superintendent at the D&H Railroad, who chose to discharge him early because of his union office and proceeded to blacklist him in the Scranton community. At this time he was forced to leave Scranton to find work and discovered that blacklisting by Dawson dogged

❖

his tracks everywhere he went. The severe depression of the seventies moved him to recognize the shortcomings of capitalism and the necessity for labor reform.

Powderly eventually returned to Scranton and worked as a machinist in spite of further blacklistings by Dawson which were overturned through the intercession of William W. Scranton, General Manager of the Lackawanna Iron and Coal Company in the city – a member of the family after whom the city was named in recognition of its pioneering iron and railroad enterprises responsible for development of the area.

These experiences, perception of the machinations of Franklin Gowen, builder of a transportation monopoly in anthracite through the Reading Railroad, awareness of antics of Vanderbilt, Gould, Drew and their associates in the stock markets, their corruptive activities in the courts and legislatures were sufficient to persuade Powderly that traditional republican values of our nation were being perverted. The federal government's huge land grants to the railroads was another element of his distrust of large corporations and blended into his Irish passion for land reform.

A receptiveness to anti-monopoly movements, monetary reform and cooperative enterprise were for Terence Powderly the legacy of his encounters with economic reality. Therefore, on becoming reestablished in Scranton he organized a local unit of the Greenback-Labor organization – a third party. In February of 1878, Powderly was elected for the first of three two-year terms as mayor of Scranton on the Greenback-Labor ticket.

In September of the year following the first mayoralty victory, he was elected leader of the Scranton district assembly of the Noble Order of Knights of Labor in which he had been initiated as a member only three years before. His rise was advanced significantly by productive service on the committee on constitution of the Knights of Labor convention in Reading. He became an influential voice on behalf of lifting the secrecy of the Knights of Labor, a cause of opposition to the Order by the Catholic Church. Finally, in September of 1879 he was elected Grand Master Workman of the Order at a convention in Chicago (Wilentz 1984, p. 14; Oestreicher 1987, pp. 34-36).

Like Powderly, Gibbons was the son of Irish immigrants. Born in Baltimore in 1834, a few years after his parents had emigrated from County Mayo (where two of his three sisters had been born) he nevertheless spent sixteen years growing up in Ireland. His father, Thomas Gibbons became a merchant's clerk in the bustling young port city of Baltimore and enjoyed prosperity sufficient to provide for the family of five children. Thomas Gibbons' success in the New World is attested by the fact that he took a sea voyage for his health with his family in tow arriving in Ireland in 1837.

Upon returning to Ireland Thomas Gibbons, for reasons unknown, decided to settle the family there and operate a grocery store in County Mayo. In 1847 in the midst of the Potato Famine, Thomas Gibbons died. The family, in straitened circumstances, remained in Ireland until 1853. In that year, they returned to

America in two separate groups and were reunited in New Orleans where they resided permanently.

James Gibbons had studied Greek and Latin in Ireland and as a boy was attracted to a priestly vocation. In New Orleans, however, he was obliged to go to work as a grocery store clerk to help support the family. By 1855, his mind firmly set on becoming a priest, he returned to Baltimore and entered the seminary.

Ordained in 1861 he began as assistant pastor of a parish in a poor section along the Baltimore waterfront. Four and a half years later his ability was recognized in his appointment as secretary to Martin Spalding, recently installed as Archbishop of Baltimore. Gibbons' rise in the American Catholic Church was no less rapid than was Powderly's in the labor movement.

Initially, as secretary to the leading American Catholic churchman, he was involved in preparations for and managing of the second Plenary Council of American Bishops held in Baltimore in 1866. Having made an excellent impression on members of the hierarchy and especially Archbishop Spalding, he was recommended for and duly appointed by Rome as Bishop of North Carolina at age thirty-four. He was, at that time, the youngest Catholic bishop in the nation.

A similar experience followed when he participated in the year and a half long Vatican Council in Rome called by Pius IX. Less than two years later he was appointed Bishop of Richmond. When Spalding's successor in Baltimore (James Roosevelt Bayley) died in 1877, Gibbons, then in his mid-forties, became head of the premier See in the United States (Ellis 1952; Gibbons 1916).

In his forty-four year tenure as shepherd of the "immigrant church" in the New World, Gibbons became well-known for his endorsement of the blessings of democracy and religious freedom in the United States. He wished to establish acceptance of the Catholic Church in America where anti-papist sentiments were still strong and periodically broke out in public. He was one of those in the church who has been labelled an Americanizer by historians. His position, his courage and his good judgment enabled him to exert great influence on the direction of the American Church. His was the voice of American Catholicism until his death in 1921.

Gibbons' decision to support the Knights of Labor was not sudden or ill-considered. It was based upon his growing conviction that workers' organizations were necessary to further the cause of justice in the workplace. In his view the Order merely sought redress for just grievances stemming from abuses of corporate employers, particularly in the railroad industry.

## III. Church Acceptance of the Knights of Labor

As leader of the Knights of Labor Powderly's dealings with the hierarchy of the American Catholic Church were historically important. They represent his most significant contribution to the development of labor organizations in America. They called for a high order of discretion and diplomacy on his part amidst vigorous

❖

pressures from opposing sides of the church and labor issue. On one side he was bedeviled by Catholic clergy and laymen for his leadership of a quasi-Masonic labor organization. When largely through his endeavors, secrecy, oaths and rituals were gradually set aside, abuse was heaped upon him by critics of the Church inside and outside the Order (particularly those in the nativist American Protective Association) who charged him with slavishly following the dictates of the Catholic hierarchy. From the time Powderly joined the Order – which had a strong religious orientation (though distinctly not a Catholic one) he was opposed to its policy of secrecy and use of quasi-sectarian rituals with Masonic overtones in initiations and other ceremonies. They were a legacy of Uriah Stephens, founder of the Order, who at one time studied in a Baptist seminary. Stephens was also a member of the Masonic Order. It should be pointed out, however, that secrecy was also a practical response to bitter employer hostility toward unions.

Powderly recognized that a large proportion of the work force was Catholic and perceived that these practices were impediments to their joining or remaining members of the Order. He estimated that two-thirds of the membership was Catholic. This estimate was included in a letter from Powderly in August of 1886, to his old Pastor Father Francis Carew of Carbondale, Pennsylvania, the town where Powderly was born and raised. It was a covering letter accompanying a copy of the constitution of the Knights of Labor which had been requested by Gibbons in a letter sent to Father Carew earlier (Browne 1949, p. 190). It is fair to say that most of the clergy and a majority of the hierarchy, had grave reservations about labor organizations and most especially secret ones. They were acutely conscious of the Molly Maguires episode of recent memory. A major conflict between the two institutions impended.

In the second half of the nineteenth century the growth of secret fraternal societies mushroomed in the United States. In many cases Catholics comprised a substantial element in them. Members of the clergy and hierarchy became concerned and no consensus evolved among them as to the appropriate response. As a result, at the Third Plenary Council of American Bishops in 1884, it was decided to lay the question before the nation's twelve archbishops, acting in concert, for their decision (Ellis).

The Knights of Labor was, of course, considered one of these secret societies. What's more its membership grew to an unprecented size of over 700,000 between 1884 and 1886. The cause was a successful strike of shopmen in 1885 against the southwest system of railroads controlled by Jay Gould. Powderly negotiated the settlement in direct talks with the powerful industrialist himself. A stampede to join the Order followed.

Only a year later Gould broke a strike on his railroads by replacing those on strike. Powderly, in efforts to find a settlement, was hoodwinked by the deceptive Jay Gould. The flood tide of new members now ebbed with equal speed.

Prospects for the conflict had heightened in October of 1883 when the Archbishop of Quebec, Alexandre Taschereau, applied to Rome for a ruling on

❖

whether the Knights of Labor should be condemned. The conflict blossomed in September of 1884 when Taschereau, with specific Vatican authorization in a message from Cardinal Giovanni Simeoni, Prefect of Congregation of Propaganda, condemned the Order.

Taschereau actively spread word of the communication he received from Cardinal Simeoni. He denounced Powderly when the leader of the Knights was in Quebec during a Canadian tour in the Spring of 1886. In April of that year he condemned the Order along with the Masons in a letter to the clergy and faithful in the Archdiocese of Quebec. The same condemnation was repeated in June through a pastoral letter in association with all ten bishops of the Provincial Council over which Taschereau presided.

On the other side Powderly was campaigning for approval. He was buoyed by reports that Archbishop Lynch of Toronto was supportive of the Order. He wrote to Archbishop Ryan of Philadelphia explaining the Order, and through Father Carew, his own pastor, communicated with Gibbons (Browne, p. 190).

Powderly also initiated efforts to make personal contact with Cardinal Gibbons, whom he recognized was the leading Catholic churchman in the United States. He first approached Bishop Keane of Richmond in early October of 1886 when the Order was holding a general assembly in the Virginia capital and met with him twice at that time. Keane arranged a meeting with Gibbons on October 28th. This date was chosen intentionally to coincide with a conference of American archbishops called by Gibbons to consider the question of secret societies and other matters. Powderly met with the hierarchs and explained that the Order had dispensed with secrecy and eliminated sectarian rituals and its oath effective January of 1882. He provided a copy of the constitution and assured the assembled metropolitans that other objectionable aspects would be removed.

After Powderly completed his presentation and departed, the archbishops deliberated on the question of condemning the Knights of Labor. At this time Gibbons noted that there were 500,000 Catholics in the Knights of Labor (Browne, p. 215). Two of their number spoke in favor of outright condemnation. Seven opposed it for various reasons. Also, two of the three archbishops who were unable to attend had sent messages opposing condemnation. In the upshot, for lack of unanimity, it was decided that the matter should be taken up with Rome and this was to be done by Gibbons who presided over the Baltimore meeting (Browne, pp. 211-220). In June of 1886 Rome had appointed both Gibbons and Taschereau as Cardinals. Early in the following year they embarked on the same ship for the journey to Rome to receive the red hat. While in the Holy City both of them pressed their case on opposite sides of the condemnation issue.

Cardinal Gibbons was the more persuasive. His statement to the Congregation of the Holy Office was couched in diplomatic but forceful language. It was an eloquent and powerful expression of reasons why it would be gravely unwise to condemn the Knights of Labor. He emphasized the "vast importance" of the question of condemnation. His report summarized the actions of American bishops

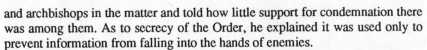

and archbishops in the matter and told how little support for condemnation there was among them. As to secrecy of the Order, he explained it was used only to prevent information from falling into the hands of enemies.

Members were free to tell all to priests inside or outside of confession. Laws of the Order required neither an oath, nor blind obedience. The organization harbored no hostility toward religion generally, the Roman Church specifically, nor was it opposed to law or authority in American government. The Knights of Labor was basically harmless in Gibbons' view (and would not last very long).

On the other hand, social evils afflicting American workers were all too real from Gibbons point of view (pp. 194-95):

> That there exist among us, as in all other countries of the world, grave and threatening social evils, public injustices which call for strong resistance and legal remedy, is a fact which no one dares to deny – a fact already acknowledged by the Congress and the President of the United States. Without entering into the sad details of these evils, whose full discussion is not necessary, I will only mention that monopolies, on the part of both individuals and of corporations, have everywhere called forth not only the complaints of our working classes, but also the opposition of our public men and legislators; that the efforts of monopolists, not always without success, to control legislation to their own profit, cause serious apprehensions among the disinterested friends of liberty; that the heartless avarice which, through greed of gain, pitilessly grinds not only the men, but even the women and children in various employments, make it clear to all who love humanity and justice that it is not only the right of the laboring classes to protect themselves, but the duty of the whole people to aid them in finding a remedy against the dangers with which both civilization and social order are menaced by avarice, oppression and corruption .

The report explained that workers form associations for mutual help and protection in lawful efforts to secure their rights. Yes, they combine with those of other religions or no religion for this purpose, but this is inevitable in American society. Nevertheless, Catholics show no inclination to lose their faith. Also inevitable are strikes and some violence when dealing with powerful and obstinate monopolies. But these also are discouraged by the Order. These unfortunate realities will not be obviated, but only worsened by condemnation. In Gibbons words (pp. 199-200):

> I repeat that, in such a struggle of the great masses of the people against the mail-clad power, which as it is acknowledged, often refuses them the simple rights of humanity and justice, it is vain to expect that every error and every act of violence can be avoided; and to dream that this

❖

struggle can be hindered, or that we can deter the multitudes from organizing, which is their only hope of success; would be to ignore the nature and forces of human society in times like ours. Christian prudence evidently counsels us to hold the hearts of the multitudes by the bonds of love, in order to control their actions by the principles of faith, justice and charity, to acknowledge frankly what is true and just in their cause, in order to deter them from what is false and criminal, and thus to turn into a legitimate, peaceable and beneficent contest what might easily, by a course of repulsive severity, become for the masses of our people a dread volcanic force like unto that which society fears and the Church deplores in Europe. (Gibbons, pp. 199-200)

Dire consequences, he believed, would flow from condemnation. The future of the Church and human society are at stake. Quoting an assertion by Britain's Cardinal Manning that "Piling up wealth like mountains, in the possession of classes or individuals cannot go on," he is convinced that the future depends upon working people. Their welfare must be improved. Lack of sympathy for them will lead to hostility toward the Church, loss of its influence and the respect it currently enjoys in America's democratic society. In an oft-quoted passage Cardinal Gibbons pointed out tellingly "to lose the heart of the people would be a misfortune for which the friendship of a few rich and powerful would be no compensation" (Gibbons, p. 203).

Gibbons warned that condemnation would cause workers not only to refuse to observe such a decree but also arouse suspicion and even anger toward their own Church in the minds of the faithful. He did not fail to remind the Sacred Congregation of the negative impact on financial support for the Church as well as undercutting the American bishops in their opposition to condemnation.

A copy of Gibbons' submission to the Holy Office was leaked to the press by persons unknown and published in the *New York Herald*. It elicited congratulations from friends of the Church and of Labor such as John Swinton, longtime labor journalist and editor; Cardinal Henry E. Manning, Archbishop of Westminster, an old friend of Gibbons; and of course Powderly who wrote a letter of thanks to the Cardinal for his defense of the Order. Needless to say opponents reacted suspiciously to the news. The latter included the *Nation*, a journal of opinion, Bishop Bernard McQuaid of Rochester and a number of Protestant religious periodicals (Browne, pp. 253, 255-258, 264).

Concrete results of Gibbons efforts were forthcoming on August 29, 1888 in the form of a communication from the Holy Office declaring "Tolerari Possunt" or conditional toleration of the Knights of Labor. The conditional nature of the decision related to the assurance by Powderly that other objectionable features of the Order would be eliminated. Although this was never accomplished in spite of Gibbons appeals to Powderly for evidence of its having been done – no more was

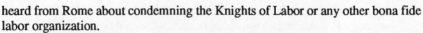

heard from Rome about condemning the Knights of Labor or any other bona fide labor organization.

Gibbons invited Powderly to Baltimore where he once again asked about elimination of the remaining objectionable features, but no further changes were forthcoming (Browne, pp. 326-327).

Powderly's leadership of a greatly diminished Knights of Labor endured until 1893 when he was unseated by a palace revolt. His life of thirty years thereafter may be sketched in brief. Unable to return to his original craft of machinist, he turned to the study of law and was admitted to the Pennsylvania Bar in 1894. His leadership skills now led him into national politics. In the campaign of 1896 he supported McKinley with whom he had become acquainted in Cleveland years before. In return the new President appointed him Commissioner General of Immigration. He remained a public servant (except for a brief interlude involving a misunderstanding with Theodore Roosevelt) until his retirement in 1921. Ironically, in later years Powderly joined the Masonic Order, abandoning the Catholic faith. He died on June 24, 1924.

## IV. The Knights of Labor and Church Teaching

The crisis had precipitated a challenge for the Church of Rome to make up its official mind on where it stood on the status of workers in the modern world and the associations workers had established for their protection and security. It is a tribute to the esteem in which James Cardinal Gibbons was held in Rome that he was able to convince the cautious tradition-bound bureaucracy of the Vatican of the wisdom of his advice. Here was a fresh voice from a relatively young and vigorous branch of the Roman Catholic Church goading its leadership away from making a decision which could alienate the working people of its democratic land.

It was Gibbons' thinking that this was a profound moral issue which should not be decided in the narrow legalistic fashion for which the Roman Curia had become known. In his mind it was a question of whether the Church should follow the example of Christ and come to the aid of ordinary working people of the new industrial age or ally itself with the side of the rich and powerful. Like other perceptive observers of his time he was conscious of the rise of corporate monopoly in the economy. He held no brief for the railroad magnates and their corrupting influence and ruthless labor policies.

I leave to others the task of recording the numerous echoes of these views which appear in *RN*, but I am convinced that the following excerpt is a lineal descendent of Gibbons ideas:

> After the old trade guilds had been destroyed in the last century, and no protection was substituted in their place, and when public institutions and legislation had cast off traditional religious teaching, it gradually came about that the present age handed over the workers, each alone

❖

and defenseless, to the inhumanity of employers and the unbridled greed of competitors. A devouring usury, although often condemned by the Church, but practiced nevertheless under another form by vicious and grasping men, had increased the evil; and in addition the whole process of production as well as trade in every kind of goods has been brought almost entirely under the power of a few, so that a very few rich and exceedingly rich men have laid a yoke almost of slavery on the unnumbered masses of non-owning workers (*RN*, #6).

Cardinal Gibbons derived great satisfaction from the publication of *RN*. He had spoken of the worker's dilemma from across the ocean and was reassured when his basic notions were reflected in the Pastoral from Rome.

*Department of Economics, Villanova University, Villanova, PA 18085 USA.

## References

Brown, Henry J. *The Catholic Church and the Knights of Labor*, Washington, DC: Catholic University of America Press, 1949.

Chandler, Alfred DuPont, Jr. *The Railroads: The Nation's First Big Business*, New York: Harcourt & Brace, 1967.

Ellis, John Tracy. *The Life of James Cardinal Gibbons*, Milwaukee: Bruce, 1952.

Gibbons, James Cardinal. *A Retrospect of Fifty Years*, Baltimore: John Murphy Co., 1916.

Leo XIII. *Rerum Novarum, Encyclical Letter on the Condition of Labor*, authorized English translation, Washington, DC: National Catholic Welfare Conference, 1942.

Lebergott, Stanley. *The Americans: An Economic Record*, New York: Norton, 1984.

Oestreicher, Richard. "Terence Powderly, The Knights of Labor and Artisanal Republicanism," in M. Dubofsky and W. Van Tine, eds., *Labor Leaders in America*, Urbana: University of Illinois Press, 1987.

Wilentz, Sean. *Chants Democratic*, New York: Oxford University Press, 1984.

❖

# Rerum Novarum and Economic Conditions in 1991

## Kishor Thanawala*

*Rerum Novarum (RN)* is considered by many scholars as the beginning of the Catholic Church's social teaching in the modern period. It has been described by Pius XI in *Quadragesimo Anno (QA)* as the *Magna Carta* on which all Christian activities on social matters are ultimately based (§ 39). Although the theme of the encyclical is sometimes narrowly interpreted as examining the condition of workers in the then industrialized countries (mainly, in Europe and North America), the document contains a statement of fundamental principles that should form the basis of any discussion pertaining to significant issues like income distribution, wealth distribution and employee-employer relationships. It is therefore not surprising that during the 100th anniversary year of the encyclical scholars find it instructive to read the pages of *RN* and learn that in some important ways the world has not changed much insofar as the relevance of *RN* is concerned.

## I. Economic Conditions in 1891 and 1991

In describing the prevailing conditions in 1891, we learn in the very first paragraph of *RN* that:

> The elements of a conflict are unmistakable; the growth of industry, and the surprising discoveries of science; the changed relations of masters and workmen; the enormous fortunes of individuals and the poverty of the masses; the increased self-reliance and the closer mutual combination of the working population; and finally, a general moral deterioration. The momentous seriousness of the present state of things just now fills every mind with painful apprehension; wise men discuss it; practical men propose schemes; popular meetings, legislatures, and sovereign princes, all are preoccupied with it—and there is nothing which has a deeper hold on public attention (§1).

—————————————————— ❖ ——————————————————

Are conditions that much different today? It is said that every great work is a product of its times. Although the above remarks depict the world in 1891, *RN* could as well have been written in 1991. Indeed it has been described by Pius IX as the "immortal document" (QA, § 39). What has made this document so timeless is its proclamation of what were perceived as the fundamental conditions for justice in the economic and social situation of 1891. But in so doing, a new and lasting paradigm was created: there can be no genuine solution of the social question without the fundamental condition of justice.

> ...when there is the question of protecting the rights of individuals, the poor and helpless have a claim to special consideration. The richer population have many ways of protecting themselves, and stand less in need of help from the State; those who are badly off have no resources of their own to fall back upon, and must chiefly rely upon the assistance of the State. And it is for this reason that wage-earners, who are undoubtedly among the weak and necessitous, should be specially cared for and protected by the common-wealth (§29).

These remarks are especially relevant today, in view of disturbing evidence about increasing poverty, both absolute and relative, to be found within countries (less developed and industrialized) as well as between countries. *RN* forcefully states that the more that individuals are helpless, defenseless within a society, the more they need and require the care of others. And, if this care is not forthcoming voluntarily from more fortunate individuals and private organizations, it is the obligation of the government to see that the basic needs of the less fortunate are met. In today's international economy, this statement can be and should be applied not merely to individuals within a particular society but also to individuals in any society and indeed to societies generally. In other words, the principle of solidarity is valid both in the internal order of each society and in the international order. (This point has been argued by John Paul II in *Sollicitudo Rei Socialis* and in *Centesimus Annus (CA)*.

In discussing "the condition of labor," *RN* was really discussing the condition of the poor and the subhuman conditions in which the people were forced to live as a direct consequence of the industrialization of societies. In 1991, conditions similar to those which prompted the birth of *RN* are being created by social, political, economic and technological changes. And unlike 1891, the poor people everywhere are painfully aware (thanks to modern telecommunications) of the vast differences in the standards of living both within and between different societies. A cursory survey of the available data indicates that a very large number of people all over the world live under conditions of absolute poverty. And these conditions have, if anything, worsened during the last ten years.

❖

## II. Condition of the Poor During the Last Decade

Intertemporal analysis of the change in the conditions under which the very poor people live is always difficult. Selection of the aspects of well-being that should be considered as well as their acceptable minimal level is very contentious both from a political and from an ethical point of view. Further, data problems make the analysis of living conditions more complicated. Apart from the fact some elements are qualitative, and therefore resist measurement, comparable and reliable time series are not always available even for developed societies. Finally, aggregation and weighing affect measurement. If we agree that a minimum threshold of consumption (and, therefore, of income) is needed for human survival and that the marginal value of income decreases with increases in the level of income, an equal reduction in income will hurt the very poor more than the relatively less poor. So the question about the relative weights of the changes in the conditions of the very poor and those of the relatively less poor arises.

With all its limitations, income is the most commonly used measure of well-being because income determines access to markets (after all, economists define demand as desire backed by purchasing power!). And markets are where one can buy goods and services, consumption of which determines one's well-being. Broad-based economic growth is a necessary condition for sustained increases in the incomes of the poor. Most reductions in poverty come from increases in average income because income distribution changes very gradually. The majority of the world's poor do not seem to have benefitted significantly in the process of economic growth during the 1980s. Per capita income decreased annually by more than 2% in Sub-Saharan Africa where almost 200 million poor live. In Latin America where approximately 75 million poor live, per capita income during the 1980s registered a smaller decline. In East Asia where almost 300 million poor reside, per capita income did increase significantly and in South Asia where more than half a billion poor live, per capita income showed a more modest annual increase. World Bank studies indicate that poverty increased in Poland and Yugoslavia also. In spite of the existence of well-established social insurance programs, the 1980s were not kind to the poor in the developed world either. Recessionary conditions coincided with increase in poverty in Great Britain and in Australia due to higher unemployment. In the United States, poverty increased mainly due to lower wages among unskilled and low-skilled workers.

The policy-makers in Third World countries face an unpleasant choice: how to square off the need for growth without letting go of social justice. A recent study ranked leading Third World countries according to the priority that their government policies give to growth and investment as opposed to egalitarian distribution of income and wealth *(World Competitiveness Report 1991)*. According to this study Singapore was ranked at the top of the list of countries whose government policies favored investment and growth rather than income distribution. Of the other nine countries studied, Hong Kong, South Korea, Taiwan, Thailand, Malay-

❖

sia, Indonesia, Mexico, Brazil and India (in that order) assigned decreasing importance to investment and increasing importance to income distribution. It would appear from these rankings that the urge to give priority to distributional aspects is greatest in countries where the incidence of poverty is highest!

The disparity in per capita incomes between countries has also increased during the 1980s. While the per capita incomes in the low-income countries increased from approximately $200 at the beginning of the decade to about $320 at the end, the group of industrialized countries experienced an increase from approximately $8,100 to over $17,000 during the same time-period. And a recent study published by a United Nations agency concluded that the world's poorest countries are also generally the least free (United Nations Development Program 1991). This conclusion is based on a "human freedom index" which ranked 88 countries according to the degree of freedom enjoyed by their citizens. According to this study, all the countries enjoying a high freedom score are industrialized ones with the exception of Costa Rica. Countries whose score indicated little freedom were among the poorest countries like China, Bangladesh, Kenya, Liberia, Tanzania and Zaire. Countries where a medium level of freedom was noted included Egypt, India and Mexico. The study noted that there seems to be a high positive correlation between development and freedom. It is argued that political freedom seems to unleash creative energies of the people and lead to higher levels of income and social progress.

## III. Attitudinal and Institutional Changes Needed to Secure Justice for the Poor

One hundred years after *RN*, Pope John Paul II observed in *CA* (§58):

Justice will never be fully attained unless people see in the poor person, who is asking for help in order to survive, not an annoyance or a burden, but an opportunity for kindness and a chance for greater enrichment. Only such an awareness can give the courage needed to face the risk and the change involved in every authentic attempt to come to the aid of another. It is not merely a matter of giving from one's surplus, but of helping entire peoples which are presently excluded or marginalized to enter into the sphere of economic and human development. For this to happen, it is not enough to draw on the surplus goods which in fact our world abundantly produces, it requires above all a change of lifestyles, of models of production and consumption, and of the established structures of power which today govern societies. Nor is it a matter of eliminating instruments of social organization which have proved useful, but rather of orienting them according to an adequate notion of the common good in relation to the whole human family.

❖

Today we are facing the so-called 'globalization' of the economy, a phenomenon which is not to be dismissed, since it can create unusual opportunities for greater prosperity. There is a growing feeling, however, that this increasing internationalization of the economy ought to be accompanied by effective international agencies which will oversee and direct the economy to the common good, something that an individual state, even if it were the most powerful on earth, would not be in a position to do. In order to achieve this result, it is necessary that there be increased coordination among the more powerful countries, and that in international agencies the interests of the whole human family be equally represented. It is also necessary that in evaluating the consequences of their decisions, these agencies always give sufficient consideration to peoples and countries which have little weight in the international market, but which are burdened by the most acute and desperate needs, and are thus more dependent on support for their development. Much remains to be done in this area.

We noted above that *RN* in 1891 postulated that there can be no genuine solution of the social question without the fundamental condition of justice. One hundred years later, we do not only still have to attain this fundamental condition, we also have yet to establish the institutional backdrop that will help us achieve the fundamental condition of justice!

*Professor of Economics, Department of Economics, Villanova University, Villanova, PA 19085 USA.

# References

John Paul II. *Centesimus Annus*, Liberia Editrice Vaticana: Vatican City, 1991.

United Nation Development Program. *Human Development Report,* NY: United Nations, 1991.

*World Competitiveness Report 1991,* Geneva: World Economic Forum, 1991.

*Seven Great Encyclicals,* Glen Rock, NJ: Paulist Press, 1963.

---------------------------------- ❖ ----------------------------------

# Collective Bargaining and
# *Rerum Novarum*

## *Larry Donnelly\**

At a conference to commemorate the one hundredth birthday of *Rerum Novarum (RN)*, it seems appropriate to have a party to celebrate the "richness of the fundamental principles" and thoughts proposed in Pope Leo XIII's Encyclical. Such a celebration is particularly appropriate to the Association for Social Economics, one of the co-sponsors of this Congress. For, we have consistently recognized that thought workshops are a critical foundation for sound socio-economic analysis and policy. As a group, we believe that thought precedes action and principles guide actions.

To help in this celebration, our panel proposes a workshop with a very narrow focus. We intend to view the U.S. system of collective bargaining in the context of basic ideas and principles articulated in *RN*. Collective bargaining has been extensively analyzed on its own merits. It has also been scrutinized under the lens of economic models, of sociological constructs, even of quantitative models. So, why not view it from the perspective of the social paradigm proposed in *RN* and expanded in succeeding Encyclicals? To be sure, this body of Christian social thought has been historically inspired and fostered by Faith. But, one need not accept the Faith-basis of the Magisterium of the Popes to reason with their thoughts. Rather, people of any nation or creed can reason along with the thought to see its logic, applicability, and validity. For Leo XIII and his successors have consistently claimed that their thoughts do stand the test of "right reason." They have invited people of goodwill to try it.

Christian social thought begins with a paradox. *Social thought* is based on the inherent *dignity of each individual person*. A celebration of *RN* really commemorates the individual beauty of each of us. Each person carries a special worth (*RN*, §8 and §27). Like other forms of life around the earth, the human person can grow, can move, can be reproductive. Like other forms of animal life around the earth, the human person can sense, can feel. But, there is something special about a person's activities. A person can know reality beyond the individual to the transcendent, a person can think beyond the present moment to the past and to the future. Further, a person is aware of some freedom of choice in growing, being reproductive, knowing and experiencing emotions. These activities and traits are not merely ontological; they directly bear upon an individual's capacity for happiness and the responsible pursuit of the same. Through their Faith, the Popes explain such dignity and capacity for happiness in terms of a person's nature and destiny as reflective of a Divine Creator. Absent such Faith, an individual's own experience offers testimony and evidence of this worth and capacity for happiness; without Faith, the person is left with unanswered questions. Still, as was recently reemphasized in *Centesimus Annus (CA)*, the foundation of Christian social thought is the inherent dignity of each individual person (*CA*, §6 and §22).

Although we people can recognize our inherent dignity, we quickly see that each of us is only a part of the material world. In fact, people cannot remain indifferent to the world around them. Each person needs the physical world for food, for shelter, for comfort, for movement, for protection — for a happy life itself. Yet, these benefits are not ready-made. Rather, through their efforts, humans must fashion the material world to meet and serve their needs. Through mental and physical efforts, the human person exercises domain over the rest of nature. These efforts, called work, are inherent and necessary to people. Papal teaching, most recently in *Laborem Exercens (LE)*, has emphasized the importance of work noting that through work, the person provides for one's needs, the person realizes one's potentials, the person exercises creative powers, the person governs in the present and plans for the future (*LE*, Part II §9). Furthermore as *RN* observes, a person's own work stands as a basic title for private ownership of both personal and productive property (*RN*, §10). Work and private ownership of property are thus basic positive expressions of the dignity of the person within a material world.

Yet, both the individual person and private ownership of property have an inherent and necessary social dimension. The social character of the person begins with the moment of conception and flows through a person's birth and education. As an adult, the person grows through communication and sharing goods with other people. Further, people manifest an inherent tendency to join with others of like interests in pursuit of some common good or goal. First in *Quadrigessimo Anno (QA)*, then in *LE*, the Popes have expanded extensively upon this social character of peoples' work (*QA*, §69; *LE*, §42 and §44). Each person has particular skills and talents. By joining with others in work, each person can be more creative, can more fully develop, can more fully provide for one's own needs as well as providing for the needs of others. In *RN* unions are explicitly and strongly endorsed as natural associations of workers formed for the common good of their members (*RN*, §§55-58). This common good involves such elementary human claims or rights of workers as a just wage, humane conditions of employment, and participation in the operation of an economic enterprise to the extent of the workers' capabilities (*RN*, §§43-51). Workers in society with their individual dignity as people have been a consistent focus within the Encyclicals.

The social character of private property ownership is also identified in *QA* and *CA* (*QA*, §§44-49; *CA*, §§31-32 and 43). Nature exists to serve all people. It serves us not only today but also for generations into the future. As noted in *RN* private ownership provides a mechanism of stewardship for orderly, responsible, and creative use of these material resources; it also offers a stimulus to human initiative in the face of the inert character of material resources to meet peoples' needs (*RN*, §§52-53). Although private ownership of property is natural for people as they pursue their happiness, it is subject to the limitations of the common good because of the dignity of all people.

The social character of people and private ownership underlies the Christian social position of the state. As an expression of peoples' natural and necessary right to associate or join together for their common good, people form the broad society of a state (*RN*, §§36-40). Through this stable society people seek to provide for themselves the environment in which they can pursue their own individual happiness. Although Christian social thought has always supported the natural need for public authority as a coordinating influence to advance the public common good, *CA* has recently re-emphasized the exercise of such authority in terms of the legislative, the executive, and the judicial roles in advancing the common good of citizens (*CA*, §44). Yet, in its social role of advancing the common good, public authority can overstep its role by pre-empting or neutralizing the efforts of intermediate societies or individuals in successfully providing the material conditions and goods which make up the public common good. Pius XI more precisely formulated a proposed balance between public authority, intermediate bodies and individuals in advancing the common good with the principle of subsidiarity (*QA*, §79). On the other hand, John Paul II explicitly addresses the needs for an active "role of the state in the economic sector," given the social character of work and property (*CA*, §48). Thus, "social prudence" is needed by the public authority as it pursues the common good on behalf of the individuals in the society.

In no way are these basic views about people, property and state restricted to any one state or political society. Regardless of specific geographic locations, people are people. Their creativity, freedom and quest for happiness can show forth in different ways and through different forms as they seek dominion over nature. Diversity of culture reflects the diversity of such expressions, especially if one adds the different ways in which different peoples seek the meaning of personal life in relation to some divine influence.[1]

Thus, this paradigm of Christian social thought can be applied to an inquiry into U.S. social customs and institutions.[2] How do our customs and institutions support and respect the dignity of the individual person, the person at work, the person as owner of property? How do they reflect the social character of people and property? Do they reflect a reasonable balance between the efforts of public authority on one hand and both private institutions and citizens on the other hand in advancing the public common good? Briefly and in broad strokes this paper next opens up such questions in the context of collective bargaining; each of the other panelists then probes more deeply into them.

Collective bargaining is clearly visible among social institutions in the U.S. In it, representatives of workers and representatives of enterprises discuss and decide wages, hours and other terms of employment for covered workers. Within the limits of each bargaining relationship and according to the interests of the Parties, labor and management jointly and freely decide matters of direct mutual interest. The system clearly relies upon effective labor unions to represent employment interests of workers within free decision-making processes. Free, independent unions represent the efforts of some 17,000,000 workers to be heard, to be protective of their employment interests, to work towards common goods at their worksites. Collective bargaining also accepts the existence and integrity of the business enterprise. Such enterprises express the normal process of people joining together to meet product and service needs of other people through use of available productive resources. Private enterprises clearly rely upon private ownership of property. In collective bargaining, management is expected to represent these interests of the owners as affected by constraints of product and factor markets at the table. In public-sector bargaining, management seems to be expected to function in ways not unlike those of private-sector management even without the existence of private ownership. The U.S. system of collective bargaining thus provides the mechanism for two intermediate groups or societies to reach free, reasoned agreements about topics of their common good. It also provides mechanisms for implementing these agreements in ways which serve the common good of the participants.

What about the role of the public authority in collective bargaining? This can be effectively illustrated by the traditions of Wagner and Taft-Hartley. In the Wagner Act, more formally known as the National Labor Relations Act *(NRLA)* Congress encourages the practice and procedure of collective bargaining with workers' associations to negotiate terms and conditions of employment *(NRLA, Section I)*. The public authority does not pre-empt or neutralize the efforts of the parties by dictating to them the terms of employment. Rather, it has fashioned ground-rules for enforcement by the National Labor Relations Board through which the parties are free to work out mutually acceptable agreements. To directly advance the public common good, Congress went a step further in Taft-Hartley, otherwise known as the Labor Management Relations Act *(LMRA)* and established the Federal Mediation and Conciliation Service to prevent and minimize interruptions of the free flow of commerce growing out of labor disputes and to assist the parties to labor disputes to settle them through conciliation and mediation *(LMRA, Section 1b. and Sections 201-203)*.

Obviously, collective bargaining is not a panacea for all U.S. social problems, nor even employment related problems. Nevertheless, it has functioned as *a* vital social institution for over a half of a century. It would be foolhardy to assert that it operates without flaws. If the people who engage in bargaining are flawed, so would we expect their works to be. That is not the point! Rather, as we pause this week to celebrate the one hundredth birthday of *RN*, it seems appropriate to look back over the Century and rejoice in the vast, positive changes in the "New Things" of 1891. Whether such improvements can be "scientifically" traced back to RN is really irrelevant. Of lasting importance is how the improvements are in harmony with the thoughts and principles of right reason based on the dignity of the person in society. Such is the understanding which *CA*, the Church's most recent review and supplementation of the principles of *RN*, offers to encourage and guide students of social affairs as they approach the "New Things of 1991" (*CA*, Chapter IV and Chapter V).

## Endnotes

*Professor of Economics and Industrial Relations and Director of Industrial RelationsPrograms, Xavier University, Cincinnati, Ohio 45207 USA.

[1] Cf. *CA*, Chapter V for applications of the basic points of Christian social thought or Christian humanism to different types of societies in the current world-scene.

[2] Within the U.S., the initial public dicussions about *CA* in the U.S. seemed to focus on similarities and dissimilarities of this document and the Bishops' Pastoral Letter on the economy under the Church's Magisterium. This presentation avoids such a "controversy"; rather, it simply tries to view one U.S. institution in the light of the basic ideas and principles of the Encyclicals. Regardless of who wrote the views and regardless of the claims of the authors, the focus here is to examine to what degree the system of collective bargaining reflects the "right reason" proposed in the Encyclicals.

## References

John Paul II. *Laborem Exercens*, Wilmington, North Carolina: McGrath Publishing, 1981.

John Paul II. *Centesimus Annus*, Vatican City: Liberia Editrice Vaticana, 1991.

Leo XIII. *Rerum Novarum*, New York: Paulist Press, 1939.

Pius XI. *Quadrigesimo Anno*, America Press Edition, undated.

United States Congress. *National Labor Relations Act*, 49 Stat. 449-57 (1935).

United States Congress. *Labor Management Relations Act*, 61 Stat. 136, as amended, 29 U.S.C. sections 141 et seq.

# Toward the Fulfillment of Individual and Social Welfare in the Workplace Through Collaborative Collective Bargaining

## Frederick R. Post*

The thesis of this paper is that an ethical consensual approach to collective bargaining that emphasizes openness, encourages cooperation, promotes honesty, harmonizes the legitimate interests of both parties and respects the inherent dignity of each individual person makes good business sense. This approach to bargaining rests upon ideas which are consistent with the thoughts expressed in Pope Leo XIII's Encyclical, initially proposed 100 years ago in *Rerum Novarum (RN)*. Such an approach is based upon ideas that make sense on their own merit based upon their logic, their validity and their applicability to all types of social interaction among individuals or groups, but are particularly appropriate for collective bargaining. Simply stated, an open cooperative process between the parties produces better results than a confrontational process.

Both building upon and focusing Larry Donnelly's remarks during this important occasion, it seems helpful to summarize his most salient observations from the social paradigm proposed in *RN* and expanded in succeeding Encyclicals. Christian social thought is premised upon the inherent dignity of each individual person. Unlike other forms of animal life on Earth, the human being must fashion his or her own material world through work that involves both physical and mental effort, thereby exercising domain over the rest of nature. Expressing oneself through work represents the basic title for one's private ownership of both personal and productive property and represents an expression of the dignity of each individual person within the material world. For most human beings, there is a social dimension to the process of work because usually the individual will join a group with like interests for the pursuit of some common good or some common goal. The group is utilized to harness the benefit of the combined efforts of the

—————————————————— ❖ ——————————————————

individuals within the group which creates a form of synergy because of the diverse skills and abilities of group members not possessed by each individual standing alone. By joining with others, each individual has a greater opportunity to achieve the common goal or common good because of these specialized skills and abilities. Working in the group, not only are one's own needs met, but also the needs of other members of the group are met.

In our contemporary world of work, the interests of those who own the corporate property, referred to usually as the "employers," are represented by individuals grouped together in managerial and supervisory positions. The interests of workers are represented by the entity called a "labor organization," or more commonly a "union" which constitutes a similar grouping together of individuals who serve as employees. Though many would argue that the "interests," "goals," or the "common good" sought by the employer and the union are opposed to each other, and the controlling federal law, the National Labor Relations Act (the Act), does provide a framework of legal rules and procedures to regulate the supposed confrontation "in smoke filled rooms" where the two groups are pitted against each other in a struggle over finite resources in the win/lose paradigm of adversarial collective bargaining, this need not be so.

*RN* does not advocate this approach. And, refreshingly, recent theoretical studies, empirical research and an abundance of anecdotal evidence demonstrate that optimum results during collective bargaining are not achieved by the adversarial, confrontational approach. One hundred years after the thoughts proposed in Pope Leo XIII's Encyclical, it is now being acknowledged by some scholars and practitioners of collective bargaining that the logic, validity, and applicability of *Quadrigessimo Anno (QA)* and *Laborem Exercens (LE)* as well that of *RN,* represent basic principles of social interaction that really work because they are premised upon the inherent dignity of each individual person, and, when practiced during bargaining, promote better outcomes. Recent research shows that, as common sense indicates, helping the employees does help the employer. And, making the bargaining system more open and more consensual, consistent with the ideas in the Papal Encyclicals, does make bargaining work better for all parties concerned.

Examining the important functions that collective bargaining performs will demonstrate why the teachings of the encyclicals are so relevant to the workplace and marketplace of 1991. The process of collective bargaining represents a method of negotiated joint determination by employees, through their union representatives, and employers of answers to questions which arise and can cause disputes during their employment relationship. It is a dispute resolution mechanism. The questions that are resolved include an abundant variety of different issues of operational, control, wage, fringe benefit and other matters arising during the employment relationship. The presence of a union does not cause these questions to surface since they are questions which are fundamental in any workplace. However, without the presence of a union, the employer normally resolves such questions unilaterally based exclusively upon the conceptions of fairness, attitudes about acceptable profit levels, attitudes about social responsibility and awareness of the current labor market conditions.

While collective bargaining cannot solve every individual employment problem nor provide a solution for every economic problem confronting the employer, it should be able to perform a more meaningful mission than it is presently being utilized for since it holds such potential promise as a device to harmonize interests through a candid exchange of ideas, resulting in mutually compromised positions directed toward the overall good of all parties as long as there is a *vision* of the *purpose* of the whole process. Such a vision can be derived from the teachings of *RN* and other encyclicals.

While our present legally driven process encouraged by federal labor law does bring the parties together and instructs them, by the sanction of federal law, that modifications from initial positions, i.e., "bargaining," on at least "mandatory" subjects is required, a fuller use of the process can be envisioned. This optimistic vision is not offered for the purpose of refuting or rejecting the admitted value to society of the present adversarial process. It serves as an immense improvement over the violence; the bloodshed; and the unsavory employer tactics, such as the use of yellow dog contracts; black listing; and *ex parte* injunctions practiced prior to 1935. However, despite consensus that the present adversarial system is superior compared to such lawlessness, the present adversarial system can be improved by the opening up of the bargaining agenda through the sharing of information, the encouragement of true cooperation between the parties, efforts to promote honesty and candor between the parties and an effort to respect the inherent dignity of each individual person in the work place, both members of management and members of the employee group.

This paper will explain a process by which the employer and the union can formulate and structure their respective interests so they can be better motivated and committed by ethical justification to joint action toward reaching agreement during collective bargaining. By so doing, their bargaining will produce better results and those results will be consistent with the thoughts expressed in the Papal Encyclicals.

In Section II, the fundamental principles behind the establishment of a more consensual bargaining format will be summarized by a review of the initial device used, as part of one theoretical model, to bring the parties to agreement about philosophy, process and interests to be negotiated by the drafting of the collaboration compact. In section III, it will be shown that the motivation for committing to a more ethical process of negotiations exists based upon good business sense because of the abundance of research evidence available that identifies the changed demands of the new market place, the new industrial relations system that has emerged in response to these changes and the necessity for a more open negotiation process to serve these changed needs. In Section IV, the justification for use of a new more open and ethical process of bargaining will be shown by demonstrating that such a system is superior because it is morally justifiable from several

❖

perspectives of moral philosophy. Through the use of a new theoretical paradigm set out in this paper, it will be demonstrated that the parties can come together in their negotiations to formulate a truly common enterprise, consistent with the teachings of the Papal Encyclicals.

## II. Establishing the Environment for Consensual Bargaining

In my recent article (Post 1990), I made a critical assessment of the present adversarial collective bargaining process (ACB) and then proposed a new speculative methodology entitled the Collaborative Collective Bargaining Process (CCB) which could eliminate certain negative aspects of the existing collective bargaining process which was characterized as comparable to the adversarial process used in court litigation, but without the safeguards of the judge, the jury and the elaborate body of necessary exclusory rules of evidence. ACB was described as a combat model based upon a balance of power framework and, so structured, rewarded victory in labor negotiations to the more convincing display of power in the process, but it left unacceptable casualties. Based upon having spent twelve years as a labor attorney representing management as chief negotiator in bargaining with numerous private sector international unions, I further explained that tactics emblematic of ACB often included deception, lying and the abandonment of truth as a moral value. In sharp contrast, I argued that CCB could foster an environment which would encourage candor and truthfulness and would allow the parties to avoid the negative and self-defeating elements of the existing balance of power process practiced under ACB. And further, CCB would produce a much better result for all parties affected by the outcome of the negotiations.

In CCB bargaining becomes non-adversarial due to a five stage chronologically structured process that includes facilitation by a mediator, involvement of the whole employee group and the preparation of a collaboration compact, more fully explained below, by which the parties contractually agree in advance how they will conduct themselves. The five stages are the Commitment Stage, the Explanation Stage, the Validation Stage, the Prioritization Stage and the Negotiation Stage. These stages are briefly summarized in Figure 1.

### Figure 1
### Collaborative Collective Bargaining

**Commitment Stage**
(12 & 6 months before contract expiration date)
– Initial planning meeting convened
– Follow-up planning meeting held
– Collaboration compact goals determined
– Mediator selection process completed
– CCB Agreement drafted and executed
– Summary of each meeting posted for employees

## Figure 1 (continued)

**Explanation Stage**
(1 month before contract expiration date)
– First bargaining meeting held
– Initial management proposal presented
– Initial union proposal presented
– Position basis questioning initiated
– Support documentation inquiries raised
– Timetable for remaining meetings determined

**Validation Stage**
(2 to 4 weeks before contract expiration date)
– Joint employee questionnaire prepared
– Joint employee questionnaire administered
– Questionnaire results calculated and posted
– Requested support documentation assembled
– Questionnaire results summaries analyzed
– Position validation document obtained

**Prioritization Stage**
(2 weeks before contract expiration date)
– Second bargaining meeting held
– Mediator CCB process facilitation initiated
– Prioritized validated management proposal presented
– Prioritized validated union proposal presented
– Mediator position questioning commenced
– Position validation documentation critiqued

**Negotiation Stage**
(1 week before contract expiration date)
– Continuous daily bargaining meetings commenced
– CCB process daily timetable established
– Mediator position questioning continued
– Agreements and disagreements agendas drafted and updated
– CCB process continued until settlement reached
– Settlement agreement drafted and executed.

❖

As can be noted from Figure 1, each stage moves progressively toward the negotiation of a new labor contract that has been bargained in an open, consensual, collaborative manner. Stage One involves the formulation of and agreement to participate in CCB. Stage Two involves the first face-to-face meeting of the respective negotiating teams and the preliminary exchange of proposals. Stage Three, a stage where the parties do not meet, involves the amassing of support for positions taken and the involvement of the employees through the joint employee questionnaire. Stage Four involves the resumption of bargaining in the presence of the facilitating mediator wherein the parties begin a serious prioritization of all proposals based upon support data. Stage Five involves the actual negotiation process conducted in a unique format which minimizes the use of delays, posturing, bluffing and other deceptive strategies.

The initial stage of the proposed CCB process, the "commitment stage," is described as *critical* because "CCB cannot function without voluntary consent between both parties to reject ACB and, instead, exercise candor, openness and honesty in the negotiation process" (Post 1990, p. 501). Part of this initial stage of CCB was the preparation of a CCB agreement, which would represent a legally binding contractual commitment to participate in the process.

Among other features, the CCB agreement would contain a "collaboration compact." This compact would consist of a series of lists of agreements. These agreements would harmonize negotiation philosophy, negotiation process and express the respective interests of the parties. For example, a harmonized negotiation philosophy would include statements acknowledging the necessity for achieving a multiple dimension workplace through the bargaining process that not only produces goods and/or services that are competitive in the marketplace but that also provides for procedural due process, economic justice and a clarified structure relating to the extent of managerial control over employees. Similarly, a harmonized negotiation process would include statements opening up the bargaining agenda and promoting the definition of conflicting interests as mutual problems to be solved by collaborative effort through a recognition of the legitimacy of each party's interests and of the necessity of searching for a solution that is responsive to the needs of each party.

The list of expressed interests of each party would include preserving the company, preserving the union, employee due process, rewarding employee performance, providing appropriate employee fringe benefits, rewarding employee longevity, providing employee health and welfare benefits, providing employee retirement benefits, providing a safe workplace and providing a lasting relationship. These interests are expressed in the labor agreement by appropriate contract language negotiated by the parties. Reaching an initial consensus through the expression of these interests in a written format, thereby forcing an articulation of the goals of each party, is an essential precondition to the success of CCB because later stages of the process will rely heavily upon these written interests as justification for the prioritizing of respective proposals, and would also better direct the mediator position questioning by focusing the parties' attention to their stated interests during the face-to-face bargaining occurring in the final "negotiation stage" of the CCB process.

Use of the collaboration compact to articulate negotiating philosophy, negotiating process and the nature of joint interests is a device that can help the parties decide what, for them, is a mutually satisfactory labor agreement. There is empirical evidence demonstrating that such types of initial commitments do produce better results, which can provide the motivation to engage in the process. However, before the parties can be expected to consider changing their bargaining approach by agreeing to the contractual commitment of the CCB agreement and the joint agenda envisioned in the collaboration compact, a demonstration of its preferability for the interests of all parties concerned must be presented. Evidence of this can be shown from both recent empirical research as well as from management literature. Not only does such an approach to collective bargaining make sense, and represent a consistent strain of thinking with the Papal Encyclicals, but empirical research supports both its logic, validity, and relevancy to the workplace and marketplace of today.

## III. Research Provides the Motivation for Change

Recent research demonstrates that the ACB process established by the Act is ineffective in meeting the needs of our changed industrial relations system because the assumptions upon which it is based are no longer valid (Hecksher 1988). By tracking our economic history and our industrial environment, a picture emerges of the U.S. developing rapidly as a world power based upon the invention and then refinement of mass production techniques, the availability and use of large numbers of unskilled and uneducated immigrant workers, a corporate environment consisting of small numbers of large employers, a stable economic system that was uniquely domestic, an adversarial management system based upon the "scientific management" theories of Frederick Winslow Taylor and, with the passage of the 1935 Wagner Act, a concerned and focused government support of labor organizations as the method of balancing employee power with that of corporate interests (Hecksher). Although this type of environment spawned the ACB model of collective bargaining, these conditions no longer exist. Now, the contemporary landscape shows a picture of declines in mass production, the rise of a large semi-professional sector of educated service employees, large numbers of small independent employers, an unstable economy due to foreign and non-union competition and a federal government overwhelmed by special interest groups who have co-opted much of the traditional union agenda.

The flexibility and responsiveness necessary to function competitively in the marketplace of today is deterred by the rigid, restrictive, adversarial type of labor negotiations represented by the ACB process. The response to the fundamental changes which have occurred based upon external environmental pressures, outdated public policy, internal corporate organizational changes and a new work

❖

force, has been the emergence of a new industrial relations system (Kochan, Katz and McKersie 1986). This dynamic model of industrial relations functions on three distinct levels, the workplace level, the collective bargaining level and the strategic planning level. Reviewing industrial relations from this three level model, recent research leads to the conclusion that innovative changes in any one level, standing alone, are "not sufficient to close the gap in economic performance...to regain the innovative position in industrial relations" (Kochan, Katz and McKersie, p. 204) because the system has become so dynamic and multivariable influenced that innovation must occur at all three distinct levels. Most innovation has occurred at the workplace level, including a number of different "worker participation" systems, such as: employee involvement, quality circles, quality of work life programs and semi-autonomous work teams. Without similar innovation at both the collective bargaining level and the strategic planning level, efforts to close the competitive gap that U.S. industry presently faces will ultimately fail because of the remnant of the secretiveness, the deception, the gamesmanship and the general level of adversarial posturing encouraged and nourished by existing labor legislation and prevailing management and union attitudes (Kochan, Katz and McKersie).

Former Secretary of Labor Ray Marshall asserts that "...the performance of the American economy has been weakened by poor economic policies and inefficient, obsolete management systems. America's policy problems, in turn, are due partly to the absence of mechanisms to balance the concerns of workers and other major economic interests" (Marshall 1987, p. 282). Marshall further asserts that "worker participation can contribute importantly to management systems and can help create economic policies that are more balanced and therefore more effective" (Marshall, p. 283). Worker participation is defined as "worker involvement in economic policy and workplace management decisions, as well as an equitable sharing of the benefits and costs of change" (Marshall, p. 3).

Recent research done by the M.I.T. Commission on Industrial Productivity, has led the authors to conclude that there are "five interconnected imperatives" that the U.S. must implement to achieve competitive industrial performance in the global marketplace of today. Two of these five imperatives relate directly to a greater utilization of human resources and a sharing of power with employees. One imperative is "to develop a new 'economic citizenship' in the workplace" (Berger, Dertouzos, Lester, Solow and Thurow 1989, p. 47). It is stressed that increased employee involvement and responsibility are essential in the new workplace. Employees can no longer be treated as expendable parts of a production process, but must be nurtured and developed as long-term assets. Another of the five imperatives is to "strive to combine cooperation and individualism" (Berger et al., p. 47). It is emphasized that the individualistic spirit of our culture has become largely counterproductive in the workplace of today. And, such individualism is largely absent in the most productive U.S. companies where, instead, "group solidarity, a feeling of community and a recognition of interdependence has led to important economic advantages" (Berger et al., p. 47). The authors strongly emphasize the significance of a reevaluation of the whole human resource component from both the perspective of utilization and empowerment in the U.S. corporation.

The Cuomo Commission on Trade and Competitiveness issued its report in 1987 and asserted (as per Kaden 1988, p. 169; emphasis added):

> The way Americans work is changing, and none too soon. In many workplaces, the hierarchy, chain of command and division of labor *have been replaced by a more collaborative approach* ... the experiments of the last ten years have shown that important gains in productivity can result from a commitment to promote new relationships between workers, managers, unions, and shareholders ... it is the commission's position that increasing the quantity and quality of employee participation is one of the most important actions that the nation can take to restore competitiveness.

There is compelling evidence that, as noted in the introduction about the findings in the report, "when individuals are given the chance to participate in the decisions that govern their working lives, productivity, quality and morale all rise. This has been demonstrated in company after company that has had the courage to break with rigid convention and make its workers partners, not parts. There is profit in participation – not only for individuals, but for industries and the nation as well" (Kaden, XXV). Management research reported in recent scholarly literature is supportive of the need to change directions as a necessity in the effort to regain a competitive position in the new global marketplace within which the U.S. corporation must compete. Paradoxically, an alliance may emerge that causes the vision and expressed goals of those in the legislature who drafted the Wagner Act of 1935 to see their goals being realized 55 years later. Illustrative of recent research which is supportive of collaboration is the following statement referencing the new relationship that must develop between employers and employees.

> If managers expect to receive the full commitment of employees toward improving productivity, for example, those employees must be assured a measure of employment security in return. In order to reach full potential, employees will expect and require participation in the decisions that affect their lives – in other words, a place in the governance process ... (I)mplicit in the new premise is the notion that employment security is a more competitive way to provide people with economic security than is income security, which has no reciprocal commitment to work. Our Asian competitors have shown this (Lodge and Walton 1989, p. 21).

Lodge and Walton demonstrate in their research that our country is losing its capacity to compete in the world economy. They suggest that there are two choices for U.S. corporations: "they can leave the country and establish operations offshore where costs are lower and the production environment more inviting; or they can stay and change – themselves and the environment" (Lodge and Walton, p. 9). The authors further assert that there must be a change both outside and inside, and that change must be away from the adversarial, arm's length, short-term, contractual, and rigid relationship of the past toward one which is more cooperative, intimate, long-term, consensual and flexible (Lodge and Walton). Particularly with regard to the role of the union relationship, the old role of the union to bargain with the employer as an outsider must now be "augmented by an equal concern for the health of the firm—which must be competitive or there will be no welfare, no wages, no jobs and no members. *Hence the union's task is as much to help design and govern a corporation consensus as to bargain a contract.* Since all workers must be committed to the corporate consensus, some form of effective two-way communication with employees is essential and all corporation constituencies must share the gains derived from increased competitiveness" (Lodge and Walton, p. 21; emphasis added).

There are five prerequisites offered by Lodge and Walton as necessary for the corporation to effectively make the major transition necessary to establish relationships capable of creating competitiveness in the new global marketplace. With reference specifically to the relationship with labor, the authors note:

> There must be a purging of old and deeply held sociopolitical beliefs and attitudes about the source of management authority, the prerogatives of management, the purpose of business and the most desirable way of organizing the corporation. Therefore managers must not allow themselves to be stifled in innovative efforts by old beliefs such as those expressed in for example, the National Labor Relations Act, which prescribed adversarial relations between management and workers.

Such a change in attitude toward labor is an essential prerequisite to reversing the decline in competitiveness of the U.S. in the new global marketplace. It emphasizes both the change that must occur in the relationship between employers, employees and their union representatives as well as a clear recognition of the impediment to achieving these changes caused by the Act as it is presently being interpreted.

## IV. Moral Philosophy Provides the Justification for Change

What is it about this new approach to collective bargaining that is ethically justifiable? The process strips away the use of tactics such as bluffing, misrepresentation and lying. The parties cannot acknowledge their positions in all interest areas with justifications for their positions, and defend their positions in the presence of

❖

a skilled mediator and the other party, both of whom will ask probing questions, without openness and honesty. Also, being required to produce supporting documentation for positions will require sober reflection about the basis for positions initially contemplated. Such candid expressions of positions based upon the agreed upon collaboration compact will preclude any effective use of the abovementioned most frequently criticized aspects of ACB. Due to the resulting free exchange of positions and ideas, the presence of hostility and distrust between the parties that permeates ACB will be eliminated or at least minimized. Because of employee awareness that such an approach is being utilized, there should be improved attitudes among employees. Consequently, their commitment to employer goals should improve. Better product quality can be anticipated as employees should no longer perceive themselves as separate and isolated from both the bargaining process and the employer.

Furthermore, because most bargaining table dishonesty, cynically referred to as "bluffing," is not punishable under the present legal framework because various forms of deception, agenda overloading and misrepresentations are condoned by the law as simply part of the adversarial process, acting the opposite of these ways with honest open candidness through the whole CCB process sends a powerful message to the employees. This message should result in reciprocation on their part due to the example that has been set by the employer. Dissemination of the policy, as one important element of the overall corporate mission, will enhance the image of the employer as having moral values that represent the best in corporate citizenship.

Use of the CCB process also underscores the value of the teamwork so needed in our competitive world marketplace. Use of the word "collaborate" defines the working together process. As the current literature emphasizes, the same collaboration in all other aspects of corporate endeavors is necessary to compete effectively and CCB can set the tone for both management style and overall corporate policy.

In addition, CCB satisfies a basic human need for friendship in the workplace. Through the involvement of the employees, a desirable joint allegiance to both the employer and the union now may be acceptable which can eliminate the current unsettling feeling of divided loyalties among employees.

Through the openness of CCB, the inclination to ignore stakeholders' interests other than just those of the operating officers and the Board of Directors is sharply reduced also. Justifications for positions taken will be debated in the presence of a mediator who will probe both parties as to the basis for their wants and needs. This will prevent the management group from prioritizing positions geared to their employment self-interests at the expense of the longer term interests of stockholders, customers, suppliers, the local community, and the employees.

Another value of the process is that intrinsic job variables, traditionally left unaddressed, may become a part of the negotiations. This will be to the distinct advantage of the affected employees. Elements of the job such as employee responsibility, opportunity for personal growth, recognition for good performance,

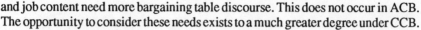

and job content need more bargaining table discourse. This does not occur in ACB. The opportunity to consider these needs exists to a much greater degree under CCB.

As to the question of the value to be placed upon employees' services, there can be more meaningful comparisons made with wage rates of competitors and a more thoughtful evaluation of cost-of-living concerns. The result will be that the union can more ably defend the need for wage and benefit increases to an employer that actually listens. In the CCB process, the employer will have to make a better effort to understand whether there is merit to positions advanced by the union. While it is difficult to determine the value of any group of employees' services, an open and frank discussion can certainly do more to promote understanding than having such matters determined by power and combat skills under ACB. Outcomes reached in that manner have little, if any, relation to the value of employees' services.

Finally, by the use of CCB, resort to the federal government for assistance against a wrongdoer's actions will normally be unnecessary. The parties will self-police their behaviors by compliance with the voluntarily agreed upon CCB process, monitored further by an impartial mediator elected by the parties to facilitate their negotiations.

The substitution of CCB can enable the parties to reorient their perspectives on labor negotiations. It should be clear by now that the value of employee services is not a predictable outcome of the combat model of ACB. By following the CCB model, the parties can avoid the negative and self-defeating elements of ACB and, in the process, work together to make the company an internally solidified entity, working toward mutually beneficial common goals, through the use of an ethically defensible approach to labor negotiations.

## V. Conclusion

While the present adversarial bargaining that is commonly practiced represents an immense improvement over the lawlessness that often prevailed prior to 1935, an abundance of research demonstrates that it is hardly an optimum way to achieve individual or social welfare in the workplace of today. Relying upon thoughts expressed 100 years ago in *RN* and in subsequent encyclicals, it seems appropriate to consider other more humane, moral and mature methods of resolving the fundamental questions of the workplace.

Collaborative Collective Bargaining represents one progressive, albeit radical, experiment for bringing the parties together for open, constructive, consensual and cooperative labor negotiations. That there are other approaches being proposed and attempted demonstrates that many scholars and practitioners recognize the need to evolve the collective bargaining process further based upon the needs of the workplace and the demands of the global marketplace.

*Assistant Professor of Business Law and Management, College of Business Administration, The University of Toledo, 2801 W. Bancroft Street, Toledo, OH 43606 USA.

# References

Berger, Suzanne, Dertouzos, Michael L., Lester, Richard K., Solow, Robert M. and Thurow, Lester C. "Toward a New Industrial America," *Scientific American,* 1989, *260,* 39-47.

Heckscher, Charles C. *The New Unionism,* New York: Basic Books, 1988.

Kaden, Lewis. *The Cuomo Commission Report,* New York: Simon and Schuster, 1988.

Kochan, Thomas, Katz, Harry and McKersie, Robert. *The Transformation of American Industrial Relations,* New York: Basic Books, 1986.

Lodge, George, and Walton, Richard. "The American Corporation and its New Relationships," *California Management Review,* 1989, *26,* 9-24.

Marshall, Ray. *Unheard Voices: Labor and Economic Policy in a Competitive World,* New York: Basic Books, 1987.

Post, Frederick R. "Collaborative Collective Bargaining: Toward an Ethically Defensible Approach to Labor Negotiations," *Journal of Business Ethics,* 1990, *9,* 495-508.

# Social Insurance and Social Justice

## George E. Rejda*

In 1991, the papal encyclical Rerum Novarum (RN) was 100 years old. This important document reflected 100 years of social teaching by the Catholic Church and prompted a reexamination of the American economic system and social justice and fairness within the system. Such a reexamination also requires an analysis of social insurance programs in the United States. Social insurance programs are an integral part of the American economy and affect millions of Americans. The various programs are designed to reduce economic insecurity from old-age, death, disability, unemployment, and occupational injury and disease. The primary purpose of this paper is to evaluate the system of social insurance in the United States to determine if the programs are consistent with or violate the principles of social justice. The major conclusion is that social insurance programs generally are consistent with the principles of social justice, but parts of certain programs clearly violate the norms of social justice.

## I. Basic Principles of Social Justice

As a starting point, the basic principles of social justice must first be established. These principles are clearly outlined in the U.S. Bishops' pastoral message marking the hundredth anniversary of *RN* in a document titled *A Century of Social Teaching: A Common Heritage, A Continuing Challenge*. The major principles of social justice are summarized as follows:

1. *The human person is central.* The fundamental test of any economic policy is whether it enhances or threatens human life and dignity.

2. *People have a fundamental right to life and to those things that make life truly human.* These basic rights include food, clothing, housing, medical care, social services, employment, and economic security.

3. *The family is the basic cell of society.* When basic human needs are not being met by private initiatives, then people must turn to the appropriate level of government to meet those needs.

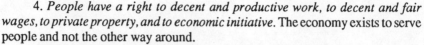

4. *People have a right to decent and productive work, to decent and fair wages, to private property, and to economic initiative.* The economy exists to serve people and not the other way around.

5. *Christian tradition calls us to put the needs of the poor and vulnerable first.* Thus, the reduction of poverty is central to this principle.

6. *Despite racial, ethnic, economic, and ideological differences, we are one human family.* Thus, our responsibility to others crosses national boundaries and involves a global dimension.

## II. Social Insurance and Social Justice

In this section we evaluate current social insurance programs in the United States based on the preceding principles of social justice. The major social insurance programs in the United States are the Old Age, Survivors, Disability, and Health Insurance (OASDHI) program; unemployment compensation; workers compensation; the Railroad Retirement Act; and compulsory temporary disability insurance laws in five states. Our discussion will be limited largely to the OASDHI program and state-federal unemployment compensation programs. These programs are extremely important and relevant in applying the principles of social justice since the vast majority of workers are affected either as taxpayers or beneficiaries under the programs. These programs also affect the economic security of large numbers of dependents and families in a meaningful way.

In general, social insurance programs are consistent with the principles of social justice if they maintain economic security by paying cash benefits to persons whose incomes are temporarily or permanently interrupted because of old-age, death, disability, or unemployment; if poverty and income inequality are reduced; if work incentives are expanded and productivity rewarded; or if the overall quality of life for individuals and families is improved. Conversely, social insurance programs violate the norms of social justice if economic insecurity is not reduced in a meaningful way after a covered loss occurs; if beneficiaries who attempt to work are unfairly penalized or their work incentives are reduced; or if cheating or other undesirable forms of social behavior are encouraged.

### A. Social Security

The OASDHI program (commonly known as Social Security) is a massive public income maintenance program that pays retirement, disability, and survivor benefits to eligible beneficiaries and their dependents. At the end of June 1991, slightly more than 40 million beneficiaries or about one in six Americans were receiving monthly cash benefits. In addition, virtually all aged persons age 65 and over and certain disabled persons under age 65 have considerable protection for their medical expenses under the Medicare program.

The following characteristics of the Social Security program are clearly consistent with the norms of social justice outlined earlier:

❖

1. *Layer of Income Protection.* The Social Security program provides a valuable layer of income protection with respect to important social risks, especially the risk of poverty and destitution during retirement. The program pays retirement benefits to virtually all retired persons age 65 and over in the United States. The monthly cash benefits tend to replace a relatively large percentage of the worker's earnings in the year prior to retirement, especially for low and middle-income workers. The gross replacement rates in 1990 were 77 percent for a minimum wage worker, about 43 percent for an average worker, and 24 percent for the maximum earner (Rejda 1991). Thus, the cash benefits provide an important base of economic security to the aged during their critical retirement years.

In addition, survivor benefits are extremely important in reducing economic insecurity for surviving family members when a family head dies. Along with earnings from employment, the survivor benefits are an important source of income to surviving spouses with eligible children under age 16 in their care. At the end of June 1991, survivor benefits were paid to about 5 million survivors and dependents. Without these benefits, the majority of these families would have been exposed to serious economic insecurity.

2. *Reduction in Poverty.* The Social Security program is extremely effective in reducing poverty and is clearly consistent with one of the most important principles of social justice—preferential treatment of the poor. Table 1 shows that before any government transfer payments, 49.1 million persons would have been counted poor in 1989. However, the addition of cash payments from Social Security and other social insurance programs removed 15.3 million persons from poverty.

**Table 1**
**Antipoverty Effectiveness of Social Insurance and Welfare Programs for All Individuals In Families or Living Alone 1989**

|  | Number of Poor Individuals (Millions) | Poverty Rate (Percent) |
|---|---|---|
| Cash income only before any government transfers | 49.1 | 19.9 |
| Plus Social Security and other social insurance programs | 33.8 | 13.8 |
| Plus means-tested cash transfers (official definition) | 31.5 | 12.8 |
| Plus food and housing benefits | 27.6 | 11.2 |
| Less federal taxes | 28.9 | 11.8 |

Source:   Calculated from U.S. Congress, House, Committee on Ways and Means, *Overview of Entitlement Programs, 1991 Green Book, Background Material and Data on Programs within the Jurisdiction of the Committee on Ways and Means* (Washington, D.C.: U.S. Government Printing Office, 1991), Table 17.

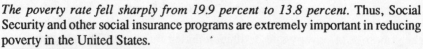

*The poverty rate fell sharply from 19.9 percent to 13.8 percent.* Thus, Social Security and other social insurance programs are extremely important in reducing poverty in the United States.

In addition, Social Security benefits are especially important in reducing poverty among the aged. For example, in 1986, 14 percent of the aged units age 65 and over whose families received Social Security cash benefits were counted poor. *If Social Security benefits had not been paid, the proportion of aged units counted poor would have increased sharply to 51 percent* (Rejda 1991).

Finally, Social Security and other social insurance are considerably more effective in reducing poverty than are public assistance and other means-tested programs. *Table 2 shows that Social Security and other social insurance programs removed 15.2 million persons from the poverty rolls in 1989. However, means-tested cash transfers and other welfare programs removed only 4.9 million from the poverty rolls.* Thus, social insurance programs are much more effective in reducing poverty than are means-tested welfare programs.

**Table 2**

| | Number of Individuals Removed From Poverty in 1989 (Millions) | Percent of Individuals Removed From Poverty in 1989 |
|---|---|---|
| From Social Security and other social insurance programs | 15.2 | 31% |
| From means-tested cash transfers, food, housing benefits, and federal taxes | 4.9 | 10 |

Source:   *Overview of Entitlement Programs, 1991 Green Book,* p. 1163.

*3. Reduction in Income Inequality.* Economists generally support a progressive income tax because income inequality is reduced. However, Social Security and other social insurance programs are much more effective in reducing income inequality than is the federal income tax.

The Gini Index is a common measure of income inequality. A value of zero indicates perfect equality of income while a value of one indicates perfect inequality. Although the federal income tax is progressive based on the Gini index, it has a relatively modest impact on the redistribution of income. A recent Bureau of the Census study shows that social insurance payments and government transfers are much more significant than taxes in redistributing income. *The study showed that in 1989 the federal income tax reduced the Gini index from .498 to .474, or a reduction of only 4.8 percent. In contrast, the payment of social insurance benefits*

❖

*plus other non-means-tested government transfers reduced the Gini index from*
*.467 to .417, or a reduction of 10.7 percent* (U.S. Bureau of the Census 1990, pp.
6-7). Thus, social insurance programs are much more effective in reducing income
inequality than is the federal income tax.

    4. *Weighted Benefit Formula.* The weighted benefit formula is another
characteristic of the Social Security program that is clearly consistent with the
principles of social justice. The weighted benefit formula weights or skews benefits
in favor of lower-income groups, which redistributes income downward in the
payment of benefits in favor of the working poor. The benefit rate applied to the
lower portion of total covered wages is substantially higher than the rate applied to
the higher portion. As a result, the working poor with limited incomes receive
preferential treatment in the payment of benefits.

## III. Violation of Social Justice Principles

    Although the characteristics of the Social Security program discussed above
are highly desirable and support the principles of social justice, certain aspects of
the program violate these norms.

    1. *Social Security Earnings Test.* The Social Security program has a complex
and onerous earnings test that clearly violates the principles of social justice in
terms of fairness and equity. If a beneficiary who is receiving monthly cash benefits
has earned income in excess of a certain annual maximum amount, part or all of the
benefits will be withheld. In 1991, beneficiaries ages 65 through 69 could earn a
maximum of $9,720 with no loss of benefits. Beneficiaries lost one dollar of
benefits for each three dollars of earnings over that amount. A more stringent test
applied to beneficiaries under age 65. Beneficiaries under age 65 lost one dollar of
benefits for each two dollars of earnings in excess of $7,080. The earnings test does
not apply to beneficiaries age 70 or older.

    The primary purposes of the earnings test are to restrict monthly cash benefits
to beneficiaries who have not retired and also to hold down the cost of the program.
However, the overall result is that the earnings test severely penalizes people who
work and receive Social Security cash benefits, especially when the taxation of
benefits is considered. Calculations by the author in an earlier study of the 1990
earnings test clearly illustrates the severe penalty that applies to the loss of benefits
if earned income exceeds the maximum allowed (Rejda 1990). Under the 1990
earnings test, the annual exempt amounts were $9,360 for beneficiaries ages 65-69
and $6,840 for beneficiaries under age 65.

    The loss of benefits under the earnings test has the same effect as a tax. As
stated earlier, earnings in excess of the maximum annual exempt amount will result
in a reduction or termination of benefits. In addition, the worker must pay a Social
Security payroll tax and a state and federal income tax. When all taxes and the loss
of benefits are considered, the marginal tax rates on excess earnings above the
exempt amount are oppressively high. For example, assume that a beneficiary is in
the 15 percent federal income tax bracket and earns an additional $1,000 above the

❖

exempt amount allowed in 1990. Also assume that the worker pays a state income tax of 3 percent and that the benefits are not taxable either before or after the additional earnings are received. A beneficiary under age 65 would pay a marginal tax of about 76 percent on the excess earnings. *A beneficiary age 65-69 would pay a marginal tax rate of about 59 percent.* The marginal tax rates are substantially higher if the beneficiary is in the 28 percent tax bracket. *A beneficiary under age 65 would pay a marginal tax rate of about 89 percent. A beneficiary age 65-69 would pay a marginal tax rate of about 72 percent.* (See Table 3.) The marginal tax rates shown would be considerably higher for workers who are in higher tax brackets or who must pay a city wage tax or live in a state with a nonoccupational

### Table 3

### Marginal Tax Rates On Taxable Wages in Excess of the Annual Maximum Earnings Test Limitation, 1990

### Case 1 – No Federal Income Tax Paid on Social Security Benefits[a]

|  | Ages 62-64<br>*($6,840 Exempt Amount)*<br>*15% Tax Bracket* | Ages 65-69<br>*($9,360 Exempt Amount)* |
|---|---|---|
| Federal income tax | 15.00% | 15.00% |
| State income tax | 3.00 | 3.00 |
| Social Security payroll tax | 7.65 | 7.65 |
| Loss of benefits from earnings test | 50.00 | 33.33 |
| Total[b] | 75.65% | 58.98% |
|  | *28% Tax Bracket* |  |
| Federal income tax | 28.00% | 28.00% |
| State income tax | 3.00 | 3.00 |
| Social Security payroll tax | 7.65 | 7.65 |
| Loss of benefits from earnings test | 50.00 | 33.33 |
| Total[b] | 88.65% | 71.98% |

[a] Social Security benefits are not taxable if the sum of adjusted gross income, plus tax free interest income, plus one-half of the Social Security benefits is less than the base amount of $25,000 for an individual and $32,000 for a couple.

[b] The true marginal tax rates are somewhat lower than those indicated. For beneficiaries under age 65, the benefits are actuarially increased at age 65 to take into account the withholding of benefits because of the earnings test. Also, the rates shown do not reflect the impact of the delayed retirement credit on beneficiaries over the normal retirement age. The true marginal tax rate would be somewhat lower because of the increase in benefits for those months in which benefits are withheld because of the earnings test. Because most beneficiaries do not consider these factors in their decision to work or not work, they are ignored in the analysis.

Source: George E. Rejda, "A Reexamination of the Controversial Earnings Test Under the OASDI Program," *Benefits Quarterly,* Vol. VI, No. 1 (Third Quarter 1990), p. 28.

temporary disability income law. Under these circumstances, few beneficiaries will want to work because their additional take-home pay is substantially reduced.

The penalty is even more severe if a federal income tax must be paid on part of the Social Security benefits solely as a result of the additional earnings. *Beneficiaries ages 65-69 in the 15 percent tax bracket who reenter the labor force and pay a federal income tax on part of their benefits solely as a result of the additional earnings would pay a marginal tax rate of about 64 percent on their excess earnings. Beneficiaries in the 28 percent tax bracket would pay a marginal tax rate of 81 percent.* (See Table 4.) The marginal tax rates are especially severe

**Table 4**

**Marginal Tax Rates on Taxable Wages in Excess of the Annual Maximum Earnings Test Limitation, 1990**

**Case 2—Federal Income Tax Paid on Part of the Social Security Benefits Solely as a Result of the Additional Wages[a]**

|  | Ages 65-69 ($9,360 Exempt Amount) | |
|---|---|---|
|  | *15% Tax Bracket* | *28% Tax Bracket* |
| Federal income tax | 15.00% | 28.00% |
| State income tax | 3.00 | 3.00 |
| Social Security payroll tax | 7.65 | 7.65 |
| Loss of benefits from earnings test | 33.33 | 33.33 |
| Taxation of Social Security benefits[b] | 5.00 | 9.34 |
| Total | 63.98% | 81.32% |

a Social Security benefits are taxable if the sum of adjusted gross income, plus tax free interest income, plus one-half of the Social Security benefits exceeds the base amount of $25,000 for an individual and $32,000 for a couple. The amount subject to taxation is the lower of (1) half of the Social Security benefits or (2) half of the excess of the taxpayer's combined income over the base amount.

b For example, a single person in the 15% tax bracket who is age 65 and has OASDI benefits of $9,000, wages of $9,360 and investment or pension income of $11,140 is just at the "limiting point" for paying an income tax on the benefits ("test income" is 50% of $9,000, plus $9,360, plus $11,140, or a total of $25,000). If wages are increased $1,000, OASDI benefits are reduced $333, and the "test income" is $25,667. Thus, $333.50 of benefits are taxable ($25,667 minus $25,000 times 50%). The 15% tax is $50.02, or 5.00% of the additional wages of $1,000. For the 28% tax bracket, the tax is $93.38, or 9.34% of the additional wages. On the other hand, if the beneficiary is well below the "limiting point" before earning the additional $1,000 in wages, the net effect would not bring him or her above it, and the taxation of OASDI benefits would not be affected. In contrast, if investment or pension income were so large before the additional wages were earned that the OASDI benefits were fully taxable, the net effect of additional wages would not result in any additional taxation of OASDI benefits, but instead would result in a lower marginal taxation of OASDI benefits, as an offset to the marginal tax rate on the additional wages.

Source:    George E. Rejda, "A Reexamination of the Controversial Earnings Test Under the OASDI Program," *Benefits Quarterly,* Vol. VI, No. 1 (Third Quarter 1990), p. 29.

## Table 5
## Marginal Tax Rates on Taxable Self-Employment Income in Excess of the Annual Maximum Earnings Test Limitation, 1990
### Case 3—No Federal Income Tax Paid on Social Security Benefits[a]

|  | Ages 62-64 ($6,840 Exempt Amount) | Ages 65-69 ($9,360 Exempt Amount) |
|---|---|---|
| *15% Tax Bracket* | | |
| Federal income tax | 15.00% | 15.00% |
| State income tax | 3.00 | 3.00 |
| Social Security payroll tax[b] | 14.15 | 14.15 |
| Loss of benefits from earnings test | 50.00 | 33.33 |
| Total[c] | 82.15% | 65.48% |
| *28% Tax Bracket* | | |
| Federal income tax | 28.00% | 28.00% |
| State income tax | 5.00 | 5.00 |
| Social Security payroll tax[b] | 13.16 | 13.16 |
| Loss of benefits from earnings test | 50.00 | 33.33 |
| Total[c] | 96.16% | 79.49% |

a Social Security benefits are not taxable if the sum of adjusted gross income, plus tax free interest income, plus one-half of the Social Security benefits is less than the base amount of $25,000 for an individual and $32,000 for a couple.

b The true marginal tax rate is slightly lower than the OASDI tax rate of 15.3% because the self-employed can deduct one-half of the self-employment tax from self-employment income for purposes of computing the income tax. Thus, as a result of this feature alone, the income for income tax purposes is lower by $76.50 (50% of 15.3% of the additional self-employment income of $1,000); the income tax reduction on the $76.50 is $11.48 at the 15% rate and $21.42 at the 28% rate, or 1.15% and 2.14%, respectively, of the $1,000 of additional earnings.

c The true marginal tax rates are somewhat lower than those indicated. For beneficiaries under age 65, the benefits are actuarially increased at age 65 to take into account the withholding of monthly benefits because of the earnings test. Also, the rates shown do not reflect the impact of the delayed retirement credit on beneficiaries over the normal retirement age. The true marginal tax rate would be somewhat lower because of the increase in benefits for those months in which benefits are withheld because of the earnings test. Because most beneficiaries do not consider these factors in their decision to work or not work, they are ignored in the analysis.

Source: George E. Rejda, "A Reexamination of the Controversial Earnings Test Under the OASDI Program," *Benefits Quarterly,* Vol. VI, No. 1 (Third Quarter 1990), p. 30.

for self-employed individuals under age 65 who are in the 28 percent tax bracket and paid a Social Security payroll tax of 15.3 percent on their covered earnings in 1990. (See Table 5.)

The preceding analysis indicates clearly the severe penalty that can result from working and earning an income in excess of the maximum allowed under the

❖

earnings test. As a result, many retired beneficiaries who would prefer to work may be dissuaded from working because of the earnings test. The overall result is a serious violation of the work ethic embodied in the Social Security program. However, the Social Security Administration has taken the position that the work disincentive effects are small since the vast majority of persons who have retired have no desire to return to the labor force and will not do so. This conclusion is questionable since the data used in their analysis say nothing about the number of persons now in the labor force who would still remain in the labor force and not retire if they could receive their Social Security benefits without penalty. Moreover, even if the questionable conclusions that the work disincentive effects are relatively small and that only a relatively small proportion of workers is affected by the earnings test are correct, the test would still penalize the small proportion of workers who would still prefer working. For that group, the loss of benefits for workers with earnings above the maximum exempt amount is certainly a serious violation of the norms of social justice.

Finally, the earnings test is objectionable because beneficiaries are encouraged to cheat and not report their earnings. In addition, the earnings test is costly to administer. Senator Robert Dole (R-Kansas) maintains that the Social Security Administration must use 8 percent of its employees to enforce the earnings test and police the income levels of beneficiaries (Rejda 1991). A program that encourages cheating and is difficult to police is inconsistent with the norms of social justice outlined earlier.

2. *Harsh Definition of Disability.* A serious long-term disability is a major cause of economic insecurity in the United States. The majority of workers are inadequately insured against the risk of long-term disability, and only a relatively small fraction of the lost wages is replaced from individual or group disability income contracts. The Social Security program pays disability income benefits only if a disabled worker can meet strict eligibility requirements and also can satisfy a harsh definition of disability. A disabled worker also must satisfy a full five-month waiting period. A disabled worker must be unable to perform any substantial gainful activity in the national economy, and the disability must be expected to last at least 12 months or result in death. As a result, a large percentage of initial applications for disability benefits are denied. *Of the 1.6 million initial application determination made in fiscal 1990, state agencies denied 61 percent of the disability claims* (Committee on Ways and Means 1991, p. 59). The overall result is an increase in economic insecurity since the vast majority of disabled workers are inadequately insured against the risk of long-term disability.

3. *Heavy Payroll Tax Burden on Working Poor.* The working poor pay little or no income tax but must pay a relatively high payroll tax on their covered earnings. In 1992, the working poor paid a Social Security payroll tax of 7.65 percent on their covered earnings. The payroll tax burden is especially oppressive on low-income self-employed persons who paid a payroll tax rate of 15.3 percent on their covered earnings.

❖

The Social Security Administration argues that the system overall is highly progressive when benefits are considered and that the working poor receive retirement benefits whose actuarial value exceeds substantially the actuarial value of their payroll tax contributions. *But this ignores the important point that a substantial time lag of several years exists between the time that taxes are paid and the time that retirement benefits are received.* The working poor receive little comfort in knowing that the actuarial value of their retirement benefits exceeds the actuarial value of their payroll taxes. The working poor have a critical need for additional income at the present time in order to survive financially.

In addition, the Social Security payroll tax also increases the number of persons who fall below the poverty line. For example, an estimated 47.7 million persons were counted poor in 1989 before any government cash transfers and other government benefits were received and before any Social Security payroll taxes were paid. *Payment of the Social Security payroll tax increased the total number of persons counted poor from an estimated 47.7 million to 50 million, or an increase of about 5 percent* (U.S. Bureau of the Census 1990, p. 10). It is difficult to justify the present financing of Social Security in view of the relatively heavy payroll tax burden that the working poor bear. Indeed, a strong case could be made for a progressive payroll tax with a relatively lighter tax burden on the working poor.

4. *No National Health Insurance.* The present social insurance system also is seriously flawed since there is no provision for a national health insurance plan covering the entire population. With the exception of South Africa, the United States is the only industrialized country in the western world that does not have some type of national health insurance plan covering all of its citizens. As a result, individuals and families in the United States who have no private or public health insurance are exposed to serious economic insecurity in the event of a severe accident or illness. A recent study shows large numbers of Americans have no public or private health insurance. In addition, there is wide variation in coverage among the states. *In 1990, 16.6 percent of the nonaged population or 35.7 million people had no health insurance coverage. The proportion of uninsured by state ranged from a low of 8.2 percent in North Dakota to a high of 26.4 percent in New Mexico* (Employee Benefit Research Institute 1992). The lack of national health insurance is a major cause of economic insecurity for many families in the United States at the present time. Our present system of health care is seriously flawed because coverage is based largely on employment. The vast majority of health insurance coverage for individuals and families is obtained through a group. If the worker loses his or her job, the group health insurance generally terminates unless the worker elects to remain in the employer's group health insurance plan under the federal Consolidated Omnibus Reconciliation Act of 1985 (COBRA). Under this law, a worker who is laid off or voluntarily quits can remain in the former employer's plan for a least 18 months if he or she pays 102 percent of the premium. However, group health insurance is expensive. Since group health insurance premiums can easily cost $300 or more monthly, the vast majority of unemployed

employees do not elect the COBRA option and lose their health insurance coverage as a result. The United States desperately needs a system of health care that extends health insurance coverage to individuals and families who are not part of a group. An analysis of national health insurance, however, is beyond the scope of this paper.

## IV. Unemployment Compensation

State unemployment compensation programs also violate the norms of social justice listed earlier. Federal-state unemployment programs exist in all states that generally pay weekly unemployment benefits for up to 26 weeks to workers who lose their jobs involuntarily. In addition, extended benefits may also be payable in those states with high unemployment rates to unemployed workers who exhaust their regular benefits.

State unemployment compensation programs are seriously flawed at the present time and violate several important principles of justice. The most important defects are the following:

1. *Relatively Small Proportion of Unemployed Receives Benefits.* One of the most serious violations of social justice is the relatively small proportion of unemployed workers who receive benefits. Although about 88 percent of all employed workers are covered under unemployment compensation programs, only a relatively small fraction of the unemployed receives benefits at any given time. *Although the United States was experiencing a recession in 1990, only about 37 percent of the unemployed received unemployment compensation benefits during an average month.* (See Table 6 and Figure 1.)

In addition, the proportion of unemployed workers who receive benefits varies widely among the states. *The proportion of unemployed receiving benefits ranged from a low of about 17 percent in South Dakota to a high of 68 percent in Alaska.* (See Table 7.)

Finally, large numbers of beneficiaries exhaust their benefits and are still unemployed. (See Table 8.) However, relatively few long-term unemployed workers who exhaust their regular benefits receive additional benefits under the extended benefits program. In December 1990, no state was qualified to receive extended benefits despite the recession that was occurring at that time. Alaska and Rhode Island were eligible for extended benefits only during the first half of 1990. Several reasons help explain why only a relatively small fraction of the unemployed receives benefits at any given time. In general, the states and federal government have imposed more restrictive eligibility requirements that make it more difficult for unemployed workers to receive benefits. A study by Mathematica Policy Research, Inc. provides valuable information on the reasons why the unemployment compensation claims ratio has declined over time. (See Tables 9 and 10.) The *unemployment insurance claims ratio* is the ratio of average weekly unemployment benefit claims under state programs during a quarter to the state's average total unemployment during the quarter. A large part of the decline can be explained by tighter and more stringent eligibility requirements. Other reasons include more

❖

### Table 6
**Unemployed Workers Receiving Unemployment Insurance National, 1955-1990**

| Year | Percentage of Unemployed Workers Receiving Benefits | Number of Unemployed Workers (thousands) | Number of Unemployed Workers Not Receiving Benefits (thousands) | Unemployment Rate |
|------|------|------|------|------|
| 1955 | 49.1 | 2,852 | 1,453 | 4.4% |
| 1956 | 48.1 | 2,750 | 1,427 | 4.1 |
| 1957 | 54.9 | 2,859 | 1,288 | 4.3 |
| 1958 | 60.3 | 4,602 | 1,829 | 6.8 |
| 1959 | 49.7 | 3,740 | 1,880 | 5.5 |
| 1960 | 53.8 | 3,852 | 1,781 | 5.5 |
| 1961 | 63.5 | 4,714 | 1,720 | 6.7 |
| 1962 | 49.8 | 3,911 | 1,965 | 5.5 |
| 1963 | 48.5 | 4,070 | 2,097 | 5.7 |
| 1964 | 46.3 | 3,786 | 2,033 | 5.2 |
| 1965 | 43.1 | 3,366 | 1,916 | 4.5 |
| 1966 | 39.3 | 2,875 | 1,746 | 3.8 |
| 1967 | 42.7 | 2,975 | 1,705 | 3.8 |
| 1968 | 42.1 | 2,817 | 1,630 | 3.6 |
| 1969 | 41.6 | 2,832 | 1,655 | 3.5 |
| 1970 | 50.6 | 4,093 | 2,023 | 4.9 |
| 1971 | 52.0 | 5,016 | 2,408 | 5.9 |
| 1972 | 44.9 | 4,882 | 2,690 | 5.6 |
| 1973 | 41.1 | 4,365 | 2,572 | 4.9 |
| 1974 | 49.6 | 5,156 | 2,598 | 5.6 |
| 1975 | 75.5 | 7,929 | 1,943 | 8.5 |
| 1976 | 67.4 | 7,406 | 2,417 | 7.7 |
| 1977 | 56.3 | 6,991 | 3,057 | 7.1 |
| 1978 | 43.3 | 6,202 | 3,517 | 6.1 |
| 1979 | 42.1 | 6,137 | 3,554 | 5.8 |
| 1980 | 50.4 | 7,637 | 3,789 | 7.1 |
| 1981 | 41.4 | 8,273 | 4,846 | 7.6 |
| 1982 | 45.3 | 10,678 | 5,846 | 9.7 |
| 1983 | 43.9 | 10,717 | 6,012 | 9.6 |
| 1984 | 34.1 | 8,539 | 5,630 | 7.5 |
| 1985 | 32.9 | 8,312 | 5,580 | 7.2 |
| 1986 | 32.7 | 8,237 | 5,545 | 7.0 |
| 1987 | 31.5 | 7,425 | 5,089 | 6.2 |
| 1988 | 31.5 | 6,701 | 4,589 | 5.5 |
| 1989 | 33.0 | 6,528 | 4,373 | 5.3 |
| 1990 | 36.8 | 6,874 | 4,342 | 5.5 |

*Table 6 (continued)*

Note: Data for the years before 1985 are from historical tables that include Puerto Rico and Virgin Islands in the tabulation of unemployment insurance beneficiaries, but not in the tabulation of the unemployed. The pre-1985 data thus overstate coverage in these years by an estimated one-half to one percentage point. None of the data for 1985 through 1990 includes beneficiaries for Puerto Rico and the Virgin Islands.
Source: Isaac Shapiro and Marion E. Nichols, *Unemployed and Uninsured, Jobless Workers, Unemployment, Insurance, and the Recession,* (Center on Budget and Policy Priorities: Washington, D.C., 1991), p. 4.

**Figure 1**

**Percentage of Unemployed Receiving Unemployment Insurance Benefits**

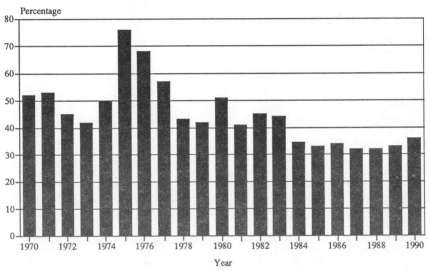

Source: Isaac Shapiro and Marion E. Nichols, *Unemployed and Uninsured, Jobless Workers, Unemployment, Insurance, and the Recession* (Center on Budget and Policy Priorities: Washington, D.C., 1991), p. 3.

restrictive federal requirements under the extended benefits program; taxation of unemployment benefits; shifts in the geographic distribution of employment; a decline in manufacturing employment; and a more accurate measurement of unemployment. Also, some labor economists believe that a large percentage of the unemployed do not apply for benefits. If correct, this indicates that public officials are derelict in their duties to inform the public about the program. Labor unions earlier made a determined effort to inform unemployed workers about the programs and encouraged them to apply for unemployment benefits. However, the decline in union membership has weakened the influence of labor unions in this regard.

❖

## Table 7
### Unemployment Insurance Protection by State, 1979 and 1990

| State | Percentage of Unemployed Workers Receiving Benefits, 1979 | Percentage of Unemployed Workers Receiving Benefits, 1990 | Percentage Point Change 1979 to 1990 |
|---|---|---|---|
| Alabama | 37.1% | 28.3% | -8.8% |
| Alaska | 79.7 | 68.1 | -11.6 |
| Arizona | 25.4 | 28.6 | +3.2 |
| Arkansas | 41.8 | 34.3 | -7.5 |
| California | 43.0 | 47.0 | +4.0 |
| Colorado | 24.6 | 26.5 | +1.9 |
| Connecticut | 39.5 | 50.0 | +10.5 |
| Delaware | 28.7 | 27.4 | -1.3 |
| District of Columbia | 44.6 | 44.4 | -0.2 |
| Florida | 23.7 | 20.6 | -3.1 |
| Georgia | 32.4 | 26.7 | -5.7 |
| Hawaii | 40.1 | 37.4 | -2.7 |
| Idaho | 49.7 | 40.6 | -9.1 |
| Illinois | 48.1 | 33.1 | -15.0 |
| Indiana | 27.6 | 22.8 | -4.8 |
| Iowa | 37.7 | 33.8 | -3.9 |
| Kansas | 36.3 | 34.4 | -1.9 |
| Kentucky | 44.5 | 29.7 | -14.8 |
| Louisiana | 29.0 | 25.2 | -3.8 |
| Maine | 44.0 | 52.5 | +8.5 |
| Maryland | 28.4 | 32.2 | +3.8 |
| Massachusetts | 48.5 | 59.6 | 11.1 |
| Michigan | 52.9 | 35.3 | -17.6 |
| Minnesota | 39.2 | 36.7 | -2.5 |
| Mississippi | 34.0 | 26.5 | -7.5 |
| Missouri | 51.7 | 35.3 | -16.4 |
| Montana | 49.6 | 34.6 | -15.0 |
| Nebraska | 30.6 | 40.8 | +10.2 |
| Nevada | 41.0 | 38.5 | -2.5 |
| New Hampshire | 33.0 | 31.1 | -1.9 |
| New Jersey | 62.7 | 51.8 | -10.9 |
| New Mexico | 24.2 | 24.9 | +0.7 |
| New York | 45.0 | 48.6 | +3.6 |
| North Carolina | 29.5 | 39.6 | +10.1 |
| North Dakota | 51.9 | 33.6 | -18.3 |
| Ohio | 40.0 | 33.1 | -6.9 |
| Oklahoma | 32.0 | 21.6 | -10.4 |
| Oregon | 41.4 | 46.5 | +5.1 |
| Pennsylvania | 52.3 | 48.2 | -4.1 |
| Rhode Island | 71.1 | 58.8 | -12.3 |
| South Carolina | 35.3 | 32.4 | -2.9 |

❖

*Table 7 (continued)*

| | | | |
|---|---|---|---|
| South Dakota | 30.4 | 16.8 | -13.6 |
| Tennessee | 45.3 | 41.2 | -4.1 |
| Texas | 24.0 | 22.8 | -1.2 |
| Utah | 43.8 | 26.5 | -17.3 |
| Vermont | 53.0 | 53.2 | +0.2 |
| Virginia | 23.7 | 20.4 | -3.3 |
| Washington | 35.3 | 51.3 | +16.0 |
| West Virginia | 48.8 | 26.4 | 22.4 |
| Wisconsin | 52.2 | 44.3 | -7.9 |
| Wyoming | 26.9 | 24.6 | -2.3 |
| U.S. Total | 42.1 | 36.8 | -5.3 |

Source: Isaac Shapiro and Marion E. Nichols, *Unemployed and Uninsured, Jobless Workers, Unemployment, Insurance, and the Recession,* (Center on Budget and Policy Priorities: Washington, D.C., 1991), p.13.

## Table 8

## Jobless Workers Who Exhausted Unemployment Benefits by State, 1990

| State | Number of Jobless Workers Who Exhausted Unemployment Benefits |
|---|---|
| Alabama | 28,100 |
| Alaska | 17,700 |
| Arizona | 22,200 |
| Arkansas | 21,000 |
| California | 332,000 |
| Colorado | 25,000 |
| Connecticut | 41,900 |
| Delaware | 2,500 |
| District of Columbia | 10,900 |
| Florida | 88,600 |
| Georgia | 51,700 |
| Hawaii | 3,500 |
| Idaho | 9,800 |
| Illinois | 111,200 |
| Indiana | 27,000 |
| Iowa | 16,600 |
| Kansas | 19,800 |
| Kentucky | 21,900 |
| Louisiana | 23,300 |
| Maine | 15,800 |
| Maryland | 26,300 |
| Massachusetts | 115,100 |
| Michigan | 125,600 |
| Minnesota | 39,900 |
| Mississippi | 18,900 |
| Missouri | 48,100 |

❖

*Table 8 (continued)*

| State | Number of Jobless Workers Who Exhausted Unemployment Benefits |
|---|---|
| Montana | 7,400 |
| Nebraska | 6,900 |
| Nevada | 10,800 |
| New Hampshire | 4,200 |
| New Jersey | 120,500 |
| New Mexico | 9,000 |
| New York | 216,700 |
| North Carolina | 32,700 |
| North Dakota | 5,500 |
| Ohio | 73,600 |
| Oklahoma | 17,000 |
| Oregon | 26,500 |
| Pennsylvania | 108,400 |
| Rhode Island | 19,800 |
| South Carolina | 19,300 |
| South Dakota | 900 |
| Tennessee | 51,000 |
| Texas | 139,800 |
| Utah | 8,500 |
| Vermont | 4,400 |
| Virginia | 21,800 |
| Washington | 44,000 |
| West Virginia | 10,900 |
| Wisconsin | 40,200 |
| Wyoming | 2,500 |
| U.S. Total | 2,266,400 |

Source: Isaac Shapiro and Marion E. Nichols, *Unemployed and Uninsured, Jobless Workers, Unemployment, Insurance, and the Recession,* (Center on Budget and Policy Priorities: Washington, D.C., 1991), p.15.

**Table 9**

**Ratio of State UI Weeks Claimed to Total Unemployment 1948-1986**

|  | Claims Ratio |
|---|---|
| 1948-49 | 0.489 |
| 1950-59 | 0.492 |
| 1960-69 | 0.426 |
| 1970-79 | 0.413 |
| 1980-86 | 0.347 |
| Overall Mean | 0.428 |

Note: Data are averages of quarterly figures.
Source: *An Examination of Declining UI Claims during the 1980s* (Princeton, N.J.: Mathematica Policy Research, Inc., 1988), Table 1.1, p.3.

### Table 10

### Major Reasons for the Decline in
### Unemployment Insurance Claims Ratio, 1980-1986

|  | Percent of Decline Explained |
|---|---|
| 1. Changes in State UI Policy | |
|   – Increased monetary eligibility requirements and reductions in the maximum potential duration of benefits | 8 to 15% |
|   – Increases in disqualifying income denials | 2 to 10% |
|   – Changes in other nonmonetary eligibility requirements | 3 to 11% |
| 2. Changes in Federal UI Policy | |
|   – More restrictive extended benefits program | 7% |
|   – Partial taxation of benefits | 11 to 16% |
| 3. Economic Effects | |
|   – Shifts in the geographic distribution of unemployment | 16% |
|   – Decline in manufacturing unemployment relative to total unemployment | 4 to 18% |
| 4. Changes in Unemployment | |
|   – More accurate measure of unemployment | 1 to 12% |

Note: The total change explained exceeds 100 percent for the high-range estimates. This result occurs because a number of estimates are made separately, and the interactions among the effects are not fully accounted for by this procedure.
Source: *An Examination of Declining UI Claims during the 1980s: Final Report* (Princeton, N.J.: Mathematica Policy Research Inc., 1988), pp. xii-xiii, 119-20.

The fact that unemployment compensation programs pay benefits to only a relatively small fraction of the unemployed at any given time violates one of the most fundamental principles of social insurance – *broad coverage of workers against well defined social risks including the risk of unemployment.* As a result, one of the fundamental principles of social justice is violated since the state clearly is not providing some economic security to all workers who experience spells of unemployment through no fault of their own.

2. *Inadequate benefits.* Unemployment compensation programs also violate the norms of social justice since they fail to pay adequate levels of income to unemployed workers who become involuntarily unemployed. Unemployment compensation benefits generally are inadequate for most middle and upper-income persons during a spell of involuntary unemployment. A commonly accepted test of benefit adequacy is that unemployment compensation benefits should restore at least 50 percent of the worker's average weekly wage. However, the average replacement rate has been roughly constant at 35 percent over time and averaged only 36 percent during the fourth quarter of 1990 (Committee on Ways and Means 1991, pp. 537-38).

❖

Although the average replacement rate is useful, it provides no meaningful information about workers with different levels of earnings. Thus, it also is useful to examine the average replacement rate for low, average, and upper-income workers. A recent federal study provides valuable information on the adequacy of unemployment compensation benefits for these groups (See Committee on Ways and Means 1990, pp. 520-21). In September 1989, all but seven jurisdictions paid benefits that met the 50 percent standard for low-income workers ($12,091 in 1989). However, a different conclusion emerges for average and upper-income workers. *In September 1989, only six jurisdictions met the 50 percent standard for average-income workers ($26,671 in 1989). No state paid benefits that met the 50 percent standard for upper-income workers ($48,364 in 1989).* As a result, it is difficult for most unemployed workers to maintain their previous standard of living without going into debt or seriously depleting their savings despite the payment of unemployment benefits.

## V. Summary and Conclusions

In summary, the Social Security and unemployment compensation programs are both consistent and inconsistent with the principles of social justice. On the positive side, the programs overall provide an important layer of income protection to the population. The benefits are paid as a matter of right with no demeaning means test. With respect to specific programs, certain characteristics of the Social Security program are consistent with the principles of social justice since the program provides a base of protection to most workers and families against important social risks; the program is extremely effective in reducing poverty among the elderly and also is more effective in reducing income inequality than is the federal income tax; finally, the Social Security program shows a preferential treatment toward the working poor by application of a weighted benefit formula that deliberately weights benefits in favor of lower-income workers.

On the negative side, however, certain characteristics of the Social Security program clearly violate the norms of social justice. The earnings test severely penalizes beneficiaries who wish to work and encourages beneficiaries to cheat and conceal their earnings. The program also imposes a harsh test of disability on disabled workers, which results in an initial denial of large proportion of disability income claims. In addition, the payroll tax imposes a relatively heavy tax burden on the working poor and increases the number of workers who fall below the poverty line. Finally, the Social Security program violates an important norm of social justice since it does not provide for a system of universal health insurance covering the entire population.

State-federal unemployment compensation programs also are seriously flawed at the present time and violate several important principles of social justice. One of the most important defects is that only a small fraction of the unemployed receives unemployment benefits at any given time. As a result, economic insecurity for many of the unemployed is substantially increased. As the present time, state governments are in violation of a fundamental principle of social justice, which is to provide basic economic security to all workers who become involuntarily unemployed.

Finally, even if unemployed workers can meet the stringent eligibility requirements and can qualify for unemployment compensation benefits, the weekly benefits are grossly inadequate for the vast majority of middle and upper-income employees. The weekly cash benefits replace less than 50 percent of the worker's average weekly wage; for upper-income workers who become unemployed, the pretax replacement rate in most states is 25 percent or less. Because of the relatively low replacement rates in most states, many unemployed workers must seriously deplete their savings or go heavily into debt. As a result, economic insecurity is substantially increased. The effectiveness of state-federal unemployment compensation as a primary income maintenance tool can be seriously questioned in view of these defects.

*V.J. Skutt Professor of Insurance, College of Business Administration, University of Nebraska-Lincoln, Lincoln, NE 68588 USA. He is a founding member of the National Academy of Social Insurance, Washington, D.C. and a past president of the American Risk and Insurance Association. He is also a former editor of *Benefits Quarterly* and a former communications and notes co-editor of *The Journal of Risk and Insurance.*

## References

Committee on Ways and Means, U.S. House of Representatives. *Overview of Entitlement Programs, 1990 Green Book, Background Material and Data on Programs Within the Jurisdiction of the Committee on Ways and Means,* Washington, D.C.: U.S. Government Printing Office, 1990.

_____. *Overview of Entitlement Programs, 1991 Green Book, Background and Data on Programs Within the Jurisdiction of the Committee on Ways and Means,* Washington, D.C.: U.S. Government Printing Office, 1991.

Employee Benefit Research Institute. *EBRI Issue Brief,* Number 123, February 1992.
Rejda, George E. *Social Insurance and Economic Security,* 4th ed., Englewood Cliffs, N.J.: Prentice-Hall, Inc. 1991.

_____. "A Reexamination of the Controversial Earnings Test Under the OASDI Program," *Benefits Quarterly,* Third Quarter 1990, *VI.,* 25-35.

Shapiro, Isaac and Marion E. Nichols. *Unemployed and Uninsured, Jobless Workers, Unemployment, Insurance, and the Recession,* Washington, D.C.: Center on Budget and Policy Priorities, 1991.

U.S. Bureau of the Census, Current Population Reports, Series P-60, No. 169-RD. *Measuring the Effect of Benefits and Taxes on Income and Poverty, 1989,* Washington, D.C.: U.S. Government Printing Office, 1990.

❖

# The Free Market and the Health of the U.S. Public (Abstract)

## Delfi Mondragón*

The objective of this analysis was to assess the effectiveness of the market system in maintaining the health of the U.S. public. Methodologies used were: development of two models of population health status, an epidemiological analysis of the major causes of U.S. mortality and morbidity, and comparison of public health status with that of societies with other modeled systems. Major findings include: health status as measured by public-health indicators increased in model one and diminished in the other, with examples such as the United States' infant mortality rate highest among all developed countries; health status is directly correlated with standard of living; the top causes of mortality, morbidity and years of life lost, (cancer, heart disease and stroke, diabetes and injuries — including violence), disproportionately affect the poor. Principal conclusions are: the market system is not effective for the health status of an increasing number of Americans, including thirty-eight million who have no access to care, and restructuring of health-care distribution must include some restructuring of the U.S. model in order to increase overall inputs to health, health status and economic growth, and therefore, decrease the need for health-care services.

*Associate Professor, Center for Health Policy and Ethics, Creighton University, Omaha, NE 68178 USA.

# The Three World Systems of Medical Care: Trends and Prospects

*Michael G. Farrall\**

It takes little prescience to recognize that there exist in the world today three basic systems of medical care: public assistance, health insurance, and national health service. These in turn are associated with and correspond to the three basic economic systems extant in the world today: precapitalist, capitalist, and socialist.

There are many individual variations among different countries that have the same medical care system. Furthermore, more than one system can be found coexistent within a single country; the type indicated for each country refers to the system by which the majority of the population obtains care.

Finally, the systems are not fixed and immovable; there is a continuing process of revision or replacement. Nor does the change from one system to another occur according to an inevitable progression. The purpose of this paper is not so much to describe the characteristics of the three systems – a necessary precondition for discussion – as to consider current trends and the prospects of transition from one system to another.

## I. Public Assistance

The public assistance system is dominant in 108 countries with 2401 million people, that is, 49 percent of the world's population. These countries are located in Asia, Africa, and Latin American and vary from colonies to semi-colonies to more independent developing nations. The economy is primarily agricultural, and the landholding system is usually feudal or semi-feudal, although a tribal economy is significant in some areas. There is an increasing growth of capitalist and socialist economic relationships in many of these countries.[1]

For the great majority of the population, whatever medical care is available is provided through a public assistance system for the poor which includes government hospitals and health centers financed by general taxation. The system

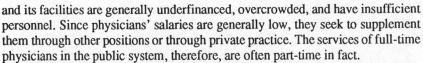

and its facilities are generally underfinanced, overcrowded, and have insufficient personnel. Since physicians' salaries are generally low, they seek to supplement them through other positions or through private practice. The services of full-time physicians in the public system, therefore, are often part-time in fact.

In addition to the public assistance system, administered by health departments, there may be programs operated by social security agencies for industrial or white-collar workers. Where they exist, these programs usually cover only a small part of the population. Some of these agencies purchase care from private physicians and hospitals, as in Chile's program for white-collar employees and Algeria's for non-agricultural workers. Most, however, provide care in their own hospitals and polyclinics because of the shortage of adequate private and public facilities; Costa Rica, Mexico, and Turkey are examples of this approach (U.S. Department of Health and Human Services 1985).

In all these countries there is a small stratum of landowners, businesspersons, officials, and professionals who use private physicians and hospitals for their care.

## II. Health Insurance

The health insurance system is dominant in 23 countries with 882 million people, that is, 18 percent of the world's population. These countries are located in Western Europe and North America and also include Australia, New Zealand, Japan, and Israel; all are industrialized nations with a capitalist economy.

There are wide variations in the insurance systems. In Israel, for example, all medical care insurance is non-governmental. In most countries, however, there is a mix of governmental and non-governmental insurance. The latter is still dominant in the United States, but governmental insurance has emerged elsewhere as the most important component. Indeed, there are a number of countries – Canada, Great Britain, Denmark, Finland, Iceland, New Zealand, and Norway – in which the entire population is covered by government medical care insurance (U.S. Department of Health and Human Services 1985).

In the other countries coverage is usually limited to employed persons, and there may be exclusions of certain occupational groups or those with salaries above a certain level. Dependents of insured persons are included, although Austria and Japan impose some cost-sharing on them. Switzerland, which subsidizes voluntary plans and, in some cantons, makes membership compulsory, does not include dependents of insured persons unless they are members of a plan in their own right. In the United States, national health insurance for those aged 65 and over does not include dependents.

Although most countries use social security taxes on employees and employers, a considerable portion of the cost is borne by general government funds. In Denmark, Iceland, Ireland, and New Zealand there are no payroll taxes on employees for medical care, while in Italy the tax on employees is extremely small (0.3 percent of earnings). Canada finances its system primarily from general federal and provincial revenues: Quebec imposes a tax of 0.8 percent on employees' earnings, and Ontario, Alberta, and British Columbia tax individuals a flat amount, but the other six provinces do not tax individuals directly for medical care. In the United States, national health insurance for the aged uses payroll taxes and individual contributions as major sources of financing.

Although the scope of service varies, practically all national health insurance programs in the industrial nations are based on fee-for-service private practice. Physicians and other practitioners are independent entrepreneurs who contract with the government or with authorized sick funds to provide care.

In some countries, such as Austria, Canada, Germany, Italy, and the Netherlands, physicians' care is provided without any additional payments by the patient. In others, such as Belgium, Finland, France, New Zealand, and Norway, patients receive a cash refund for part of their medical expenses. Denmark requires earners with incomes above the level of skilled workers to pay part of the cost of physicians' fees, while co-payments by all patients are required in Iceland, Japan, and the United States (U.S. Department of Health and Human Services 1985). The failure of most national health insurance to cover the full cost of care is a major deficiency of fee-for-service programs.

An interesting exception to the reliance on private practice is Spain, where, because of the shortage of other facilities, the social security system provides comprehensive medical services through its own institutions. The social security medical program covers 65 percent of the population; they are served by 88 hospitals with more than 39,000 beds, and 187 permanent and 365 temporary outpatient clinics. The social security system employed more than 30,000 physicians in 1991 (Segovia de Arana 1991).

In the countries with national health insurance, the administrative agencies are those concerned with social security as a whole, namely, Ministries of Social Welfare and their Social Insurance Institutes. The only exceptions are New Zealand, where the Department of Health administers the medical benefits, and Canada, where the Department of National Health and Welfare administers the program at the federal level, and health departments predominate at the provincial level (Terris 1986). The anomalous and thoroughly illogical situation whereby a health services program is administered by a finance-oriented agency is generally characteristic of national health insurance.

## III. National Health Service

The national health service is dominant in 14 countries with 1,617 million people, that is, 33 percent of the world's population. They include the formerly-Soviet republics in Europe, four in Asia, and Cuba in the Americas – the so-called Second World. All these countries are either industrialized or undergoing rapid industrialization.

Unlike the public assistance systems and most of the insurance systems, national health services cover the entire population. Financing is by taxation. Like most of the public assistance systems, and unlike most of the insurance systems,

❖

services are provided by salaried physicians and other health personnel who work in government hospitals and health centers. Practically all services are included and provided free of charge. A common exception is drugs prescribed in ambulatory care, where the practice in different countries varies from no charge at all to different proportions of actual cost.

The architect of the first national health service was Nikolai A. Semashko, the People's Commissar of Health of the Soviet Union from 1918 until 1930. In his book on *Health Protection in the U.S.S.R.* published in England in 1934, Semashko stated three basic principles of the Soviet national health service: 1) unity in the organization of the health service; 2) participation of the population itself in the entire work of health protection; and 3) preventive (prophylactic) measures as the basis of the entire health service in the country. Preventive measures have been greatly emphasized in all of the national health services. These include not only the control of environmental and occupational hazards, and the campaigns directed to infectious diseases and maternal and child health, but a great emphasis on early detection, with many millions of people being screened every year, and on dispensarization (from the Russian word dispanser or follow-up center) for preventive supervision of vulnerable groups in the population and of persons with chronic diseases (Popov 1971; Lisitsin 1972). One other characteristic of the national health services should be mentioned. This is the great emphasis on ambulatory care through the construction of community and factory health centers close to the people being served.

## IV. Prospects for Transition

In the United States, which because of its political conservatism and ideological commitment to private practice would seem to be completely refractory to such ideas, there is a growing interest in a national health service. The widely respected Cambridge Survey offered four alternatives to those interviewed in a national poll and found that 8 percent were undecided; 13 percent were for keeping things as they are; 23 percent favored giving medical insurance to poor people and major medical insurance to all; 35 percent were for comprehensive national health insurance for everyone; and 22 percent favored a totally nationalized system in which comprehensive care is provided for all and doctors and hospitals are taken over by the government (*Chicago Sun-Times*, 1975). According to a 1991 ten nation survey published in *Health Affairs*, only 10 percent of Americans surveyed say their health system functions "pretty well," while 89 percent say their system needs "fundamental changes" or "complete rebuilding" (Marmor and Mashaw 1990).

Some proponents of national health insurance in the United States have taken the position that a national health service is premature and that a prior stage of comprehensive national health insurance is inevitable. This ignores the fact that the United States has already lived through national health insurance, for those 65 years and older, with unsatisfactory results. Furthermore, if those who believe in inevitable stages were consistent, they would support government subsidy of voluntary plans. This was, after all, the usual progression in Europe: first, the growth of voluntary plans; second, government subsidy and regulation of the plans; and third, government health insurance (Perrott 1984).

Indeed, there is a very real danger that the proponents neither of national health insurance nor of a national health service will have their way in the United States. The likelihood of this outcome has nothing to do with stages of inevitability, but with political power; the insurance companies exercise tremendous economic and political leverage. In the absence of a political party of labor such as exists in every other industrial nation, it will take heroic efforts to avoid the establishment of subsidized private insurance, or of government health insurance administered by private insurance companies.

In the industrial capitalist countries with well-entrenched health insurance systems – in which practitioners are essentially small businesspeople selling their services – the resistance to change to a salaried service is very great. Nevertheless, the trend is unmistakably toward the national health service. The latter not only has demonstrated its superiority in terms of quality and cost effectiveness but has shown that it is unnecessary to submit to the blind forces of the medical marketplace; nations can plan rationally for their health services, and can plan them well. A national health service, finally, makes it possible to plan democratically and humanely, not for a minority but for all citizens and with all citizens.

## Endnotes

*Department of Sociology and Anthropology, Creighton University, Omaha, NE, 68178-0117 USA.

[1] Countries with less than 100,000 population are excluded from this and subsequent tallies.

## References

"Americans Want Health Care Reform," *Chicago Sun-Times,* 12 October 1975, 7.

Lisitsin, Y. *Health Protection in the USSR,* Moscow: Progress Publishers, 1972.

Marmor, Theodore and Mashaw, Jerry. "Canada's Health Insurance and Ours," *The American Prospect,* Fall 1990, 18-29.

Perrot, G. "Voluntary Health Insurance in Western Europe," *Public Health Reports,* 1984, *62,* 733.

Popov, G., *Principles of Health Planning in the USSR,* Geneva: World Health Organization, 1971.

Segovia de Arana, J., in J. Bowers and E. Purcell, eds., *National Health Services,* NY: Josiah Macy Jr. Foundation, 1991.

Terris, M. "The Epidemiologic Revolution, National Health Insurance and the Role of Health Departments," *American Journal of Public Health,* 1986, 66, 1155.

U.S. Department of Health and Human Services. *Social Security Programs Throughout the World,* Washington, D.C.: U.S. Government Printing Office, 1985.

# The Federal Budget Deficit:
# The Sins of the 1980s Crippling the
# Nation in the 1990s

## Christopher A. McLean*

I am pleased to put today's discussion of health care and the social needs of the nation into perspective vis-à-vis, the federal budget. The largest single impediment to addressing the "social questions" of the 1990s is the federal budget deficit and the national debt so enlarged during the 1980s.

The federal budget deficit and the accumulated national debt now hover over every decision in Washington, D.C. Whether it be in developing a health care strategy or helping the new democracies in Eastern Europe. The very existence of the debt and deficit stifles any agenda for substantial change. The nation's fiscal condition limits our nation's options in terms of what the economy can bear and what the American people will tolerate.

When President Reagan took office, the accumulated national debt was just under one trillion dollars.[1] That figure represented all the remaining debt accumulated from George Washington's administration through President Carter's administration. Today, the national debt exceeds $3.5 trillion.[2] Such a figure is almost impossible to comprehend. Let me put it another way, in 1980, per capita share of the national debt was $4,014. Today, it is over $14,300.[3] By the end of 1992 fiscal year, it will be $15,831.[4]

This time last year, you may remember what was then an approaching fiscal crisis. The Gramm-Rudman law was about to shut down the government, slice budgets and make everyone's life miserable. In the face of this created crisis, the Congressional leadership and the President's key economic advisors met for weeks at Andrews Air Force Base, the Capital and other locations to hammer out "the deal of the century" to finally fix the budget deficit. Through weeks of facing an imminent shut down of the federal government and several days where the monuments and parks were actually closed, the Congress and the President did come to an agreement coincidentally in time for the 1988 elections. The collapse of the government was avoided.

Rather than embark on an era of fiscal austerity, the Congress and the President simply changed the Gramm-Rudman law. They left town congratulating themselves on the single largest deficit reduction package in history. What they really did was give each other a nudge and a wink. The budget summit agreement which dictated the last two Congressional budgets and will control at least the next budget created three caps on appropriated spending, (one for defense, one for international affairs and one for domestic discretionary) and it allowed entitlements to go on automatic pilot after the first year of the agreement. It locked in spending in those categories and prevented inter-category transfers, so savings in defense could not be used to fund new spending in education, for example. The five year budget summit agreement was intentionally designed to put any re-consideration or renegotiation of the budget agreement beyond the 1992 presidential election.[5]

Under the structure of the budget reforms, the agreement will explode just after the next election. By the architecture of the agreement, from now until the fiscal year 1994 budget submission, the deficit is a political safe zone.

Expected and unexpected budget busters such as spending for the war, the savings and loan bailout or the banking bailout were simply placed outside of the agreement through off-budget accounts and emergency spending requests. I am proud to report, however, that Senator Exon would have no part of the budget summit charade and repeatedly voted and spoke against the measure.[6]

Today, more than half way through President Bush's term in office, the deficit is larger than ever but the silence from the financial markets, the nation's economists and the American people could not be quieter.

But, I submit, deficits do matter. They are the single largest impediment to a progressive agenda. They are a mortgage on the nation's future. They are a time bomb which, I fear with my party's luck, will go off in the next Democratic administration.

As governors and mayors across the country are discovering, borrowing is not an alternative to taxes, borrowing is simply a future tax, made more expensive by the accumulation of interest expense.

In the next budget which the Congress will consider, the single largest spending program will be gross interest, exceeding $300 billion alone in the fiscal year 1993.[7] That spending does not build bridges, resurface roads, educate students, finance health care reform or feed the hungry, that money pays for the fiscal and economic sins of the past.

In a real sense, the economic policies of the 1980s created a wealth transfer program. The essence of that program was to transfer wealth from the debtor classes to the lender classes. There are a number of ways this transfer has expressed itself. America's strength has always been its solid middle class. The 1980s helped the rich, hurt the poor and did no favors for the middle class. Distribution of income in 1989 was more unevenly divided than anytime since the Second World War.[8]

According to the Congressional Budget Office, from 1977 to 1988 the average after tax income of the poorest fifth of American households fell 10 percent. The middle fifth saw a gain of less than 4 percent and the top fifth saw their after tax income increase 34 percent.[9]

That same study indicated that in 1988, the richest one percent in America had more pre-tax income than the entire bottom 40 percent.[10]

While average wages and salaries more than doubled for the richest one percent from 1977 to 1988, average wages and salaries for the bottom 90 percent fell by 3.5 percent.[11]

As a nation, we have also sold assets at an unprecedented pace to foreign interests to meet the payments on our budget and trade deficits. The U.S. net foreign asset position declined by about $600 billion over the last decade, making the United States by the mid 1980s a net debtor nation for the first time since the First World War.[12] Seventeen percent of U.S. Federal debt is now held by foreign investors.

The failure of the Reagan and Bush administration to regulate economic activity created a financial crisis in banking, insurance, pensions and Savings and Loans. Thanks to the Reagan/Bush regulatory policies, it is now possible for any American in any part of the nation to fly coast to coast on a bankrupt airline!

The frustrating thing about working with the budget on a daily basis is that there are no quick solutions, no silver bullets, no painless cures. It is clear that the present course is unsustainable.

Over the decade of the 1980s, for the average American there has been a decline in the standard of living. Some may have not noticed because, while they may have their house and their job, what they have lost is their options. Millions of Americans are only a pink slip away from total economic disaster. A college degree, or an advanced degree, for that matter, no longer guarantees success. For the half of adult America that did not attend college, the opportunities and job prospects are growing more limited every day. We now have an economy where community boosters brag about how low wages are, and states give away untold riches to attract and hold business.

During the 1980s the nation surrendered many of the industries which provided those willing to work hard for a pathway out of poverty to foreign competitors. There is a terrible "job-lock" because the opportunities for advancement and transfer are limited or health insurance is unavailable in a new position.

The social problems of the 1990s are in part the manifestations of the economic irresponsibility of the 1980s. That very irresponsibility makes it difficult for the federal government to deal with the domestic problems including comprehensive health care reform in a meaningful and immediate way. The accumulation of $3.5 trillion of debt, and the addition of $300 to $500 billion more debt each and every year for as far as the eye can see, cripple the government from spending the money needed to address the growing unmet social needs of the nation.

I doubt that the public will accept higher taxes for more spending. What is the solution? What can be done? I submit, the solution lies in political action and Presidential leadership.

There are many individual leaders in Congress, and I am very proud to say, of somewhat immodestly, my boss, Jim Exon, has been one of the warning voices throughout the 1980s about the dangers of the supply side experiment. But the Congress as an institution can not be expected to lead a nation. The Congress is an institution of 535 members which largely responds to the public and the President.

If our nation is to reverse the deterioration of the 1980s, make resources available for new initiatives such as health care reform, and embark on a path towards future prosperity in the next century, this President or, more likely, the next President must be willing to ask for *present* sacrifice of the American people.

Until that time, the American people should get smart and angry about the nation's fiscal condition. Rather than reading the President's lips, they should read his budget. They should be willing to say that if an economic agenda sounds too good to be true (such as cutting taxes, increasing spending and reducing the deficit) it probably is.

Most of all, Americans should take their anger to the polls and start voting. America has one of the lowest voting rates of any democracy in the world.[13] About half our nation's eligible voters do not go to the polls. Until those who have been hurt by the supply side policies of the 1980s go to the polls and vote their interest and the nation's interest, there is little chance that the policies of the 1990s will be any different than the policies of the past decade.

What is needed is a sustained, and yes, painful period of total fiscal austerity. Value must be derived from every tax dollar spent. Productivity gains must be demanded from all levels of government, be it Congressional staff, defense procurement officers, postal clerks, social workers, tax collectors or first grade teachers. Budgets from the Department of Defense to the Department of Health and Human Services must be scrubbed.

Old programs will have to be traded in for new programs and investments must be made in the nation's human and industrial capital to assure that our nation and its economy is ready for the next century. It will be difficult. Special interests from all corners will fight.

I believe that the American people will accept sacrifice to reduce the deficit and prepare for the future if they are convinced that the burdens of austerity are shared fairly and that there will be a visible reward for their sacrifice. The problem to date has been that the President and most in the Congress have been unwilling to ask.

❖

# Endnotes

*Christopher A. McLean is Legal Counsel and Legislative Assistant to United States Senator J. James Exon. The opinions expressed in this paper reflect the views of Mr. McLean and do not necessarily reflect the views or positions of Senator Exon.

¹ *The Budget of the U.S. Government, Fiscal Year 1992*, Table 7.1, Part Seven-71 (1991).

² *Ibid.*

³ *News From NASCACT* (The National Association of State Auditors, Comptrollers and Treasurers), July 24, 1991 and NASCAT's Quarterly Report on the "Federal Deficit...Mortgaging our Children's Future," July 22 1991.

⁴ Ibid.

⁵ See *The Omnibus Budget Reconciliation Act of 1990, Conference Report to Accompany H.R. 5835,* (House Report 101-964).

⁶ See, for example, *Congressional Record,* September 25, 1990, S 13700-02, October 6, 1990, S. 14676, October 8, 1990 S 14735-6, October 17, 1990 S 15504-5, October 27, 1990 S 17513-4.

⁷ See the *Mid-Session Review of the Budget,* July 15, 1991, by the Executive Office of the President, Office of Management and Budget and testimony of Richard Darman before the Senate Budget Committee, July 17, 1991.

⁸ Shapiro and Greenstein, *Selective Prosperity: Increasing Income Disparities Since 1977,* (The Center on Budget Policy and Priorities), July 1991.

⁹ The top 1% saw their income increase 122% over the same period. See, The Committee on Ways and Means, U.S. House of Representatives, 1991 *Green Book: Background Material and Data on Programs within the Jurisdiction of the Committee on Ways and Means,* May 7, 1991, p. 1301; see also, *Shapiro and Greenstein* p. 2.

¹⁰ *The Green Book,* pp. 1312 and 1293, respectively.

¹¹ *Current Economic Conditions,* prepared by the Majority Staff of the Joint Economic Committee of Congress, Paul S. Sarbanes, Chairman, August 2, 1991, p. 8.

¹² C.J. Lawrence, *Portfolio Strategy Service,* July 29, 1991 p. 17.

¹³ See, *United States General Accounting Office, Voting: Some Procedural Changes and Informational Activities Could Increase Turnout;* Nov. 1990, 26-27. Northern and Western states ranked highest in voter participation. Minnesota lead the nation with an impressive 66.3% turnout in 1988. Nebraska ranked 14th with 56.7%. In 1980, the United States ranked 20th among the world's 21 industrialized democracies in voter participation. That year 52.6% of the voting age population participated in the 1980 elections in the United States. Italy, in comparison, had 94% voter participation.

# Proceedings

❖

PROGRAM

---

# SIXTH WORLD CONGRESS OF SOCIAL ECONOMICS

---

On the Condition of Labor and the Social Question:
One Hundred Years Later

Sponsored by the **International Institute of Social Economics** in collaboration with the **Association for Social Economics, Creighton University** and **Marquette University**

Commemorating

The 100th Anniversary of
the "Great Social Encyclical",
**Rerum Novarum:   De Conditione Opificum**
of **Pope LEO XIII**

and the

Fiftieth Anniversary of the Founding of the
**Association for Social Economics**

---

**Red Lion Hotel * Omaha, Nebraska  USA * 9-11 August 1991**

# Prefatory Note

The "Apostolic Blessing" presented on page 1 supra originally appeared inside the front cover of the Program, and is not re-produced again here. The present is an annotated facsimilie of the original Program, wherein the following code ( ) will be employed:

(1a)  —  paper presented, but published in J.C. O'Brien (ed.), *FESTSCHRIFT in Honour of John E. Elliott, Parts I & II* = (1a/i; 1a/ii), IJSE, 19/7-12, 1992; abstracted here.

(1b)  —  ibid.; not abstracted here.

(2a)  —  paper presented, but published in P.L. Danner (ed.), *Anniversary issue of the RSE*, XLIX:4 (Winter 1991); abstracted here.

(2b)  —  ibid.; not abstracted here.

(3a)  —  paper presented, but appearing in J.B. Davis and E.J., O'Boyle (eds.), *The Social Economics of Human Material Need* (forthcoming), SIU Press, 1994; abstracted here.

(3b)  —  ibid.; not abstracted here.

(4a)  —  paper presented but only abstracted here.

(4b)  —  presentation made but not published or abstracted here.

(5a)  —  paper submitted/accepted but not presented.

(5b)  —  paper (comment, etc.) not submitted/presented.

Absent any of the above (or other) notations, the paper (comment, etc.) was presented and is published herewith, though titles might differ somewhat as between submission, presentation, and/or publication.

## INVITED LECTURES & SPECIAL EVENTS;
## ACADEMIC PROGRAM SUMMARY

*Friday 09 August 1991*

08:00-10:00 a.m. -- **Registration**; Coffee, Tea and Rolls          *MEZZANINE*

10:00-12:00 noon -- **Plenary Session:** Inaugural & Welcoming          *NEBRASKA*
Remarks (Tom Nitsch, Coordinator; Michael G. Morrison, SJ,
President, Creighton University, Host; Barrie O. Pettman,
Director, IISE; Kishor Thanawala, President, ASE; Guy R. Banville,
Dean, College of Business Administration, Creighton University;
and, Thomas A. Bausch, Dean, College of Business
Administration, Marquette University); **Opening Address** by
Archbishop John R. Roach of Saint Paul and Minneapolis,
introduced by Archbishop Daniel E. Sheehan of Omaha,
"The Call to Community and the Common Good."

01:15-03:15 p.m. -- **Simultaneous Individual Sessions 1-5**

03:30-05:30 p.m. -- **Simultaneous Individual Sessions 6-10**

06:30-09:00 p.m -- **Social Hour** (no-host bar); Dinner, and          *MIDLANDS*
**Keynote Address** by William J. Byron, SJ, President,
The Catholic University of America, introduced by
Michael G. Morrison, SJ, President, Creighton University,
"The Social Question: Who Asks, Who Answers?"

*Saturday 10 August 1991*

08:00-10:00 a.m. -- **Simultaneous Individual Sessions 11-14**

10:15-12:15 p.m. -- **Simultaneous Individual Sessions 15-19**

12:30-01:45 p.m. -- **Luncheon & Invited Presentation honoring**          *MISSOURI/*
**the ASE:** Peter L. Danner, Marquette University,          *IOWA*
Chair; Henry W. Briefs, Georgetown University,
introduced by William R. Waters, DePaul University, "Götz
Briefs and the Association: What Did He Contribute and How?"

02:00-04:00 p.m. -- **Simultaneous Individual Session 20-23**

04:30-09:00 p.m. -- **Riverboat Dinner Cruise** (Optional)

*Sunday 11 August 1991*

10:00-12:15 p.m. -- **Plenary Session (#24):** Invited Panel on          *LEWIS/CLARK*
"Socioeconomic Security, National Health Insurance
and Medical Care Systems: Programs and Proposals."

12:15-12:30 p.m. -- **Closing Remarks** (etc.) by Tom Nitsch (et al.)

# SESSION 1

## *ANCIENT/EARLY CHRISTIAN SOCIAL ECONOMY*

*Friday 9 August      1:15 - 3:15 P.M.        BELAIR*

| | |
|---|---|
| **Chairperson** | **Frank Brown**, DePaul University. |

**PAPER 1**      **Anastassios D. Karayiannis**, University of Piraeus, Greece.
"Redistribution of Wealth: Some Suggestions and Justifications
from the Eastern Christian Father (350-400 A.D.)." (5a)

**PAPER 2**      **Barry Gordon**, University of Newcastle, Australia.
"Rich, Poor and Slave in the Socio-Economic Thought of the
Later Church Fathers."

**PAPER 3**      **Bruce J. Malina** and **Thomas O. Nitsch**, Creighton University.
"The Bishops' Pastoral Letter and the Poverty Problem: Early vs.
Contemporary Concerns and Doctrines." (4a)

**PAPER 4**      **Giuseppe Gaburro**, University of Verona, Italy.
"Christian Anthropology as a Foundation for a New Economics."

# SESSION 2

## *CURRENT SOCIOECONOMIC POLICY ISSUES*

*Friday 9 August    1:15 - 3:15 P.M.        CAPITOL*

**Chairperson**      **Hans E. Jensen**, University of Tennessee, Knoxville.

**PAPER 1**      **Robert F. Allen**, Creighton University.
"The 'New Capitalism' and Recent U.S. Antitrust Policy."

**PAPER 2**      **Edward L. Fitzsimmons**, Creighton University.
"Deregulation in the Transportation Sector of the U.S. and Its
Effect on Labor."

**PAPER 3**      **Carl P. Kaiser**, Washington and Lee University.
"Sickness Absence in the Welfare State."

**PAPER 4**      **Auke Rein Leen**, Leiden University, Netherlands.
"Creativity, Entrepreneurship and Consumer Policy."

# SESSION 3

## *THE SOCIAL ECONOMICS OF HUMAN NEEDS:  ROUND-TABLE* [*]

*Friday 9 August      1:15 - 3:15 P.M.          DAKOTA*

**Chairperson**          **Edward J. O'Boyle,** Louisiana Tech University. (3a)

**Introductory
  Remarks**          **John B. Davis,** Marquette University.

**COMMENT 1**          **Kishor Thanawala,** Villanova University.
"The Person and the Social Economy:   Need, Values and
Principles." ("Comment" appears in <u>Papers</u> supra.)

**COMMENT 2**          **William R. Waters,** DePaul University. (4b)
"The Historical Dynamics of the Concept of 'Need.'"

**COMMENT 3**          **Wallace C. Peterson,** University of Nebraska - Lincoln. (4b)
"Human Physical Need:  A Concept that at Once is Absolute
and Relative."

**COMMENT 4**          **John E. Elliott,** University of Southern California. (4b)
"The Need for Work as Such:  Self-Expression and Belonging."

**COMMENT 5**          **Robert H. Deans,** California State University - Long Beach.
"Social Management and the Self-Managed Firm." (5b)

**COMMENT 6**          **Lewis E. Hill,** Texas Tech University. (4b)
"Government Participation to Address Human Material Need."

---

[*] On J.B. Davis and E.J. O'Boyle (eds.), <u>The Social Economics of Human
Material Need</u>, SIU Press, forthcoming. (Ed./TN)

❖

# SESSION 4

## *LABOR ISSUES IN THE SOCIAL ECONOMY*

*Friday 9 August   1:15 - 3:15 P.M.      KANSAS*

Chairperson   **Michael J. Schuck,** Loyola University, Chicago.

PAPER 1     **Rev. Vincent P. Mainelli,** St. Cecilia's Cathedral, Omaha.
             "Worker Participation and Catholic Social Teaching -- 100 Years."

PAPER 2     **Michael Naughton,** University of St. Thomas.
             "Practical Applications of the Papal Social Teachings on Workers
             Participation."

PAPER 3     **Joseph M. Phillips, Jr.,** and **Robert R. Johnson,** Creighton University;
             and **Gerald R. Jensen,** Northern Illinois University.
             "Catholic Social Teaching and Human Resource Policy: Implications
             for Equity Investors."

PAPER 4     **Dennis A. O'Connor,** Loras College.
             "Economic Democracy, Employee Ownership, and Pay Equity: A
             Pattern of Convergence."

# SESSION 5

## *ALTERNATE ECONOMIC PARADIGMS, ETC.*

*Friday 9 August   1:15 - 3:15 P.M.      WYOMING*

Chairperson   **Jack Schwartzman,** Nassau Community College.

PAPER 1     **Morris Altman,** University of Saskatchewan, Canada. (4b)
             "Human Action as a Determinant of Material Welfare: Economics on
             the Margin."

PAPER 2     **Albino Barrera, O.P.,** Dominican House of Studies. (4b)
             "Anthropological Assumptions and the Right Economic Order."

PAPER 3     **Monroe Burk,** U. S. Foreign Service (Ret.). (4a)
             "Economics and Morality."

PAPER 4     **Charles K. Wilber,** University of Notre Dame.
             "Trust, Moral Hazards and Social Economics."

# SESSION 6

## *RSE SPECIAL ISSUE (1991) ON CENTENNIAL OF <u>RN</u> AND SEMICENTENNIAL OF ASE*

*Friday 9 August   3:30 - 5:30 P.M.   BELAIR*

**Chairperson   Peter L. Danner**, Marquette University.

**PAPER 1**     **Gladys W. Gruenberg**, Saint Louis University.
               "The American Contribution to Social Action and Social Order after
               <u>Rerum Novarum</u>." (2b)

**PAPER 2**     **Kishor Thanawala**, Villanova University.
               "Toward a Just World Economy." (2a)

**PAPER 3**     **Edward J. O'Boyle**, Louisiana Tech University.
               "On Justice and Charity." (2b)

**PAPER 4**     **Charles K. Wilber**, University of Notre Dame.
               "Catholic Social Thought:  An Agenda for the Future." (2b)

# SESSION 7

## *CATHOLIC SOCIAL ECONOMY AND THE SOCIAL QUESTION:  PRE-RN*

*Friday 9 August   3:30 - 5:30 P.M.   CAPITOL*

**Chairperson   Hans E. Jensen**, University of Tennessee, Knoxville.

**PAPER 1**     **Thomas O. Nitsch**, Creighton University.
               "Catholic Social Economy and the Social Question: Founders and First
               Positors." (4a)

**PAPER 2**     **Ernst J. Brehm**, Creighton University.
               "Catholic Social Economy and the Social Question in Spain in the
               Mid-19th Century: La Sagra et al."

**PAPER 3**     **Paul Misner**, Marquette University.
               "Antecedents of <u>Rerum Novarum</u> in European Catholicism."

❖

## SESSION 8

### *SOCIAL ECONOMICS IN THE CURRICULUM*

*Friday 9 August     3:30 - 5:30 P.M.        DAKOTA*

**Chairperson   John C. O'Brien**, California State University - Fresno.

**PAPER 1**     **Bryce J. Jones**, Rockhurst College.
"Social Economics in the Principles Course." (4b)

**PAPER 2**     **Gerard L. Stockhausen, S.J.**, Creighton University.
"Teaching Social Economics in the Principles Course."

**PAPER 3**     **James S. Richard, S.J.**, Regis College.
"Teaching the Social Encyclicals." (4b)

**PAPER 4**     **Edward L. Fitzsimmons**, Creighton University.
"Comments on Presentations." (4b)

## SESSION 9

### *SOCIAL ECONOMICS & THE NATURAL ENVIRONMENT*

*Friday 9 August   3:30 - 5:30 P.M.   KANSAS*

**Chairperson   Michael G. Farrall**, Creighton University.

**PAPER 1**     **F. Gregory Hayden**, University of Nebraska - Lincoln. (4b)
"Values and Beliefs Integrated into the Valuation of Ecosystems."

**PAPER 2**     **Mark Haggerty**, Clarion University and **Stephanie Welcomer**, Pennsylvania State University. (4b)
"Socio-economic Perceptions of Hazardous Waste."

**PAPER 3**     **Thomas O. Nitsch**, Creighton University. (4a)
"Orthodox Economics, Papal Social Teaching, and the Environment."
(Cf. supra, "OIKONOMIA & the Environment (&c.).")

## SESSION 10

### *PROBLEMS OF CENTRAL EUROPEAN TRANSFORMATION*

*Friday 9 August   3:30 - 5:30 P.M.   WYOMING*

**Chairperson   Rev. Charles D. Skok**, Gonzaga University.

**PAPER 1**      **Priyatosh Maitra**, University of Otago, New Zealand.
"Imported Technology and Return to Market Economy in the USSR."

**PAPER 2**      **Elena G. Mickhailova**, Cheboksary Branch, Moscow Co-operative Institute, USSR.
"Perestroika of the Soviet Economy and the Experience of the USA."

**PAPER 3**      **Helmut Jenkis**, Verband Niedersachsisch - Breimischer, Germany.
"Economic and Social Problems of German Unification." (4b)

**PAPER 4**      **Mircea N. Sabau**, University of Chicago.
"Revolution and Counterrevolution in Romania." (5b)

## SESSION 11

### *ESSAYS IN HONOR OF JOHN E. ELLIOTT:  I*

*Saturday 10 August   8:00 - 10:00 A.M.   BELAIR*

**Chairperson   John C. O'Brien**, California State University - Fresno.

**PAPER 1**      **John B. Davis**, Marquette University. (1b/ii)
"Keynes and the Socialization of Investment."

**PAPER 2**      **Thomas O. Nitsch**, Creighton University. (1a/i)
"Marx on Man's Sociality by Nature:  An Inexplicable Omission?"

**PAPER 3**      **Edward J. O'Boyle**, Louisiana Tech University. (1a/ii)
"Inter-firm and Supra-firm Cooperation in the Workplace and the Marketplace."

# SESSION 12

## *CATHOLIC SOCIAL TEACHING*

*Saturday 10 August   8:00 - 10:00 A.M.   CAPITOL*

**Chairperson   Joseph M. Phillips, Jr.**, Creighton University.

**PAPER 1**     **Charles D. Skok**, Gonzaga University.
                "Models of Papal Social Thought."

**PAPER 2**     **Michael J. Schuck**, Loyola University, Chicago.
                "The Centrality of Faith for Catholic Social Teaching." (4b)

**PAPER 3**     **Fr. Ralph Powell**, St. Louis;   per **Rev. William D. Virtue**, Diocese of
                Peoria, Illinois.
                "The Common Good." (Cf. supra, "Mechanistic Justice (&c.).")

**PAPER 4**     **Frank Brown**, DePaul University.
                "Education and Human Capital." (4a)


# SESSION 13

## *TRANSFER SPENDING, TAXES, AND THE AMERICAN WELFARE STATE*

*Saturday 10 August   8:00 - 10:00 A.M.   DAKOTA*

**Chairperson   Robert F. Allen**, Creighton University.

**PAPER 1**     **Wallace C. Peterson**, University of Nebraska - Lincoln.
                "Introductory Remarks and Overview." (4b)

**PAPER 2**     **George E. Rejda**, University of Nebraska - Lincoln.
                "Reaction/Commentary # 1." (4b)

**PAPER 3**     **Kishor Thanawala**, Villanova University.
                "Reaction/Commentary #2." (4b)

**PAPER 4**     **Chris McClean**, Legal Counsel and Legislative Assistant to United
                States Senator J. James Exon, Nebraska.
                "Human Needs and Budget Constraints." (Moved to Sess. 24.)

# SESSION 14

## *LABOR ISSUES: INDIA AND SOUTH AFRICA*

*Saturday 10 August    8:00 - 10:00 A.M.    KANSAS*

Chairperson   **Mark Haggerty**, Clarion University.

PAPER 1    **Gabriella A. Bucci**, DePaul University and **Beswajit Banerjee**,
International Monetary Fund.
"On-the-Job Search after Entering Urban Employment:
An Analysis Based on Indian Data on Migration." (5b)

PAPER 2    **Ila Chakrarorti**, Sukhadia University, India.
"Employment and Wage Structure of Unskilled Migrant Labour and the
Development of the Textile Industry in Bhilwara, India." (5a)

PAPER 3    **Brian Dollery**, Creighton University.
"The Origins, Nature and Effects of Labour Apartheid in South
Africa."

PAPER 4    **P. N. Palmer**, University of South Africa.
"A Systems Approach to Manpower Modelling and the Interregional
Mobility of Labour."

# SESSION 15

## *ESSAYS IN HONOR OF JOHN ELLIOTT: II*

*Saturday 10 August    10:15 A.M. - 12:15 P.M.    BELAIR*

Chairperson   **John C. O'Brien**, California State University - Fresno.

PAPER 1    **Ernest Raiklin**, University of Northern Iowa.
"From A Ricardian to a Marxian Ranking of Economic Goals and
Means." (1b/i)

PAPER 2    **Kishor Thanawala**, Villanova University.
"Exploitation and International Development." (1a/ii)

PAPER 3    **Lewis E. Hill**, Texas Tech University.
"A Comparative Analysis of Selected Economic Methodologies:
Proxeology, Positivism, and Institutionalism." (1b/ii)

# SESSION 16

## *CENTESIMUS ANNUS -- ROUND-TABLE*

*Saturday 10 August     10:15 A.M. - 12:15 P.M.     CAPITOL*

Chairperson          **Larry Donnelly**, Xavier University.

COMMENTATOR 1        **Richard J. Coronado**, Benedictine College. (4b)

COMMENTATOR 2        **Rev. Michael F. Gutgsell**, Archdiocese of Omaha, Nebraska. (4b)

COMMENTATOR 3        **Rev. Vincent P. Mainelli**, St. Cecilia's Cathedral (4b)

COMMENTATOR 4        **Gerard L. Stockhausen, S.J.**, Creighton University.

COMMENTATOR 5        **Charles K. Wilber**, University of Notre Dame. (5b)

# SESSION 17

## *ISLAMIC AND OLD TESTAMENT SOCIAL ECONOMY*

*Saturday 10 August     10:15 A.M. - 12:15 P.M.     DAKOTA*

Chairperson        **Brian Eggleston**, Augustana College.

PAPER 1            **Musa Al-Hindi**, Creighton University (MAIR Candidate). "Recent Developments in Islamic Economic Thought."

PAPER 2            **Masudul Choudhury**, University College of Cape Breton, Canada. "An Islamic Theory of Moral Entitlement (etc.)."

PAPER 3            **John E. Elliott**, University of Southern California. "Domination, Exploitation and the Condition of Labor in the Old Testament." (1b/ii)

# SESSION 18

## *POLICY ISSUES*

*Saturday 10 August    10:15 A.M. - 12:15 P.M.    KANSAS*

Chairperson        **Morris Altman,** University of Saskatchewan, Canada.
PAPER 1            **Glen Alexandrin,** Villanova University.
                   "E.F. Schumacher's Work and Impact in the U.S.A."
PAPER 2            **J.A.C. van Ophem,** Agricultural University Wegeningen,
                   Nederland. "Poverty in the Netherlands."
PAPER 3            **Joseph M. Phillips, Jr.,** Creighton University, and **Jeff A. Ankrom,**
                   Wittenberg University. "Catholic Social Teaching and Family
                   Income across Countries."
PAPER 4            **Li-Tech Sun,** Moorhead State University. "Economics of the
                   Golden Mean: A Preliminary Inquiry." (4a)*

# SESSION 19

## *COMPARATIVE ECONOMIC SYSTEMS*

*Saturday 10 August    10:15 A.M. - 12:15 P.M.    WYOMING*

Chairperson        **Mircea N. Sabau,** University of Chicago.

PAPER 1            **Michael Hletsos,** Athens, Greece. (5a)
                   "The State and the Wage-Labour Relation in the Eastern
                   Countries."

PAPER 2            **Siegfried G. Karsten,** West Georgia College.
                   "Social Encyclicals and Social Market Economics."

PAPER 3            **Priyatosh Maitra,** University of Otago, New Zealand.
                   "Technology Transfer and the Capitalist Transformation in
                   Economic Development: A Hundred Years Later."

PAPER 4            **William R. Waters,** DePaul University.
                   "The Influence of the Encyclicals on Solidarist Economic Theory."

---

*Cf. IJSE, 19:1 (1992), pp. 47-59.

# SESSION 20

### *ESSAYS IN HONOR OF JOHN E. ELLIOTT: III*

*Saturday 10 August    2:00 - 4:00 P.M.    BELAIR*

**Chairperson    Barrie O. Pettman,** International Institute of Social Economics, Hull, England.

**PAPER 1**      **John C. O'Brien,** California State University - Fresno. (1b/ii) "Schmoller's Political Economy:  Self-Interest vs. the Higher Law."

**PAPER 2**      **Hans E. Jensen,** The University of Tennessee, Knoxville. (1b/ii) "Alfred Marshall on the Structural and Behavioral Properties of Institutions."

**PAPER 3**      **Siegfried G. Karsten,** West Georgia College. (1b/ii) "Walter Eucken:  Social Economist."

# SESSION 21

### *SOCIAL ECONOMICS:  RETROSPECT AND PROSPECT -- ROUND-TABLE*

*Saturday 10 August    2:00 - 4:00 P.M.    CAPITOL*

**Chairperson**              **John B. Davis,** Marquette University.

**CONTRIBUTOR-**           **Lewis E. Hill,** Texas Tech University. "Some Observations
**COMMENTATOR 1**      Concerning the Institutionalist Approach (etc.)."

**CONTRIBUTOR-**
**COMMENTATOR 2**      **Thomas O. Nitsch,** Creighton University. (4b)

**CONTRIBUTOR-**           **Edward J. O'Boyle,** Louisiana Tech University. "Catholic Social
**COMMENTATOR 3**      Economics: A Response (etc.) (Abstract)."

**CONTRIBUTOR-**
**COMMENTATOR 4**      **William R. Waters,** DePaul University. (4b)

## SESSION 22

### RERUM NOVARUM: LABOR AND LAND; THE U.S. AND GLOBAL ECONOMIES

Saturday 10 August   2:00 - 4:00 P.M.   DAKOTA

Chairperson   Rev. Vincent P. Mainelli, St. Cecilia's Cathedral, Omaha.

PAPER 1   Dennis A. O'Connor, Loras College.
"One Hundred Years Later: The Magna Carta for Labor -- Rerum Novarum Revisited." (4b)

PAPER 2   Jack Schwartzman, Nassau Community College.
"Henry George and Rerum Novarum."

PAPER 3   L. A. O'Donnell, Villanova University.
"Rerum Novarum and the American Connection."

PAPER 4   Kishor Thanawala, Villanova University.
"Rerum Novarum and the World Economy in 1991."

## SESSION 23

### CONTEMPORARY LABOR ISSUES IN THE U.S.

Saturday 10 August   2:00 - 4:00 P.M.   KANSAS

Chairperson   Larry Donnelly, Xavier University.

PAPER 1   Larry Donnelly, Xavier University.
"Collective Bargaining and Rerum Novarum."

PAPER 2   Frederick R. Post, University of Toledo.
"U.S. Labor-Management Relations 100 Years After: A Management Viewpoint." (Cf. supra, "Toward the Fulfillment (etc.).")

PAPER 3   Thomas J. Kircher, Kircher, Robinson, Cook, Newman and Welch.
"U.S. Labor-Management Relations 100 Years After: A Labor Viewpoint." (4b)

PAPER 4   Maureen E. Labenski, Federal Mediation and Conciliation Service.
"The Role of Mediative Activities."(4b)

---

❖

---

## SESSION 24

### PLENARY MEETING -- SOCIOECONOMIC SECURITY, NATIONAL HEALTH INSURANCE AND MEDICAL CARE SYSTEMS: PROGRAMS AND PROPOSALS *

*Sunday 11 August    10:00 A.M. - 12:15 P.M.    LEWIS/CLARK*

**Chairperson  Lewis E. Hill**, Texas Tech University.

**PAPER 1**      **George E. Rejda**, University of Nebraska - Lincoln.
                 "Social Insurance and Social Justice."

**PAPER 2**      **Charles J. Dougherty**, Creighton University. (4b)
                 "Health Care Policy and Moral Philosophy."

**PAPER 3**      **Jeremiah Hurley**, McMaster University. (4b)
                 "Decentralization within Publicly-Funded Health Care Systems."

**PAPER 4**      **Delfi Mondragón**, Creighton University. (4a)
                 "The Free Market and the Health of the U.S. Public."

**PAPER 5**      **Michael G. Farrall**, Creighton University.
                 "The Three World Systems of Medical Care: Trends and Prospects."

## CLOSING REMARKS

*Sunday 11 August    12:15 - 12:30 P.M.    LEWIS/CLARK*

**Chairperson  Tom Nitsch**

---

*Chris McClean's Sess. 13 Paper (#4) was rescheduled to this meeting.

# PARTICIPANTS

| | |
|---|---|
| Alexandrin, G. | #18 |
| Al-Hindi, M. | #17 |
| Allen, R.F. | ##2,13 |
| Altman, M. | #18 |
| Ankrom, J. | #18 |
| Banerjee, B. | #14 |
| Banville, G.R. | P. 1 |
| Barrera, A., O.P. | #5 |
| Bausch, T.A. | P.1 |
| Brehm, E.J. | #7 |
| Briefs, H.W. | P.1 |
| Brown, F. | ##1,12 |
| Bucci, G.A. | #14 |
| Burk, M. | #5 |
| Chakrarorti, Ila | #14 |
| Choudhury, M. | #17 |
| Coronado, R.J. | #16 |
| Danner, P.L. | P.1;#6 |
| Davis, J.B. | ##3,11,21 |
| Deans, R.H. | #3 |
| Dollery, B. | #14 |
| Donnelly, L. | ##16,23 |
| Dougherty, C.J. | #24 |
| Eggleston, B. | #17 |
| Elliott, J.E. | #3,17 |
| Farrall, M.G. | #9,24 |
| Fitzsimmons, E.L. | ##2,8 |
| Gaburro, G. | #1 |
| Gordon, B. | #1 |
| Gruenberg, G.W. | #6 |
| Gutgsell, M.F. | #16 |
| Haggerty, M. | ##9,14 |
| Hayden, F.G. | #9 |
| Hill, L.E. | ##3,15,21,24 |
| Hletsos, M. | #19 |
| Hurley, G. | #24 |
| Jenkis, H. | #10 |
| Jensen, G.R. | #4 |
| Jensen, H. | ##2,7,20 |
| Johnson, R.R. | #4 |
| Jones, B.J. | #8 |
| Kaiser, C.P. | #2 |

❖

| | |
|---|---|
| Karayiannis, A.D. | #1 |
| Karsten, S.G. | ##19,20 |
| Kircher, T.J. | #23 |
| Labenski, M.E. | #23 |
| Leen, A.R. | #2 |
| Mainelli, V.P. | ##4,16,22 |
| Maitra, P. | ##10,19 |
| Malina, B.J. | #1 |
| McClean, C. | #13 → #24 |
| Mickhailova, E.G. | #10 |
| Misner, P. | #7 |
| Mondragón, D. | #24 |
| Morrison, M.G. | P.1 |
| Naughton, M. | #4 |
| Nitsch, T.O. | P.1; ##1,7,9,11,21,24 |
| O'Boyle, E.J. | ##3,6,11,21 |
| O'Brien, J.C. | ##8,11,15,20 |
| O'Connor, D.A. | #4,22 |
| O'Donnell, L.A. | #22 |
| Palmer, P.N. | #14 |
| Peterson, W.C. | ##3,13 |
| Pettman, B.O. | P.1;#20 |
| Phillips, Jr., J.M. | ##4,12,18 |
| Post, F.R. | #23 |
| Powell, R. | #12 |
| Raiklin, E. | #15 |
| Rejda, G.E. | ##13,24 |
| Richard, J.S. | #8 |
| Roach, Abp., J.R. | P.1 |
| Sabau, M.N. | ##10,19 |
| Schuck, M.J. | ##4,12 |
| Schwartzman, J. | ##5,22 |
| Sheehan, Abp., D.E. | P.1 |
| Skok, C.D. | ##10,12 |
| Stockhausen, G.L. | ##8,16 |
| Sun, L. | #18 |
| Thanawala, K. | P.1;##3,6,13,15,22 |
| Virtue, W.D. | #12 |
| Waters, W.R. | P.1;#3,#19,#21 |
| Wilber, C.K. | ##5,6,16 |
| *Ophem, J.A.C. van | #18 |
| *Byron, William J. | #1 |

## ASE Luncheon Meeting:  Résumé

The Luncheon and Invited Presentation honoring the ASE (former CEA) on its semicentennial was held on Saturday 10 August, and was very well attended. Pete Danner chaired and Bill Waters — also one of the "older guard" — gave a personal introduction of our invited speaker, Henry Briefs of Georgetown University. Henry, in his turn, gave us an intimate and informative account of his father's role in and relationship with the ASE/CEA from the early days on, under the caption, "Götz Briefs and the Association: What Did He Contribute and How?" It is this presentation which — though it was made from "hard copy" — will, for the time being at least, remain consigned to our "Oral Tradition."

## Co-ordination and Editing

**Co-ordinating Committee at Creighton University**
    Tom Nitsch, Chair (Coordinator)
    Ed Fitzsimmons
    Joe Phillips
    Gerry Stockhausen, S.J.
        Department of Economics and Finance
    Bryan LeBeau, Director
        Center for the Study of Religion and Society

**Editorial Committee at Creighton University**

    Thomas O. Nitsch, Professor of Economics, General Editor
    Joseph M. Phillips, Jr., Associate Professor of Economics, Editor
    Edward L. Fitzsimmons, Assistant Professor of Economics, Editor
    Bryan F. LeBeau, Associate Professor of History, Associate Editor
    Eugene L. Donahue, S.J., Associate Professor of Business and Society, Associate Editor
    N.R. Vasudeva Murthy, Associate Professor of Economics, Associate Editor

# TORONTO STUDIES IN THEOLOGY

47. Douglas J. Davies, Frank Byron Jevons, 1858-1936: An Evolutionary Realist

48. John P. Tiemstra (ed.), Reforming Economics: Calvinist Studies on Methods and Institutions

49. Max A. Myers and Michael R. LaChat (eds.), Studies in the Theological Ethics of Ernst Troeltsch

50. Franz G. M. Feige, The Varieties of Protestantism in Nazi Germany: Five Theopolitical Positions

51. John W. Welch, A Biblical Law Bibliography: Arranged by Subject and by Author

52. Albert W. J. Harper, The Theodicy of Suffering

53. Bryce A. Gayhart, The Ethics of Ernst Troeltsch: A Commitment to Relevancy

54. David L. Mueller, Foundation of Karl Barth's Doctrine of Reconciliation: Jesus Christ Crucified and Risen

55. Henry O. Thompson (ed.), The Contribution of Carl Michalson to Modern Theology: Studies in Interpretation and Application

56. David G. Schultenover (ed.), Theology Toward the Third Millennium: Theological Issues for the Twenty-first Century

57. Louis J. Shein, The Philosophy of Lev Shestov (1866-1938)

58. Hans Schwartz, Method and Context as Problems for Contemporary Theology

59. William C. Marceau, The Eucharist in Théodore de Bèze and St. Francis de Sales

60. Ronald D. Srigley, Eric Voegelin's Platonic Theology: Philosophy of Consciousness and Symbolization in a New Perspective

61. John Musson, Evil - Is it Real?: A Theological Analysis

62. Kenneth Cauthen, Theological Biology: The Case for a New Modernism

63. Robert S. Osborn, The Barmen Declaration as a Paradigm for a Theology of The American Church

64. A. James Reimer (ed.), The Influence of the Frankfurt School on Contemporary Theology: Critical Theory and the Future of Religion, Dubrovnik Papers in Honour of Rudolf J. Siebert

65. Lesley Armstrong Northup, The 1892 Book of Common Prayer

66. J. Crewdson, Christian Doctrine in the Light of Michael Polanyi's Theory of Personal Knowledge

67. James Langelaan, The Philosophy and Theology of Love According to St. Francis de Sales

68.

69. Thomas O. Nitsch, Joseph M. Phillips, Jr., Edward L. Fitzsimmons (eds.), On the Condition of Labor and the Social Question One Hundred Years Later: Commemorating the 100th Anniversary of Rerum Novarum, and the Fiftieth Anniversary of the Association for Social Economics